T0305355

Financial
Risk Management

The Wiley Finance series contains books written specifically for finance and investment professionals, as well as sophisticated individual investors and their financial advisors. Book topics range from portfolio management to e-commerce, risk management, financial engineering, valuation and financial instrument analysis, as well as much more. For a list of available titles, visit our website at www.WileyFinance.com.

Founded in 1807, John Wiley & Sons is the oldest independent publishing company in the United States. With offices in North America, Europe, Australia and Asia, Wiley is globally committed to developing and marketing print and electronic products and services for our customers' professional and personal knowledge and understanding.

Financial Risk Management

Applications in Market, Credit, Asset and Liability Management and Firmwide Risk

JIMMY SKOGLUND
WEI CHEN

WILEY

Library of Congress Cataloging-in-Publication Data:

Skoglund, Jimmy, 1971–
   Financial risk management : applications in market, credit, asset and liability management and firmwide risk / Jimmy Skoglund, Wei Chen.
      pages cm. — (Wiley finance series)
   Includes bibliographical references and index.
   ISBN 978-1-119-13551-7 (cloth)—ISBN 978-1-119-15723-6 (epdf)—ISBN 978-1-119-15724-3 (epub)
1. Financial institutions–Risk management. 2. Banks and banking–Risk management. 3. Financial risk management. I. Chen, Wei, 1968 November 10– II. Title.
   HG173.S575 2015
   658.15′5–dc23

                                                                                            2015020152

Cover Design: Wiley
Cover Image: © barbol88/iStockphoto

Printed in the United States of America

10 9 8 7 6 5 4 3 2 1

Contents

Preface

ABOUT THIS BOOK

In recent years risk management has become one of the fastest growing disciplines in the banking industry. It is certainly fueled by the fundamental intermediary role that banks play in the economy that expands globally with significant complexity. It is also driven by more risk-seeking behavior of the industry in order to achieve more profits. Another important reason is the increasing sophistication of the quantitative capability, including both methodology and technology. There have been many books on quantitative risk management. Most of them focus on specialized subjects. Only few advanced financial risk management books are application-oriented.

This book evolved over a number of years as the authors worked in banks and software companies with risk management analytics development and risk systems implementation. Our experiences with development and implementation of risk analytics in banks globally have inspired us to write a comprehensive quantitative oriented risk management book from a practitioner's point of view. The book discusses models and applications in the areas of market, credit, asset and liability management, and firmwide risk. An introductory chapter also reviews the economic foundation of modern risk management and how it has reached the current stage, the evolution of regulatory practices, the construction of financial risk systems, and the growing importance of model risk management as banks are required to perform more and more complex risk calculations that involve many models.

After the introduction, we continue with two chapters on market risk followed by chapters on portfolio credit risk, counterparty credit risk, liquidity risk, and funds transfer pricing and profitability analysis. While this book is mostly organized around the traditional market, credit, and other risk categories to provide contexts for the presentation of the risk methodologies, we cross reference different methodologies and risks, and dedicate two chapters to firmwide risk. These are the last chapters in the book, which discuss firmwide risk aggregation and firmwide scenario analysis and stress testing. Our intention is to provide a holistic view of the modern integrated yet modularized risk management practice.

In the past, quantitative methods were largely considered to be useful for risk measurement only and rarely served as input to the risk-based decision process. Quantitative methods are now frequently used to provide guidance to the risk management itself as well as assist in risk-based business decisions. This is another aspect of the comprehensiveness that we wish to demonstrate in this book. An important motivation of the book is to bring together the methodologies that can be applied across risk types and establish a common ground of quantitative approaches on which firmwide risk analysis can be established.

Since risk regulations have driven a lot of the recent practices, we also relate the concepts in the book to the most recent regulations in each risk area. In many cases the relation explains the risk-modeling foundation and in some cases also drawbacks of the risk regulations. However, this book is not a regular textbook overview on risk analysis in the sense that we have chosen to only include risk models and risk applications where we have acquired significant experience from both our research and actual implementations at banks. Hence, the book is significantly biased to the risk methods and models that we have found practically useful.

To put emphasis on the practical use of risk models the book includes many application examples illustrating how the models are used in practice. Therefore, our aim is to provide enough details that readers can actually implement the methods if they follow the discussions in this book. The book represents the collective experience of not only the authors but also the people we have worked with in the past—both in banks and in risk technology.

WHOM IS THIS BOOK FOR?

While this book emphasizes the financial risk management methods and models, we approach all the subjects from application aspects. Because the book is written with application in mind, we have skipped a lot of theoretical derivations and provide references for those who are interested in finding these details. The book still assumes maturity with mathematics and statistics as well as previous exposure to financial risk analysis concepts. It is therefore not a book for beginners. Consistent with the intended audience for this book we do not provide background chapters or appendices that introduce basic statistical and mathematical concepts. There are already several excellent books that can be used for that purpose if the reader needs a reminder on concepts. However, readers with a strong quantitative background should find no trouble following the details in the book. In each subject we also include discussions on the economic insights behind the methods for those who are interested in the rationale for the modern risk management methods. Therefore, we believe the book provides value to practitioners as well as researchers and students who seek to get more insights and implementation details of risk analytics in practice. The outline of the book that follows should help readers navigate through the book.

OUTLINE OF THE BOOK

The first two chapters of the book, following the introduction chapter, are devoted to market risk. Market risk is clearly one of the most well-known and studied risk areas. The modernization of the risk management concept started in the application of market risk. Even today, market risk is still a major driver of many innovations in risk management. The techniques used in the market risk context can be often easily transferred to the other risks as well. The style of the book builds on this history and introduces many risk concepts that are subsequently reused in the other chapters on credit, asset and liability management, and firmwide risks.

The first market risk chapter focuses on the once-popular linear and quadratic approach to portfolio risk management—assuming multivariate normal or log-normal distribution of the underlying risk factors. It also focuses on the multivariate normal or log-normal simulation-based approach to market risk analysis. For many risk practitioners the material in this first chapter is partly known. However, as we mentioned earlier, the market risk chapters still serve as an introduction where we also introduce core concepts that will be reused and expanded on throughout the book. For example, risk contributions: In the discussion of the simulation-based approach to market risk, key practical concepts such as how to reduce the calculation times by either or both of (i) reducing the number of scenarios and (ii) reducing pricing time are also discussed.

The second market risk chapter is focused on more advanced topics, but is still of significant practical importance. Here we consider extensions of risk measures to a general portfolio profit-and-loss distribution and in particular how one can decompose risk into contributing subportfolios and instruments as well as into risk factors of relative importance. It is by now well-known that the multivariate normal or log-normal model for risk factors is a simplifying assumption in practice and does not meet the stylized facts of financial risk returns. We therefore focus in depth on what are the stylized facts of returns and which models can capture the stylized facts and perform well in terms of backtesting. Other important practical topics discussed in this chapter include how to scale risk over time in risk models as well as how to incorporate market illiquidity in market risk models. Stress testing has quickly emerged as one of the core risk activities in banks and we discuss a structured approach to stress testing as well as how to integrate model- and stress testing–based views. Another important topic for risk analysis is optimal risk-based decision making. This is one of the core activities of risk managers: specifically, to analyze and understand optimal portfolio hedges and replicate portfolios for subsequent risk measurement and management. The advanced market risk chapter ends with a note on the very recent developments in the regulation for market risk.

The fourth and fifth chapters of the book move the focus to credit risks. The fourth chapter focuses on issuer portfolio credit risk—for exposures in both the trading book and the banking book. In practice, portfolio credit risk economic capital for large corporate exposures uses models founded on the structural Merton approach to corporate claims. In the portfolio setting, multifactor models are often used to describe the credit index of the corporate and referred to as *latent variable models* as the credit index itself is unobserved. Economic capital and capital allocation for bond exposures in the trading book usually have to account for trading behavior and liquidity horizons. With the relatively recent regulatory incremental risk charge for credit exposures in the trading book, economic capital models and regulatory capital are becoming more aligned.

Portfolio credit risk models for the banking book are usually founded in the reduced form credit scoring or credit state transition models used at account or customer level. The models are typically calibrated on large pools. The transition models can be dynamic and include macroeconomic variables or be static and rely on an ex-post inclusion of macroeconomic variables describing default and migration behavior over time. The inclusion of macroeconomic variables is a prerequisite for building an economic capital model for credit risk. Consequently, we focus on extending credit scoring models to include time series information and how the models can be subsequently used in calculating economic capital. A specific credit scoring–based portfolio credit risk model that is quite popular due to avoiding simulation is the CreditRisk$^+$ model.

The distinction between structural and reduced form models is, however, largely artificial and is more driven by a calibration approach rather than model formulation. For example, with a large portfolio we can identify the latent credit index in the structural approach with the historical empirical default frequencies of the large portfolio. Because of this relation between models and also because both models derive default correlations from correlated macroeconomic drivers the models can be easily integrated for a firmwide portfolio credit risk economic capital view. The correlated macroeconomic driver approach to specifying dependence in credit risk models is often referred to as a *conditional independence approach*. This is because conditional on the macroeconomic factors defaults are independent. Another, more direct way to introduce default correlation is to link the default events explicitly, for example, assigning a jump in default probability of one firm conditional on default for another firm. Such models are referred to as *contagion* or *feedback models*.

An important application of portfolio credit risk models is stress testing. While the second market risk chapter reviews general structured approaches to stress testing, applicable also in the contex of portfolio credit risk, we also consider explicit examples of credit stress testing with macroeconomic scenarios in the portfolio credit risk chapter. Due to the recent firmwide stress testing regulation in both Europe and the United States, the credit book stress testing has gained increasing importance. This has also called for an extension of the credit portfolio models originally developed for internal economic capital calculations.

After a brief discussion on credit risk mitigation and transfer we end the portfolio credit risk chapter with a recap of the regulatory capital for credit risk with a focus on the Basel II/III capital charge for banking book exposures.

The fifth chapter of the book is again focused on credit risk but now the focus is on counterparty credit risk in derivative trades and the associated pricing. While credit risk in bonds is usually accounted for with market risk spreads in discounting of bond cash flows the credit risk adjustment for derivatives is more complex. This is due to the bilateral nature of credit risk and the fact that exposure is random. The recent financial crisis has brought the counterparty risk in the trading book into the limelight. Exposure risk profiling accounting for netting, margin agreement, and counterparty credit quality is key to counterparty credit risk measurement and pricing. A particularly important topic is how to account for wrong-way risks, that is, the expectation that high counterparty default rates will likely occur at the same time that exposure is high. Counterparty risk managers and trading desks not only need to price the credit risk but also need to manage the tail credit risk. With mitigation tools like frequent collateral posting, the counterparty credit risk is reduced but also creates other financial risks such as the liquidity risk of funding collateral requirements and potential funding costs of collateral. Recently, more opportunities for banks to clear counterparty credit risk centrally are available and the decision whether to pass a certain trade or a set of trades to central clearing can be a delicate one in practice. We end the chapter with a discussion of the recent Basel III regulation for counterparty credit risk.

The sixth and seventh chapters of the book are dedicated to advanced topics in asset and liability management with emphasis in liquidity risk and profitability. There are already many books that give a good introduction to the classical asset and liability management concepts, such as liquidity and interest rate risk measurement with gap reports, net interest margin analysis, and economic value views on the balance sheet. In these chapters we therefore assume the reader already has a basic understanding of classical asset and liability management.

The sixth chapter is focused on the now more than ever important topic of liquidity risk. Liquidity risk is essentially a consequential risk but by itself can lead to insolvency as was experienced in the 2007 financial crisis. Our approach to liquidity focuses on quantitative methods that are not just for risk measurement and monitoring but are also key to risk hedging, risk-based performance analysis, and optimal decision making. We discuss both the rationale and the practice of scenario-based approaches to liquidity and how liquidity risk can be measured and managed. The focus is on the structural mismatch liquidity risk as well as the contingency liquidity risk. The core of the management of contingency liquidity risk is to earmark a liquidity hedging portfolio and test its sufficiency frequently. The decision on the size and composition of the liquidity hedging portfolio is of importance. This is because the portfolio carries opportunity costs that can directly impact the banks' competitiveness in product pricing. Using advanced analysis and optimal models of liquidity hedging and structural liquidity planning is therefore an emerging core activity in banks. While liquidity risk measurement and allocation is usually more complex than for market and credit risk—largely due to the inherent path-dependent nature of solvency liquidity risk—it can still be allocated consistently. The consistent allocation of liquidity risk is also of significant importance in creating pricing incentives that reward providers of liquidity and penalize users of liquidity. We end the liquidity risk chapter with discussion of recent regulatory developments and regulatory-required reporting metrics.

The seventh chapter is dedicated to transfer pricing of risks and the associated profitability analysis of cash flows and how banks use transfer pricing in practice to create incentives for value creation. The funds transfer price includes all the perceived risk costs and expenses to signal the required spread for customer profitability. Funds transfer rates are also key in expanding banks' traditional asset and liability management from an aggregate level to granular levels, in particular in profitability analysis such as net interest margin analysis and economic value views. With synthetic funds transfer instruments the banks' profit and loss is essentially split up into the branch net interest margin and the residual profit and loss of treasury. The treasury manages centrally the residual portfolio of issued synthetic funds transfer instruments to branches versus the actual funding. For most banks, there is structural interest rate risk and liquidity risk arising in the residual portfolio due to the fact that customers in general want both long-term loans and quick access to the deposits they made. The funds transfer instruments balance balance sheets and allow profitability views to be decomposed to granular levels such as account, product type, and branch.

Firmwide risk management breaks the traditional silo approach to risk and allows banks to have a holistic view of the risk. This is our focus in the concluding eighth and ninth chapters of this book. The firmwide risk chapters also serve as good concluding chapters of the book as we refer back to the specific risk models and methods discussed in the previous chapters and apply them to the firmwide-level risk management.

In Chapter 8 we focus on the firmwide risk aggregation, which enables banks to measure, allocate, and manage risk from a global optimal instead of a local optimal view. Risk aggregation methods have recently developed significantly with more flexible models to capture the exact granular dependence between risk types and business lines.

Another aspect of firmwide risk management is firmwide scenario analysis and stress testing, which is our focus in the final chapter of this book. Two approaches can in practice be used for the firmwide scenario analysis and stress testing. First, one can aggregate the results of different scenarios from the specific, granular modeling systems used to calculate market risk, credit risk, and so forth. Second, one can create a macroeconomic firmwide risk model that captures the main risks for integrated scenarios across risk types and different portfolios. Usually, in this second approach, the firmwide risk is approximated using the core risk drivers for the different risks and portfolios. The benefit of the approach is an integrated view of firmwide risk and that comprehensive scenarios across risk types can be created in one system. The downside is of course that it is hard to fully capture all risks and positions in the specific systems such as the market risk system.

The firmwide stress testing—with the aim of forward-looking the banks' balance sheet and income statement and thus the capital adequacy under stress—has picked up relatively recently with the introduction of the Comprehensive Capital Analysis and Review (CCAR) and European Banking Authority (EBA) stress tests. It requires banks to create so-called satellite models to materialize the impact of the macroeconomic stress on the specific bank risk factors impacting the earnings and balance sheet. The firmwide macroeconomic stress testing approach also necessitates a close collaboration between the bank's risk experts responsible for generating earnings and loss projection under stress, as well as financial and capital management experts responsible for analyzing the bank's available capital and planning future capital needs. The comprehensive results of firmwide risk measurement and stress testing give a unique opportunity to integrate the risk and finance view with firmwide projected risk being used in forward-looking balance sheet and income statement, hence being essential for scenario-based financial planning.

Acknowledgments

Both authors would like to thank their families for their patience and support during the writing of this book. Jimmy would like to thank his wife, Ann-Louise, and his children, Izabel, Ellen, Nelly, and Leo. Wei would like to thank his wife, June I-Chun, and his daughter, Vivian. We also appreciate the support of our colleagues during the writing of this book. The authors have also benefited from idea exchanges with risk professionals in various seminars and conferences. Since this book is based partly on earlier published risk research, we would also like to thank our previous research coauthors.

Finally, we would also like to thank the Wiley copy editor for the patience in the editing of this book and SAS Institute (our current employer) for allowing us to write this book and granting us the right to use SAS software to develop all the examples in this book. The opinions expressed in this book are, however, those of the authors and do not necessarily reflect the view of SAS Institute.

CHAPTER 1

Introduction

BANKS AND RISK MANAGEMENT

Risk management has gone through a long journey in the history of corporate development. Modigliani and Miller (1958) proposed that in an environment without contracting cost, information asymmetry, and taxes, risk management among other financial policies is irrelevant to firm value creation. Sometimes it even lowers the value of the firm because it is seldom free. In the last decades the topic on the role of risk management in a value creation–oriented corporate world—especially in banks—has driven the evolution of the risk management practice. With the development of the computational technology and the witness of several major financial distresses, a sound infrastructure of the risk management systems becomes not only a regulatory concern but also corporate competitive advantage reality. However, the debate of the value and role of risk management in a financial institution still goes on. Some institutions retain the thought that risk management is just an answer to regulatory compliance or a defense system. The modern financial theory based on the capital asset pricing model and other related models is fundamental to the no-arbitrage principle. That is, excess returns can only be achieved by taking risks. This principle makes it necessary to recognize that risk management is not just a preference but is accompanied by the profit-chasing mandate of corporations.

The discussion on bank-specific risk management topics has to be picked up from the existence of banks as intermediary between borrowers and investors. The development of banks and the reliance on banks in the economic activities show that banks are a special corporate that provide unique services for parties from both sides. Banks in general provide special value to the corporate world by playing the role of three major intermediations: information, risk, and liquidity. As the intermediary between borrowers and investors, banks have more information about the type of resource available and wanted as well as the preferences of the two sides. This information asymmetry gives banks dominant roles in the resource allocation of the economy. Banks get their rewards by creating efficiency in the allocation process. In addition, banks are viewed as delegated monitors or evaluators of their borrowers. Because of the scale of economy and specialty, banks can provide monitoring services at a lower cost than the non-bank lenders. A bank must be responsible for the safety of the money from their lenders. Banks also offer insurance against shocks to a consumer's consumption by smoothing the resource allocation along a multihorizon path for the consumer. When the consumer has excess money, the money can be lent through banks to earn returns for the future. In case the consumer runs into a money crunch, emergency funds can be borrowed from the bank, which will have to be paid back from future income. Hence, banks' payment systems effectively connect the spatially and temporally separated trades.

The primary obligation of corporate entities, including banks, is to create value for their shareholders. However, through the intermediation service a bank provides to its customers, risk management in banks also brings social benefits as well. This is because banks not only create value for their shareholders but also have strong impact on the value of their customers. It is obvious that a bank's insolvency can bring the loss of its creditors. Risk management is in the core of the banking value creation and also a public benefit. Risk management is not just a certain methodology in a bank. It is about a culture and an end-to-end process that spirally moves a bank up into a value chain that demonstrates its core competitive advantage against its peers. A sound risk management process spans from identification, to measurement, to monitoring, to control, to optimal decision making, and back to identification.

As an information, risk, and liquidity intermediary, banks possess unique information on the general macroeconomic condition and customer and market status. Hence, banks have a unique position in risk identification. A well-known fact in any social science study is that past experience is not a guaranteed prediction to the future—although history does tend to repeat itself in disguised fashion. One of the prominent difficulties is the discovery of so-called "black swan" risks. In his famous book on the topic, Taleb (2007) borrows the term "black swan" for the situation where seemingly impossible or nonexistent events actually occur. Sometime overreliance on past experience will lead to loss of sight of a forthcoming crisis. One of the lessons learned from the 2007 financial crisis is to engage a forward-looking risk discovery practice that can identify risks that may not have existed in the past.

Traditionally financial risk measurement has been categorized into market, credit, liquidity, and other risks. Market risk represents the risks that are primarily driven by market variables including interest rates, foreign exchange rates, equities, and commodity prices. Credit risk is the risk underlying the default risk of counterparties ranging from retail customers to trading counterparties. Market risk and credit risk have traditionally been separately managed in most banking institutions. In traditional asset and liability management, market risk and credit risk have been separated in the way that the asset and liability committee manages interest rate risk impacts on profitability, and liquidity risks while the business units are concerned with the credit risk. It is an increasing trend to look at comprehensive risks in a more holistic way. All the potential risks in a particular business line or book are analyzed together without an artificial separation into driving risk types. For some risks this is also a prerequisite, for example, liquidity risk, which is usually a consequential risk from other risks.

Risk assessment includes both qualitative and quantitative measurement of the risk exposures of a bank. Such assessments require a joint effort of expert knowledge and scientific discovery techniques. Diebold et al. (2010) provide a knowledge theory that classifies risks into known, unknown, and unknowable. From a measurement point of view, a known risk is both identified and completely modeled. Note that a known risk is not deterministic but can be well measured. Diebold et al. (2010) specifically refer the models to fully specified probability distributions of potential profit and losses. An unknown risk is known to exist but cannot be modeled properly. A consumer behavioral risk such as prepayment risk serves as a simple illustration of the difference between these two risk types. The prepayment risk is certainly a well-identified risk. For consumer portfolios the well-specified statistical prepayment models can only be claimed to be known to a pool of a large number of such exposures. But it is much harder to predict the prepayment for a particular consumer. Unknowable events are events we experience as a surprise, arising from unseen events that are not identified.

One important factor to successful risk identification and measurement is data. Data quality is critical to identification and measurement of risks. Statistical analysis methodologies are often used in practice to overcome the issues in the observed data. For example, actual loss data are often censored and truncated to cause only partially available data for the study of a loss. In risk measurement the main target is often to estimate the probability of extreme losses. This is of course a much more difficult problem than estimating average losses and puts strong reliance on the model at hand being approximately a correct descriptor of potential extreme losses that can happen. Clearly, in risk measurement the analysis of model risk is central to the risk measurement process. In practice, data scarcity and disparateness also affect the measurement of the tail risk and are central components in practice in validating specific model assumptions.

The risks identified and assessed by a bank, as part of the financial disclosure, are subject to monitoring and reporting that must serve three different audiences: management, regulator, and the market. Shareholders, management, and debt holders are all motivated to manage risk, but they all have their own incentives, which are in some cases not aligned. For banks, given the role they play as financial intermediary in the society, they may also be viewed as having an obligation to the stability of the entire financial system. Due to the importance of banking stability to the entire economic system, bank regulators and the market also demand risk management disclosure of banks. Regulators want to make sure each individual bank operates fairly and responsibly. At the same time, regulators are also responsible to make sure the entire banking system remains stable under contagion effects.

To manage the level of risk in a portfolio, banks use risk mitigation tools. For example, for market risk, various hedging strategies are available to reduce the risk level in the portfolio. For credit risk, financial and physical collaterals and guarantees are popular risk mitigations. For liquidity risk, the ultimate risk mitigation tool is cash to neutralize the funding gap. With the recent development of the financial system and capital markets banks also have more innovative ways of risk mitigation. This includes credit derivatives to transfer the risk. Governments and central banks can also offer banks risk mitigation vehicles through guarantees and liquidity facilities.

A bank cannot merely control risk passively. It must offer its expertise in the risk intermediation area to remain valuable. One of the goals of risk management is to find an efficient way to mitigate risk so that the bank can have a tolerable risk level. For each identified risk, risk measurement helps measure the risk level and finds the right mitigation approach to protect the bank from taking unsustainable risk. For example, traditionally banks borrow short and lend long term to earn the term premium of interest rates. In this practice banks face both liquidity risk (as the bank must guarantee to be able to roll over its short-term funding) and interest rate risk (as the bank has to make sure, over the life of the lending instrument, the average short-term funding rate can be effectively lower than the long-term lending rate). In an economy full of uncertainty, it is almost impossible to fully secure any of these two guarantees. Banks must use dedicated hedging instruments like interest rate derivatives and liquidity facilities. Of course, hedging risk usually comes at a cost, reducing the inherent expected term premium to the bank.

As many of a bank's investment decisions are made under uncertainty, the ultimate decision weighs in the expected profits as well as the risks associated with the investment. Traditional value creation in a bank focuses on risk-adjusted returns and the bank's thresholds for investments contributing favorably. However, a bank's risk appetite, referred to as the level of risk the institution is willing to take in its value creation process, may also exclude the bank from participating in certain types of investments regardless of current market premiums. To implement the risk appetite in the business operations, a bank must monitor the materialized risk level in the bank against the risk limits and set strategic objectives optimally following the risk policies, all established by the risk appetite. Risk-based performance analysis of a business unit should preferably reflect the risk contribution of the unit to the entire organization.

Besides the economic motivations and regulatory requirements, the fast evolution of the computation technology contributes greatly to the shaping of the modern risk management practice. Modern technology allows banks to reduce risk calculation times and respond faster in business operations to new risk levels. It also allows more granular risk analysis and risk decompositions to account, trade, and position level, enabling more accurate views on exactly where in the bank's books shareholder value is created. The modern technology also allows banks to adopt more sophisticated approaches to scenario analysis and risk-based portfolio optimization.

Although this book focuses on the quantitative aspects of risk management we must emphasize that quantitative methodology and risk analytics are by no means the whole spectrum. At the very core of risk management is risk governance. It governs the entire risk management process. At the same time, it connects risk management to the entire business operations of a bank. Transparency is also an important factor. The key stakeholders must understand the assumptions and business rationale of the risk methodologies— although they do not have to know mathematical model details. Risk model development, validation, and deployment teams have responsibility to make sure models are soundly developed, implemented, and validated. However, they also have the important responsibility of communication.

EVOLUTION OF BANK CAPITAL REGULATION

Regulation is of course a strong driver for banks' evolution in risk management practices and the implementation of sound risk management systems. The costs of meeting regulatory compliance for banks have been significantly increasing over the years. The costs are both direct and operational related to implementation of sophisticated risk and compliance systems, disclosure processes, and retaining skilled people. In addition, there are significant indirect opportunity costs faced by banks as the new regulations have increased the minimum regulatory capital buffers. Over the three generations of the Basel accord, banks have seen ever-increasing capital requirements for the different risk types.

The first Basel accord in 1988 (Basel Committee, 1988) did not have a substantial impact on operational costs and risk systems; it simply required banks to slot credit exposures into gross tiers of risk-weighted assets. The next generation of the regulation focused on amending the regulatory standardized and internal models approach to market risk in 1996 (Basel Committee, 1996). At this time, many banks implemented internal value at risk (VaR) models on which capital requirements were based. The more sophisticated use of simulation models to calculate and price market risk for many banks drove investment into specialized risk technology and risk systems as well as skilled people. For the first time many banks recruited large teams of risk quants to manage the market risk models. In day-to-day business operations traders found their risk limits on books transitioning from simple delta and gamma limits to more sophisticated VaR limits.

The Basel I accord had a very gross assignment of risk-weighted assets for credits and had been criticized by many banks for not being risk sensitive since its inception. The next major update to the regulation therefore came with Basel II in 2005 (Basel Committee, 2005a), which required banks to report more sophisticated risk-weighted assets for credit risk than in the first accord. Basel II also brought necessary sophistication into the regulatory capital paradigm by introducing three pillars that set the minimal capital requirement (pillar 1), a supervisory review that encourages banks to improve their internal risk management practice in credit risk (pillar 2), and proper disclosure and market disclosure (pillar 3). Many banks were required to adopt the advanced internal ratings-based approach for retail and small and medium-sized-firm credits. For large corporates the foundation internal ratings–based approach was used and was largely based on external ratings. With Basel II the Basel accord for credit risk was model based for the first time and required banks to estimate model input parameters such as the probability of default, loss given default, and exposure at default for all its credit exposures. Basel II hence drove a significant investment of banks into credit scoring models, processes, and systems. The statistical modeling approach to analyze credit quality created a demand for skilled statisticians in banks. Large credit scoring model development and validation teams were built. At the same time the relative importance of the traditional qualitative credit analyst departments in banks decreased and credit lending was largely industrialized. The Basel II accord also instituted a standard practice for banks in risk-adjusted pricing of their credits. Hence, regulation drove significant investment not only in risk systems but also in implementing processes in the day-to-day use of traditional banking systems like loan systems. Banks were also looking for ways to arbitrage on their required capital, which contributed to a rising interest in packaging and issuing securitization instruments on some of the credit portfolios.

At the time of implementation of Basel II an important discussion arose between banks and regulators about the potential countercyclicality of the new credit capital buffers. This referred to the situation that, at good times, when the probability of default and loss given default inputs to the risk-weighted assets model was low capital requirements were also low. At bad times the opposite situation would occur and increase capital requirements. Potentially, this situation could lead to banks having to raise capital and increase offered customer rates at the exact time of a recession, contributing to countercyclicality. The regulatory response to stabilize capital requirements and avoid the countercyclicality was to demand the use of stressed and long-run probability of defaults and loss given defaults in calculation of capital requirements.

A remaining critique of the Basel II accord for credit risk is the fact that risk-weighted assets are summable and hence the regulatory capital does not take into account concentration and diversification. Many banks therefore have developed their own economic capital models for credit risk. At the time banks were implementing the Basel II accord for credit risk there was also a lively discussion about whether one should use the regulatory risk capital versus the economic capital model allocated risk when pricing credits.[1]

While Basel II certainly had the most significant impact on banks' credit risk analysis methods and lending processes the Basel II accord also instituted new capital requirements for operational risk, and in its second pillar focused also on banks' general process for capital assessment, with, for example, general guidelines on specific topics such as liquidity risk.

In 2005 the Basel II accord also added more advanced capital requirements for over-the-counter (OTC) derivatives counterparty exposure at default (Basel Committee, 2005b). The original 1988 amendment to Basel I used simplified current exposure and regulatory prescribed add-on factors. The new regulation allowed banks to use either an updated current

---

[1]While the economic capital model, regulatory required capital levels, and actual held capital were quite different in practice, some banks rescaled the economic capital model capital allocation so that they summed to the actual capital, achieving a full allocation of capital with concentration effects.

exposure approach, a standardized method, or an internal models approach to estimate the exposure. The calculated exposure was subsequently used in the Basel II prescribed model for risk capital. In the internal model method banks could use advanced multihorizon simulation-based approaches to price OTC derivatives at future times and subsequently aggregate exposure per netting set agreement. In addition banks could take into account collateral such as margining when estimating regulatory exposures. The regulatory exposure measure was subsequently adjusted by a regulatory assigned or internally calibrated alpha parameter to control for wrong-way risk and model risk. The regulatory assigned alpha was 1.4 and the internal model floor for alpha was set at 1.2. At this time many of the larger banks expanded their current market risk systems or invested in completely new systems to calculate the regulatory exposure measures for the OTC derivatives book. Hence, again significant investments were made in systems, processes, and skilled people. It also became standard practice to apply and monitor limits on counterparty exposures using a worst-case exposure measure—usually referred to as potential future exposure. Significant time was also spent on calibrating internal estimates of alpha to bring capital requirements down. These estimates focused on deriving an implied bank-specific alpha using the economic capital model as comparison to the regulatory exposure model.

The same Basel paper that introduced new capital requirements methods for OTC derivatives in 2005 also opened up a way for banks to more effectively account for credit hedges in Basel II. Previously, a hedged credit exposure could use the credit quality of the credit hedge issuer instead of the credit itself in the Basel II risk-weighted asset formula. This was of course only beneficial if the credit quality of the credit hedge issuer was better than on the credit itself. The substitution approach was criticized for being too conservative—essentially assuming perfect correlation between default events of the credit hedge issuer and the credit. The new double default formula allowed a more favorable approach than substitution by explicitly incorporating the correlation between the credit and the credit hedge issuer credit quality.

The next major change to the Basel regulation appeared in 2009, called Basel 2.5 (Basel Committee, 2009a, b) and was focused on updated capital requirements for market risk in trading book and a new capital charge for credit risk in the trading book, called the *incremental risk charge*. The new market risk charge added a stressed value at risk charge to the current charge for internal market risk models,[2] substantially increasing market risk capital requirements. The incremental risk charge was focused mainly on bonds in the trading book with liquidity trading horizons assigned to credits. No model was prescribed but since the regulatory requirement concerned the trading book and hence large counterparties, many banks used their existing portfolio credit risk models for large firms inspired by the Merton (1974) structural model. A particular popular implementation was the multifactor approach describing the firm's credit quality in terms of observed financial indices. Initially, some banks deemed the new incremental risk charge model as too complex, especially the required mapping of trading book credit exposures to liquidity trading horizons. This was because many banks' existing credit portfolio models at this time did not have a concept of trading and liquidity horizon, hence meeting the regulation required enhancements to existing systems.

While Basel 2.5 was being implemented in banks the regulators were also working on a more comprehensive response to the experiences in the 2007 financial crisis. The new

---

[2]The stressed VaR charge was implemented as the VaR obtained when market risk models were calibrated on a stressful period in the past.

Basel III accord—initiated in 2010–2011—introduced new, complementary capital and liquidity requirements (Basel Committee, 2011a, 2013a). On the firmwide capital side existing Basel II rules for capital were strengthened with, for example, new, more conservative levels of Tier 1 capital and requirements on countercyclical capital buffers.[3]

In Basel III a completely new capital requirement was introduced for OTC derivatives that was in addition to the 2005 method, founded in calculating default loss–based capital based on banks' exposures. The new credit valuation adjustment charge capitalized mark-to-market changes in counterparty exposures in addition to the 2005 default charge.[4] The rationale was that during the 2007 crisis a large part of the losses observed in the OTC derivative books of banks were due to mark-to-market and not realized. Still, banks had to devalue their OTC books in the crisis by substantial amounts due to sharply increasing market credit spreads of deal counterparties. The pricing and hedging of credit risk valuation adjustment was not a new practice. Many of the large investment banks had already adopted special credit valuation adjustment desks and invested in cutting-edge technology risk systems to actively price and manage credit valuation adjustments after the 2007 financial crisis. With the new regulation the investment in new credit valuation systems also spread to banks with smaller OTC books. However, the need for dynamic hedging of credit valuation adjustment was not as imminent as for the investment banks and many of the smaller banks still view credit valuation adjustments as a reserve component rather than a market-priced and hedged component.[5]

Alongside the new Basel III charge for credit valuation adjustments the most significant new Basel III charge was the requirement for banks to hold dedicated liquidity buffers. The new Basel III liquidity risk regulation underscores the importance of managing a liquidity contingency buffer. The focus is on maintaining a high-quality liquidity portfolio that can hedge liquidity outflows under stress scenarios, that is, to generate sufficient counterbalancing capacity. The key minimum reporting standards in the Basel III liquidity risk framework are a short-term, 30-day liquidity coverage ratio, and a longer-term structural ratio to address structural liquidity mismatches. There are also metrics for monitoring liquidity, for example, the monitoring of maturity mismatch, funding concentration, and unencumbered assets available (available for sale). Holding a liquidity buffer incurs opportunity cost just as holding capital does. Hence, one of the core activities by banks in their approach to Basel III liquidity risk is to institute a pricing of liquidity risk and hence pass the buffer costs to the consumers of the buffer. Contingent liquidity risk—which is what the liquidity buffer is held for—is mainly attributed to off–balance sheet commitments such as facilities that can be drawn by the bank's counterparties, but also for other items such as sudden funding withdrawals.

In 2012, 2013, and 2014, the Basel 2.5 2009 market risk updates were further enhanced (Basel Committee, 2012, 2013b, 2014a). New proposed market risk requirements included a move from value at risk to expected shortfall as a risk measure (also referred to as conditional value at risk, or CVaR, which is the term we will use in this book), introduction

---

[3]For example, there is both a 2.5% general capital conservation buffer as well as a 2.5% discretionary countercyclical capital buffer. The capital conservation buffer is designed to ensure that banks build up capital buffers outside periods of stress that can be drawn down as losses are incurred. Hence, outside periods of stress, banks should hold buffers of capital above the regulatory minimum.

[4]The credit valuation adjustment prices the fair mark-to-market adjustment of trades due to counterparty credit risk.

[5]However, the regulators have been clear in this matter. The Basel III credit valuation adjustment charge should be computed based on market credit spreads and not based on historical default information.

of longer liquidity horizons than the current 10 days for illiquid trades,[6] and a newly revised mandatory standardized approach—even for banks currently using the internal models approach. As CVaR is the expected tail loss beyond VaR market risk capital can increase with this new measure, although the regulators tend to agree to reduce the confidence level from 99% to 97.5% for the internal model–based approach.[7] However, the introduction of longer liquidity horizons than 10 days will surely increase market risk capital requirements for illiquid portfolios.

In addition to the evolution of the Basel regulation there have been several regional initiatives requiring banks to analyze capital sufficiency. These initiatives are especially focused on stress testing as the vehicle for analyzing the soundness of banks' current capital base. For example, in Europe EBA has required banks to report comprehensive stress tests, and in the United States, CCAR also requires banks to stress test their firmwide capital, in contrast to model-based charges, where the stress tests focus on putting capital limits under prescribed regulatory stress scenarios. The stress tests are by nature macroeconomic firmwide and focus on projected income and capital statements under stress. The relatively recent focus of regulators on stress testing as a key tool for analyzing risk and capital sufficiency is founded in the view that classical model-based charges represent mainly a historical view—either in terms of calibrating model parameters on history, or directly as in historical simulation approaches. It can also be viewed as a regulatory trend in distrust of models. Stress testing is viewed as a forward-looking risk analysis tool that should complement risk analysis based on historically calibrated models. Compared to model-based risk charges the stress tests and scenario analysis impacts can also be easier to communicate to the different stakeholders.

The focus on stress testing as a complementary supervisory tool followed quickly after the 2007 financial crisis. In the United States, the Supervisory Capital Assessment Program (SCAP) started in 2009 to focus on comprehensive stress test programs for US banks. It was followed by today's CCAR stress tests. Both SCAP and CCAR surely inspired the more recently introduced European EBA stress tests. The Basel regulation also promoted stress testing as a complement to model-based charges after the 2007 financial crisis. In 2009 the Basel committee paper on principles for sound stress testing practices and supervision promoted a comprehensive stress testing approach in banks (Basel Committee, 2009c), the concept of *reverse stress testing*. That is, identification of the still plausible but severe impact scenarios was made into stress testing practice in banks.

Guidelines on banks' capital planning process were introduced already in pillar 2 of the Basel II 2005 accord. However, the 2007 financial crisis and the stress test initiatives by (for example) EBA after the crisis have increased the importance of regulators promoting a sound capital planning process. Basel 2014 (Basel Committee, 2014b) focuses on guidelines for firmwide capital planning and in particular that banks take a forward-looking scenario-based approach to capital planning. As a response there is an increasing practice in banks to integrate the risk view into traditional financial statements such as profit-and-loss statements and capital views (balance sheet views). For profit-and-loss statements this requires banks to convert risk systems stress test outputs such as scenario expected losses into effects on banking book net interest margins, trading book profit and loss, and subsequently into scenario

---

[6]The original market risk VaR requirement considers a 10-day holding period for all positions. The introduction of liquidity horizons between 10 days and 1 year allows a segmentation on position close-out times connected to the position's market liquidity.

[7]For a normal distribution CVaR at confidence level 97.5% is equal to the VaR at 99% confidence level.

operating profit from stressed revenues and expenses. This integration of risk analysis into the finance view is important as it explicitly links the results of complex risk analysis to future potential income and balance sheet statements. Hence, it enhances the understanding and communication of risk analysis impacts on traditional financial measures, both within the bank and with external stakeholders.

As regulations have evolved and surely will continue to evolve banks need to further invest in systems, processes, and skilled people to minimally meet the regulation. However, regulatory capital requirements are only the minimal risk benchmarks. Banks must have a clear risk appetite definition that serves as internal management guidelines. Business policies and growth strategy must adhere to these guidelines. A natural question is whether a bank that invests more in risk management analytics and risk management processes can take advantage of this in business and hence give a return on the added investment. That is, can banks compete on risk analytics and the embedding of sound risk analytics in day-to-day processes such as product pricing?

CREATING VALUE FROM RISK MANAGEMENT

The use of sophisticated risk models and stress tests in understanding aggregate currency amounts at risk for the bank's portfolios is only one of the applications of risk analysis. Perhaps of even more importance is to understand the relative risks of positions and sub-portfolios. This is because relative risks are important in the process of risk-based value creation for banks. A clear understanding of risk costs down to granular levels improves the bank's understanding of which current products, customers, and counterparties are profitable. Moreover, with granular knowledge on risk costs the bank can be more competitive in product pricing. It can also avoid participation in markets where the risk compensation is not sufficient to cover the bank's risk costs. Clearly, banks that invest more in scientific data and economic rationale investigations on their customers and the market behavior are better prepared to capture such aspects in their risk models and hence subsequently take advantage of the knowledge.

The ultimate value creation from risk analytics is realized when it is deployed in day-to-day business strategy. As a result of regulation but also driven by market competitiveness banks are investing more in systems and processes to accurately price products and create strong incentives for value creation in their business lines. For example, branches' loans and deposits carry funds transfer rates with associated risk costs to signal the minimal customer rate needed for profitability. For traders, the fair values of the swap deals carry credit valuation adjustments and funding cost adjustments to signal to the trader the client spread needed to be profitable. It is also an increasing trend to centralize the hedging and risk management of more and more of the risk costs experienced in business. A centralization allows banks to better understand their exact concentration in certain markets, counterparties, and products, and, depending on a bank's risk appetite, measures can be taken to increase internal product charges or making changes to the product design. However, the centralization of risk measurement and management must also factor in that in some cases at least part of the risk responsibility has to be decentralized, both because of information asymmetry and to create the right incentives within the organization to actively manage the risk. For example, branches may possess unique information about local business that central credit models cannot capture. Removing the branches' responsibility for credit risk losses may therefore not be optimal.

Banks' risk models and risk analytics cannot be too simple. They must capture all the relevant risks down to the relevant level they are used and in particular the stylized facts that have been experienced in the past. Risk models must also include elements of forward-looking behavior—not relying solely on model validation—based on history. Since much of the business value from risk analytics derives from risk-based pricing there are strong demands that risk analytics can appropriately rank the relative risks of products. Banks with poor granular-level risk models and risk analytics run the risk of mispricing relative to the market and eventually end up with the nonprofitable portfolios. Banks with strong granular-level risk analytics and empirically and economically vetted risk models can be more competitive and can also avoid creating excessive risks in portfolios. They also create more trust in the organization for the use of risk analytics. It has become a practice sometimes to refer to model simplicity itself as an absolute good. The relevant concept is relative simplicity. For example, we would favor a more simplistic model instead of a more complex model if sufficient evidence is not available for the added complexity. As Albert Einstein once said, everything should be kept as simple as possible but not simpler than that.

Throughout this book readers can find numerous topics on risk-adjusted performance and risk-constrained optimization methodologies that help banks create value from proper risk management methods and models. Accurate risk measurement and monitoring of risk levels is clearly one core objective of risk management models. Using risk management models to also aid risk-based decision making, especially the performance analysis and profit maximization, also makes risk management models central to the business.

FINANCIAL RISK SYSTEMS

Besides all the economic and business drivers, the advance in the modern risk management is greatly indebted to innovations in technology. In fact the birth of the financial theories underlying the modern risk management practice, including Markowitz portfolio theory, Sharpe's capital asset pricing theory, Ross arbitrage pricing theory, and Black-Scholes option pricing, coincided with the commercialization of the computer technology. It is not an exaggeration to say that the growth of risk management goes hand-in-hand with the development of computational technology.

A financial risk management system is certainly the platform where the quantitative risk management methodologies materialize in practice. It usually refers to a computer system that can be used to

- manage risk models and risk data,
- construct risk scenarios,
- evaluate the bank portfolio under the risk scenarios,
- report on risk measures, and,
- in some cases also assist in risk based decision making.

Traditionally banks have employed silo risk systems to calculate the different types of risks such as market, credit, and asset and liability management risk. Risk aggregation to firmwide capital levels is then a post-process on the silo system's risk distributions or risk measures.

While the risk calculation itself is the core of a financial risk management system the system capabilities also rely on its risk infrastructure and what risk technology the system can use. The risk infrastructure should support the use of the system, for example, with proper workflows and configuration capabilities. The risk technology should be aligned to the requirements of the risk calculation. In many cases the development of the risk calculation algorithms and methods themselves must also take into account the risk technology to take full advantage of the computer resources such as processors and memory. In our discussion of the financial risk system's capabilities we will decompose the system capabilities into three components:

1. Risk analytics or risk calculation capabilities
2. Risk infrastructure capabilities
3. Risk technology capabilities

While we hope this book provides enough detailed discussion of the risk analysis methods to be successfully implemented in banks' current financial risk management systems, we would also like to give some explicit instructions on the core components to consider when constructing or implementing new financial risk systems. Indeed, constructing or implementing a new risk system is not a trivial task. Banks often face many competing challenges, such as a balanced decision weighing the trade-off between cost and performance, short-term and long-term needs, regulatory and internal compliance, security and new technology, and risk and finance reconciliation.

Risk Analytics

A risk system can be designed to only calculate (for example) market risk or can be designed more comprehensively to be able to calculate risk across many risk types. In general, a financial risk system implements a risk calculation flow where at each step in the flow risk analysts can assign or create new methods or models that are used in the risk analysis. Examples include pricing functions, market simulation models, and credit risk evaluation models. Many modern risk systems are designed to be comprehensive in the analysis of financial risk. That is, cover all the financial risks of a position that can come from market, credit, and liquidity risks. To accommodate the required risk analytics the risk calculation flow follows a few core sequential steps:

1. The calibration of risk factor models and joint scenario generation from risk factor models such as models for equity prices, interest rates, credit drivers, behavioral risk factors, etc. The scenario generation also includes the creation of ad-hoc stress scenarios.
2. The transformation of risk factors used in scenario models or ad-hoc stress scenarios to actual risk factors used for pricing and other risk calculations. For example, transformation of bond price and yield curve risk factors to zero-coupon curves used in pricing of cash flow instruments such as swaps, bonds, or loans. Other examples include currency triangulations for currency pairs that can be derived from existing currency pair scenarios, and factor models used for generating comprehensive risk factor scenarios from a core reduced set of macroeconomic risk factor scenarios.
3. The credit model rating assessment or probability of default calculation on instrument (loan), counterparty, or pool level needed to price or assign default and migration losses.

In case of credit model calculations on counterparty or pool level, all the associated pool or counterparty exposures inherit the credit characteristics.[8] The credit model rating assessment is conditional on the (credit) risk factors.

4. The pricing and cash flow generation of the financial instruments, conditional on rating model assessments and the market risk factors. The pricing and cash flow generation of traditional banking book instruments can also depend on behavioral risk factors such as deposit withdrawal behavior and prepayment rates.

5. Aggregation of pricing and cash flows and computation of relevant measures such as exposure. Aggregation examples include counterparty or netting set.

6. The application of collateral agreements or hedge strategies to reduce instrument-level exposures as well as aggregated exposure levels such as at counterparty or netting sets. Here, the collateral or hedge can itself be stochastic and depend on the risk factors and hence be priced in step 4 together with the exposures. Examples include market risk and liquidity hedging portfolios as well as credit collaterals such as mortgage property collateral and other collateral agreements with counterparties.

7. The application of risk and statistical summary measures on profit-and-loss results as well as on cash flows—for example, value at risk or other measures on profit-and-loss or traditional cash flow–based asset and liability management measures such as hedged and unhedged interest rate and liquidity gap.

8. The application of post-aggregation processing measures such as risk-adjusted returns that depend on the computed risk measures.

The eight steps in the risk calculation flow in a financial risk system are also illustrated in Figure 1.1. Of course, in this process we have assumed the necessary portfolio and market data are prepared for the models and the risk analytics. This process is not just pure data management but rather a joint effort between data and risk modeling teams to define a standardized risk data model.

Regulatory requirements and the fast evolution of market practices in risk analysis require risk systems to perform more and more risk calculations faster and faster, cover more risk

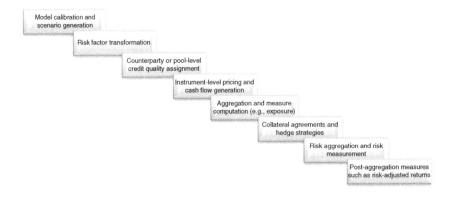

FIGURE 1.1   Risk Calculation Flow in a Financial Risk System

---

[8]In some cases a counterparty credit risk is also constrained by its parent entity credit risk. For example, a counterparty in a country is subject to the country risk and a subsidiary is subject to the parent company counterparty risk.

types (i.e., be more comprehensive), and be able to communicate results with other bank (risk) systems. For example, requirements such as CCAR and EBA stress testing exercises promote banks to analyze firmwide stress results in the context of impacts on projected future income statements and balance sheet statements. There can also be a feedback effect to the risk calculation when management actions are taken based on the projected income and balance sheet statements that affects the portfolios in the next risk analysis horizon.

Risk Infrastructure

Apart from the risk analytics and the risk calculation flow, a financial risk system needs a risk infrastructure. The risk infrastructure should both support the current use of the system as well as being able to adapt to future needs. We approach the requirements on a financial risk management systems risk infrastructure from a few core principles that the system should support. These core principles include:

- Comprehensiveness and relevance
- Accuracy
- Timeliness
- Governance
- Transparency
- Extensibility

The comprehensiveness and relevance principle means that the risk system must be able to capture all material risks that are in the scope of the system. That is, the system must have access to all the material risk data, by business line, legal entity, asset type, industry, region, and other groupings, as relevant for the risks in question. The system must also implement the risk models and analytics that are appropriate for the mission of the system, adequate to allow identifying and reporting risk exposures, concentrations, and emerging risks and adaptive to the granularity of the data. The data comprehensiveness should also encompass the multiple configurations the system is commissioned to do. Oftentimes a risk system has to be adaptive to multiple configurations even for a single risk type. Such configuration can be due to:

- Multi-jurisdictions that the institution has to respond to:
  This typically happens to a multinational institution that runs business in different countries or regions. Any international accord of risk regulation like Basel accords is subject to local modifications. Sometimes the modification can be quite significant due to the local business practice. In this case institutions have a choice to build different systems for different jurisdictions, which is not ideal for economic and integrity reasons, or have one system that can cater to different configurations on subset portfolios and economic data for the jurisdictions. A good example is the Basel II and Basel III regulations; many multinational banks that operate directly or indirectly through subsidiaries in very diverse regions face the challenge of being compliant with different jurisdictions. These international holding companies also need to aggregate and reconcile group risk measures to report to the group home regulators.
- Multiple business environments the institution operates in:
  Even for a non-regulatory risk analyses the need for multiple configuration settings can also easily come up because of different local business environments. First, different

countries have different governing laws that forbid a company doing certain things. For example, in the development and applications of the credit assessment models in some countries certain private customer information cannot be collected or used in the internal rating models even if the information is generally known as good predictors of the credit quality of customers. Another example is that the loan tenor can be different in different countries; some can be quite long (e.g., 30 years or longer) while the others can be short. Therefore, the analysis horizon can be of various length. Business calendars also vary across regions that call for different payment convention, pricing, and rate resetting models.

- Playpen, testing, and production:
  A risk system is not only designed to submit a set of final production results, but also needs to generate intermediate, testing, validation, and what-if results. Can the data and the system accommodate multiple sets of models, such as the champion and challengers? Can the data and the system sustain evolving regulations especially during the transition periods when different versions of the regulatory settings have to be accommodated?

Obviously accuracy is a key requirement for a risk system. Regulators and a bank's senior management must understand the risk profile of the bank in order to make informed risk-based decisions. Accuracy does not necessarily mean that every balance sheet and off–balance sheet item has to be evaluated or projected up to a certain precision. There are many approximation-based risk methodologies still actively used. However, banks must be able justify the validity of any approximation methods within the system.

The timeliness principle is related to the fact that risk analysis should reflect the current market situation and current portfolios to enable risk decisions to be taken on current risk information. With the important role of risk management in the value creation process in the banks, the delayed risk analysis is obviously not good for a bank to remain competitive. Meeting timeliness for a market risk application in trading book with frequent portfolio and market changes may require frequent intraday updates of risk while meeting timeliness for a credit risk application on the retail and commercial banking side may require less frequent updates due to relatively slowly changing portfolio compositions and credit conditions of borrowers. Timely analysis of a customer's risk profile, the bank's aggregated exposure to the customer, can help the bank to make a risk-based decision on customer retention and cross-sell and up-sell strategy based on the credit risk analysis and risk-based pricing. Timely monitoring of the bank's concentration, risk exposure, and cash flow projection in terms of regions, products, and currency can also help the bank to set optimal capital and liquidity hedging plans to proactively prepare for the possible downturn of the business.

A risk management process is not just about data and analytic results. The governance of the entire risk process is critical. A good risk system should therefore implement a workflow process that duly reflects the bank's risk governance policy. The workflow should clearly define the process and the staff's responsibility in the system. The same requirement also imposes security policies to the system. For example, when a data or risk analyst logs into the system, what kind of data and analysis does the analyst have access to? Another example is that not all the available data may be at the required quality for risk analytics. Banks usually have to approve the variables whose data can be used in modeling. The governance should also include approval and report submission workflows. When an analyst has a risk result ready the result should be validated and approved before reports are created and distributed.

Transparency is a core principle for a risk system. An analyst must be able to explain what the system does, including the data used, specific model assumptions, and risk calculations.

That the risk system is transparent is a key requirement for the bank to be able to understand the specific models and assumptions used in the system and hence to be able to validate them, either by data, expertise judgment, or both.

Connected to both the governance and transparency principles of the risk systems are critical requirements for a risk system to be able to trace, audit, and reproduce the results:

- Traceability means that the system provides a way to trace a result back to the right version of input in a particular incidence of a process. The scope of the traceability depends on how the user manages the input. That means the system should archive the inputs, including portfolio, market data, configuration, and models. Traceability also includes lineage. The lineage information can provide useful impact analysis results. The input data or a model parameter change lineage helps to trace which part of results or intermediate results would be affected. Another usage of lineage is to trace a risk result to see how it is attained.
- Reproducibility means that the system keeps enough information for the user to reproduce the same result when the user applies the exact same situation where the result of interest was created. Traceability is a prerequisite for reproducibility but the system has to now make sure all inputs are correctly restored and retrievable back to the system in order to reproduce the same input environment required by the result.
- Auditability for a system applies information in a shared data space in terms of who and what made changes to the system, and when.

Transparency, process, and governance are certainly critical to decision making. A decision must sustain questions, validation, and examination. Traceability, auditability, and reproducibility are obviously directly applicable. Risk-based decision making and performance analysis are in fact the ultimate purpose of risk management. In practice two categories of decision support are expected from a risk system. The first category of decision support is made almost completely by the system with minimal human intervention. Such decisions are usually based on well-established models and market practice. Decisions in this category can include automated approval/rejections of credit applications based on credit models and loan pricing models. Automated market-hedging strategies can fall into this category as well. The second system-generated decision support type is more referential and provides guidance to the decision makers. Accuracy and timeliness are two critical characteristics of a good decision-making framework.

Risk management is a quickly evolving discipline. This is not only because the methodology and technology change rapidly but is also due to the fast-changing economic and market environment in which banks are running business. The risk system should be adaptive to newly identified risks, new methodologies, and new reporting requirements. For example, during the Greek debt crisis, global and European banks were demanded to submit their total exposures to Greek counterparties and a few other European countries that had similar debt size concerns to the senior management and regulators. It turned out to be a difficult task for many banks. This was because the aggregated risk to such a level was never calculated and reported before. If a system cannot support quick extensibility, it will not only induce more operational cost and risk at the time of the new risk analysis requirement but also disable the accuracy and timeliness of the risk analysis.

Risk Technology

The proper use of the technology is key to financial risk systems and the actual implementation of the quantitative methods discussed in this book. It is also decisive for meeting the timeliness principle we discussed in the context of risk infrastructure. Just as any computer system, a risk system faces the constraint of four major computer resources:

- Processor capacity
- Memory capacity
- Storage capacity
- Network bandwidth in distributed calculation and storage on a grid of multiple computer nodes

The first obvious way to reduce calculation time for a risk analysis is to deploy the risk calculation on parallel processors. However, the first challenge is to ensure that the algorithm itself, if possible, is not deployed as a sequential calculation. Parallel programming can in principle be achieved even in this case if multiple such algorithms can be executed simultaneously. Many portfolio risk analyses are naturally deployed in parallel. For example, the pricing of positions can be done independently across a set of scenarios. For a fixed number of processors the optimal distribution of exposure valuation to processors may depend on the analysis type. For example, for many scenarios such as a model simulation it may be optimal to distribute the scenarios while for just a few scenarios such as a stress test it may be optimal to distribute the positions. Even so-called nested simulation pricing methods, where simulation is used to price the position for every risk scenario, can in principle be distributed. This is because, for a given risk scenario, the nested simulation position can be distributed in sub-positions with independent, smaller, nested simulation samples that are eventually aggregated to an average nested simulation price for the position.

The parallel processing can also be more complex to implement. For example, in credit risk applications one frequently needs to first calculate the credit quality of the counterparty, then price the exposures belonging to the counterparty, aggregate exposures, and then allocate the collateral to the exposures. That is, perform steps 3–6 in the risk analytics flow in the financial risk system discussed above. The easiest solution is to distribute by counterparties and hence by all the exposures and collateral belonging to a counterparty. However, such a distribution approach may not be optimal as the pricing time for counterparty exposures may vary significantly, either due to portfolio size, pricing complexity, or both. While distributing exposures with one single counterparty onto different computer threads may result in simultaneous access to the counterparty data the independent exposure evaluation may still be optimal. Of course, in this case, at the time of collateral allocation the counterparty exposures and priced collateral on different threads may need to be aggregated back. This is one example that calls for full understanding of the analysis sequence when designing the parallel computation.

Processing capacity is not the only constraint. The second is on the memory. Faster processing time achieved through parallelism increases the demand on memory. Individual machines can only have a certain amount of memory. When the risk calculation requires many more folds of memory for the input and intermediate data, increasing parallel processing will run into the obstacles of memory requirement. For this reason traditional systems constantly upload and unload data between memory and the hard disk, which can create a lot of bottlenecks. Writing and reading information to and from the storage trades off with the memory usage. However, the introduction of grid computing makes available not only more processors but also memory from a cluster of multiple computers. Holding data in memory and not writing it to disk can avoid the writing and reading bottlenecks. This in-memory technology can be applied not only to a system with complicated calculation logic but also to systems for large-scale query of risk results. Holding the lowest level of risk data in memory, such as profit and loss per position for every scenario, makes the risk system more flexible in terms of the risk measures and risk results that can be queried on demand. Because memory is not an unlimited resource, it is imperative to optimize the implementation of an algorithm to decide what information should be held in memory for fast access and what should be written to the storage and release the memory for that information.

Storage technology has also vastly advanced just as the other computing resources. Now it is not difficult to find hard drives that can hold terabytes of data but even this size on one single computer can easily be obsolete for a risk system. In contrast to the traditional direct storage to each individual computer, network storage has become the standard for many risk systems. However, it is not necessarily optimal for the application if a large volume of data is required within a short period of time (i.e., high data velocity). There are a couple of solutions to high velocity. The first is through a high-velocity, low-latency data event stream processing technology; the other is to leverage a distributed file system. Both solutions are mostly applicable to a grid computing setting where a large number of computer nodes are available for an application. A risk application can interact with data storage in several ways. Traditionally, risk systems require data to physically move out of the storage for input to the risk analysis, and also later to physically move the risk results to storage for subsequent reporting. The physical movement of data not only can be time consuming but can also create unnecessary staging data copies that can quickly fill the storage. Another approach for risk systems to consume and deliver data is to leverage in-memory. In-memory views of data can in principle also include transformations. The benefit is the potential speed of data delivery and that a physical duplicate of data is prevented.

Another factor that affects the choice of distributed calculation and storage on a grid of multiple computer nodes is the network bandwidth. Network bandwidth is a scarce resource even when a dedicated network is set up for the grid. Nowadays multigigabytes of data can be transmitted among computers. However, oftentimes multiple nodes share one network cable. If a lot of data are transmitted through the network, it can easily saturate the network bandwidth capacity. Therefore, one should consider the network factor in risk system architecture.

MODEL RISK MANAGEMENT

Risk analytics is the core of a risk system. It is also this book's focus. In a book that focuses heavily on risk analysis models it is appropriate to discuss model risk management even before going into detailed discussion of any models.

A risk system contains many different models used in the risk calculations. Models have their lifecycles and need to be frequently validated and tested. The need for more risk calculations and their growing complexity also means that banks need to manage and validate more and more models that are deployed in the risk system(s). Sometimes models are managed on a firmwide level even if certain risk calculations are executed on a silo risk system level. A firmwide model risk management approach is motivated by the firmwide stress test requirements from CCAR and EBA. Given the many different models that are involved in banks' regulatory calculations, banks' practice in model risk management is also a serious concern for regulators. For example, in 2011, the US Federal Reserve and the Office of the Comptroller of the Currency (OCC) issued joint guidance on model risk management practices.

Model risk can arise from many points in an analytical risk process. It cannot be completely avoided but it can be managed. Model risk can arise and thus ought to be managed in the following aspects:

- Model data:
  The first source of model risk is data. We are familiar with the garbage-in-garbage-out rule. When the input data have major flaws, even the best model can generate misleading results. Data flaws can occur not only due to the data quality but also from a partial selection of the data history. For example, in the years preceding the 2007 financial crisis, housing price statistics displayed upward trending for many years with only sporadic default losses. When banks used this part of the historical data in the housing price models and the credit default risk models it was impossible to obtain tail risk levels anywhere close to the losses in the 2007 financial crisis. Even if data are available that cover a full business cycle with both up- and downturns it is still just *one* observation of a business cycle. The future business cycle swings will most likely not be similar to the last one. This observation is relevant not only in the context of using data for model calibration such as how probability of default depends on the business cycle but also in selection and design of (macroeconomic) stress scenarios for the portfolios.[9] Another well-studied data flaw subject in the econometrics literature is the survivorship bias, which leads to overly optimistic beliefs of the future. Therefore, in many institutions there is strict governance on the data that can be used for model development and application.
- Model assumptions:
  A famous quote from Box and Draper (1987) is, "All models are wrong; the practical question is how wrong do they have to be to not be useful." Every model is an approximation. In order to reach a parsimonious view of the world but still remain useful proper assumptions have to be made. First, it is important that the assumptions are practically reasonable. Second, when the model is applied the model assumption should still hold. Of course, the readers of this book are urged to understand the assumptions of the models presented in this book and validate the model assumptions against the specific application purpose when a model is adopted.
- Model development:
  There are many examples in this book where models are developed with clear assumptions and sound economic and mathematical theory. These are the foundations of a good model. As mentioned before, the design and choice of a model must fit the actual use case. Therefore, the model development is a collaborative work between model developers and the business experts. Testing the fit of a model is also an integral part of the model development. However, good model fit on historical data is not necessarily a good indicator that the model will be able to generate relevant future risk scenarios. Good model fit should be complemented with expert judgment. A model with less statistical fit may outperform as a risk model. When fitting models it is also important to be prudent in what history is chosen for the model fit. Model parameters estimated on data can also be overridden with more prudent estimates. Because of the changing business environment a model is always subject to reexamination, redevelopment, and revalidation.

---

[9]It is a relevant question to ask if a model that has been calibrated over a specific business cycle can be confidently used to predict behavior in other types of stressed tail events.

- Model documentation:

  The Basel 2005 document explains the assumption, insight and derivation of the Basel II risk weight functions for the internal model–based approaches (Basel Committee, 2005c). This document also sets a good example of model documentation. Every model employed in a risk system should be clearly documented for its assumptions, economic insights, mathematical justification, and reasons to be adopted for a particular risk analysis. Besides these elements, it should also document the history of the model updates to give information on how a model has evolved. Other information related to model governance such as developer, modification date, version number, and so on can also be included in the model documentation. A model document not only helps explain the model to the stakeholders, including the regulators and senior management, but also allows better transition of the model knowledge when there is any staff change. The latter is important because it warrants the continuation of the knowledge of the model.

- Model validation:

  Model validation is getting more and more attention in the financial institutions. Independent validation groups are established to examine the models from assumption all the way to production. There are several tasks a model validation function is responsible for. The first is to examine the key elements of a model as discussed above. Second, the model validation group applies statistical tools to validate the model outcome. On some occasions the model validation function also creates overlapping models to cross-check the developed models. The validation group can also check the computer programs and the documentation of a model. Techniques familiar to mathematicians and statisticians are widely used in model validation. For example, pricing models and the parameters are constantly calibrated to the market values and peer models. In-sample and out-of-sample performance tests are performed on the statistical models and risk measures are back-tested. In many cases, champion and challengers models are set up in the model repository to diversify model risk and enhance the governance. This book contains several examples of model validation, especially on backtesting. One example is the backtesting study of the time aggregation of market risk with and without trading, which challenges the regulatory time scaling risk approach for the market risk capital.

- Model execution:

  All the models are created to be used. Therefore, model execution usually is the last step in a modeling process. This stage is where all the models are put together to accomplish a certain risk analysis. The prerequisite of this stage is to make sure required data and assumptions of the model are suitable. This is when the data, the analysis of interest, and model assumptions must be aligned. A common source of model execution risk is the loss of fidelity when models are translated from the model development platform to the model execution platform. It is not unusual for banks to have models in actual use being several versions behind the models just developed. Another challenge in this stage is whether the system can efficiently accommodate the sophistication of the models. Such sophistication includes both the mathematical complexity and the granularity of the data the model applies to. For example, a bank that moves from a pooled analysis of banking book credit losses and cash flows to loan level models not only faces the challenge of more granular model validation. This increased granularity requires the risk system to be able to execute models against millions of loans. The capturing of credit losses and cash flows over long horizons leads to challenges in computer processing, memory, input and output capability, as well as storage. To solve this challenge, banks must find balance between the efficiency of the risk system and the models to be used.

- Model governance:

  There is rarely a case that one risk system actually carries out all the modeling functions covered in this section. Sometimes these functions are dispatched in different systems. For that very reason model governance becomes essential to minimize the model risk in the entire modeling lifecycle. Although model execution is usually the last stop in a modeling cycle, it should not be the end of the process. The result of model execution should be validated and serve as a trigger for model updates. To minimize the model risk, it is preferable to automate the entire model risk management workflow. This workflow typically requires a clear management policy in terms how a model, from its inception and development, can finally get into the production and participate in any risk analysis. Rigorous examination and approval should be put in place. A good model governance capacity should also be able to track all the issues and actions about all the models in its specific usage, for example, all the stress testing models or market risk capital models. When the model validation team discovers an issue, they should be able to track who owns the issue, what is the current status, and if/how it was resolved.

Market Risk

CHAPTER 2

Market Risk with the Normal Distribution

Regarding modern risk management, it is fair to say research and practice in market risk have played a very important role. The major financial economics breakthroughs were due to a rich body of contributions by academic researchers and practitioners. In 1990, Harry Markowitz, Merton Miller, and William Sharpe were jointly awarded the Nobel Prize in Economic Sciences for "their pioneer work in the theory of financial economics" in the 1950s and 1960s. They laid down a foundation of risk-based asset pricing and portfolio decision theory. Fisher Black, Myron Scholes, and Robert Merton's work on options successfully applied risk-based concepts such as replicating portfolio for hedging and law of no-arbitrage in asset pricing. Their work laureated Scholes and Merton (with an honorable mention of the late Black) the Nobel Prize in Economic Sciences in 1997.

Since the early risk researches and practice the multivariate normal distribution assumption for the changes in all the market risk and macroeconomic factors such as equity, foreign exchange, and interest rates is one of the most popular quantitative approaches. We will therefore start with market risk management using a multivariate normal distribution assumption. We will consider three different cases for the portfolio representation: first, the case of linear portfolios such as plain stock portfolios or portfolios that can be approximated well by a first-order sensitivity; second, a quadratic portfolio representation that includes also second-order sensitivities for portfolios with convexity; and third, using simulation-based valuation of the portfolio.

In advance of this chapter we need to remark that the assumption that financial risk factors return series are normal and independent over time is one of the most common simplifying assumptions in finance.[1] The stylized facts of financial return series depend in practice on the temporal aggregations such as daily or monthly returns. The typical time horizon for market risk management is, however, counted in days. For daily returns, the stylized facts of financial return series show that the assumption of a normal distribution is questionable due to the observed fat-tailed nature of financial time series. It is typically also a feature of financial time series that they display volatility clusters, which is inconsistent with a simple multivariate normal distribution. Notwithstanding the fact that the stylized facts of financial returns may deviate from the multivariate normal assumption, it is an important benchmark model, especially for introducing core concepts that we later can extend to more general settings. In addition, the assumption of a multivariate normal distribution for risk factors enables some simple analytical representations with straightforward interpretation that are useful for understanding more general cases.

---

[1]See, for example, Taleb (2007), is highly critical of the use of the normal distribution as it cannot explain the extreme "black swan" outliers observed in practice.

LINEAR PORTFOLIOS

The classical and simplest method for portfolio risk analysis relies on the assumption of multivariate normal risk factor returns and approximation of instrument price changes using a first-order Taylor approximation. The method is usually referred to as the *delta method*. The delta sensitivities of a position are related to the changes in the value of an underlying asset in a position such as an equity. The changes in the underlying asset is the primary source of market risk. Hence, the delta sensitivities are important in risk management.

Basic Model

To introduce the basic delta model we denote by **U** an $n \times 1$ vector of sensitivities to the $j = 1, \ldots, n$ portfolio risk factors $S(t)$. Here, the vector $S(t) = [S_1(t), \ldots, S_n(t)]$ contains market risk factors like equity, foreign exchange, and interest rates. We denote the pricing function for a specific portfolio instrument $i = 1, \ldots, m$ by

$$p_i = F_i[S(t)] \tag{2.1}$$

where each F_i is a function of (typically a subset of) the $j = 1, \ldots, n$ portfolio risk factors $S(t)$. The total portfolio value, $V(t)$, is a weighted sum of the $i = 1, \ldots, m$ instruments in the portfolio such that

$$V(t) = \sum_{i=1}^{m} h_i F_i[S(t)]$$

where h_i is the current position in instrument $i = 1, \ldots, m$. Each position number, h_i, is an element of the $1 \times m$ holding vector, $\mathbf{h} = (h_1, \ldots, h_m)$.

To calculate the portfolio risk sensitivity to the market risk factors we let the j:th element of the n-dimensional sensitivity vector, $\vec{\Delta}$, be defined as

$$\Delta_j = \sum_{i=1}^{m} h_i \frac{\partial F_i(S(t))}{\partial S_j(t)}.$$

Collecting all Δ_j elements in matrix format,

$$\vec{\Delta} = \begin{bmatrix} \Delta_1 & \cdots & \Delta_{n-1} & \Delta_n \end{bmatrix}'$$

defines the n-dimensional vector $\vec{\Delta}$. We can write this as

$$\Delta_j = \sum_{i=1}^{m} h_i \Delta_i^j$$

where Δ_i^j indicates the delta for position i with respect to risk factor j. The portfolio value at a future time T, with current positions (i.e., time t positions), $\{h_i(t)\}_{i=1}^{m}$, can now be written as

$$V(T) = \sum_{i=1}^{m} h_i(t) F_i[S(T)].$$

We may now approximate $V(T) - V(t)$ by the approximate change in portfolio value between $(t, T]$ as

$$V(T) - V(t) \approx \vec{\Delta}'[S(T) - S(t)]. \tag{2.2}$$

For example, if we have two positions ($m = 2$) and three risk factors ($n = 3$), we have that

$$V(T) - V(t) \approx \begin{bmatrix} \Delta_1 & \Delta_2 & \Delta_3 \end{bmatrix} \begin{bmatrix} S_1(T) - S_1(t) \\ S_2(T) - S_2(t) \\ S_3(T) - S_3(t) \end{bmatrix}$$

$$= \begin{bmatrix} h_1\Delta_1^1 + h_2\Delta_2^1 & h_1\Delta_1^2 + h_2\Delta_2^2 & h_1\Delta_1^3 + h_2\Delta_2^3 \end{bmatrix} \begin{bmatrix} S_1(T) - S_1(t) \\ S_2(T) - S_2(t) \\ S_3(T) - S_3(t) \end{bmatrix}$$

or, expressed differently, in terms of the $m = 2$ positions,

$$V(T) - V(t) \approx h_1 \begin{bmatrix} \Delta_1^1 & \Delta_1^2 & \Delta_1^3 \end{bmatrix} \begin{bmatrix} S_1(T) - S_1(t) \\ S_2(T) - S_2(t) \\ S_3(T) - S_3(t) \end{bmatrix}$$

$$+ h_2 \begin{bmatrix} \Delta_2^1 & \Delta_2^2 & \Delta_2^3 \end{bmatrix} \begin{bmatrix} S_1(T) - S_1(t) \\ S_2(T) - S_2(t) \\ S_3(T) - S_3(t) \end{bmatrix}$$

where again Δ_i^j indicates the delta for position i with respect to risk factor j.

To obtain the distribution of $V(T) - V(t)$ it therefore remains to specify the distribution of $S(T) - S(t)$. In this chapter we focus on the case when the increment (returns) vector $S(T) - S(t)$ is multivariate normal. That is,

$$S(T) - S(t) \sim N(\boldsymbol{\mu}, \boldsymbol{\Sigma})$$

where $\boldsymbol{\mu}$ is the $n \times 1$ expected returns vector over the $(T - t)$ horizon for the risk factors, $S(t) = [S_1(t), \ldots, S_n(t)]$, $\boldsymbol{\Sigma}$ is the corresponding $n \times n$ covariance matrix for the $(T - t)$ horizon of the n-dimensional vector of risk factors $S(t)$. Using the basic properties of the normal distribution we have that

$$\vec{\Delta}'(S(T) - S(t)) \sim N(\vec{\Delta}'\boldsymbol{\mu}, \vec{\Delta}'\boldsymbol{\Sigma}\vec{\Delta}). \tag{2.3}$$

The approximate portfolio is hence distributed as univariate normal with mean $\mu_p = \vec{\Delta}'\boldsymbol{\mu}$ and variance $\sigma_p^2 = \vec{\Delta}'\boldsymbol{\Sigma}\vec{\Delta}$. Henceforth in the analysis we however set $\boldsymbol{\mu} = \mathbf{0}$ and hence $\mu_p = 0$ for notational convenience. This case is also practical for a short-term risk horizon, which is the usual case in market risk analysis.

In the above simple linear normal market risk model, we note that there are two core inputs to measure portfolio risk:

1. Position sensitivities to the risk factors
2. The covariance matrix of the risk factors

We will first focus on the computation of sensitivities as well as the computation of risk measures and risk contributions in the linear normal model. After that we will return to the issue of how to estimate the covariance matrix of the risk factors.

Computing Sensitivities We consider three examples of computing position sensitivities: first, a simple, stock portfolio; second, a bond position; and third, a stock option position. Of course, the simplest case of the model is when it is applied to linear positions such as stock positions or spot foreign exchange positions. In this case, because of position linearity the distribution of $V(T) - V(t)$ in equation (2.2) is exact rather than an approximation when the market risk factors are multivariate normal.

Equity Portfolio Sensitivities We consider an equity portfolio with 5 different equity positions. Each equity position has a corresponding market risk factor, $S_1, \ldots, S_5$ being the stocks. We assume that current stock values are given by

$$S_1 = 46.75$$
$$S_2 = 55.75$$
$$S_3 = 178.25$$
$$S_4 = 1119.25$$
$$S_5 = 263.75$$

in units of a common currency. The corresponding portfolio holding vector, $\mathbf{h}$, in the 5 stocks is given by

$$\mathbf{h} = \begin{bmatrix} 20 & 18 & 6 & 1 & 4 \end{bmatrix}. \tag{2.4}$$

Since equity positions are linear the sensitivity vector, $\vec{\mathbf{\Delta}}$, is hence

$$\vec{\mathbf{\Delta}} = \begin{bmatrix} 20 & 18 & 6 & 1 & 4 \end{bmatrix}'.$$

The current mark to market of the portfolio sums the position-adjusted current equity values. That is,

$$V(t) = \sum_{i=1}^{5} h_i S_i = 5,182.25. \tag{2.5}$$

If we assume the stock values all increase 5% between time t and T, then because portfolio value is linear in the stock prices, the change of the portfolio value is

$$\Delta V = \sum_{i=1}^{5} h_i \Delta S_i \approx 259.11.$$

When portfolio value is not linear in the position, risk factor sensitivities can be calculated analytically from the functional form of the pricing function in equation (2.1), or use a numerical approximation to the analytic sensitivity. For example, both bonds and European stock options have analytic sensitivities.

Bond Sensitivity For bond instruments the pricing function (2.1) is based on present value (PV) of cash flows. Assuming discrete compounding, it is the practice to make use of the modified duration, MOD, as the first-order sensitivity, defined as

$$\text{MOD} = -\frac{\partial \text{PV}}{\partial y} \frac{1}{\text{PV}} = \frac{1}{\text{PV}(1+y)} \sum_{t_i \in \mathbb{C}} t_i \frac{C_i}{(1+y)^{t_i+1}}.$$

Here PV is the present value of the bond, y the yield to maturity, C_i the cash flow amount at t_i, and t_i a cash flow date such that $t_i \in \mathbb{C}$ the set of all cash flow dates. The (modified) duration hence corresponds to a normalized weighted average cash flow measure with y the yield solved from

$$\text{PV} = \sum_{t_i \in \mathbb{C}} \frac{C_i}{(1 + y)^{t_i}}.$$

The duration in absolute values, also known as dollar duration, DUR, is given by

$$\text{DUR} = \text{MOD} \times \text{PV}$$

and the traditional Macaulay duration, MCDUR,

$$\text{MCDUR} = \text{DUR} \times (1 + y).$$

The duration can be shown to correspond to the first term in a Taylor series expansion of the bond price with respect to y. That is,

$$\Delta\text{PV} \approx -\text{DUR} \times dy = -\text{MOD} \times \text{PV} \times dy = \frac{\partial\text{PV}}{\partial y} \times dy.$$

A drawback of the duration as sensitivity measure is that it assumes a parallel term-structure (through y). To include nonparallel shifts of the term-structure of interest rates we may therefore define a series of partial durations, that is derivatives, with respect to yield curve points, $\{y_{t_i}\}_{t_i \in \mathbb{C}}$. The series of partial durations then correspond to the derivatives of the bond price with respect to the vertices of the discount curve.

For credit-risky bonds the discount term, r, is often decomposed as $r = r_y + r_c$ where r_y is the discount rate for default-free bonds and r_c is the credit spread.[2] In that case

$$\Delta\text{PV} \approx \frac{\partial\text{PV}}{\partial r_y} \times dr_y + \frac{\partial\text{PV}}{\partial r_c} \times dr_c$$

which allows a decomposition in terms of traditional interest rate risk and spread risk. We refer to Fabozzi (1997, ch. 13) for many examples of bond price sensitivity analysis using duration.

Option Sensitivity   For a European call option maturing at T on a single underlying stock, S, priced at time t by the standard Black and Scholes (1976) formula we obtain the arbitrage-free option premium, denoted by c, as

$$c = S(t)N(d_1) - \exp(-r(T - t))KN(d_2)$$

where $N(\cdot)$ is the cumulative normal distribution function, r is the risk-free rate, σ is the volatility of the stock, and K is the strike price. The inputs to the cumulative normal distribution function, d_1 and d_2, are given by

$$d_1 = \frac{1}{\sigma\sqrt{T - t}} \ln\left[\frac{S(t)}{K} + \left(r + \frac{\sigma^2}{2} \right)(T - t) \right]$$

$$d_2 = d_1 - \sigma\sqrt{T - t}.$$

---

[2]We will discuss in more detail the credit spread in the credit risk chapters of the book.

The first-order derivatives with respect to the underlying stock, volatility, and interest rate are then given by (denoting by $\phi(\cdot)$ the normal density),

$$\frac{\partial c}{\partial S} = N(d_1)$$

$$\frac{\partial c}{\partial \sigma} = S(t)\phi(d_1)\sqrt{T-t}$$

$$\frac{\partial c}{\partial r} = K(T-t)\exp(-r(T-t))N(d_2).$$

These first-order derivatives are denoted respectively the delta, the vega, and the rho of the option. We can now write, assuming a unit position in the European call option,

$$\Delta c \approx \frac{\partial c}{\partial S}\Delta S + \frac{\partial c}{\partial \sigma}\Delta\sigma + \frac{\partial c}{\partial r}\Delta r.$$

Risk Measures

Previously we have defined the delta method portfolio distribution as normal in equation (2.3). The normal portfolio distribution variance, σ_p^2, depends on the covariance of market risk factors, $S(t) = [S_1(t), \dots, S_n(t)]$, and the portfolio position sensitivities to the market risk factors. The portfolio variance, σ_p^2, or volatility, σ_p, is a classical measure of risk. Markowitz (1952, 1959) used portfolio variance in the optimal mean-variance frontier construction. However, quantile and other tail-based measures of risk are now more commonly used in risk measurement. Let therefore ρ be a risk measure. If ρ is a worst-case quantile of the portfolio distribution, we obtain the well-known value at risk measure, denoted VaR(α) and defined by

$$\text{VaR}(\alpha) \equiv \inf\{\varsigma \mid P(-\Delta V(T) \geq \varsigma) \geq \alpha\}$$

where $\Delta V(T) = V(T) - V(t)$.[3] In this normal distribution setting VaR(α) is simply given by

$$\text{VaR}(\alpha) = N^{-1}(\alpha)\sigma_p = Z_\alpha\sigma_p$$

where N is again the cumulative distribution of the normal, N^{-1} its inverse, and $Z_\alpha = N^{-1}(\alpha)$ is an α quantile of the univariate standard normal distribution.

Another popular tail risk measure is the risk measure that computes the expected losses beyond VaR. The conditional value at risk, denoted CVaR(α), is defined by the average tail integral,[4]

$$\text{CVaR}(\alpha) = E(-\Delta V(T) \mid -\Delta V(T) \geq \text{VaR}(\alpha)) = \frac{1}{1-\alpha}\int_\alpha^1 \text{VaR}(u)du. \qquad (2.6)$$

---

[3]Note that in the definition of VaR(α) we are concerned with the positive tail loss in $-\Delta V(T)$. This is because we are concerned about negative return contributions to $\Delta V(T)$.

[4]Here we use the terminology conditional value at risk. However, this measure is also frequently termed expected shortfall.

To have an explicit representation for CVaR(α), we note that for a normally distributed variable X with mean μ, variance σ^2 and truncation point a,

$$E[X \mid X > a] = \mu + \sigma \lambda \left(\frac{a - \mu}{\sigma} \right).$$

The function $\lambda(v) = \frac{\phi(v)}{1 - N(v)}$ is the well-known hazard function for the normal distribution.[5] Using the fact that $\mu = 0$ and VaR $= Z_\alpha \sigma_p$, we get

$$\mathrm{CVaR}(\alpha) = \sigma_p \lambda \left(\frac{\mathrm{VaR}(\alpha)}{\sigma_p} \right)$$

$$= \mathrm{VaR}(\alpha) \left(\frac{\phi(Z_\alpha)/(1 - N(Z_\alpha))}{Z_\alpha} \right). \tag{2.7}$$

We can therefore conclude that VaR(α) and CVaR(α), as well as the portfolio volatility, σ_p, are equivalent risk measures in this setting since they only differ by constants.

Example Risk Measures   Below we illustrate numerically the calculation of risk measures for an equity portfolio and a bond.

Computation of VaR and CVaR Risk Measures for a Sample Equity Portfolio   We consider the sample equity portfolio, introduced above when considering equity portfolio sensitivities, with risk factors, $S_1, \ldots, S_5$, and holding vector as in (2.4), For this portfolio we now specify the covariance matrix, Σ, of the risk factors, $S_1, \ldots, S_5$, as

$$\Sigma = \begin{bmatrix} 4 & 0.45 & 0.85 & 0.35 & 0.15 \\ 0.45 & 5 & 0.45 & 0.45 & 0.15 \\ 0.85 & 0.45 & 11 & 0.45 & 0.15 \\ 0.35 & 0.45 & 0.45 & 47 & 0.15 \\ 0.15 & 0.15 & 0.15 & 0.15 & 13 \end{bmatrix}. \tag{2.8}$$

Note that this is the covariance matrix of the arithmetic returns of the risk factors (i.e., $S_j(T) - S_j(t)$ for $j = 1, \ldots, 5$), since we have assumed that the arithmetic returns are normally distributed in equation (2.3). From the covariance matrix, Σ, we obtain, for example, that the daily standard deviation of equity risk factor S_1 arithmetic returns is equal to $\sqrt{4} = 2$.

With this covariance matrix the portfolio profit and loss is distributed as normal with

$$N(0, \vec{\Delta}' \Sigma \vec{\Delta}) = N(0, 4, 585.8)$$

---

[5]The hazard function for a probability density function, $f(x)$, and cumulative density function, $F(x)$, is given by

$$\frac{f(x)}{1 - F(x)} = \frac{P(X = x)}{1 - P(X \leq x)}.$$

The hazard function is hence a conditional density function.

for the time horizon of $T - t = 1$. Hence, portfolio volatility, σ_p, is approximately 67.72. For a 99% confidence level we now have that portfolio VaR(0.99) and CVaR(0.99) are given by respectively

$$\text{VaR}(0.99) = Z_{0.99} \times \sigma_p = 157.54$$

$$\text{CVaR}(0.99) = \text{VaR}(0.99) \times \left(\frac{\phi(Z_\alpha)/(1 - N(Z_\alpha))}{Z_\alpha} \right) = 180.48.$$

The portfolio VaR(0.99) is hence 3.04% of the total portfolio market value of $5,182.25$ (see equation (2.5)). The corresponding percentage for CVaR(0.99) is 3.48%.

To obtain risk measures for $T - t > 1$ one can estimate the covariance matrix on the appropriate risk factor returns time horizon, for example, weekly arithmetic returns. Alternatively, one can adjust the daily covariance matrix by $\sqrt{T - t} = \sqrt{5}$ to obtain the weekly risk measures from the 1-day risk measures. That is, use scaling with the square root of time. In our example the weekly VaR(0.99), denoted by $\text{VaR}^5(0.99)$, is given by

$$\text{VaR}^5(0.99) = \text{VaR}(0.99) \times \sqrt{5} = 352.27.$$

Hence, for a weekly time horizon VaR(0.99) as a percentage of the portfolio market value is 6.79%. In practice, banks frequently calculate the 1-day horizon VaR and subsequently scale the 1-day VaR to obtain an n-day VaR estimate such as a 10-day regulatory VaR estimate. For example, this simple scaling holds true in case of a normal independent and identical distribution and a buy-and-hold trading strategy, which is the case we are concerned with here. See Diebold et al. (1997).[6] We now turn to a bond example.

Computation of Bond Risk Consider a 5-year bond with Macauley duration equal to 5 years. The current yield, y, is 5% and the standard deviation of (absolute) change in interest rates is 0.25%. Assuming the bond price is 100 units of currency we get that

$$\text{VaR}(0.99) \approx \text{MCDUR} \times \text{PV} \times \left(\frac{1}{1 + y} \right) \times Z_{0.99} \times \sigma_p$$

$$= 5 \times 100 \times \left(\frac{1}{1 + 0.05} \right) \times 2.33 \times 0.0025$$

$$\approx 2.77.$$

Risk Factor Returns and Risk Measures So far we have assumed that arithmetic risk factor returns are normal in our analysis. That is,

$$S(T) - S(t) \sim N(0, \Sigma)$$

is multivariate normal. If instead relative returns are assumed multivariate normal,

$$[S(T) - S(t)]./S(t) \sim N(0, \Sigma)$$

---

[6]In the next chapter on market risk we will discuss the issues with using the square root of scaling method more generally and possible remedies.

with "./" indicating component by component division, then equation (2.3) holds with the sensitivity component $\vec{\Delta}_j$ for risk factor $j = 1, \ldots, n$ being replaced by $\overline{\Delta}_j = \Delta_j S_j$. Hence, we get

$$\overline{\Delta}' ([S(T) - S(t)]./S(t)) \sim N(\overline{\Delta}' \mu, \overline{\Delta}' \Sigma \overline{\Delta}).$$

The mixed case with some risk factors arithmetic normal and some relative normal is obtained by defining, for risk factor j, $\overline{\Delta}_j = \Delta_j S$ or $\overline{\Delta}_j = \vec{\Delta}_j$ as appropriate. Of course, for consistency, the assumed format for returns for a risk factor should be respected when calculating the joint covariance matrix, Σ, of risk factor returns.

The relative return of a risk factor is often identified with the logarithmic return. Specifically, the relative return of a risk factor j, is denoted r_j, such that

$$r_j = \frac{S_j(T) - S_j(t)}{S_j(t)} = \frac{S_j(T)}{S_j(t)} - 1$$

and is usually referred to as the simple net return. Clearly, $r_j \approx \log(1 + r_j)$. With continuous compounding the simple net return is just the logarithm of $(1 + \bar{r}_j)$ such that

$$\bar{r}_j = \log S_j(T) - \log S_j(t).$$

We refer to Campbell et al. (1997, ch. 1) for a discussion of the different definitions of returns.

Simple Extensions to the Normal Distribution Assumption We finally note in this subsection on risk measures that the explicit formulas for VaR and CVaR under the multivariate normal distribution assumption for risk factors and first-order sensitivities can be extended quite easily in some cases. For example, using a multivariate t-distribution for risk factors such that $S(T) - S(t) \sim t(\mu, \Sigma, v)$ with degrees-of-freedom parameter v the VaR is expressed as

$$\text{VaR}(\alpha) = t_v^{-1}(\alpha) \sigma_p$$

with $t_v^{-1}(\alpha)$ the inverse of the t-distribution function with degrees-of-freedom parameter v. For example, if $\alpha = 99\%$ and $v = 4$, then $t_v^{-1}(\alpha) \approx 3.74$. Compared to the normal distribution case risk has hence increased by 60% since $\frac{t_v^{-1}(\alpha)}{N^{-1}(\alpha)} \approx \frac{3.74}{2.33} = 1.6$. See Sadefo-Kamdem (2003).

Risk Contributions

Given the portfolio distribution and a risk measure ρ, an interesting question is how we attribute the overall portfolio risk to sources of risks. That is, how can we decompose risk? This is an important issue to the risk manager and the management of an institution because they need to know not only the total portfolio risk but also the breakdown of the total portfolio risk into contributing positions. The breakdown allows the risk manager to find which positions and risk factors contribute to the portfolio risk and hence which positions need to be adjusted to (for example) decrease portfolio risk. Identifying the major positions and risk factors that concentrate risk in the portfolio and hedge out portfolio risk is hence at the core of risk management activities. Another use case of the risk contribution analysis is to fairly account each position's contribution to the total portfolio risk for risk-adjusted performance analysis and capital allocation purposes.

Risk attribution usually comes up from two dimensions. One is the physical holdings of a particular security, which is known as position. The other refers to risk position, which represents the exposure to a particular risk. For example, a bank may hold one unit of a bond denominated in a currency different to the bank's reporting currency. Therefore, the bank has a position of one unit in the bond; at the same time the bond may be mapped to a risk position for foreign exchange risk, a number of risk positions for interest rate risk (in the foreign currency), and one or more risk positions for credit risk. The Basel Committee also uses the risk position as a unit in the trading book capital requirement calculation.

The Euler Decomposition When decomposing portfolio risks we naturally want the decomposed risks to satisfy the condition that the sums of decomposed risks equal the total risk. Of course, this does not naturally happen for standalone risk measures and hence we need to consider another measure of risk, still based on the portfolio-level risk, that naturally reflects the risk contribution of portfolio items. For our linear portfolio we consider a portfolio-level risk measure ρ, which has the properties that

- ρ is continuously differentiable (i.e., $\rho \in C^1$).
- ρ is homogeneous of degree 1 (i.e., the risk measure satisfies $\rho(t\mathbf{X}) = t\rho(\mathbf{X})$ for scalar $t = 1$ and a stochastic vector $\mathbf{X}$).

We then have a natural risk decomposition by the famous *Euler formula*[7]

$$\rho = \sum_{i=1}^{m} h_i \frac{\partial \rho}{\partial h_i}$$

and, by normalization

$$1 = \frac{\sum_{i=1}^{m} h_i \frac{\partial \rho}{\partial h_i}}{\rho} = \sum_{i=1}^{m} a_i.$$

The Euler decomposition hence provides us with a risk decomposition that satisfies the full allocation property. That is, all the portfolio risk (capital) obtained using risk measure ρ is allocated. In order to obtain Euler decompositions of the portfolio volatility risk measure, σ_p, that we have discussed above we first differentiate the standard deviation of the portfolio, σ_p, obtaining

$$\frac{\partial \sigma_p}{\partial \vec{\Delta}} = \left(\vec{\Delta}'\Sigma\vec{\Delta}\right)^{-\frac{1}{2}} \Sigma\vec{\Delta} = \sigma_p^{-1}\Sigma\vec{\Delta}. \tag{2.9}$$

The equation (2.9) is hence an n-dimensional vector of risk contributions to the $j = 1, \ldots, n$ portfolio risk factors. By additivity we can of course also calculate the contribution of a

---

[7]The Euler formula states that a function f of n variables $x_1, \ldots, x_n$ with continuous partial derivatives is homogeneous of degree k if and only if the following equation holds for all $x_1, \ldots, x_n \in D$, an open domain

$$\sum_{i=1}^{n} x_i \frac{\partial f}{\partial x_i} = kf.$$

portfolio position, $i = 1, \ldots, m$. Specifically, denote the delta vector for the specific position i to the $j = 1, \ldots, n$ risk factors by $\widetilde{\boldsymbol{\Delta}}_i$ such that

$$\widetilde{\boldsymbol{\Delta}}_i = \begin{bmatrix} h_i \Delta_i^1 & \cdots & h_i \Delta_i^n \end{bmatrix}'$$

then

$$\sum_{i=1}^{m} \sigma_p^{-1} \left(\vec{\boldsymbol{\Delta}}' \boldsymbol{\Sigma} \widetilde{\boldsymbol{\Delta}}_i \right) = \sigma_p.$$

A Numerical Example of Euler Risk Contributions Consider a portfolio with three positions in two risk factors, S_1 and S_2, where $\vec{\boldsymbol{\Delta}} = (3, 5)$, $\widetilde{\boldsymbol{\Delta}}_1 = \widetilde{\boldsymbol{\Delta}}_3 = (1, 1)$, and $\widetilde{\boldsymbol{\Delta}}_2 = (1, 3)$. Using the covariance matrix, $\boldsymbol{\Sigma}$, such that

$$\boldsymbol{\Sigma} = \begin{bmatrix} 1 & 0.5 \\ 0.5 & 2 \end{bmatrix}$$

we obtain from equation (2.9) the contribution from each risk factor (i.e., portfolio risk position),

$$\sigma_p = \sqrt{74}$$

$$\vec{\boldsymbol{\Delta}}_1 \frac{\partial \sigma_p}{\partial \vec{\boldsymbol{\Delta}}_1} = 0.22297 \sqrt{74}$$

$$\vec{\boldsymbol{\Delta}}_2 \frac{\partial \sigma_p}{\partial \vec{\boldsymbol{\Delta}}_2} = 0.77703 \sqrt{74}$$

such that

$$\vec{\boldsymbol{\Delta}}_1 \frac{\partial \sigma_p}{\partial \vec{\boldsymbol{\Delta}}_1} + \vec{\boldsymbol{\Delta}}_2 \frac{\partial \sigma_p}{\partial \vec{\boldsymbol{\Delta}}_1} = \sqrt{74}.$$

For the portfolio (physical) position view of the contributions we have,

$$\sigma_p^{-1} \left(\vec{\boldsymbol{\Delta}}' \boldsymbol{\Sigma} \widetilde{\boldsymbol{\Delta}}_1 \right) = \sigma_p^{-1} \left(\vec{\boldsymbol{\Delta}}' \boldsymbol{\Sigma} \widetilde{\boldsymbol{\Delta}}_3 \right) = 0.22973 \sqrt{74}$$

$$\sigma_p^{-1} \left(\vec{\boldsymbol{\Delta}}' \boldsymbol{\Sigma} \widetilde{\boldsymbol{\Delta}}_2 \right) = 0.54054 \sqrt{74}$$

and, hence we have that,

$$\sum_{i=1}^{3} \sigma_p^{-1} \left(\vec{\boldsymbol{\Delta}}' \boldsymbol{\Sigma} \widetilde{\boldsymbol{\Delta}}_i \right) = \sqrt{74}$$

as expected. We can therefore conclude that for this portfolio the percentage volatility contribution of risk factor 1, S_1, is approximately 23% and for risk factor 2, S_2, it is approximately 77%. As we have mentioned above, the risk contributions in terms of the portfolio risk factors are usually referred to as the risk positions of the portfolio. This is different than the actual physical portfolio positions contributions, and in terms of the three portfolio positions, we have that position 1 and 3 each contribute an approximate 23% of total portfolio risk while position 2 contributes approximately 54% to total portfolio risk. Hence, closing out or hedging position 2 should reduce portfolio volatility the most.

From Volatility Contributions to VaR and CVaR Contributions Now, by the equivalence of the volatility risk measure, σ_p, with value at risk, VaR, in this case, we have that

$$\frac{\partial \text{VaR}(\alpha)}{\partial \vec{\Delta}} = Z_\alpha \frac{\partial \sigma_p}{\partial \vec{\Delta}}. \tag{2.10}$$

Similarly, by the equivalence of VaR(α) and CVaR(α) in this setting,

$$\frac{\partial \text{CVaR}(\alpha)}{\partial \vec{\Delta}} = \left(\frac{\phi(Z_\alpha)/(1 - N(Z_\alpha))}{Z_\alpha} \right) \frac{\partial \text{VaR}(\alpha)}{\partial \vec{\Delta}}$$

where, again, these decompositions satisfy the full allocation property. For example, we have that

$$\text{CVaR}(\alpha) = \vec{\Delta}' \frac{\partial \text{CVaR}(\alpha)}{\partial \vec{\Delta}}.$$

We now continue with our equity portfolio example focusing on the computation of risk contributions.

Computation of Risk Contributions for the Sample Equity Portfolio Table 2.1 displays the VaR(0.99) and CVaR(0.99) risk measures for the aggregate equity portfolio and the equity positions, $P_1, \ldots, P_5$, using the covariance matrix in (2.8) and holding vector (2.4). It also displays the VaR(0.99) and CVaR(0.99) Euler risk contributions, denoted Cont VaR(0.99) and Cont CVaR(0.99) respectively, with respect to the positions, $P_1, \ldots, P_5$.

Table 2.1 shows that risk is diversified in the context of the portfolio since risk contributions are significantly lower than standalone risk for the equity positions. One can also measure the degree of diversification obtained by an instrument or subportfolio when put in the context of the portfolio by dividing the risk contributions by the standalone risk. For example, for VaR(0.99) risk contributions divided by standalone VaR(0.99) we obtain portfolio diversification percentages, for positions $P_1, \ldots, P_5$, as

$$P_1 = 69.5\%$$

$$P_2 = 67.8\%$$

TABLE 2.1 The VaR(0.99) and CVaR(0.99) Risk Measures for the Aggregate Portfolio and the Equity Positions, $P_1, \ldots, P_5$. The Table also Displays the VaR(0.99) and CVaR(0.99) Euler Risk Contributions with Respect to the Positions $P_1, \ldots, P_5$

Equity position	VaR(0.99)	CVaR(0.99)	Cont VaR(0.99)	Cont CVaR(0.99)
P_1	93.05	106.61	64.69	74.11
P_2	93.63	127.27	63.54	72.79
P_3	46.29	53.04	18.99	21.76
P_4	15.95	18.27	2.25	2.57
P_5	33.55	38.44	8.07	9.25
Portfolio	157.54	180.48	157.54	180.48

$$P_3 = 41.0\%$$

$$P_4 = 14.1\%$$

$$P_5 = 24.0\%.$$

Clearly, equity position, P_4, has the largest diversification benefit in the portfolio. This might seem unintuitive because, for example, position P_5 has a lower correlation with the other portfolio positions. However, position size also matters because of the delta component in the risk contribution equations and equity position P_4 only has one holding. This shows that diversification is not only a function of the covariance matrix but also the position sensitivity that contains the holding.

If position sensitivity is the same for all positions, then the covariance matrix is the sole source of diversification effects. Consider therefore a modified sample equity portfolio with unit holding in each of the equities, $P_1, \ldots, P_5$, and, using the covariance matrix

$$\Sigma = \begin{bmatrix} 1 & 0.45 & 0.85 & 0.35 & 0.15 \\ 0.45 & 1 & 0.45 & 0.45 & 0.15 \\ 0.85 & 0.45 & 1 & 0.45 & 0.15 \\ 0.35 & 0.45 & 0.45 & 1 & 0.15 \\ 0.15 & 0.15 & 0.15 & 0.15 & 1 \end{bmatrix}$$

where all variances are equal to unity but with same covariances as before in the covariance matrix (2.8). With the modified unit holding and the new covariance matrix we obtain that each equity position standalone VaR(0.99) = $Z_{0.99} \approx 2.33$ since each equity return is standard normal distributed.

Calculating the portfolio diversification percentages for this case we obtain,

$$P_1 = 79.8\%$$

$$P_2 = 71.6\%$$

$$P_3 = 82.8\%$$

$$P_4 = 68.6\%$$

$$P_5 = 45.9\%.$$

This shows that the equity position with the lowest correlation to the other portfolio positions, P_5, indeed now has the largest diversification effect in the portfolio context, or, put differently, the lowest concentration in the context of the portfolio.

Euler Risk Decompositions and Hedging The Euler risk decomposition is a convex function of the sensitivity vector $\vec{\Delta}$. Hence, we can differentiate to find the minima of the risk contribution. Let σ_{jl}^2 be the risk factor covariance between risk factor j and risk factor l; then, for VaR as risk measure, this entails solving for $\vec{\Delta}_j$ in the equation

$$\frac{\partial \text{VaR}(\alpha)}{\partial \vec{\Delta}_j} = Z_\alpha \left(\frac{\sigma_{jj}^2 \vec{\Delta}_j + \sum_{l \neq j}^n \sigma_{jl}^2 \vec{\Delta}_l}{\sigma_p} \right) = 0$$

yielding,

$$\vec{\Delta}_j^b = \frac{-\sum_{j\neq i}^n \sigma_{jl}^2 \vec{\Delta}_l}{\sigma_{jj}}.$$

The obtained $\vec{\Delta}_j^b$ may be referred to as the *best hedging position* of risk factor j. We note that in this setting this best hedging position is independent of whether the risk measure is volatility, VaR, or CVaR. By plotting the portfolio risk measure for a local grid of holdings in a particular instrument, i, we can trace out how the portfolio risk profile changes with different holdings. The minimum of this profile is the best hedging position. The reader is referred to Litterman (1996) for further examples of risk contributions and best hedging position applications to simple linear portfolios. Litterman also discuss the fact that in large portfolios with many risk factors and positions it may be useful to find a small (delta) replicating portfolio with just a few positions and risk factors to obtain a simplified view of the portfolio risk profile.

Interpretation as Regression The Euler risk decompositions also has a useful regression, or equivalently, conditional expectation interpretation. This is because for the normal distribution the conditional expectation and linear regression coincide. In particular for the j:th risk factor we obtained above (see equation (2.10)) that

$$\frac{1}{Z_\alpha} \frac{\partial \text{VaR}(\alpha)}{\partial \vec{\Delta}_j} = \frac{\Sigma_j \vec{\Delta}}{\sigma_p} = \frac{\sigma_{jj}^2 \vec{\Delta}_j + \sum_{l\neq j}^n \sigma_{jl}^2 \vec{\Delta}_l}{\sigma_p}$$

Σ_j denoting the j:th row of the covariance matrix Σ and σ_{jl}^2 the (j,l):th component of Σ. Notice therefore that $\Sigma_j \vec{\Delta}$ corresponds to the covariance between risk factor j and the set of all risk factors. By the definition of the classical linear regression coefficient, β, as covariance divided by variance we therefore have

$$\frac{1}{Z_\alpha \sigma_p} \frac{\partial \text{VaR}(\alpha)}{\partial \Delta_j} = \beta_j \qquad (2.11)$$

where β_j is the least squares regression coefficient from the regression of risk factor j returns on the total portfolio returns. That is,

$$\beta_j = \frac{\text{COV}(r_j, r_p)}{\sigma_p}$$

where

$$r_j = \Delta_j(S_j(T) - S_j(t))$$

is the risk factor j returns, and

$$r_p = \vec{\Delta}'(S(T) - S(t))$$

is the portfolio returns. The β parameter here is the same as in the famous capital asset pricing model (CAPM). According to CAPM one can write the expected return of an asset j as a function of the risk-free rate of interest, r_f, the asset's β with respect to the market portfolio such that

$$E(r_j) = r_f + \beta E(r_p - r_f). \qquad (2.12)$$

See Sharpe (1964). To gain insight into this result consider first the case when $\beta = 0$. That is, the risk factor contribution is null, or in CAPM terminology, the risk factor is uncorrelated with the portfolio. In our case, since the risk factor itself is always included in the portfolio $\beta = 0$ typically happens in the degenerate case with $\sigma_{ij} = 0$ as well as when $\sigma_{ij} > 0$ is exactly offset by the covariances with the portfolio. If $\beta < 0$, this means the risk factor is, on average, negatively related to the portfolio and hence provides a form of insurance or hedge. Garman (1997) and Hallerbach (2003) contain further discussions on risk contributions or so-called component risk as well as the relation of the risk contributions to CAPM β:s in this linear, delta normal, model setting.

Decomposing Risk Factor Contributions into Systematic and Idiosyncratic Risk Especially in the asset management industry it is practice to decompose risk not only per risk factor (that is per risk position) but also in the systematic and idiosyncratic component of the risk factor. The asset returns for factor $j = 1, \ldots, n$ is modeled as a multifactor model

$$r_j(t) = \alpha_j + a_{1j}X_1(t) + a_{2j}X_2(t) + \ldots + a_{Kj}X_K(t) + \varepsilon_j(t) \tag{2.13}$$

where $\{X_k(t)\}_{k=1}^K$ are the common factors (e.g., country and industry factors), $\{a_{kj}\}_{k=1}^K$ are the factor loadings (factor betas) for asset j on the common factors. Finally, $\varepsilon_j(t)$ is the asset j specific factor. For example, Fama and French (1993) model stock and bond returns with multifactor models. In matrix format we have that

$$\mathbf{r}(t) = \mathbf{A}\mathbf{X}(t) + \varepsilon$$

with $\mathbf{X}$ a $1 \times K$ vector and $\mathbf{A}$ a $K \times n$ matrix, being the factor loading matrix, and ε the $n \times 1$ vector representing the idiosyncratic risks where $\varepsilon \sim N(0, \mathbf{\Omega}_\varepsilon)$. Since by definition the asset-specific factor is independent of the common factors the joint covariance of returns, $\mathbf{r}(t)$, is given by

$$\widetilde{\mathbf{\Sigma}} = \mathbf{A}'\mathbf{\Omega}_X\mathbf{A} + \mathbf{\Omega}_\varepsilon = \widetilde{\mathbf{\Sigma}}_X + \mathbf{\Omega}_\varepsilon$$

where $\mathbf{\Omega}_X$ is the $K \times K$ covariance matrix of $\mathbf{X}$ and $\mathbf{\Omega}_\varepsilon$ is the $n \times n$ covariance matrix of ε. Replacing $\mathbf{\Sigma}$ by $\widetilde{\mathbf{\Sigma}}$ in our Euler risk decomposition formulas we obtain, for example, for portfolio volatility, σ_p,

$$\frac{\partial \sigma_p}{\partial \vec{\mathbf{\Delta}}} = \frac{\widetilde{\mathbf{\Sigma}}_X \vec{\mathbf{\Delta}}}{\sqrt{\sigma_p^2}} + \frac{\mathbf{\Omega}_\varepsilon \vec{\mathbf{\Delta}}}{\sqrt{\sigma_p^2}} \tag{2.14}$$

where

$$\sigma_p^2 = \vec{\mathbf{\Delta}}'\widetilde{\mathbf{\Sigma}}_X\vec{\mathbf{\Delta}} + \vec{\mathbf{\Delta}}'\mathbf{\Omega}_\varepsilon\vec{\mathbf{\Delta}}.$$

The first term in equation (2.14) represents the risk factor contribution from systematic risk explained by the common factors. The second term is attributed to a risk factors idiosyncratic risk.

Economic Interpretation of Euler Decomposition We remarked above that the Euler decomposition has the full allocation property. That is, exactly the total risk is allocated. However, any risk decomposition method can be adapted to this property by simple normalization. This leads to the question of why we should consider the Euler decomposition and not just any other decomposition. The answer lies in the economic interpretation of the Euler decomposition and its role in portfolio optimization.

Consider an equity portfolio with holdings $\{b_j\}_{j=1}^n$ in the $\{S_j\}_{j=1}^n$ equity risk factors. The Sharpe ratio (Sharpe, 1994), denoted by S, relates the expected portfolio returns to a risk measure in ratio form and is defined for a portfolio as

$$S = \frac{\mathbf{h}'\boldsymbol{\mu}}{\rho}$$

where $\mathbf{h} = (b_1,\ldots,b_n)'$ is the holdings vector and $\boldsymbol{\mu} = (\mu_1,\ldots,\mu_n)'$ is the expected returns vector for the equities. Furthermore, ρ is a continuously differentiable and homogeneous of degree 1 risk measure. By homogeneity of our risk measure, we can decompose ρ as above with the Euler formula,

$$\rho = \sum_{j=1}^n b_j \frac{\partial \rho}{\partial b_j}$$

and, by normalization

$$1 = \frac{\sum_{j=1}^n b_j \frac{\partial \rho}{\partial b_j}}{\rho} = \sum_{j=1}^n \pi_j.$$

Now, as in Nyström and Skoglund (2003a), since the Sharpe ratio is given by S it is natural to define

$$S_j^* = \frac{b_j \mu_j}{b_j \frac{\partial \rho}{\partial b_j}}$$

as the marginal Sharpe ratio of equity position j, $j = 1,\ldots,n$. Then,

$$S = \sum_{j=1}^n S_j^* \pi_j$$

where $\pi_j \in [0,1]$ for $j = 1,\ldots,n$ is the fraction allocated to equity position j. The investor optimization problem can then be formulated as, with π_j^0 indicating initial allocation,

$$\max_{\pi} \sum_{j=1}^n S_j^* \pi_j - f\left[\sum_{j=1}^n \left(\pi_j - \pi_j^0\right)^2\right]$$

where $f(\cdot)$ is a penalty function for the costs associated with reallocation and subject to the constraint $\sum_{j=1}^n \pi_j = 1$. Taking $f(V) = V$ we obtain from the first-order condition

$$\pi_j - \pi_j^0 = \frac{1}{2}\left(S_j^* - \frac{1}{n}\sum_{j=1}^n S_j^*\right).$$

Hence it is optimal to allocate π_j in relation to equity position (risk factor) j:s marginal Sharpe ratios deviation from the mean marginal Sharpe ratio of the portfolio. Hence for a given equity to be considered for inclusion in the portfolio we require that the expected return divided by the marginal risk should be larger than the corresponding mean of the portfolio. The inputs to the portfolio manager's optimization process are therefore a (normalized) vector of Euler risk contributions and the expected returns vector. The optimal portfolio has the characteristic that

$$S_j^* = \overline{S}^*, \quad j = 1, \ldots, n$$

where $\overline{S}^* = \frac{1}{n}\sum_{j=1}^{n} S_j^*$ is the average marginal Sharpe ratios. Tasche (1999) proves that the Euler decomposition is the only risk decomposition that is consistent with (local) portfolio optimization. For a second economic justification of Euler risk contributions as the only fair allocation in cooperative game theory we refer to Denault (2001).

Estimating the Covariance Matrix of Risk Factors

Having calculated the position sensitivities to the risk factors, the second important model component in the linear delta normal model is an estimate of the covariance matrix of the risk factors. Let $R \equiv (R_1, R_2, \ldots, R_t)'$ be an independent and identically distributed size t sample of returns from the $j = 1, \ldots, n$ risk factors that are distributed as multivariate normal with $R_t \sim N(\mu, \Sigma) \; \forall t$. The log likelihood function takes the form

$$l(\mu, \Sigma, R) = c - \frac{nt}{2}\log(2\pi) - \frac{t}{2}\log(\det[\Sigma]) - \frac{1}{2}\sum_{s=1}^{t}(R_s - \mu)'\Sigma^{-1}(R_s - \mu). \qquad (2.15)$$

Solving for the first-order conditions $\frac{\partial l(\mu, \Sigma, R)}{\partial \mu} = 0$ and $\frac{\partial l(\mu, \Sigma, R)}{\partial \Sigma^{-1}} = 0$ respectively, yields the well-known two-step maximum likelihood estimators

$$\hat{\mu} = \frac{1}{t}\sum_{s=1}^{t} R_s$$

$$\hat{\Sigma} = \frac{1}{t}\sum_{s=1}^{t}(R_s - \hat{\mu})(R_s - \hat{\mu})'.$$

From a risk management perspective it is useful to understand the uncertainty in these estimates and hence the *model estimation risk or parameter risk*. First, since $\hat{\mu}$ is a linear combination of normals, it is itself normally distributed with

$$\hat{\mu} \sim N\left(\mu, \frac{1}{t}\Sigma\right).$$

The distribution of the covariance matrix estimate, $\hat{\Sigma}$, is a direct generalization of the well-known χ^2-distribution (chi-square) to a matrix distribution, the so-called Wishart distribution with $(t-1)$ degrees of freedom. We write

$$t\hat{\Sigma} \sim W_n(\Sigma, t-1)$$

where $W_n(\Sigma, t-1)$ denotes an n-dimensional Wishart distribution with $t-1$ degrees of freedom. The Wishart distribution hence plays a central role in estimation of the covariance matrix of the multivariate normal distribution. The estimated averages and the variances and covariances are independent with the estimated averages normally distributed and the estimated variances and covariances Wishart distributed. See Anderson (1958).

The sample covariance matrix above is the standard estimator of the covariance matrix. A true covariance matrix should be positive definite in general. However, the sample covariance matrix can be poorly estimated in two typical situations. First is when the number of risk factors, $j = 1, \ldots, n$, is large in proportion to the number of historical observations, $s = 1, \ldots, t$, which may result in a matrix that is not full rank. The other, even harder situation may arise because the extreme covariances are unreliable with a tendency for large values to become even larger and for small values to become even smaller. Typical remedies for a poorly estimated covariance matrix include reducing ranks or shrinkage. The reduction of ranks can use principal component analysis, which we will discuss later in this chapter in the section on simulation-based valuation. The idea behind the shrinkage estimator is to pull the extreme coefficients toward some central value. Though the shrinkage approach introduces some bias, the estimated covariance matrix has a smaller variance than the sample covariance matrix. See, for example, Jorion (1986) and Ledoit and Wolf (2003, 2004) on shrinkage estimators.

Distribution of Risk Measures

Using the Wishart distribution, obtained above as the distribution of the covariances, we can now consider the distribution of the portfolio risk measures. First, substituting estimates for population counterparts we have for the estimated portfolio volatility, $\hat{\sigma}_p$,

$$\hat{\sigma}_p = \sqrt{\vec{\Delta}'\Sigma\vec{\Delta}} \sim W_1(\sigma_p, t) \equiv \sigma_p \chi_t^2$$

with χ_t^2 the chi-square distribution with t degrees of freedom, and hence the estimated VaR(α), denoted $\widehat{\text{VaR}}(\alpha)$, has the distribution

$$\widehat{\text{VaR}}(\alpha) \sim Z_\alpha \sigma_p \chi_t^2$$

with a symmetric $\delta\%$ coverage interval defined by

$$\frac{\widehat{\text{VaR}}(\alpha)}{Z_\alpha \sigma_p} \in (\chi_t^2(1 - \delta/2), \chi_t^2(\delta/2))$$

and similarly for CVaR(α).

To consider also confidence intervals for Euler risk contributions we recall that the beta (β) or least squares regression coefficient from the regression of risk factor j returns on the portfolio returns was the main component. From classical linear regression analysis and the model,

$$y = \mathbf{X}'\gamma + u, u \sim N(0, \sigma_u^2)$$

it is well known that the estimated γ, denoted $\hat{\gamma}$, has the property that

$$\hat{\gamma} \sim N(\gamma, \sigma_u^2(\mathbf{X}'\mathbf{X})^{-1}).$$

Applying this in our setting, denoting by r_p the period realized portfolio return,

$$r_j = \beta r_p + v, v \sim N(0, \sigma_v^2)$$

with

$$\hat{\beta} \sim N\left(\beta, \frac{\sigma_v^2}{\sum_{s=1}^{t} r_{p,s}^2}\right)$$

and, for example, a $\delta\%$ coverage interval for VaR(α) risk contributions is defined by

$$\frac{\hat{\beta} - \beta}{Z_\alpha \sigma_p \sigma_v^2 / \sum_{s=1}^{t} r_{p,s}^2} \in (N(1 - \delta/2), N(\delta/2))$$

where N denotes the normal cumulative density function. Again, there is a similar expression for a coverage interval of CVaR(α) risk contributions.

Probabilistic Stress Testing

Finally in this section on the linear delta normal risk model we shall consider an attractive method for stress testing discussed in, for example, Nyström and Skoglund (2002) that uses conditional distributions and stress events. In the case of a linear portfolio with multivariate normal risk model, the conditional probabilistic stress tests are analytical due to the fact that the normal distribution is closed under conditioning. For an n-dimensional multivariate normal vector $\mathbf{X}$ decomposed as an $n_1 + n_2$-dimensional vector, we can write

$$\begin{bmatrix} \mathbf{X}_1 \\ \mathbf{X}_2 \end{bmatrix} \sim N\left(\begin{bmatrix} \boldsymbol{\mu}_1 \\ \boldsymbol{\mu}_2 \end{bmatrix}, \begin{bmatrix} \boldsymbol{\Sigma}_{11} & \boldsymbol{\Sigma}_{12} \\ \boldsymbol{\Sigma}_{21} & \boldsymbol{\Sigma}_{22} \end{bmatrix}\right).$$

where the mean vector, $\boldsymbol{\mu}$, and the covariance matrix, $\boldsymbol{\Sigma}$, has been partitioned accordingly. Now, conditioning on $\mathbf{X}_2 = \mathbf{x}_2$ we have that,

$$\mathbf{X}_1 \mid \mathbf{X}_2 = \mathbf{x}_2 \sim N(\boldsymbol{\mu}_1 + \boldsymbol{\Sigma}_{12}\boldsymbol{\Sigma}_{22}^{-1}(\mathbf{x}_2 - \boldsymbol{\mu}_2), \boldsymbol{\Sigma}_{11} - \boldsymbol{\Sigma}_{12}\boldsymbol{\Sigma}_{22}^{-1}\boldsymbol{\Sigma}_{21})$$

where $\boldsymbol{\Sigma}_{22}^{-1}$ is the inverse of the matrix, $\boldsymbol{\Sigma}_{22}$. See, for example, Greene (1993, p. 90). Setting mean values to zero we can simplify further to get

$$\mathbf{X}_1 \mid \mathbf{X}_2 = \mathbf{x}_2 \sim N(\boldsymbol{\Sigma}_{12}\boldsymbol{\Sigma}_{22}^{-1}\mathbf{x}_2, \boldsymbol{\Sigma}_{11} - \boldsymbol{\Sigma}_{12}\boldsymbol{\Sigma}_{22}^{-1}\boldsymbol{\Sigma}_{21}). \tag{2.16}$$

We can now think of the conditioning events, $\mathbf{X}_2 = \mathbf{x}_2$, as, for example, the event that one or a few stocks experiences a downturn by 10% or the event that short-term interest rates rise by 100 basis points at the same time as a downturn by 10% in a stock. Using a conditional distribution we can estimate the risk in our portfolio contingent on such stress events. This is because we can use equation (2.16) and obtain the conditional distribution of our risk factors.

In general, the stress events themselves can be defined from expert knowledge or actual historical stress events. In practice one may object to using the normal distribution assumption and an estimated covariance matrix when conditioning on stress events. Indeed, during stress it is common that volatilities and correlations tend to grow. This observation is certainly not consistent with the simple multivariate normal distribution and we will discuss this issue later in the context of stylized univariate and multivariate risk factor returns. For now it suffices to notice that we may condition the covariance matrix, Σ, on the extremity of stress events or, phrased differently, on the expected experienced volatility and correlations under the stress.

A Numerical Example of Probabilistic Stress Testing We now consider a numerical example of probabilistic stress testing reusing again our equity portfolio example. In the example we consider the case of unit holdings in each of the 5 equity positions, $P_1, \ldots, P_5$, in the portfolio and a covariance matrix, for the time horizon $T - t$, given by the covariance matrix, Σ, in (2.8). Now, if we condition on an extreme negative return for position P_5 such that

$$S_5(T) - S_5(t) = -50$$

we can use the covariance matrix, Σ, to get

$$\Sigma_{11} = \begin{bmatrix} 4 & 0.45 & 0.85 & 0.35 \\ 0.45 & 5 & 0.45 & 0.45 \\ 0.85 & 0.45 & 11 & 0.45 \\ 0.35 & 0.45 & 0.45 & 47 \end{bmatrix} \tag{2.17}$$

$$\Sigma_{22} = [13]$$

$$\Sigma'_{12} = \Sigma_{21} = \begin{bmatrix} 0.15 & 0.15 & 0.15 & 0.15 \end{bmatrix}$$

where Σ'_{12} denotes the transpose of the matrix Σ_{12}. Here $\Sigma'_{12} = \Sigma_{21}$ contains the covariances of portfolio position 5 to the other positions in the portfolio. We therefore have a conditional normal distribution as

$$\vec{S}(T) - \vec{S}(t) \mid S_5(T) - S_5(t) = -50$$

$$\sim N \left(\begin{bmatrix} -0.576\,92 \\ -0.576\,92 \\ -0.576\,92 \\ -0.576\,92 \end{bmatrix}, \begin{bmatrix} 3.998\,3 & 0.448\,27 & 0.848\,27 & 0.348\,27 \\ 0.448\,27 & 4.998\,3 & 0.448\,27 & 0.448\,27 \\ 0.848\,27 & 0.448\,27 & 10.998 & 0.448\,27 \\ 0.348\,27 & 0.448\,27 & 0.448\,27 & 46.998 \end{bmatrix} \right)$$

where

$$\vec{S}(T) - \vec{S}(t) = \begin{bmatrix} S_1(T) - S_1(t) \\ S_2(T) - S_2(t) \\ S_3(T) - S_3(t) \\ S_4(T) - S_4(t) \end{bmatrix}.$$

Using the properties of the normal distribution as in equation (2.3) we now obtain the conditional 99% VaR, denoted $\text{VaR}^C(0.99)$, as given by

$$\text{VaR}^C(0.99) = 2.3077 + Z_{0.99} \times \sigma_p = 2.3077 + 2.33 \times \sqrt{72.9} \approx 22.22.$$

In contrast, the unconditional distribution $\text{VaR}(0.99)$ for equity positions, $P_1, \ldots, P_4$, is

$$\text{VaR}(0.99) = 2.33 \times \sqrt{73} \approx 19.82.$$

Knowing that equity position 5 has a large negative return of -50 VaR for positions, $P_1, \ldots, P_4$, has hence significantly increased. Note here that the -50 absolute return of equity position 5 is equivalent to an almost -19% relative return. Specifically,

$$S_5(T) - S_5(t) = 213.75 - 263.75 = -50$$

and hence

$$\frac{S_5(T) - S_5(t)}{S_5(t)} = \frac{-50}{263.75} \approx -0.1895.$$

If we now increase the common covariance factor of portfolio position 5 to the rest of the portfolio from 0.15 to 0.95 (i.e., $\Sigma'_{12} = \Sigma_{21} = \begin{bmatrix} 0.95 & 0.95 & 0.95 & 0.95 \end{bmatrix}$), we get that

$$\text{VaR}^C(0.99) = 14.615 + Z_{0.99} \times \sigma_p = 14.615 + 2.33 \times \sqrt{71.89} \approx 34.35$$

and hence conditional VaR, VaR^C, has increased even more compared to the unconditional case. Note, however, that the increase in conditional VaR comes mainly from a change in conditional mean of the portfolio profit-and-loss distribution and not from a significant change in conditional portfolio volatility. In fact, portfolio volatility, σ_p, has reduced from $\sqrt{72.9} \approx 8.54$ to $\sqrt{71.89} \approx 8.47$ when portfolio position 5 common covariance factor to the rest of the portfolio has increased.

While conditional VaR, VaR^C, represents one way to integrate stress events into the risk calculation one can also consider expected portfolio losses only. In our example above this corresponds to focusing on the conditional expected mean of portfolio profit and loss with risk factors $S_1(t), \ldots, S_4(t)$ while conditioning on the stressed return for risk factor $S_5(t)$. For example, we calculated the conditional expected portfolio loss above as 2.3077 and 14.615 respectively with the covariance of equity risk factor 5 returns to the other risk factors being either 0.15 or 0.95. This observation reveals that stress events affect not only the unexpected loss but also the expected loss. Oftentimes the impact on the expected loss can be even bigger.

QUADRATIC PORTFOLIOS

For option portfolios as well as bonds with a significant amount of nonlinearity, the approximation errors from using only a first-order sensitivity might be considered too high. Our focus in this section is therefore to consider a quadratic portfolio approximation capturing the second-order sensitivity of the portfolio instruments as well. However, we still maintain the assumption of normally distributed risk factors.

Our analysis of the quadratic portfolio risk will focus on the derivation of a representation for the quadratic form distribution. This is to provide intuition on the change of distribution from the simple normal distribution in the linear model to a more complex distribution in the quadratic case. In fact, the distribution is not explicit in general, although the Fourier transform is, and calculating risk measures for the quadratic portfolio hence requires numerical techniques such as Fourier inversions or other tail approximations. We will highlight the most frequently used numerical techniques for calculating quadratic portfolio risk measures but refer to the literature for details on implementation and examples.

Quadratic Portfolio Representation

Using a quadratic approximation of our portfolio we consider the probability of portfolio loss exceeding a fixed loss level, y, such that $P(Q(X) \leq -y)$ where $Q(X) = \Delta X + X'\Gamma X$ is a quadratic form in the multivariate normal vector $X \sim N(\mathbf{0}, \Sigma)$. Using our previous risk factor notation,

$$X \equiv S(T) - S(t) \sim N(\mathbf{0}, \Sigma)$$

is multivariate normal with $j = 1, \ldots, n$ portfolio risk factors. Here Δ is the delta vector of the portfolio and Γ is the Hessian matrix of second-order and cross-derivatives.

After a diagonalization procedure that we describe below we obtain that the portfolio is distributed as a sum of independent, scaled, non-central chi-square variables. The distribution is not explicit in general but the Fourier transform of the distribution can be obtained using the independence. We can then either invert the transform numerically or make some type of approximation of the transform in order to be able to invert explicitly.

Various solutions have been proposed in the literature. For example, Fallon (1996) and Pichler and Selitsch (2000) use a Cornish-Fisher expansion. Rouvinez (1997) uses the trapezoidal rule to invert the characteristic function. Cardenas et al. (1997) use the fast Fourier transform and Duffie and Pan (2001) use an inversion formula due to Gil-Pelaez (1951) and control the approximation errors in the numerical inversion of the Fourier transform using the Poisson summation.[8] Using either of these methods, approximate Euler risk contributions can be obtained as ε-perturbations on the holdings. For m portfolio instruments this of course requires m recomputations with the perturbed holdings. It can be quite time consuming for a large portfolio.

A simpler method to approximate the quadratic portfolio risk is the method of moments. However, the method of moments implies that one only makes use of, for example, the information contained in the first four moments of the distribution. However, the few moments may very well contain little information about the tail behavior of the distribution. Moreover, since the reference distribution is arbitrary there is no way to obtain probabilistic error bounds on the estimates.

Yet another approach is to use the method of stationary phase to develop an asymptotic expansion. One can after manipulation make use of a Taylor expansion at the stationary points of the phase, hence developing an asymptotic expansion for the integral. This route has been followed by Nyström and Skoglund (2003b) for VaR and Nyström (2008) for CVaR.

Computation of Second-Order Sensitivities Using a quadratic portfolio approximation requires second-order and cross-derivatives for the positions. We therefore extend our previous example of sensitivities for bonds and options to compute the second-order sensitivities.

Bond Convexity For bonds a quadratic expansion entails including also the so-called modified convexity term in the approximation, yielding

$$-\frac{\partial PV}{\partial y} \frac{1}{PV(1+y)} \times dy + \frac{1}{2} \frac{\partial^2 PV}{\partial y^2} \frac{1}{PV(1+y)^2} \times (dy)^2$$

---

[8]Duffie and Pan (2001) consider a more general setting than the multivariate normal distribution for assets we consider. They also consider exogenous jump intensities for assets in a jump diffusion model.

with y the yield. We see that for a yield increase of 1 basis point the modified duration (first term) gives a negative price impact whereas the modified convexity (second term) corresponds to a positive price impact. Common values for modified duration and modified convexity found in practice are respectively 10 and 100. For such values the approximate bond price change of a 1 basis point increase of the yield is a price decrease of 0.095%.

Option Second-Order Sensitivities To achieve a quadratic approximation of the European call option price we include second-order versions of delta, vega, and rho as well as cross-derivatives, resulting in a Hessian matrix of second-order effects. We therefore define

$$
\Gamma = \begin{bmatrix} \frac{\partial^2 c}{\partial S^2} & \frac{\partial^2 c}{\partial S \partial \sigma} & \frac{\partial^2 c}{\partial S \partial r} \\ \frac{\partial^2 c}{\partial \sigma \partial S} & \frac{\partial^2 c}{\partial \sigma^2} & \frac{\partial^2 c}{\partial \sigma \partial r} \\ \frac{\partial^2 c}{\partial r \partial S} & \frac{\partial^2 c}{\partial r \partial \sigma} & \frac{\partial^2 c}{\partial r^2} \end{bmatrix}
$$

as the Hessian matrix of the option. In common financial jargon the first and second derivatives of option prices are referred to as the Greeks. For European call options, we have that

$$
\frac{\partial^2 c}{\partial S^2} = \frac{\phi(d_1)}{S(t)\sigma\sqrt{T-t}}
$$

$$
\frac{\partial^2 c}{\partial S \partial \sigma} = \frac{d_2 \phi(d_1)}{\sigma}
$$

denoting by $\phi(\cdot)$ the normal density and d_1 and d_2, are given by

$$
d_1 = \frac{1}{\sigma\sqrt{T-t}} \ln\left[\frac{S(t)}{K} + \left(r + \frac{\sigma^2}{2}\right)(T-t)\right]
$$

$$
d_2 = d_1 - \sigma\sqrt{T-t}.
$$

The reader may consult Haug (2007, ch. 2) for explicit formulas for all the equity option Greeks.

Quadratic Portfolio Views Having illustrated the computation of second-order effects for the bond and equity option we now proceed to derive a tractable expression for the quadratic portfolio. As in the case for the linear normal model we emphasize that the risk can be viewed from both a physical position view as well as a risk (factor) position view.

Physical Position View Consider a quadratic portfolio with $i = 1, \ldots, m$ instruments and $j = 1, \ldots, n$ risk factors. Denoting by Δ_i the $n \times 1$ sensitivity vector for instrument i such that

$$
\Delta_i = \begin{bmatrix} \Delta_i^1 & \cdots & \Delta_i^n \end{bmatrix}'
$$

and by Γ_i the corresponding $n \times n$ second-order sensitivity matrix for instrument i the change in portfolio value between $T - t$ is given by

$$
V(T) - V(t) \approx \delta + \sum_{i=1}^{m} h_i \Delta_i' [S(T) - S(t)] + \frac{1}{2} \sum_{i=1}^{m} h_i [S(T) - S(t)]' \Gamma_i [S(T) - S(t)] \tag{2.18}
$$

where $V(T)$ denotes portfolio value at T, δ is a constant, that is, the time derivatives, and $\mathbf{h} = (h_1, \ldots, h_m)'$ is the position vector for the m instruments.

For example, if we have 2 positions ($m = 2$) and 3 risk factors ($n = 3$), we have that

$$V(T) - V(t) \approx \delta + h_1 \begin{bmatrix} \Delta_1^1 & \Delta_1^2 & \Delta_1^3 \end{bmatrix} \begin{bmatrix} S_1(T) - S_1(t) \\ S_2(T) - S_2(t) \\ S_3(T) - S_3(t) \end{bmatrix}$$

$$+ h_2 \begin{bmatrix} \Delta_2^1 & \Delta_2^2 & \Delta_2^3 \end{bmatrix} \begin{bmatrix} S_1(T) - S_1(t) \\ S_2(T) - S_2(t) \\ S_3(T) - S_3(t) \end{bmatrix}$$

$$+ h_1 \frac{1}{2} \begin{bmatrix} S_1(T) - S_1(t) \\ S_2(T) - S_2(t) \\ S_3(T) - S_3(t) \end{bmatrix}' \begin{bmatrix} \Gamma_1^{11} & \Gamma_1^{12} & \Gamma_1^{13} \\ \Gamma_1^{21} & \Gamma_1^{22} & \Gamma_1^{23} \\ \Gamma_1^{31} & \Gamma_1^{32} & \Gamma_1^{33} \end{bmatrix} \begin{bmatrix} S_1(T) - S_1(t) \\ S_2(T) - S_2(t) \\ S_3(T) - S_3(t) \end{bmatrix}$$

$$+ h_2 \frac{1}{2} \begin{bmatrix} S_1(T) - S_1(t) \\ S_2(T) - S_2(t) \\ S_3(T) - S_3(t) \end{bmatrix}' \begin{bmatrix} \Gamma_2^{11} & \Gamma_2^{12} & \Gamma_2^{13} \\ \Gamma_2^{21} & \Gamma_2^{22} & \Gamma_2^{23} \\ \Gamma_2^{31} & \Gamma_2^{32} & \Gamma_2^{33} \end{bmatrix} \begin{bmatrix} S_1(T) - S_1(t) \\ S_2(T) - S_2(t) \\ S_3(T) - S_3(t) \end{bmatrix}$$

where Δ_i^j indicates the delta for position i with respect to risk factor j and Γ_i^{jl} indicates the second-order derivative for position i with respect to risk factor $j = 1, 2, 3$ and $l = 1, 2, 3$.

The quadratic expansion above is also frequently used for ex-post breakdown and explanation of the profit-and-loss components for a portfolio or a position. This practice is referred to as "P/L explain" and in this case $V(T) - V(t)$ as well as $S(T) - S(t)$ is observed and the right-hand side of equation (2.18) is hence the decomposition of the observed profit or loss into $S(T) - S(t)$ first- and second-order effects.

Risk Position View Summing up all the first- and second-order positions per risk factor $j = 1, \ldots, n$ we have

$$V(T) - V(t) \approx \delta + \vec{\Delta}'[S(T) - S(t)] + \frac{1}{2}[S(T) - S(t)]'\vec{\Gamma}[S(T) - S(t)] \qquad (2.19)$$

where

$$\Delta_j = \sum_{i=1}^{m} h_i \Delta_i^j$$

$j = 1, \ldots, n$ indexing risk factors, and

$$\vec{\Gamma}_{jl} = \sum_{i=1}^{m} h_i \Gamma_i^{jl}$$

where j, l indexes the elements of the n-by-n matrix $\vec{\Gamma}$. Expressed in our previous example with 2 positions ($m = 2$) and 3 risk factors ($n = 3$),

$$\vec{\Delta}' = \begin{bmatrix} h_1 \Delta_1^1 + h_2 \Delta_2^1 & h_1 \Delta_1^2 + h_2 \Delta_2^2 & h_1 \Delta_1^3 + h_2 \Delta_2^3 \end{bmatrix}$$

$$\vec{\Gamma} = \begin{bmatrix} b_1\Gamma_1^{11} + b_2\Gamma_2^{11} & b_1\Gamma_1^{21} + b_2\Gamma_2^{21} & b_1\Gamma_1^{13} + b_2\Gamma_2^{13} \\ b_1\Gamma_1^{12} + b_2\Gamma_2^{12} & b_1\Gamma_1^{22} + b_2\Gamma_2^{22} & b_1\Gamma_1^{23} + b_2\Gamma_2^{23} \\ b_1\Gamma_1^{13} + b_2\Gamma_2^{13} & b_1\Gamma_1^{32} + b_2\Gamma_2^{32} & b_1\Gamma_1^{33} + b_2\Gamma_2^{33} \end{bmatrix}.$$

In practice an institution's portfolio can be delta hedged such that the sum of risk factor $j = 1, \dots, n$ deltas across all the positions, $i = 1, \dots, m$ is close to zero. In equation (2.19) the delta, Δ_j, for risk factor j is the sum of all position deltas with respect to risk factor j. For example, if risk factor j is a stock and the institution has one European call option position in the stock and a short stock position with holding equal to the option delta, the portfolio delta with respect to the stock is zero. In those cases only the quadratic terms will contribute to risk and the delta normal model is of course not a good description of risk as it will indicate the portfolio as risk-free.

Quadratic Portfolio Diagonalization Procedure We now focus on the derivation of a representation for the quadratic form distribution using a diagonalization procedure of the covariance matrix that will eventually simplify the quadratic form to a sum of independent random variables. There are three steps in the procedure: First, we decompose the covariance matrix using the Cholesky decomposition. Second, we use the eigenvalue decomposition to obtain independence between the risk factors. Third, we expand the quadratic form to finally obtain the (relatively) simple distribution representation.

Step 1: Cholesky Decomposition Now, since $S(T) - S(t) \sim N(\mathbf{0}, \mathbf{\Sigma})$, in equations (2.18) and (2.19), and assuming that $\mathbf{\Sigma}$ is positive definite, we can do a Cholesky decomposition of $\mathbf{\Sigma}$ as

$$\mathbf{\Sigma} = \mathbf{C'C} \tag{2.20}$$

and write $\mathbf{CZ} \sim N(\mathbf{0}, \mathbf{\Sigma})$ where $\mathbf{Z} \sim N(\mathbf{0}, \mathbf{I})$ and $\mathbf{I}$ is the identity matrix. As a simple example of the Cholesky decomposition consider the case of $n = 2$ risk factors. Using the definition of a covariance matrix,

$$\mathbf{\Sigma} = \begin{bmatrix} \sigma_1^2 & \rho\sigma_1\sigma_2 \\ \rho\sigma_1\sigma_2 & \sigma_2^2 \end{bmatrix}$$

with σ_1^2 the variance of risk factor 1, σ_2^2 the variance of risk factor 2, and, ρ, the correlation between risk factors. We can now obtain the Cholesky decomposition as

$$\mathbf{C} = \begin{bmatrix} \sigma_1 & \frac{\rho\sigma_1\sigma_2}{\sigma_1} \\ 0 & \sqrt{\frac{\sigma_2^2 - (\rho\sigma_1\sigma_2)^2}{\sigma_1^2}} \end{bmatrix}. \tag{2.21}$$

In case $\sigma_1^2 = \sigma_2^2 = 1$ this simplifies to

$$\mathbf{C} = \begin{bmatrix} 1 & \rho \\ 0 & \sqrt{1 - \rho^2} \end{bmatrix}$$

which shows that the Cholesky matrix is not defined if $|\rho| = 1$, which is the case of perfect correlation between the risk factors. This is why the common algorithm to calculate the unique Cholesky matrix, **C**, assumes that the matrix is positive definite. That is, all of its eigenvalues are positive, meaning that two or more risk factors cannot be perfectly correlated. Of course, a large covariance matrix for risk factors may not be positive definite in practice due to collinearity. In those cases one can create a so-called modified Cholesky matrix. An alternative is to apply the principal component factorization that effectively reduces the rank of the covariance matrix, that is, to remove the collinearity in the system. We will discuss such methods later in this chapter when we discuss simulation using the multivariate normal distribution. For now we assume that the covariance matrix, $\mathbf{\Sigma}$, is positive definite and use the Cholesky decomposition to simplify the quadratic form in equation (2.19),

$$V(T) - V(t) \approx \delta + \vec{\Delta}' \mathbf{C} \mathbf{Z} + \frac{1}{2} \mathbf{Z}' \mathbf{C}' \vec{\Gamma} \mathbf{C} \mathbf{Z}$$

$$= \delta + \overline{\Delta}' \mathbf{Z} + \frac{1}{2} \mathbf{Z}' \overline{\Gamma} \mathbf{Z} \tag{2.22}$$

with $\overline{\Delta}' = \vec{\Delta}' \mathbf{C}$ and $\overline{\Gamma} = \mathbf{C}' \vec{\Gamma} \mathbf{C}$.

Step 2: Eigenvalue Decomposition   The eigenvalue decomposition of $\overline{\Gamma}$ is given by $\overline{\Gamma} = \overline{\mathbf{E}} \mathbf{\Lambda} \overline{\mathbf{E}}'$ with $\overline{\mathbf{E}}$ orthogonal and $\mathbf{\Lambda}$ diagonal. Specifically,

$$\mathbf{\Lambda} = \begin{bmatrix} \Lambda_{11} & 0 & \dots & 0 \\ 0 & \Lambda_{22} & \dots & 0 \\ \dots & \dots & \dots & \dots \\ 0 & 0 & \dots & \Lambda_{nn} \end{bmatrix}$$

is the matrix with eigenvalues on the diagonal, $\Lambda_{jj} = \lambda_j$, and $\overline{\mathbf{E}}$ has the eigenvectors, $\{E_{jl}\}_{j=1,l=1}^{n,n}$, such that

$$\overline{\mathbf{E}} = \begin{bmatrix} E_{11} & E_{21} & \dots & E_{1n} \\ E_{21} & E_{22} & \dots & E_{2n} \\ \dots & \dots & \dots & \dots \\ E_{n1} & E_{n2} & \dots & E_{nn} \end{bmatrix}.$$

Here $\overline{\mathbf{E}}$ is orthogonal. That is, $\overline{\mathbf{E}}\overline{\mathbf{E}}' = \mathbf{I}$ and we have that both $\mathbf{Z} \sim N(\mathbf{0}, \mathbf{I})$ and $\overline{\mathbf{E}}\mathbf{Z} \sim N(\mathbf{0}, \mathbf{I})$. Further, due to the orthogonal properties of $\overline{\mathbf{E}}$ we also have that $\mathbf{Z}'\overline{\Gamma}\mathbf{Z} \simeq \mathbf{Z}'\mathbf{\Lambda}\mathbf{Z}$, where "$\simeq$" indicates equal in distribution.

Step 3: Expanding the Quadratic Form   Using the eigenvalue decomposition we can now expand to obtain a quadratic form in $\mathbf{Z}$, writing equation (2.22) as

$$V(T) - V(t) \approx \delta + \frac{1}{2}[\mathbf{Z} + \mathbf{\Lambda}^{-1}\overline{\Delta}]'\mathbf{\Lambda}[\mathbf{Z} + \mathbf{\Lambda}^{-1}\overline{\Delta}] - \frac{1}{2}\overline{\Delta}'\mathbf{\Lambda}^{-1}\overline{\Delta}$$

$$= \overline{\delta} + \frac{1}{2}[\mathbf{Z} + \mathbf{\Lambda}^{-1}\overline{\Delta}]'\mathbf{\Lambda}[\mathbf{Z} + \mathbf{\Lambda}^{-1}\overline{\Delta}]$$

$$= \overline{\delta} + \frac{1}{2}\sum_{j=1}^{n}\sum_{l=1}^{n}(Z_j + u_j)(Z_l + u_l)\Lambda_{jl}$$

$$= \overline{\delta} + \frac{1}{2}\sum_{j=1}^{n}(Z_j + u_j)^2 \lambda_j \tag{2.23}$$

where u_j is the j:th element of $\Lambda^{-1}\overline{\Delta}$, and the last line follows since Λ is diagonal. Hence, we have reduced the initially complex quadratic form to a sum of scaled squared shifted normally distributed variables, $\{Z_j + u_j\}_{j=1}^n$, that are also independent. We now use equation (2.23) to calculate quadratic VaR for the case of an equity option position.

Sample Quadratic VaR for an Equity Option Consider a single position in an at-the-money European call equity option with strike price, K, 100, annual implied option volatility, σ, of 30%, risk-free rate, r, 5%, and a time to maturity, $T - t$, of 1 year. Using the Black and Scholes pricing formula we arrive at the option premium, c,

$$c = S(t)N(d_1) - \exp(-r(T - t))KN(d_2) = 14.23.$$

We also obtain the option delta,

$$\frac{\partial c}{\partial S} = N(d_1) = 0.624$$

and gamma,

$$\frac{\partial^2 c}{\partial S^2} = \frac{\phi(d_1)}{S(t)\sigma\sqrt{T - t}} = 0.0126.$$

We can then write, ignoring the time derivative,

$$V(T) - V(t) \approx \frac{\partial c}{\partial S} \times (S(T) - S(t)) + \frac{1}{2}\frac{\partial^2 c}{\partial S^2} \times (S(T) - S(t))^2.$$

Based on this we can conjecture that

$$\text{VaR}(\alpha) \approx \frac{1}{2}\left[Z + \frac{\Delta}{\lambda\sigma_S}\right]^2 \lambda\sigma_S^2 - \frac{1}{2}\frac{\Delta^2}{\lambda} \tag{2.24}$$

where

$$\Delta = \frac{\partial c}{\partial S}$$

$$\lambda = \frac{\partial^2 c}{\partial S^2}$$

and where $\left[Z + \frac{\Delta}{\lambda\sigma_S}\right]^2$ is distributed as the non-central chi-square distribution. That is,

$$\left[Z + \frac{\Delta}{\lambda\sigma_S}\right]^2 \sim \chi_1^2(\upsilon)$$

with $\upsilon = \left(\frac{\Delta}{\lambda\sigma_S}\right)^2$ the non-centrality parameter. Hence, if daily absolute stock volatility, σ_S, is 1 unit of currency,

$$\text{VaR}(0.99) \approx 0.0063 \times \overleftarrow{Z}_{0.99} + 15.451 = 1.4175$$

where $\overleftarrow{Z}_{0.99} \approx 2,227.60$ is the 99% quantile of the $\chi_1^2(\upsilon)$ distribution. For comparison the delta-only VaR component is approximately 1.4516. Clearly, the delta VaR portion is the main risk component in this case, and if we instead assume the option is perfectly delta hedged by a short position in the underlying stock, we obtain the delta-hedged VaR(α) from (2.24) as

$$\text{VaR}(\alpha) = \frac{1}{2}Z^2\lambda\sigma_S^2 = \frac{0.0126}{2}\chi_1^2$$

such that VaR(0.99) $\approx$ 0.0418.

To see that this simple quadratic option position VaR expression is consistent with our general n-dimensional risk factor derivation in equation (2.23) we set

$$V(T) - V(t) \approx \frac{1}{2}\left[Z + \left(\lambda\sigma_S^2\right)^{-1}\Delta\sigma_S\right]\left(\lambda\sigma_S^2\right)\left[Z + \left(\lambda\sigma_S^2\right)^{-1}\Delta\sigma_S\right] - \frac{1}{2}\Delta\sigma_S\left(\lambda\sigma_S^2\right)^{-1}\Delta\sigma_S$$

$$= \frac{1}{2}Z\lambda\sigma_S^2 Z + Z\left(\lambda\sigma_S^2\right)\left(\lambda\sigma_S^2\right)^{-1}\Delta\sigma_S + \frac{1}{2}\Delta(\lambda)^{-1}\Delta - \frac{1}{2}\frac{\Delta^2}{\lambda}$$

$$= \frac{1}{2}Z^2\lambda\sigma_S^2 + Z\Delta\sigma_S$$

$$= \frac{1}{2}\left[Z + \frac{\Delta}{\lambda\sigma_S}\right]^2\lambda\sigma_S^2 - \frac{1}{2}\frac{\Delta^2}{\lambda}.$$

For most options with sufficient time to maturity the second-order effect is significantly smaller than the first-order delta effect. However, as time to maturity becomes shorter the second-order component becomes larger. We had in the example above that for an at-the-money European call equity option with strike price 100, annual implied option volatility of 30%, risk-free rate 5%, and a time to maturity of 1 year, the option delta is 0.624 and the option gamma is 0.0126. Reducing the time to maturity to a 0.01 fraction of a year (that is, a few days using a daycount of remaining days/365) we get the option delta and gamma respectively, 0.517 and 0.1329. Hence, gamma has significantly increased. This leads us to think that unless the European call option portfolio is delta hedged or very close to maturity the simple delta normal representation works quite well as an approximation. It is also the case that significantly in-the-money European call options (stock value significantly above strike) display a large delta and a very small gamma and are hence well approximated by the delta normal. In contrast, significantly out-of-the-money European call options (stock value significantly below the strike) have a relatively small delta component and a relatively large gamma component. See Britten-Jones and Schaefer (1999) for an in-depth analysis of option positions where linear and quadratic approximations performs well versus less well.

Quadratic Portfolio Distribution

The obtained quadratic representation in equation (2.23) of the portfolio value distribution is not explicit in general for $n > 1$ risk factors but the Fourier transform of the distribution can be obtained using the independence of the $j = 1,\ldots,n$ chi-square distributions. Our next step in the analysis is therefore to derive the Fourier transform of the distribution. For that purpose recall that for a univariate random variable X the function $\psi(\varphi) = E(\exp^{i\varphi X})$ where $i^2 = -1$, that is, the complex i, is called the Fourier transform or characteristic function of X. Using a power series expansion of $\exp^{i\varphi X}$ we arrive at the representation

$$\psi(\varphi) = \int_{-\infty}^{\infty}\cos(x\varphi)\,dF(x) + i\int_{-\infty}^{\infty}\sin(x\varphi)\,dF(x)$$

where each of the integrals is referred to as a Fourier transform of $f(x)$. Because $|\cos xt|$ and $|\sin xt|$ do not exceed 1, each of the Fourier integrals exists and hence $\psi(t)$ always exists.

Using the Fourier transform we can now write

$$V(T) - V(t) \approx \xi + \vec{\Delta}'\mathbf{CZ} + \frac{1}{2}\mathbf{Z}'\mathbf{C}'\vec{\Gamma}\mathbf{CZ}$$

$$= \xi + \vec{\Delta}'\mathbf{Z} + \frac{1}{2}\mathbf{Z}'\vec{\Gamma}\mathbf{Z}$$

$$= \xi + \sum_{j=1}^{n} a_j Z_j + \sum_{j=1}^{n} b_j Z_j^2$$

yielding,

$$\psi(\varphi) = \exp\left[i\xi\varphi - \frac{1}{2}\left(\sum_{j=1}^{n} \frac{\varphi^2 a_j}{\sqrt{1 - 2i\varphi b_j}} \right) \right] \Pi_{j=1}^{n} \frac{1}{\sqrt{1 - 2i\varphi b_j}}$$

by the well-known independence property of Fourier transforms.

We can also obtain the moment generating function, $M(\varphi)$, which is also referred to as the Laplace transform, as

$$M(\varphi) = \exp\left[\xi\varphi - \frac{1}{2}\left(\sum_{j=1}^{n} \frac{\varphi^2 a_j}{\sqrt{1 - 2\varphi b_j}} \right) \right] \Pi_{j=1}^{n} \frac{1}{\sqrt{1 - 2\varphi b_j}} \qquad (2.25)$$

and the cumulant generating function, $\ln M(\varphi)$,

$$\ln M(\varphi) = \xi\varphi - \frac{1}{2}\sum_{j=1}^{n} \ln(1 - 2\varphi b_j) + \frac{1}{2}\sum_{j=1}^{n} \frac{\varphi^2 a_j}{\sqrt{1 - 2\varphi b_j}} \qquad (2.26)$$

from which the cumulants, $\varkappa$, are derived by differentiation. See Feuerverger and Wong (2000). It remains now to devise a method for computing a quantile, that is, value at risk of the corresponding density.

Calculation of Risk Measures for the Quadratic Portfolio

Fourier Inversion Having derived an explicit Fourier transform it is natural to try to invert the transform to obtain the portfolio distribution. The classical Fourier inversion formula for a continuous distribution, $F(x)$ with Fourier transform, $\psi(t)$, can be inverted for any $a < b$ as

$$F(b) - F(a) = \frac{1}{2\pi} \lim_{g \to \infty} \int_{-g}^{g} \frac{\exp(\varphi a) - \exp(\varphi b)}{\varphi} \psi(\varphi) d\varphi.$$

See, for example, Davidson (1994, p. 168). To obtain the portfolio distribution we may hence utilize a version of the above inversion formula, or an inversion formula directly for $F(b)$ due to Gil-Pelaez (1951),

$$F(b) = \frac{1}{2} - \frac{1}{\pi} \int_0^\infty \frac{\cos(\varphi \overline{b}) \operatorname{Im}(\psi(\varphi)) - \sin(\varphi \overline{b}) \operatorname{Re}(\psi(\varphi))}{\varphi} d\varphi$$

$$= \frac{1}{2} - \frac{1}{\pi} \int_0^\infty I(\varphi) d\varphi$$

where

$$I(\varphi) = \cos(\varphi \overline{b}) \operatorname{Im}(\psi(\varphi)) - \sin(\varphi \overline{b}) \operatorname{Re}(\psi(\varphi))$$

and, $\psi(\varphi)$, is as defined above. Of course, in practice the indefinite integral needs to be approximated, that is, discretized and truncated to compute the cumulative density. Introducing the step size h and the truncation point K, setting

$$\varphi = \left(k + \frac{1}{2}\right) h, \quad d\varphi = h$$

we may write

$$F(b) \approx F^h(b) \equiv \frac{1}{2} - \frac{1}{\pi} \sum_{k=0}^\infty \frac{I\left(\left(k + \frac{1}{2}\right) h\right)}{k + \frac{1}{2}}$$

$$\approx F^{h,K}(b) \equiv \frac{1}{2} - \frac{1}{\pi} \sum_{k=0}^K \frac{I\left(\left(k + \frac{1}{2}\right) h\right)}{k + \frac{1}{2}}$$

and the approximation errors introduced are

1. Discretization error due to step size h
2. Truncation of the infinite sum at $K < \infty$

For details on how to control the approximation errors in the numerical inversion of the Fourier transform above using the Poisson summation formula we refer to Duffie and Pan (2001).

Tail Approximations Instead of using the Fourier transform to numerically calculate the distribution function one can consider tail approximations using, for example, the Cornish-Fisher expansion or the saddle point approximation by Lugannani and Rice (1980).

Cornish-Fisher Expansion The Cornish-Fisher expansion approximates the quantiles of a distribution using a polynomial expansion for standardized percentiles of a general distribution in terms of its standardized moments and the corresponding percentiles of the standard normal distribution. Specifically, denoting by $\varkappa_i$ the i:th cumulant, which is obtained from equation (2.26) by differentiation, the first four terms in the expansion are

$$\tilde{Z}_\alpha = Z_\alpha + \frac{1}{6}(Z_\alpha^2 - 1)\varkappa_3 + \frac{1}{24}(Z_\alpha^3 - 3Z_\alpha)\varkappa_4 - \frac{1}{36}(2Z_\alpha^3 - 5Z_\alpha)\varkappa_3^2$$

where $Z_\alpha = N^{-1}(\alpha)$ is an α quantile of the univariate standard normal distribution such that

$$\text{VaR}(\alpha) \approx \widetilde{Z}_\alpha \sqrt{\mu_2} + \mu_1$$

with μ_1 the mean of $V(T) - V(t)$ and μ_2 the variance. See Mina and Ulmer (1999). Mina and Ulmer (1999) also compare Fourier inversion and Cornish-Fisher expansion quadratic VaR using test portfolios and favor the Fourier inversion method. See also Castilacci and Seclari (2003) on quadratic VaR with the Cornish-Fisher expansion.

Saddle Point Method The saddle point method approximates the cumulative distribution function, $F(b)$, using

$$F(b) \approx N(r) - \phi(r) \left(\frac{1}{u} - \frac{1}{r} \right) \tag{2.27}$$

where N is the normal cumulative density and ϕ the normal probability density, and

$$r = \sqrt{2}\sqrt{\varphi b - \ln M(\varphi)}$$
$$u = \varphi \sqrt{\varkappa_2(\varphi)}.$$

The saddle point, φ, solves

$$\varkappa_1(\varphi) = b.$$

We refer to Feuerverger and Wong (2000) on the application of saddle point approximation to quadratic VaR.

SIMULATION-BASED VALUATION

As risk measurement based on even quadratic approximations can be too crude for many portfolios, in practice it is common in market risk management to employ simulation-based valuation, that is, applying full or approximate valuation of the portfolio under each scenario to construct a profit-and-loss distribution. This of course generates an empirical profit-and-loss distribution from the realized portfolio profit and loss obtained under the scenarios. Subsequently risk measures are obtained from the simulated profit-and-loss distribution.

It is important to understand that even if on an aggregate level the market risk portfolio is dominated by relatively simple instruments such as bonds and vanilla options that may be well approximated with linear or quadratic expansions, a large risk exposure may still arise from the more complex instruments in the portfolio. The oversimplification of complex instruments, for example, using a delta approximation, may also result in a nonrepresentative decomposition of the risks in the portfolio using risk contributions and hence resulting unfair capital allocations. Hence, even if a smaller part of the portfolio has complex positions one may resort to a simulation-based approach to enable full valuation of the complex positions. Of course, to reduce valuation time for the simpler instruments their pricing can be approximated by a first- or second-order approximation in the simulation-based scenario valuation. Enabling the choice of best valuation representation per position is of course a key advantage of the simulation-based approach to market risk.

Another key advantage with a simulation-based approach to risk management is that one can consider general distributions for the portfolio risk factors, $S(t)$. However, consistent with previous sections on the linear and quadratic portfolios we will here still assume that the distribution of risk factors is multivariate normal and will defer the discussion of more general risk factor distributions and models to the next chapter on advanced market risk analysis. Hence the focus in this section is on the simulation of samples from the multivariate normal distribution and the corresponding valuation scheme.

Clearly, even if the risk factors are multivariate normal the resulting portfolio profit-and-loss distribution does not need to be normal and hence the set of empirical portfolio loss samples $\{L_d\}_{d=1}^{D}$ for $d = 1, \ldots, D$ scenarios can come from an arbitrary distribution. The deviation from nonnormality of the portfolio distribution is driven by the functional form of the pricing functions for the instruments. For example, we have seen that when the portfolio instruments are priced using a quadratic approximation, the resulting portfolio distribution is no longer normal (as it still is in the delta case) and is distributed as a sum of scaled squared shifted normally distributed variables.

In the simulation-based approach to market risk, we can allow any functional form for the pricing function for a specific portfolio instrument $i = 1, \ldots, m$. In principle, the pricing function does not have to be analytic but we assume a functional representation as,

$$p_i = F_i[S(t)] \qquad (2.28)$$

as a function of the $n \times 1$ vector of risk factors, $S(t)$, with

$$S(T) - S(t) \sim N(\mu, \Sigma).$$

As we have discussed above, the pricing function in equation (2.28) may in practice be non-linear and not well approximated by either a linear or even a quadratic portfolio. As a few motivating examples of position nonlinearity we now consider the profit-and-loss profiles for three common barrier stock options using a grid of values for the underlying stock. It is well-known that the representation of barrier options in terms of its Greeks is not without problems. For example, standard barrier options will typically have a large gamma component when the stock value is close to the barrier value. See Derman and Kani (1996). This also makes barrier options difficult to hedge.

Example of Barrier Stock Options and Position Nonlinearity[9]

Single-Barrier Option   Our first example is a single-barrier option with current stock price at 46.75 units of currency and option volatility at 25%. The single-barrier option is an up and in put option with barrier level 60 and strike level 50. Being an up and in put a standard Black and Scholes European put option is knocked in if the stock value breaches the barrier. The option maturity date is approximately 3 years and 4 months from the valuation date. Table 2.2 and Figure 2.1 display the single-barrier option profit-and-loss profile for the different stock values. We note that the option value increases as underlying stock price moves closer to the barrier value of 60. However, for stock values far above the barrier value the

---

[9]All our barrier stock option examples have analytical pricing. For details on the pricing functions for the barrier options we refer to Merton (1973), Reiner and Rubinstein (1991), and Hart and Ross (1994).

TABLE 2.2 Profit-and-Loss Profiles for Barrier Options for a Grid of the Underlying Stock Value

Stock value	Profit and loss profiles for barrier options		
	Single barrier option	Binary barrier option	Soft barrier option
35	−0.81	−1.09	−1.01
42.50	−0.36	−0.41	−0.46
46.75	0	0	0
50	0.35	0.32	0.45
57	1.32	1	1.56
65	1.83	2.72	1.16
72	0.91	2.72	0.26
80	0.28	2.72	−0.31
88	−0.15	2.72	−0.67
95	−0.44	2.72	−0.9

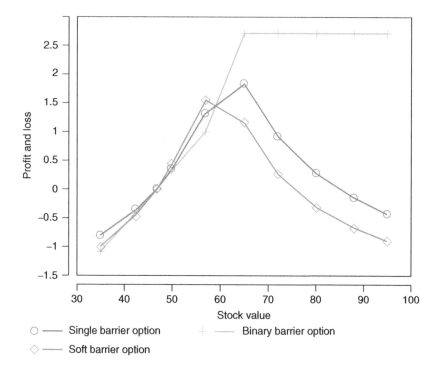

FIGURE 2.1 Profit-and-Loss Profiles for Barrier Options for a Grid of the Underlying Stock Value

barrier option profit and loss decreases. This is because while the barrier has been breached, and the standard Black and Scholes European put has been knocked in, it becomes less likely that the option will have an intrinsic value at maturity.

Binary Barrier Option Our second example is a binary barrier option. The option is an up and in cash-or-nothing call that pays at the maturity date, which is approximately 2 years and 10 months from valuation date. The option strike level is 50 and the barrier level is 60. As for the single-barrier option the current stock value is 46.75 and the option implied volatility is 25%. The binary barrier option pays out a cash amount of 5 units of currency. Hence, if the option is knocked in, the option holder receives at maturity the cash payout (today the discounted value of the cash payout). The profit-and-loss profile for the binary barrier option is also displayed in Table 2.2 and Figure 2.1. For the binary barrier option the profit-and-loss profile rises with higher values of the stock value as the option is knocked in, and at barrier level 60 there is a fixed, discounted value of final cash payout.

Soft Barrier Option   Our final barrier option example is a put soft barrier option. Being a soft barrier option this means that the put is knocked in proportionally as we move from the lower barrier level to the upper barrier level. The put strike level is 50 and the lower and upper soft barriers are 55 and 65, respectively. Hence, to knock in the put 100% we require the stock value to breach the upper barrier. The maturity date is approximately 2 years and 7 months from the valuation date. Again, the current stock value is 46.75 and the option volatility is 25%. The put soft barrier option profit-and-loss profile, displayed in Table 2.2 and Figure 2.1 as for the other examples, does not increase monotonically as the put is knocked in. This is because while the soft barrier option gets knocked in further the intrinsic value of the knocked-in put option decreases as the stock value increases. The profit-and-loss profile for the soft barrier option is hence similar to the profit-and-loss profile for our first example put barrier option.

Simulation from the Multivariate Normal Distribution

In the simulation-based approach to market risk analysis, the first step is to simulate $d = 1, \ldots, D$ samples of the $n \times 1$ vector of risk factors, $S(t)$. As before we assume the multivariate normal risk factor model,

$$S(T) - S(t) \sim N(\mu, \Sigma)$$

where Σ, μ has been estimated from historical data using the normal log-likelihood in equation (2.15). We can now define the simulation samples as follows:

1. Decompose Σ as $\Sigma = E \Lambda E'$ using the eigenvalue decomposition where Λ is a diagonal matrix with eigenvalues on the main diagonal,

$$\Lambda = \begin{bmatrix} \lambda_1 & 0 & \cdots \\ 0 & \cdots & 0 \\ \cdots & 0 & \lambda_n \end{bmatrix}$$

and E is orthogonal, with the eigenvectors,

$$E = \begin{bmatrix} E_{11} & E_{21} & \cdots & E_{1n} \\ E_{21} & E_{22} & \cdots & E_{2n} \\ \cdots & \cdots & \cdots & \cdots \\ E_{n1} & E_{n2} & \cdots & E_{nn} \end{bmatrix}$$

such that $EE' = I$, the identity matrix.
2. Define $C = \Lambda^{\frac{1}{2}} E$ and generate samples from CZ where $Z \sim N(0, I)$.
3. Transform to sampled values for $S(T)$, $\hat{S}(T)$, by translation of CZ by μ.

Having available the simulation samples, $\widehat{S}(T)$, we can now value the portfolio conditional on the realized samples. That is, we transform to portfolio sampled profit-and-loss values by evaluation of

$$\widehat{V}(T) = \sum_{i=1}^{m} h_i F_i \left[\widehat{S}(T)\right] \qquad (2.29)$$

where h_i is the holdings of instrument i. The loss distribution is now the distribution of

$$L_d = -\left(\widehat{V}_d(T) - V(t)\right)$$

for $d = 1, \ldots, D$ samples of $\widehat{V}(T)$ and hence also $\widehat{S}(T)$.

The eigenvalue decomposition in step 1 does not require the covariance matrix to be positive definite—only positive semi-definite.[10] Besides the collinearity issue discussed previously in the context of estimating the covariance matrix of risk factors in section 2.1.4, in practice, numerical precision might also result in a covariance matrix that is not positive semi-definite. We refer to Rebonato and Jackel (1999) for a spectral decomposition method to adjust the non-positive–semidefinite covariance matrix.

To generate the standard normals in step 2 above we make use of a random number generator. There are basically two types of random number generators available, pseudo-random generators and quasi-random generators. These generators realize a uniform random number (i.e., a number between 0 and 1). Traditionally high discrepancy pseudo-random number generators are used to generate the uniform innovations to Monte Carlo simulations. Loosely translated, a high-discrepancy pseudo-random number generator is a *random* generator in which there is very little correlation between current and past numbers generated. In contrast to pseudo-random generators, quasi-random generators are *deterministic*. That is, they produce random numbers that have no random component. Well-known quasi-random number generators include the Sobol and Faure sequences. It has been shown that for some problems quasi-random number generators converge to the true distribution with a smaller number of draws than the pseudo-random generators. However, a problem with quasi-random generators is that they typically induce restrictions on the dimensionality (e.g., ≤ 40), which typically requires restrictive dimension reduction methods on the risk factor models. We refer to Glasserman (2003) for more details on pseudo- and quasi-random number generators. For the purpose of illustration Figure 2.2 displays 100 simulated normal points from a pseudo-random number generator (left panel) and a quasi-random number generator (right panel).

Having generated a uniform $[0, 1]$ random number u we may transform to a random number x where the distribution $F(x)$ is continuous using the inverse function transformation. Specifically, denote by $F(x)$ the cumulative distribution function of x. If x is strictly increasing, then the inverse function F^{-1} is defined as

$$F^{-1}(u) = x$$

whereas if $F(x)$ is constant on some interval, we define the inverse function as

$$F^{-1}(u) = \inf\{x : F(x) \geq u\}.$$

---

[10]This is in contrast to the standard Cholesky decomposition we used in equation (2.20) that requires the matrix to be positive definite.

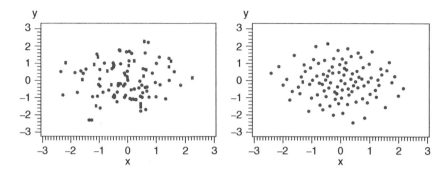

FIGURE 2.2   100 Normal Simulated Points from a Pseudo-Random Number Generator (Left) and a Quasi-Random Number Generator (Right)

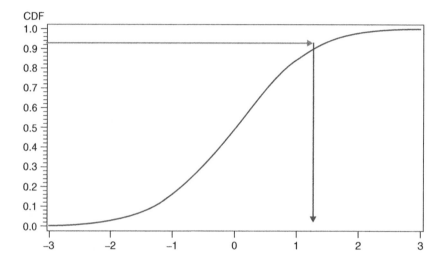

FIGURE 2.3   The Inverse Function Transformation for the Normal Distribution

Figure 2.3 displays the inverse function transformation for the normal distribution. Note that in case of the normal distribution, $F(x) = u$ is strictly increasing on the domain and hence the definition $F^{-1}(u) = x$ with F^{-1} the inverse normal distribution suffices.

    Once we have generated $j = 1, \ldots, n$ independent random normal variables, representing the $j = 1, \ldots, n$ risk factors, the next step is to construct corresponding correlated random normal variables, that is, to generate a sample from the distribution, $S(T) - S(t) \sim N(\mathbf{\mu}, \Sigma)$. If the covariance matrix, Σ, is positive definite, we can use the Cholesky decomposition for this purpose. For example, if $n = 2$

$$\Sigma = \begin{bmatrix} \sigma_1^2 & \rho\sigma_1\sigma_2 \\ \rho\sigma_1\sigma_2 & \sigma_2^2 \end{bmatrix}$$

with σ_1^2 the variance of risk factor 1, σ_2^2 the variance of risk factor 2, and $|\rho| < 1$, the correlation between risk factors. We can then decompose the covariance matrix as in (2.21)

$$C = \begin{bmatrix} \sigma_1 & \dfrac{\rho\sigma_1\sigma_2}{\sigma_1} \\ 0 & \sqrt{\dfrac{\sigma_2^2 - (\rho\sigma_1\sigma_2)^2}{\sigma_1^2}} \end{bmatrix}$$

where $\Sigma = C'C$ is the Cholesky factorization. We can now generate risk factor, S_1 and S_2, return samples as follows (assuming zero mean returns):

$$S_1(T) - S_1(t) = \sigma_1 Z_1$$

$$S_2(T) - S_2(t) = \frac{\rho \sigma_1 \sigma_2}{\sigma_1} Z_1 + \sqrt{\frac{\sigma_2^2 - (\rho \sigma_1 \sigma_2)^2}{\sigma_1^2}} Z_2$$

where Z_1 and Z_2 are two independent standard normal variables.

In case $\sigma_1 = \sigma_2 = 1$ we can simplify to get

$$S_1(T) - S_1(t) = Z_1$$

$$S_2(T) - S_2(t) = \rho Z_1 + \sqrt{1 - \rho^2} Z_2.$$

When risk factor returns are relative and continuously compounded we have instead that

$$S_1(T) = S_1(t) \times \exp(Z_1)$$

$$S_2(T) = S_2(t) \times \exp\left(\rho Z_1 + \sqrt{1 - \rho^2} Z_2\right).$$

which is appropriate, for example, for stocks since the stock price is bounded below by 0. A true geometric Brownian motion has contribution from the volatility to the growth rate.

Note here that due to dealing with the normal distribution and independent increments we can scale the variance of the sampled normal variables to simulate risk factor values at different horizons. For example, if we have $n = 2$ risk factors and the covariance matrix of absolute returns is estimated at an horizon of 1 day but we require simulation at an horizon of 10 days, the simulated risk factor value at the 10-day horizon is simply obtained as

$$S_1(T) - S_1(t) = \sqrt{10} \times Z_1$$

$$S_2(T) - S_2(t) = \sqrt{10} \times \left[\rho Z_1 + \sqrt{1 - \rho^2} Z_2\right].$$

Here we have assumed a unit variance for both risk factors. That is, $\sigma_1 = \sigma_2 = 1$.

Below we consider several methods of adjusting the simple simulation process sketched above.

- First, we recognize that the dimension of $j = 1, \ldots, n$ risk factors may be very large and that dimension reduction techniques can be useful in practice.
- Second, we consider the introduction of parameter uncertainty in the simulation process by factoring in the estimation risk in μ and Σ.
- Third, we consider two commonly used methods to enable reduction of the computation time in Monte Carlo simulation.

The first method is a variance reduction scheme using importance sampling suggested by Glasserman et al. (2000a, b). It allows the reduction of the number of scenarios required to achieve a given accuracy, and hence, the number of potentially time-consuming instrument valuations. As described here this method is specific to the multivariate normal distribution for risk factors as we will make use of the linear and quadratic expansions of the portfolio detailed previously. However, Glasserman et al. (2002) also consider variance reduction for simulation of samples from the multivariate t-distribution.

The second method is focused on simplifying the portfolio pricing and hence reducing pricing time for a given set of scenarios. We consider several portfolio approximations as well as specific instrument pricing simplification methods that enable the reduction of valuation time for a portfolio. These portfolio valuation time reduction methods are certainly not specific to the assumption of a multivariate normal distribution for returns. We still include the description of their method in this section.

Risk Factor Dimension Reduction

A typical market risk model for a financial institution has thousands of risk factors that affect the portfolio value. The risk factor types include:

- Equity
- Interest rate
- Foreign exchange
- Commodity
- Credit spread
- Volatility factors

The large dimension of $j = 1, \ldots, n$ risk factors can make it difficult to understand what risk factors are the core factors driving the portfolio risk.[11] In practice the number of risk factors $j = 1, \ldots, n$ is also considerably larger than the number of time series observations used to estimate the covariance matrix. This means that a covariance matrix for a large number of risk factors can contain relatively little information and there may only be a few sets of independent principal components that can explain close to 100% of the distribution. Risk factor dimension reduction with factor models is therefore often used in practice. It is useful to make a distinction between observed factor models and unobserved factor models. The observed factor models use actual market indices such as broad equity market indices to reduce risk factor dimensions. The unobserved factor model uses statistical techniques to infer a few principal components that can largely explain the variability in large-dimensional data.

Observed Factor Models The observed factor model decomposes the n risk factors into a reduced set $K < n$ observed risk factors that we can model instead of the original n factors. An observed factor model, generally known as Arbitrage Pricing Theory (APT) model as in equation (2.13), decomposes the n risk factor returns into $K < n$ factors such that

$$r_j(t) = \alpha_j + a_{1j}X_1(t) + a_{2j}X_2(t) + \ldots + a_{Kj}X_K(t) + \varepsilon_j(t) \tag{2.30}$$

where $\{X_k(t)\}_{k=1}^{K}$ are the common factors such as market indices, $\{a_{kj}\}_{k=1}^{K}$ are the factor loading (factor betas) for risk factor j on the common factors. Finally, $\varepsilon_j(t)$ is the risk factor j specific factor returns.

This decomposition of a large number of $j = 1, \ldots, n$ risk factors into K common factors allows scenario and simulation analysis to focus on the reduced set of K factors. We note especially that the risk factor covariance matrix we need to estimate is now K-dimensional instead of n-dimensional. Once the scenarios for the K factors have been obtained the factor

---

[11]Although in the advanced market risk chapter we will discuss a measure referred to as the risk factor information measure that is useful for understanding which specific risk factors are important in determining portfolio profit and loss.

model is used to convert the K factor scenarios into the actual portfolio risk factor returns, $\{r_j(t)\}_{j=1}^n$. The conversion has two components:

- First, the risk factor transformation in equation (2.30) has an expected value of the actual portfolio risk factor returns, $\{r_j(t)\}_{j=1}^n$.

  This expected value is obtained by setting $E[\varepsilon_j(t)] = 0$. Hence, capturing only the systematic portion of risk factor $j : s$ return.
- The second component is the specific risk.

  The specific risk samples $\{\varepsilon_j(t)\}_{j=1}^n$ independently for each $j = 1, \dots, n$ risk factor. An often-used special case of the observed factor model is the single-index CAPM model introduced in equation (2.12).[12] In the CAPM model each risk factor return is expressed as reference to a "beta" risk factor. The beta of the single factor is calculated by regression analysis as the return of the individual risk factor on the risk-free rate of return and the return on the single market index. The model is often used for equity returns. See Elton and Gruber (1995, ch 7, 8) for an overview of equity factor models used in practice.

Unobserved Factor Models The multivariate normal distribution has the property that the eigenvalue decomposition of the covariance matrix produces independent eigenvectors, $\mathbf{EE}' = \mathbf{I}$, and that the eigenvalues basically explain the variance attributed to eigenvector j. Assume therefore that Λ, the diagonal matrix with eigenvalues on the diagonal, is ordered such that the eigenvalues of Λ appear in descending order. To measure the ability of the $J < n$ first principal components to explain the variability we write $\sum_{j=1}^{J} \lambda_j / \sum_{j=1}^{n} \lambda_j$ as the total variability explained by the first J principal components. To obtain a representation of the covariance matrix in terms of the $J < n$ main principal components we have that

$$\Sigma_J = \mathbf{E}_J' \Lambda_J \mathbf{E}_J$$

where the subscript J indicates that the ordered matrices have been truncated accordingly. To generate random numbers for the J principal components we now set

$$\mathbf{Y}_J = \mathbf{C}_J \mathbf{Z}_J$$

where

$$\mathbf{C}_J = \Lambda_J^{\frac{1}{2}} \mathbf{E}_J$$

and $\mathbf{Z}_J \sim N(\mathbf{0}, \mathbf{I}_J)$. The representation in terms of the original n-dimensional risk factors,

$$\mathbf{Y} = S(T) - S(t)$$

is obtained as

$$\mathbf{Y} = \widetilde{\mathbf{E}}' \mathbf{Z}_J \tag{2.31}$$

where $\widetilde{\mathbf{E}}$ is partitioned such that $\widetilde{\mathbf{E}}$ is J by n-dimensional and conformable with $\mathbf{Z}_J$.

---

[12]Both the CAPM and the APT are influential models on asset pricing. Although mathematically the CAPM can be viewed as a special case of the APT model, the APT model is by and large considered more general than the CAPM because it allows any observed factors in addition to the only market index factor in the original CAPM.

As a numerical example of principal component analysis consider $n = 3$ risk factors and a covariance matrix, Σ, given by

$$\Sigma = \begin{bmatrix} 1 & 0.9971 & 0.9848 \\ 0.9971 & 1 & 0.9941 \\ 0.9848 & 0.9941 & 1 \end{bmatrix}.$$

The corresponding eigenvalues are

$$\begin{bmatrix} \lambda_1 = 2.9840 \\ \lambda_2 = 0.0154 \\ \lambda_3 = 0.0006 \end{bmatrix}.$$

Hence, the first eigenvalue explains almost 99.5% of the variability since

$$\lambda_1 / \sum_{j=1}^{3} \lambda_j \approx 0.995$$

and the first two eigenvalues 99.98% since

$$(\lambda_1 + \lambda_2)/ \sum_{j=1}^{3} \lambda_j \approx 0.9998.$$

The corresponding eigenvectors are

$$E = \begin{bmatrix} 0.576\ 94 & 0.578\ 74 & 0.576\ 36 \\ -0.654\ 07 & -0.095\ 28 & 0.750\ 41 \\ 0.489\ 21 & -0.809\ 92 & 0.323\ 57 \end{bmatrix}.$$

The dominant first eigenvector (first row) now corresponds to an almost equal shift of the three risk factors. Generating random numbers, using only the first principal component, we have that

$$Y = \tilde{E}'Z_1 = \begin{bmatrix} Y_1 \\ Y_2 \\ Y_3 \end{bmatrix} = \begin{bmatrix} 1.7216 \\ 1.7270 \\ 1.7199 \end{bmatrix} [Z_1] = \begin{bmatrix} 1.7216 \times Z_1 \\ 1.7270 \times Z_1 \\ 1.7199 \times Z_1 \end{bmatrix}.$$

Principal component analysis is traditionally applied to interest rates and specifically yield curve dimension reductions. In case of yield curves one often talks about the main principal components being

- A parallel shift of the curve (first eigenvector)
- A twist of the curve (second eigenvector)
- A butterfly move, that is, a bend of the yield curve (third eigenvector)

This is illustrated in the following yield curve principal components example.

Yield Curve Principal Components Example   We consider the historical monthly US Treasury yield curve from February 2006 to January 2013. The yield curve has yields for the maturities

TABLE 2.3 Mean and Standard Deviation of US Treasury Historical Yields

Yield maturity	Mean	Standard deviation
1 month	1.48	2.01
3 months	1.54	2.03
6 months	1.65	2.05
1 year	1.72	1.97
2 years	1.80	1.79
3 years	2.10	1.66
5 years	2.58	1.44
7 years	3.00	1.24
10 years	3.42	1.05
20 years	4.06	0.87
30 years	4.14	0.73

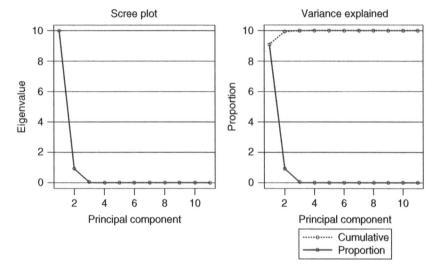

FIGURE 2.4 Eigenvalues and Variance Explained by Principal Components Analysis of the US Treasury Curve

of 1 month, 3 months, 6 months, 1 year, 2 years, 3 years, 5 years, 7 years, 10 years, 20 years, and 30 years. Table 2.3 displays the historical means and standard deviations of the yields. Figure 2.4 shows the eigenvalues of the covariance matrix for these 11 yields and the variance explained by these eigenvalues. The first three eigenvalues can cumulatively explain more than 99% of the total variance.

In a simulation of the US Treasury yield curve scenarios one can consider to model only the first three principal components. There are two immediate benefits gained from modeling the principal components rather than all of the curve components.

- First, the number of factors to be modeled reduces from 11 to 3.
- Second, the principal components can be modeled independently because they are orthogonal.

As a final step we can transform back to the original interest rate curve using the simulated principal components and equation (2.31).

Table 2.4 and Figure 2.5 display the obtained first three principal components in our interest rate principal components example. We notice from Table 2.4 and Figure 2.5 that the first three principal components indeed reflect a parallel shift, a curve twist, and a butterfly move as expected. We refer the interested reader to Litterman and Scheinkman (1991) for a thorough discussion of the principal components factors affecting bond returns.

TABLE 2.4 First Three Principal Components of the US Treasury Yield Curve

Yield maturity	Component 1	Component 2	Component 3
1 month	0.300171	−0.310751	0.374625
3 months	0.301668	−0.302667	0.283004
6 months	0.303280	−0.289463	0.132895
1 year	0.305486	−0.264530	0.003473
2 years	0.310740	−0.186357	−0.189603
3 years	0.314063	−0.097946	−0.317344
5 years	0.314850	0.068967	−0.327312
7 years	0.309681	0.197286	−0.266078
10 years	0.302882	0.292970	−0.153138
20 years	0.280849	0.467022	−0.081825
30 years	0.269726	0.515868	0.645877

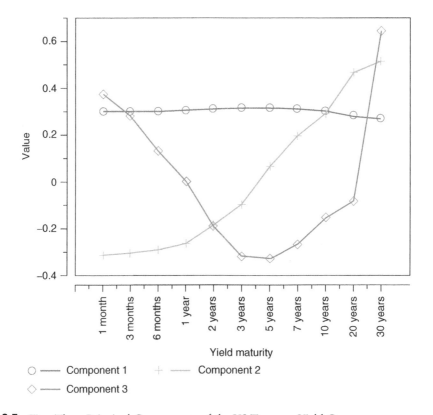

FIGURE 2.5 First Three Principal Components of the US Treasury Yield Curve

A Few Words of Caution When Using Principal Component Analysis Note that when applying principal component analysis on a larger scale for the $j = 1, \ldots, n$ risk factors in the portfolio the large sample covariance matrix used as basis for principal component analysis can be poorly estimated. As we have discussed previously this is especially the case when the number of risk factors is large in proportion to the number of historical observations. Since the principal components themselves are derived from the estimated covariance matrix, it is important that one validates the empirical covariance matrix, for example, using a shrinkage estimator of the covariance matrix.

Finally, caution is necessary when using principal component analysis in risk management. Since risk management focuses on tail risks one needs to be careful in focusing on only a few principal component shifts. For example, in tail risk analysis of a bond portfolio unlikely yield curve shifts may still give rise to large tail risks. It is therefore useful to have in mind that principal component analysis finds the factors that can explain *historical* yield curve movements the most and not necessarily the yield curve movements that can *explain* portfolio profit and loss best. Methods that attempt to "rank" which risk factors can explain most of portfolio profit and loss for general nonlinear portfolios include the risk factor information measure, based on Kullback-Leibler information and partial least square analysis. We will return to a discussion of these measures in the next chapter on advanced market risk analysis.

Incorporating Model Estimation Error in the Simulation Scheme

The previously discussed multivariate normal risk factor simulation process ignores the estimation risk in the parameters μ, Σ. To incorporate the uncertainty in the estimates $\hat{\mu}, \hat{\Sigma}$ we consider a simple modification to the scheme above. First, we replace step 2 by the following:

2*. Generate samples from $Z \sim N(0, I)$ and $B \sim W_n\left(\hat{\Lambda}^{\frac{1}{2}}\hat{E}, t - 1\right)$ and construct $V = BZ$.

Here W_n is the n-dimensional Wishart distribution with $t - 1$ degrees of freedom introduced previously as the distribution of the estimated covariance matrix of the normal distribution.

Second, we replace step 3 by:

3*. Transform to samples for $S(T), \hat{S}(T)$, by translation of V by samples from $N(\hat{\mu}, \Sigma_\mu)$ where Σ_μ is the covariance matrix of the μ parameters.

By construction the distributions for the covariances and the averages are independent. Hence these modified steps 2 and 3 can still be done independently.

While this approach accounts for *risk factor model parameter uncertainty* it does not represent a comprehensive approach to model risk. Indeed, the model itself may be wrong and/or the historical data on which the model is calibrated may not be representative of the future. There are also other aspects of the portfolio risk model that may be exposed to model risk. For example, there can be model risk inherent in the pricing models used to value the positions. Especially complex financial products may carry significant model risk in their pricing.[13] An important part of the model validation process for financial institutions is to

---

[13]For example, in the subprime mortgage crisis in the United States, the value of mortgage-backed securities quickly dropped because of the rise in mortgage defaults, hence questioning the pre-crisis credit default correlation assumptions used in pricing models.

perform stress testing as well as backtesting of the risk measures produced by the market risk model. Both stress testing and backtesting will be discussed extensively in the next chapter on advanced market risk analysis.

Variance Reduction by Importance Sampling

Importance sampling is a powerful tool that in general allows the number of scenarios to achieve a given accuracy in risk measures such as value at risk to be far fewer than otherwise. It is especially useful in situations where losses may happen with a very low probability such that the portfolio profit and loss resembles insurance-style contracts where there is a steady earning at a very high probability and extreme losses with a very low probability. This feature is typically reminiscent of speculative market risk portfolios and portfolios with issued credit insurance. A classical example in the market risk context is a portfolio that earns income through selling deep out-of-the-money options. To earn a sizable income stream the portfolio holding itself needs to be sizable since each out-of-the-money contract carries a relatively small market premium. Of course, the larger the portfolio of sold deep out-of-the-money options the larger the tail risk payout amount. Clearly, in such portfolio situations the bulk of the normal scenarios from the $j = 1, \ldots, n$ risk factors carry no or little information about the portfolio risk, and one could be better off by focusing sampling directly in the tail.

General Methodology We start by describing the general methodology of importance sampling and then proceed to discuss the specific case of interest in this chapter, namely using the normal linear or quadratic portfolio approximation to guide the sampling of scenarios. Let the expectation

$$E[h(\mathbf{X})] = \int h(\mathbf{X}) \, dF(\mathbf{X})$$

be the quantity of interest, with $\mathbf{X}$ an $n \times 1$-dimensional independent vector with $dF(\mathbf{X}) = f(\mathbf{X})d\mathbf{X}$. Supposing we have available a function $g(\mathbf{X})$ with the property that $g(\mathbf{X}) = 0$ whenever $f(\mathbf{X}) = 0$, we can write

$$E[h(\mathbf{X})] = \int \frac{h(\mathbf{X}) f(\mathbf{X}) g(\mathbf{X}) \, d\mathbf{X}}{g(\mathbf{X})}.$$

It seems therefore that we can estimate $E[h(\mathbf{X})]$ by generating samples from $g(\mathbf{X})$ and computing $\frac{h(\mathbf{X})f(\mathbf{X})}{g(\mathbf{X})}$. Following this program we could enable a variance reduction if $\frac{h(\mathbf{X})f(\mathbf{X})}{g(\mathbf{X})}$ has small variance. Note here that

$$\frac{f(\mathbf{X})}{g(\mathbf{X})}$$

is a likelihood ratio and as we would like to reduce variance in $h(\mathbf{X})$ we should obviously try to choose the function g such that the likelihood ratio is small when h is large and possibly large only when h is small. Still, we require

$$E\left[\frac{f(\mathbf{X})}{g(\mathbf{X})}\right] = 1.$$

The requirement that to be successful in our variance reduction we must have h exceedingly small sometimes so that the likelihood ratio is allowed large sometimes suggests that importance sampling will work best for estimating small probabilities. That is, probabilities of large thresholds are our main concern here. The question is now how we could choose g in practice. A generic density that satisfies the properties referred above is the following:

$$g(\mathbf{X}, \zeta) = \frac{\exp^{\zeta X} f(\mathbf{X})}{M_X(\zeta)}$$

where $M_X(\zeta)$ is the Laplace transform (moment generating function) of $f(\mathbf{X})$. Then $g(\mathbf{X}, \zeta) > f(\mathbf{X})$ for $\zeta > 0$ and the reverse for $\zeta < 0$.

Estimating Tail Probabilities Consider now the specific case of estimating $\alpha = \chi_{(S \geq a)}$ where $S = \sum_{k=1}^{m} X_j$. Here $\chi_{(S \geq a)}$ denotes the indicator function such that $\chi_{(S \geq a)} = 1$ if the condition $S \geq a$ is fulfilled and zero otherwise. Using the tilted density the importance sampling estimator of α is

$$\alpha = \chi_{(S \geq a)} \frac{f(S)}{g(S, \zeta)} = \chi_{(S \geq a)} M_S(\zeta) \exp^{-\zeta S}. \tag{2.32}$$

Since $\zeta > 0$ we have that

$$\exp^{-\zeta a} \geq \chi_{(S \geq a)} \exp^{-\zeta S}$$

and hence

$$\alpha \leq M_S(\zeta) \exp(-\zeta a)$$

where this bound is minimized at $\zeta = \zeta^*$. It can be shown that the minimizing ζ^* satisfies $E_g[S] = a$ where the expectation here is taken with respect to the density g. That is, the (independent) elements of S have density g_i.

To summarize we therefore have the following importance sampling estimator of α:

1. Generate random samples from $g(X_j, \zeta^*)$, $j = 1, \ldots, n$, that is, from their tilted density functions.
2. Evaluate the importance sampling estimator (2.32).

We now consider an explicit example using the normal distribution where $X_j \sim N(\mu_j, \sigma_j^2)$ is independent for $j = 1, \ldots, n$, then

$$g(X_j, \zeta) \sim N(\mu_i + \sigma_i^2 \zeta, \sigma_i^2)$$

and, by independence between components,

$$g(S, \zeta) \sim N\left(\sum_{j=1}^{n} \left(\mu_i + \sigma_i^2 \zeta \right), \sum_{j=1}^{n} \sigma_i^2 \right).$$

Hence, estimating α we generate random samples from $g(S, \zeta)$ and compute the likelihood ratio $\frac{f(S)}{g(S, \zeta)}$ times $\chi_{(S \geq a)}$ in each run. The minimizing choice of ζ is

$$\zeta^* = \frac{a - \sum_{i=1}^{n} \mu_i}{\sum_{j=1}^{n} \sigma_i^2}.$$

Variance Reduction Using the Quadratic Portfolio Approximation Focusing on our main objective of the importance sampling estimation of the probability of portfolio loss over a large threshold a we are, as above, interested in the quantity

$$\alpha = E_g\left[\chi_{(L \geq a)}\frac{f(X)}{g(X)}\right]$$

where L denotes the (positive) portfolio loss. According to the above we may choose the Laplace transform in g as approximating L and still have an unbiased estimator. In particular denoting the approximative portfolio value by $-Q$, where Q is the quadratic portfolio approximation, and the corresponding transform by $M(\zeta)$ (see equation (2.25)), we get

$$\alpha = \chi_{(L \geq a)}\frac{f(L)}{g(Q,\zeta)} = \chi_{(L \geq a)}M(\zeta)\exp^{-\zeta Q}$$

as the importance sampling estimator when we sample from the tilted density. From equation (2.22) we have that the quadratic portfolio approximation can be written

$$V(T) - V(t) \approx Q = \delta + \vec{\Delta}'\mathbf{CZ} + \frac{1}{2}\mathbf{Z}'\mathbf{C}'\vec{\Gamma}\mathbf{CZ} \tag{2.33}$$

$$= \delta + \vec{\Delta}'\mathbf{Z} + \frac{1}{2}\mathbf{Z}'\overline{\Gamma}\mathbf{Z}$$

$$= \delta + \sum_{j=1}^{n} a_j Z_j + \sum_{j=1}^{n} b_j Z_j^2$$

with approximate quadratic portfolio loss, $\widetilde{L}$,

$$\widetilde{L} = -Q \approx L \tag{2.34}$$

such that a large loss contribution for risk factor j occurs, for example, when Z_j is a large negative number (negative return) with a large a_j (large delta and volatility component) and small b_j (small gamma component).

Glasserman (2003) shows that the tilted density is obtained if we set the parameters of the normal simulation vector $\mathbf{Z}$ as

$$\mu_j = \zeta a_j/(1 - 2b_j\zeta) \tag{2.35}$$

$$\sigma_j^2 = 1/(1 - 2b_j\zeta)$$

$$\sigma_{ij} = 0 \text{ for } i \neq j$$

and follow the scheme:

- Generate a $\mathbf{Z}$ scenario from the tilted distribution (2.35) and compute an approximate portfolio loss scenario, $-Q = \widetilde{L}$, as in equation (2.34) using the approximation (2.33).
- Calculate a true portfolio loss scenario, L, by using the regular covariance matrix simulation scheme above (with $\mathbf{\Sigma}$ decomposed as $\mathbf{\Sigma} = \mathbf{C}'\mathbf{C}$ and the actual portfolio pricing functions).

- Calculate $\chi_{(L \geq a)} M(\zeta) \exp^{\zeta \tilde{L}}$ where $M(\zeta)$ is the Laplace transform in equation (2.25).
- Obtain the estimate of the probability $P(L \geq a)$ as the average over the replications of weighted portfolio loss exceeding a, $\chi_{(L \geq a)} M(\zeta) \exp^{\zeta \tilde{L}}$.

For a discussion on the optimal choice of the ζ parameter as the VaR of the quadratic approximation as well as an extension of the importance sampling method to post-stratification we refer to Glasserman (2003).

Reducing Pricing Time

In a simulation-based approach to market risk the portfolio valuation step is usually by far the most time-consuming task. Indeed, for each scenario $d = 1, \ldots, D$ each portfolio instrument has to be repriced. Here the number of scenarios, D, is usually counted in the order of thousands, such as 10,000 scenarios. The portfolio size is usually counted in the order of hundreds of thousands or even millions. As a first dimension reduction for pricing we note that there is no need to price different positions held by, for example, different desks in the same instrument separately. This is because pricing is linear in the holding (see equation (2.29)). Hence, it suffices to obtain the instrument market price under a unit holding and then construct the position value(s) by multiplication of the position holding(s). This also means that, for no change in market scenarios, the incremental risk of adding a position in an instrument does not require a portfolio resimulation—just a reaggregation of unit position profit and losses using the new position holding scaling.[14] Once basic portfolio dimension reduction principles such as position scaling have been applied it is natural to try to reduce a given portfolio or instrument's pricing time through various approximation techniques.

Grid Pricing A sometimes useful method to reduce pricing time for simulation-based risk measurement is through so-called grid pricing. In this method a grid of instrument prices is pre-computed as a function of n risk factors. Write

$$F_i = F_i(S_1, \ldots, S_n)$$

as the pricing function for a particular instrument i as a function of $j = 1, \ldots, n$ risk factors and define a particular discretization r_j for S_j such that

$$S_j^{[1]} \leq S_j^{[2]} \leq \cdots \leq S_j^{[r_j]}.$$

We may then, for $j = 1, \ldots, n$ risk factors, evaluate the instrument pricing function F_i under all the possible combinations. Denoting the resulting pricing surface by Θ we may now, for a given realization of $S_1, \ldots, S_n$, obtain a value for F_i using n-dimensional interpolation. In practice, however, one typically works with a reduced risk factor dimension (e.g., $n = 2$) to allow a feasible interpolation scheme.

A practical example of grid pricing is the standard practice in risk management to compute so-called risk matrices or stress matrices for options by computing the variation in the

---

[14]Note, however, that an instrument's price may not be linear in holding when market liquidity is considered as well. For example, a very large position may not carry the same intrinsic value as a small position due to the market costs of liquidating a large position.

option price due to a deterministic bivariate grid for the underlying asset and the implicit volatility of the option. To make use of such a risk matrix in the approximate grid pricing method amounts to, for a value pair of the underlying asset price and its implied volatility respectively, applying bivariate linear interpolation to retrieve a price associated with the pair. Obviously, for highly nonlinear instruments, such as the single and soft barrier option examples in Table 2.2, the demands on the grid fineness are higher to capture profit-and-loss turning points. For multidimensional products with n large, such as basket options, the requirements on the number of risk factors in the pricing surface may also restrict its use in practice.[15] However, the grid pricing method is still a very simple, yet potentially powerful, method to reduce computation time in risk management. The method has been discussed in Rowe (1993, 1995) and Rowe and Mulholland (1999).

Example of Grid Pricing for an American Option   Consider a single position in an at-the-money American call equity option with strike price 100, annual implied option volatility of 30%, risk-free rate 5%, and a time to maturity of 1 year. The continuous dividend yield of the stock is 5%. The valuation of the option uses a binomial lattice (Cox, Ross, and Rubinstein, 1979) with 100 steps.[16] We calculate the value of the option for a grid of underlying stock values, S, and implied volatilities, σ, as

$$\Theta = \begin{bmatrix} & \sigma = 20\% & \sigma = 25\% & \sigma = 30\% & \sigma = 35\% & \sigma = 40\% \\ S = 80 & 20.683 & 21.657 & 22.838 & 24.146 & 25.545 \\ S = 90 & 13.155 & 14.749 & 16.433 & 18.151 & 19.864 \\ S = 100 & 7.646 & 9.549 & 11.446 & 13.336 & 15.218 \\ S = 110 & 4.129 & 5.932 & 7.839 & 9.741 & 11.636 \\ S = 120 & 2.064 & 3.562 & 5.192 & 7.007 & 8.830 \end{bmatrix}. \tag{2.36}$$

For realized risk factor scenario values of $S = 117$ and $\sigma = 33\%$ we then obtain the bivariate linear interpolated option price, c, as $c = 7.09076$. The scenario pricing time for the American option using the lattice technique has hence been replaced with the time to perform a bivariate linear interpolation.

We finally note two important things to consider when applying the grid pricing method.

- First, it may be applied to a (sub)portfolio as well and not just specific instruments.

    For example, in our American option grid pricing the pricing grid may be constructed for the portfolio of options with S as the underlying risk factor.
- Second, when applying the grid pricing approximation it is important that the risk factor scenarios, $S_1, \ldots, S_n$, are covering the space of possible risk factor values in the scenarios and include extreme shifts of risk factors as well for correct pricing of the tail risk.

    For example, if we think the 99.9% worst-case equity fall is 40% for an option instrument or portfolio, we may want to also use equity scenarios that cover a 50% fall in equities for some safety.

---

[15]For basket products one can potentially map the risk factors to one or a few indices using CAPM $\beta : s$ to reduce the dimension of the risk factor pricing grid. However, such simplifications may be too crude in practice.
[16]If the stock would have a zero dividend yield, the American call price would reduce to the Black and Scholes analytical European call price.

Grid Pricing and Curve Fitting Instead of using linear interpolation directly in the grid pricing we can use K-dimensional polynomials for curve fitting based on the grid prices. For a pricing grid with a single risk factor S we have the K-polynomial pricing approximation, $P(S)$, as

$$P(S) = \sum_{k=0}^{K} a_k S^k.$$

The Weierstrass approximation theorem provides the foundation for this choice of approximation of the pricing grid. That is, we can approximate any function arbitrarily well using a polynomial. For multiple risk factors, say S_1 and S_2, with nonlinear dependence the polynomial, $P(S_1, S_2)$, of course needs to capture cross-terms of the risk factors as well,

$$P(S_1, S_2) = \sum_{k=0}^{K} a_k S_1^k + \sum_{k=0}^{K} b_k S_2^k + \sum_{k=1}^{K} \sum_{l=1}^{L} c_{kl} S_1^k S_2^l.$$

In practice a second- or third-order polynomial may be sufficient.

Using the grid pricing and curve fitting approach we have hence replaced the pricing time with the evaluation of a polynomial function. Of course, as we increase the number of core risk factors the polynomial function, $P(S)$, becomes increasingly more complex, especially if there are nonlinear interactions between the risk factors. Both plain grid pricing and grid pricing with curve fitting methods can therefore benefit from an initial risk factor dimension reduction using factor models and/or principal component analysis. Below we will discuss a few literature references that combine grid pricing with risk factor dimension reduction methods.

Literature References Using Grid Pricing with Risk Factor Dimension Reduction Jamshidian and Zhu (1997) propose grid pricing together with principal component analysis and discrete stratified sampling of risk factors for fixed-income portfolios. Chishti (1999) contains a case study of the method applied to a portfolio of callable bonds. Gibson and Pritsker (2000) also apply the grid pricing method to fixed-income portfolios. However, they challenge both the use of discrete simulation of risk factors and the use of principal component analysis for dimension reduction as proposed in Jamshidian and Zhu (1997). Indeed, as we have discussed above, principal component analysis to reduce the number of interest rate factors for the fixed-income portfolio may be dangerous for some portfolios. This is because principal components analysis is based on selecting yield curve components that have high explanation of historical yield curve movements and not necessarily yield curve components that can actually explain portfolio profit and loss. Gibson and Pritsker (2000) suggest replacing principal component analysis with the use of partial least squares to define the reduced yield curve components for grid pricing. The benefit of partial least squares is that it focuses on selecting reduced components that can actually explain portfolio loss.

Quadratic Pricing The quadratic portfolio approximation in equation (2.18) allows us to write the approximate scenario price for a position i (or portfolio), p_i, as,

$$p_i(T) \approx p_i(t) + \xi_i + h_i \Delta_i'[S(T) - S(t)] + \frac{1}{2} h_i [S(T) - S(t)]' \Gamma_i [S(T) - S(t)] \tag{2.37}$$

where $p_i(t)$ is the current mark-to-market value and $S(T) - S(t)$ are the scenario realized risk factor returns. In contrast to the grid pricing method this price approximation efficiently deals with large dimensions for risk factors and can be used for basket option products with many underlying assets as well as subportfolios that depend on a large number of risk factors, $j = 1, \ldots, n$.

Of course, in practice, the instrument approximately valued using a delta gamma approximation may not have analytical Greeks. However, the pre-computation of numerical Greeks and a scenario evaluation of equation (2.37) may still take considerably less time. Still, as we have mentioned before the delta gamma representation may not be that good for certain instruments, for example, barrier options where option payoff depends on the path of the asset price and either a knock-in or knock-out with respect to the barrier. An in-the-money knock-out barrier option can have very large delta and gamma values close to the barrier because the option value can jump from an intrinsic value to zero when the barrier is breached. Of course, in such cases where Greeks are not smooth in changes of the underlying risk factors the quadratic pricing approximation fails.

Nested Stochastic Valuation—Least Squares Monte Carlo   The pricing of many financial instruments requires simulation by itself for pricing. This is usually referred to as *nested simulation valuation*. For example, many basket options and the path-dependence of exotic options naturally lead to a simulation-based approach to valuation. This results in a nested stochastic problem with a large number of "inner" risk-neutral scenarios that are used for valuation for each "outer" risk analysis scenario $d = 1, \ldots, D$. An important method to reduce the number of inner scenarios in valuation of American options is the Least Squares Monte Carlo approach (LSMC) introduced by Longstaff and Schwartz (2001). In this method the outer scenarios are used to calibrate the optimal, American exercise, decision functions using only the cross-sectional information in the simulated outer scenario paths, $d = 1, \ldots, D$. With LSMC the potentially very expensive nested simulation pricing of the American option for each outer scenario has hence been replaced by a global calibration of regression functions based on the outer scenarios and the associated evaluation of the optimal exercise decision. We refer the reader to the paper by Longstaff and Schwartz (2001), which contains an excellent introduction to the rationale of LSMC using an American put option example. It also contains several practical examples of the LSMC approach.

Nested Stochastic Valuation—Proxy Pricing   A similar idea to the LSMC approach to avoiding expensive nested valuation of instruments is to perform the expensive risk-neutral pricing only a few times per outer risk scenario d. For example, for a given scenario d the pricing can be based on only 2 inner risk-neutral pricing scenarios. Of course, for each outer scenario $d = 1, \ldots, D$ the pricing will then be very inaccurate. However, if there are many inaccurate pricings very close to each other one could argue that the average of many inaccurate pricings in a region is still a consistent estimator of the price in the region. As a second step we could fit a polynomial regression to the many inaccurate valuations, similar to the grid pricing and curve fitting approach. Again, the idea is that since there are so many points close to each other the local region contribution to the regression is a consistent estimator of market price. The consistency of the regression hence relies on having many outer scenarios very close to each other everywhere.

To ensure that the polynomial regression estimates consistently can retrieve market prices for a wide range of outer scenarios—including large shifts—it is advisable to ensure that outer scenarios are created evenly on a multidimensional cube and include the extreme risk factor levels. Hence, in this method, the outer polynomial fitting scenarios are not created as economical risk scenarios but rather designed to achieve many fitting points uniformly in the relevant range of each risk factor. Because of this required uniform feature of the outer fitting scenarios they can preferably use deterministic quasi-random number generators such as the Sobol and Faure sequences on a predefined range multidimensional cube for the risk factors. The second step of the method, that is, the polynomial fitting, is equivalent to the polynomial fitting in the grid pricing and curve fitting method. Although, since in this method each grid point is an inaccurate pricing we require many more local pricing points to fit the polynomial on. The third step in this method is the use of the polynomial regression in actual instrument or portfolio valuation based on the economical risk factor scenarios. This step is equivalent to the curve fitting use of the polynomial regression.

The curve fitting approach and the current LSMC inspired proxy pricing method is frequently used in insurance stochastic liability evaluation. See Wieland (2011) for an overview and literature references. However, the method is slowly finding its use in banking.

We finally note here that the grid pricing and curve fitting approach can also be used for nested simulation cases. The method then approximates the price using a large number of inner risk-neutral scenarios to yield very accurate valuations at just a few outer fitting points on the grid. In contrast, the LSMC-inspired proxy pricing methods use much more outer fitting points but just a few inner risk-neutral valuation points for each outer point such that each pricing is inaccurate. Improvement of the method focuses on increasing the number of inner risk-neutral valuation scenarios—to yield less inaccurate valuations for each outer fitting point—as well as increasing the density of the outer fitting points. The improvement of the grid pricing and curve fitting approach extends the number of outer fitting points on which accurate valuations are obtained. A benefit is that the choice of the outer fitting points can be carefully made to regions where exact prices are needed more.

Replicating Portfolios Instead of approximating the pricing itself for a portfolio we can try and replicate the portfolio with a simpler and, preferably, dimension reduced representation. The replication method can use a mapping procedure or use more advanced optimization methods. The most well-known replicating portfolio mapping is probably the bond portfolio dimension reduction used in RiskMetrics (1996). The idea is to map bond cash flows into a stream of zero-coupon bond flows that are assigned to cash flow buckets. The bond portfolio has hence been replaced with a single bond representation. The use of advanced optimization techniques in portfolio replication is, however, an increasing practice. Essentially, in a portfolio replication optimization we define a set of scenarios on which we want to evaluate the portfolio replication error. We can then perform a scenario-based optimization to find the minimum deviation portfolio using a deviation measure. It is of course important that the scenarios include large shocks to the risk factors and that we explicitly control the fit for these large shocks of the risk factors. We will return to the discussion on portfolio optimization and replication in the next chapter on advanced market risk analysis.

CHAPTER 3

Advanced Market Risk Analysis

In this second market risk chapter we focus on a few important advanced topics in market risk analysis.

First, we consider an arbitrary set of portfolio profit-and-loss samples $\{L_d\}_{d=1}^{D}$ for which we wish to apply risk measures. The empirical portfolio loss distribution can come from any underlying model and the focus is hence on general simulation-based risk measures.

Second, we analyze the univariate and multivariate stylized facts of financial time series and discuss risk factor models that can capture these stylized facts. As we have mentioned before the multivariate normal distribution assumption for market risk factors is in general a simplifying assumption rather than an empirically vetted assumption. We show that models that do not capture the stylized facts tend to underestimate risk, sometimes severely. They may also fail to account for the fact that portfolio losses from one day to another can be correlated.

The third topic in this chapter is concerned with measurement horizons for market risk. In practice, financial institutions measure market risks on relatively short-term horizons such as a day. However, for regulatory reporting and other purposes, longer horizon market risk measures are also needed. We therefore discuss the concept of scaling risk measures as well as temporal aggregation of data to obtain longer horizon risk analysis. A complicating factor with temporal aggregation of data and scaling of risk measures is that intervening portfolio trading decisions may occur and significantly impact the risk profile.

Fourth, we consider the important and often overlooked issue in market risk analysis of market liquidity risk. Indeed, the style of liquidity execution can have a significant effect on the risk, as we discuss.

Our fifth topic is concerned with scenario analysis and stress testing. This is an increasingly important topic in risk analysis. One challenge is the design of stress tests that can have a significant impact on the financial institution's portfolio profit and loss. With an increased regulatory focus on stress tests financial institutions need a comprehensive integrated approach to model-based and scenario-based risk analysis. Such an approach also allows stress scenarios to be a part of advanced risk management decision-making analysis, such as scenario-based portfolio optimization.

The sixth topic in this chapter is focused on risk-based portfolio optimization. Optimizations is used frequently in market risk management to find risk and return optimal portfolios, and best hedge portfolios, as well as to replicate portfolios.

Finally, we discuss recent developments in the regulation for market risk.

RISK MEASURES, RISK CONTRIBUTIONS, AND RISK INFORMATION

Here we consider an arbitrary set of portfolio loss samples $\{L_d\}_{d=1}^{D}$ for which we wish to apply risk measures. In particular, we may wish to compute an empirical VaR(α) or CVaR(α) estimate using the portfolio loss samples.

Denote the empirical cumulative density function of $\{L_d\}_{d=1}^D$ by F_L and the desired quantile by x_α; we can then define the empirical estimate of VaR(α) by

$$\text{VaR}(\alpha) = L_\alpha = F_L^{-1}(\alpha)$$

where F_L^{-1} denotes the inverse of the empirical cumulative density function of $\{L_j\}_{d=1}^D$.

Here we have assumed that $\{L_d\}_{d=1}^D$ is sorted from the smallest loss to the largest loss and that the number of discrete samples, D, and the confidence level, α, are chosen such that D times α is an integer such that the empirical VaR(α) does not split the atoms of the discrete probability distribution. Of course, if D times α is not an integer, then a weighted VaR(α) can be defined.[1]

Rockafellar and Uryasev (2002) define a general discrete convex CVaR(α) as a weighted average of

$$\text{CVaR}(\alpha) = \lambda \text{VaR}(\alpha) + (1 - \lambda)\text{CVaR}^+(\alpha)$$

with average CVaR$^+$(α) losses strictly exceeding VaR(α) such that

$$\text{CVaR}^+(\alpha) = E(L \mid L > \text{VaR}(\alpha)).$$

Assuming VaR(α) is not at the end point of the distribution such that CVaR$^+$(α) exists, $\lambda = 0$ when $D \times \alpha$ is an integer and we can define an empirically convex (smooth) CVaR(α) as

$$\text{CVaR}(\alpha) = \frac{\sum_{d=1}^D \chi_{(L_d > L_\alpha)} L_d}{\sum_{d=1}^D \chi_{(L_d > L_\alpha)}} \tag{3.1}$$

where $\chi_{(L_d > L_\alpha)}$ is the unit indicator function for the set of loss samples $(L_1, \ldots, L_D)$ that are greater than L_α. Again, our assumption that D times α is an integer will ensure convexity of CVaR(α) in equation (3.1).

It is easy to see that equation (3.1) is a particular choice of numerical approximation to its continuous counterpart in equation (2.6). While CVaR(α) as defined above in the discrete case is convex, VaR(α) is not necessarily convex. For elliptical portfolio distributions (e.g., the normal and t-distribution) VaR(α) is still convex. This is a consequence of the linear form of VaR(α) for elliptical distributions and the fact that the sum of elliptical distributions is an elliptical distribution. See, for example, Embrechts, McNeil, and Straumann (2001), Hult and Lindskog (2001), and Sadefo-Kamdem (2003).

VaR Interval Estimation

In practice VaR is an estimate of the portfolio loss quantile and as any other statistical estimate its uncertainty depends on the number of data points used in estimation. As the loss distribution in general does not have a known distribution it is especially useful if one could devise a confidence interval for VaR that does not rely on knowing the loss distribution. Fortunately, it turns out that to obtain a nonparametric confidence interval for the empirical VaR estimate we can make use of the probabilities of order statistics.

---

[1]In terms of statistics VaR(α) is the $\alpha \times 100$ percentile of the simulated empirical distribution. In statistics there are a number of different methods for percentile calculation. The definition we use is the simple empirical distribution function approach.

Consider a general discrete random sample $x_1, \ldots, x_n$ where $x_1 < x_2 < \ldots < x_n$ are the possible values in ascending order with probability density function $f_X(x_i) = p_i$. We can then obtain the probability that the j:th-order statistic, $X_{(j)}$, is less than or equal to x_i as

$$P[X_{(j)} \leq x_i] = \sum_{k=j}^{n} \binom{n}{k} P^k (1-P)^{n-k}$$

where $P = P(X_j \leq x_i)$. See, for example, Cassella and Berger (1990). Using this we can obtain that an interval of the form $[X_{(s)}, X_{(r)}]$, $s < r$ covers an estimate of VaR$(\alpha) = X_{(j)}$ with probability

$$P(X_{(s)} \leq X_{(j)} \leq X_{(r)}) = \sum_{k=s}^{r} \binom{n}{k} P^k (1-P)^{n-k}$$

$$= \sum_{k=s}^{r} \frac{n!}{k!(n-k)!} P^k (1-P)^{n-k}.$$

Example Calculation of Nonparametric Probabilistic VaR(α) Bounds Let $L_1, \ldots, L_{100}$ be an ordered profit-and-loss sample of size 100. Then VaR$(0.95) = L_{(95)}$ and a probabilistic VaR bound based on $L_{(91)}$ and $L_{(98)}$, $P(L_{(91)} \leq$ VaR$(0.95) \leq L_{(98)})$, is given by

$$P\left(L_{(91)} \leq \text{VaR}(0.95) \leq L_{(98)}\right) = \sum_{k=91}^{98} \binom{100}{k} 0.95^k 0.05^{100-k}$$

$$= 0.93473.$$

That is, with approximately 93.5% probability the true 95% VaR is contained within the interval created by the ordered observations $[L_{(91)}, L_{(98)}]$.

In practice, for a desired β level confidence interval we can find the values of $[X_{(s)}, X_{(r)}]$ that minimize the equation

$$g(r, s) = \sum_{k=s}^{r} \binom{n}{k} P^k (1-P)^{n-k} - \beta.$$

Of course, the nonparametric VaR bound does not directly answer, for a given number of scenarios $d = 1, \ldots, D$, the practical question of how many scenarios D are required to, with a given confidence level, reach a certain desired maximum VaR sampling error of say n units of currency. Finding an answer to that question in general still requires experimentation with different scenario sample sizes. A real portfolio example calculating simulation-based VaR and CVaR as well as the nonparametric probabilistic bounds on VaR is helpful at this stage.

We consider the calculation of VaR, CVaR, as well as nonparametric VaR confidence intervals for a market risk horizon of 1 day using a sample equity portfolio. The portfolio consists of unit holdings in two stocks, denoted A and B, and unit holdings in at-the-money European options on the stocks. On both stock A and stock B we have a European call (EuC) and a European put (EuP).[2] Table 3.1 displays the portfolio and its characteristics.

---

[2]Buying a put and call option on the same stock at the same strike price and exercise time is referred to as a straddle position, which gains from market volatility. See Hull (2006).

TABLE 3.1 Sample Equity Portfolio

Instrument type	Equity	Time to maturity	Equity quote	Strike price	MtM
Equity spot	A	.	50	.	50
Equity spot	B	.	280	.	280
Equity option (EuC)	A	1 year	50	50	6.64
Equity option (EuP)	A	1 year	50	50	5.16
Equity option (EuC)	B	1 year	280	280	37.19
Equity option (EuP)	B	1 year	280	280	28.92

Assuming that equity A and B relative returns are jointly normal distributed with equity A and B relative returns standard deviations, 0.1168 and 0.0355 as well as correlation 0.075, we simulate 1,000, 10,000, 100,000, and 1,000,000 scenarios. In the simulation we also use a slightly positive mean return for the equities. Specifically, equity A has a mean return of approximately 0.011 and equity B has a mean return of approximately 0.010. When pricing the equity options under the scenarios, we assume a fixed volatility of 30% and a fixed 3% interest rate for discounting.[3]

Table 3.2 displays the portfolio mark to market (MtM) and portfolio level VaR(0.99), VaR(0.99) 95% confidence lower and upper bounds (VaR(0.99) LB and VaR(0.99) UB respectively), and CVaR(0.99) for the different number of scenarios.

We notice that the VaR(0.99) 95% confidence interval lower and upper bounds is closer and closer to the VaR(0.99) as the number of scenarios increase. Hence, we are getting more and more certain about our VaR estimate. While more scenarios yield more confidence in the VaR number, one must of course remember that this certainty is always conditional on the model used being correct. The CVaR(0.99) in Table 3.2 is always larger than VaR(0.99) consistent with our definition of CVaR(α) as the average losses strictly exceeding VaR(α).

Probability Bounds Using the Central Limit Theorem An alternative method to obtain a confidence bound on the nonparametric VaR estimate relies on the central limit theorem and

TABLE 3.2 Sample Equity Portfolio Risk Measures for 1,000, 10,000, 100,000, and 1,000,000 Scenarios

Scenarios	MtM	VaR(0.99)	VaR(0.99) LB	VaR(0.99) UB	CVaR(0.99)
1,000	407.92	27.19	24.09	29.93	30.46
10,000	407.92	27.90	27.20	28.39	31.69
100,000	407.92	27.96	27.78	28.19	31.60
1,000,000	407.92	27.88	27.82	27.94	31.37

---

[3]In practice one typically includes the option-implied volatility as well as the discount rates as risk factors. However, for simplicity we treat them as fixed here. In addition, a volatility smile adjustment may be used when pricing to capture market observed option smile effects for equity scenarios that are significantly in or out of the money.

the expression for the density of order statistics. Serfling (1980) shows that the estimated empirical quantile, $X_{(j)}$, converges to the true quantile, $\overline{X}_{(j)}$, and that

$$\sqrt{D}(X_{(j)} - \overline{X}_{(j)}) \Rightarrow \frac{\sqrt{P(1-P)}}{f_{X_{(j)}}} Z, \text{ where } Z \sim N(0,1).$$

Here, $f_{X_{(j)}}$ denotes the density of the order statistic $X_{(j)}$. As shown in Casella and Berger (1990) the (continuous limit) density of $X_{(j)}$ is given by

$$f_{X_{(j)}} = \frac{D!}{(j-1)!(D-j)!} f_X [F_X]^{j-1} [1 - F_X]^{D-j}$$

where f_X is the (continuous limit) density of $X_1, \dots, X_n$ and F_X the corresponding cumulative density function. We note that for j close to D (i.e., a high quantile) we have $f_{X_{(j)}} \approx f_X [F_X]^{j-1}$, which is potentially large for small j (i.e., small D), inflating the variance of the estimator in the central limit theorem above. Although this limit result is useful for understanding qualitative properties of the estimator, it is not very useful in practice since it involves the density of the quantile itself, which is typically unknown.

A Note on Interval Estimation for General Risk Measures To obtain nonparametric confidence bounds for other risk measures than VaR (e.g., CVaR) the bootstrap re-sampling method is often used—employing re-sampling with replacement from the simulated portfolio distribution to construct a bootstrap distribution for the risk measure. Confidence bounds on the risk measure are then obtained by application of empirical probabilistic bounds on the bootstrap distribution. The nonparametric confidence interval estimations of the risk measures are based on the simulated empirical distribution with equal probability weight on every sample point. The interested reader may find a good introduction to the bootstrap method in Efron and Tibshirani (1993).

Coherent Measures of Risk

We now consider the important concept of *coherent measures of risk* introduced by Artzner et al. (1999) as a characterization of reasonable properties or axioms that a risk measure should satisfy. A risk measure ρ is said to be coherent if it has the following properties:

1. Subadditive. That is, for two portfolios X and Y

$$\rho(X + Y) \leq \rho(X) + \rho(Y).$$

2. Homogeneous, such that for a scalar t

$$\rho(tX) = t\rho(X).$$

3. Monotonous. That is, for $X \gg Y$ almost everywhere

$$\rho(X) > \rho(Y).$$

4. Risk-free condition. For a risk-free position r we have

$$\rho(X + r) = \rho(X) + r.$$

Property 1 is also known as the diversification effect, which says that merging two risky assets together cannot create more risk than the sum of their standalone risks. Property 2 implies that the risk measure is linear in positions. Property 1 and 2 together imply that the risk measure is *convex* and hence is amenable for use in portfolio optimization programs, as we shall discuss below. Loosely speaking, a convex risk measure is also a smooth risk measure enabling interpretation of its risk contributions. Property 3 is obvious, stating that portfolios that lead to higher losses in every state of the world should be considered riskier by the risk measure. Finally, property 4 states that by adding or subtracting a deterministic quantity we shift the magnitude of the risk by that amount.

The coherent properties are by no means always correct in practice. For example, property 1 can be violated when two firms merge together; the integration of the two business operations may introduce additional operational risk to the existing risks the two firms are facing. Property 2 can be criticized in case of market illiquidity because the market liquidation value of a concentrated position (large holding) may be less than the market value of a single holding scaled by the actual large holding. However, the coherent risk measure properties can at least establish a risk measurement standard. In addition, the convexity implied by the coherence provides a desired mathematical property for many risk analysis results. However, coherence is not necessary for convexity.

Föllmer and Schied (2002) define a convex risk measure as a so-called monetary risk measure that is satisfying properties 3 and 4, and also has the convexity property

$$\rho(tX + (1 - t)Y) \leq t\rho(X) + (1 - t)\rho(Y)$$

for $0 \leq t \leq 1$. A convex risk measure is then also coherent if it satisfies property 2 for $t \geq 0$. However, as we have mentioned, property 2 may be violated in practice due to concentrated positions liquidity risk.

As shown by Artzner et al. (1999), and perhaps not so surprisingly due to the fact that the tail information beyond a certain point is ignored, $VaR(\alpha)$ is not necessarily convex and hence not subadditive, implying that

$$VaR(X_1) + VaR(X_2)$$

is not in general an upper bound on

$$VaR(X_1 + X_2).$$

In contrast $CVaR(\alpha)$ is convex and moreover is necessarily smooth, making it more easily interpreted as a risk measure. CVaR is therefore the preferred risk measure for risk managers even though VaR is still frequently used due to the intuition it brings. However, regulators are recently also considering replacing VaR with CVaR (termed *expected shortfall* by regulators) for internal market risk models to better capture tail risk. This replacement of VaR by CVaR is part of the Basel fundamental review of the market risk in the trading book (Basel Committee, 2012, 2014a).

Simulation-Based Risk Contributions

Recall that in case of the linear normally distributed portfolio the Euler risk contribution to risk measure ρ of instrument i with holding h_i is defined by the derivative,

$$\frac{\partial \rho}{\partial h_i}.$$

In the discrete (simulation) setting the derivative does not exist, so how do we then define a risk decomposition? Following Tasche (2000) the answer lies in the interpretation of risk contributions as conditional expectations (regressions) put forward in the linear normal portfolio case (see equation (2.11)). We consider the following situation:

Let $F(L_1, \ldots, L_D) = F(\mathbf{L})$ be the discrete portfolio distribution with m instruments and m-dimensional holding vector $\mathbf{h}$ with loss components $\{L_{i,d}\}_{i=1,d=1}^{m,D}$, $\mathbf{L}_{i,\cdot} = (L_{i,1}, \ldots, L_{i,D})'$ having VaR(α) equal to the portfolio loss sample point L_s and define

$$D_{\text{VaR}(\alpha)}(h_i) = E(\mathbf{L}_{i,\cdot} \mid L = L_s) \tag{3.2}$$

as the VaR(α) risk contribution for position i.

Note that by definition equation (3.2) sums to VaR(α) over the $i = 1, \ldots, m$ instruments as the discrete VaR(α) contribution is the realized loss of the specific instrument or subportfolio in the loss scenario corresponding to total risk as measured by VaR(α).

Similarly we can consider risk contributions for empirical CVaR(α). For that purpose recall the integral relation for continuous distributions in equation (2.6),

$$\text{CVaR}(\alpha) = \frac{1}{1-\alpha} \int_\alpha^1 \text{VaR}(u) du,$$

and, taking the derivative inside the integral, we can write,

$$\frac{\partial \text{CVaR}(\alpha)}{\partial h_i} = \frac{1}{1-\alpha} \int_\alpha^1 \left[\frac{\partial}{\partial h_i} \text{VaR}(u) \right] du.$$

It seems therefore that we can interpret CVaR(α) contributions as the average of a sequence of VaR contributions. This is formalized in Tasche (2000) and we now have the following situation:

As above, we let $F(L_1, \ldots, L_D) = F(\mathbf{L})$ be the discrete portfolio distribution with m instruments and m-dimensional holding vector $\mathbf{h}$ with loss components $\{L_{i,d}\}_{i=1,d=1}^{m,D}$, $\mathbf{L}_{i,\cdot} = (L_{i,1}, \ldots, L_{i,D})'$ having VaR(α) equal to the portfolio loss sample point L_s and define

$$D_{\text{CVaR}(\alpha)}(h_i) = \frac{\sum_{d=1}^{D} E(\mathbf{L}_{i,\cdot} \mid L_d > L_s)}{\sum_{d=1}^{D} \chi_{(L_d > Ls)}}. \tag{3.3}$$

The equation (3.3) makes it clear that CVaR(α) risk contributions may be interpreted as average VaR(α) contributions. Note that equation (3.3) yields CVaR(α) contributions as the average strictly above VaR(α). This is consistent with our definition of discrete CVaR(α) above, ensuring a coherent and in particular convex risk measure.

The empirical risk contribution to CVaR is a statistical consistent estimator. However, in small scenario samples, due to tail truncation, downward bias of CVaR itself should be expected. In those cases loss tail extrapolation by extreme value theory using the generalized Pareto distribution should be expected to decrease variance and bias compared to the empirical sample estimator of CVaR. However, it is harder to argue for the use of extreme value theory for the CVaR contributions as the corresponding instrument or subportfolio loss contributions may not reside in the tail of their $i = 1, \ldots, m$ sub-loss distributions, $\{L_{i,d}\}_{i=1,d=1}^{m,D}$. We will discuss the use of extreme value theory for extrapolation of density tails later in this chapter.

TABLE 3.3 Example Ordered Loss Matrix

Scenario	Loss 1	Loss 2	Loss 3	Portfolio loss
1	0.701	101.73	0.727	103.158
2	−0.086	101.365	0.453	101.732
3	−0.086	87.150	1.073	88.137
4	−0.086	72.572	−1.875	70.611
5	−0.086	44.043	−4.281	39.676

Examples Illustrating the Calculation of VaR and CVaR Risk Contributions Table 3.3 displays the five highest portfolio losses in units of currency in descending order, ordered by the total portfolio loss, together with the realized loss in the scenarios for the three instruments that comprise the portfolio. For a portfolio sample of size 1000 the table corresponds to the 0.05% highest ordered loss scenarios. Hence, considering the 99.5% VaR, we obtain portfolio VaR as the ordered scenario 5 loss for the portfolio (i.e., 39.676) and the VaR risk contributions as the corresponding scenario losses for the instruments (i.e., Loss 1 contribution equal to −0.086, Loss 2 contribution equal to 44.043, and Loss 3 contribution −4.281). For CVaR at the 99.5% confidence level we obtain, at the portfolio level, $CVaR = \frac{1}{4}\sum_{i=1}^{4} L_i \approx 90.90$ where L_i is the total portfolio loss in scenario $i = 1, \ldots, 4$. The CVaR risk contributions are obtained by averaging the individual losses in scenario $i = 1, \ldots, 4$, yielding Loss 1 contribution as 0.1107, Loss 2 contribution as 90.704, and finally Loss 3 contribution as 0.0945.

Our next example of risk contributions reuses the sample equity portfolio in Table 3.1. We also refer to Table 3.2 for the sample equity portfolio mark to market (of 407.92 units of currency) and aggregate VaR and CVaR numbers obtained previously for the portfolio.

Table 3.4 displays the VaR(0.99), CVaR(0.99) as well as the incremental risk (Inc) and Euler risk contributions (Contr) for the equity and equity option positions in the portfolio in Table 3.1.[4] We also display the risk measures for the portfolio aggregated to the equity

TABLE 3.4 VaR and CVaR 99% Confidence Level Risk Measures, Incremental Risk, and Risk Contributions for the Portfolio Instruments

Instrument type	Equity	VaR	Inc-VaR	Contr-VaR	CVaR	Inc-CVaR	Contr-CVaR
Equity	A	11.90	4.10	4.97	13.35	4.64	6.87
Equity	B	22.25	16.90	20.56	25.32	19.56	22.95
Equity option (EuC)	A	5.12	2.50	2.64	5.44	2.84	3.26
Equity option (EuP)	A	3.78	−3.66	−2.33	4.05	−4.18	−3.61
Equity option (EuC)	B	12.13	10.50	11.30	13.59	11.95	12.43
Equity option (EuP)	B	8.43	−9.30	−9.27	9.47	−10.79	−10.52
Aggregate equity	.	26.22	25.60	25.54	29.92	29.04	29.82
Aggregate options	.	2.28	1.66	2.34	2.34	1.45	1.55
Portfolio	.	27.88	27.88	27.88	31.37	31.37	31.37

---

[4]The incremental risk is the additional risk obtained when adding the particular instrument to the portfolio. Specifically, denote the incremental risk of position i, X_i, with risk measure ρ as

$$\rho(X_i) = \rho(X) - \rho(X - X_i)$$

where X is the portfolio with all positions.

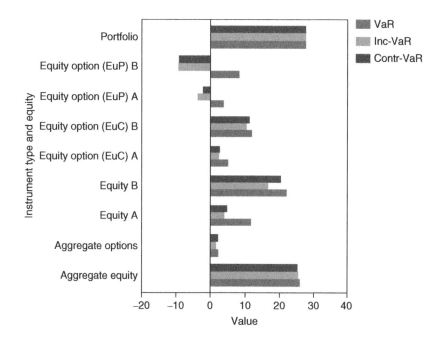

FIGURE 3.1 VaR 99% Confidence Level Risk Measures, Incremental Risk, and Risk Contributions for the Portfolio Instruments

positions, the equity option positions, and the portfolio. In the calculation of the risk measures we have used 1,000,000 scenarios.[5] We note from Table 3.4 that the put options have a negative incremental risk and risk contribution in the context of the portfolio as they represent hedges in the portfolio to the long equity and option call positions. Specifically, the value of the put options increases when stock prices decrease while the plain equity and equity call option position values increase when stock prices increase. For both VaR and CVaR the incremental risk and contribution risks are relatively close to each other for all the portfolio instruments. Practically, we can think of incremental risk measures as a global effect and risk contribution measures as a local effect. That the two are similar is hence an indication that the portfolio loss is a smooth function of all the instruments in the portfolio. Of course, this is not surprising given the simple portfolio instruments. Figure 3.1 displays graphically the VaR, incremental VaR, and contribution VaR for the portfolio obtained from Table 3.4.

To illustrate the smooth risk profiles for the portfolio instruments, Table 3.5 and Figure 3.2 display the portfolio VaR(0.99) as we vary the holding of the European call option on stock A from 1 to −1. Note that a negative holding is a short position in the option and that for the current portfolio holding of 1 unit we retrieve the current portfolio VaR(0.99) being 27.88. The smooth risk profile is due to the simplicity of our sample portfolio. Therefore, for illustration, Figure 3.3 displays a non-convex trade risk profile. Just as in Figure 3.2 the *x*-axis displays the number of holdings and the *y*-axis the risk measure value. The non-convex trade risk profile is also overlaid by a smoothed, convex curve—being representable of the corresponding trade risk profile for a convex risk measure (e.g., CVaR). Clearly, estimates of

---

[5]Hence, we obtain the same aggregate portfolio VaR and CVaR here as in Table 3.2 for the case of 1,000,000 simulations.

TABLE 3.5 Portfolio Trade
Risk Profile for the European
Call Option on Stock A as we
Vary Its Holding from 1 to −1

Holding	VaR(0.99)
1	27.88
0.5	26.52
0.25	25.93
0	25.38
−0.25	24.97
−0.5	24.58
−1	24.26

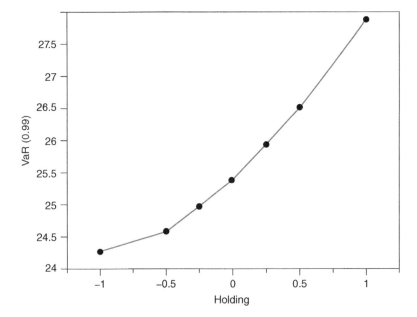

FIGURE 3.2 Portfolio Trade Risk Profile for the European Call Option on Stock A as We Vary Its Holding from 1 to −1

risk contributions from non-convex risk measures can provide no or little information on the curvature, rendering its use doubtful. Hence, the convexity requirement on risk measures is instrumental not only in theory.

Smoothing VaR Contributions   We have seen that in a sample of losses the natural estimator of VaR contribution is the conditional realization of loss. However, as VaR can be non-convex as discussed above it is practical to smoothen the VaR contributions. One approach is to define the VaR contributions using CVaR contributions such that one calculates contributions to CVaR($\widetilde{\alpha}$) where $\widetilde{\alpha} \leq \alpha$ is chosen such that

$$\text{VaR}(\alpha) = \text{CVaR}(\widetilde{\alpha}).$$

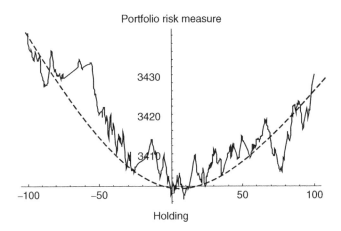

FIGURE 3.3 Trade Risk Profile for Convex and Non-convex Risk Measures

Similarly, one may choose an interval of nearest neighbors to VaR(α), say [VaR(α_1), VaR(α_2)] where $\alpha_1 < \alpha < \alpha_2$. In this case VaR($\alpha$) contributions are obtained for all VaR in the interval and averaged.

Smoothed VaR Examples Using the example computation of VaR and CVaR above with scenario loss Table 3.3 we choose to smoothen VaR(α) at confidence level of 99.7% using the two nearest neighbors. First, VaR(0.997) = 88.137 and hence the smoothened VaR contribution for loss 1 is: −0.086, for loss 2: $\frac{261.09}{3}$ = 87.03, for loss 3: $\frac{-0.349}{3}$ = −0.116 33. Clearly, the smothered VaR contributions do not add to portfolio VaR. However, we can rescale them such that they sum to portfolio VaR.

Our next example calculates smoothed VaR(0.99) contributions for the sample equity portfolio in Table 3.1.

Table 3.6 displays the non-smoothed VaR contributions (obtained from Table 3.4) and the VaR contributions smoothed with the 20 and 40 nearest neighbors ($n = 20$ and $n = 40$ respectively). The smoothed VaR contributions have been re-scaled to sum to portfolio VaR.

TABLE 3.6 VaR Risk Contributions and Smoothed Risk Contributions for the Portfolio Instruments

Instrument type	Equity	Contr-VaR	Contr-VaR($n = 20$)	Contr-VaR($n = 40$)
Equity	A	4.97	6.48	6.14
Equity	B	20.56	19.71	19.88
Equity option (EuC)	A	2.64	3.10	3.00
Equity option (EuP)	A	−2.33	−3.39	−3.13
Equity option (EuC)	B	11.30	10.84	10.94
Equity option (EuP)	B	−9.27	−8.86	−8.94
Aggregate equity	.	25.54	26.19	26.02
Aggregate options	.	2.34	1.69	1.86
Portfolio	.	27.88	27.88	27.88

Due to the smooth profit-and-loss behavior of the simple instruments in the portfolio the smoothened VaR contributions are similar to the empirical VaR contribution. While this behavior is observed in the context of a simple market risk portfolio it cannot be extrapolated to, for example, simple credit risk portfolios. Loosely speaking VaR is a dubious risk measure when portfolio instruments yield no loss (or profit) with a very high probability, though with very low probability losses are large. We will see several examples of this when we discuss portfolio credit risk.

Trading Off Bias and Variance in Smoothed VaR Contributions Hallerbach (2003) similarly proposes calculating VaR contributions using an adjusted conditional mean estimator that involves setting the VaR contribution equal to the mean of contribution VaR, which are close to the VaR threshold. Calculating the mean contribution using a small number of contributions offers less bias but results in a higher variance. Using more contributions gives a lower variance but higher bias. Epperlein and Smillie (2006) consider a Kernel estimator to smoothen the VaR contributions and evaluate the bias and variance of the Kernel smoothing versus using the exact VaR contribution. Another approach is to use regression to estimate the VaR contribution. This is because conditional expectations as in equation (3.2) appear naturally as solutions in regression problems. In practice, linear or quadratic regressions are often used to fit the relationship between the position profit and loss and the portfolio profit and loss—with quadratic regression being preferred for nonlinear portfolios. The regression function estimate of the VaR contribution is the value of the fitted regression function at the portfolio VaR point.

Concentration and Diversification Risk contributions are useful for understanding the instrument or subportfolio local contribution to total risk and hence are critical for risk managers in decomposing risk and understanding the most risky components of the portfolio, taking into account portfolio diversification effects. One can also take this one step further and consider specific measures of subportfolio diversification and concentration in the context of the portfolio. Specifically, we can define a diversification index for position or subportfolio i, $I_{\rho(\alpha)}(h_i)$, as

$$I_{\rho(\alpha)}(h_i) = \frac{D_{\rho(\alpha)}(h_i)}{\rho(\alpha)(h_i)}$$

where $D_{\rho(\alpha)}(h_i)$ is the Euler contribution to position or subportfolio i for risk measure ρ, $\rho(\alpha)(h_i)$ is the standalone risk for position or subportfolio i for risk measure ρ.

For a risk measure ρ that is subadditive, homogeneous of degree 1, and co-monotonic (that is, for perfectly dependent risks X and Y, $\rho(X + Y) = \rho(X) + \rho(Y)$), we have that

$$I_i \leq 1.$$

The CVaR(α) risk measure satisfies these properties and hence

$$I_{\text{CVaR}(\alpha)}(h_i) \leq 1.$$

See Tasche (2006, 2007), Memmel and Wehn (2006), and Garcia Cespedes et al. (2006). The diversification index measures the degree of diversification obtained by an instrument or subportfolio when put in the context of the portfolio. A subportfolio with a diversification index close to 100% might be considered to have high concentration risk, whereas a subportfolio with a low diversification index might be considered well diversified in the context of the portfolio.

Examples of Calculation and Interpretation of Diversification and Concentration Consider a portfolio with two equities. Portfolio CVaR is 1 unit of currency and standalone CVaR for equity 1 and 2 is 0.6 and 0.78. The portfolio CVaR contributions are 0.35 and 0.65 respectively for equity 1 and 2. We hence obtain the diversification for equity 1 as $I_1 = \frac{0.35}{0.6} \approx$ 0.583 and for equity 2 as $I_2 = \frac{0.65}{0.78} \approx 0.833$. Equity 1 has therefore a diversification index, when put in the context of the portfolio, close to 50%. The diversification of equity 2, when put in the context of the portfolio, is much less.

We also consider diversification measures for our sample equity portfolio in Table 3.1.

Using Table 3.4, we can calculate the VaR(0.99) and CVaR(0.99) diversification indices for the sample equity portfolio in Table 3.1. This is done in Table 3.7. Note that according to the diversification indices, in the context of the portfolio, the equity B position is more concentrated than the equity A position. The European put equity option on stock B has a diversification index less than −1. It is hence adding a stronger negative contribution to the portfolio than its standalone risk. As in our linear delta-normal model example on risk contributions and diversification in the previous chapter diversification depends on the position size. For example, if we increase the holding of the equity A position to 10 units instead of the current 1 unit, we obtain a diversification VaR and CVaR of equity A in the context of the portfolio of 0.937 and 0.972 respectively. As a consequence of the portfolio change in relative position sizes we also obtain a significant reduction in the equity B position concentration with diversification VaR and CVaR now being 0.456 and 0.321. In general a position or subportfolio diversification is hence a function of both covariance (or more generally codependency) and position scaling.

Implied Normal Risk Contributions—Betas In the linear normal model discussed in the previous chapter we had that risk contributions could be analytically expressed as scaled betas (see equation (2.11) for the case of VaR). For example, the contribution of asset j to the portfolio volatility is given by $\beta_j \sigma_p$ where

$$\beta_j = \frac{\text{cov}(r_p, r_j)}{\sigma_p^2} \tag{3.4}$$

TABLE 3.7 VaR and CVaR 99% Confidence Level Diversification Indices

Instrument type	Equity	Div-VaR	Div-CVaR
Equity	A	0.418	0.515
Equity	B	0.924	0.906
Equity option (EuC)	A	0.516	0.599
Equity option (EuP)	A	−0.616	−0.891
Equity option (EuC)	B	0.932	0.915
Equity option (EuP)	B	−1.100	−1.111
Aggregate equity	.	0.974	0.997
Aggregate options	.	1.026	0.662
Portfolio	.	1	1

and hence β_j is the covariance between portfolio and asset j returns divided by the portfolio variance. In case the portfolio returns are not normal we can still compute equation (3.4) using the realized simulated portfolio returns and instrument or subportfolio j returns. We can hence construct what we can call "implied normal" portfolio risk contributions for an arbitrary set of portfolio loss samples.

As we shall discuss below in the context of copulas the covariance may not be a good measure of codependency in general. One can therefore consider the implied normal beta as being estimated on the simulated portfolio returns and instrument or subportfolio j returns transformed to normal.[6] Since implied normal beta contributions will not sum up to the risk measure they can be scaled by, for example, aggregate portfolio VaR to sum up.

Risk Information Measures

The Euler risk contribution decomposition applies to the portfolio instruments $i = 1, \ldots, m$ and, of course, optionally to subportfolios of instruments by aggregation as risk contributions have the additive property by construction. However, if $X_1, \ldots, X_m$ denotes the m instruments, then, in general, for n risk factors $S_1, \ldots, S_n$ we have that $X_i = f(S_1, \ldots, S_n)$, that is, instrument i is a function of the n underlying risk factors. Having obtained a decomposition of risk in $X_1, \ldots, X_m$ as above, the question is then how we can further decompose risk in attributions to $S_1, \ldots, S_n$.

This is clearly a key concern of risk managers—that is, how they can further decompose risk into contributions of the portfolio risk factors such as equity, foreign exchange, and economy-wide systematic and interest rate components. In the linear normal model case discussed in the previous chapter we saw that this decomposition of risk is in fact obtained by the Euler risk contributions. This was of course due to the linear property of the portfolio and does not hold generally when each of the instruments $X_1, \ldots, X_m$ are nonlinear functions of the portfolio risk factors $S_1, \ldots, S_n$.

Following Skoglund and Chen (2009) we will approach this problem from the perspective of what *information* is generated in $S_1, \ldots, S_n$ and for this purpose we introduce the concept of information (Fisher, 1956; Shannon, 1956; Wiener, 1956). Following Kullback (1959) denote by H_i, $i = 1, 2$, the hypothesis that X comes from a population with probability measure μ_i, $i = 1, 2$. Using elementary conditional probability rules

$$P(H_i \mid X) = \frac{P(H_i)f_i(X)}{P(H_1)f_1(X) + P(H_2)f_2(X)}, \quad i = 1, 2$$

yielding

$$\log \frac{f_1(X)}{f_2(X)} = \log \frac{P(H_1 \mid X)}{P(H_2 \mid X)} - \log \frac{P(H_1)}{P(H_2)}$$

which measures the logarithm of the odds in favor of H_1 after and before the observation that $X = x$. Alternatively, we say that $\log \frac{f_1(X)}{f_2(X)}$ describes the weight of evidence for H_1 given $X = x$.

---

[6]That is, we could transform the empirical density of the portfolio return and the asset or subportfolio j return first to uniform and then to normal, applying the beta calculation (3.4) to the transformed normal returns.

The mean information for discrimination in favor of H_1 against H_2, given $x \in E$, is

$$I(1:2) = \frac{1}{\mu_1(E)} \int_E \log \frac{f_1(x)}{f_2(x)} d\mu_1(x)$$

$$= \frac{1}{\mu_1(E)} \int_E f_1(x) \log \frac{f_1(x)}{f_2(x)} d\lambda(x)$$

since $d\mu_1(x) = f_1(x) d\lambda(x)$. Specifically, suppose that the sample space is the Euclidean space $\mathbb{R}^2$ with elements (x, y) and H_1 is the hypothesis that x, y are dependent, whereas the hypothesis H_2 is that the variables are independent. In that case we may write $I(1:2)$ as

$$I(1:2) = \iint f(x,y) \log \frac{f(x,y)}{h(x)g(y)} dx dy. \tag{3.5}$$

The information measure $I(1:2)$ in equation (3.5) has the property that $I(1:2) \geq 0$ and is zero if and only if $f(x,y) = h(x)g(y)$. Furthermore equation (3.5) is additive for independent events (see Kullback, 1959, ch. 2). The fact that the information measure is nonnegative and additive for independent events makes it useful for measurement of relations or dependence.

Risk Information in the Linear Portfolio Model Having previously discussed Euler risk contributions in the classical linear normal risk model in Chapter 2 we now consider the equivalence of the Kullback information measure and the Euler risk contribution in that setting. Above we defined the mean (risk) information in x about y by equation (3.5). If x, y are both univariate normal and we consider the hypothesis H_1 of a bivariate normal density and H_2 a product of normal densities, we find that

$$I(1:2) = -\frac{1}{2} \log(1 - \rho^2) \tag{3.6}$$

with $\rho \in (-1, 1)$ the correlation coefficient of the bivariate normal distribution, and

$$f(x,y) = \frac{1}{2\pi\sigma_x\sigma_y\sqrt{(1-\rho^2)}} \exp\left[-\frac{1}{2(1-\rho^2)} \left(\frac{x^2}{\sigma_x^2} - 2\rho\frac{xy}{\sigma_x\sigma_y} + \frac{y^2}{\sigma_y^2} \right) \right]$$

$$h(x) = \frac{1}{\sqrt{2\pi}\sigma_x} \exp\left[-\left(\frac{x^2}{\sigma_x^2}\right) \right], \; g(y) = \frac{1}{\sqrt{2\pi}\sigma_y} \exp\left[-\left(\frac{y^2}{\sigma_y^2}\right) \right]$$

being the joint and marginal densities of x and y. Note that $I(1:2)$ in equation (3.6) ranges from $[0, \infty)$ as $|\rho|$ ranges between $[0, 1)$. Moreover $I(1:2)$ is zero if and only if $\rho = 0$.

For y an n-dimensional vector $\mathbf{y} = (y_1, \dots, y_n)'$ with weights $\mathbf{w} = (w_1, \dots, w_n)'$ we similarly have

$$I(1:2) = -\frac{1}{2} \log(1 - \delta^2)$$

where δ is now the correlation between x and the weighted linear combination of the n-dimensional vector $\mathbf{y} = (y_1, \dots, y_n)'$. By the definition of correlation,

$$\delta = \frac{\mathrm{cov}(x, \mathbf{w}'\mathbf{y})}{\sigma_x\sigma_y} = \frac{\sum_{i=1}^{n} w_i \, \mathrm{cov}(x, y_i)}{\sigma_x\sigma_y}$$

with σ_x^2 the variance of x, and

$$\sigma_y^2 = \mathbf{w}'\mathbf{\Sigma}_y\mathbf{w}$$

the variance of the weighted linear combination of the vector $\mathbf{y}$. Here, $\mathbf{\Sigma}_y$ is the covariance matrix of the vector $\mathbf{y}$.

Using our linear portfolio definition in equation (2.2) and in correspondence with the scaled β representation of linear model risk contributions in equation (3.4) we can therefore write

$$I(U_j:U) = -\frac{1}{2}\log\left(1 - \left[\beta_j\sigma_p\sigma_{jj}\right]^2\right) \tag{3.7}$$

where

$$U_j = \Delta_j[S_j(T) - S_j(t)]$$

and

$$U = \vec{\mathbf{\Delta}}'[\mathbf{S}(T) - \mathbf{S}(t)]$$

with $\vec{\mathbf{\Delta}}$ the n-dimensional sensitivity vector and Δ_j the j:th element of the sensitivity vector. The Kullback information measure is hence closely related to the Euler risk contributions in this linear normal portfolio setting. However, while the Euler allocation has the desirable property that dependent risks are additive no such concept is available for the Kullback information measure. That is, there is no total portfolio information that the information of the U_j components in equation (3.7) can be compared with. For each U_j component the comparison in equation (3.7) is with respect to the possible minimum and maximum information, that is, $[0, \infty)$ and for two components U_j and $U_{j'}$ we can compare the relative importance of U_j versus $U_{j'}$ in determining portfolio value by comparing $I(U_j:U)$ and $I(U_{j'}:U)$.

Risk Information for Discrete Distributions Dealing with general simulated discrete loss distributions we now consider a discrete version of the $I(1\!:\!2)$ information measure.

Let $f(i,j)$ be the frequency of the joint occurrences of x belonging to quintile i and y belonging to quintile j and let s represent the number of quantile cutoff factors for the distributions of x, y. We then define a discrete version of the information measure in equation (3.5) as

$$I_D(1\!:\!2 \mid s) = \sum_{i=1}^{s}\sum_{j=1}^{s} f(i,j)\log\frac{f(i,j)}{g(i)h(j)}. \tag{3.8}$$

Clearly $f(i,j) \in [0,1]$ where unity corresponds to the case where x belonging to quintile i is always matched with y belonging to quintile j. The maximum of $I_D(1\!:\!2 \mid s)$ is hence $\log s$.

The discrete information measure is seen to be a measure of the amount of covariation between quintiles of the distributions and hence a (nonparametric) measure of codependency. A normalized information measure, by $\log s$, therefore expresses this degree of codependency on a $[0, 1]$ scale.

Examples of Risk Information Measures As a simple example of the discrete information measure $I_D(1\!:\!2 \mid s)$ we set $s = 2$ giving a 50% quantile (median) cutoff for x and y, and

$$I_D(1\!:\!2 \mid 2) = f(1,1)\log\frac{f(1,1)}{g(1)h(1)} + f(2,1)\log\frac{f(2,1)}{g(2)h(1)}$$

$$+ f(1,2)\log\frac{f(1,2)}{g(1)h(2)} + f(2,2)\log\frac{f(2,2)}{g(2)h(2)}. \tag{3.9}$$

TABLE 3.8 Sample Distributions of X and Y (Bold Sample Numbers Indicate the Sample Belonging to the Left Part of the Distribution, i.e., the First Quintile for $s = 2$)

Sample	$g(X)$	$h(Y)$
1	15	−7
2	7	−5
3	9	7
4	10	3
5	4	2
6	13	5

It remains to specify the sample distributions to complete equation (3.9) numerically. Employing the sample distribution numbers in Table 3.8 gives

$$
\begin{aligned}
I_D(1:2 \mid 2) &= \frac{2}{6} \log \frac{2/6}{(3/6)(3/6)} + \frac{1}{6} \log \frac{1/6}{(3/6)(3/6)} \\
&\quad + \frac{1}{6} \log \frac{1/6}{(3/6)(3/6)} + \frac{2}{6} \log \frac{2/6}{(3/6)(3/6)} \\
&= \frac{4}{6} \log \frac{2/6}{(3/6)(3/6)} + \frac{2}{6} \log \frac{1/6}{(3/6)(3/6)} \\
&\approx 0.327.
\end{aligned}
$$

A normalized information measure for the samples in Table 3.8 is now obtained by dividing the $I_D(1:2 \mid 2) \approx 0.327$ by $\log 2$, yielding a $[0, 1]$ normalized information measure of approximately 0.472. Note that changing place of the sample points 1 and 3 for the distribution of y. That is, exchanging places of the sample points −7 and 7 would yield a normalized information measure of 1. This is because, this change, within the sample knowledge of which part of the distribution x belongs to, would allow us to predict with certainty the part of the distribution for the corresponding sample of y.

Our next example uses the sample equity portfolio in Table 3.1.

For the sample equity portfolio in Table 3.1 we compute the equity A and B Risk Factor Information measures (RFI) as well as correlation (Corr) of the equity risk factors to the portfolio profit and loss at the aggregate equity, option, and portfolio level. The results are displayed in Table 3.9 and use the same 1,000,000 scenarios for equity A and B as we used in Table 3.4.[7] Table 3.9 shows that equity B has the highest RFI measure of the two equities.

---

[7]The portfolio profit and loss and risk factor values are decomposed in 5 20% percentile buckets as 0%–20%, 20%–40%, 40%–60%, 60%–80%, and 80%–100%, such that

$$
\mathrm{RFI} = \sum_{i=1}^{5} \sum_{j=1}^{5} f(i, j) \log \frac{f(i, j)}{g(i)h(j)}
$$

where $f(i, j)$ is the joint frequency of portfolio profit and loss being in percentile bucket i and the risk factor being in percentile bucket j. Here $g(i)$ is the marginal frequency of the portfolio profit and loss being in percentile bucket i and $h(j)$ is the marginal frequency of the risk factor being in percentile bucket j.

TABLE 3.9 Risk Factor Information Measures and Correlation of
Equity Risk Factors to Portfolio Profit and Loss

Instrument type	RFI		Corr	
	Equity A	Equity B	Equity A	Equity B
Aggregate equity	0.090	0.328	0.557	0.871
Aggregate options	0.112	0.341	0.539	0.740
Portfolio	0.092	0.335	0.564	0.862

TABLE 3.10 Risk Factor Information Measures and Correlation of
Equity Risk Factors to Portfolio Profit and Loss When Holding in
Equity A is Changed to 10 Units Instead of 1 Unit

Instrument type	RFI		Corr	
	Equity A	Equity B	Equity A	Equity B
Aggregate equity	0.661	0.015	0.986	0.239
Aggregate options	0.112	0.341	0.539	0.740
Portfolio	0.625	0.018	0.981	0.265

As for diversification measures the risk factor information measures are dependent on the position size. For example, changing the holding in equity A to 10 units from the current 1 unit of holding we obtain new risk factor information measures (RFI) and correlations (Corr) in Table 3.10. Note that equity A now has the highest RFI at both the aggregate equity and portfolio level while at the aggregate options level we of course obtain the same risk factor information as in Table 3.9.

For a more extensive, market risk focused application of information measures to a portfolio of equity derivatives we refer to Skoglund and Chen (2009). Further numerical examples of the risk factor information measure are also considered later in this chapter as well as in the chapter on portfolio credit risk.

Practical Use of the Risk Factor Information Measure Clearly, the risk factor information measures give the ranking of which risk factors are important for determining profit and loss. Depending on the specific portfolio characteristics two different situations typically arise in practice:

- First, there are cases where many combinations of risk factors can give rise to the same or almost the same profit and loss.

    In this case there is typically a common low level of risk factor information among many of the risk factors.
- Second, there are cases where a small subset of risk factors are truly more important to determine portfolio loss.

    In this case a few risk factors would have a high risk factor information measure and other risk factors a low measure.

In the second situation the risk factor importance ranking feature of the Kullback information measure can allow a risk manager to extract very useful information on the value of so-called reverse stress tests where a certain loss is identified with certain risk factor values and, in particular, any key risk factors that seem to have a predictive impact on loss. This is a topic that we will return to later in this chapter when we discuss stress testing.

While risk factor information measures are computed at the risk factor level it is also useful to look at the risk factor information measures per risk factor categories such as per equity, interest rate, and foreign exchange categories. If just a few risk factor categories have large risk factor information measures, one can try to extract summarized portfolio risk factor exposure information like "for severe losses we would be exposed to very high interest rates simultaneously with dramatically falling equity prices."

We also note that while we here choose to focus on the information as the measure to rank risk factors' relative importance on portfolio profit and loss, various other techniques can also be used in practice to assess the most influential factors. Post-simulation one has available both risk factor scenarios and portfolio profit-and-loss scenarios; it is hence natural to consider regression-based techniques to infer the most influential risk factors. For example, in Tables 3.9 and 3.10 we also computed the correlation between portfolio profit and loss and the risk factor as another measure indicating the importance of a risk factor in explaining profit and loss. A closely related example to using correlation measures is the partial least squares method used by Gibson and Pritsker (2000) to achieve a risk factor dimension reduction for a fixed income portfolio that we discussed in the previous chapter. Gibson and Pritsker (2000) use partial least squares as an advancement over principal component analysis, extracting principal factors that are potentially truly influential on portfolio profit and loss rather than only influential on historical risk factor variation. The partial least squares method can hence also be interpreted as a factor importance analysis.

The benefit of the risk information measure discussed here is that it is nonparametric (and hence not based on normal correlation matrices). Moreover, it produces ranked factor importance analysis in terms of the actual portfolio risk factors. Therefore, the risk factor information measure can also be used as a risk factor dimension reduction method in terms of the observed risk factors.

Finally, a word of caution is warranted in using any risk factor importance analysis method. As with any statistical method what is measured is essentially the degree of covariation and not causality. This means that risk factors that may not even influence the portfolio but still have a strong covariation with portfolio profit and loss may seem important using the statistical measures. We will see an example of this in the next chapter on portfolio credit risk.

Risk Distortion Measures

So far we have focused on VaR and CVaR as the measures of risk. More generally one can consider defining risk measures using a so-called risk distortion function. A risk distortion function allows one to define a risk measure that gives different weights to specific parts of the loss distribution.

Consider a given realized discrete loss distribution $\{L_d\}_{d=1}^{D}$ from which we can construct the empirical cumulative density function, F_L. Now, define a distortion function, g, $g(F_L)$, such that

- g is non-decreasing and right-continuous
- $g(0) = 0$
- $g(1) = 1$

The expected value of this distorted distribution g is then called a distortion risk measure; see Wang (1996). A risk distortion measure is not necessarily coherent. For example, VaR(α) is a distortion function that enables you to compute value at risk at the α confidence level. The corresponding distortion function is

$$g = 0 \quad \text{if } t \le \alpha \quad \text{and} \quad g = 1 \quad \text{if } t > \alpha$$

where t denotes the cumulative probability of F_L. The distortion function for VaR(α) is hence a step function that jumps from zero to 1. Similarly, for CVaR(α) the distortion function is

$$g = 0 \quad \text{if } t \le \alpha \quad \text{and} \quad g = \frac{t - \alpha}{1 - \alpha} \quad \text{if } t > \alpha$$

such that when the cumulative probability passes the α threshold the distortion function increments a step for each observation until reaching the cumulative probability 1 for the last maximum observed loss.

In practice, various different weights can be used on the distribution function of losses and we will just consider a few common risk distortion functions below. For example, the block maxima distortion function is given by

$$g(t, n) = t^n$$

where if $n > 1$, it is convex. Clearly, as $n > 1$ increases more weight will be given to extreme losses.

Figure 3.4 displays a sample empirical cumulative distribution function (denoted CDF) and the block maxima distortion function for n equal to 5, 10, or 20 for a loss sample. It is clear from the figure that with increasing n the block maxima distortion function resembles

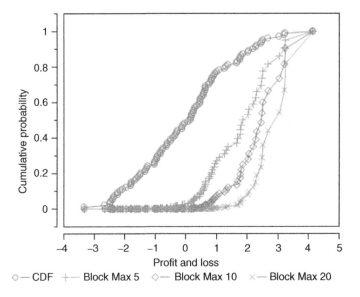

FIGURE 3.4 Empirical Distribution Function (CDF) and Block Maxima Distortion Function for n Equal to 5, 10, and 20 for a Loss Sample

more and more a tail-based risk measure as more of the weight is given to the VaR(α) loss observations with α large.

Yet another distortion function is the dual block minima function. It distorts the distribution function as follows

$$g(t, n) = 1 - (1 - t)^n$$

where if n is between $(0, 1)$, it is convex. In this case as n decreases more weight is given to losses.

The Wang q transformation is defined by the following distortion function:

$$g(t, q) = N[N^{-1}(t) - q]$$

for $q > 0$ where N is the normal cumulative distribution function, and N^{-1} its inverse.

Risk distortion measures can be seen as a risk measure framework where one can simply and elegantly implement new risk measures with user-defined loss weighting. Since distortion measures represent weighted portfolio losses we can also calculate Euler risk contributions to the risk distortion measure. Indeed, a distortion risk measure can be viewed as a weighted function of the portfolio VaR : s associated with different risk confidence levels α. In practice different distortion functions (different VaR(α) loss weights) are useful to assess the sensitivity of risk and risk contributions to the risk measure itself.

Example Calculation of Risk Distortion Measures as Well as Euler Contributions and Risk Without Measures to Risk Distortion Measures

We consider a simple linear normal portfolio of two equities with variance 0.1 for equity 1 and variance 0.2 for equity 2. The covariance between the equities is zero and current equity value is unity for both equities. Using 10,000 simulations we calculate a realized discrete loss distribution, $\{L_d\}_{d=1}^{10,000}$, and the cumulative loss density, F_L.

Table 3.11 displays the aggregate risk, the standalone risk, the Euler risk contributions, and the "risk without" for five different risk distortion measures (VaR(0.95), CVaR(0.95),

TABLE 3.11   Risk Distortion Measures

Instrument	VaR(0.95)	CVaR(0.95)	BM(2)	DBM(0.5)	W(1.96)
			Risk distortion measure		
			Aggregate risk		
Portfolio	0.67	0.81	0.18	0.18	0.73
			Stand alone risk		
Equity 1	0.40	0.47	0.13	0.13	0.43
Equity 2	0.52	0.60	0.17	0.15	0.54
			Euler risk contributions		
Equity 1	0.24	0.33	0.06	0.07	0.29
Equity 2	0.43	0.48	0.12	0.11	0.44
			Risk without		
Equity 1	0.52	0.60	0.17	0.15	0.54
Equity 2	0.40	0.47	0.13	0.13	0.43

Block maxima(2) BM(2)), Dual block minima(0.5) (DBM(0.5)), and Wang(1.96) (W(1.96)). The risk without is simply the risk remaining when the instrument is removed from the portfolio. It is the counterpart of the incremental risk used in Table 3.4.[8]

Table 3.11 shows that the aggregate risk for block maxima and dual block minima risk distortion functions are much lower than for CVaR(0.95). However, we can change the weighting in these measures such that more weight is given to large losses and hence they more resemble tail risk measures. For example, increasing the block maxima parameter to 50 we get an aggregate risk of 0.86, and increasing to 500 we now have an aggregate risk of 1.06. This is relatively close to the maximum simulated loss of 1.14 and hence the bulk of the loss weights are now with a few large losses.

Considering the risk without measure we have, for example, that the VaR(0.95) portfolio risk is 0.67 and corresponding risk without for equity 1 is 0.52. This translates into an incremental risk of adding instrument 1 of 0.15 since one can always obtain incremental risk from total risk and risk without and vice versa.

The Euler risk contributions for all the risk distortion measures sum to aggregate risk as expected and for all the measures the higher variance of equity 2 is captured in a larger risk contribution for equity 2.

Spectral Risk Measures Risk distortion measures also includes a large family of general risk measures. If g is convex, the distortion measure is also convex (subadditive). Acerbi (2002) therefore introduced a subset of risk distortion measures, called spectral risk measures, that are coherent. Spectral risk measures (SRM) are in a family of risk measures that generalize CVaR by allowing non-negative weights assigned to the β-VaRs with $\beta \geq \alpha$. That is,

$$\text{SRM} = \int_0^1 w(u)\text{VaR}(u)du \tag{3.10}$$

where $w(\cdot)$ is an increasing weight function $w:[0, 1] \rightarrow [0, \infty)$ and

$$\int_0^1 w(u)du = 1.$$

Comparing to equation (2.6) CVaR is a special case of SRM where $w(u) = \frac{1}{1-\alpha}$ with $(\alpha \leq u \leq 1)$.

In addition to being coherent, the spectral risk measures offer a couple of nice properties.

- First, the weight function allows a financial institution to assign a different tolerance to different loss severities.

  The increasing weights on the severity reflects the institution's risk aversion as higher weights have to be placed on more severe losses. However, the actual sizes are still choices by the institution.
- The second advantage is that the SRM does not really impose a specific confidence level.

  It basically allows any loss to be counted toward the risk measure, and therefore potentially makes itself react to changes in the loss distribution more smoothly than to any specific confidence level–based measure like VaR that may cause a jump effect between the losses slightly below and above the confidence level.

---

[8] Specifically, we have that the total portfolio risk minus risk without for an instrument is the equivalent incremental risk of adding the instrument.

MODELING THE STYLIZED FACTS OF FINANCIAL TIME SERIES

Univariate Time Series

The assumption that financial return series are normal and independent over time is one of the most common assumptions in finance. Stylized facts of financial return series show, however, that both of these assumptions are questionable. In particular, the independence assumption is questionable due to the tendency of financial return series to display volatility clusters and the assumption of a normal distribution is questionable due to the observed fat-tail nature of financial time series—even after correcting for volatility clusters.

It is by now well-known that financial time-series (after suitable transformation) display a number of so-called stylized facts that can be summarized as follows:[9]

1. They tend to be uncorrelated but dependent.
2. Volatility is stochastic and the autocorrelation function of **absolute** (or squared) returns tend to decay very slowly.
3. They tend to be heavy tailed and asymmetric. In particular large negative returns occur more frequently than predicted by the normal distribution.

Figure 3.5 displays the typical volatility clustering behavior of a financial return series where a large return (of either sign) is typically followed by another large return (of either sign).

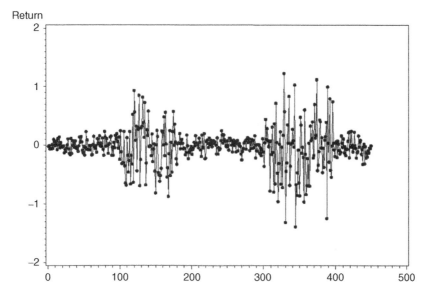

FIGURE 3.5 A Typical Financial Time Series of Returns that Displays the Well-Known Property of Volatility Clustering

---

[9]Of course these stylized facts depend on the time scale chosen. What we have in mind here is daily data as is often the case for market risk analysis. Financial market data returns aggregated to lower frequencies such as month or year benefit from the central limit theorem as daily returns are summed and hence may be close to normally distributed in practice.

TABLE 3.12 Unconditional Moments
of Returns to the SP 500 Index

Mean	0.01821
Variance	1.32377
Skewness	−0.48725
Kurtosis	25.4164

As a concrete example we consider the distributional properties of the returns to the daily S&P 500 index between 1928 and 1991. Table 3.12 gives the estimates of the first four unconditional moments of the distribution of logarithmic returns to the S&P 500 index. The table shows that the S&P 500 returns display both negative skewness and excess kurtosis compared to a normal distribution. Figure 3.6 displays the autocorrelations of the S&P 500 daily returns and the squared returns respectively. The autocorrelation of returns display very little structure but the autocorrelations for squared returns decay extremely slowly consistent with stylized fact 2. The properties of the S&P 500 returns have been analyzed extensively in Mills (1999, ch. 5) and Granger and Ding (1995) investigated the properties of absolute returns.

The lack of autocorrelation in financial returns implied by stylized fact 1 suggests that *linear* association between consecutive observations is not large. Linear time series models, such as autoregressive moving average (ARMA) models, may therefore not be expected to perform very well in terms of returns forecasting availability. However, the predictability of financial returns is a debated issue. Financial returns series may be predictable to some extent. See Campbell et al. (1997). It is fair to say that there is more evidence of predictability of financial returns series at longer horizons when fundamental macroeconomic factors can provide explanation for performance. For example, McMillan (2001) analyzes the S&P 500 monthly returns using linear and nonlinear time series models and finds evidence of linear predictability from macroeconomic factors and nonlinear predictability from interest rates.

At shorter time horizons, such as daily returns, linear and nonlinear models for returns may not improve significantly on the simple random walk hypothesis. Hence, for the short-term market risk management there is no compelling reason to go beyond simple parametric conditional mean specifications such as the growth or mean-reverting model.

Ignoring stylized facts 2 and 3 above for the moment one can model equities using a standard growth model such as the geometric Brownian motion,

$$dS(t) = \mu_S S(t)dt + \sigma_S S(t)dW_S(t)$$

where μ_S and σ_S are the mean growth rate and instantaneous volatility respectively and with $W_S(t)$ the Wiener process. This model is of course equivalent to the normal covariance simulation of logarithmic (relative) returns that we have discussed previously. It is a natural model for stocks since stock values are bounded below by 0. However, risk factors such as interest rates are usually assumed to have a long-term mean reversion to an equilibrium rate. We can capture such mean reversion effects using, for example, a Cox-Ingersoll-Ross model (Cox, Ingersoll, and Ross, 1985),

$$dr(t) = a_r[b_r - r(t)]dt + \sigma_r \sqrt{r(t)}dW_r(t)$$

where $W_r(t)$ is the Wiener process. Here the parameter b_r is the mean reversion level at which all future trajectories will evolve around in the long run. The parameter a_r characterizes the

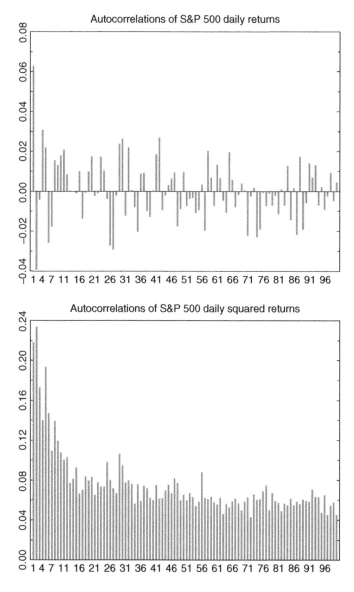

FIGURE 3.6 Autocorrelation of Returns and Squared Returns for the S&P 500 Index

speed at which trajectories will regroup around the mean reversion rate b_r over time, and σ_r is the instantaneous volatility of the short-rate model. While mean reversion also in foreign exchange rates is supported by the purchasing power parity, empirical evidence of mean reversion, especially at shorter time horizons, is a discussed issue. See, for example, Cheung and Lai (1994), Sweeney (2000), and Taylor and Taylor (2004). Similar to the discussed issue about the degree of mean reversion in forward foreign exchange rates there is a discussion about the rationale for mean reversion in credit spreads—specifically, if the observed mean reversion is due to survival effects. See, for example, Bhanot (2005).

In practice for short-term horizon market risk analysis (e.g., 1–10 days) the choice of whether to include long-term mean reversion in the model for the asset class is not that important. The short-term behavior is dominated by the volatility and the distribution of the random shocks to the model, that is, by stylized facts 2 and 3. Hence, for short-term market analysis we can essentially focus on modeling the arithmetic or relative returns of a risk factor directly with no mean-reversion component.[10] Below, we therefore focus our discussion on univariate financial time series on the key aspects of the market risk model for the risk factors, S(t), that is, how to capture stylized fact 2 and stylized fact 3.

Capturing the Volatility Clustering Regarding stylized fact 2 it is well-known when considering financial time series that the modeling and forecasting of volatility is a key issue. If volatility is stochastic and forecastable (as implied by stylized fact 2), then an accurate modeling of volatility improves the measurement of risk as the risk increase in volatility clustering periods is captured. When considering one-day returns the generalized autoregressive conditional heteroskedasticity (GARCH) family of stochastic processes tends to explain much of the dependence structure referred to in stylized fact 2, and the GARCH filtered residuals displays little or no dependence, being approximately independent and identically distributed.

GARCH Models To introduce the GARCH family of processes we consider the following simple univariate model describing the returns, y_t,

$$y_t = \mu + \varepsilon_t$$

$$\varepsilon_t = z_t h_t, z_t \sim iid(0, 1)$$

denoting by $X_t = X(t)$. The dynamic variance is parametrized as

$$h_t^2 = h(\varepsilon_{t-1}, \ldots, \varepsilon_{t-k}, h_{t-1}, \ldots, h_{t-k}; \Upsilon) > 0 \ \forall t.$$

with Υ the parameter vector. The following properties are obtained using that $z_t \sim iid(0, 1)$,

$$E(\varepsilon_t) = 0,$$

$$E(\varepsilon_t, \varepsilon_{t-k}) = 0 \ \forall k > 0,$$

$$E(\varepsilon_t^2) = E(h_t^2),$$

and hence the process is uncorrelated. However, $E(\varepsilon_t^2, \varepsilon_{t-k}^2) \neq 0$ as well as $E(|\varepsilon_t|, |\varepsilon_{t-k}|) \neq 0$ and the process has the ability to generate excess kurtosis. That is, it has the potential to address not only stylized fact 2 but also some of the heavy tailed nature of financial time series referred to in stylized fact 3. This can be easily seen by applying Hölder's inequality to the kurtosis of ε_t, $k(\varepsilon_t)$:

$$k(\varepsilon_t) = \frac{E\varepsilon_t^4}{(E\varepsilon_t^2)^2} = k(z_t)\frac{Eh_t^4}{(Eh_t^2)^2} \geq k(z_t).$$

---

[10]Of course, for longer-term risk analysis such as analyzing counterparty exposure over the lifetime of a 10-year maturity swap portfolio the specific choice of parametric model for interest rates (mean reversion or not) has a significant effect. On the other hand, for longer time horizons, the importance of capturing stochastic volatility and nonnormality becomes less important due to the central limit theorem.

Intuitively, the unconditional distribution of ε_t (hence y_t) is a mixture, some with small variances that concentrate mass around the mean and some with large variances that put mass in the tails of the distribution.

The classical ARCH(q) parametrization of this model by Engle (1982) is

$$h_t^2 = \alpha_0 + \sum_{j=1}^{q} \alpha_j \varepsilon_{t-j}^2$$

for which a necessary and sufficient condition for $P(h_t^2 > 0) = 1$ is $\alpha_0 > 0$, $\alpha_j > 0 \ \forall j$. The class of stochastic volatility models (see Shephard, 1996) generalize this model further by adding an unobserved error component, η_t being, for example, χ^2-distributed. However, we confine ourselves to ARCH-type models in this exposition. Writing for the ARCH(q) process,

$$E(\varepsilon_t^2) = E(z_t^2)E(h_t^2) = v_2 E\left(\alpha_0 + \sum_{j=1}^{q} \alpha_j \varepsilon_{t-j}^2\right) = \frac{v_2 \alpha_0}{1 - \sum_{j=1}^{q} \alpha_j}$$

we find that the ARCH(q) model is covariance-stationary if $\sum_{j=1}^{q} \alpha_j < 1$ and $v_2 < \infty$ such that $E(\varepsilon_t^2) < \infty$. Assuming further that $k(z_t) < \infty$ and $q = 1$,

$$E(\varepsilon_t^4) = k(z_t)E(h_t^4) = \frac{\alpha_0(1 + v_2 \alpha_1)}{(1 - v_2 \alpha_1)(1 - k(z_t)\alpha_1^2)}$$

which gives the following condition for existence of the fourth moment of the ARCH(1) process:

$$(1 - k(z_t)\alpha_1^2) > 0 \Rightarrow k(z_t)\alpha_1^2 > 1 \Rightarrow \alpha_1 < \sqrt{k(z_t)}.$$

Hence if $z_t \sim N(0,1)$, then $k(z_t) = 3$ and the requirement on α_1 for existence of $E(\varepsilon_t^4)$ is $\alpha_1 < \frac{1}{\sqrt{3}} \approx 0.577$.

Considering the temporal dependence of the ARCH(1) process,

$$E(\varepsilon_t^2 \varepsilon_{t-1}^2) = \frac{\alpha_0^2 v_2 (v_2 + k(z_t)\alpha_1)}{(1 - v_2 \alpha_1)(1 - k(z_t)\alpha_1^2)}$$

yielding by induction that

$$E\left(\varepsilon_t^2 \varepsilon_{t-k}^2\right) = v_2 \alpha_1 E\left(\varepsilon_t^2 \varepsilon_{t-(k-1)}^2\right).$$

This form of the temporal dependence reveals a fundamental problem with the ARCH process as an empirical model for financial time series. In particular, to capture the slowly decaying temporal dependence observed in practice (see Figure 3.6) we require α_1 high. Unfortunately α_1 high is infeasible with the existence of a fourth moment and hence the autocorrelation function of squared observations. Hence, there is a motivation to generalize the ARCH process.

Bollerslev (1986) suggested the GARCH(p,q) process where

$$h_t^2 = \alpha_0 + \sum_{j=1}^{q} \alpha_j \varepsilon_{t-j}^2 + \sum_{i=1}^{p} \beta_i h_{t-i}^2.$$

Here $\alpha_0 > 0, \alpha_i > 0, \beta_i > 0 \; \forall j, i$ are sufficient for $P(h_t^2 > 0) = 1$ and necessary conditions are provided by Nelson and Cao (1992). The GARCH model is commonly used in its most simple form, the GARCH$(1, 1)$ model, in which the conditional variance is given by

$$h_t^2 = a_0 + a_1 \varepsilon_{t-1}^2 + \beta_1 h_{t-1}^2$$
$$= a_0 + (a_1 + \beta_1)h_{t-1}^2 + a_1(\varepsilon_{t-1}^2 - h_{t-1}^2).$$

The term

$$(\varepsilon_{t-1}^2 - h_{t-1}^2) = h_{t-1}^2(z_{t-1}^2 - 1)$$

has zero mean conditional on past information and can be interpreted as the shock to volatility. The coefficient a_1 therefore measures the extent to which a volatility shock in period j feeds through into the volatility in period $j + 1$, while $(a_1 + \beta_1)$ measures the rate at which this effect dies out, that is, the discount rate. Hence the GARCH model has greater potential to satisfy the observed slowly decaying autocorrelation function of squared observations since two parameters are involved.

Forecasting with GARCH Models   Assuming that $\alpha_1 + \beta_1 < 1$ in the GARCH$(1, 1)$ model we obtain the k step ahead forecast as,

$$E[h_{t+k}^2 \mid h_t^2] = (\alpha_1 + \beta_1)^k \left(h_t^2 - \frac{\alpha_0}{1 - \alpha_1 - \beta_1} \right) + \frac{\alpha_0}{1 - \alpha_1 - \beta_1}. \tag{3.11}$$

Hence, the forecast of h_{t+k}^2 reverts to its unconditional mean at rate $(\alpha_1 + \beta_1)^k$. Nelson (1990) considered the properties of the integrated GARCH model (i.e., the case where $\alpha_1 + \beta_1 = 1$). He showed that if $\alpha_1 + \beta_1 = 1$ and $\alpha_0 = 0$, $E[h_{t+j}^k \mid h_t^2]$ dies out in finitely many steps, that is, it degenerates, whereas if $\alpha_1 + \beta_1 = 1$ and $\alpha_0 > 0$, $E[h_{t+k}^2 \mid h_t^2]$ explodes as $k \to \infty$. In particular, for the integrated GARCH model $E[h_{t+k}^2 \mid h_t^2] = h_t^2 + k\alpha_0$. In its integrated form the GARCH model has therefore some nondesirable features, which makes it questionable as a model for financial time series. Nevertheless the model appears as a reasonable alternative in estimation in finite samples where estimated parameters, $\hat{\alpha}_1 + \hat{\beta}_1$, are very often close to unity. However, obtaining estimated parameters consistent with integrated GARCH does not necessarily mean that an integrated GARCH model is an accurate description. In particular it is well-known that time-varying parameter models, for example, through structural breaks of the process, give rise to "integrated type behavior" in finite samples of fixed parameter specifications. Lundbergh (1999) contains a simulation example of this feature in the context of GARCH models.

The RiskMetrics Model—A Special Case   Ignoring the theoretical deficiencies of the integrated GARCH model, acknowledging simply that it behaves reasonably over short time periods such as a one-day or one-week forecast, a special case of the integrated GARCH model (termed the RiskMetrics model) is often used in practice. The RiskMetrics (1996) model is defined by

$$h_t^2 = (1 - \lambda)\varepsilon_{t-1}^2 + \lambda h_{t-1}^2 \tag{3.12}$$

corresponding to an exponentially weighted moving average model. In practice λ is here pre-set, avoiding the cumbersome estimation stage, to, for example, 0.97. The rationale for this approach to avoiding estimation is that the range of useful GARCH parameters is often very small and $\hat{\alpha}_1 + \hat{\beta}_1 \approx 1$.

Asymmetric GARCH Models   The GARCH(1,1) model is symmetric in the sense that negative and positive shocks have the same impact on volatility. There is much stronger evidence that positive innovations to volatility are correlated with negative innovations to returns than with positive innovations to returns; see Black (1976) and stylized fact 3 above. To capture this potential asymmetry we may follow Glosten, Jagannathan, and Runkle (1993) and specify a GARCH(1,1) model as

$$h_t^2 = a_0 + a_1 \varepsilon_{t-1}^2 + a_2 \, \text{sgn}(\varepsilon_{t-1}) \varepsilon_{t-1}^2 + \beta h_{t-1}^2.$$

Here $\text{sgn}(\varepsilon_t) = \text{sgn}(z_t) = 1$ if $z_t < 0$ and 0 if $z_t \geq 0$ and the difference between the symmetric GARCH and the present model is that the impact of a shock and its discounting is captured by the term $a_2 \text{sgn}(\varepsilon_{t-1})$ as well.

Calibration of GARCH Models   To estimate GARCH-type models the method of normal maximum likelihood is often applied regardless of whether the conditional distribution is assumed normal. The resulting estimator is termed a *quasi-maximum likelihood estimator* and is still generally consistent (see Bollerslev and Wooldridge, 1992). However, the application of the normal likelihood in a setting where it is not valid may of course result in a large loss of efficiency relative to the true but unknown maximum likelihood estimator. In response Engle and Gonzales-Rivera (1991) introduced the semi-parametric maximum likelihood estimator of GARCH models. The semi-parametric estimator is a two-step estimator. In the first step consistent estimates of the parameters are obtained using the quasi-maximum likelihood estimator and are used to estimate a nonparametric conditional density. The second step consists of using this nonparametric density to adapt the initial estimator. As our main concern is cases where we have deviations from normality, that is, deviations from $z_t \sim N(0, 1)$ as emphasized by stylized fact number 3, we may also consider estimators that use information about the moments of z_t. Skoglund (2001) analyzes the efficient GMM estimator of GARCH(1,1) regression models in detail and in particular establishes the asymptotic efficiency of GMM relative to quasi-maximum likelihood estimator. Skoglund (2001) also evaluates the finite-sample properties of the GMM estimator of a GARCH(1,1) process through a Monte Carlo study and shows that the asymptotic relative efficiency is realized for sample sizes encountered in practice.

The Exponential GARCH Model   A vast array of different GARCH models have been proposed in the literature. See He and Teräsvirta (1999), which contains many examples of GARCH models and their statistical properties. There is a GARCH model that deserves special consideration due to its popularity in applications. This is the exponential GARCH model proposed by Nelson (1991). Nelson criticized the GARCH(p,q) model on several grounds: first, the complexity of positivity restrictions required to ensure that $P(h_t^2 > 0)$; second, the symmetry of the model and the fact that persistence is difficult to evaluate. Given stylized facts of financial return series the relevant range of the standard GARCH parameters has been shown in applications to be very small. To overcome some of these deficiencies Nelson's idea was to propose a logarithmic version of the GARCH model, formulated as

$$\ln h_t^2 = \alpha_0 + \sum \Psi_j g(z_{t-j})$$

where $z_t \sim iid(0, 1)$ and

$$g(z_t) = \theta z_t + \gamma(|z_t| - E|z_t|).$$

The first part of $g(z_t)$ is the asymmetry term and the second the symmetric term where, in particular, $E|z_t| = \frac{\pi}{2}$ if $z_t \sim N(0, 1)$. Write

$$\ln h_t^2 = \alpha_0 + \frac{1 + \Psi_1 L + \cdots + \Psi_q L^q}{1 - \beta_1 L - \cdots - \beta_p L^p} g(z_{t-j})$$

where L^s is the lag operator for lag s. Replacing $1 - \sum \Psi_j$ by an approximating rational polynomial obtains

$$\ln h_t^2 = \alpha_0 + \sum_{j=1}^{q} \Psi_j g(z_{t-j}) + \sum_{l=1}^{p} \beta_j \ln h_{t-j}^2$$

which is the exponential GARCH(p, q) model proposed by Nelson. If $z_t \sim iid(0, 1)$ and normally distributed, then $\sum_{l=1}^{p} \beta_j < 1$ is a necessary condition for all the moments to exist for the exponential GARCH model, which is to be compared with the complex necessary parameter restrictions required on the classical GARCH model.

Capturing Tail Behavior   Having estimated a GARCH model for the risk factor we can construct the empirical residuals

$$\widehat{z}_t = \frac{\widehat{\varepsilon}_t}{\widehat{h}_t} \tag{3.13}$$

which are in practice approximately independent and identically distributed over time. As observed in practice, however, the distribution of model residuals, z_t, does not seem to support the symmetry or the exponentially decaying tail behavior, exhibited by the normal distribution. Hence, using the normal distribution approximation for z_t the high quantiles may be severely underestimated.

An immediate alternative to the normal distribution may be to consider a Student's t-distribution, being only slightly more complex. For example, Bollerslev (1987) considers an application of GARCH with Student's t-errors. The Student's t-distributions have heavier tails than the normal, displaying polynomial decay in the tails. It may therefore be able to capture the fat tails although it maintains the hypothesis of symmetry, which is troublesome because many financial returns residuals are found to be asymmetric, having a much fatter left tail than right tail.

In contrast, purely nonparametric methods (e.g., kernel methods or the empirical distribution function) make no assumptions concerning the nature of the empirical distribution function but have several drawbacks, especially their poor behavior in the tails. Extreme value theory and in particular the generalized Pareto distribution give an asymptotic theory for the tail behavior. Based on a few assumptions the theory shifts the focus from modeling the whole distribution to the modeling of the tail behavior and hence the symmetry hypothesis may be examined directly by estimating the left and right tail separately. In addition, application of extreme value theory has the advantage of requiring just a few degrees of freedom.

We now turn to using extreme value theory in extrapolation of density tails. Our exposition is brief and focused on the practical application of extreme value theory in tail extrapolation of the conditional GARCH residuals, z_t, as in McNeil and Frey (2000) and Nyström and Skoglund (2005). See also Kourouma et al. (2011) for an analysis of performance of univariate extreme value theory models during the 2007 financial crisis. For a comprehensive textbook account on extreme value theory we refer to Embrechts et al. (1997).

Extreme Value Theory and the Generalized Pareto Distribution To introduce the extreme value theory we recall that the central limit theorem states a 1–1 asymptotic correspondence between (properly normalized) sums and the normal distribution. The essence of extreme value theory is that it gives similar results as the central limit theorem but for the maximum of random variables. We introduce the following distribution,

$$\Gamma_{\xi,\mu,\sigma}(z) = \exp\left(-\left(1 + \xi\frac{(z-\mu)}{\sigma}\right)_+^{-1/\xi}\right)$$

where $\sigma > 0$, ξ and μ are parameters and $(z)_+ = \max\{z,0\}$. This is the general form of the extreme value distribution. We also let

$$\Gamma(z) = \exp(-\exp(-z))$$

and $\Gamma_\xi(z) = \Gamma_{\xi,0,1}(z)$. Here $1/\xi$ is referred to as the tail index as it indicates how heavy the upper tail of the underlying distribution is. The parameters μ and σ represent a translation and scaling respectively. Obviously the distribution $\Gamma_{\xi,\mu,\sigma}(z)$ is non-zero if and only if $(1 + \xi\frac{(z-\mu)}{\sigma}) > 0$. As σ by definition is positive the subset of the real axis where this inequality is true is depending on the sign of ξ. If $\xi = 0$, the distribution spreads out along all of the real axis and in this case the distribution is often called a Gumbel distribution. If $\xi > 0$, the distribution has a lower bound (often the distribution is called Frechet in this case), and if $\xi < 0$, the distribution has an upper bound (usually referred to as the Weibull case).

Concentrating on the conditional distribution function F_u, defined in the following manner for $z > u$,

$$F_u(z) = P(Z \leq z \mid Z > u) = \frac{F(z) - F(u)}{1 - F(u)}$$

we also introduce the generalized Pareto distribution, GP,

$$GP_{\xi,\beta}(z) = 1 - \left(1 + \xi\frac{z}{\beta}\right)_+^{-1/\xi}.$$

Extreme value theory now states a 1–1 correspondence between extreme value distributions and the generalized Pareto distribution. The formal connection can be stated

$$1 - GP_{\xi,\beta}(z) = -\ln\Gamma_{\xi,0,\beta}(z).$$

The relation is that excesses over a threshold is asymptotically (large threshold) described by the generalized Pareto distribution. See Embrechts et al. (1997) for details.

Applying Extreme Value Theory We can now make use of extreme value theory in an estimate of the tail for large z. In order to do so we have to make a choice for the threshold u. That is, we have to decide where the tail starts. Consider a sample of $t = 1,\ldots,T$ points sorted according to their size, $Z_n \leq \ldots \leq Z_1$. Suppose that we let the upper tail be defined by an integer $k < n$, hence considering $Z_k \leq \ldots \leq Z_1$ to be the observations in the upper tail of the distribution. This implies that we choose $u = Z_{k+1}$ to be our threshold. A natural estimator for $1 - F(u)$ is k/n. Using the generalized Pareto distribution for the tail we get, for $z > u$, the following estimator of the distribution function $F(z)$

$$\widetilde{F}(z) = 1 - \frac{k}{n}\left(1 + \widetilde{\xi}\frac{(z - Z_{k+1})}{\widetilde{\beta}}\right)_+^{-1/\widetilde{\xi}}$$

where $\widetilde{\xi}$ and $\widetilde{\beta}$ are estimates of the parameters in the generalized Pareto distribution. Given this as an estimate for the upper tail of the distribution function we solve the equation $q = F(z_q)$ for $q > 1 - k/n$ (i.e., for high quantiles). Using the formula above we get

$$\widetilde{z}_q = Z_{k+1} + \frac{\widetilde{\beta}}{\widetilde{\xi}}\left(\left(\frac{1-q}{k/n}\right)^{-\widetilde{\xi}} - 1\right).$$

The maximum likelihood estimator is consistent and asymptotically normal provided that $\xi > -1/2$; see Smith (1987). When estimating ξ one could assume a priori that $\xi > 0$ (Frechet case) combined with a maximum-likelihood method. In this case we get a maximum likelihood estimator of the parameter $\xi > 0$ only. This estimator is referred to as the Hill estimator. Specifically, Hill (1975) proposed the estimator

$$\widetilde{\alpha}_H = \frac{1}{\widetilde{\xi}} = \left(\frac{1}{k}\sum_{j=1}^{k}\log\frac{Z_j}{Z_{k+1}}\right)^{-1} \tag{3.14}$$

where α_H is referred to as the Hill tail index.

For $z \leq u$ we may choose the empirical distribution as an estimate for $F(z)$. Of course, all the estimates are depending on the size of the sample, $t = 1, \ldots, T$, and on the threshold u implicitly through k. There is furthermore a trade-off when choosing the size of the quotient k/n. If this quotient is too small, we will have too few observations in the tail, giving rise to large variance in our estimators for the parameters in the GP-distribution. If the quotient is very large, the basic model assumption, that is, the fact that from the point of view of the asymptotic theory $k(n)/n$ should tend to 0, may be violated. One therefore has to understand the stability of any estimator with respect to the choice of k.

Nyström and Skoglund (2005) consider a Monte Carlo evaluation of the finite sample properties of the maximum likelihood and Hill estimator using a reference t-distribution. They find that maximum likelihood is the preferred estimator. It always performs better than the Hill estimator. In addition it has the useful property of being almost invariant to the choice of threshold, u. This is in sharp contrast to the Hill estimator, which is very sensitive to the threshold. There are also theoretical reasons to prefer the maximum likelihood estimator. The maximum likelihood estimator is applicable to light-tailed data as well, whereas the Hill estimator is designed specifically for the heavy-tailed case. Since the Hill estimator can be sensitive to the threshold the so-called Hill plot is often used. It plots the Hill estimator for a range of different thresholds u and can be used to judge the sensitivity of the Hill estimator to the threshold for particular data. See, for example, Bensalah (2000).

Estimating Risk Using Extreme Value Theory   To estimate risk at time $t + 1$ using the generalized Pareto extrapolation of tails, we denote by Z a random variable having as its distribution function the distribution function constructed using the filtered residuals. Then,

$$y_{t+1} = \mu + h_{t+1}Z \tag{3.15}$$

where the volatility factor h_{t+1} is a forecast obtained from the GARCH process. Hence, y_{t+1} is a random variable with randomness quantified by the random variable Z. If we apply the risk measure ρ to y_{t+1}, we get (assuming that ρ is homogeneous of degree 1 and fulfills the risk-free condition)

$$\rho(y_{t+1}) = \mu + h_{t+1}\rho(Z).$$

Hence, the risk in y_{t+1} is completely determined by the risk in Z and we see that a higher forecasted volatility gives higher risk. For VaR(α) we therefore have as an estimate

$$\mathrm{VaR}_{y_{t+1}}(\alpha) = \mu + h_{t+1}\mathrm{VaR}_Z(\alpha). \tag{3.16}$$

We now consider an example of using equation (3.16) to compute VaR for a simple equity and an exchange rate. The different models considered for the tails of Z are the empirical distribution function, the normal density, the t-density, and the generalized Pareto density.

Figure 3.7 displays the 1-day VaR for different quantiles $1 - \alpha$ such that $(1 - \alpha) \in [0.05, 0)$ for the USD/SEK exchange rate and using different models for the tail of the

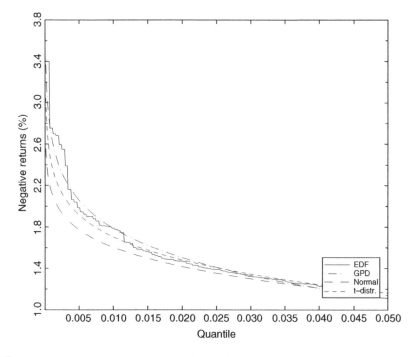

FIGURE 3.7   GARCH Filtered Lower Tail Residuals of the USD/SEK Exchange Rate. The Fitted Tail Distributions are the Empirical Distribution Function, Normal Density, t-Density, and the Generalized Pareto Distribution

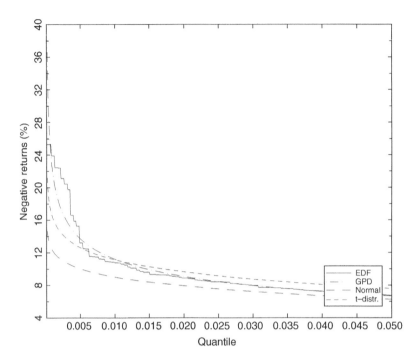

FIGURE 3.8 GARCH Filtered Lower Tail Residuals of the ABB Stock. The Fitted Tail Distributions are the Empirical Distribution Function, Normal Density, t-Density, and the Generalized Pareto Distribution

obtained standardized residuals in equation (3.13). Figure 3.8 displays the same for the ABB (Asea Brown Boveri) stock quoted on the Stockholm exchange. In both cases a GARCH(1,1) model has been estimated on daily returns between January 1, 1993, and September 6, 2001. Different tail models are then fitted to the standardized GARCH residual tails, specifically, the empirical distribution function (EDF), the normal density (Normal), the t-density (t-distr.), and the generalized Pareto density (GPD). The VaR for the different quantiles, expressed in % returns, are then obtained using equation (3.16). Note that in both cases (though more pronounced for the ABB stock) the normal and t-model underestimates the risk for high quantiles, whereas the generalized Pareto density provides a good in-sample fit to the empirical density with the added benefit of providing consistent estimates of out-of-sample quantiles.

We also consider an example of using the simplified Hill extreme value estimator in equation (3.14) for portfolio risk in the context of our sample equity portfolio in Table 3.1. Danielson and De Vries (1997) proposed the following estimator of tail probabilities given an estimated tail index, $\widetilde{\alpha}_H$,

$$\widetilde{F}(z) = \frac{k}{n}\left(\frac{z}{Z_{k+1}}\right)^{-\widetilde{\alpha}_H}$$

such that

$$\widetilde{z}_q = \widetilde{F}^{-1}(z) = Z_{k+1}\left(\frac{k}{n\widetilde{F}(z)}\right)^{1/\widetilde{\alpha}_H}$$

which can be used to compute a Hill based VaR estimate. To gain intuition on the VaR(α) estimate we can write

$$\text{VaR}(\alpha) = \text{VaR}(1 - \lambda)\left(\frac{1 - \lambda}{1 - \alpha}\right)^{1/\widetilde{\alpha}_H}$$

where λ is the percentage cutoff point for the estimator. Hence, for a given cutoff percentage λ we can calculate VaR(α) for any $\alpha \geq \lambda$. We can also obtain a Hill-based CVaR(α) for $\widetilde{\alpha}_H > 1$ as

$$\text{CVaR}(\alpha) = \frac{\widetilde{\alpha}_H}{\widetilde{\alpha}_H - 1}\text{VaR}(\alpha).$$

For our sample equity portfolio in Table 3.1 we now compute the aggregate portfolio loss tail index, $\widetilde{\alpha}_H$, using the Hill estimator. We also compute the VaR(0.99) and CVaR(0.99) based on the Hill tail index, denoted VaR^H(0.99) and CVaR^H(0.99) respectively. This is done for different percentages of sample points in the tail of 10%, 7%, 5%, 3%, and 1% and using 1,000,000 scenarios. Table 3.13 displays the results. For reference, the portfolio empirical VaR(0.99) and CVaR(0.99) from Table 3.2 are 27.88 and 31.37, respectively. We note that the Hill estimator is quite sensitive to the number of sample points in the tail, that is, the choice of threshold. This is consistent with the findings in Nyström and Skoglund (2005).

We finally emphasize that in this univariate setting the GARCH model filtering of the financial returns yields a transformed return series, $\hat{z}_t$, that should be close to independent and identically distributed. Hence, we have transformed the return series to a distribution that is amenable for random sampling using the bootstrap methodology, requiring independent and identically distributed observations. The bootstrap re-sampling of $\hat{z}_t$ instead of y_t (that is, sampling from the density of Z in equation (3.15)) is often referred to as a filtered historical simulation, introduced by Barone-Adesi et al. (1998, 1999). Filtered historical simulation improves on the naive historical simulation of y_t, which does not take into account that returns are in general dependent (see stylized fact 2). It is also natural, as we have done here, to address also stylized fact 3 (i.e., that the returns are in general fat-tailed). Consequently, we have used extreme value theory for the tails of the (standardized) returns, $\hat{z}_t$, while we can of course retain the empirical distribution function in the center as in filtered historical simulation since there are sufficient empirical observations there.

In a multivariate context with n risk factors we of course also need to model the dependence between the financial returns. Barone-Adesi et al. (1998, 1999) use a nonparametric estimation of dependence by re-sampling, for random t, multivariate $j = 1, \ldots, n$ standardized

TABLE 3.13 Hill-Based Exteme Value Portfolio Risk for Different Percentage Sample Points in the Tail

Sample points in tail	Tail index ($\widetilde{\alpha}_H$)	VaR^H(0.99)	CVaR^H(0.99)
10%	3.84	29.99	40.92
7%	4.63	28.45	36.56
5%	5.39	27.75	34.31
3%	6.54	27.41	32.54
1%	9.11	27.88	31.45

residuals, $\{\hat{z}_{jt}\}_{j=1}^{n}$. While addressing multivariate dependencies in standardized residuals by using bootstrap re-sampling of the observed dependence is one way to consider codependency we will focus below on using explicit parametric dependence structures with copulas.[11] A benefit of many copula models of explicit parametric dependence is that they have parameters that can be used to stress the degree of dependence that has been calibrated on history. This is useful since historically calibrated dependence relationships may change quickly in distress, and in practice there is a lot of uncertainty about whether historically observed dependencies will hold true going forward.

Multivariate Time Series

We now focus on the codependency of the (univariate GARCH filtered) residual vector, $\mathbf{z}_t = (z_{1t}, \ldots, z_{nt})$ where z_{jt} $\forall j$ is approximately independent and identically distributed over time t.

Among parametric copulas the elliptic copulas such as the normal and t-distribution copulas are the most frequently used copulas in practice. This is because these copulas can handle the scale of financial applications and use the well-known correlation approach to modeling dependency. Here, we shall also make the assumption that the dependence between the random variables $(z_{1t}, \ldots, z_{nt})$ is time-independent. Denoting by Ξ a measure of correlation between components of $\mathbf{z}$ we assume that $\Xi_s = \Xi_l$ $\forall s, l$. Note that the present specification allows for GARCH models for each of the univariate return series $y_{1t}, \ldots, y_{nt}$ and the assumption that $\Xi_s = \Xi_l$ $\forall s, l$ does not imply time-independent correlation between the financial return series themselves. In what follows we denote the model with $\Xi_s = \Xi_l$ $\forall s, l$ the constant conditional correlation model. In a multivariate normal framework this model was originally proposed by Bollerslev (1990), who used it as a parsimonious multivariate specification to model exchange rates. The constant conditional covariance matrix model can be represented in the form

$$\Sigma_t = \lambda_t \Xi \lambda_t$$

where λ_t is a diagonal volatility matrix with univariate GARCH specifications on the diagonal.

Implicit in the use of copula as a model of codependency is the separation of the modeling of univariate marginal distributions and the dependence structure. In this setting the model specification framework consists of two components.

- The first component is the specification and estimation of models for univariate marginal distributions including, for example, parametric GARCH specifications and fitting of (non)parametric densities to the (tails of the) univariate residuals as we have discussed above.
- The second component is the specification of a model for codependency between financial time series in terms of copula for the vector $\mathbf{z}_t$.

Copulas Traditionally dependence between real-valued random variables $Z_1, \ldots, Z_n$ is described by the joint distribution function. The idea of the copula is to decouple the construction of multivariate distribution functions into the specification of marginal distributions

---

[11]The approach to modeling codependency in the multivariate filtered historical simulation can be thought of as using the empirical dependence.

and a dependence structure. Suppose that $Z_1, \ldots, Z_n$ have continuous marginals $F_1, \ldots, F_n$. Then for each $j \in \{1, 2, \ldots, n\}$, $U_j = F_j(Z_j)$ is a uniform $(0, 1)$-variable. By definition

$$F(z_1, \ldots, z_n) = P(Z_1 \leq z_1, \ldots, Z_n \leq z_n)$$
$$= P(F_1(Z_1) \leq F_1(z_1), \ldots, F_n(Z_n) \leq F_n(z_n)). \tag{3.17}$$

Hence

$$F(z_1, \ldots, z_n) = P(U_1 \leq F_1(z_1), \ldots, U_n \leq F_n(z_n))$$

and if $F_i^{-1}(\alpha)$, $\alpha \in [0, 1]$, denotes the inverse of the marginal, the copula may be expressed in the following way

$$C(u_1, \ldots, u_n) = F(F_1(Z_1), \ldots, F_n(Z_n)).$$

The copula is hence the joint distribution function of the vector of transformed marginals. Independence between the components is equivalent to

$$C(u_1, \ldots, u_n) = \Pi_{j=1}^n u_j.$$

We also introduce the copulas C^- and C^+, usually referred to as the lower and upper Frechet bounds, respectively:

$$C^-(u_1, \ldots, u_n) = \max \left\{ \sum_{j=1}^n u_j - n + 1, 0 \right\},$$

$$C^+(u_1, \ldots, u_n) = \min\{u_1, \ldots, u_n\}.$$

The lower Frechet bound is not a copula for $n > 2$. For $n = 2$ it may be interpreted as the dependence structure of two counter-monotonic random variables. The upper Frechet bound is always a copula and symbolizes perfect dependence as its density has no mass outside of the diagonal.

Figure 3.9 displays the bivariate Frechet bounds (counter-dependence and perfect dependence, respectively) and the independence copula respectively. The bivariate lower Frechet bound copula has no mass outside the northeast corner, whereas the upper Frechet bound has no mass outside the diagonal. In contrast the independence copula has mass almost everywhere.

The most commonly used copulas include the elliptic and Archimedean copula families and some of their members. As we have mentioned above the elliptic family includes the well-known normal and t-copulas. The Archimedean class of copulas displays three well-known members. They are the Clayton, Gumbel, and Frank copula. All of these Archimedean copulas have an explicit copula representation, which makes them easy to use for simulation purposes. The Clayton two-dimensional copula is represented as

$$C(u, v) = (u^{-\theta} + v^{-\theta} - 1)^{-\frac{1}{\theta}}$$

and as θ approaches 0 we obtain the independence copula, whereas as θ approaches ∞ we obtain the perfect dependence copula. The Clayton copula displays lower tail dependence. The Gumbel copula has two-dimensional representation

$$C(u, v) = \exp \left\{ -((-\log u)^\theta + (-\log v)^\theta - 1)^{\frac{1}{\theta}} \right\}$$

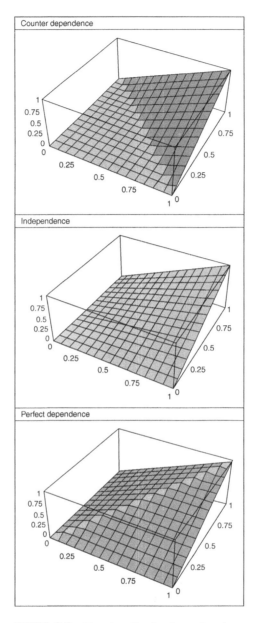

FIGURE 3.9 Bivariate Frechet Bound and
Independence Copulas

where $\theta = 1$ implies the independence copula and as θ approaches ∞ we obtain the perfect dependence copula. The Gumbel copula displays upper tail dependence. Finally, the Frank copula has the bivariate representation

$$C(u, v) = -\frac{1}{\theta} \log \left\{ 1 + \frac{(\exp(-\theta u) - 1)(\exp(-\theta v) - 1)}{(\exp(-\theta) - 1)} \right\}.$$

The Frank copula displays perfect negative dependence for θ equal to $-\infty$ and perfect positive dependence for θ equal to ∞. The Frank copula has both upper and lower tail dependence.

Since both the Clayton and Frank copula display lower tail dependence ($\theta < 0$ for Frank copula) they are natural copulas for risk analysis since our main interest is in modeling tail loss. However, these Archimedean copulas parametrize dependence in a single parameter and are usually difficult to make use of in practice with many financial risk factors due to the limitation of the single dependence parameter.[12]

Measuring Copula Dependence The most well-known copula dependence measures are the Spearman's rho, the Kendall's tau, and the coefficients of upper and lower tail dependence. See Embrechts et al. (2002). These are all bivariate notions that can be extended to the multivariate case by applying them to all pairs of components in the vector. The linear correlation, ρ, between Z_1, Z_2 is

$$\rho(Z_1, Z_2) = \frac{\mathrm{cov}(Z_1, Z_2)}{\sqrt{\mathrm{var}(Z_1)}\sqrt{\mathrm{var}(Z_2)}}.$$

Linear correlation is, as the word indicates, a linear measure of dependence. For constants α, β, c_1, c_2 it has the property that

$$\rho(\alpha Z_1 + c_1, \beta Z_2 + c_2) = \rho(Z_1, Z_2)$$

and hence is invariant under strictly increasing *linear* transformations. However, in general

$$\rho(Z_1, Z_2) \neq \rho(F(Z_1), G(Z_2))$$

for strictly increasing transformations and hence the linear correlation ρ is not a copula property as it depends on the marginal distributions.

For two independent vectors of random variables with identical distribution function (Z_1, Z_2) and $(\tilde{Z_1}, \tilde{Z_2})$ Kendall's tau is the probability of concordance minus the probability of discordance,

$$\tau(Z_1, Z_2) = P[(Z_1 - \tilde{Z_1})(Z_2 - \tilde{Z_2}) > 0] - P[(Z_1 - \tilde{Z_1})(Z_2 - \tilde{Z_2}) < 0].$$

Kendall's tau is a copula property. Spearman's rho is the linear correlation of the variables $(F_1(Z_1), F_2(Z_2))$,

$$\rho_S(Z_1, Z_2) = \rho(F_1(Z_1), F_2(Z_2))$$

and Spearman's rho is a property of only the copula C and not the marginals. Often the Spearman's rho is referred to as the correlation of ranks. We note that Spearman's rho is simply the usual linear correlation, ρ, of the probability transformed random variables.[13]

---

[12]However, see Chapter 8 on firmwide risk aggregation where a risk aggregation is decomposed in n subset partial aggregations where each partial aggregation has a lower dimensional copula than all the risks.

[13]See Figure 2.3, which displays the inverse function transformation for the normal distribution, $F^{-1}(u) = x$, and equivalently, $F(x) = u$.

Another important copula quantity is the coefficient of upper and lower tail dependence. The coefficient of upper tail dependence $\Lambda_U(Z_1, Z_2)$ is defined by

$$\Lambda_U(X_1, X_2) = \lim_{u \nearrow 1} P[Z_1 > F_1^{-1}(u) \mid Z_2 > F_2^{-1}(u)].$$

The coefficient of lower tail dependence $\Lambda_L(Z_1, Z_2)$ is similarly defined by

$$\Lambda_L(X_1, X_2) = \lim_{u \searrow 0} P\left[Z_1 < F_1^{-1}(u) \mid Z_2 < F_2^{-1}(u)\right].$$

If $\Lambda_U(Z_1, Z_2) \in (0, 1]$, then Z_1 and Z_2 are said to have asymptotic upper tail dependence. If $\Lambda_U(Z_1, Z_2) = 0$, then Z_1 and Z_2 are said to have asymptotic upper tail independence. The obvious interpretation of the coefficients of upper and lower tail dependence is that these numbers measure the probability of joint extremes of the copula.

Elliptic Copulas Elliptic copulas are copulas derived from the elliptic class of distributions such as the normal, Student's t, and logistic distribution. The elliptic copulas that will concern us below are the normal copula and the Student's t-copula.

The Gaussian or normal copula is the copula of the multivariate normal distribution. The random vector $Z = (Z_1, \dots, Z_n)$ is multivariate normal if and only if the univariate margins $F_1, \dots, F_n$ are Gaussians and the dependence structure is described by a unique copula function C, the normal copula, such that

$$C(u_1, \dots, u_n) = \Phi(N^{-1}(u_1), \dots, N^{-1}(u_n)), \tag{3.18}$$

where Φ is the standard multivariate normal distribution function with linear correlation matrix Σ and N^{-1} is the inverse of the standard univariate Gaussian distribution function.

For the Gaussian copula there is an explicit relation between the Kendall's tau, τ, the Spearman's rho, ρ_S, and the linear correlation, ρ of the random variables X_1, X_2. In particular,

$$\tau(X_1, X_2) = \frac{2}{\pi} \arcsin \rho,$$

$$\rho_S(X_1, X_2) = \frac{6}{\pi} \arcsin \frac{1}{2}\rho.$$

The copula of the multivariate Student's t-distribution is the Student's t-copula. Let Z be a vector with an n-variate student-t distribution with v degrees of freedom, mean vector μ (for $v > 1$), and covariance matrix $\frac{v}{v-2}\Sigma$ (for $v > 2$). It can be represented in the following way,

$$Z \overset{d}{=} \frac{\sqrt{v}}{\sqrt{S}} E \tag{3.19}$$

where $S \sim \chi_v^2$ and the random vector $E \sim N(0, \Sigma)$ is independent of S. The copula of the vector Z is the Student's t-copula with v degrees of freedom. It can be analytically represented as

$$C_{v,\Sigma}^t(u) = t_v(t_v^{-1}(u_1), \dots, t_v^{-1}(u_n))$$

where t_ν denotes the multivariate distribution function of the random vector $\frac{\sqrt{\nu}}{\sqrt{S}}Z$ and t_ν denotes the margins. For the t-copula there is an explicit relation between the Kendall's tau and the linear correlation of the random variables Z_1, Z_2. Specifically,

$$\tau(Z_1, Z_2) = \frac{2}{\pi} \arcsin \rho.$$

However, the simple relationship between the Spearman's rho, ρ_S, and the linear correlation, ρ, that we had for the Gaussian copula above does not exist in the t-copula case.

To capture different tail dependencies between risk factors an enhancement of the t-copula to a mixture of degrees of freedoms, ν, is useful. Therefore, the grouped t-copula was introduced by Daul et al. (2003) and Demarta and McNeil (2005). The basic idea is to construct a t-copula for a random vector Z such that subvectors of Z are allowed to have different levels of the degrees-of-freedom parameter.[14] We know from equation (3.19) that $Z = \frac{\sqrt{\nu}}{\sqrt{S}}E$. We can hence partition Z into $\{1, \ldots, d\}$ subgroups with degrees-of-freedom parameters $\nu_1, \ldots, \nu_d$. Denoting subgroup j by Z_j we set $Z_j = \frac{\sqrt{\nu_j}}{\sqrt{S}}E_j$. The obtained sample vector Z is referred to as a sample from a grouped t-copula.

Above we defined the upper tail dependence of a copula as the limiting conditional probability,

$$\Lambda_U(Z_1, Z_2) = \lim_{u \nearrow 1} P\left(Z_1 > F_1^{-1}(u) \mid Z_2 > F_2^{-1}(u)\right).$$

The normal copula is well-known to be asymptotically independent while the t-copula displays asymptotic tail dependence with

$$\Lambda_U(Z_1, Z_2) = 2t_{\nu+1}\left(-\sqrt{\frac{(\nu+1)(1-\rho)}{1+\rho}}\right).$$

See McNeil et al. (2005). Although these asymptotic notions are interesting from a practical perspective it might be more interesting to investigate the finite tail-dependence for the normal and t-copula.

Figure 3.10 displays the (for $u \leq 1$) tail dependence of the bivariate normal and t-copula for different values of the correlation parameter and different values for u. We note from the figure that the decay of tail dependence is quite fast for the normal copula and hence in risk applications, especially for very high quantiles, real differences between the copulas are expected.

Estimation of Copulas To estimate the parameters of the normal and t-copulas there is, due to the explicit relationships between Kendall's tau and linear correlation, a simple method based on Kendall's tau. The method consists of constructing an empirical estimate of linear correlation for each bivariate marginals and then using the relationship between the linear correlation and Kendall's tau stated above to infer an estimate. Obviously, there is no

---

[14]As we will discuss below the degrees-of-freedom parameter is important for the tail dependence.

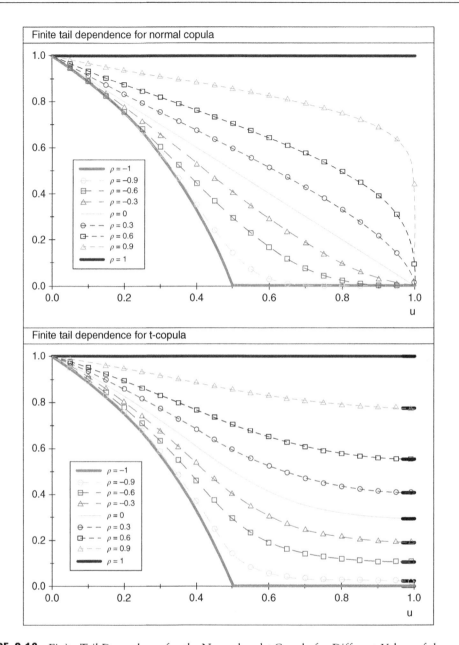

FIGURE 3.10 Finite Tail Dependence for the Normal and t-Copula for Different Values of the Correlation Parameter and Threshold

guarantee that the componentwise transformation of the empirical Kendall's tau matrix will be positive definite. However, it can be fixed by using a procedure such as the eigenvalue adjustment method of Rousseeuw and Molenberghs (1993). An alternative method employs the linear correlation of the probability transformed random variables, that is, the Spearman's rho, or, in the case of the Gaussian, the explicit relation between linear correlation and Spearman's rho.

In addition to the nonparametric approaches to estimation of correlation we can also employ the familiar method of maximum likelihood. For that purpose consider the fundamental relation

$$F(z_1, \ldots, z_n) = C(F_1(z_1), \ldots, F_n(z_n)).$$

Taking derivatives the density of the copula is given by

$$c(u_1, \ldots, u_n) = \frac{\partial^n C(u_1, \ldots, u_n)}{\partial u_1 \ldots \partial u_n}$$

and fulfills

$$f(z_1, \ldots, z_n) = c(F_1(z_1), \ldots, F_n(z_n)) \prod_{j=1}^{n} f_j(z_j)$$

such that

$$c(F_1(z_1), \ldots, F_n(z_n)) = \frac{f(z_1, \ldots, z_n)}{\prod_{j=1}^{n} f_j(z_j)}$$

$$= \frac{f(F^{-1}(u_1), \ldots, F^{-1}(u_n))}{\prod_{j=1}^{n} f_j(F^{-1}(u_j))}.$$

Hence the log-likelihood can be written as

$$l = f(F^{-1}(u_1), \ldots, F^{-1}(u_n)) - \sum_{j=1}^{n} \ln f_j(F^{-1}(u_j))$$

$$\simeq f(F^{-1}(u_1), \ldots, F^{-1}(u_n))$$

since the second term only depends on the margins and is not relevant for estimation of correlation.

Focusing on the Gaussian copula we have $F^{-1} = N^{-1}$ the standard normal inverse function. The maximum likelihood estimate is hence recognized as simply the covariance matrix estimate for the normalized univariate margins—albeit under the restriction that the estimate is a true correlation matrix, that is, the components of the estimated matrix, p_{ij}, satisfying $p_{ij} \in [-1, 1]$ and $p_{ii} = 1$ for $i, j = 1, \ldots, n$. To a close approximation this is expected to be satisfied by the normalized univariate margins. If this is not the case in practice, normalization to a true correlation matrix can be used. The maximum likelihood estimation of the Gaussian copula hence proceeds as follows.

1. Transform the univariate model residuals z_j to uniforms using the cumulative density function of z_j:s, $u_j = F_j(z_j)$.
2. Transform the obtained uniforms to normals using the inverse normal cumulative distribution function, N^{-1}. That is, $x_j = N^{-1}(u_j)$ where $x_j \sim N(0, 1)$.
3. Estimate the correlation matrix Ψ_N of the normalized vector $\mathbf{x} = (x_1, \ldots, x_n)$ where $\hat{\Psi}_N$ is an estimate of the normal copula.

For the *t*-copula the log likelihood can be maximized with respect to the correlation parameters and the degrees-of-freedom parameter using numerical optimization. However, when the dimension of the data increases the numerical optimization can become infeasible. One can then estimate the t-copula correlation matrix using the explicit relation between the Kendall's tau and the linear correlation. Then, conditional on the correlation matrix the degrees-of-freedom parameter can be estimated. In practice it is possible that the estimate of the correlation matrix is not positive definite. In this case one can use the eigenvalue adjustment method of Rousseeuw and Molenberghs (1993). See also algorithm 5.55 in McNeil et al. (2005) that uses this method.

The Gumbel and Clayton copula parameter θ has closed-form explicit representation in terms of Kendall's tau. Specifically, for the Gumbel copula

$$\theta = \frac{1}{1 - \tau}$$

and, for the Clayton copula,

$$\theta = \frac{2\tau}{1 - \tau}$$

One method to estimate the parameters is therefore to calibrate with Kendall's tau.[15] Alternatively, one can use maximum likelihood method to estimate θ.

Empirical Example of Estimation and Simulation from Copulas   We consider a 10-day sample of returns from four equities in Table 3.14. Figure 3.11 displays the bivariate scatter plots between the equities returns.

We now estimate the normal copula using the maximum likelihood method above, yielding a correlation matrix Ψ_N,

$$\Psi_N = \begin{bmatrix} 1 & 0.7120 & 0.7696 & 0.6144 \\ 0.7120 & 1 & 0.4774 & 0.7880 \\ 0.7696 & 0.4774 & 1 & 0.3999 \\ 0.6144 & 0.7880 & 0.3999 & 1 \end{bmatrix}.$$

TABLE 3.14   Sample Equity Returns for 10 Days

Day	Equity 1	Equity 2	Equity 3	Equity 4
1	0.004182	0.010367	0.002002	0.003503
2	−0.027960	0.001913	−0.035861	−0.000582
3	0.006732	0.023607	−0.010671	0.025611
4	−0.033435	0.004239	−0.024610	−0.002838
5	0.029560	0.026680	0.007301	0.010814
6	−0.003054	0.004441	0.016414	−0.001689
7	−0.012255	−0.027346	−0.022546	−0.012408
8	0.013958	0.008418	0.053857	0.003427
9	−0.011318	−0.010851	−0.010689	−0.017075
10	−0.022587	−0.015021	−0.001955	0.002316

---

[15]The Frank copula has functional relation between Kendall's tau and the θ parameter; see McNeil et al. (2005, p. 222). This functional form can be inverted numerically to obtain θ as a function of Kendall's tau.

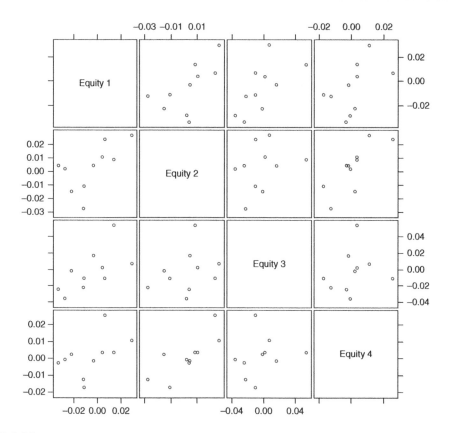

FIGURE 3.11   Bivariate Scatter Plots of Equity Returns

We also estimate the *t*-copula using Kendall's tau and subsequent maximum likelihood to find the degrees of freedom, v. The corresponding Kendall's tau *t*-copula correlation matrix, Ψ_t^K, is

$$
\Psi_t^K = \begin{bmatrix} 1 & 0.7660 & 0.8090 & 0.6691 \\ 0.7660 & 1 & 0.5000 & 0.8440 \\ 0.8090 & 0.5000 & 1 & 0.3746 \\ 0.6691 & 0.8440 & 0.3746 & 1 \end{bmatrix}
$$

with v estimated to 100. The corresponding full maximum likelihood estimate of the *t*-copula gives the same estimate for the degrees of freedom. However, the full maximum likelihood correlation matrix, Ψ_t^{ML}, is estimated as

$$
\Psi_t^{ML} = \begin{bmatrix} 1 & 0.8099 & 0.8470 & 0.7407 \\ 0.8099 & 1 & 0.6374 & 0.8637 \\ 0.8470 & 0.6374 & 1 & 0.5758 \\ 0.7407 & 0.8637 & 0.5758 & 1 \end{bmatrix}.
$$

For the Archimedean copulas Clayton, Gumbel, and Frank we fit the θ parameter using both the Kendall's tau and maximum likelihood. The estimates are given in Table 3.15.

TABLE 3.15 Estimation of Theta Parameter for
Archimedean Copulas Clayton, Gumbel, and Frank Using
Kendall's Tau and Maximum Likelihood Method

Estimation method	Copula		
	Clayton	Gumbel	Frank
Maximum likelihood	1.228	1.949	5.232
Kendall's tau	2.087	2.043	5.801

The reader may have observed that there may be significant differences between the estimates using Kendall's tau and maximum likelihood for the t-copula and the Archimedean copulas. However, this is largely due to the small sample size we use for the equity returns (only 10 days).

Having estimated the copula parameters we can simulate from the copulas. Figures 3.12 and 3.13 display the bivariate scatter plots of 10,000 copula simulations for equity 1

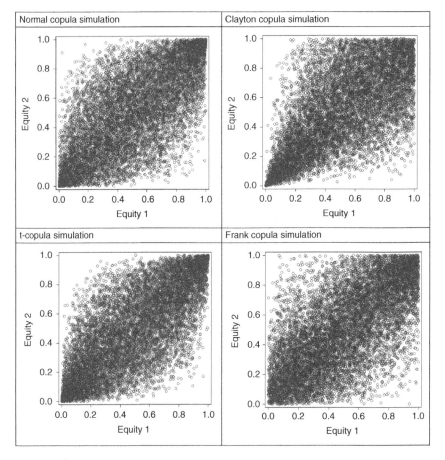

FIGURE 3.12 Bivariate Scatter Plots of 10,000 Uniform Copula Simulations of Returns for Equity 1 and and Equity 2 from the Normal Copula, the t-Copula (Estimated with Kendall's Tau), and Archimedean Copulas Estimated with Kendall's Tau (Clayton and Frank)

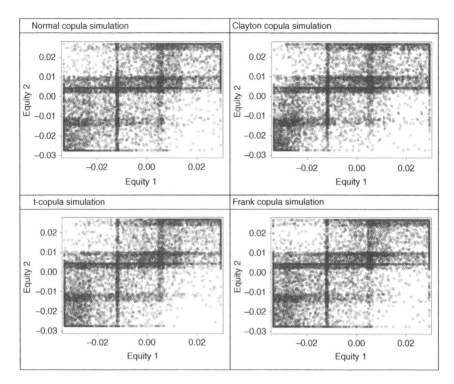

FIGURE 3.13 Bivariate Scatter Plots of 10,000 Empirical Density Copula Simulations of Returns for Equity 1 and Equity 2 from the Normal Copula, the *t*-Copula (Estimated with Kendall's Tau), and Archimedean Copulas Estimated with Kendall's Tau (Clayton and Frank)

and equity 2 from the normal copula, the *t*-copula (estimated with Kendall's tau), and Archimedean copulas estimated with Kendall's tau (Clayton and Frank). Specifically, Figure 3.12 displays the copula simulated uniforms and Figure 3.13 displays the corresponding empirical values (transformed back to empirical distribution from the copula simulated uniforms using the empirical distribution function). In Figure 3.12 the normal and *t*-copula display similar behavior as the degrees-of-freedom parameter of the *t*-distribution is 100 and hence the *t*-distribution is close to normal. The Clayton copula simulation displays the characteristic lower tail dependence while the Frank copula has both lower and upper tail dependence. The copula simulations transformed to the empirical densities in Figure 3.13 concentrate mass due to the fact that we have only 10 observations for the empirical density.

Normal Mixture Copulas and Copula Asymmetry Having considered the normal and *t*-copulas as unique copulas we will now consider a more general copula, termed the normal mixture copula, that contains the two as a special case. The normal mixture copula representation is also an economically relevant representation of dependence as it introduces essentially different states of dependence. This is consistent with financial markets behavior with stressed and normal states of dependence.

To introduce the normal mixture copula we consider a normal mixture distribution as the distribution of the random vector

$$\mathbf{Z} \cong f(\mathbf{W}) + \mathbf{W}\mathbf{E}$$

where $f(\mathbf{W}) \in R^n$, $W \geq 0$ is a random variable and the random vector $\mathbf{E} \sim N(0, \mathbf{\Sigma})$ is independent of W. In particular, if $f(\mathbf{W}) = \boldsymbol{\mu}$ and W is distributed as an inverse gamma with parameters $(\frac{1}{2}v, \frac{1}{2}v)$, then $\mathbf{Z}$ is distributed as a t-distribution. Another type of normal mixture distribution is the discrete normal mixture distribution, where $f(\mathbf{W}) = \boldsymbol{\mu}$ and W is a discrete random variable taking values w_1, w_2 with probability p_1, p_2. By setting w_2 large relative to w_1 and p_1 large relative to p_2, one can interpret this as two states—one ordinary state and one stress state. The normal mixture distribution where $f(\mathbf{W}) = \boldsymbol{\mu} + \mathbf{W}\boldsymbol{\gamma}$ and $\boldsymbol{\gamma}$ is different among at least one of the components $\gamma_1, \ldots, \gamma_n$ is a non-exchangeable normal mixture distribution, and $\boldsymbol{\gamma}$ is called an asymmetry parameter. Negative values of $\boldsymbol{\gamma}$ elements produce a greater level of tail dependence for joint negative returns. This is the case that is perceived as relevant for many financial time series where joint negative returns show stronger dependence than joint positive returns. The copula of a normal mixture distribution is a normal mixture copula.

Model Validation and Backtesting

All models are created in a context of proper assumptions, historical data, and target use case. Therefore, they are all subject to validation of this context and performance of model during its life cycle. Model validation has attracted a lot of attention recently, partly due to the 2007 financial crisis. In general, model validation methodology includes

1. *Expert examination:* Financial economic models must follow sound economic intuition, ensure mathematical justification, and meet business practice. Expert examination usually focuses on these aspects. The examination is also accompanied by thorough documentation of the model. The topics of VaR scaling for risk horizons longer than the typical 1-day market risk horizon, the impact on VaR with trading activities, as well as incorporation of market illiquidity premiums discussed later in this chapter are a few examples how models and risk measurement can be complicated by practical factors.
2. *Stress testing and scenario analysis:* Stress testing and scenario analysis provide forward-looking capabilities to capture any substances that models based on historical data may miss. They not only provide a validation function versus expert estimates but also often complement the existing models to help the management or regulator to capture any unseen scenarios.
3. *Backtesting:* Backtesting is the most direct validation of a model. It is also a widely studied subject in the modeling practice. In the discipline of time series modeling and forecasting it is usually related to the study of goodness of fit. However, in risk management the performance focus is usually not on the forecasted value but the out-of-sample accuracy of the confidence interval.

Clearly, model validation and model management play a vital role in financial institutions since both valuation and risk management are based on models and the associated model assumptions.

In the simulation-based approach market risk measures are obtained in steps.

- First, statistical risk factor models are used to generate future possible scenarios.
- Second, portfolio valuation is performed under the scenarios to generate a portfolio profit-and-loss distribution.
- Third, risk measures are obtained from the portfolio profit-and-loss distribution.

Model risks can arise mainly from the first two stages. In the first step of generating scenarios from risk factor models one faces the risk of incorrect risk factor model assumption, specification, and implementation. In the second step of valuation there may be uncertainty around whether the pricing model fairly represents the scenario obtainable market values, especially when markets are not liquid or portfolios are concentrated.

Pricing models may depend on risk factors that are not liquidly quoted with significant bid–offer spreads. For example, a long-term swap depends on both the relatively liquid short-term money market quotes as well as the long-term swap rates, which may be less liquid. Pricing models may also include risk factors that more resemble model assumptions than actual liquid market quotes. Examples include correlations in basket products.

General model risk management has been discussed in the introduction to this book. We also refer the reader to Derman (1996) and Rebonato (2001) on model risk management. Our focus in this subsection will be mainly on statistical backtesting models used to test the accuracy of the final risk measures obtained from the market risk model.

Statistical backtesting models can potentially reveal incorrect model assumption and specification risk, for example, if we are using the wrong risk factor model or an incomplete model that ignores important risk factors. Portfolio-level backtesting methods can potentially also reveal whether we use an incorrect model for specifying risk factor dependence. We will discuss both VaR and CVaR backtesting starting with VaR since the backtesting methodology for VaR lays the foundation for backtesting techniques of CVaR.

The VaR measure is essentially an interval forecast of the maximum portfolio loss that could occur over a given period of time at a specific confidence level. Intuitively this can be tested by an exceedance test. We define a VaR exceedance indicator I_t at time t as

$$I_t = \begin{cases} 1 & \text{if } \text{VaR}_t \text{ is exceeded} \\ 0 & \text{otherwise} \end{cases}.$$

The expected exceedance rate is therefore $E(I_t) = \alpha$. I_t is also called "hit sequence" by Christoffersen (1998). Since VaR is a quantile measure, backtesting can be done with the statistical evaluation of an interval estimator. A VaR estimation is considered accurate if it satisfies both unconditional and independence properties.

Unconditional Coverage Unconditional coverage is a critical property of the VaR because it makes VaR true at the promised confidence level α. With the observed actual losses in the past T periods, one can count how many times the VaR computed for that period was exceeded. If there are too many exceedances, then the VaR underestimates the risk; on the other hand, if there are too few exceedances, then the VaR estimation is too conservative. Therefore, the hypothesis test can use the classical Bernoulli trials by assuming a binomial distribution for the number of exceptions x:

$$f(x) = \binom{T}{x} \alpha^x (1 - \alpha)^{T-x}.$$

For a large number T, the above binomial distribution can be approximated by the normal distribution $N(\alpha T, \alpha(1 - \alpha)T)$.[16]

---

[16]However, if the total number of observed losses is not large enough, then the test will rely on the bootstrap method. See Dufour (2006).

Christoffersen (1998) formulates a likelihood test based on the assumption of a correctly specified model. The likelihood function of independent and identically distributed Bernoulli(π) random variables, I_t, is

$$L(\pi) = \Pi_{t=1}^{T}(1 - \pi)^{1-I_t}\pi^{I_t}$$

which simplifies to

$$L(\pi) = (1 - \pi)^{T_0}\pi^{T_1}$$

where T_0 is the number of periods where no violations occurred and T_1 is the number of violation periods. The maximum likelihood estimate of π is $\hat{\pi} = \frac{T_1}{T}$. Hence, the null hypothesis is simply H_0: $\pi = \alpha$, which amounts to test whether on average the coverage rate is consistent with the VaR model. The likelihood ratio statistic is

$$LR_{UC} = -2\log\left(\frac{L(\alpha)}{L(\hat{\pi})}\right)$$

and the p-value of the statistic is obtained from the χ_1^2-distribution.

The Basel regulatory backtesting of the market risk VaR measure uses the coverage test to specify three supervisory review zones based on the number of exceedance of the 99% confidence level VaR.

Independence Christoffersen (1998) has shown that the failure rate–based test performs poorly in financial risk management where higher-moment dynamics such as clustering of volatility are often present. It may produce a correct overall "unconditional" evaluation but incorrect local evaluation at any given time. The basic idea is that if the VaR prediction is conditional, it must exhibit serial independence. The independence property is the other important property of a risk measure like VaR. There are several independence test methods. The most used are the independence and duration tests.

Independence Test Christoffersen (1998) proposes the independence (IT) likelihood ratio test of the validity of the independence assumption. If the exceedances, I_t, are dependent random variables, then it is assumed that their sequence is a first-order Markov process with a transition matrix

$$\Psi = \begin{bmatrix} 1 - \pi_{01} & \pi_{01} \\ 1 - \pi_{11} & \pi_{11} \end{bmatrix}.$$

Here π_{01} is the probability that a no-violation is followed by a violation and π_{11} is the probability that a violation is followed by a violation. The likelihood function of the Markov process is

$$L(\Psi) = (1 - \pi_{01})^{T_{00}}\pi_{01}^{T_{01}}(1 - \pi_{11})^{T_{10}}\pi_{11}^{T_{11}}$$

where T_{ij} is the number of times an i event is followed by a j event. The maximum likelihood estimates of the transition probabilities are

$$\hat{\pi}_{01} = \frac{T_{01}}{T_{00} + T_{01}}$$

and

$$\hat{\pi}_{11} = \frac{T_{11}}{T_{10} + T_{11}}.$$

If the exceedances are independent, then $\hat{\pi}_{01} = \hat{\pi}_{11} = \hat{\pi}$ where

$$\hat{\pi} = (T_{01} + T_{11})/T.$$

The likelihood ratio statistic of the null hypothesis of independence is, hence,

$$LR_{IT} = -2 \log \left(\frac{L(\hat{\pi})}{L(\hat{\Psi})} \right)$$

and the p-value of the statistic is obtained from the χ_1^2-distribution.

Duration Test Another test for independence of the exceedances is the duration test (DT) proposed by Christoffersen and Pelletier (2004). The test is based on the distribution of the periods between exceedances (i.e., the durations). With a correctly specified VaR model the durations should have mean of $\frac{1}{\beta}$ with $\beta = 1 - \alpha$ and, moreover, be exponentially distributed and hence memoryless. Under the alternative hypothesis the exceedances follow a Weibull distribution where a special case of the Weibull distribution is the exponential. The Weibull distribution,

$$f(x) = a^b b x^{b-1} \exp[-(ax)^b]$$

has the property that when $b < 1$ the distribution of durations has memory, which indicates that the violations are not independent. However, when $b = 1$ the Weibull distribution reduces to the exponential distribution, which is memoryless. Under the null hypothesis of independence we have the likelihood,

$$L(\beta) = \Pi_{t=1}^{T_1 - 1} [\beta \exp(-\beta D_t)]$$

where T_1 are the number of periods in which a violation occurred and D_t are the durations. The likelihood ratio test statistic is hence,

$$LR_{DT} = -2 \log \left(\frac{L(\beta)}{L(\hat{\beta}, 1)} \right)$$

and the p-value is obtained by comparison with the χ_1^2-distribution.

Density Forecast and CVaR Backtesting Despite the increasing popularity of CVaR it is harder to backtest than the quantile-based VaR. Since CVaR is the conditional expectation in the tail of the loss distribution the test can start from a density estimate evaluation. Several density estimate evaluation methods have been introduced into financial risk management. Crnkovic and Drachman (1996) suggest using the Kuiper and related statistics to test the distance between the observed density and the projected density. Diebold, Gunther, and Tay (1998) propose a variety of graphical approaches. The basic idea is that the transformed data should be uniformly distributed and thus the histograms should be relatively flat.

In general the density test evaluation starts with a transformation of observed losses, $\{L_d\}_{d=1}^{D}$, to uniform using the empirical distribution function. A density forecast evaluation can then test the null hypothesis that the density is uniform independent and identically distributed using nonparametric density tests such as Anderson-Darling and Kolmogorov-Smirnov. We can also transform the uniform losses to normal and test that the observations are indeed normal using the Jarque-Berra normality test. A test of CVaR(α) can then be considered, testing that the loss points beyond the VaR(α) point are indeed normal independent and equally distributed.

Berkowitz (2001) consider likelihood-based density forecast evaluation methods. Specifically, let the predicted cumulative distribution function be $\widehat{F}(.)$. Under the null hypothesis that the prediction is correct, the transformation $z_t = N^{-1}[\widehat{F}(L_d)]$ is independent and identically distributed $N(0, 1)$ where $N^{-1}(.)$ is the inverse of the standard normal distribution. The test against a first-order autoregressive alternative with mean and variance different than 0 and 1 uses the well-known log-likelihood construction:

$$L(\mu, \sigma^2, \rho) = -\frac{1}{2}\left[\ln(\sigma^2)/(1 - \rho^2) + \frac{(z_1 - \mu/(1 - \rho))^2}{\sigma^2/(1 - \rho^2)} \right.$$

$$\left. + (T - 1)\ln(\sigma^2) + \sum_{t=2}^{T} \frac{(z_t - \mu - \rho z_{t-1})^2}{\sigma^2} \right].$$

Here ρ is the autoregressive parameter. The log-likelihood ratio test of independence across observations, $\rho = 0$, and $(0, 1)$ mean-variance can now be formulated as

$$LR_{ind} = 2[L(\widehat{\mu}, \widehat{\sigma}^2, \widehat{\rho}) - L(0, 1, 0)]$$

which is distributed as $\chi^2(3)$ under the null hypothesis.

Similarly one can construct a hypothesis test for the CVaR based on a censored normal distribution. Let $c(\alpha) = N^{-1}(\alpha)$ be the cutoff point and define a new variable

$$z_t^* = \begin{cases} c(\alpha) & \text{if } z_t \geq c(\alpha) \\ z_t & \text{otherwise} \end{cases}.$$

The log-likelihood function for z_t^* is

$$L(\mu, \sigma^2) = \sum_{z^*=c(\alpha)} \ln\left[1 - \Phi\left(\frac{c(\alpha) - \mu}{\sigma}\right)\right] - \frac{1}{2}\sum_{z^*<c(\alpha)}\left[\ln(2\pi\sigma^2) + \frac{(z_t^* - \mu)^2}{\sigma}\right].$$

A log-likelihood ratio test against the null hypothesis that $\mu = 0$ and $\sigma^2 = 1$ to assuming the match in the first two moments of the tail is

$$LR_{tail} = 2[L(\mu, \sigma^2) - L(0, 1)]$$

which is $\chi^2(2)$ distributed.

Other Backtesting Methods in the Literature Several backtesting methods have been proposed in the literature that we do not cover here. This includes the functional delta approach of Kerkhof and Melenberg (2004), and the saddlepoint technique by Wong (2008). More recently introduced backtesting methods include the dispersion of a truncated distribution test by Righi and Ceretta (2013) and the VaR composition approximation by Emmer et al. (2014). Colletaz et al. (2013) propose taking into account also the size of the VaR(α) exceedance in the test. This allows one to distinguish two models, having the same number of exceedances, based on their relative size of exceedance. Their approach is based on introducing a second VaR(β) measure with a higher confidence level $\beta > \alpha$ referred to as the VaR super-exception.

In the next subsection we will put the VaR-based tests for unconditional coverage and independence discussed above to use in comparing performance of different VaR models.

A Multivariate Model of Risk Factor Returns

Having considered both the univariate risk factor model and copula models to model the codependency of the multivariate filtered residual vector,

$$\mathbf{z}_t = (z_{1t}, \dots, z_{nt})$$

we can now join these two components together to arrive at a multivariate model of asset returns. Specifically, consider an n-dimensional sample of asset returns $\{y_{jt}\}_{j=1,\dots,n}^{t=1,\dots,T}$ where y_{jt} can be decomposed as

$$y_{jt} = \mu_j + \varepsilon_{jt}$$

$$\varepsilon_{jt} = z_{jt} h_{jt}$$

and $\{z_{jt}\}_{j=1,\dots,n}^{t=1,\dots,T}$ are independent and identically distributed over time. The parametrization of the sequences $\{h_{jt}\}_{j=1,\dots,n}^{t=1,\dots,T}$ is by n univariate GARCH models,

$$h_{jt}^2 = h(\varepsilon_{jt-1}, \dots, \varepsilon_{jt-k}, h_{jt-1}, \dots, h_{jt-k}; \Upsilon_j) > 0 \ \forall t \ \text{and,}$$

$$j = 1, \dots, n, t = 1, \dots, T.$$

Having estimated the univariate GARCH parameters $\{\Upsilon_j\}_{j=1,\dots,n}$ we obtain the filtered residual vectors $\{\mathbf{z}_j\}_{j=1,\dots,n}$.

We can now specify a univariate model for each of the $j = 1, \dots, n$, $t = 1, \dots, T$ samples of $\{z_{jt}\}_{j=1,\dots,n}^{t=1,\dots,T}$. For example, we can choose a t-distribution. We can also consider a mixed distribution with a normal or empirical density in the center and another distribution for the tails. Using extreme value theory for the tails we should consider a choice of lower and upper thresholds z_j^l, z_j^u and fit a generalized Pareto density to the excesses over the thresholds. Having estimated the left and right tail parameters of the generalized Pareto density, obtaining estimates of (ξ_j^l, β_j^l) and (ξ_j^u, β_j^u) for the lower and upper tail respectively, the marginal distribution of $\{\mathbf{z}_j\}_{j=1,\dots,n}$ is defined by:

$$
F_j(z_{jt}) =
\begin{cases}
\dfrac{k_j^l}{T}\left(1 + \xi_j^l \dfrac{|z - z_{jt}^l|}{\beta_j^l}\right)^{-1/\xi_j^l} & \text{if } z_{jt} < z_j^l, t = 1, \dots, T \\[3mm]
1 - \dfrac{k_j^u}{T}\left(1 + \xi_j^u \dfrac{|z - z_{jt}^u|}{\beta_j^u}\right)^{-1/\xi_j^u} & \text{if } z_{jt} > z_j^u, t = 1, \dots, T \\[3mm]
\widetilde{F}_j(z_{jt}) & \text{if } z_j^l < z_{jt} < z_j^u, t = 1, \dots, T
\end{cases}
$$

where $\widetilde{F}_j$ is the empirical cumulative density function of $\mathbf{z}_j$ or, for example, a kernel estimator.

Having calibrated the univariate models for each of the asset return vectors, $\{\mathbf{y}_j\}_{j=1,\ldots,n}$, it remains to specify the cross-dependence between $\mathbf{z}_i, \mathbf{z}_j \; \forall i \neq j$, that is, to estimate the copula. To obtain a scenario for the n asset returns we now proceed as follows:

1. Simulate uniform random variates from the copula.

$$(u_1, \ldots, u_n) \sim C.$$

2. Transform the simulated random variates using the inverse marginal distributions, F_j^{-1}, where F_j^{-1} is the (generalized) inverse of the cumulative distribution functions $F_j(z_{jt})$ above.

3. Apply a location (μ_i) and scale transformation, that is, multiply by $\widetilde{h}_{j,T+1}$ (where $\widetilde{h}_{j,T+1}$ is defined by the conditional expectation $\widetilde{h}_{j,T+1}^2 = E(h_{j,T+1}^2 \mid h_{j,T}^2)$ as in equation (3.11)) to the simulated z_j:s in order to obtain a scenario for the asset returns, y_j.

Backtesting Performance of the Multivariate Model   We will now focus on two examples where the above model has been applied in risk analysis, and the historical performance has been compared with simpler models such as the multivariate normal model or historical simulation.

The first example we consider is a master thesis by Josefsson (2004), who considers the evaluation of the performance of several models using a portfolio of stocks and exchange rates. The second example is a VaR backtesting comparison for several multivariate models using data that include the 2007 financial crisis by Skoglund et al. (2010).

VaR Model Performance Analysis by Josefsson (2004)   Josefsson (2004) considers the evaluation of the performance of several models using a portfolio of stocks and exchange rates. The portfolio includes holdings in five exchange rates and 23 stocks traded on the Stockholm exchange, each consisting of 2,786 samples quoted on business days from the beginning of March 1993 to the beginning of February 2004.[17] The following models are considered:

(a) The simple multivariate normal distribution
(b) The multivariate conditional normal distribution with fitted univariate GARCH models
(c) A model with univariate GARCH, generalized Pareto distribution for the tails (and empirical density in the center) with a normal copula
(d) A model with univariate GARCH, generalized Pareto distribution for the tails (and empirical density in the center) with a t-copula with 4 degrees of freedom
(e) A model with univariate GARCH, generalized Pareto distribution for the tails (and empirical density in the center) with a t-copula with 10 degrees of freedom

For each of these financial series the logarithmic returns were computed and a GARCH(1,1) model was fitted. Except for the simple multivariate normal model and the multivariate conditional normal model generalized Pareto distributions to the tails of the standardized GARCH residuals were estimated for all the financial time series using a

---

[17]The specific exchange rates are DKK, GBP, JPY, NOK, USD with respect to SEK. The specific stocks are ABB, ATCO A, ATCO B, AZN, BILI A, ELUX B, ERIC B, GAMB B, HEXA B, HOLM B, HUFV A, INDU A, INVE A, NCC B, SAND, SDIA, SEB C, SECO B, SHB B, SKF B, SSAB B, TREL B, VOLV B.

TABLE 3.16 VaR Exceedances for the Models

Model	VaR(0.99)	VaR(0.995)	VaR(0.999)
Expected	12.85 (1%)	6.43 (0.5%)	1.29 (0.1%)
(a) Normal	527 (41.08%)	518 (40.37%)	499 (38.89%)
(b) Conditional normal	16 (1.25%)	7 (0.55%)	1 (0.08%)
(c) Copula EVT-normal	9 (0.7%)	2 (0.16%)	1 (0.08%)
(d) Copula EVT-t_4	18 (1.4%)	7 (0.55%)	2 (0.16%)
(e) Copula EVT-t_{10}	11 (0.86%)	5 (0.39%)	1 (0.08%)

uniform threshold of 5%. The normal and t-copula were fitted using the nonparametric Kendall's tau estimator of the correlation. Using an equally weighted portfolio and starting with the 1,500th observation in the sample of 2,785 returns, each day different models were reestimated using the last 1,500 day's returns (rolling forward) and 5,000 samples were generated. By using each of the models' (one-day) VaR-forecasts for the following day a total of 1,285 forecasts were produced. These VaR-forecasts were then compared to the actual return on that particular day, and the number of days when the actual loss was larger than the VaR-forecast was counted. This is called the number of exceedances and the results are presented in Table 3.16. The expected number of exceedances are stated on the first row for the 99%, 99.5%, and 99.9% VaR confidence level.

As expected the simple normal model underestimates the risk severely while the conditional normal and the elliptic copula EVT models are quite close to the expected exceedances. From this, one can conclude that the GARCH-based conditional volatility seems to be of great importance for the accuracy of the VaR-forecast because of the performance improvement between model (a) and (b). Considering the choice of copula we note that the choice of copula has much less impact on the accuracy of the VaR-forecast than the choice of using GARCH models. This can be seen by comparing the (c) normal, (d) student's t_4, and (e) student's t_{10} copula models.

In Table 3.17 are the number of days between exceedances of VaR(0.99) for the models (a)–(e) tested in Josefsson (2004). The table reveals that the elliptic copula EVT model with normal and student's t_{10} copula are the best models in terms of spreading the exceedances over time. None of them had two exceedances in a row and both of them had only one pair of exceedances within three days. Neither the conditional normal nor the copula EVT t_4 model were able to avoid consecutive exceedances.[18] Since the simple linear normal model produces

TABLE 3.17 Days Between VaR Exceedances for the Models

Model	1 day	≤2 days	≤3 days	≤5 days
(a) Linear normal	249	334	408	484
(b) Conditional normal	2	2	2	4
(c) Copula EVT-normal	0	1	1	2
(d) Copula EVT-t_4	2	2	2	4
(e) Copula EVT-t_{10}	0	1	1	3

---

[18]It may seem unintuitive that the t_4 copula can yield lower risk than, for example, the t_{10} copula. However, this depends on the choice of confidence level. While the t_4 copula can produce heavier tails at very high confidence levels the tail loss at lower confidence intervals may be smaller.

VaR-forecasts that do not react to changing market conditions (that is, it does not update volatility) it is not surprising to see that 249 pairs of exceedances occur in consecutive days.

VaR Model Performance Analysis by Skoglund et al. (2010)   Using a portfolio of plain equity holdings as well as forward agreements and European and American option holdings on the stocks Skoglund et al. (2010) perform a backtesting comparison of the VaR risk measure for several multivariate models. The models performance comparison is based on empirical data from 7 stocks. The stocks are traded on New York Stock Exchange (ABB, Astra Zeneca, FORD, AIG), Nasdaq (Microsoft, Ericsson), and OTC (Volvo), each consisting of 2,063 samples quoted on business days from April 6, 2001, to June 17, 2009. The data period hence includes the 2007 financial crisis turbulence, which allows model performance under a period of significant stress. The models considered are:

(a) The portfolio delta approximation normal model using either an arithmetic covariance matrix or a RiskMetrics covariance matrix[19]
(b) The covariance simulation model using either an arithmetic covariance matrix or a Risk-Metrics covariance matrix
(c) The historical simulation model
(d) Several multivariate copula models based on GARCH filtering and models for the standardized residuals

Specifically, for model (d), we consider the normal, t, and normal mixture copula and the different models for the standardized GARCH residuals are the normal distribution, the t-distribution, and the empirical distribution function with t-distributed tails. For the t-copula we consider 10 or 5 degrees of freedom and the discrete normal variance mixture copula has parameters $w_1 = 1$, $w_2 = 400$, $p_1 = 0.9$, $p_2 = 0.1$. The copula correlation matrix parameters are estimated using Kendall's tau on the historical data. Each of the t- and normal mixture copulas can also have asymmetry with common asymmetry parameter -0.8 for the stocks.

Using the models each of the one-day VaR-forecasts were compared to the actual return on that particular day, and the number of days when the actual loss was larger than the VaR-forecast was counted. This is hence the number of exceedances and the results are presented in Table 3.18.

In the table we have used the model notation "copula type (GARCH residual model type)" to describe the different copula models where the abbreviations N, t, NM refer to the normal, t, and normal mixture copulas, and the GARCH residual model abbreviations N, t, and E(t) refer to the normal, t, and empirical model with t-distributed tails. The expected number of exceedances are stated on the first row for the 99% VaR confidence level.

In Table 3.18 the unconditional coverage likelihood ratio test (UC) tests if the VaR violations occur with expected probability. By assumption, exceedances are independent and identically distributed Bernoulli random variables. The p-values of the unconditional coverage test for all the models and for the 99% VaR confidence level are found in Table 3.18.

---

[19]We have previously discussed the univariate RiskMetrics model as a special case of a GARCH model with predefined parameters. See equation (3.12). The multivariate RiskMetrics model is similarly a special case of multivariate GARCH. We refer to our subsequent dicussion on multivariate GARCH models and equation (3.20) below on the definition of the multivariate RiskMetrics covariance matrix as a special case of multivariate GARCH.

TABLE 3.18 VaR Backtesting Comparison of the Models, Comparing Expected Number of Exceedances Versus Actual and p-Values from the Unconditional Coverage Test, the Independence and the Duration Test

Model	VaR(0.99)	UC p-value	IT p-value	DT p-value
Expected	1.00%	.	.	.
Delta-normal	2.85%	0.0000	0.0000	0.0000
Delta-normal (RiskMetrics)	1.66%	0.0123	0.0008	0.0009
Historical simulation	1.84%	0.0018	0.0020	0.0013
Covariance simulation	3.09%	0.0000	0.0000	0.0000
Covariance simulation (RiskMetrics)	2.02%	0.0002	0.0042	0.0036
N copula (N)	1.48%	0.0615	0.3846	0.0699
t10 copula (N)	1.30%	0.2255	0.2911	0.3048
t10 asym copula (N)	0.17%	0.0000	0.9175	0.2636
t5 copula (N)	1.30%	0.2255	0.2911	0.3048
t5 asym copula (N)	0.17%	0.0000	0.9175	0.2636
NM copula (N)	0.83%	0.4766	0.6278	0.8947
NM asym copula (N)	0.53%	0.0355	0.7556	0.1195
N copula (t)	0.71%	0.2131	0.6779	0.8532
t10 copula (t)	0.65%	0.1279	0.7035	0.9637
t10 asym copula (t)	0.005%	0.0000	0.9724	0.9999
t5 copula (t)	0.65%	0.1279	0.7035	0.9637
t5 asym copula (t)	0.00%	0.0000	0.9999	0.9999
NM copula (t)	0.41%	0.0064	0.8088	0.0803
NM asym copula (t)	0.17%	0.17	0.9175	0.2636
N copula (E(t))	1.54%	0.0372	0.4182	0.1394
t10 copula (E(t))	1.36%	0.1514	0.3210	0.1841
t10 asym copula (E(t))	0.17%	0.0000	0.9175	0.2636
t5 copula (E(t))	1.24%	0.3240	0.2625	0.2670
t5 asym copula (E(t))	0.17%	0.0000	0.9175	0.2636
NM copula (E(t))	1.01%	0.9648	0.5557	0.6192
NM asym copula (E(t))	0.53%	0.0355	0.7556	0.1195

From Table 3.18 we observe that the simple risk models such as the delta-normal model and the covariance simulation model underestimate risk quite severely. The models' ability to capture the expected exceedances are rejected at low levels of significance. However, using a RiskMetrics covariance matrix improves the situation for both models even though risk is still underestimated with more exceedances than expected. The historical simulation model also underestimates risk quite severely.

The results for the copula models are mixed. While none of the copula models underestimate risk by more than either of the delta-normal, covariance simulation models (with or without RiskMetrics covariance matrix), or the historical simulation model, some copula models overestimate risk quite severely, for example, the model with a t5 copula and *t*-distributed GARCH residuals. On the other hand the model with a normal mixture copula with empirical GARCH residuals and *t*-distributed tails is very close to the expected number of exceedances. The copula models with *t*- and normal mixture asymmetry generally overestimate risk at the 99% level.

In addition to the requirement that the VaR model should be able to match closely the number of realized exceedances with the expected number one would prefer a VaR model that distributes the exceedances randomly rather than a model where exceedances are correlated over time.

Table 3.18 contains the p-values for the independence test (IT) for all the models for 99% VaR. Table 3.18 also displays the p-values for the duration-based test calculated using the continuous Weibull distribution for 99% VaR.

Comparing the models' ability to spread exceedances over time we note that models with no stochastic volatility component (no GARCH or RiskMetrics) are not able to have independent exceedances. For example, the *p*-values of the independence (IT) and duration (DT) tests indicate that the delta-normal model and the covariance-based simulation model are rejected at any significance level. This is not surprising as the models do not react to high-volatility regimes and exceedances are expected to come in clusters. The delta-normal model with RiskMetrics covariance matrix and the covariance simulation model with Risk-Metrics covariance are also rejected, albeit the covariance simulation model with RiskMetrics covariance matrix is rejected at slightly lower levels of confidence. This indicates that the RiskMetrics covariance matrix is not able to capture volatility regimes adequately with its "predefined" GARCH parameters that are not updated. For historical simulation the independence and duration tests in Table 3.18 indicate that the model is not able to spread the exceedances independently and hence is not a realistic model of VaR.

In contrast the copula models with GARCH univariate models are not rejected at the 5% significance levels for any of the models. This is a clear indication that the GARCH models are able to capture volatility clusters and respond to volatility increases with higher risk estimates, hence avoiding producing correlated exceedances. In the judgment of an adequate model for VaR one must take into account the unconditional coverage of the model as well as the ability of the model to produce independent VaR exceedances.

Learnings from the Models Backtesting Performance   We can now summarize the findings from the above two backtesting examples as follows:

- First, simple models that do not capture the stylized fact of volatility clustering in financial returns tend to both underestimate the risk level as well as display significant correlation in exceedances.

  Using the simple, exponentially moving average, RiskMetrics model improves the situation. However, due to the fact that parameters are not estimated on data and hence tailored to current volatility regimes the current volatility level may not be captured well enough and correlated exceedances may still be produced. The first-order (most important) correction of simple models is therefore to consider a model for stochastic volatility with parameters that are updated regularly such as the GARCH model.

- Second, taking into account fat tails for the standardized GARCH residuals may improve the model further but is a second-order (less important) effect.

- Third, another second-order correction is to consider other copulas than the normal. However, the *t*-copulas and normal mixture copulas may outperform the normal copula only by a small margin.

Apart from the two backtesting examples above there are several empirical studies in the literature on the performance of VaR models. See, for example, Bao et al. (2004), Brooks et al. (2005), and Kuester et al. (2006) for applications to different financial returns. Berkowitz and O'Brien (2002) use the expected frequency of exceedances to evaluate the performance of VaR risk models for six banks. Barone-Adesi et al. (2000) do an extensive backtesting analysis on the multivariate filtered historical simulation model. Pritsker (2006) compare various historical simulation methods, including filtered historical simulation.

A Note on Dynamic Codependency and Multivariate GARCH We now briefly consider a method of generalizing the time-invariant elliptic copula models studied above. Recall that in the constant conditional correlation case the covariance matrix of multivariate financial returns could be represented in the form $\Sigma_t = \lambda_t \Xi \, \lambda_t$ where λ_t is a diagonal volatility matrix with univariate GARCH specifications on the diagonal,

$$\lambda_t = \begin{bmatrix} h_{1t} & \cdots & 0 \\ \cdots & \cdots & \cdots \\ 0 & \cdots & h_{nt} \end{bmatrix}.$$

Hence, for that model the correlation matrix of rescaled innovations, $\mathbf{z}$, is time-invariant. Potential drawbacks of the assumption of a constant correlation matrix for $\mathbf{z}$ include

- Multivariate financial returns may display evidence of dynamics in covariances as well as in volatility.
- The plausible effect that a volatility shock to a financial return series may create spillover effects to other financial returns series is ruled out with a constant conditional correlation matrix.

To test these potential drawbacks empirically we note that the assumption of constant conditional correlation implies that

$$z_{it} z_{jt} = \frac{\varepsilon_{it} \varepsilon_{jt}}{\sqrt{h_{iit} h_{jjt}}}, \quad i \neq j$$

should be serially uncorrelated (note that this does not apply to $\varepsilon_{it}\varepsilon_{jt}$ for $i \neq j$). Hence, traditional Ljung-Box type tests of the null hypothesis of no serial correlation in the estimated $\hat{z}_{it}\hat{z}_{jt}$ may be constructed. See Bollerslev (1990) and Tse (2000) for discussions of tests of the null hypothesis of no serial correlation in cross-covariances.

Rejecting the null hypothesis of constant conditional correlation requires the modeling of the correlation matrix Ξ_t as dynamic (e.g., using a multivariate GARCH model for $\Xi = \Xi_t$). It is clear that given the scale of applications in market risk management with hundreds or thousands of risk factors the functional form chosen for Ξ_t must still enable the separation of the estimation stage in two steps, and moreover, have a parsimonious parameter specification for feasible estimation. This is in general not the case for the multivariate GARCH models found in the literature, which are designed for full information maximum likelihood estimation, for example, the multivariate GARCH model with time-varying covariances proposed by Bollerslev, Engle, and Wooldridge (1988).

However, Engle (2002) and Tse and Tsui (2002) consider parsimonious models, enabling the separation of the estimation stage in two steps, of the form

$$\Xi_t = \Xi \left(1 - \sum_{l=1}^{q} \alpha_l - \sum_{s=1}^{p} \beta_s \right) + \sum_{l=1}^{q} \alpha_l z_{t-l} z'_{t-l} + \sum_{s=1}^{p} \beta_s \Xi_{t-s}$$

for multivariate GARCH(p, q). A special case is the multivariate exponentially weighted moving average RiskMetrics model, where

$$\Xi_t = (1 - \lambda)\mathbf{z}_{t-1}\mathbf{z}'_{t-1} + \lambda\Xi_{t-1}. \tag{3.20}$$

For an empirical comparison of the case of constant conditional correlation versus the case of dynamic conditional correlations using the t-copula see Kang and Babbs (2012), who apply the two models to funds returns.

TIME SCALING VAR AND VAR WITH TRADING

When institutions are concerned with obtaining T-period risk measures from t-period risk measures (e.g., t is 1 day and T is 10 days) they can consider one of the following:

- Scale an already calculated t period ($t < T$) risk measure using an appropriate method.
- Use temporal aggregation to aggregate financial returns data to T-period intervals and specify models on the T-period interval data obtaining the 1 period risk.
- Estimate T period risk by simulating paths of returns for $t = 1, \ldots, T$ and calculate risk at T.

While market risk models typically forecast 1-day risk measures, risk measures at multiple horizons are needed in practice, both for regulatory reporting purposes as well as for internal economic capital models.

It is important to understand which of the three methods are appropriate in practice. For example, the methods of scaling and temporal aggregation may be appropriate in case we assume a constant portfolio for the time horizon T. However, if the portfolio is traded during the time interval $T - t$, then, of course depending on the actual trading strategy impact on risk, both of these methods may be inappropriate and the simulation of paths of $t = 1, \ldots, T$ returns together with the trading strategy may be needed to accurately assess T-period risk.

Time Aggregation of VaR with Constant Portfolios

In practice many financial institutions use the method of scaling to obtain T-period risk measures from $t = 1$ day period risk measures. If we assume that

(i) the portfolio returns are normal independent and identically distributed, and
(ii) a buy-and-hold trading strategy between $T - t$, we can obtain the T-period VaR, $\overrightarrow{\text{VaR}}$, as

$$\overrightarrow{\text{VaR}} = \text{VaR}\sqrt{T}.$$

See Diebold et al. (1997) and McNeil et al. (2005). The square root of time result for VaR also extends to CVaR as in the normal iid case CVaR is obtained via a constant scaler on VaR (see equation (2.7)).

In case the distribution is not normal, such as a GARCH model for volatility, or the portfolio composition changes, the square root of time scaling is inappropriate. While this is well-known by industry practitioners the square root of time model is still in wide use for obtaining T-period VaR estimates from corresponding t-period forecasts.

The impact of the distribution deviating from normal independent and identically distributed as a source of error for the square root of time scaling has been extensively studied in the literature. Danielsson and De Vries (1997) discuss the VaR scaling with heavy tailed distribution with tail index α being given by $T^{\frac{1}{\alpha}}$—which is less than the normal scaling rule of $T^{\frac{1}{2}}$ in case $\alpha > 2$ (which corresponds to the finite variance case).[20] McNeil and Frey (2000) study the behavior of multiple-day returns from a mixture of GARCH and extreme value theory models for the tail and find evidence in favor of a power law of scaling for multiple-day quantiles. Danielsson and Zigrand (2004) study time scaling of quantiles when returns follow a jump-diffusion process. More recently Menkens (2007) studied the feasibility of using self-similarity of underlying profit and loss distribution and the Hurst coefficient to derive T-period VaR estimates from 1-period VaR estimates.

The questionable use of the simple square root of time method to obtain 10-day VaR from 1-day VaR for regulatory reporting has also been recognized by the Basel Committee in 2002 (Basel Committee, 2002, p. 93) where the Basel Committee state that to obtain VaR at higher frequencies financial institutions must use an "analytically appropriate method supported by empirical evidence."

A simple method to consider in validating the scaling method used is to use temporal aggregation of the data to T-period intervals and compute T-period risk measures that can be compared with their scaled counterparts. For example, Christofferson et al. (1998) study the square root of time scaling model versus the exact method of temporal model aggregation and Kauffman and Patie (2003) compare different methods of studying long-term risks such as scaling short-term risks versus estimating risks on the desired measurement frequency. Of course, temporal aggregation of data still, as with the case of scaling, relies on an assumption that portfolios are constant even for T-period intervals. Consequently, the Basel Committee, in a working paper (Basel Committee, 2011b) also discuss the problems with scaling short-horizon VaR to longer horizons since this rule ignores future changes in portfolio composition. Indeed, to firmly understand long-term risks in case of management intervention the short-term trading behavior needs to be incorporated.

Time Aggregation of VaR with Trading

When market risk portfolios are traded more frequently than the target risk horizon T we have to consider the simulation of paths of $t = 1, \ldots, T$ returns together with the trading strategy to accurately assess T-period risk. This potential source of error for the simple square root of time rule is at least as important to validate considering the fact that banks rarely operate under a buy-and-hold strategy for their market risk portfolios. Indeed, the bulk of the market risk portfolio for which risk is calculated is actively traded at least daily.

As we have discussed above, in case of buy-and-hold portfolios, a potential solution to the problem of using the square root of time rule in calculating VaR is to use temporal aggregation of data. The temporal aggregation approach does not solve the problem of the inconsistency if the composition of the portfolio changes. In this case the risk model should incorporate the trading behavior and T-day risks should be estimated from path-dependent simulations over days $t = 1, \ldots, T$.

To analyze the trading impact of T-period risks Skoglund et al. (2011) consider a Monte Carlo simulation comparison of the 10-day VaR using different daily trading strategies.

---

[20]We can use the Hill estimator, $\widetilde{\alpha}_H$, in equation (3.14) to estimate the tail index.

Three basic trading methods are applied. They are the convex, the concave, and the volatility-based trading method. Convex trading means that traders buy winners, that is, instruments with increasing value (return), and sell instruments with decreasing value (return). Concave trading is opposite of convex trading such that traders sell winners, that is, instruments with increasing value (return), and buy instruments with decreasing value (return). In volatility trading, traders sell (or buy) nonvolatile stocks (low absolute returns) and buy (or sell) volatile stocks (high absolute returns). Hence, we consider two types of volatility trades. One that trades into high-volatility instruments and one that trades into low-volatility instruments.

These trading strategies are parametrized as filter-based strategies with filter parameter ϕ. This means, for example, for the convex trading strategy that if the daily return has exceeded ϕ, then further positions are bought using cash from instruments that are sold based on the filter strategy (i.e., stocks for which the daily return is lower than $-\phi$). Similarly, for the buy volatility strategy the filter ϕ is used such that instruments with daily returns above $|\phi|$ are bought and instruments with daily returns between $(-\phi, \phi)$ are sold.

Applying these strategies Skoglund et al. (2011) find that severe underestimates of risk may result from scaling the risk of actively traded volatility buying portfolios using a square root of time rule, which incorporates an implicit buy-and-hold portfolio assumption. Moreover, in general the longer the scaling period the more severe is the underestimation of risk. In contrast, for actively traded portfolios that trade into low volatility one should not expect a severe overestimation of risk by scaling (i.e., by assuming a buy-and-hold portfolio). The risk reduction achieved by minimizing portfolio volatility is strictly bounded, whereas the order of risk increase by maximizing portfolio volatility can be significant, especially in extremely volatile markets such as the 2007 crisis.

The analysis is notwithstanding whether the square root of time scaling is appropriate for the model at hand. That is, even if the portfolio model is normal independent and identically distributed scaling is in general not appropriate when the portfolio composition changes. This is an important point because the square root of time approach is often used in situations where the underlying model assumptions are not valid, accepting that the method is a generally fairly accurate approximation to T-day VaR under small deviations from the normal independent and identically distributed assumption.

MARKET LIQUIDITY RISK

Market liquidity of an instrument can be measured from the trading buy-and-sell executions, the executed order volumes, and the associated market prices for a given order volume corresponding to the liquidity depth in a market situation. The primary source of the market liquidity of an instrument is the demand-and-supply inequilibrium. Market liquidity may have a nonnegligible effect on the pricing and risk of a financial instrument.

Bangia et al. (1999) and Bervas (2006) argue that there are two types of market illiquidity. The first type is exogenous and the second type is endogenous.

The exogenous market liquidity is common to all market players. It is independent of each individual trading activity. It can happen in both normal market conditions and a systematic crisis in the market. Especially low-quality instruments such as non-investment-grade bonds or complex financial instruments such as structured products may suffer from a flight to quality in case of market distress.

An asset may encounter significant illiquidity even in a normal market situation. This illiquidity is said to be endogenous. For example, when unloading a large size position in an asset comparing to the market depth of the asset a trader may have to pay extra cost for the convenience of unloading it fast. Clearly, this type of illiquidity is inconsistent with coherent risk measures, in particular property 2 stating that the risk measure is linear in positions.

Traditionally illiquidity is incorporated in market risk models using an extended closeout time for the portfolio. Lawrence and Robinson (1995) proposed to incorporate illiquidity within the VaR framework by matching the VaR time horizon with the time horizon it could take to liquidate the portfolio. Another approach to incorporate liquidity risk is to assume that the full position is executed immediately (with no closeout time) and incorporate the resulting liquidity spread in the risk measurement. Bangia et al. (1999) added the risk of the bid–ask spread to the market-based risk assuming additivity of risks to obtain a liquidity-adjusted VaR model. Such additivity can be motivated by the fact that the worst liquidity spread for the instrument likely happens at the same time as market distress. Angelidis and Benos (2006) also included endogenous liquidity by including the position size in the liquidity-adjusted VaR model. We also refer the reader to Ernst et al. (2009) for a useful overview of liquidity VaR models based on the liquidity spread and an empirical comparison of models.

In practice, liquidity execution cannot be characterized as being captured with either an extended closeout period with no liquidity spread or a full immediate closeout with a liquidity spread. The trader is faced with market execution limits and anticipated execution costs that may depend on the execution size relative to the market. Of course, the liquidity execution program itself will be a trade-off between either incurring immediate larger liquidity costs by executing large positions versus holding onto the position and incur larger market risk. For a given risk preference the exact trade-off depends on how the risk grows over time and on how liquidity execution costs can change over time. That is, incurred liquidity risks depend on the exact trading strategy.

Here, in the context of market risk models, we will mainly focus on the inclusion of illiquidity in market risk models using closeout times for positions. However, we will return to consider more complex trading execution models of liquidity risk in our chapter on liquidity risk management, specifically, in the context of optimal hedging of funding liquidity risk using tradable assets. Our current focus on position closeout times is motivated by current practice, specifically the current regulatory use of market risk VaR models with an extended closeout period of 10 days. It is also motivated by Basel Committee (2012, 2014a) proposing an extended and more granular liquidity adjustment to the regulatory market risk capital calculation than the 10-day risk horizon. The adjustment is more granular because it requires institutions to allocate positions into different liquidity buckets corresponding to liquidity horizons. The allocated liquidity bucket is connected to the market liquidity of the risk factors, $S(t)$, that drives the position value. At the same time the standard 10-day position horizon becomes a lower bound for the most liquid positions.

An added advantage of the extended closeout time model for handling illiquidity is that CVaR is still a coherent risk measure within this model of illiquidity.

Closeout Time with No Liquidity Cost

We can assume that an asset can be traded within a trading period up to a certain trading threshold known as market depth at a market bid–ask spread $c_0 = 0$. In order to execute the trading in a bigger volume, market price moves unfavorably at a cost rate c_1 where $c_1 > 0$. The execution cost c_1 can be interpreted as fire sale cost. To avoid liquidity execution costs a trader can execute the position over multiple days. For example, we noted above that VaR for T days (with $t = 1$ day) can, in the normal independent and identically distributed model setting, be obtained as

$$\overrightarrow{\text{VaR}} = \text{VaR}\sqrt{T}.$$

This is a special case when the trader holds onto the position for $T - t$ more days and then executes the full position with no liquidity cost. We can interpret this case as the trader is holding onto the position until markets have calmed and liquidity costs are no longer significant.

Another case is when the trader executes the position in smaller portions over T days with no liquidity execution costs—that is, not above the market depth. In case of equal portions over the T days we have that

$$\overline{\text{VaR}} = \text{VaR}\sqrt{\sum_{i=0}^{T-1}\left(\frac{T-i}{T}\right)^2}.$$

Clearly,

$$\overrightarrow{\text{VaR}} \geq \overline{\text{VaR}}$$

and when $T = 10$ days we have specifically that

$$\sqrt{T} = 3.1622 > \sqrt{\sum_{t=0}^{T-1}\left(\frac{T-i}{T}\right)^2} = 1.9621.$$

Hence, the style of liquidity execution can have a significant effect on the risk.

Instead of having a single liquidity execution portion per asset one can classify the positions into different liquidity buckets with associated daily execution percentages at no significant liquidity cost.

Example of Partial Portfolio Closeout Over Time We consider a portfolio of 7 unit holding stocks with different daily execution percentages of the initial holding as in Table 3.19.

The executed portion of the stock is put in a risk-free cash account with no return and carries no risk after being sold. Using a logarithmic stock returns variance of 0.01 and zero covariance for each of the 7 stocks we perform the trading execution on the path of 1 day up to 15 days. Of course, because of the iterative percentage daily trades the positions will not close out fully after 15 days and a very small, insignificant holding will still remain even for the stocks with 30% and 40% daily execution. For the stocks with 10% and 20% daily execution an approximate 20% and 3.5% respectively of the initial holding will still reside

TABLE 3.19 Stock Allocation to Liquidity Groups

Stock	Daily execution %
1	10
2	10
3	20
4	20
5	30
6	30
7	40

TABLE 3.20 Percent Closeout VaR Profile and the No-Closeout VaR Profile on Either of Days 1, ..., 15

Liquidity horizon (days)	Percent VaR(0.99)	
	Partial closeout	Full closeout
1	8.07	8.07
2	9.98	11.12
3	10.86	13.15
4	11.36	14.87
5	11.72	16.36
6	11.92	17.56
7	12.03	18.81
8	12.10	19.70
9	12.17	20.70
10	12.18	21.46
11	12.21	22.29
12	12.23	23.14
13	12.23	23.74
14	12.24	24.44
15	12.26	25.09

after 15 days. The current stock values are respectively 1 unit of currency for all 7 stocks. The portfolio mark-to-market is hence, with unit positions in the stocks, 7 units of currency.

Table 3.20 displays the partial closeout 99% confidence level VaR profile and the corresponding VaR profile obtained with full closeout on any of days 1, ..., 15. The 99% VaR numbers are here expressed in percent of the mark-to-market value of the portfolio. Table 3.20 shows that the partial closeout portfolio is, for all practical purposes, almost fully closed out after 10 days as VaR is almost constant after that. The liquid 1-day portfolio VaR is 8.07% and hence with 15-day percent closeout as in Table 3.19 the risk has increased by a factor of approximately 1.51 (that is 12.26/8.07). If on the other hand the portfolio is held fixed until day 15 and then closed out in full, it results in portfolio risk increase by a factor of approximately 3.10 (that is, 25.09/8.07). Again, this shows that the closeout assumption for the portfolio significantly impacts the risk. For illustration Figure 3.14 displays the VaR(0.99) profiles in Table 3.20 graphically.

Example of Tiered Portfolio Closeout Over Time   The Basel Committee (2012, 2013b, 2014a) proposal for the illiquidity adjustment does not assume a partial portfolio closeout over time. Instead, portions of the portfolio are tiered with full closeout at a specific horizon.

We now consider a tiered closeout example using the same portfolio as in the example above but with tiered full closeout for the stocks as indicated in Table 3.21. In Table 3.21 when the closeout horizon is n days the stock holding is zero at horizon $n + 1$. All the stocks except stock 7 are closed out before the risk horizon of 15 days.[21]

---

[21]The Basel Committee gives a specific liquidity adjustment equation for CVaR that we will discuss later in this chapter in the section on the developments in the market risk internal models capital regulation. The adjustment equation is based on CVaR rather than VaR consistent with the intended move to CVaR as risk measure. In addition the liquidity horizons in this example are for illustration only and are not those assigned by Basel, which range from 10 days to 1 year.

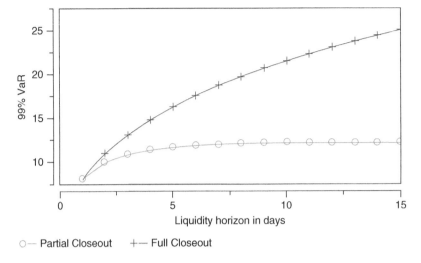

○— Partial Closeout   +— Full Closeout

FIGURE 3.14   VaR at the 99% Confidence Level for Partial and Full Closeout at the Liquidity Horizons

TABLE 3.21   Stock Allocation to Full Closeout Horizons

Stock	Full closeout (horizon)
1	3 days
2	3 days
3	5 days
4	5 days
5	10 days
6	10 days
7	15 days

The obtained 99% VaR, in percent of the mark-to-market value of the portfolio, is given in Table 3.22. We can now compare the 15-day VaR with tiered full closeout (as per Basel proposal) to the case with full portfolio closeout on either of the horizons. From Table 3.20 we obtain the full portfolio closeout 15-day VaR as 25.09%. By portfolio tiering the full closeout, as in Table 3.21, VaR has decreased by approximately 25% compared to the full portfolio closeout case (18.57/25.09). On the other hand, the position tiered full closeout VaR is approximately a factor of 2.3 times higher than would be the case if all the stocks in the portfolio had a liquidity horizon of 1 day (18.57/8.07).

Figure 3.15 displays graphically the VaR(0.99) profiles over the $1, \ldots, 15$ liquidity horizons for the tiered closeout by horizon as in Table 3.21 versus the full portfolio closeout of all positions on either of the horizons. We note that as stock positions closeout at the horizons the VaR profile increases at a slower rate compared to the no-closeout case.

A Note on General Market Illiquidity Models

Clearly, while our position liquidity closeout examples above have been simple, the incorporation of liquidity risk in market risk models is nontrivial in general. The liquidity cost

TABLE 3.22 Percent Tiered Full Closeout VaR Profile on Days 1, ..., 15

Liquidity horizon (days)	Percent VaR(0.99)
1	8.07
2	11.12
3	13.15
4	14.39
5	15.43
6	16.01
7	16.61
8	17.00
9	17.46
10	17.91
11	18.06
12	18.19
13	18.32
14	18.44
15	18.57

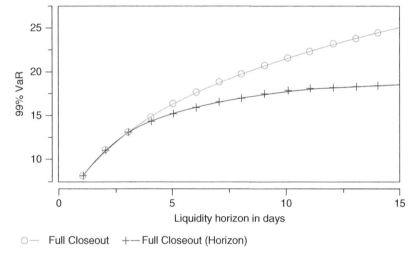

○— Full Closeout +—Full Closeout (Horizon)

FIGURE 3.15 VaR at the 99% Confidence Level for Full Closeout for Different Stocks at the Liquidity Horizons and Full Closeout at the Liquidity Horizons

incurred is a function of both the market liquidity of the instrument as well as the trader execution style of the position in the market. There are two extreme scenarios available.

- First, trade the full position immediately at a current known, but probably high cost.
- Second, trade in smaller portions over a fixed time at relatively lower or no cost.

The latter strategy may lower expected cost; however, it is also more uncertain because it includes waiting to unwind the portfolio over a longer time. Hence, market risk increases and there is also uncertainty about future liquidity spreads. It is also an undesirable strategy if an institution must close out the position as soon as possible for the reasons of market timing or funding shortage.

Our analysis here has focused on the case when a trader can wait to execute at minimal liquidity cost but at higher incurred market risk. However, as mentioned previously, we will return to the issue of (forced) immediate liquidity execution with large execution costs when we discuss funding liquidity risk. See also Almgren and Chriss (2000) on the analysis of optimal liquidity execution for a given level of risk. The authors trace out the equivalent of an efficient frontier for liquidity execution strategies.

SCENARIO ANALYSIS AND STRESS TESTING

Capturing tail events, especially those that incur severe loss at rare chance, is an important objective in modern risk analysis. Historically, a substantial part of finance research has been devoted to the development of models that extend beyond the normal distribution and that capture the stylized facts of financial time series. However, past performance is no guarantee of future results.

Regardless of methodology, VaR-type risk models rely almost exclusively on history—either in terms of calibrating model parameters or directly as in historical simulation and other approaches that re-sample from empirical distributions. Stress testing is viewed as a forward-looking risk analysis tool that should complement risk measures based on historical calibration such as VaR.

Many recent risk regulations, including Basel III liquidity requirements, CCAR firmwide stress testing, EBA firmwide stress testing, and the Solvency II regulation for insurers, have either included stress testing as a complementary risk analysis or directly employed a stress scenario–based approach to measure tail risk. Stress scenarios are also a key element in the widely adopted Standardized Portfolio Analysis of Risk (SPAN) exchange margin system where the required exchange margin on futures options is based on the maximum one-day loss using 16 prescribed scenarios for the underlying futures price and volatility.

Basel Committee (2009c) provides several principles for sound enterprise stress testing. Stress testing plays an important role in many enterprise functions, including:

- Providing forward-looking assessment of risk that overcomes limitations of models and historical data
- Supporting internal and external communication
- Feeding into provision, capital, and liquidity analysis and planning process
- Supporting a bank's risk tolerance and facilitating risk mitigation and contingency planning

In our discussion of stress testing we find it convenient to structure a financial institution's approach to scenario analysis and stress testing in four components. This includes:

1. Portfolio sensitivity analysis
2. Systematic portfolio stress test programs
3. Implied stress scenarios
4. Integration of stress and model-based analysis

We will review each of these approaches and discuss their role in a comprehensive market risk stress testing program for financial institutions.

Arguably, in many cases a joint stress testing across risk types is required for firmwide stress testing where market risk is only one of the loss contribution items in the bank's projected income statement under stress. We will return to the issue of firmwide stress testing later in this book in Chapter 9.

Portfolio Sensitivity Analysis

The main idea of portfolio sensitivity analysis is to systematically construct portfolio sensitivity to each of the $j = 1, \ldots, n$ portfolio risk factors $S(t)$. The purpose of the analysis is to be able to identify portfolio impacts from isolated univariate and potentially bivariate risk factor movements. There is no notion of joint market stress as all risk factors except the univariate risk factor or the bivariate pair of risk factors are held constant. Hence, the method is essentially a portfolio risk factor sensitivity method although we are concerned also with large changes in the underlying risk factor(s) such as a range of -30% to 30% of changes in a stock price. Depending on the portfolio characteristics we may use approximation methods or full valuation to obtain the risk factor sensitivity.

Linear Portfolio   Using the linear delta model approximation as in equation (2.2) we can attribute a portfolio sensitivity to each of the $j = 1, \ldots, n$ portfolio risk factors $S(t)$ for small changes in the risk factor, δ. If the portfolio is truly linear, such as a stock portfolio, the delta impacts on portfolio profit and loss can of course be extrapolated to large risk factor shocks as well.

Quadratic Portfolio   For nonlinear portfolios the quadratic approximation model in equation (2.18) allows second-order risk factor effects as well as potential cross-risk-factor effects to be captured in the local portfolio sensitivity analysis. As in the linear model case such sensitivities may be used in extrapolation to large risk factor shifts.

Full Valuation   When the portfolio is significantly nonlinear it can be dangerous to extrapolate the Greeks local sensitivity analysis, with small δ risk factor shifts effect on portfolio profit and loss, to large risk factor shifts effect on portfolio profit and loss. In those cases a full valuation approach is used, applying stressed shocks to a single or a few risk factors across a grid of values for which the portfolio value is calculated.

For example, for an equity option portfolio it is appropriate to calculate the portfolio profit-and-loss impact from varying underlying equity value and the equity implied volatility through a range of values. The result is a pricing matrix, similar to the grid pricing matrix (2.36), though mark-to-market values are on a portfolio level rather than for a specific instrument. In the univariate risk factor case, that is, variation of a single risk factor, j, a vector of mark-to-market values or portfolio profit and losses are obtained.

Systematic Portfolio Stress Tests

In systematic portfolio stress test programs we are interested in joint market scenarios for all the $j = 1, \ldots, n$ portfolio risk factors, $S(t)$. The scenarios can be inspired from historical events with historical values for the portfolio risk factors or be forward looking. The scenario definition can involve all the $j = 1, \ldots, n$ portfolio risk factors or a subset $S_2(t)$ with

$S(t) = \begin{bmatrix} S_1(t) \\ S_2(t) \end{bmatrix}$. In case the scenario definition only includes a subset of the risk factors one of course has to transfer the stress scenario from the $S_2(t)$ risk factors to all portfolio risk factors, $S(t)$. This stress transfer to all the portfolio risk factors can be done using models or by searching the history for relevant $S_1(t)$ risk factor shifts conditional on assumed $S_2(t)$ shifts. If the core scenario for the $S_2(t)$ risk factors are inspired from an historical event it is natural to search for the experienced $S_1(t)$ risk factor shifts during the same historical period. However, in practice the risk factor may not be observed historically such that one has to resort to models for generating $S_1(t)$ risk factor shifts conditional on $S_2(t)$ shifts.

Using Models to Transfer Stress   We have previously seen, in the context of normally distributed risk factor returns, how we can potentially use conditional distributions to calculate the expected behavior of all risk factors conditional on a scenario for a few risk factors. Specifically, with historical mean returns zero, we can obtain, as in equation (2.16), the expected returns of the risk factors $S_1(t)$ from scenarios conditional on the risk factors $S_2(t) = s_2$, from the conditional distribution

$$S_1 \mid S_2 = s_2 \sim N\left(\Sigma_{12}\Sigma_{22}^{-1}s_2, \Sigma_{11} - \Sigma_{12}\Sigma_{22}^{-1}\Sigma_{21}\right). \tag{3.21}$$

Another type of model that is relevant to transfer stress from the $S_2(t)$ risk factors to $S_1(t)$ risk factor shifts is the observed factor model in equation (2.30). When the model expresses risk factors $S_1(t)$ returns in terms of stress defined $S_2(t)$ returns we can obtain the expected stress return of $S_1(t)$ risk factors. That is, if $r_2(t)$ is the returns of the stressed risk factors, $S_2(t)$, we have that

$$\mathbf{r}_1(t) = \mathbf{A}\mathbf{r}_2(t) + \epsilon \tag{3.22}$$

with $\mathbf{r}_1(t)$ the returns vector of the $S_1(t)$ risk factors, $\mathbf{A}$ the factor loading matrix, and ϵ the vector representing the idiosyncratic risks of $S_1(t)$.

Of course, in practice, in either of these models to transfer stress, the stressed factors may not affect the portfolio directly at all. This happens if the initial stressed factors are only high-level macroeconomic scenarios such as GDP and unemployment. However, we can still use the model approaches above to transfer stress to the portfolio risk factors. The interpretation is then that the $S_1(t)$ factors are the actual portfolio risk factors and $S_2(t)$ are the macroeconomic variables.

Both factor model and conditional distribution model approaches to stress transfer rely on covariances to specify the relationship between risk factors. In the conditional distribution model it is explicit since one specifies a joint covariance matrix of $S_1(t)$ and $S_2(t)$ risk factors. In the factor model approach covariance information is implicit in the factor loading matrix, $\mathbf{A}$, of the regression.

When the core scenarios are high-level macroeconomic factors several hierarchical factor models may in practice be used to transform to a specific portfolio risk factor. For example, if the macroeconomic scenario specifies an unemployment rate shift and the portfolio risk factor is a specific stock, there may be a factor model linking first the unemployment rate shift to a broad market equity index shift. A second factor model may link the market equity index implied shift to a stock industry specific index shock. Finally, a third factor model may link the industry index shock to a shock in the specific stock.

A few caveats are necessary when using models to transfer stress.

First, for the purpose of stress testing it is prudent to use model parameters estimated on volatile subperiods. In extreme stress situations it may also be relevant to abandon historical implied model parameters and assume, for example, a perfect positive correlation between all risk factors. Each risk factor may still maintain its own volatility in this case and hence the response to the market shock is based on its relative volatility to the stressed factors, $S_2(t)$. In the case of the conditional distribution model one can also generalize the multivariate normal risk factor model to one of the more advanced copula models we have discussed. However, while the conditional expectation is explicit in the normal case it may have to be simulated for more elaborate models.

Second, both the conditional distribution model and the observed risk factor model yield a distribution for the $S_1(t)$ risk factor shifts conditional on the stress scenario for $S_2(t)$. Instead of using the conditional expected $S_1(t)$ risk factor shifts, hence ignoring the idiosyncratic risk in $S_1(t)$, it may be relevant to use the full conditional stress distribution and calculate a tail risk measure from the profit-and-loss distribution as the stress scenario. This is relevant because conditional on the stressed factors, $S_2(t)$, there can still be a significant variation in the conditional stress distribution. The more the stressed $S_2(t)$ risk factors explain the $S_1(t)$ risk factors systematic risk the less variation in the conditional stress distribution.[22]

Regulatory Provided Scenarios Systematic portfolio stress tests are not only internally developed by financial institutions. A useful application in practice of systematic portfolio stress is to assume $S_2(t)$ contains the prescribed macroeconomic variables evolution in regulatory stress testing, for example, the CCAR exercise required by the Federal Reserve in United States. At the end of every year, Federal Reserve Board releases supervisory scenarios for the following year submission. These scenarios include macroeconomic factors ranging from interest rates, housing price index, unemployment rate to major economic indices outside the United States. The bank holding companies that are subject to CCAR must expand these macroeconomic scenarios to their specific portfolio risk factors. Another example is EBA stress tests in Europe.

Both CCAR and EBA also require major European banks to apply instantaneous global market risk shocks to their trading portfolios and compute the resulting portfolio profit and loss.[23] The risk factors are relatively granular—spanning interest rates, foreign exchange, equity, commodity and volatility factors for major currencies and indices. However, banks still have to transform the predefined risk factors into the actual portfolio risk factors. For example, EBA favors a transformation approach from the stressed $S_2(t)$ risk factors to all the portfolio risk factors, $S(t)$, using:

- First, similar historical relationships if available
- Second, statistical transformation models (sometimes referred to as satellite models in this context, see ECB (2013, p. 20)) such as the conditional distribution or factor models
- Third, theoretical arguments

---

[22]Conditional stress may have a significant effect on expected portfolio loss. However, it may still have significant conditional portfolio loss volatility remaining. See the probabilistic stress testing example in the chapter on market risk analysis with the multivariate normal distribution.
[23]In CCAR the global market risk shock is mandatory for the bank holding companies with large trading operations.

Finding equivalent historical shifts for the $S_1(t)$ risk factors is of course more likely for historically inspired scenarios while in case of forward-looking scenarios the bank may have to resort to statistical models. Ultimately, when the bank has inferred all the portfolio risk factors, $S(t)$, shifts from the core scenarios they can run the scenarios through the market risk system to obtain portfolio profit and loss. In both CCAR and EBA the market risk shock profit and loss is subsequently used as an add-on component in the CCAR and EBA *firmwide* stress testing.[24] In EBA the market risk loss is distributed over the stress horizon of three years while in CCAR the full market risk loss is allocated to the first stress quarter of a total of nine stress quarters.

The EBA stress testing includes all the bank's positions exposed to market risk and uses full valuation of the portfolio instruments in the stress scenario. However, for the subset of market risk positions held for trading EBA also requires banks to perform further risk factor decomposition analysis using the simple linear delta model. This includes a sensitivity analysis to all the EBA specified risk factors and a decomposition of scenario profit and loss into EBA risk factors. The stress approach has the following steps:

- First, all trading positions are decomposed into risk factor asset classes (e.g., equity, foreign exchange) and then to the specific regulatory shock risk factor using the linear delta model approach.

    This approach is termed the risk position approach and was discussed in the previous market risk chapter in the context of risk attribution. A risk position of a physical position represents the exposure to a particular risk factor. For example, an equity option has risk positions in equity, interest rate, and volatility. Each of these risk positions are then referred to as asset class exposures for the physical position. Since the regulatory prescribed risk factors may not match the actual risk positions, as we have discussed above, a model may be needed to transfer from actual portfolio risk positions to regulatory risk positions.

- Second, a linear profit and loss is computed based on the prescribed regulatory risk positions shocks.

    Note here that since the risk position model is linear the profit-and-loss contribution from a physical positions risk positions sums to aggregate impact. Because of the linearity we can also decompose aggregate portfolio impact into summable contributions from asset class.

- Third, compute full valuation profit and loss at an aggregated level, for example, books of business.

    In this case the aggregate profit and loss cannot be easily decomposed in summable components to regulatory risk factors or risk factor asset classes because of the nonlinearity. However, we can aggregate the profit and loss to higher levels, for example, from books of business to firmwide profit and loss.

- Fourth, aggregate the linear risk positions profit and loss to the reporting level(s).

    Here, reporting levels can be granular such as regulatory risk positions but also aggregated such as asset class.

---

[24]The CCAR and EBA firmwide stress testing focuses on the firmwide earnings and loss with contributions from market risk, credit risk, income and expense, etc. In this book we discuss the CCAR and EBA stress testing both in the context of the chapters of specific risk types as well as at the firmwide level in Chapter 9.

▪ Fifth, apply a nonlinearity adjustment to the risk positions profit and loss using the full valuation at the reporting level(s).

For example, we can infer a nonlinearity adjustment at the firmwide level comparing the firmwide full valuation profit and loss to the firmwide risk positions profit and loss.

Systematic Stress Test Programs vs. Portfolio Sensitivity Analysis We can conclude that the purpose of systematic stress test programs is quite different from portfolio sensitivity analysis. Systematic stress test programs typically include stressed values for a large number of risk factors that affect the portfolio and try to replicate potential market stresses that could happen. Core risk factor shifts can be derived from previous historical scenarios or expert knowledge of potential stresses. Since stress scenarios are usually defined only for the reduced set of core risk factors, as it is usually too complex to specify the behavior of all risk factors that can affect the portfolio, a model or historically implied values are frequently used to spread the core risk factor scenarios to all the portfolio risk factors. Since the use of models to transfer risk factor stress is central in systematic portfolio stress tests the models used need to be vetted. Moreover, different scenarios may use different models or approaches.

Hypothetical Scenario from Reverse Stress Testing

In the systematic portfolio stress tests we assumed that core risk factor scenarios were derived from historically relevant events or forward looking—based on economic conjecture. However, in practice, with a large and complex portfolio, it is hard to know a priori which scenarios could potentially cause the largest portfolio losses. A complementary method to design systematic portfolio stress tests is to infer, from the portfolio profit and loss under many scenarios, which hypothetical scenarios could be affecting the portfolio most using a reverse impact analysis.

The idea of a hypothetical stress scenario is to specify potentially large shifts in risk factors that have significant impact on (sub) portfolio profit and loss. Regulators, for example, Basel Committee (2009c) and CEBS (2009, 2010), also require banks to base stress tests on the key scenarios that could challenge the bank (called reverse stress tests), thereby uncovering hidden risks and interactions among risks. The hypothetical stress scenario is in its nature forward looking and has usually not materialized historically yet. Still, it is an economically plausible scenario.

In practice, in order to derive quantifiable hypothetical stress scenarios, several of the tools we have discussed previously are useful. Specifically,

▪ Portfolio risk contribution analysis (through Euler contribution allocations) can be used to identify the current most risky and concentrated subportfolios where stress could be focused.
▪ The risk factor information measure that ranks the most influential risk factors that determine portfolio profit and loss.

An important component in a hypothetical stress scenario is hence to use reverse impact analysis to identify the key portfolios and risk factors to focus on in systematic stress test programs.

The concept of reverse stress testing is focused exactly on finding the risk factor scenarios that could contribute to large losses. The purposes of reverse stress tests are hence clear:

Uncover which risks contribute the most to portfolio profit and loss and use that information subsequently to design plausible stress scenarios. In practice this can be done in many ways. For example:

(a) Identify implied values of risk factors with (for example) a VaR scenario.
(b) Identify implied (average) extreme values of risk factor values for tail losses above a certain quantile (use CVaR as base).
(c) Devise a measure that ranks which risk factors contribute the most to portfolio profit and loss.

A naive approach of extracting the risk factor values contributing to a certain loss and subsequently using this information to define a stress event may or may not be meaningful. In reality (a) may not be that useful in practice because for many portfolios there are many different combinations of risk factor values that can give the same or almost the same loss. Hence, using (a) one may not extract *systematic* information about which risk factor extreme values are also associated with extreme loss.

A similar approach to using VaR of the simulation as a reference point is to attempt a goal-seek scenario optimization to see which combinations of risk factor values can give a certain loss. However, this is potentially practical for a few risk factors only. Moreover, there is typically no single solution to such an optimization and the number of potential solutions may be very large even for a small number of risk factors. That is, there are many combinations of risk factor values that can give (almost) the same loss.

Grundke (2011, 2012) classifies a reverse stress scenario as a scenario where the capital buffer is exactly exhausted (and not more severe than that) and hence uses VaR as the reference point. A risk factor grid search finds the most likely reverse stress test that exhausts the capital base. Likelihood of a scenario is here based on the multivariate distribution of risk factors (using the grid points). Solving the inversion problem to find the set of risk factor values and determining the scenario probabilities is of course mathematically more demanding the greater the number of risk factors. The method hence relies on a small risk factor dimension. See also McNeil and Smith (2012), who use the statistical concept of depth of the distribution to find the most likely ruin event among a set of possible ruin events.

Using CVaR as base, that is, (b) above may be more useful because it averages the realized risk factor values for exceeding a given tail loss and may give more *systematic* information about which (extreme) risk factor values contribute to loss. This approach is taken by Glasserman et al. (2013). In their approach to reverse stress testing they first estimate the conditional mean of the risk factors conditional on portfolio loss exceeding a certain loss level. Second, the conditional mean is adjusted to obtain the *most likely loss scenario* for risk factors. Specifically, this amounts to solving for

$$\max_{S} f(S|L < l)$$

where f is the conditional density of the S $j = 1, \ldots, n$ portfolio risk factors—being conditional on the portfolio loss, L, exceeding the threshold, l. Glasserman et al. (2013) show that for the normal and Laplace distribution the most likely loss scenario coincides with the conditional mean asymptotically as the loss threshold, l, becomes larger. For the t-distribution the most likely loss can be obtained, as the loss threshold grows large, as a simple scaler on the conditional mean loss using $\frac{v-1}{v}$ with v the degrees of freedom for the t-distribution. An important contribution by Glasserman et al. (2013) is not only to solve for the most likely scenario but to also propose a method, due to Owen (2001), that computes a confidence interval around the conditional loss and, approximately, the most likely scenario. Indeed, as we have discussed, reliance on a single or just a few scenarios can be misleading for reverse stress testing. Once the confidence interval is obtained one can in principle sample from the region to obtain extreme scenarios as discussed in Glasserman et al. (2013). However, in practice for many risk factors the information still needs to be ranked. That is, we have to reduce the dimensions of the risk factors.

An example of (c) is the risk factor information measure that ranks the most influential risk factors that determine portfolio profit and loss. It can also be seen as a dimension reduction tool to enable goal-seek reverse stress testing approaches such as Grundke (2011, 2012) and n-dimensional confidence region methods such as Glasserman et al. (2013) as it ranks the top $k < n$ risk factors. Practically therefore reverse stress test information is extracted from history or the scenario simulation itself, which should have all the information, assuming enough scenarios are generated. It can also use smoothing, through a smoothed risk measure like CVaR, and dimension reduction techniques, such as the risk factor information measure, to extract systematic information about tail behavior.

Finding Hypothetical Stress Scenarios Example As a simple example of finding hypothetical stress scenarios we consider a market risk portfolio profit and loss that is described by 5 market indices risk impact on 3 market risk sub-books using the simple delta approach. Table 3.23 displays the delta approximation of the books with respect to the 5 market indices. Because we approximate the profit and loss rather than the portfolio values the current or base case value is naturally zero for each of the market indices. In this model it is assumed that each of these market indices have a zero mean univariate t-distribution with an estimated degrees of freedom and volatility as in Table 3.24.

The correlation matrix between the market indices, Σ, is given by

$$\Sigma = \begin{bmatrix} 1 & & & & \\ 0.2664 & 1 & & & \\ 0.5421 & -0.4032 & 1 & & \\ 0.5829 & -0.4015 & 0.8858 & 1 & \\ 0.3071 & 0.6816 & -0.2041 & -0.078 & 1 \end{bmatrix}.$$

TABLE 3.23 Delta Approximation of 3 Market Risk Books

Market risk book	Index 1	Index 2	Index 3	Index 4	Index 5
1	0	827,460	489,933	520,311	464,642
2	604,489	898,281	564,033	127,557	114,749
3	10,224	46,760	727,901	519,575	743,446

TABLE 3.24 Market Indices Volatility and Degrees of Freedom

Distribution feature	Index 1	Index 2	Index 3	Index 4	Index 5
Volatility	5.34	2.41	5.12	2.30	5.05
Degrees of freedom	15	22	5	16	16

TABLE 3.25 VaR and CVaR 99% Confidence Level Risk Measures, Incremental Risk, and Risk Contributions for the Approximate Firmwide Market Risk Portfolio

Market risk book	VaR	Inc-VaR	Contr-VaR	CVaR	Inc-CVaR	Contr-CVaR
			Copula = $t(5)$			
1	13,391,122.29	14,772,122.39	12,883,506.74	16,213,554.69	15,830,175.93	16,040,022.11
2	17,997,112.34	18,387,021.12	17,078,082.90	21,013,276.74	20,347,863,28	20,643,241.88
3	18,174,018.67	18,110,011.01	20,107,508.94	21,068,021.60	20,746,604.16	20,746,604.16
Aggregate	50,069,098.57	50,069,098.57	50,069,098.57	57,429,868.16	57,429,868.16	57,429,868.16
			Copula = Normal			
1	12,701,340.01	12,313,697.89	16,373,462.53	15,241,712.42	14,588,949.11	14,768,745.59
2	17,814,839.07	15,493,950.26	11,530,123.11	21,830,006.63	20,598,953.45	21,423,694.18
3	16,487,802.13	14,176,886.05	16,457,928.02	20,414,988.60	19,433,543.35	19,613,357.90
Aggregate	44,361,513.66	44,361,513.66	44,361,513.66	55,805,797.67	55,805,797.67	55,805,797.67

TABLE 3.26 Risk Factor Information Measures and Portfolio Profit-and-Loss Correlations for the Equity Indices

Measure	Index 1	Index 3	Index 4	Index 5	Index 2
RFI	0.281	0.146	0.143	0.094	0.040
Corr	0.828	0.705	0.685	0.518	0.342

Clearly, the distribution of the market indices is a mixture of t-distributions. Hence, we cannot easily obtain market risk measures analytically and resort to a simulation-based approach. Using 1,000 scenarios Table 3.25 displays the VaR(0.99), CVaR(0.99), as well as the incremental risk (Inc) and Euler risk contributions (Contr) for the 3 market risk books and the aggregate risk using either a t-copula with 5 degrees of freedom or a normal copula. As expected the risk is higher for the books and the aggregate portfolio when we use a $t(5)$ copula instead of a normal copula. The aggregate market risk VaR with the $t(5)$ copula is a bit above 50,000,000 units of currency compared to a bit above 44,000,000 units of currency using a normal copula.

Our next step is to examine the impact of stress tests on the market risk loss. For that purpose we first compute the market indices risk factor information (RFI) measure and correlation (Corr) with the aggregate profit and loss in Table 3.26. The market indices RFI suggests that index 1 is the main driver of the aggregate risk with index 3 second, closely followed by index 4. To confirm the relative impact of the market indices Table 3.27 displays the market indices values in the 10 worst scenarios where the 10th worst scenario is the realized VaR(0.99) scenario as we have 1,000 scenarios. The numbers in the table indeed verify that in all worst-case aggregate portfolio losses market index 1 has a large negative value. This is however also true for index 3 and index 4, while index 2 and 5 mix large negative values with positive and small negative values. Looking only at the sizes of deltas for the indices in Table 3.23 and the indices distributional characteristics in Table 3.24, we would probably have guessed that index 3 would be the main source of risk. However, correlations matter as well and index 1 is the only index that has positive correlations to all the other indices.

TABLE 3.27 Realized Equity Index Values in the 10 Worst Aggregate Portfolio Loss Scenarios

Worst scenario	Index 1	Index 2	Index 3	Index 4	Index 5
1	−18.02	−6.03	−12.28	−6.37	−17.63
2	−13.83	−6.87	−12.75	−2.48	−12.27
3	−12.41	1.39	−22.12	−7.65	−5.98
4	−15.19	−2.06	−13.17	−5.26	−10.01
5	−11.50	3.28	−22.19	−6.86	−5.20
6	−16.92	1.40	−25.08	−5.85	4.34
7	−11.99	−3.18	−9.54	−4.12	−12.69
8	−13.94	−1.90	−12.89	−4.04	−8.72
9	−10.67	−4.29	−10.52	−3.21	−10.51
10 VaR(0.99)	−9.56	2.32	−21.97	−7.46	−0.34

With this information we can now continue to focus on stressing the portfolio. Focusing initially only on stressing index 1 we find that when index 1 is –20 and the other indices remain at zero the portfolio loss impact is 12,294,268.83 units of currency. If we stress all indices to –20 the portfolio loss is instead 133,187,265.81 units of currency. This is significantly above the VaR(0.99) and CVaR(0.99), partly because of the relatively unlikely event of all indices being –20 with the assumed univariate distributions for the indices, but also because the correlation matrix has offsetting negative correlations, for example, between index 2 and index 3 and 4. This makes it even more unlikely that all indices will be very large negative at the same time. On the other hand, stress scenarios are model independent and should focus on unlikely but still plausible events. Hence, even if a model is used to derive information on hypothetical stress scenarios, we may abandon the model in the final systematic stress design. We may also experiment with different stressed distributions and correlations for the indices, especially since we now know from this example that correlations can have a large impact in determining the main risk driver(s).

A Reverse Stress Test Example Using the Glasserman et al. (2013) Approach Our next example on hypothetical stress scenarios uses the approach by Glasserman et al. (2013) to compute the conditional mean of the risk factors conditional on a certain portfolio loss level as well as the most likely loss scenario and confidence intervals around these points. The data used are historical weekly returns data for the indices S&P 500, FTSE, DAX, Nikkei 225, Hang Seng, and Bovespa, ranging from May 3, 1993, to December 26, 2011. This data set is also used by Glasserman et al. (2013). To construct a portfolio we use a weight for all the indices' risk factors and the resulting portfolio returns are displayed in Figure 3.16.[25] Having the portfolio returns we define a loss threshold of –0.05, that is, –5%. Using this loss threshold we can now compute the conditional mean of the risk factors as well as the most likely loss scenario. In Table 3.28 we display the 19 historical dates where the portfolio loss exceeded the loss threshold of –0.05. Table 3.28 also displays the conditional mean loss of the indices'

---

[25]We use the same relative portfolio weights as in Glasserman et al. (2013) corresponding to the market capitalization of the index traded on the exchanges. For the S&P 500, FTSE, DAX, Nikkei 225, Hang Seng, and Bovespa the portfolio weigths used are respectively 0.5050, 0.136, 0.0539, 0.1443, 0.1022, 0.0583.

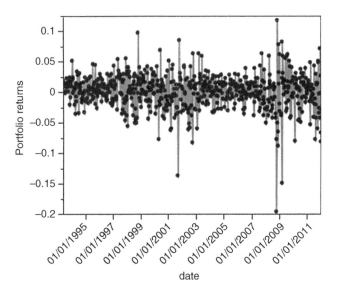

FIGURE 3.16 Index Portfolio Returns Between May 3, 1993, and December 26, 2011

TABLE 3.28 The 19 Historical Dates Where the Portfolio Loss Exceed the Loss Threshold of −5%, the Conditional Loss, and the Most Likely Loss

Date	Portfolio	S&P 500	FTSE	DAX	Nikkei 225	Hang Seng	Bovespa
1/5/1998	−0.0547	−0.04856	−0.01063	−0.02899	−0.0173	−0.16722	−0.12996
4/10/2000	−0.07612	−0.10538	−0.05964	−0.04086	0.00898	−0.04716	−0.1553
3/5/2001	−0.06194	−0.06187	−0.04007	−0.04504	−0.05922	−0.10577	−0.05923
3/12/2001	−0.05874	−0.0672	−0.05991	−0.07574	−0.03127	−0.04736	−0.05495
9/10/2001	−0.13637	−0.14801	−0.11023	−0.20666	−0.06577	−0.12939	−0.2186
6/3/2002	−0.06119	−0.07144	−0.05703	−0.08463	−0.0345	−0.05761	−0.03276
7/8/2002	−0.05136	−0.06913	−0.09284	−0.05745	−0.00192	0.00469	−0.01544
7/15/2002	−0.05811	−0.07992	−0.02978	−0.05784	−0.03764	−0.03032	−0.03501
9/30/2002	−0.08259	−0.10028	−0.04845	−0.19239	−0.0232	−0.06213	−0.09046
1/27/2003	−0.0593	−0.05821	−0.10926	−0.11158	−0.01541	−0.0339	−0.05681
9/29/2008	−0.07698	−0.09399	−0.02126	−0.04395	−0.0803	−0.05351	−0.12339
10/6/2008	−0.19568	−0.18195	−0.21047	−0.2161	−0.24334	−0.16319	−0.20008
11/10/2008	−0.0646	−0.09854	−0.03297	−0.05568	−0.01336	−0.0305	−0.0394
11/17/2008	−0.08705	−0.08389	−0.10678	−0.12374	−0.06518	−0.06524	−0.1268
3/2/2009	−0.14813	−0.1735	−0.15727	−0.16925	−0.07794	−0.12049	−0.10964
2/1/2010	−0.07998	−0.06881	−0.08552	−0.09992	−0.06864	−0.11803	−0.10674
3/14/2011	−0.05196	−0.03175	−0.04546	−0.07167	−0.13905	−0.04736	−0.01664
8/1/2011	−0.07702	−0.07189	−0.09771	−0.12888	−0.05422	−0.06658	−0.09986
9/26/2011	−0.05934	−0.06956	−0.04469	−0.01283	−0.01849	−0.09575	−0.0854
Conditional mean	−0.08111	−0.08863	−0.07474	−0.09596	−0.05462	−0.07562	−0.09245
Most likely loss	−0.06489	−0.0709	−0.05979	−0.07677	−0.0437	−0.0605	−0.07396

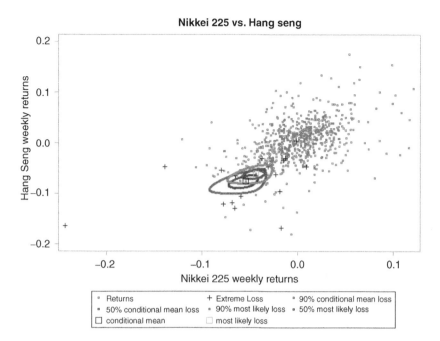

FIGURE 3.17 Conditional Mean, Most Likely Loss and 50% and 90% Confidence Intervals Around the Points for the Nikkei 225 and Hang Seng Index Risk Factors

risk factors and the most likely loss scenario. To compute the most likely loss scenario from the conditional mean of the risk factors we have assumed a *t*-distribution for the portfolio returns with $v = 5$ degrees of freedom.

Our next step in this example is to compute the confidence intervals for the indices' risk factors around the conditional mean loss and the most likely loss. The confidence intervals are computed as the empirical likelihood confidence regions and use a numerical optimization scheme. As an example of the confidence intervals, we display the confidence intervals for the risk factors Hang Seng and Nikkei 225 in Figure 3.17. In Figure 3.17 we have computed both 50% and 90% coverage confidence intervals. Figure 3.17 shows that extreme portfolio losses are often associated with joint negative returns for Hang Seng and Nikkei 225. Remember that the portfolio is linear and therefore this is a well-behaved situation. More complex and nonlinear portfolios can show a greater range of risk factor values that yield the same or almost the same portfolio loss. Sometimes a risk factor can display positive as well as negative values that contribute to portfolio extreme loss values. The complexity also increases with the risk factor dimension, both in terms of solving for the *n*-dimensional confidence regions numerically as well as displaying and interpreting results.

Practical Approaches to Reverse Stress Tests for Large Portfolios In practice, for a large portfolio with many risk factors, portfolio-based risk factor dimension reduction methods such as the risk factor information measure and the partial least squares method can be the first step in reverse stress testing. Next, assuming one can identify a set of significantly reduced core risk factors that contribute to the majority of the portfolio loss, one can hold constant the other risk factors and apply the Grundke (2011, 2012) or the Glasserman et al. (2013)

reverse stress test approach to the core risk factors. Hence, we can consider the following two-step method of reverse stress testing:

1. Use a portfolio-based risk factor dimension reduction method to reduce number of risk factors to the top $k < n$ risk factors.
2. Holding constant the "non-top" $n - k$ risk factors, perform the Grundke (2011, 2012) goal-seek for the top k risk factors or compute the Glasserman et al. (2013) confidence intervals for the k risk factors.

Another approach to dimension reduction in step 1 is the use of economic factor models or unobserved factor models such as principal component analysis. However, as we have discussed previously, such models are often based on selecting risk factor components that have high explanation of historical movements and not necessarily movements that can actually explain portfolio loss. For example, principal component analysis is based on selecting yield curve components that have high explanation of historical yield curve movements and not necessarily yield curve components that can actually explain portfolio profit and loss. Post-simulation one has available both risk factor scenarios and portfolio profit-and-loss scenarios. It is therefore natural to consider dimension reduction methods that actually try to infer the most influential risk factors on the portfolio (and not historical variation). Using portfolio-based risk factor dimension reduction methods is also more credible for being applied to real portfolios with hundreds or thousands of risk factors.

Once one has obtained reasonable reverse stress test scenarios for the top k risk factors one can spread the reverse stress test to all the n risk factors using a suitable method—for example, conditional distribution approaches.

Integration of Stress and Model Analysis

The integration of stress and model analysis, our fourth item in our stress testing components above, is a practice of increasing importance. Integration of stress- and model-based analysis is an important issue because it allows a comprehensive tail risk analysis based on both information from historical data and forward-looking hypothesis of stress events. It also allows stress scenarios to be a part of advanced risk management decision-making analysis such as scenario-based portfolio optimization, which we will discuss below. More importantly perhaps, integration of stress and model analysis provides one solution to how to aggregate the results of different stress tests, and how to reconcile a stress test risk charge with a model-based VaR or CVaR-type charge. Simply summing stress risk charges for multiple stress tests and model based risk charges is not a solution.[26]

Berkowitz (2000) proposed a single period model that superimposes probability weighted exogenous rare event scenarios to a VaR-type risk model. In Berkowitz's model, stress-testing

---

[26]Rebonato (2010) considers aggregating the loss of a stress event using conditional loss events and conditional probabilities. He also proposes an event risk charge based on the maximum of conditional losses. In this setting the stress test charge is, however, still a standalone charge separated from model-based risk charges.

is embedded within the VaR model such that a random sample of asset returns $1, \ldots, n$, $\mathbf{y} = (y_1, \ldots, y_n)$ is realized as

$$\begin{bmatrix} \mathbf{y} & \sim & g_0(\mathbf{y}) & \text{with probability } 1 - \sum_{i=1}^{m} \alpha_i \\ \mathbf{y} & = & g_1(\mathbf{y}) & \text{with probability} & \alpha_1 \\ & \cdots & \\ \mathbf{y} & = & g_m(\mathbf{y}) & \text{with probability} & \alpha_m \end{bmatrix}$$

where $g_0(\mathbf{y})$ is the base risk model, $g_1(\mathbf{y}), \ldots, g_m(\mathbf{y})$, are point mass (stress) events, and "with probability" denotes the probability of the base risk model and the stress events. Clearly, $\{\alpha_i\}_{i=1}^{m} \geq 0$ and $\sum_{i=1}^{m} \alpha_i < 1$. This model integration is motivated by the fact that stress events represent potential future economic states that are not captured by the base model. The base risk model is based on financial economic models calibrated from data while the complementing stress scenarios, $g_1(\mathbf{y}), \ldots, g_m(\mathbf{y})$, are forward-looking based on hypothetical assumptions and expert knowledge.

Recently, Chen and Skoglund (2013) extends the Berkowitz model to a multi-period switching simulation model framework to integrate both model- and event-based stress. This means that multi-period stress tests and model-based views can naturally be integrated in a comprehensive risk model. We refer to Chen and Skoglund (2013) for an application of the model to an equity portfolio with multi-period, dynamic, rare stress events and switching models in stressed periods using an equity index correlated with the portfolio as indicator. The integrated stress model framework is of course more broadly applicable than market risk. For example, credit risk models, as we will discuss in the next chapter, usually have limited data for calibration and validation and hence rely on both expert judgment in calibration as well as on complementary, forward-looking scenarios to model-based views.

Of course, market risk VaR-type risk models may also contain an inherent element of stress in calibration—for example, by calibration of the risk factor models on stressful periods such as recent crisis, and Basel Committee (2009a) introduced an added stressed VaR component into the market risk capital requirement. However, the basis of the model is still historical with no forward-looking stress events complementing the historical view.

PORTFOLIO OPTIMIZATION

Optimization is used frequently in market risk management to find risk and return optimal portfolios as well as to replicate portfolios. In this section we will focus on the classical problems of portfolio mean risk optimization and cash flow replication. Portfolio replication optimization is also used frequently as a pre-process to model-based VaR-type analysis to extract positions from partial information on funds or portfolios. One example is revealing the most likely holdings of a hidden fund investment in the portfolio. See Markov et al. (2004) for an application of dynamic style analysis for detecting portfolio's hidden dynamics. Another example is when the risk manager may only have portfolio sensitivity information available such as portfolio delta and gamma information only. In this case optimization can be used to find the best replicating positions that can subsequently be used as input to a VaR risk model.

Portfolio Mean Risk Optimization

The traditional portfolio optimization is mean-variance optimization, which was originated by Markowitz (1952). The decision rule is to maximize the expected return of the portfolio while keeping the return variance to a certain level (or to minimize the return variance for a given expected return). The resulting portfolios for different desired variance levels make a so-called mean-variance efficient frontier. The efficient frontier concept is useful as a criterion for investor decision making—presenting the investor with a curve that shows the maximum feasible expected return that can be obtained per unit of risk. The Markowitz efficient portfolio is the portfolio that has holdings that maximize the portfolio expected return subject to a constraint on the portfolio volatility.

Traditional Markowitz Efficient Portfolio   Let $\mathbf{y} = (y_1, \ldots, y_n)$ be a vector of multivariate normal random returns of n assets in a portfolio and $\lambda = (\lambda_1, \ldots, \lambda_n)$ is the vector of the proportion of the portfolio invested in these assets. The covariance matrix of returns on these n assets is Σ. The mean-variance optimization seeks to find an optimal vector λ such that

$$\underset{\lambda}{\text{Max}} \sum_{i=1}^{n} \lambda_i \bar{y}_i$$

is subject to:

$$\lambda' \Sigma \lambda \leq \theta$$

$$\sum_{i=1}^{n} \lambda_i = 1$$

$$l_i \leq \lambda_i \leq u_i \text{ for } i = 1, \ldots, n$$

where $\bar{y}_i$ are the expected returns of the n assets in the portfolio. Here, θ is a preset tolerance of the variance of portfolio return, and l_i and u_i are the lower and upper bounds of weight on the asset i in the portfolio. The optimal solutions from a range of θ constraints result in a mean-variance efficient frontier.

The Markowitz mean-variance optimization is important theoretically. However, in practice, as we have seen, the multivariate normal model may not be a good descriptor of financial returns, and in addition market risk portfolios typically contain significantly nonlinear products such as options. This assumption deviation imposes challenges to the mean-variance optimization model above. Indeed, in the practical setting of a nonlinear portfolio and a deviation from the multivariate normal distribution for the risk factors the variance can no longer be considered a good measure of risk. Therefore, we consider using CVaR as an alternative risk measure to variance, and employ a scenario-based approach to optimization.

Scenario-Based Portfolio Optimization   Scenario-based optimization can use any multivariate model for the portfolio risk factors and full valuation of nonlinear portfolio instruments. The method is hence useful in practice for portfolio optimization. To introduce the more generally applicable scenario-based optimization we denote by $\mathbf{y}$ the portfolio returns with distribution $f(\mathbf{y})$ and express CVaR as the conditional expectation of the portfolio return associated with choice of asset weights λ as

$$\delta_\alpha = \gamma + \frac{1}{1-\alpha} \int [-\mathbf{y}'\lambda - \gamma]^+ f(\mathbf{y}) d\mathbf{y} \tag{3.23}$$

where $[a]^+ = a$ if $a > 0$ and 0 otherwise, and γ is the smallest solution to

$$\omega(\lambda, \gamma) = \int I(-\mathbf{y}'\lambda \leq \gamma)f(\mathbf{y})d\mathbf{y} = \alpha$$

where $I(b \leq c) = 1$ if true and 0 otherwise. Rockafellar and Uryasev (2000) proved that equation (3.23) is a convex and continuously differentiable function. In a sample space of $d = 1, \ldots, D$ equiprobable simulated samples from the distribution $f(\mathbf{y})$ we can further approximate equation (3.23) by a convex and piecewise linear function

$$\overline{\delta}_\alpha(\lambda, \gamma) = \gamma + \frac{1}{(1-\alpha)D} \sum_{d=1}^{D} [-\mathbf{y}'\lambda - \gamma]^+.$$

Therefore, the minimum CVaR conditional on a target return μ is approximated as

$$\operatorname*{Min}_{\lambda, \gamma} \left(\gamma + \frac{1}{(1-\alpha)D} \sum_{d=1}^{D} z^d \right)$$

subject to

$$E[\mathbf{y}'\lambda] \geq \mu$$

$$z^d \geq 0$$

$$\mathbf{y}'\lambda^d + \gamma + z^d \geq 0$$

$$\sum_{i=1}^{n} \lambda_i = 1$$

as well as including potentially upper and lower bounds on optimal holdings and linear holding constraints.

Krokhmal et al. (2002) showed duality of the mean CVaR optimization in the sense that finding the minimum CVaR conditional on a target return generates the same efficient frontier as maximizing the mean return subject to a preset tolerance of CVaR.

The major advantage of the above linear program formulation, due to Rockafellar and Uryasev (2000, 2002), is that even large-scale programs can be solved very efficiently.[27] Having obtained an efficient linear programming formulation for a CVaR risk constraint the reader may also want to optimize the expected return using a VaR constraint. However, as noted previously, VaR is not a coherent risk measure in general. Optimization with a VaR constraint is therefore potentially a non-convex program with many local extrema. For these reasons direct VaR optimization may be nontrivial and the approach taken by Larsen, Mausser, and Uryasev (2002) is to approximate the VaR optimization using a series of CVaR constraints.

Scenario-Based Portfolio Optimization Example Using the sample equity portfolio in Table 3.1 we compute the Markowitz efficient frontier using 1,000 simulations. We perform

---

[27]However, see Alexander et al. (2004) for an example of an ill-posed optimization problem for a derivative portfolio where derivatives are evaluated with the delta-gamma approximation.

TABLE 3.29 Efficient Frontiers for the
Unconstrained and the Constrained Case Across
CVaR 99% Confidence Risk Ranging Between 1%
and 15% of Portfolio Mark to Market

CVaR constraint (%)	Unconstrained optimal return (%)	Constrained optimal return (%)
1	8.42	5.19
2	8.71	5.47
3	8.94	5.66
4	9.13	5.82
5	9.29	5.96
6	9.44	6.08
7	9.58	6.19
8	9.71	6.30
9	9.83	6.40
10	9.99	6.49
11	10.0	6.58
12	10.1	6.60
13	10.2	6.73
14	10.3	6.81
15	10.4	6.88

both an unconstrained and a constrained portfolio optimization. In the constrained case we have enforced a minimum and maximum portfolio weight for each instrument, being 10% and 50%, respectively. The efficient frontier has been calculated for CVaR(0.99) risk ranging from 1% to 15% of the portfolio mark to market. Table 3.29 and Figure 3.18 display the efficient frontiers obtained by applying the Rockafellar and Uryasev (2000, 2002) approach to portfolio optimization of CVaR. The unconstrained and constrained efficient frontiers in Table 3.29 and Figure 3.18 should be compared with the current portfolio CVaR(0.99) percentage of the market value and expected return of the absolute portfolio being approximately 7.5% (see Table 3.2 for the previously computed CVaR of 30.46 with 1,000 scenarios) and 0.621%.

Focusing first on the unconditional case then, conditional on the simulations as the representation of potential future returns and risk, the current portfolio weights are clearly suboptimal. From Table 3.29 we can reduce risk from the current 7.5% to 1% and still achieve a 13.5 times higher expected return (8.42% / 0.621%).

The current and optimal portfolio weights as well as net amount to buy and sell are displayed in Table 3.30 when the CVaR(0.99) constraint is 7%. The unconstrained optimal portfolio hence prefers no weight in either of the stock positions or the European options on stock B. It allocates a weight of approximately 61% to the European call on stock A and 32% to the European put on stock A. The optimal allocation for the other CVaR(0.99) constraints is similar in the sense that the optimal portfolio weights always choose the European options on stock A as the only instruments in the optimal portfolio. For example, for CVaR(0.99) constrained to 1% the weights are close to 50% for each of the options on stock A.

As we increase the CVaR constraint a progressively larger weight gets allocated to the European call option on stock A. At the CVaR constraint 15% the European call weight is

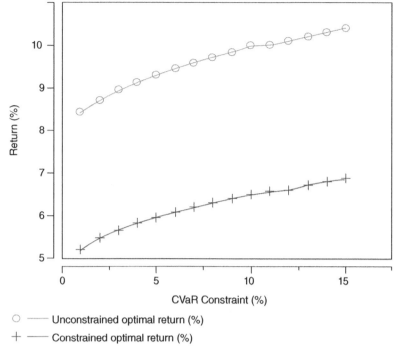

FIGURE 3.18 Efficient Frontiers for the Unconstrained and the Constrained Case Across CVaR 99% Confidence Risk Ranging Between 1 and 15% of Portfolio Mark to Market

TABLE 3.30 Optimal Net Buy-and-Sell Amounts—Unconstrained Portfolio with CVaR Constrained at 7%

Instrument type	Equity	MtM	Current weight (%)	Optimal weight (%)	Net buy (+)/sell(−)
Equity spot	A	50	12.257	0	−50
Equity spot	B	280	68.641	0	−280
Equity option (EuC)	A	6.64	1.628	61.361	243.66
Equity option (EuP)	A	5.16	1.266	38.639	152.45
Equity option (EuC)	B	37.19	9.118	0	37.19
Equity option (EuP)	B	28.92	7.089	0	28.92

68.357% and the European put weight is 31.643%. We can interpret these optimal portfolios such that at low CVaR risk levels the optimal portfolio is a so-called straddle. A straddle gives a profit if the stock price of A moves away sufficiently from the strike price. If the stock A price is close to the strike, it gives a loss. It is hence a volatility bet. As we increase the CVaR risk tolerance level the weight on the European call option increases. This is close to a so-called strap option position with two calls and one put. The strap position bets on volatility as the straddle position but the larger weight on the call option bets higher on a stock A price increase than a decrease.[28]

---

[28]See Hull (2006) for a discussion on straddle and strap option strategies.

The obtained optimal portfolios can be explained by the volatilities and expected returns for stock A and stock B used in the simulation. Stock A has a higher volatility than stock B. Specifically, stock A has volatility of 0.1168 while stock B has a volatility of 0.0355. Stock A also has a higher expected return of 0.11 compared to 0.10 for stock B.

Now, considering the constrained optimization, Table 3.29 shows that the constrained optimal return is significantly lower than the unconstrained. This is because we have forced a minimum portfolio weight of 10% for each of the portfolio instruments while the optimal portfolio has no holding in either of the stocks or the European options on stock B. In the constrained case the optimal portfolios for the different CVaR constraints allocate the minimum portfolio weights of 10% to the stocks and the options on stock B. The remaining weights are allocated to the European options on stock A. As for the unconstrained case, as the CVaR constraint increases, more of the weight is given to the European call option on stock A. Table 3.31 displays the current and optimal portfolio weights as well as net amount to buy and sell for the constrained case when the CVaR(0.99) constraint is 7%.

Model Risk and Portfolio Optimization A common approach to measure the uncertainty due to estimation error in portfolio optimization is the statistical bootstrapping approach (portfolio re-sampling) to obtaining confidence bounds. See Scherer (2004, ch. 3) in this regard. Of course, this approach does not solve the general question of model risk—that is, differences between different models—as it only attempts to take into account the uncertainty in a specific model, specifically the estimation risk. Different model assumptions such as expected returns, volatilities, and correlations can have a significant effect on the outcome of the optimization as we have seen in the example above. One is therefore advised to consider not only a single model but a set of plausible models in the efficient frontier approach to optimal portfolio construction.

Another approach to model risk in portfolio optimization is robust optimization approaches. The robust optimization models can be used both in the traditional mean-variance optimization to cater for uncertainty in the mean and variance estimates as well as in scenario-based optimization—accounting for model distribution uncertainty. We refer to Bertsimas et al. (2011) for an overview of robust optimization methods and applications in finance.

When the optimization is based on simulated scenarios it is an advantage as not only model-based scenarios but also expert views and specific, forward-looking stress scenarios can be integrated. As we have discussed in the context of scenario analysis and stress testing, there are integrated models that can join model-based views as well as forward-looking

TABLE 3.31 Optimal Net Buy-and-Sell Amounts—Constrained Portfolio with CVaR Constrained at 7%

Instrument type	Equity	MtM	Current weight (%)	Optimal weight (%)	Net buy (+)/sell(−)
Equity spot	A	50	12.257	37.873	−9.21
Equity spot	B	280	68.641	22.127	−239.21
Equity option (EuC)	A	6.64	1.628	10	147.85
Equity option (EuP)	A	5.16	1.266	10	85.09
Equity option (EuC)	B	37.19	9.118	10	3.60
Equity option (EuP)	B	28.92	7.089	10	11.87

expert views, for example, the Berkowitz (2000) model and its generalization in Chen and Skoglund (2013).

Cash Flow Replication

Cash flow replication models stem from the classical problem of bond portfolio immunization. See Hawawini (1982), Granito (1984), Christensen and Fabozzi (1987), and Elton and Gruber (1995, ch. 21) for textbook accounts on bond portfolio immunization. In this approach the bond portfolio is immunized from interest rate shifts by a portfolio that replicates the bond portfolio's duration and convexity. However, we focus here on immunization achieved by an exact cash flow matching optimization. The cash flow matching is accomplished by finding the minimum cost portfolio such that the matching portfolio cash flows satisfy the constraint of being sufficient to meet the liabilities. Specifically, in this approach the model takes as objective function the deviation to be minimized over a set of M, $m = 1, \ldots, M$ of discrete time buckets with weights $\{w_m\}_{m=1}^{M}$. The cash flow time buckets are there to reduce the complexity of the problem by grouping cash flows into different time spans and treating them as one. The weight on each time bucket is used to indicate the importance of the time bucket mismatch contribution to the final decision. When deciding on the weights on the time buckets it is in general advisable to consider the possibility of being able to trade the replication portfolio. Indeed if the replicating portfolio is liquidly traded, then immediate cash flow mismatches are most important to close. The choice of the time buckets and their weights therefore depends on both the time horizon and the mispricing tolerance.

Cash Flow Deviation Optimization   To represent the cash flow deviation minimization problem we denote by B the set of all instruments whose shares in the replicating portfolio are to be determined. We also denote by L the set of cash flow instruments (liabilities) that are to be replicated.[29] Denoting the shares for instrument i by h_i and the shares vector for all instruments in B by $\mathbf{h}$, we then have

$$\min_{\mathbf{h}} E \left\{ \sum_{m \in M} w_m f \left[\sum_{i \in B, j \in L} \left(h_i C_{m,i} - C_{m,j} \right) d_m \right] \right\} \qquad (3.24)$$

where d_m is the discount factor for time bucket m.

In a simulation with D scenarios equation (3.24) becomes

$$\min_{\mathbf{h}} \sum_{d=1}^{D} p_d \sum_{m \in M} w_m f \left[\sum_{i \in B, j \in L} \left(h_i C_{m,i}^d - C_{m,j}^d \right) d_m^d \right] \qquad (3.25)$$

where D is the number of scenarios and p_d is the scenario probability, w_m is the weight of the cash flow bucket $d = 1, \ldots, D$, $C_{m,i}^d$ is the cash flow from instrument i in time bucket d in

---

[29]The set of cash flow instruments that are to be replicated are traditionally referred to as the liabilities. However, in practice they do not have to be liabilities of course. The term originates from the classical application of cash flow mismatch to the assets and liabilities in the bank's balance sheet.

scenario $d = 1, \ldots, D$, d_m^d is the discount factor for time bucket m in scenario d.[30] Finally, f is determined according to the matching rule, for example,

$$f = |.|$$

represents the absolute mismatch or an L1-norm deviation, and

$$f = (.)^2$$

the least squares cash flow mismatch or L2-norm deviation.

In practice, all the liabilities can be aggregated to a single liability when performing the optimization. This is because the decision criterion is only with respect to the best replicating asset holdings.

Example Cash Flow Deviation Optimization Using the Least Squares Criterion   We consider 5 scenario cash flows, $d = 1, \ldots, 5$, from asset 1, asset 2, and a liability across $m = 1, \ldots, 8$ time buckets. Table 3.32 displays the asset and liability cash flow scenarios for the 8 time buckets, denoted CF 1, $\ldots$, CF 8. To further illustrate the mismatch of asset and liability cash flows with unit holdings of the assets Figure 3.19 displays graphically the cash flow scenarios for asset 1 and the corresponding negative liability scenario cash flows.

Using an equal weight for all time buckets (w_m) and the least squares cash flow mismatch as criterion for selecting optimal asset weights we find the optimal replicating asset weights, h_1 and h_2, for asset 1 and 2, respectively, as 3.488 and 0.2483. The quadratic optimization yields the optimal least squares objective function as $12,085.75$ and hence the replication comes with significant error.

TABLE 3.32   Asset and Liability Cash Flow Scenarios for the 8 Time Buckets

Asset/Liability	Scenario	CF 1	CF 2	CF 3	CF 4	CF 5	CF 6	CF 7	CF 8
Asset 1	1	5	10	8	7	9	12	11	23
Asset 1	2	2	13	6	7	18	12	11	23
Asset 1	3	9	10	8	1	9	12	4	2
Asset 1	4	12	10	8	1	9	12	17	23
Asset 1	5	31	3	5	21	11	1	11	12
Asset 2	1	1	1	4	11	3	9	5	3
Asset 2	2	1	1	2	3	3	2	5	3
Asset 2	3	1	1	9	21	3	9	5	3
Asset 2	4	1	8	4	11	3	9	19	6
Asset 2	5	2	1	0	1	33	9	0	3
Liability	1	99	150	43	11	31	9	15	3
Liability	2	103	100	22	18	2	2	16	3
Liability	3	93	19	95	2	3	8	9	3
Liability	4	117	58	41	1	3	94	102	6
Liability	5	200	10	33	120	31	68	0	32

---

[30]Here, discount factors are explicitly kept in the objective function to match the present value calculations.

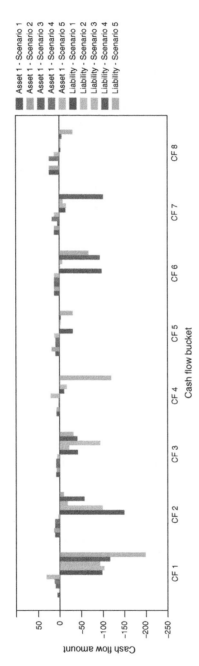

FIGURE 3.19 Asset 1 and Liability Cash Flow Scenarios for the 8 Time Buckets

Cash Flow Mismatch as a Constraint vs. Naive Cash Flow Replication The previous numerical example shows that one needs to be careful with a naive approach to replicating cash flows. The replication error can in practice be significant. In particular, the main drawbacks of the replicating portfolio model in equation (3.25) are:

1. It doesn't allow control of how well the asset portfolio should match the liabilities that are to be replicated for the purpose of pricing and/or hedging. Specifically, the optimization only finds the best match based on the given set of tradable instruments.
2. Because the difference between the replicating portfolio and the liabilities is provided as it is, there is no way to check a priori if the tradable instruments are good candidates for the replicating portfolio, even when the minimal mismatch is reached. This is because the returned minimized mismatch may remain at a very high magnitude.
3. Valuation is done separately from the replicating process in equation (3.25). The process of finding the replicating portfolio doesn't calculate the replicating value at all. This is problematic because if there are several asset portfolios that are able to match the liabilities equally well, then from a pricing perspective we would prefer the least cost portfolio.

To address these deficiencies Chen and Skoglund (2012) recast the naive cash flow replication in equation (3.24) to a cash flow mismatch as a constraint of the objective to find the minimal cost replicating portfolio. This gives the optimization problem,

$$\min_{\mathbf{h}} E\left[\sum_{m \in M} \sum_{i \in B} \left(h_i C_{m,i} d_m\right)\right] \tag{3.26}$$

subject to the mismatch constraint for each time bucket $m \in M$

$$f\left[\sum_{i \in B, j \in L} \left(h_i C_{m,i} - C_{m,j}\right)\right] \leq \sigma_m \tag{3.27}$$

where the constraint function f can be absolute or squared deviation. Neither the absolute nor least square cash flow mismatch criterion is designed to effectively capture large tail mismatches. Chen and Skoglund (2012) therefore also include risk constraints such as CVaR constraints—expanding on the return CVaR optimization from Rockafellar and Uryasev (2000) to cash flow mismatches. The cash flow mismatch as constraint model formulation now explicitly controls—using $\{\sigma_m\}_{m=1}^{M}$—how well the asset portfolio should match the liabilities that are to be replicated for the purpose of pricing and/or hedging. It also includes valuation as part of the process to find the least cost, or alternatively, the maximum return portfolio. Another advantage of the cash flow mismatch as constraint formulation is that the optimization is now an efficient linear program for absolute and CVaR constraints.

Applications of Cash Flow Replication Cash flow replication optimization has many potential applications. The most well-known is probably as finding best cash flow hedging portfolios. However, cash flow replication optimizations also allows us to replace certain cash flow assets with other, tradable cash flow assets that we have a fundamental understanding of and hence may be able to analyze using traditional risk measurement and hedging techniques applied to market instruments. For example, replication of deposits with tradable bonds allows the treasurer to determine an approximate fair value of deposits and implement market hedging schemes. In these applications, the replication of deposits with tradable instruments is crucial as this restates the problem of pricing and hedging deposits into, for the treasury trader, well-known, standard market instrument valuation and hedging.

Cash flow replication optimization can also be used as a portfolio dimension reduction tool for risk analysis, for example, replacing a large dimensional fixed income portfolio with just a few best replicating fixed income instruments. In risk management applications using cash flow replication the cash flow mismatch as a constraint approach is beneficial as it explicitly constrains tail deviation in addition to expected deviation. We will return to cash flow optimization models later in this book in the chapter on liquidity risk. Specifically, we will consider the use of cash flow mismatch optimization models in determining efficient liquidity hedging portfolios and liquidity execution strategies.

DEVELOPMENTS IN THE MARKET RISK INTERNAL MODELS CAPITAL REGULATION

The classical regulatory model for internal market risk VaR, founded in 1996, requires estimation of the 10-day 99% VaR. The capital requirement, $C(T)$, is based on

$$C(T) = \max \left[\text{VaR}\,(T-1), M \sum_{i=1}^{60} \text{VaR}(T-i) \right] \tag{3.28}$$

with M a regulatory multiplier between 3 and 4 that depends on the model's backtesting performance. The capital charge hence takes the largest of the most recent VaR and the 60-day average of VaR:s scaled with the regulatory multiplier. In 2009, about 13 years after the 1996 introduction of a model-based VaR approach to regulatory capital for market risks, the regulators introduced an additional market risk VaR charge as part of the so-called Basel 2.5. This charge required a stressed period calibration of the market risk models. The resulting market risk charge is the sum of the regular and stressed VaR. However, this was only the starting point for a revision to a new market risk regulation. Recently, the market risk regulation is going through its most substantial revision ever (Basel Committee, 2012, 2013b, 2014a). The current regulatory proposal for a fundamental review of the market risk in the trading book includes, for example:[31]

- A move to CVaR at the 97.5% confidence level as the risk measure—replacing 99% VaR.[32] This move to CVaR would also undo the Basel 2.5 introduced double counting of VaR + stressed VaR and base the capital requirement on a single stressed CVaR.
- A mapping of positions to liquidity horizons ranging between 10 days and 1 year. The liquidity horizons are derived from the liquidity of the risk factors that the positions depend on. This move to a position specific liquidity horizon removes the need for the regulatory M multipliers minimum value of 3.

---

[31]The fundamental review also proposes changes to the Basel 2.5 default and migration risk in the trading book. While this capital charge is part of the total market risk capital charge we will discuss credit risk charges in the credit risk chapters.

[32]For a normal distribution CVaR at confidence level 97.5% is equal to the VaR at 99% confidence level.

- A focus on stressed market period analysis, model approval, and model performance measurement on trading desk level—rather than on just aggregate (entity) portfolio level.
- A mandatory standardized approach that also needs to be disclosed on the trading desk level.
- A revised, stricter boundary for trading book allocated positions with the purpose to restrict banks from moving positions from banking to trading book and vice versa for more favorable treatments.
- A restriction on banks in the modeling of cross-asset class diversification—with diversification level controlled by a diversification parameter, ρ.

We have already discussed some of these items, for example, the use of CVaR instead of VaR, and the introduction of liquidity horizons. Basel Committee proposes five liquidity horizon categories ranging from the current 10 days to 1 year to which positions can be allocated. Specifically, the regulators put forward risk factor categories with preassigned liquidity horizons that banks need to map their risk factors to. Not surprisingly, credit risk factor categories are typically allocated the longest liquidity horizons. The specific regulatory adjustment equation is defined as

$$
\text{CVaR} = \sqrt{\left(\text{CVaR}\left(Q_1\right)\sqrt{\frac{LH_1}{T}}\right)^2 + \left(\sum_{j<1}^{5}\text{CVaR}\left(Q_j\right)\sqrt{\frac{LH_j - LH_{j-1}}{T}}\right)^2}. \tag{3.29}
$$

Here $T = 10$ days is the base risk measurement horizon and Q_j for $j = 1, \ldots, 5$ corresponds to the five regulatory liquidity horizons, which range from 10 days to 1 year (250 days) and are 10, 20, 60, 120, and 250 days. The LH_j also corresponds to the liquidity horizon in days such that $LH_j - LH_{j-1}$ correspond to the incremental liquidity horizon in days. In the calculations $\text{CVaR}(Q_1)$ includes all the risk factors while $\text{CVaR}(Q_j)$ only shocks the subset of the risk factors that have a liquidity horizon at least as long as j.[33] For example, if $j = 2$, this corresponds to risk factors with a liquidity horizon greater than or equal to 20 days. This means that the regulatory CVaR is obtained from the base horizon for all risk factors, $\text{CVaR}(Q_1)$, plus a collection of incremental CVaR for subsets of risk factors with longer liquidity horizons. In this approach, for each successive $\text{CVaR}(Q_j)$ calculation one hence "turns-off" successively more risk factors that do not have a liquidity horizon at least j.[34]

A major change in the new proposal is the move of the model validation and approval to desk level and that the model validation (backtesting) is now, presumably, with respect to CVaR. This of course raises the question if a VaR validated internal model, at portfolio level, is automatically approved for CVaR at the desk level or if model approval at the trading desk level will require major revalidation. It is obvious that a VaR model can perform well in $\text{VaR}(\alpha)$ testing but fail at a higher confidence level, β. A further complication with CVaR

---

[33]That is, the risk factors with liquidity horizon less than j are held constant.
[34]The regulatory liquidity adjustment equation (3.29) can be seen as an approximation to a multi-horizon simulation over the liquidity horizons with tiered portfolio closeout by liquidity horizon, that is, as in our example of tiered portfolio close out by liquidity horizon in Table 3.22. The benefit of using equation (3.29) for the liquidity adjustment is that it can be easily implemented in an existing market risk system as multiple risk calculations while implementing portfolio closeout (trading) over horizons may be harder.

is that backtesting methods are more developed and empirically tested for VaR. The current regulatory proposal is therefore to validate the CVaR model using backtesting of 97.5% and 99% VaR quantiles. In addition to the backtesting requirements banks are also required to do profit-and-loss attribution analysis, comparing the model profit and loss versus actual profit and loss.[35]

Consistent with the requirement on desk-level model validation and approval the regulators also institute a mandatory standardized approach—on trading desk level—that in principle allows a switch on/off on internal model approvals at desk level. The new standardized approach has its basis in the delta-normal model and the RiskMetrics (1996) mapping approach of cash flows onto vertices or buckets. The method requires mapping of all instruments to a specified set of risk factors with a regulatory specified covariance matrix. For greater comparability across banks the new regulatory proposal also includes a requirement to disclose the standardized approach capital down to trading desk level publicly.

Perhaps the most debated proposed change is to restrict the cross-asset class diversification in banks internal market risk models. This is done by a calculation of the total capital requirement as a weighted sum of the single diversified capital, and the marginal capital numbers per risk factor asset class with the weight being the diversification parameter ρ for the single diversified capital and $1 - \rho$ for the capital numbers per asset class. For regulatory capital purposes the aggregated charge for an approved trading desk is then equal to the maximum of the most recent capital and a weighted average of the capital from the previous 12 weeks—scaled by a multiplier that depends on the backtesting performance, similar to equation (3.28).[36] The proposed adjustment to market risk capital as a weighted sum of diversified and nondiversified capital indicates that the regulators do not trust the banks in modeling diversification themselves. It also requires banks to compute market risk capital per asset class in addition to portfolio level. This is in addition to the incremental risk calculations already needed for the regulatory liquidity adjustment in equation (3.29).

---

[35]We discussed profit-and-loss attribution in the context of the quadratic portfolio model in the previous market risk chapter. The quadratic expansion is frequently used for such ex-post breakdown and explanation of the profit- and-loss components for a portfolio or a position.

[36]There can also be adjustments to the capital charge for the so-called non-modellable risk factors. Risk factors that are considered non-modellable are capitalized via an add-on.

Credit Risk

CHAPTER 4

Portfolio Credit Risk

For many financial institutions the credit risk in the banking and trading book represents by far the largest financial risk exposure. The 2007 financial crisis is of course a prominent example of the importance of managing credit risk and as a result of the experiences in the 2007 financial crisis regulators have been very active in developing new, stricter regulations for credit risk under the heading of Basel III. Many of the new regulations were driven by reports on the (failed) risk management practices during the crisis. See, for example, the Senior Supervisors Group (2008) and Financial Stability Forum (2008) reports.

As we have discussed in the introduction to this book credit risk capital requirements have a long history. The larger banks use the advanced internal ratings based approach originating from Basel II to calculate risk weighted assets for credit risk. The advanced Basel charge for credit risk is model based, though the model is prescribed by regulators, and require banks to estimate model input parameters such as the probability of default, loss given default and exposure at default for the credit exposures. In 2009, with Basel 2.5, banks were also allowed to develop fully internal model based charges for bond trading exposures termed the incremental risk charge. The incremental risk charge assigns liquidity trading horizons to the bonds and uses the banks own bond portfolio credit risk model. Credit risk is also a main part of the CCAR and EBA firmwide stress tests and requires banks to project expected credit losses and risk weighted assets under regulatory, multi-horizon, macroeconomic stress scenarios.

A financial institutions credit risk exposure includes both issuer credit risk in the banking and trading book as well as counterparty credit risk in derivatives transactions such as swaps. Our focus in this chapter is however only on the issuer credit risk while we will return to counterparty credit risk in the next chapter. The issuer credit risk can be divided into

- Retail exposures such as mortgages, loans, and credit cards[1]
- Large corporate (wholesale) exposures such as commercial loans and credit facilities
- Trading exposures such as bonds

As we mentioned above, for the larger banks the banking book retail and wholesale credit exposures uses the prescribed Basel model framework while the (bond) trading book exposures use an internal model VaR based charge similar to the internal model based VaR charge for market risk.

A complicating factor for measurement of issuer credit risk is that default data are relatively rare, which obviously makes statistical validation of credit risk models difficult. For consumers and small companies one can consider credit risk models estimated on large pools of obligors and thereby derive relatively accurate estimates of probability of default. The situation for large corporates is of course more difficult and usually relies on external ratings

---

[1]We also count the small corporate exposures into the retail class of exposures.

and structural credit risk models such as the Merton (1974) model for credit risk assessment. Due to scarcity of default data it is especially complex to validate correlations in credit risk models. Indeed, one of the main failures of the credit risk models used before the 2007 crisis was the underestimation of default correlations versus the realized number of joint defaults during the crisis. A low credit portfolio default correlation implies that senior tranches of mortgage backed securities are "safe" even with thin subordinate tranches. See Jorion (2009) for an interesting discussion of deficiencies in risk models used during the crisis.

In the context of market risk we have seen that it is generally a first-order important component of a model to capture the stylized fact of univariate financial returns volatility clustering (and to some extent fat tails of the conditional residuals). The specific model for the codependency (the copula) is generally a second order important effect. This result can, however, not be applied to credit risk models. This is because credit risk models are in general based on monthly, quarterly, or even yearly financial data versus daily data for market risk. Temporal aggregation of data enforces the central limit theorem such that financial returns on, for example, a monthly basis are closer to (unconditionally) normal. However, since defaults are rare events we should in the context of credit risk expect the model for correlated defaults and in particular the tail dependency to have a significant impact on credit risk. Moreover, since credit risk default and migration models usually focus on risk measurement over a long period such as a year or multiple years the credit correlation is driven by co-movement of economic variables during business cycle swings rather than day to day co-movements as in market risk analysis.

The fact that correlated defaults in a portfolio credit risk model arises from long-term joint behavior of financial economic indicators complicates the use of traditional market risk backtesting methods for validating portfolio credit risk models as they require many time series observations. Expert examination and scenario testing is therefore critical in the validation of portfolio credit risk models default correlation.[2]

The analysis of credit migration and default is usually viewed as distinct from the analysis of the short-term credit spread risk (with no credit migration) of a financial instrument which is treated as a market risk factor. Credit migration and default risk models can of course include credit spread variation risk in the analysis framework but then the models for credit spread volatility uses the relatively long time horizons of the portfolio credit risk model.

Portfolio credit risk models proposed in the literature can roughly be divided into structural models and reduced form or intensity based models.

In the structural approach corporate liabilities are contingent claims on the assets of the firm and the firm defaults when its assets falls below its liabilities. The approach is hence based on the specific balance sheet of the firm. Consequently, the model is usually applied to large corporates and hence to large corporate issued loans and bonds. Portfolio models based on the structural approach specify dependence between the default events of firms based on dependence between firms assets or proxies such as firm equity or financial indices factor models for firms.

The reduced form approach does not attempt a microeconomic-based explanation of default but rather a macroeconomic view of the key factors that can drive default risk.

---

[2]Pessimistically we can say that for the equivalent of a years backtesting history for market risk models we require observing the portfolio credit risk model performance in 250 business cycle swings rather than 250 business days. On the other hand, for large (homogenous) credit portfolios, we generally have sufficient defaults to validate the portfolio default rate prediction at a given point in time. That is, conditional on a given point in the business cycle.

The default intensity is exogenously modeled, for example using a Poisson process. The reduced form approach is frequently used for consumer and small business portfolios as regression evidence of which economic factors that drive default can be established for large cohorts. In reduced form portfolio models default dependence is traditionally modeled using codependency between the driving economic factors. However, the distinction between structural and reduced form models may not be that important in practice. For example, Duffie and Lando (2001) show the link between intensity and structural-based models by assuming that firm asset values are imperfectly observed.

Another categorization of the credit risk models, as used by Basel (1999), is the default-only mode versus mark-to-market model. The mark-to-market model approach is frequently used for bonds and wholesale exposures. In the mark-to-market approach, the financial institution can suffer credit losses not only from the default event but also from the rating migrations. In default mode models the credit loss is only realized in the event of the default and based on the loss given default. Moreover, there is no credit migration that can over time eventually lead to a default. Historically, this approach has been widely used in the retail banking book assuming the loans are held until maturity. Many traditional credit scoring models and portfolio credit risk models—for example, the actuarial approach models like the CreditRisk$^+$ model—are default only models. However, after the 2007 financial crisis financial institutions have started to use credit migration models in the retail banking books as well. Sometimes with an associated model for measuring (unexperienced) loss in the event of downgrade. That is a mark-to-model method of assigning loan value.[3] Multiple credit states also arise naturally in retail credit models that capture the delinquency status of loans. For example, a loan may be delinquent 30 days or delinquent 90 days but not yet in default. The tracking of loan delinquency also has implications for how state cash flows and losses are booked. Clearly, when the loan is delinquent, scheduled cash flows accrue and may be lost. The loan may, however, also go back to current and repay the accruals.

In this chapter we consider market standard models used to price and risk manage credit risk portfolios. We first focus on market pricing of issuer credit risk in trading book and credit portfolio models for trading book exposures and wholesale loan exposures. Consistent with large corporate exposures, the model we employ for portfolio credit risk has its foundation in the Merton structural model of the firms balance sheet. We then consider credit models and credit analysis for the retail banking book exposures. For retail and the small business segment of the banks credit exposures, reduced form credit scoring models, with the addition of common economic factors, are the natural basis for credit portfolio models.

At the end, a financial institution also needs to consider its firmwide portfolio credit risk and combine the different credit risk models. Consequently, we explain how the structural and reduced form models can be integrated using correlation and more generally copulas.

Other important topics we cover in this chapter include stress testing using the credit models and a summary of the required features of new generation credit portfolio models. For many banks the portfolio credit risk models that are in use today were largely developed

---

[3]The mark-to-model method for loans can use the funds transfer pricing rates in the discounted "fair" value of loan cash flows. Hence, yielding a model based fair value for the banking book items. This approach to fair value is motivated by the fact that the funds transfer rates capture the key risk components and costs attributed to the loan cash flows. They represent the banks best estimates of the risk spreads in absence of a market where risk spreads are embedded in the market quotes. We refer the reader to the chapter on funds transfer pricing and profitability for details on loan fair value using the funds transfer rates.

about 10 years ago with the introduction of Basel II risk weighted assets. However, new regulations such as the CCAR and EBA stress tests require for example multi-horizon models, the prediction of both loss and revenue as well as regulatory capital impact.

The introduction of credit derivatives has allowed financial institutions to hedge their credit risk exposure. Single name credit default swaps or credit guarantees allow financial institutions to hedge an issuers specific credit risk—both from a market value perspective and default loss perspective. Index based credit default swaps such as the iTraxx and CDX indices can be used for approximate macroeconomic hedging of credit portfolios. This is also true for basket credit default swaps. In basket credit default swaps the assumed credit correlations are the most important driver of the market price.

Finally, we end the chapter with a discussion of the Basel II capital requirements for credit risk with a focus on banking book requirements.

ISSUER CREDIT RISK IN WHOLESALE EXPOSURES AND TRADING BOOK

In the presence of default risk fixed income investors take the additional risk of realizing a downward jump in the value of the asset due to worsening credit quality of the issuer. From a modeling perspective capturing the default and migration risk amounts to considering a model that can incorporate these potential jumps as well as their monetary implication in terms of losses.

Traded bonds are typically marked to market for the different rating grades using market observed or market implied credit spreads. Wholesale exposures can be marked to model for different rating grades using a similar methodology. Alternatively, a default mode only approach can be used for wholesale loans. Note, however, that if wholesale exposures are treated with a default loss only model this is still a special case of the mark to market model. It simply means that wholesale exposures experience no market value change in non-default states.

For both traded bonds and wholesale exposure counterparties external ratings are generally available as well as corporate equity prices. The corporate equity prices can be used as basis for approximate firm value estimates in a structural model approach to credit risk.

Market Pricing of Corporate Bonds

In the fixed income modeling it is convention to focus on the models of zero-coupon bonds. This is because any coupon bond can be expressed as a series of cash flows from zero-coupon bonds. The value of the coupon bond is the value of all the zero coupon bonds. See for example Fabozzi (1997, ch. 7). As a result, we will primarily focus on the zero coupon bonds as the bond credit exposure.

The Bond Pricing Equation   Considering a model for the market pricing of corporate bonds we denote the bond price as $P(t, T; R)$ for a bond maturing at T and being priced today at t. We now write the bond price at t as,

$$P(t, T; R) = F(t, T; R(t), N(t))$$

where $R(t)$ is the short-rate of interest and $N(t)$ is a Poisson process that produces default jumps $\Delta F(t, T; R(t), N(t))$ such that,

$$\Delta F(t, T; R(t), N(t)) = [F(t, T; R(t), N(t)) - c]$$

at the Poisson events, where $c \geq 0$ is a variable capturing the recovery value in default.

Assuming fractional recovery of market value. That is, $c = rF$ where $r \in [0, 1]$, Duffie and Singleton (1999) derive the credit-risky bond discounting formula[4]

$$F(t, T; R(t), N(t)) = E_{t,R} \left[\exp \left(- \int_t^T \left(R(s) + h(s)(1 - r) \right) ds \right) \right].$$ (4.1)

Here $h(s)$ denotes the default intensity of the Poisson process. The pricing equation (4.1) is derived under the assumption that we hedge only the market risk component. That is, $R(t)$, and not the jump risk. This is achieved by taking expectations of the Poisson events which is justified in a "large homogeneous portfolio" situation where only systematic credit risk remains. The expectation is taken under the so-called risk-neutral dynamics of the short-rate process, $R(t)$. If the default intensity, $h(s)$, is assumed stochastic (referred to as a Cox process) this means that we cannot directly factor the intensity, $h(s)$, outside the expectation in the pricing equation (4.1) and we interpret the expectation as being over the realizations of $h(s)$ as well.

The pricing equation (4.1) shows that, with fractional recovery of market value, the price of a defaultable bond is the price of a default-free in a world where the discount factor is

$$\exp \left(- \int_t^T (R(s) + \xi(s)) ds \right)$$

rather than simply

$$\exp \left(- \int_t^T R(s) ds \right)$$

where $\xi(s)$ is the credit spread. From a theoretical pricing perspective the only difference between pricing a credit-risky debt and a credit risk-free debt is hence on the choice of discount curve.

In practice, we might define

$$\widetilde{R}(s) = R(s) + \xi(s)$$

as the credit-risky rate and bootstrap a zero curve from similar traded (credit risky) instruments.[5] For example, a credit discount curve may be derived from corporate issues with different maturities. In case there are not enough issues (maturities) from the same corporation, one can approximate credit discount factors at different terms using prices of similar credits (e.g., bonds with same external rating and belonging to the same industry).

Bond Prices and Default Rates In principle, market implied default rates on issuers can also be derived from bond prices. As a simple example of implied zero-coupon bond default rates, consider a zero-coupon bond with maturity 1 year that is issued by a firm. The coupon rate is 6% such that for a notional principal of 100 units of currency we have that

$$P(t, T; \widetilde{R}) = \exp(-0.06) \times 100 = 94.176.$$

---

[4]See also Jarrow and Turnbull (1995), Jarrow et al. (1997), Lando (1998). The credit-risky discounting formula applies to general interest rate derivatives with payoff, χ, say. However, we focus our discussion on credit-risky bonds.

[5]See Ron (2000) on the bootstrapping of zero curves from traded market instruments.

using a continuously compounded rate. Assume now that an equivalent credit risk free zero coupon bond pays the coupon rate 3%. Hence, its price is

$$P(t, T, R) = \exp(-0.03) \times 100 = 97.045.$$

Assuming a recovery rate of 50% for the default risky bond, $P(t, T; \tilde{R})$, the implied 1-year default rate from the bond is 6%. That is, $h(1 - r) = 3\%$ such that $h = 6\%$.

Market Risk VaR Models and the Credit Spread When a credit-risky bond is analyzed for short-term market risk the risk is usually decomposed into the variation of the credit risk free zero rate, $R(t)$, and the credit-risky spread, $\xi(s)$. This is motivated by the fact that for short-term market risk horizons jump to default or migration is unlikely and hence the main credit risk component is the market credit spread risk. The market credit spread already has the short-term market perspective of default and migration information built into it.[6]

Internal regulatory models for market risk VaR may include the bond spread risk components as risk factors subject to the institutions approval for interest rate specific risk. We now illustrate the market risk effect of including the spread risk of a corporate bond on risk measures—using different correlations between zero coupon rates and credit spread rates.

Consider a corporate bond paying coupons semi-yearly with 1 year left to maturity. Next coupon payment is 6 months from today and the final coupon payment and redemption of principal value occurs at maturity. The bond principal value is 1,000,000 of currency and the coupon rate is 8.322%. The bond is valued using a zero curve plus a credit spread. The current zero curve and spread curve are displayed in Table 4.1.

In our analysis we set the daily returns volatility of each zero curve and credit spread curve component as 0.1. The correlation between the points *within* the curves are set high to 0.999, yielding an almost collinear behavior within the curve with essentially parallel shifts only. Now, to consider the behavior *between* the curves we introduce the correlation parameter ρ which captures the correlation between the zero curve and credit curve components. We will vary this correlation parameter between $(-0.70, 0, 0.70)$ as we compute risk measures for the corporate bond.

Results on the empirical co-variation between zero rates and credit spreads have been mixed in the literature, see Neal et al. (2012). The structural Merton (1974) model, that we will discuss in detail below, implies a negative relationship between zero rates and credit spreads because as risk-free rates increase the implied risk neutral growth rate of the firm increases.

TABLE 4.1 Corporate Bond Zero Curve and Credit Spread Curve Current Values for Maturities 1 Month, 3 Months, 6 Months, and 12 Months (1 Year)

	Maturity			
Curve type	1 month	3 months	6 months	12 months
Zero curve	0.0456	0.0462	0.0469	0.0481
Credit spread curve	0.0318	0.0348	0.0350	0.0375

---

[6]See Jagannathan et al. (2011) where the authors take a reduced form anatomy of the credit spread.

TABLE 4.2 99% VaR and CVaR for the Corporate Bond Using Different Risk Factors and Different Values for the Correlation Parameter, Rho

	Risk measure (%)	
Risk factors used	VaR(0.99)	CVaR(0.99)
Zero rates only	1.29	1.51
Credit spreads only	1.33	1.55
Both zero and credit ($\rho = 0$)	1.87	2.13
Both zero and credit ($\rho = -0.70$)	0.94	1.07
Both zero and credit ($\rho = 0.70$)	2.49	2.87

Using our assumed volatilities and correlations, we compute VaR and CVaR for the corporate bond using:

1. Only simulation for the risk free rates (conditional on current spread curve)
2. Only simulation for the spread rates (conditional on current zero curve)
3. Joint simulation of the zero rates and the spread rates using the different values for the correlation parameter, ρ

Table 4.2 displays the obtained 99% VaR and CVaR in percent of the corporate bond mark to market value when the number of simulations used is 10,000. The corporate bond mark to market value is 1,011,128 in units of currency.

Table 4.2 shows that in the case of $\rho = -0.70$ (i.e., a negative co-variation between risk free rates and credit spreads) the corporate bond risk is reduced by using both zero and credit rates in the simulation. Hence, the inclusion of specific issuer risk in the market risk model may reduce portfolio risk. When $\rho = 0$ or $\rho = 0.70$ bond risk has increased compared to using zero rates only.

We can also consider the risk factor information measure, introduced in the previous chapter in the context of market risk, for the zero and credit spread curve components. Due to the almost perfect correlation within the curves the risk factor information measure for the curve components within a curve are the same. This is essential since they have the same correlation with portfolio profit and loss. For the case of $\rho = 0$ we obtain that the credit spread curve components have a risk factor information measure of 0.1758 while the zero curve components risk factor information measure is 0.1654. The corresponding risk factor information measures for $\rho = -0.70$ are 0.0466 and 0.0350, and, finally for the case of $\rho = 0.70$ we obtain the risk factor information measures as 0.452 and 0.437 for the credit curve and zero curve components respectively. The risk factor information levels for the two curves are hence driven by the correlation while their relative impact is similar as expected.

The fact that the risk factor information measure for the curve components within a curve are the same shows a weakness of the empirical risk factor information measure. Specifically, since the bond payments occur only 6 months and 1 year from today the only real risk factors affecting the bond value is the 6-month and 1-year maturities for the zero and credit curve. However, the risk factor information measures for the 1-month and 3-month components of the curve still have the same risk factor information measures as the corresponding 6-month and 1-year components. This is because they are also strongly correlated with portfolio loss—even though they do not really impact portfolio loss. Hence, one needs to be careful with interpreting risk factor information measures as causal relationships between risk factors and portfolio profit and loss.

Components of Credit Spreads In practice quoted bond credit spreads and credit default swap premiums are due not only to default risk but also other components such as liquidity risk.[7] Indeed, empirical default loss rates are significantly smaller than implied by credit spreads. The difference is especially large for good credit quality counterparties. See Manning (2004), who finds that only 8%–11% of the variability in default rates for the top investment grades can explain the variability in credit spreads. The remaining part of the market credit spread is attributed to other market factors such as liquidity.

The fact that market implied default rates—obtained through either credit default swaps or credit spreads—may contain an estimate well in excess of actual default rates is a concern for using market implied credit spreads for bond lifetime (hold to maturity) empirical default loss estimation. However, not for pricing which uses the market credit spreads.

Merton's Structural Model for Corporate Bond Pricing

We now turn our attention to the Merton structural model of corporate bond pricing. As we will see, it will be able to yield a very similar pricing formula as in equation (4.1)—albeit with endogenously given expressions for the default rate, h, and recovery rate, r.

The Merton Pricing Model In the Merton (1974) structural bond pricing model the objective is to provide the fair price of a zero-coupon bond issued by a defaultable firm with face value K. In the setup of the model it is supposed that the firm has only two classes of claims:

1. A single zero coupon debt
2. The residual claim, equity

The firm promises to pay a total of K amounts of currency to the bondholders at the bond maturity date T. In the event that this payment cannot be met, the bondholders recover what is available and the shareholders receive nothing. Hence, on the maturity date, T, the firm must either pay the debt to the bondholders or else the current equity will be useless. Note that since the debt is a simple zero coupon bond this allows the firm to be technically insolvent for any $t < T$ since default can only happen at maturity. Extensions to this simple capital structure will be discussed later.

In the Merton model, $V(t)$, the value of the assets of the firm, follows a geometric Brownian motion,

$$dV(t) = \mu V(t)dt + \sigma V(t)dW(t)$$

where μ and σ are the mean growth rate and instantaneous volatility respectively and with $W(t)$ the Wiener process.

---

[7]There is a theoretical relationship between credit default swap premiums and bond spreads. Specifically, a credit-risky bond with credit spread ξ should have a credit default swap premium approximately ξ as well. This is because the portfolio of the credit-risky bond and the credit default swap should earn the risk-free rate. See Hull et al. (2004) on this theoretical relationship in practice.

On the liability side of the balance sheet of the firm, the total value is financed by equity, $S(t)$, and the zero-coupon debt contract, maturing at time T, with face value K. This gives the balance sheet identity

$$V(t) = P(t, T; R) + S(t) \qquad (4.2)$$

where $P(t, T; R)$ is the credit-risky bond value, using the notation $P(t, T; R)$ to denote that at this point of the analysis the paying rate is still the credit risk-free short-rate, R.

Using the identity in equation (4.2) we note the following:

- If $V(T) \leq K$, the zero-coupon bond is worth $V(T)$, that is, the recovery value.
- If $V(T) > K$, the zero-coupon bond is worth K.

Hence, the value of the risky zero coupon debt at time T is

$$P(T, T; R) = \min(V(T), K)$$

or,

$$P(T, T; R) = K - \max[K - V(T), 0]. \qquad (4.3)$$

Here we recognize the last term as the terminal value of a standard Black and Scholes European put option on the firms assets with strike price K and maturity T.

By the no-arbitrage principle we have, for $t < T$, that a risk-free debt position $K \exp(-R(T - t))$ is equivalent to a risky debt position, $P(t, T; R)$, with paying interest rate R as the non-credit-risky debt, and a long position in a put on the value of the firm, p. We can therefore write

$$K \exp(-R(T - t)) = P(t, T; R) + p$$

and

$$P(t, T; R) = K \exp(-R(T - t)) - p. \qquad (4.4)$$

The holders of the risky debt have hence, with paying rate R, issued a free of charge put option on the firms assets with strike K. The price of the put option can therefore be interpreted as the cost of eliminating the credit risk, or, the required premia on R for taking on credit risk.

Applying now the Black and Scholes European call option pricing formula to equation (4.4) we arrive at

$$P(t, T; R) = K \exp(-R(T - t)) - [K \exp(-R(T - t))N(-d_2) - V(t)N(-d_1)] \qquad (4.5)$$

$$= K \exp(-R(T - t))(1 - N(-d_2)) + V(t)N(-d_1)$$

$$= K \exp(-R(T - t)) \left[N(d_2) + \frac{V(t)}{K \exp(-R(T - t))} N(-d_1) \right]$$

where N is the cumulative distribution function of the stochastic variable $Z \sim N(0, 1)$ and

$$d_1 = \frac{\ln\left(\frac{V(t)}{K}\right) + \left(R + \frac{\sigma^2}{2}\right)(T - t)}{\sigma\sqrt{T - t}},$$

$$d_2 = d_1 - \sigma\sqrt{T - t}.$$

Clearly $P(t, T; R) \leq K \exp(-R(T - t))$.

Bond Value in Terms of Spread The above analytical expression of the value of credit-risky debt expressed in prices can be simpler to interpret when expressed as an interest rate spread on R. We denote the resulting credit-risky interest rate by $\tilde{R}$ and consider the credit-risky equivalent bond value,

$$P(t, T; \tilde{R}) = K \exp(-\tilde{R}(T - t)) \tag{4.6}$$

with,

$$\tilde{R} = -\frac{\ln(P(t, T; \tilde{R})/K)}{T - t}. \tag{4.7}$$

This enables us to solve for the required $\tilde{R}$ in equation (4.6), yielding

$$
\begin{aligned}
\tilde{R} &= \frac{-1}{T - t} \ln \frac{K \exp(-R(T - t)) \left[N(d_2) + \frac{V(t)}{K \exp(-R(T-t))} N(-d_1) \right]}{K} \\
&= \frac{-1}{T - t} \left((-R(T - t)) + \ln \left[N(d_2) + \frac{V(t)}{K \exp(-R(T - t))} N(-d_1) \right] \right) \\
&= R - \frac{1}{(T - t)} \left(\ln \left[N(d_2) + \frac{V(t)}{K \exp(-R(T - t))} N(-d_1) \right] \right).
\end{aligned}
\tag{4.8}
$$

The required credit spread, in excess of R, is then a function of:

- The leverage ratio, $\frac{V(t)}{K \exp(-R(T-t))}$, or inversely of the debt ratio, $\frac{K \exp(-R(T-t))}{V(t)}$
- The volatility of the firms assets σ (the firms business risk)
- Maturity of the debt issue $(T - t)$

As expected, the credit spread is for fixed maturity increasing in K/V and σ.[8]

Example of Merton Model Credit Spreads As an example of Merton model implied credit spreads, Table 4.3 and Figure 4.1 display the percent implied credit spread, in excess of the risk-free rate R, when $R = 0.05$, $\sigma = 30\%$ and for $1, \ldots, 10$ years bond maturity as the quasi debt ratio, K/V, varies between 50%, 65%, and 75%. As expected, with a higher debt ratio the bond credit spread increases. For a fixed debt ratio the credit spread first increases with bond maturity and then decreases slightly. This behavior is consistent with the geometric Brownian motion model of asset price and the default barrier, K, at maturity time T. For short maturity times $V(t)$ will likely not cross the default barrier, K. As we increase maturity time it becomes more likely due to the increased volatility over time. However, for very long maturity times the drift, R, of the geometric Brownian motion process ensures the geometric

---

[8]If we allow for stochastic interest rates in the Merton model then this amounts to using the Black and Scholes option pricing model with stochastic interest rates as in Merton (1973). Shimko et al. (1993) derive the price of a defaultable corporate bond using stochastic interest rates. In this case the model credit spread, due to stochastic bond prices, involves two additional parameters. First, the instantaneous correlation between the asset price process and the bond price process, and, second, the volatility of the bond price process. The effect of increasing either of these new parameters is to (almost monotonically) increase the credit spread.

TABLE 4.3 Merton Credit Spreads in Percent as the Debt Ratio, K/V, Varies Between 50, 65, and 75% and for 1,..., 10 Years Bond Maturity

Bond maturity	K/V=50%	K/V=65%	K/V=75%
1	0.18%	1.50%	3.72%
2	0.75%	2.54%	4.41%
3	1.19%	2.92%	4.45%
4	1.47%	3.05%	4.33%
5	1.64%	3.07%	4.16%
6	1.74%	3.04%	3.99%
7	1.80%	2.97%	3.81%
8	1.82%	2.90%	3.64%
9	1.83%	2.81%	3.48%
10	1.82%	2.72%	3.33%

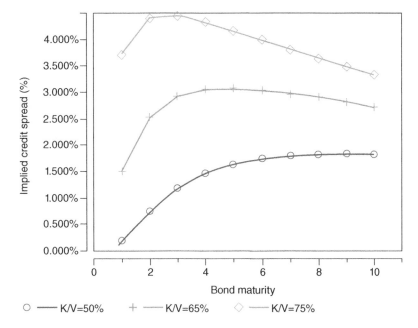

FIGURE 4.1 Merton Credit Spreads in Percent as the Debt Ratio, K/V, Varies Between 50, 65, and 75% and for 1,..., 10 Years Bond Maturity

Brownian motion drifts away from the default barrier. This hump-shaped behavior of credit spreads from the Merton model is also consistent with survival contingent effects.

Solving for the Unobserved Claims Value of the Firm In practice, determination of the credit spread and hence pricing risky debt requires knowledge of K, $V(t)$, and σ. But, all the claims of the firm are in general not publicly traded and an indirect approach has to be taken. For example, one could estimate the face value of the debt, K, from accounting data. Given knowledge of K and assuming that the equity value, $S(t)$, and its volatility, σ_S, is observable one could then infer the asset value, $V(t)$, and volatility of the firm, σ, from the equation system

$$S(t) = \left[V(t)N(d_1) - K \exp\left(-R\,(T-t)\right) N(d_2) \right] \qquad (4.9)$$

$$\sigma_S = \sigma \frac{V(t)}{S(t)} \frac{\partial S(t)}{\partial V(t)} = \sigma \frac{V(t)}{S(t)} N(d_1)$$

where the first equation is the price of a European call option on the firms assets with strike price K and the second equation results from applying Ito's lemma. Since we now have two equations and two unknowns, $(V(t), \sigma)$, a solution can be found using numerical techniques. See Ronn and Verma (1986) for a practical application.

Empirical Market Spreads Versus the Merton Model Spreads Empirically, comparing the observed market spreads with the theoretical spreads obtained from the Merton model one generally finds too low theoretical spreads, see for example Jones et al. (1984), Gemming (2002), and Manning (2004). However, although the level of the credit spreads obtained from the Merton model does not match actual market data the general shape of the theoretical spreads seem to accord very well with the zero-coupon bond market spreads, see Sarig and Warga (1989). However, recall from our previous discussions that the market credit spreads, especially for investment grade credits, are also attributed to other market factors than credit risk.

To make the Merton model fit market spreads, in practice, a very high value of the volatility of assets, σ, must be chosen. Another approach is to extend the Merton model for a better fit. In the literature two standard approaches to remedy some of the discrepancy between market and theoretical spreads have emerged. Either one assumes that the terminal distribution of the asset process has fatter tails than the normal or one introduces a default barrier before T, allowing for the possibility of default before the maturity of the bond. We will discuss both of these approaches below. However, first we will consider the connection between the reduced-form pricing formula in equation (4.1) and the structural pricing formula obtained from the Merton model.

Deriving a Structural Equivalent of the Reduced Form Pricing Approach By declaring a firm to be in default at time T if $V(T) - K < 0$, and using the corresponding risk-neutral asset process,

$$dV(t) = RV(t)dt + \sigma V(t)dW_t$$

we can find

$$P(V(T) < K) = P\left(V(t)\exp\left(\left(R - \frac{\sigma^2}{2}\right)(T-t) + \sigma Z\sqrt{(T-t)} \right) < K \right)$$

denoting the standard normal component of the increments of the Wiener process, W_t, as $Z \sim N(0,1)$. Hence,

$$P(V(T) < K) = P\left(\ln V(t) + \left(\left(R - \frac{\sigma^2}{2}\right)(T-t) + \sigma Z\sqrt{(T-t)} \right) < \ln K \right) \qquad (4.10)$$

$$= P\left(Z < \frac{\ln \frac{K}{V(t)} - \left(R - \frac{\sigma^2}{2}\right)(T-t)}{\sigma\sqrt{(T-t)}} \right) = N(-d_2)$$

is the (risk-neutral) default probability.

By rearranging equation (4.5),

$$P(t,T) = K\exp(-R(T-t)) - \left[K\exp(-R(T-t))N(-d_2) - V(t)N(-d_1)\right] \quad (4.11)$$

$$= K\exp(-R(T-t)) - \text{PD} \times \left[K\exp(-R(T-t)) - V(t)\frac{N(-d_1)}{N(-d_2)}\right]$$

$$= K\exp(-R(T-t)) - \exp(-R(T-t))\text{PD}(1-r)K$$

where now PD $= N(-d_2)$ is the probability of default, K is the exposure at default (face value of debt) and

$$(1-r) = \left[1 - \frac{V(t)}{K\exp(-R(T-t))}\frac{N(-d_1)}{N(-d_2)}\right] \quad (4.12)$$

is one minus the recovery rate, r. Hence, we can now interpret the value of risky-debt as the value of secure debt minus the risk-neutral expected loss due to default. We note the following:

- PD and Loss Given Default (LGD) are not constant through time.
- They depend on the same factors. Hence PD and LGD are highly codependent and LGD cannot be assumed to be exogenously determined.

The above result, in the setting of the Merton model, implies that it is not possible to easily separate out the market (risk-neutral) probability of default from the observed market credit spreads. However, we can back out expected loss.

By approximating the spread equation (4.8) as follows

$$\tilde{R} = R - \frac{1}{(T-t)}\left(\ln\left[N(d_2) + \frac{V(t)N(-d_1)}{K\exp(-R(T-t))}\right]\right)$$

$$= R - \frac{1}{(T-t)}\left(\ln\left[1 + \left(\frac{V(t)N(-d_1)}{K\exp(-R(T-t))} - N(-d_2)\right)\right]\right)$$

$$\approx R - \frac{1}{(T-t)}\left(\frac{V(t)N(-d_1)}{K\exp(-R(T-t))} - N(-d_2)\right)$$

$$= R + \frac{1}{(T-t)}N(-d_2)\left(1 - \frac{V(t)}{K\exp(-R(T-t))}\frac{N(-d_1)}{N(-d_2)}\right)$$

$$= R + \frac{1}{(T-t)}\text{PD}(1-r) = R + \frac{1}{(T-t)}\text{PD}\times\text{LGD}.$$

We can now price risky debt using the equation

$$P(t,T) \approx \exp(-(R+\pi)(T-t))K,$$

where $\pi = \text{PD}\times\text{LGD}$ is the added particle due to credit risk.[9] We can now recall that this expression also forms the basis for the reduced form, market based, approach to pricing issuer credit risk in equation (4.1) where PD and LGD are exogenously given from market rather than obtained from a structural model.

---

[9]The approximation $\ln(1+x) \approx x$ is certainly valid here since $\text{PD}(1-r) \leq \text{PD}$ is usually very small.

Matching Market Credit Spreads   Recall that it was empirically found that the Merton model produce too low credit spreads. As mentioned above two standard approaches to remedy some of the discrepancy between market and theoretical spreads have emerged. Either one assumes that the terminal distribution of the asset process has fatter tails than the normal or one introduces a default barrier, allowing for the possibility of default before the maturity of the bond.

Adjusting the Asset Value Distribution   Following the first route Zhou (1997) consider a jump-diffusion process for the asset value. More specifically he considers the process

$$dV(t) = \mu V(t)dt + \sigma V(t)dW(t) + (\Pi - 1)dN(t)$$

where $\Pi > 0$ is the jump amplitude expressed in %. For example, if $\Pi = 0.9$ the jump amplitude is a 10% fall in the asset price and $N(t)$ is a Poisson process with intensity h so that $dN(t) = 0$ with probability $(1 - h)dt$ and $dN(t) = 1$ with probability hdt. There is therefore a probability of hdt of a jump in $N(t)$ of size $(\Pi - 1)$ in time-step dt. More generally Π may be drawn from a distribution independent of the Poisson process.

The resulting credit spread equation has a similar form as the formula for European option prices when the underlying follows a jump-diffusion, derived by Merton (1974). This approach can answer the problem that a perfectly healthy firm, having credit spread almost zero in the original Merton model, can have systematically a positive credit spread. Since the model also has more degrees of freedom (more parameters) it may also be used to fit a wider diversity of credit spread shapes. In some sense these additional degrees of freedom is also a weakness of the model since their calibration to data is non-trivial.

Similarly, Madan, Carr, and Chang (1998) consider a stochastic volatility model for the asset value. More specifically, they consider a Brownian motion process where volatility is evaluated at an independent random time given by an increasing process with increments that have gamma distribution with mean 1 and variance v. They argue that the model calibrates well. In particular the short-maturity credit spread is substantial in contrast to what would be found in the Merton model.

The above approaches basically relies on the well-known deficiency of the Black and Scholes model in equity derivative pricing and market risk management. That is, that the log-normal distribution fails to calibrate to the empirical observed stochastic volatility and excess kurtosis and skewness. Hence, one may argue that this method of "fixing the spread" relies rather on the stylized facts of equity returns and not on the stylized facts of the asset return process. For example, one may argue that it is rather the complex debt structures and the real-life dynamics of debt that is non-trivial to capture in the basic model.

Debt Adjustments   The second route to remedy the low market credit spreads obtained from the Merton model is therefore to introduce a more realistic debt scheme (e.g., allowing for default before maturity such as introducing a default barrier so that the firm can default should this barrier be reached before the maturity of the contract). This corresponds basically to a knockout (down-and-out) barrier option. For example, Longstaff and Schwartz (1995) price a zero-coupon bond as (compare equation (4.11))

$$P(t, T) = K[1 - P(V(t) < \overline{K}, \forall s \in [t, T]) \times \text{LGD}]$$

$$\approx K \exp(-P(V(t) < \overline{K}, \forall s \in [t, T]) \times \text{LGD})$$

where $\overline{K}$ is an exogenously given constant default barrier. No reference is given to the face-value of the risky debt so that the recovery rate is assumed exogenously given as well. Clearly this is now akin to a reduced form model.

Extensions of the Longstaff and Schwartz model include allowing for a stochastic default barrier. This yields the bond price as

$$P(t, T) = K[1 - P(V_t < \overline{K}(t), \forall s \in [t, T]) \times \text{LGD}]$$

where, for example, the $\overline{K}(t)$ dynamics is described by

$$d\overline{K}(t) = \mu_K \overline{K}(t)dt + \sigma_K \overline{K}(t)dW^{\overline{K}}(t).$$

This is done in for example Saa'-Requejo and Santa Clara (1997) who introduce two stochastic processes, one for the assets dynamics and one for the debt dynamics. That is, the dynamics of the default barrier to price debt.

Other Extensions and Further Reading   The interested reader is referred to Cossin and Pirotte (2001) for an extensive account on the Merton model and its subsequent generalizations. For example Geske (1977) extends the Merton model to coupon bonds. Since, as we have discussed, market credit spreads also contain liquidity premiums it is also natural to add a liquidity component to the Merton model. This is done in for example Chen et al. (2013) who extends the Geske (1977) model.

The Multivariate Merton Model

In the previous subsection we derived the Merton bond pricing model which provided us with structural estimates of the bond issuer PD as well as the ultimate losses, should default occur. The probability of default of a single issuer was obtained as,

$$\text{PD} = N(-d_2)$$

where

$$d_2 = \frac{\ln\left(\frac{V(t)}{K}\right) + \left(R + \frac{\sigma^2}{2}\right)(T - t)}{\sigma\sqrt{T - t}} - \sigma\sqrt{T - t}$$

and with K being the nominal debt value, $\frac{V(t)}{K}$ the leverage ratio with $V(t)$ the value of assets. Further R and σ are respectively the short-rate of interest and the volatility of the asset process.

For a portfolio of N bond issuers we are now concerned with the probability that the sum of N Bernoulli loss indicators, $\{L_i\}_{i=1}^N$ attain the value of $n \leq N$,

$$P\left(\sum_{i=1}^{N} L_i = n\right). \tag{4.13}$$

As an extension of the univariate case consider therefore an N-dimensional geometric Brownian motion process for the asset values, $\{V_{it}\}_{i=1}^N$

$$d\mathbf{V}_t = D[\mathbf{V}_t]\boldsymbol{\mu}dt + D[\mathbf{V}_t]\boldsymbol{\sigma}d\mathbf{W}_t \tag{4.14}$$

where $\mu = (\mu_1, \ldots, \mu_N)'$, $D[\mathbf{x}]$ is an N by N diagonal matrix with the vector $\mathbf{x}$ on the diagonal, $\mathbf{W}_t = (W_{1t}, \ldots, W_{Nt})'$ are N independent standard uncorrelated Wiener processes. The matrix σ is an N by N square root matrix such that $\sigma\sigma' = \Sigma$ is the covariance matrix in the Cholesky decomposition. It is defined as,

$$\sigma = \begin{bmatrix} \sigma_{11} & \cdots & \sigma_{1N} \\ \vdots & \vdots & \vdots \\ \sigma_{N1} & \cdots & \sigma_{NN} \end{bmatrix}$$

with (i, j):th element σ_{ij}. By construction

$$\left(\sum_{j=1}^{N} \sigma_{ij}^2 \right)^{\frac{1}{2}} = 1$$

for all $i = 1, \ldots, N$. Note that while $\mathbf{W}_t = (W_{1t}, \ldots, W_{Nt})'$ are N independent standard uncorrelated Wiener processes $\overline{\mathbf{W}}_t = \sigma \mathbf{W}_t$ are N correlated Wiener processes.

The instantaneous correlation between $\overline{W}_{it}$ and $\overline{W}_{jt}$ is given by

$$\rho_{ij} dt = E(d\overline{W}_{it} d\overline{W}_{jt}) - E(d\overline{W}_{it})E(d\overline{W}_{jt})$$

$$= \frac{\sigma_i' \sigma_j}{\sigma_{ii} \sigma_{jj}} dt.$$

In full analogy with the probability of default in the univariate case we here find for an issuer i,

$$P(V_{iT} < K_i) = P\left(V_{it} \exp\left(\left(\mu_i - \frac{\sum_{j=1}^{N} \sigma_{ij}^2}{2} \right)(T - t) + \sum_{j=1}^{N} \sigma_{ij} Z_j \sqrt{(T - t)} \right) < K_i \right)$$

with $Z_j \sim N(0, 1)$ yielding,

$$P\left(\widetilde{Z}_i < \frac{\ln \frac{K_i}{V_{it}} - \left(\mu_i - \frac{(\sigma_i)^2}{2} \right)(T - t)}{\left(\sum_{j=1}^{N} \sigma_{ij}^2 \right)^{\frac{1}{2}} \sqrt{(T - t)}} \right) = N(-d_2^i)$$

where

$$\widetilde{Z}_i = \frac{\sum_{j=1}^{N} a_{ij} Z_j}{\left(\sum_{j=1}^{N} \sigma_{ij}^2 \right)^{\frac{1}{2}}} \sim N(0, 1) \tag{4.15}$$

and $a_{ij} = \dfrac{\sigma_{ij}}{\left(\sum_{j=1}^{N} \sigma_{ij}^2 \right)^{\frac{1}{2}}}$.

We can refer to equation (4.15) as the standardized asset returns of the multivariate Merton model. Practical applications of the multivariate Merton model express this standardized asset return either in terms of approximating equity returns or using a multifactor model. Standard industry models such as the KMV model and CreditMetrics use factor models where the underlying factors are macroeconomic variables. The KMV model uses historical default data to calibrate the default threshold while CreditMetrics (1997) use multiple states corresponding to rating classes. The different states cutoff levels are calibrated based on empirical default and transition data.

Applied Portfolio Migration and Default Risk Models

We now consider portfolio migration and default risk models inspired by the multivariate Merton model for N firms and how we can practically use these models for estimating portfolio credit risk. Extensive examples are given for two approaches: First, using equity data as proxy for asset values, and, second, using multifactor models for each firm where the factors are relevant drivers for the credit quality of the firms such as country indices, sector indices and other economic factors. We also study a model proposed originally by Li (2000) focusing the modeling on the default times of issuers.

Applying the Multivariate Merton Model Using Equity Data To estimate the probability defined in equation (4.13) requires the calibration of the asset process parameters μ and Σ. However, as in the univariate model, in practice we face the problem that asset values are non-traded and hence unobserved. In practical implementation of the multivariate Merton model one can therefore use equity data as a proxy for asset values—that is, assuming that the correlations and volatilities of asset returns and equity returns are comparable. It is also the practice to estimate the default threshold, as given by the debt level, K_i, in the multivariate Merton model by using the empirically observed default frequency (CreditMetrics, 1997). That is for a given observed default probability, p, the threshold is obtained as $N^{-1}(p)$ where N^{-1} is the inverse normal distribution function. The driver of the asset quality of the firm in the multivariate Merton model is equation (4.15) where $\widetilde{Z}_i \sim N(0,1)$. Hence, realized values of $\widetilde{Z}_i$ should be compared with the default threshold $N^{-1}(p)$ to determine if the firm is in default or not.

For different classes of rating categories we have $\widehat{K}$ distinct transition probabilities to the $\widehat{K}$ classes. For an issuer belonging to class k we have hence $p_{k1}, p_{k2}, \ldots, p_{k\widehat{K}}$ transition probabilities. In this case the $\widehat{K}$ thresholds are obtained from the $\widehat{K}$ transition probabilities and the realized rating is determined by the realized return and the thresholds. Figure 4.2 illustrates the decomposition of the thresholds for a firm rated BBB using the Standard and Poor's rating grade scale.

In practice the thresholds in Figure 4.2 are easily calculated from a given transition matrix. Consider for example a bond having current rating grade BBB. Employing the one-year sample transition matrix in Table 4.4 we can obtain the implied one-year—standard normal distribution—rating thresholds for the bond. This is done in Table 4.5. Hence, for the bond to default a standard normal variable would have to be smaller than −2.82. If the sampled standard normal variable is not greater than 1.56 and not smaller than −1.53 the bond remains rated BBB in the sampled scenario.

An Illustration: Risk Measures for a Bond Portfolio Having a basic understanding of the multivariate Merton model and how one can use transition probabilities to define default and rating migration thresholds of a firm we now consider an extensive example of bond portfolio migration and default risk that illustrates the main model components. The example also illustrates the risk sensitivity to model assumptions such as copula used and the typically different behaviors of VaR and CVaR risk measures in the context of credit portfolios.

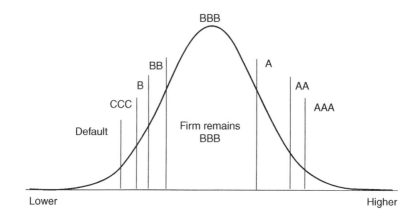

FIGURE 4.2 Example of Obtained Rating Grade Thresholds Using the Transition Probabilities of the Standard and Poor's Rating Grade Scale

TABLE 4.4 Sample Transition Matrix

Rating	AAA	AA	A	BBB	BB	B	CCC	Default
AAA	0.91939194	0.07460746	0.00480048	0.00080008	0.00040004	0	0	0
AA	0.00639936	0.9180082	0.06749325	0.0059994	0.00059994	0.00119988	0.00029997	0
A	0.0007	0.0227	0.9169	0.0511	0.0056	0.0025	0.0001	0.0004
BBB	0.00039996	0.00269973	0.05559444	0.87871213	0.04829517	0.01019898	0.00169983	0.00239976
BB	0.00040004	0.0010001	0.00610061	0.07750775	0.81488149	0.07890789	0.01110111	0.01010101
B	0	0.001	0.0028	0.0046	0.0695	0.828	0.0396	0.0545
CCC	0.00189981	0	0.00369963	0.00749925	0.02429757	0.12128787	0.60443956	0.23687631
Default	0	0	0	0	0	0	0	1

TABLE 4.5 Implied One-Year Rating Thresholds for a Bond Rated BBB

Threshold	BBB bond
Z_{AAA}	+inf
Z_{AA}	3.35
Z_A	2.73
Z_{BBB}	1.56
Z_{BB}	−1.53
Z_B	−2.19
Z_{CCC}	−2.64
Z_{Def}	−2.82

We have previously seen that for simple market risk portfolios the choice of VaR or CVaR as risk measure may not be fundamental. However, this is not true for simple credit portfolios.

We consider a portfolio of 7 corporate bonds with 3 years remaining to maturity for each bond and each bond is paying annual coupons. The corporate bonds $1, \ldots, 7$ are rated in, respectively, the categories AAA, AA, A, BBB, BB, B and CCC corresponding to the rating grades in the transition matrix in Table 4.4.

Each bond has an associated firm equity return that is observed and denoted, $e_1, \ldots, e_7$. The joint distribution of equity returns is given by (see the definition of copula in equation (3.17)),

$$F(e_1, \ldots, e_7) = P(U_1 \leq F_1(e_1), \ldots, U_7 \leq F_7(e_7))$$

where $U_1, \ldots, U_7$ are uniform such that $U_i = F_i(e_i)$. We will focus on the case when e_i is standard normal such that $F_i = N_i$ with N_i the standard normal distribution function. We can now write the copula as,

$$C(u_1, \ldots, u_7) = F(F_1(e_1), \ldots, F_7(e_7)).$$

Initially, we will consider the normal copula such that the random vector $\mathbf{e} = (e_1, \ldots, e_7)$ is multivariate normal and the dependence structure is described by a normal copula as in equation (3.18),

$$C(u_1, \ldots, u_7) = \Phi(N^{-1}(u_1), \ldots, N^{-1}(u_7)), \tag{4.16}$$

where Φ is the standard multivariate normal distribution function with linear correlation matrix Σ and N^{-1} is the inverse of standard univariate Gaussian distribution function.

Using an equicorrelation matrix with common correlation 0.45 between firm returns we now generate 100,000 correlated standard normal scenarios for the $1, \ldots, 7$ firms returns, $\mathbf{e} = (e_1, \ldots, e_7)$. The return scenarios are translated to actual realized ratings using the inverse normal distribution applied to the 1 year transition matrix in Table 4.4. Hence, in each scenario we have available a realized, standard normal, firm return and a set of rating thresholds converted to normal as in Table 4.5. This information is used to determine the rating in a given scenario.[10]

Let now the realized, non-default, scenario rating, AAA, $\ldots$, CCC be denoted k for a particular bond. We then have the bond is valued—conditional on the realized rating, k, as

$$V_c = \frac{f}{(1 + r_k(1))} + \frac{f}{(1 + r_k(2))^2} + \frac{K + f}{(1 + r_k(3))^3} \tag{4.17}$$

$$\approx \sum_{s=1}^{3} f \times \exp(-r_k(s) \times s) + K \exp(-r_k(3) \times 3)$$

where f is the fixed bond coupon rate, K the bond principal value being 100 in units of currency for all the bonds, and, $r_k(s)$ the credit-risky discount rate at year $s = 1, 2, 3$ conditional on rating k.

---

[10]Note that while we here transform the transition matrix thresholds to normal to arrive at the scenario realized rating when comparing the thresholds with the sampled standard normal return we could, equivalently, have converted the sampled standard normal return to uniform and directly compared to the transition matrix thresholds in Table 4.4.

TABLE 4.6 Credit-Risky Discount Rates for the Bonds for Years 1, 2, and 3 for the Different Rating Categories as Well as Fixed Coupon Rates for the Bonds in Different Rating Categories

Rating	Year 1	Year 2	Year 3	Coupon (%)
AAA	0.036	0.0417	0.0473	4
AA	0.0365	0.0422	0.0478	4.5
A	0.0372	0.0432	0.0493	5
BBB	0.041	0.0467	0.0525	6
BB	0.055	0.0602	0.0678	6.5
B	0.0605	0.0702	0.0803	7
CCC	0.1505	0.1502	0.1403	8

The credit-risky discount rates used in our example for the different ratings and for the years 1, 2, and 3 are given in Table 4.6. The table also displays the fixed coupon rate, f, for each bond assigned to the different rating categories. We can already note that the origination coupon rate for the bond in the CCC rating category is significantly lower than the current CCC rating category market spreads. Hence, for the CCC rated bond we should expect a current mark to market significantly less than the bond principal value of 100 units of currency.

To continue with our example we also have to specify the recovery rate of the bonds in case of default. We simply assume a cash recovery rate of 0% of the bond value. That is, no recovery. This means that the maximum bond and portfolio loss is easily obtained as the current mark to market. This is because we do not incorporate the effect of aging of the bond in the valuation in equation (4.17) when we simulate future possible bond market values induced by simulated future bond ratings. Hence, we isolate the effect of credit migration and default on the portfolio from the discounting effect.

Table 4.7 displays the calculated risk measures for the bond portfolio as well as for the individual bonds at the 98% confidence level, the 99% confidence level, and, at the 99.9% confidence level. Specifically, Table 4.7 displays the VaR, CVaR as well as the VaR and CVaR contributions (denoted in the table by Cont VaR and Cont CVaR, respectively). It also displays the incremental VaR and CVaR (denoted Inc VaR and Inc CVaR, respectively) and the bonds and portfolio mark to market values (denoted MtM). In Figure 4.3 we also display graphically the VaR at the 98%, the 99%, and the 99.9% confidence level for the bonds and the portfolio.

In Table 4.7, we have marked risk measures that imply a maximum loss by *. For example, at the 98% confidence level the VaR for the bond rated B and CCC have a VaR and CVaR equal to the maximum loss. In addition, CVaR has a maximum loss for the bond rated BB. At the 99% level this is also the case for the bond rated BB and the VaR risk measure, and, at the 99.9% level also for the bond rated BBB and the VaR risk measure.

For the higher rated bonds in rating category AAA, AA, and A we observe a significant difference between the VaR and CVaR risk measures for all the confidence levels. Specifically, CVaR is much higher than VaR. This is because for the higher quality bonds significant downgrades and default are extremely rare events (see the transition matrix in Table 4.4). As a consequence of the bond value changing only because of rating migration, the bonds and the portfolio profit and loss distributions, are discrete—corresponding to the rating events.

TABLE 4.7 Corporate Bond Portfolio Risk Measures

Bond rating	MtM	VaR	CVaR	Cont VaR	Cont CVaR	Inc VaR	Inc CVaR
			98% confidence level				
AAA	98.08	0.13	0.96	0	0.17	0.40	0.84
AA	99.33	0.40	3.34	0.40	0.71	0.40	1.35
A	100.30	0.87	10.40	0	2.87	0.40	2.45
BBB	102.16	4.07	24.68	0	13.79	1.73	9.08
BB	99.42	17.02	99.42*	3.14	31.03	3.14	19.02
B	97.58	97.58*	97.58*	97.58*	82.41	87.54	67.27
CCC	85.84	85.84*	85.84*	85.84*	82.43	84.91	81.92
Portfolio	682.70	186.96	213.42	186.96	213.42	186.96	213.42
			99% confidence level				
AAA	98.08	0.13	0.96	0	0.23	0.16	0.23
AA	99.33	0.40	3.34	8.27	1.11	0.92	0.53
A	100.30	0.87	10.40	0.87	4.61	1.42	3.64
BBB	102.16	7.18	68.41	0	18.58	4.73	13.08
BB	99.42	99.42*	99.42*	0	50.94	4.67	33.34
B	97.58	97.58*	97.58*	97.58*	81.51	81.76	50.17
CCC	85.84	85.84*	85.84*	85.84*	79.22	82.97	78.15
Portfolio	682.70	192.56	236.20	192.56	236.20	192.56	236.20
			99.9% confidence level				
AAA	98.08	1.39	5.31	0.13	0.56	0.58	0.50
AA	99.33	8.27	21.53	0	3.01	1.01	2.18
A	100.30	7.94	82.62	4.87	17.45	2.27	10.65
BBB	102.16	102.16*	102.16*	4.07	55.32	7.67	29.66
BB	99.42	99.42*	99.42*	99.42*	75.05	8.06	33.75
B	97.58	97.58*	97.58*	97.58*	90.79	91.14	80.58
CCC	85.84	85.84*	85.84*	85.84*	84.03	85.44	83.38
Portfolio	682.70	291.91	326.21	291.91	326.21	291.91	326.21

For reference, Table 4.8 displays the possible discrete profit and loss for the bonds $1, \ldots, 7$ for the different possible realized rating categories.

Turning now to the risk contributions in Table 4.7 we note that the empirical VaR contributions are not a good choice for risk allocation in this case. In fact as the natural estimator of VaR contribution is the conditional realization of loss the contributions can vary significantly with confidence level. Especially at the lower confidence intervals 98% and 99% the VaR contributions are zero for some of the higher quality bonds. In contrast, the CVaR contributions, being based on average tail losses, are smooth and produce well-behaved and economically intuitive contributions. For example, the CVaR contributions are never zero and ranks the bonds contribution risk accurately according to their rating. Moreover, the CVaR contributions vary smoothly across confidence levels. As we have discussed previously

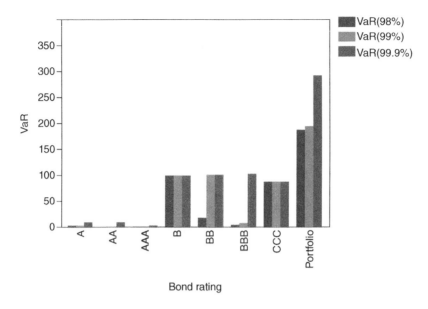

FIGURE 4.3 Corporate Bond Portfolio VaR at Different Confidence Levels

TABLE 4.8 Bond Discrete Profit and Loss for Different Rating Categories

Bond/Rating	AAA	AA	A	BBB	BB	B	C	Default
AAA	0	−0.13	−0.53	−1.39	−5.31	−8.33	−21.44	−98.08
AA	0.14	0	−0.40	−1.27	−5.23	−8.27	−21.53	−99.33
A	0.54	0.40	0	−0.87	−4.87	−7.94	−21.36	−100.30
BBB	1.44	1.30	0.89	0	−4.07	−7.18	−20.92	−102.16
BB	5.56	5.42	5.01	4.11	0	−3.14	−17.02	−99.42
B	8.77	8.63	8.22	7.31	3.16	0	−14.04	−97.58
CCC	23.27	23.13	22.71	21.78	17.56	14.35	0	−85.84

in the advanced market risk chapter, it is practice to smooth VaR contributions, or, use the naturally smoothed CVaR contributions when conditional (VaR) contribution to portfolio loss is not smooth.[11]

Using the risk contributions and the stand-alone risk measures, we can also compute diversification indices for the bonds. For example, the AAA rated bond has a CVaR diversification index of $\frac{0.23}{0.96} \approx 0.24$ at the 99% confidence level.

In Table 4.7, we also display the incremental VaR and CVaR risk measures for the different confidence levels. The interpretation of these measures for the bonds is the risk measure increase when the bond is added to the portfolio. Naturally, at the portfolio level, incremental

[11]Heuristically, the conditional portfolio loss contribution is not considered smooth if it can jump significantly for small changes in the confidence level. For example, for the bond rated AA the conditional portfolio loss contribution at the 98% confidence level is 0.40, at the 99% confidence level 8.27, and, at the 99.9% confidence level 0.

TABLE 4.9 Risk Factor Information Measures for the Firm Returns

Firm return	RFI	Corr
CCC	0.3823	0.731
B	0.0954	0.541
BB	0.0880	0.457
BBB	0.0773	0.430
A	0.0697	0.419
AA	0.0675	0.416
AAA	0.0672	0.415

risk is also the portfolio risk. Note that the incremental VaR risk measure seems to produce more economically intuitive results than the empirical VaR contribution.

We now recall that risk factor information measures calculate the relative importance of risk factors in determining aggregate portfolio loss. While the risk factor information measure is not a contribution measure it gives a relative ranking of risk factors. In our example, the relevant risk factors are the firm equity returns, $e_1, \ldots, e_7$, for the rating categories AAA, $\ldots$, CCC of the bonds.

Table 4.9 displays, at the 98% confidence level, the risk factor information measures (RFI) for the firm returns as well as the correlation (Corr) between the firm return risk factor and the portfolio profit and loss. The risk factor information measure orders the influential risk factors naturally by ranking the firm returns in reverse order of credit quality. That is, the firm returns for the firm rated CCC gives the largest loss information while the firm returns for the firm rated AAA are ranked as having the lowest loss information.

Extension to the *t*-Copula So far in our example of corporate bond migration and default risk, we have used the multivariate normal distribution. That is, we have used the normal copula in equation (4.16) for the firms returns. We could of course also consider another copula to join the univariate standard normal firm returns. A natural choice is the *t*-copula such that

$$C(u_1, \ldots, u_7) = \mathbf{t}_v(t_v^{-1}(u_1), \ldots, t_v^{-1}(u_7)) \tag{4.18}$$

where t_v denotes the multivariate *t*-distribution function with degrees of freedom parameter v and t_v denotes the margins. As we have discussed previously, the *t*-copula, in contrast to the normal copula, displays (asymptotic) tail dependence.

Table 4.10 displays corporate bond portfolio risk measures as in Table 4.7 but now using the *t*-copula with 3 degrees of freedom and at the 99.9% confidence level only. Clearly, the stand-alone risk for the bonds has not changed since each bond still has the same marginal distribution. However, with the *t*-copula portfolio VaR has increased from 291.91 to 315.49 and portfolio CVaR has increased from 326.21 to 402.64. The most significant increase is hence for CVaR with about a 23% increase in risk.

The increase in the VaR and CVaR risk measures with the *t*-copula can be broken down into the contributions of the bonds to total risk. For VaR the main contribution increase is seen to come from the bonds in categories AAA, $\ldots$, BBB with main contribution increase from the BBB bond compared to the normal copula case. With the *t*-copula the contribution VaR is now the maximum loss. For CVaR the main contribution increase includes the same bonds as for VaR but also the BB-rated bond.

TABLE 4.10 Corporate Bond Portfolio Risk Measures Using the *t*-Copula with 3 Degrees of Freedom

Bond rating	MtM	VaR	CVaR	Cont VaR	Cont CVaR	Inc VaR	Inc CVaR
			99.9% confidence level				
AAA	98.08	1.39	5.31	0.13	1.34	1.64	1.05
AA	99.33	8.27	21.53	8.27	6.04	3.67	4.73
A	100.30	7.94	82.99	7.94	28.79	9.94	24.44
BBB	102.16	102.16*	102.16*	102.16*	92.24	23.79	86.38
BB	99.42	99.42*	99.42*	99.42*	94.83	24.69	89.27
B	97.58	97.58*	97.58*	97.58*	95.68	26.81	90.26
CCC	85.84	85.84*	85.84*	0	83.71	15.81	78.69
Portfolio	682.70	315.49	402.64	315.49	402.64	315.49	402.64

This analysis shows that the choice of copula in general have a significant effect on portfolio credit risk models risk measures. We also refer to Frey et al. (2001) for further analysis of the normal copula versus the *t*-copula in this simple equity version of the Merton based credit portfolio model. However, we will also return to the comparison of the normal and *t*-copula for Merton-based models when we discuss the multifactor version of the model below.

Extension to Multiple Horizons Risk Analysis For bond credit portfolio analysis for longer periods than 1 year one needs to adjust the transition matrix accordingly in order to capture rating migrations for the longer period. It is practice in this model to assume that the transition probabilities are exogenously given long-run rates. The credit correlation derives from the equity correlation with a time homogeneous transition matrix. A time homogeneous transition matrix is estimated as if it is not dependent on the business cycle and is generally referred to as a Through the Cycle (TTC) credit transition matrix or a long-run transition matrix. A transition matrix that is not time homogeneous depends on the business cycle and is generally referred to as a Point in Time (PIT) estimate of the credit transition matrix. See Schuermann and Jafry (2003) on the estimation of the different transition matrices using Standard and Poor's rating data.

A time homogeneous transition matrix can be used to obtain, for example, the 2-year transition matrix, by using matrix powers. Assuming we have available a 1-year long-run transition matrix, denoted by **A**, we can now obtain the 2-year transition matrix using the matrix multiplication **A** × **A**. Similarly, the 3-year transition matrix is obtained with the matrix multiplication **A** × **A** × **A**. Using this matrix power principle, we can extend our corporate bond default and migration risk example to analyze aggregate portfolio risk at year 2 and 3 as well.

In general, two important steps are needed to extend our bond portfolio analysis to multiple horizons.

- First, as discussed above, we use the matrix power to obtain the transition matrices at year 2 and 3 from the transition matrix in Table 4.4.
- Second, since we now analyze portfolio risk across time we also need to consider a stochastic process for the firm returns random vector, $e = (e_1, \ldots, e_7)$.

We therefore construct the marginal process for firm returns as zero expected returns processes across year 1, 2, and 3 such that

$$\Delta e_1(t) = \Delta W_{e_1}(t) \tag{4.19}$$

$$\Delta e_2(t) = \Delta W_{e_2}(t)$$

$$\cdots\cdots$$

$$\Delta e_7(t) = \Delta W_{e_7}(t)$$

where, for example, $\Delta e_1(t) = e_1(t) - e_1(t-1)$, and with $e_1(0) = 0$. Here $W_{e_i}(t)$ is the standard Wiener process for firm i equity returns such that $\Delta W_{e_i}(t) = Z_{e_i} \sim N(0, 1)$ is a standard normal variable. For example, with a multivariate normal distribution for $Z_{e_1}, \ldots, Z_{e_7}$ we have that

$$\Delta \mathbf{W}_e(t) = (\Delta W_{e_1}(t), \ldots, \Delta W_{e_7}(t)) \sim N(\mathbf{0}, \Sigma) \tag{4.20}$$

where Σ is the correlation matrix.

As in the single horizon version of the model, we assume an equicorrelation matrix having equicorrelation 0.45. Note also that with this multi-horizon model specification we have introduced path-dependence in simulated firm returns over the years with dependent increments. With dependent increments of firm returns a large positive return in period 1 gives a relatively low (conditional) probability of default in period 2. Similarly, a large negative return in period 2 gives a relatively high (conditional) probability of default in period 3. An argument against this model specification of multi-horizon firm returns is that it does not capture a firms response behavior conditional on the observed yearly high positive or high negative returns. That is, for large positive returns the firm can add more debt and for large negative returns the firm can take measures to avoid default. Using such an argument we should simulate returns directly at the 1-, 2-, and 3-year horizon with a static, one-period, model. We refer to Morokoff (2003) for a discussion on the use of dependent increments versus independent increments in multi-horizon simulation of firm returns.

Another natural question when one moves from a single period model to a multi-horizon model is whether one should include path-dependence in the firms ratings across years 1, 2, and 3. Here path-dependence in ratings means that a firm rated in a particular rating category in a scenario at year 1 starts year 2 with that rating and so on. Using path-dependence in ratings we should use the 1 year transition matrix for each year rather than a cumulative transition matrix for years 2 and 3. Path-dependence in ratings is important if one focuses on the marginal risk within a year. However, if the focus is instead only on the cumulative risk at years 1, 2, and 3, path dependence in ratings is not necessary.

Our example here focuses on the cumulative risk across years and also uses a t-copula with 3 degrees of freedom. That is, instead of the multivariate normal distribution in equation (4.20) we use the t-copula for the transformed uniforms as in equation (4.18). We compute the portfolio level VaR and CVaR at the cumulative intervals of 1 year, 2 years, and 3 years. To obtain bond rating migrations and defaults across years we hence proceed as follows:

- For the first year horizon simulated firm returns we use the 1-year transition matrix in Table 4.4 to evaluate the 1-year realized rating as before.

- For the second-year horizon we use the second power of the transition matrix in Table 4.4 and the simulated returns for year 2 to evaluate the second-year ratings.
- Finally, for the third year we use the third power of the transition matrix in Table 4.4 and the simulated returns for year 3.

Using a confidence level of 99.9% the obtained $t(3)$ copula portfolio VaR and CVaR for the first year is of course 315.49 and 402.64 as in Table 4.10. For the second year we obtain VaR and CVaR as 586.01 and 625.70, and, for the third year we obtain both VaR and CVaR as the mark to market of the portfolio 682.70. Hence, at the 99.9% confidence level, both VaR and CVaR achieves the maximum portfolio loss at year 3.

A Multifactor Model for Asset Returns Having analyzed the multivariate Merton model implemented on the basis of single equity proxies to asset values, we now consider a popular implementation of the multivariate Merton model that employs a factor model as an approximation to the issuers vector asset process.

Using a multifactor model the standardized returns for issuer i, $\widetilde{Z}_i$ in equation (4.15), is driven by observed indices such as country indices, sector indices and other economic factors. The returns of an issuer i is described by the following linear multifactor model

$$\widetilde{Z}_i = \sum_{j=1}^{N} \beta_{ij} Z_j + \lambda_i \varepsilon_i \tag{4.21}$$

where the Z_j:s are interpreted as returns of the common credit factors $j = 1, \ldots, n$, $Z_j \sim N(0, \sigma_j)$ and with β_{ij} the sensitivity of issuer i to the j:th index factor. The ε_i:s are the idiosyncratic factors that represents the specific risk to issuer i. The ε_i:s are assumed to be independent and identically distributed standard normal variables which are independent of the Z_j:s.

Since the Z_j:s are not necessarily standardized we can obtain the standardized $\widetilde{Z}_i$:s as

$$\widehat{Z}_i = \phi_i \left(\sum_{j=1}^{N} \beta_{ij} Z_j \right) + \lambda_i \varepsilon_i \tag{4.22}$$

$$\phi_i = \sqrt{\frac{1 - \lambda_i^2}{\beta \Sigma \beta'}}$$

where Σ is the covariance matrix of $(Z_1, \ldots, Z_N)$ and $\beta = (\beta_1, \ldots, \beta_N)$. Note here that the horizon of the covariance matrix, Σ, in equation (4.22) must be consistent with the simulation horizon of the standardized factor, $\widehat{Z}_i$. For example, if Σ is calculated on monthly data and the simulation horizon is yearly then Σ must be scaled by $\sqrt{12}$ for consistency in equation (4.22).

Denoting the transformed (to normal) default threshold by I for issuer i we have that the conditional (on $\mathbf{Z}$) default probability is,

$$P(\widehat{Z}_i < I) = N \left(\frac{I - \phi_i \left(\sum_{j=1}^{N} \beta_j Z_j \right)}{\sqrt{1 - R_i^2}} \right). \tag{4.23}$$

where $R_i^2 = 1 - \lambda_i^2$.

We have assumed here that $Z \sim N(\mathbf{0}, \Sigma)$ although in principle we can consider other cases. For example, using equation (3.19) we can have a multivariate t-distribution for $\hat{Z}$ such that

$$\hat{Z}_i = \frac{\sqrt{v}}{\sqrt{S}} \left(\phi_i \left(\sum_{j=1}^{N} \beta_{ij} Z_j \right) + \lambda_i \varepsilon_i \right)$$

with $S \sim \chi_v^2$, $(Z_1, \ldots, Z_N) \sim N(\mathbf{0}, \Sigma)$ and ε_i is independent of S. Further, v is the degrees of freedom parameter for the t-distribution. See Schönbucher (2000) on using the t-distribution in the multifactor model. Having a t-distributed standardized return for the normalized credit index, $\hat{Z}_i$, we of course also need to use the t-distribution when we transform the standardized returns to uniforms to compare with the actual transition matrix thresholds. Alternatively, we use the inverse t-distribution to transform the actual transition matrix transition probabilities to t-distributed thresholds.

A generalization often used in practice is to retain the normal distribution for each $\hat{Z}_i$ and use a copula for $(Z_1, \ldots, Z_N)$ such that we simulate from

$$C(u_1, \ldots, u_N) = F(F_1(Z_1), \ldots, F_N(Z_N)) \tag{4.24}$$

and then transform back to normal using, $N^{-1}(u_i)$, where N^{-1} is the inverse normal distribution function.

Below we will consider using the t-copula as an alternative to the implied normal copula in equation (4.22). The t-copula is useful in this credit risk context since it still maintains the flexibility of using a full correlation matrix between the credit factors, $(Z_1, \ldots, Z_N)$, and still, for low values of the degrees of freedom parameter, v, displays significant tail dependence. Hence, it can generate more extreme tail events (i.e., more joint defaults than the normal). The same flexibility is provided by the normal mixture copula and the grouped t-copula introduced by Daul et al. (2003).

A Numerical Example of Multifactor Models   As a concrete example of a multifactor model, consider a firm with a credit index driven by four monthly observed return factors. We denote these return factors by $Z = (Z_1, Z_2, Z_3, Z_4)$ where the factors are distributed as multivariate normal with the standard deviation of the return factors being 0.078, 0.084, 0.049, and 0.069, respectively. The correlation matrix between the returns is given by

$$\Sigma = \begin{bmatrix} 1 & 0.58 & 0.74 & 0.72 \\ 0.58 & 1 & 0.68 & 0.69 \\ 0.74 & 0.68 & 1 & 0.87 \\ 0.72 & 0.69 & 0.87 & 1 \end{bmatrix}.$$

The factor parameters, β, and the idiosyncratic parameter, λ, are given by

$$\beta = \begin{bmatrix} 0.62 & 0.33 & 0.03 & 0.02 \end{bmatrix}$$
$$\lambda = 0.89.$$

Note here that $\sum_{j=1}^{4} \beta_j = 1$ and that each β_j can be interpreted as the percentage exposure to that factor.

It is natural to think of these factors as influencing the firms credit health in different ways. For example, a manufacturing firm with significant export may be exposed to a local index for similar firms as well as indices that indicate the potential revenue in exports (e.g., foreign countries' GDP deviations from trend and foreign exchange rates). The idiosyncratic parameter λ captures the part of the firm's credit health that cannot be explained by the factors.

From classical linear regression theory we have that the R^2 is defined as 1 minus the variance of the error term divided by the variance of the dependent variable. In terms of equation (4.22), the dependent variable is $\hat{Z}_i$ and by definition the variance of $\hat{Z}_i$ is unity. Hence, in this model the classical linear regression R^2 is given by $R^2 = 1 - \lambda^2$. Note, however, that for the original regression equation (4.21) the regression R^2 is given by,

$$R^2 = 1 - \frac{\lambda^2}{\lambda^2 + \beta\Sigma\beta'} = \frac{\beta\Sigma\beta'}{\lambda^2 + \beta\Sigma\beta'}$$

For our numerical example we then have that the standardized model R^2 for the firm is 0.2079 and that the unstandardized model R^2 for the firm is 0.5574. The remaining explanatory part is attributed to the unknown idiosyncratic factor, ε. Henceforth, when we refer to the R^2 we will mean the standardized model R^2.

Calibration of Multifactor Models   The expression of the multifactor model in terms of R^2 such that

$$\hat{Z}_i = \phi_i \left(\sum_{j=1}^{N} \beta_{ij} Z_j \right) + \sqrt{1 - R_i^2} \, \varepsilon_i$$

$$\phi_i = \sqrt{\frac{R_i^2}{\beta\Sigma\beta'}}$$

is convenient for expert-based calibration of the firm parameters (β, λ). However, β and λ can also be statistically calibrated based on time series of approximate asset returns, $\tilde{Z}_i$, for firm i. Two approaches are generally used:

1. Calibration to asset values or approximate asset values.

    For example, Dullman, Scheicher, and Schmieder (2007) use monthly time series of Moody's KMV produced approximate asset values (inferred from the Merton model from equity prices, see equation (4.9)) to estimate single and multifactor sector models for about 2,000 European firms returns. They find substantial variation in asset correlations over time, suggesting that at least the model covariance matrix between credit factors, Σ, should be regularly updated.
2. Another, simpler approach, is to use directly the equity returns as proxy for asset values.

    For example, Mashal et al. (2003) find that the dependence of equity and inferred asset returns is similar. Using equity returns directly as $\tilde{Z}_i$ in model calibration clearly simplifies the regression analysis, as market observed equity returns can be regressed on several credit factors to find the best fit.

Simulation of Multifactor Models   Having obtained the model parameters for the firms credit index we can now easily construct a firm scenario for $\hat{Z}$ by joint simulation of the return factors $\mathbf{Z}$ as well as an independent normal factor, ε. Finally, using equation (4.22) we obtain the realized firm credit index, $\hat{Z}$. The obtained $\hat{Z}$ then needs to be compared with the ratings thresholds implied by the transition matrix to determine the firm rating in the scenario.

Note that in this model (assuming a multivariate normal distribution and hence a normal copula between firm returns), the firms credit quality correlation (and hence default and migration correlation) is completely driven by the correlation between the firms factors and the firm factor parameters. Specifically, for two firms with factor models

$$\hat{Z}_1 = \phi_1 \left(\sum_{j=1}^{N} \beta_{1j} Z_j \right) + \sqrt{1 - R_1^2} \varepsilon_1$$

$$\hat{Z}_2 = \phi_2 \left(\sum_{j=1}^{N} \beta_{2j} Z_j \right) + \sqrt{1 - R_2^2} \varepsilon_2$$

we obtain, since the idiosyncratic components are independent,

$$\text{COV}(\hat{Z}_1, \hat{Z}_2) = \text{COV} \left(\phi_1 \left(\sum_{j=1}^{N} \beta_{1j} Z_j \right), \phi_2 \left(\sum_{j=1}^{N} \beta_{2j} Z_j \right) \right) = \phi_1 \phi_2 \beta_1 \Sigma \beta_2'. \tag{4.25}$$

Application of the Multifactor Models We now consider an extensive application of the multifactor model in a dynamic setting where credit portfolio loss is path dependent across horizons. The path dependency of credit loss implies that the rating is made path dependent across horizons. That is, next horizon starts with the previous horizons rating and once a default has occurred at a certain horizon the firm remains in default as the default state is absorbing.

Our sample portfolio is composed of 8 bond-issuing firms where each firm has a current rating in the rating categories A1 to A9, A1 being the highest quality rating grade and A9 the lowest quality rating grade. Table 4.11 displays the 8 firms in the portfolio and their current rating.

Each firm has a monthly horizon multifactor model describing its asset returns. The multifactor models for the 8 firms (see equation (4.21)) describes the dynamics of the firms asset returns, $\{\tilde{Z}_i\}_{i=1}^8$, and depends on $\{Z_i\}_{i=1}^{18}$ normal credit factors. The specific asset returns models for the 8 firms hence use $\mathbf{Z} = (Z_1, \ldots, Z_{18})$ unique credit factors that we for now assume are distributed as multivariate normal. That is, $\mathbf{Z} \sim N(\mathbf{0}, \Sigma)$.

Focusing on the specific sample multifactor models for the firms, we have that firm 1:s multifactor model uses the same parameters as our numerical example above and is given by

$$\tilde{Z}_1 = 0.62 \times Z_1 + 0.33 \times Z_2 + 0.03 \times Z_3 + 0.02 \times Z_4 + 0.89 \times \varepsilon_1$$

TABLE 4.11 Firms' Ratings

Firm	Rating
1	A6
2	A4
3	A6
4	A2
5	A7
6	A5
7	A4
8	A5

such that its exposure is mainly to the credit factors Z_1 and Z_2 with minimal exposure to credit factors Z_3 and Z_4. The explained portion of the model is

$$R_1^2 = 1 - \lambda_1^2 = 0.2079.$$

Firms 2, 3, and 4 multifactor models use only two factors and are described by

$$\widetilde{Z}_2 = 0.67 \times Z_5 + 0.33 \times Z_2 + 0.89 \times \varepsilon_2,$$
$$\widetilde{Z}_3 = 0.67 \times Z_6 + 0.33 \times Z_7 + 0.89 \times \varepsilon_3,$$
$$\widetilde{Z}_4 = 0.67 \times Z_8 + 0.33 \times Z_9 + 0.77 \times \varepsilon_4.$$

Hence, for firms 2, 3, and 4, two thirds of the exposure is attributed to a single credit factor. The explained portion of the model for firms 2 and 3 is the same as for firm 1 while firm 4 explained portion of the model is higher with $R_4^2 = 0.4071$. This is because firm 4 has a lower idiosyncratic λ parameter, λ_4.

Firm 5 has a 5-factor model that is given by

$$\widetilde{Z}_5 = 0.33 \times Z_{10} + 0.30 \times Z_{11} + 0.22 \times Z_{12} + 0.09 \times Z_{13} + 0.06 \times Z_{14} + 0.89 \times \varepsilon_5$$

with main exposure to 3 factors, Z_{10}, Z_{11}, and, Z_{12}. The model R^2 is 0.2079 as for firms 1, 2, and 3.

Firm 6 has a 7-factor model given by

$$\widetilde{Z}_6 = 0.33 \times Z_{10} + 0.30 \times Z_4 + 0.212 \times Z_3 + 0.092 \times Z_{15} + 0.033 \times Z_{12}$$
$$+ 0.023 \times Z_{14} + 0.01 \times Z_{16} + 0.89 \times \varepsilon_6.$$

However, main exposure is just toward 3 factors as for firm 5. Firm 6 also has the same model R^2 as firm 5.

Finally, for firm 7 and 8 we have respectively a 4-factor and a 7-factor model given by

$$\widetilde{Z}_7 = 0.33 \times Z_{10} + 0.323 \times Z_4 + 0.19 \times Z_3 + 0.157 \times Z_{15} + 0.89 \times \varepsilon_7$$

and

$$\widetilde{Z}_8 = 0.33 \times Z_{10} + 0.23 \times Z_{11} + 0.165 \times Z_{13} + 0.095 \times Z_{17} + 0.085 \times Z_4$$
$$+ 0.06 \times Z_3 + 0.035 \times Z_{18} + 0.89 \times \varepsilon_8.$$

Both models, R^2 is 0.2079, as is the case for all firms except firm 4, which has a higher R^2 of 0.4071.

Our next step is to specify the distribution parameters for the credit factors, $\mathbf{Z} = (Z_1, \ldots, Z_{18})$, that drive systematic risk in the $1, \ldots, 8$ firms asset returns. Recall that we assumed a multivariate normal distribution with $\mathbf{Z} \sim N(\mathbf{0}, \boldsymbol{\Sigma})$. Each $\{Z_i\}_{i=1}^{18}$ has a monthly standard deviation that is displayed in Table 4.12. The credit factors, $\mathbf{Z} = (Z_1, \ldots, Z_{18})$, corresponding correlation matrix is given in Table 4.13. Note that we only display numbers for the upper triangular part of the correlation matrix in Table 4.13 as correlation matrices are symmetric.

TABLE 4.12 Credit Factors Monthly Returns Standard Deviation

Credit factor	Standard deviation
1	0.0785
2	0.0848
3	0.0497
4	0.0696
5	0.0346
6	0.0762
7	0.0726
8	0.1088
9	0.0888
10	0.0569
11	0.0688
12	0.0647
13	0.0602
14	0.0510
15	0.0565
16	0.0558
17	0.0860
18	0.0738

TABLE 4.13 Credit Factors Monthly Asset Returns Correlation Matrix

	2	3	4	5	6	7	8	9	10	11	12	13	14	15	16	17	18
1	0.54	0.74	0.72	0.51	0.80	0.76	0.68	0.76	0.71	0.78	0.62	0.79	0.67	0.61	0.55	0.70	0.99
2		0.69	0.69	0.47	0.62	0.74	0.56	0.63	0.78	0.66	0.65	0.65	0.61	0.62	0.54	0.62	0.58
3			0.87	0.67	0.78	0.78	0.56	0.63	0.78	0.83	0.80	0.81	0.89	0.95	0.83	0.82	0.75
4				0.58	0.77	0.84	0.54	0.67	0.87	0.88	0.78	0.77	0.79	0.78	0.73	0.72	0.72
5					0.44	0.43	0.39	0.51	0.57	0.56	0.50	0.55	0.58	0.61	0.50	0.53	0.52
6						0.85	0.62	0.75	0.79	0.83	0.67	0.82	0.70	0.68	0.60	0.79	0.80
7							0.64	0.76	0.90	0.84	0.72	0.76	0.71	0.66	0.62	0.73	0.76
8								0.73	0.65	0.65	0.59	0.63	0.56	0.49	0.46	0.52	0.68
9									0.79	0.78	0.54	0.84	0.52	0.48	0.39	0.54	0.76
10										0.88	0.75	0.77	0.69	0.68	0.60	0.69	0.71
11											0.75	0.87	0.74	0.74	0.64	0.77	0.78
12												0.66	0.87	0.76	0.76	0.74	0.63
13													0.70	0.68	0.57	0.69	0.79
14														0.86	0.95	0.79	0.67
15															0.84	0.79	0.62
16																0.70	0.54
17																	0.70

Knowing the exact distribution of the credit factors, $\mathbf{Z} = (Z_1, \ldots, Z_{18})$, we now have all information needed to simulate equation (4.22) for each firm. We break down the process in steps:

1. First, we simulate each Z_i, $i = 1, \ldots, 18$ using a model as in equation (4.19). That is,

$$d\mathbf{Z}(t) = \sigma d\mathbf{W}(t)$$

where σ is the 18 by 18 square root matrix ($\sigma\sigma' = \Sigma$ the covariance matrix) that is obtained from Tables 4.12 and 4.13. The initial value of each $\{Z_i\}_{i=1}^{18}$ is zero with dependent increments in factor returns between horizons (see our discussion above on dependent versus independent firm returns).

2. Second, at each horizon and scenario we construct the normalized asset returns, $\hat{Z}_i$, using equation (4.22). We now have obtained the realized standard normal firm return that we can use to compare with the transition matrix thresholds to obtain a new rating.

3. Consequently, in step 3, we can either use the normal distribution transformation, $u_i = N(\hat{Z}_i)$, on the realized standardized firm return, $\hat{Z}_i$, to compare the uniform u_i with the uniform transition matrix thresholds. This will allow us to decide the new rating at the horizon. Equivalently, we can retain the realized standardized firm return, $\hat{Z}_i$, as normal and transform the transition matrix thresholds to normal instead.

In our example we will focus on risk at the horizons of 3, 6, 9, and 12 months. Hence, we need a 3-month transition matrix since the interval length between horizons is 3 months. The 3-month transition matrix we use is displayed in Table 4.14.

Having simulated the firms rating transitions using the realized standardized firm return, $\hat{Z}_i$, and the transition matrix thresholds we can now calculate portfolio profit and loss using the bond exposures for each firm. We assume that each firm can have multiple exposures (which all inherit their rating from the firm) and that all firm exposures are zero-coupon bonds with 5 years remaining to maturity.[12] For example, firm 1 has 3 zero-coupon bond exposures with currency notional amounts 50,000, 400,000, and 600,000. Each exposure also has a recovery rate. That is, recovery rates are assigned to exposure level rather than

TABLE 4.14 The 3-Month Transition Matrix for Rating Classes A1, ..., A9 and Default

Rating	A1	A2	A3	A4	A5	A6	A7	A8	A9	Default
A1	0.981076	0.01373	0.002432	0.002071	0.000628	0.000028	0.000014	0.000003	0.000001	0.000017
A2	0.000346	0.955995	0.02981	0.008782	0.003894	0.000572	0.000479	0.000089	0.000009	0.000024
A3	0.000166	0.002461	0.926368	0.05613	0.008105	0.004032	0.002067	0.00041	0.000236	0.000025
A4	0.000002	0.00046	0.010864	0.931403	0.039692	0.010823	0.00489	0.001245	0.000535	0.000086
A5	0.000036	0.000218	0.001883	0.029349	0.92279	0.030815	0.011152	0.002666	0.000676	0.000415
A6	0.000061	0.000081	0.000495	0.007339	0.031295	0.914282	0.035751	0.008994	0.000987	0.000715
A7	0.000001	0.000004	0.000428	0.003203	0.010665	0.03582	0.910908	0.029834	0.005681	0.003456
A8	0.000001	0.000003	0.000796	0.002731	0.006292	0.015428	0.044812	0.879731	0.024703	0.025503
A9	0	0.000001	0.000024	0.000138	0.002276	0.004656	0.020566	0.038688	0.856389	0.077262
Default	0	0	0	0	0	0	0	0	0	1

---

[12] We use relatively simple zero-coupon bond exposures here as illustration. In practice, one can think of the zero-coupon bond exposure as an approximation to the actual exposure.

TABLE 4.15   Firm Zero-Coupon Bond Exposures and Percent
Recovery Rates

Firm	Exposure	Notional amount	Recovery rate (%)
1	1	50,000	0
1	2	400,000	0
1	3	600,000	0
2	1	1,000,000	0
3	1	100,000	69
3	2	75,000	69
3	3	80,000	69
4	1	100,000	76
4	2	25,000	76
5	1	125,000	69
6	1	90,000	69
6	2	325,000	69
6	3	210,000	69
7	1	112,000	80
7	2	29,000	80
8	1	56,000	80
8	2	95,000	69
8	3	10,000	80
8	4	245,000	80

firm level. Table 4.15 displays the portfolio exposures and their assigned recovery rates in percent of the current value of the exposure.

In order to value the exposures we also need the zero coupon rates as well as the credit spread curves for the rating classes, $A1, \ldots, A9$. As our portfolio only consists of zero coupon bonds with 5 years to maturity and our maximum analysis horizon is 1 year we only need the zero and credit spread rates between years 4 and 5. For simplicity we specify the rates at years 4 and 5 only and use linear interpolation between the years for the 3, 6 and 9 month analysis horizons. The 4 and 5 year zero rates are given by 3.048% and 3.257%, respectively. The 4- and 5-year credit spread rates for rating category A1 is 2.915% and 3.121%. For other rating categories than A1, we use an upward scaling on the A1 rating category spreads. Specifically, rating category A2 spreads are scaled A1 category spreads by a factor of 1.2. We then use an incremental scaling of 0.2 for each additional rating downgrade such that for example rating category A9 has the A1 rating category spreads scaled by 2.6 yielding 4- and 5-year spread rates for rating category A9 as 7.579% and 8.1146%, respectively.

Having all the information about the firms exposures we can now proceed to step 4 in our process:

4. Given the realized ratings for firms in a given scenario and horizon, we compute bond value as the discounted value of the notional amount at the horizon using the zero coupon rates and appropriate risk spreads for the realized rating.

Here a specific credit exposure profit and loss is defined as the deviation between the value of the exposure holding fixed the initial rating versus the value of the exposure at the scenario rating. The calculation of the exposure-based value, holding fixed the initial rating, is done at each horizon as well as the value based on the scenario rating. Hence, at any time, the profit and loss measure based on the two exposure values is concentrated on credit migration profit and loss and not time effects such as portfolio aging.[13] With this definition of profit and loss, the loss, holding fixed the rating, may actually decrease across horizons. For example, consider a downgrade of a firm after 6 months. Holding fixed the firm's 6-month new rating at the 9-month horizon, the 6-month exposure loss is greater than the 9-month exposure loss. This is because the profit and loss difference, for a fixed rating, will decrease as time to maturity decreases. The opposite situation will occur for a firm that defaults at a horizon earlier than 12 months with cash recovery and no reinvestment or interest earned on the recovery amount. While the firm stays in default at all future horizons, the loss will grow over time as the base value, with no credit migration, will increase over horizons due to aging.

Once we have available exposure-level empirical profit and losses, we can perform the last step in our process. That is step 5.

5. Aggregate the empirical profit and losses at each horizons to portfolio and other levels such as firm level and compute risk measures such as VaR on the empirical profit and loss.

Table 4.16 displays the obtained portfolio VaR and CVaR risk metrics for horizons 3, 6, 9, and 12 months using 100,000 scenarios and a confidence level of 99%. In Table 4.16, we also display the mark to market (MtM) and the VaR and CVaR contributions (Cont VaR and Cont CVaR) as well as the incremental risk measures for VaR and CVaR (Inc VaR and Inc CVaR, respectively). Figure 4.4 also displays graphically the 99% VaR for the firms and the portfolio for the horizons of 3, 6, 9, and 12 months. We can notice several important points from Table 4.16.

- First, both on portfolio level and firm level there is generally a significantly higher CVaR than VaR. This is because there is in general a low probability of severe losses (less than 1%) and hence the tail loss contribution beyond the 99% significance level is substantial.
- Second, the individual firm CVaR and CVaR contributions seem to reflect fairly the relative differences in risks between firms.

For example, comparing the firm 1 and firm 2 CVaR contributions, at either of the horizons, which have similar exposures and the same exposure recovery rate of zero, we find that firm 1 has a larger CVaR contribution that we can attribute to the firm's lower rating. In contrast, the VaR contributions allocate a zero contribution to firm 1 and a non-zero contribution to firm 2 at all horizons. This VaR allocation is not consistent with the firms relative risk profiles and seems unintuitive. Indeed, as we have discussed previously, the empirical VaR contribution may not be a good estimate of portfolio risk contribution as it relies on a single realization. Since the CVaR risk contribution represents a realized average of tail losses it captures more information about the loss contributions in the tail.

- Third, incremental CVaR, at least for the longer horizons, match relatively well the CVaR contributions.[14] This is useful since (Euler) contributions can be seen as a local measure of risk contribution whereas the incremental measure is global. Note also that the incremental VaR measure seems to produce more intuitive results than the empirical VaR contribution. At least beyond the 3-month horizon.

---

[13]The profit and loss measure that takes as base value for all the horizons the initial market value of the bond contains profit and loss effects from both credit migration and portfolio aging.

[14]Although, at the 3-month horizon the incremental CVaR produces unintuitively negative results for firms 3, . . . , 8. The interpretation is that the portfolio is hedged by adding one of these firms.

TABLE 4.16 Firm Portfolio Risk Measures at Horizons 3, 6, 9, and 12 Months

Firm	MtM	VaR	CVaR	Cont VaR	Cont CVaR	Inc VaR	Inc CVaR
				3 months horizon			
1	652,796	38,183	366,805	0	70,253	9,514	61,578
2	661,783	38,551	71,253	56,999	44,173	18,816	18,207
3	214,729	4,087	33,561	0	5,354	0	-6,280
4	88,055	5,109	8,484	0	851	0	-2,854
5	75,324	2,240	11,821	0	1,553	0	-3,305
6	530,736	10,400	36,830	0	11,062	0	-575
7	93,311	5,436	9,039	0	948	0	-2,770
8	284,017	12,942	23,993	0	4,318	0	-6,590
Portfolio	2,600,752	56,999	138,782	56,999	138,872	56,999	138,872
				6 months horizon			
1	652,796	36,758	388,082	0	176,422	11,677	159,242
2	661,783	54,708	136,338	71,973	63,757	25,823	47,409
3	214,729	3,608	34,979	0	7,779	3,345	3,240
4	88,055	7,221	11,189	0	1,575	1,289	1,491
5	75,324	4,258	25,628	0	2,915	2,033	2,374
6	530,736	9,063	38,302	9,063	25,487	5,429	17,783
7	93,311	7,714	11,683	0	1,786	1,410	798
8	284,017	12,206	26,086	0	7,678	4,506	5,061
Portfolio	2,600,752	81,036	287,400	81,036	287,400	81,036	287,400
				9 months horizon			
1	652,796	35,206	404,830	0	338,132	36,327	305,920
2	661,783	52,243	168,215	35,267	97,124	32,768	86,652
3	214,729	3,118	39,128	0	8,340	11,682	5,176
4	88,055	6,869	11,062	0	2,012	2,237	1,966
5	75,324	25,724	28,224	4,087	3,519	5,588	2,980
6	530,736	11,484	101,532	7,693	46,871	21,540	27,566
7	93,311	7,366	11,950	2,518	2,249	2,578	2,205
8	284,017	16,967	48,264	70,694	8,733	11,944	6,357
Portfolio	2,600,752	120,258	506,979	120,258	506,979	120,258	506,979
				12 months horizon			
1	652,796	49,767	735,915	0	565,360	166,340	463,492
2	661,783	65,458	381,372	65,458	162,278	70,938	126,286
3	214,729	3,916	74,919	0	4,892	11,518	4,542
4	88,055	8,573	12,855	0	2,308	1,778	2,306
5	75,324	28,332	30,833	1,975	3,817	14,147	3,741
6	530,736	9,450	110,279	186,357	13,349	96,249	10,647
7	93,311	9,230	16,294	4,723	2,554	4,723	2,554
8	284,017	15,810	51,832	15,810	6,848	13,298	6,543
Portfolio	2,600,752	274,323	761,406	274,323	761,406	274,323	274,323

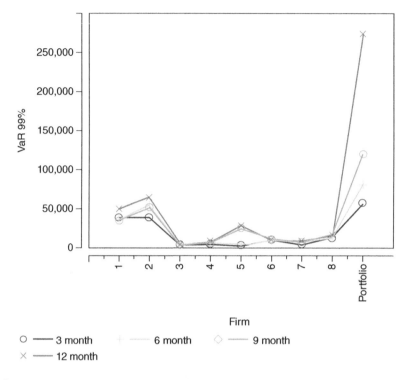

FIGURE 4.4 Firm Portfolio VaR at Horizons 3, 6, 9, and 12 Months

It is also interesting to decompose the portfolio risk factors. That is, the $\{Z_i\}_{i=1}^{18}$ normal credit factors, relative importance using their risk factor information measures. Indeed, it can be especially complex with many credit factors to understand which factors that are relatively more important in determining portfolio profit and loss.

Table 4.17 displays the 5 top risk factors according to the risk factor information measure (RFI) and their correlation (Corr) with portfolio profit and loss at the horizon of 12 months. The highest risk factor information measure is 0.09425 attributed to credit factor Z_{10} and hence there does not seem to be a single risk factor which is significantly more important than other risk factors. Many of the $\{Z_i\}_{i=1}^{18}$ risk factors have a similar risk factor information measures. This result complicates reverse stress testing for the portfolio as many risk factors can

TABLE 4.17 Risk Factor Information Measures for the Top 5 Ranked Credit Factors at the Horizon of 12 Months

Credit factor	RFI	Corr
Z_{10}	0.09425	0.278
Z_{11}	0.09104	0.273
Z_3	0.08876	0.274
Z_5	0.08837	0.269
Z_8	0.08565	0.271

contribute almost equally to portfolio loss. Hence, reverse stress testing for this portfolio can in general not focus on a significantly dimension reduced set of risk factors.

Extensions to the *t*-Copula We now continue the above example to examine the impact of a *t*-copula with tail dependence on the portfolio VaR and CVaR. That is, we assume the copula function in equation (4.24) is used to simulate correlated uniforms with the *t*-copula. Subsequently, the uniforms are transformed to normal marginal distributions such that we still have that each $Z_j \sim N(0, \sigma_j)$.

Considering the aggregate portfolio risk impact of using a *t*-copula Table 4.18 displays the portfolio 99% confidence level VaR and CVaR at the 12 month horizon using a *t*-copula with 3 degrees of freedom versus the normal copula we have implicitly used above.

We notice that the largest relative risk measure increase from using the *t*-copula is on the VaR risk measure. This can be explained by analyzing the empirical portfolio tail loss using the normal and the *t*-copula. For illustration, Figure 4.5 displays the portfolio credit loss tail, at the 12-month horizon, using the normal and t(3) copula for confidence levels 99% and

TABLE 4.18 VaR and CVaR at the 12-Month Horizon for the Portfolio with the Normal and the *t*-Copula with 3 Degrees of Freedom

Copula	VaR	CVaR
Normal	274,323	761,406
t(3)	738,303	940,309

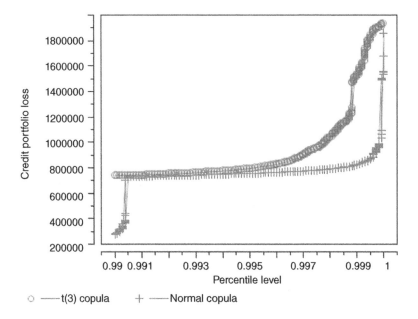

FIGURE 4.5 Credit Portfolio Loss Tail for the Normal and *t*(3) Copula for Confidence Levels 99% and Higher

higher. While the tail loss amounts for the $t(3)$ copula are higher than for the normal copula we note that for some confidence levels the normal and t(3) copula would give a similar VaR. For example, at the 99.1% to the 99.5% confidence level. In contrast, at the 99.9% confidence level there are significant differences in VaR.

The reader interested in further applications comparing the t- and normal copula for the multifactor credit risk models may consult Daul et al. (2003) who compare the grouped t-copula (which allows different degrees of freedoms for the credit factors) to the regular t-copula (that we used here with 3 degrees of freedom) and the normal copula.

Recovery   In our portfolio credit risk analysis so far we have taken bond exposure recovery rates as exogenously given rates. However, in the structural Merton model framework the recovery rate is explicit. See equation (4.12).

Several empirical studies have focused on estimating observed historical recovery rates dependence on core factors such as bond seniority and industry of bond issuer. For example, Altman and Kishore (1996) measure recovery rates from quoted defaultable bond prices. For traded bonds the recovery rate is usually measured as the quoted defaultable bond price rather than the ultimate recovery rate. The ultimate recovery rate is the realized (discounted) amount paid by the firm to the bondholders. More recently, Jankowitsch et al. (2014) analyze the determinants of US bond recovery rates between 2002 and 2010 (measured using quotable bond prices in default) and find that bond characteristics, firm fundamentals, macroeconomic variables and liquidity measures are key factors in explaining recovery rates. Both Altman and Kishore (1996) and Jankowitsch et al. (2014) find that average bond recovery rates are about 40% of bond face value, which is a numerical recovery value often used in practice.

Recovery and Macroeconomic Factors   There is also evidence for a general macroeconomic negative correlation between default rates and recovery rates such that recovery rates are at their lowest when default rates are high. See Altman et al. (2005). Altman et al. (2002), in a Basel working paper study, investigate the effect of different recovery models assumption on the credit portfolio risk as measured by VaR. Using a portfolio of 250 loans and a single common one factor model for the loans they compare three different recovery models:

1. A fixed recovery rate of 70%.
2. A stochastic recovery rate drawn from a truncated Beta distribution with mean 70% and with lower and upper bound 50% and 90%.[15]
3. A stochastic recovery rate drawn from a truncated Beta distribution where the common factor influences the recovery such that if the common factor indicates a strong recession then recovery rates take their minimum value of 50%. Similarly, if the common factor indicates a strong economy the recovery rates increase to 90%.

---

[15]The Beta distribution is often used for stochastic recovery rates as it is defined on the interval $[0, 1]$. The probability function is parametrized as

$$f(\alpha, \beta) = \frac{\Gamma(\alpha + \beta)}{\Gamma(\alpha)\,\Gamma(\beta)} y^{\alpha-1}(1 - y)^{\beta-1}$$

where $y \in [0, 1]$ is the revovery rate and $\Gamma(\cdot)$ is the Gamma function. The parameters, α and β, of the Beta function can be fitted to empirical recovery data using maximum likelihood.

Their results indicate that there is no significant difference between risk—as measured by VaR—when one moves from a fixed recovery rate (case 1) to a stochastic recovery rate that is independent of default rates (case 2).

This shows that even if the portfolio is relatively small with 250 loans the law of large numbers effectively ensures the aggregate portfolio level losses are similar. In contrast, the case with correlated default and recovery rates (case 3) yields significantly larger VaR than the other recovery models. Of course, this is not surprising as the correlated recovery and default rate model tends to generate more tail events where loss rates are higher. See also Rösch and Scheule (2005) who uses a multifactor model with negative correlation between default rates and recovery rates applied to Moody's global corporate default and recovery rates. The model is generalized by Hamerle et al. (2007) using a simultaneous model of probability of default and loss given default.

Double Default and the Factor Model   In addition to modeling outright recovery rates bond issues and corporate loans can also be hedged with credit products. The rise in trading volumes of credit-risky assets has caused a market need for credit derivatives to hedge counterparty defaults. Credit derivatives pay off based on events such as bankruptcy, failure of a payment obligation or downgrade. Several credit events are now standard definitions by International Swap and Derivatives Association (ISDA).

At the credit event the protection payer typically receives either a cash amount or a physical delivery of a market instrument (such as a non-defaulted bond). The most common credit derivative is the single-name credit default swap which protects the buyer against a specific counterparty default on a certain agreed notional amount. In return, the protection buyer pays a periodic premium to the protection seller. A protected exposure is hence lost only if both the issuer and the guarantor counterparty default. This is termed double-default.

Basel II (Basel Committee (2005b)) added a specific correlation based treatment of double default to the Basel II accord in response to the bank's concern on the adequacy of a simple substitution rule. Under the simple substitution rule, if the guarantor counterparty has a lower probability of default, it could be used in place of the issuer probability of default. The rule is simple because it assumes

(i) If the guarantor defaults, then the exposure counterparty should have already defaulted, but
(ii) If the exposure defaults, the guarantor would still have the same probability of default unconditionally.

Let E denote the exposure and G the guarantee protection then $P(E, G)$ is the joint default probability of the exposure and the guarantee. In the first situation, when the exposure and guarantor have very close credit quality, from

$$P(E|G) = \frac{P(E, G)}{P(G)}$$

then substitution rule implies that if $P(G) = 1$, then $P(E|G) = P(E, G) = 1$, which discourages banks to seek credit protection against the exposure of high credit quality. This is because it would be very costly to find a credit protection that has a lower probability of default that can effectively replace the probability of default of the exposure itself. On the other hand, when the exposure has a very poor credit quality, from $P(G|E) = \frac{P(E,G)}{P(E)}$, the substitution approach leads to $P(E) = 1$, and

$$P(G|E) = P(E, G) = P(G)$$

which ignores the situation that when the exposure defaults the guarantor may become more vulnerable.

Basel II credit risk capital requirements are based on a special case of the multifactor model—specifically, a one-factor model version of equation (4.22). Heitfield and Barger (2003) use the single-factor model and explain the difference between the substitution approach and the double-default approach. The double-default formula assumes a one-factor model for both the exposure and the guarantee counterparty. It results in an analytic formula based on the bivariate normal distribution. The model credit correlation, however, derives from two sources. First, the common systematic factor. The second source of correlation is introduced as a common factor in the idiosyncratic terms for the exposure and the guarantee counterparty. The double-default formula is consistent with the simple substitution rule when assets of the obligor and guarantor are perfectly correlated, they share the same exposure to the systematic risk factor, and, the recovery rate of the lowest credit quality counterparty is zero. Heitfield and Barger (2003) provide numerical examples to illustrate how the substitution approach compares to the double default formula.

In the context of the multifactor portfolio model we can easily model the double default case. Specifically, if an issuer exposure is hedged by a guarantor counterparty we can model the guarantor counterparty credit index model together with the issuer model and thereby capture default correlations between the issuer and the guarantor. For example, if issuer i has multifactor model

$$\widetilde{Z}_i = \sum_{j=1}^{N} \beta_{ij} Z_j + \lambda_i \varepsilon_i$$

and guarantor G has multifactor model

$$\widetilde{Z}_G = \sum_{j=1}^{N} \beta_{Gj} Z_j + \lambda_G \varepsilon_G$$

we can calculate the correlation between credit indices using equation (4.25).

Consistent with the Basel double-default formula we could also introduce a second source of correlation through a common factor in the idiosyncratic terms, ε_i, ε_G. For example, replace ε_i, ε_G by

$$\varepsilon_i = E\alpha + e_i \sqrt{1 - \alpha^2}$$

$$\varepsilon_G = E\alpha + e_G \sqrt{1 - \alpha^2}$$

where now e_i, e_G are the independent components and E is the common idiosyncratic component.

An Example Using Multifactor Models for Double Default We continue our example on the dynamic multifactor model focusing only on firm 2 in Table 4.15 with its single exposure of 1,000,000 units of currency and a recovery rate of zero. We introduce a guarantor counterparty that guarantees a notional recovery of 900,000 in case firm 2 defaults. In the example below, we will assume that all issuer and guarantor credit correlations derives from the common systematic factors. Hence, there is no common factor in the idiosyncratic terms.[16]

In our example, firm 2 keeps its current multifactor model such that

$$\widetilde{Z}_2 = 0.67 \times Z_5 + 0.33 \times Z_2 + 0.89 \times \varepsilon_2$$

while the new multifactor model for the guarantor, $\widetilde{Z}_G$, is

$$\widetilde{Z}_G = 0.57 \times Z_{G1} + 0.33 \times Z_2 + 0.05 \times Z_{G2} + 0.05 \times Z_{14} + 0.90 \times \varepsilon_G$$

where Z_2 and Z_{14} have already been used in our example above and Z_2 is a common factor for firm 2 and the guarantor. The guarantor also has two new factors, Z_{G1} and Z_{G2}.

The credit factors monthly standard deviation is given in Table 4.19 while Table 4.20 displays the correlation between the credit factors used here. Note that, as before, we only display numbers for the upper triangular part of the correlation matrix in Table 4.20 as correlation matrices are symmetric.

Clearly, all else equal, the stronger the correlation between the firm 2 and the guarantor credit indices the stronger is the default correlation between firm 2 and the guarantor. This is essentially the situation that the Basel double-default treatment wants to capture. When a protection has strong positive correlation with the exposure, a wrong-way risk type of situation arises. We know from Table 4.11 that firm 2 is rated in category A4 and we also assume that the guarantor is currently rated in category A4. Hence, we assume that the guarantor has

TABLE 4.19 Credit Factors Monthly Returns Standard Deviation

Credit factor	Standard deviation
2	0.0848
5	0.0346
14	0.0510
G1	0.0648
G2	0.0620

TABLE 4.20 Credit Factors Monthly Returns Correlation Matrix

Credit factor	5	14	G1	G2
2	0.47	0.61	0.39	0.53
5		0.58	0.48	0.50
14			0.35	0.71
G1				0.52

---

[16]In the Basel double-default formula this case reduces the capital charge to the product of capital charges for the unhedged exposures.

TABLE 4.21 Firm 2 Hedged and
Unhedged Risk Measures at Horisons 3,
6, 9, and 12 Months

Case	VaR	CVaR
	3 months horizon	
Unhedged	38,551	71,253
Hedged	38,551	63,513
	6 months horizon	
Unhedged	54,708	136,338
Hedged	54,708	77,261
	9 months horizon	
Unhedged	52,243	168,215
Hedged	52,243	74,703
	12 months horizon	
Unhedged	65,458	381,372
Hedged	49,662	72,075

the same current rating as firm 2. Of course, this means that if we were following a simple Basel substitution approach in this case the guarantee would have no value. We now compute the 3 months, 6 months, 9 months, and 12 months horizon VaR and CVaR risk at the 99% confidence level—with and without firm 2's exposure being hedged by the guarantee. We can of course obtain the case when firm 2's exposure is unhedged directly from Table 4.16 and Table 4.21 displays the case when firm 2's exposure is hedged compared with the unhedged case.

While there is no effect on VaR until the final horizon of 12 months (due to the fact that there is not enough amounts of firm 2 defaults and hence not enough significant recoveries due to the guarantee) we notice that there is an effect on CVaR at all horizons. The effect is more significant the longer the risk horizon. For example, at the 12-month horizon hedged CVaR, at the 99% confidence level, is less than 19% of the unhedged CVaR. Clearly, at this confidence level a joint default of firm 2 and the guarantor becomes more unlikely. However, if we compare the hedged and unhedged CVaR at a higher confidence level of 99.9% we find a less substantial risk reduction (not shown in Table 4.21). Specifically, at the 99.9% confidence level the 12-months horizon unhedged and hedged CVaR are both 734,364, yielding no hedge reduction. At this high confidence level, the tail events include the double default case.

The above example shows that the portfolio risk accredited value of default protection depends heavily on the choice of risk measure, as well as on the confidence level for a given model. Another important factor is, of course, also the joint default probability or the default correlation. As we have seen previously, using a t-copula for joint defaults with a low degrees of freedom can significantly impact the risk measure due to more frequent joint defaults. While using a t-copula with low degrees of freedom between factors, $(Z_1, \ldots, Z_N)$, can increase the dependence of firms i and j factors $\hat{Z}_i$ and $\hat{Z}_j$ and hence joint default probability the probability of joint default also depends on the factor loadings through β.

Probability of Joint Defaults and Default Correlation in the Multifactor Model The multifactor model expresses dependence between firms default probability indirectly through the factor correlations. Intuitively, the higher the correlation between two firms factor models the higher the default correlation. Following Schönbucher (2000) the joint default probability between firms A and B, p_{AB}, is

$$p_{AB} = p_A p_B + \rho \sqrt{p_A(1 - p_A)p_B(1 - p_B)}$$

where p_A and p_B are the individual default probabilities of firm A and B respectively and ρ is the default correlation between firm A and B.[17] Similarly, the conditional default probability of firm A defaulting conditional on a firm B default, $p_{A|B}$, is

$$p_{A|B} = p_A + \rho \sqrt{\frac{p_A}{p_B}(1 - p_A)(1 - p_B)}.$$

Hence, if $p_A = p_B = 0.5\%$ and $\rho = 20\%$ then

$$p_{AB} = 0.1\,02\%.$$

$$p_{A|B} = 20.4\%.$$

We note here that $p_{A|B}$ is almost invariant to the individual default probabilities of firm A and B. Specifically, if $p_A = p_B = 0.05\%$ then $p_{A|B} = 20.04\%$, and, if $p_A = p_B = 5\%$ then $p_{A|B} = 24\%$.

In principle, one could consider a credit risk model where one would specify the default correlation directly between firms. However, it is in practice more convenient to work with multifactor models that implicitly specify default correlations using the factor correlations and factor model parameters. However, in general, default correlations implied from multifactor models are much lower than the actual correlations between the multifactor models (see equation (4.25)). It is also in general the case that the more the number of factors that are used in multifactor models, the more diluted becomes the correlation between multifactor models and hence the default correlation. This is because the factors are usually less than perfectly correlated and increasing the number of factors therefore contributes to diluting the correlation. We refer to Schönbucher (2000) for a detailed account on default correlations in factor models for portfolio credit risk.

Firm Pooling and the Conditional Law of Large Numbers Until now, we have focused on modeling the credit index for specific firms. However, sometimes there are enough firms (or bonds and loans if the model is applied on that level) such that one can create approximately homogenous pools. When the multifactor model is applied to a set of firms that are homogeneous with respect to (i) current rating, and (ii) the multifactor model (which drives migration and default), one can consider using an approximation method to derive the pools empirical transition and default frequencies—conditional on the credit factors, $\{Z\}$.

---

[17]Specifically, ρ is the correlation between the default events for firms A and B.

Finger (1999) considers, in the context of a one-factor model and a default only assumption with no migration, three different approaches to derive an approximation to the full credit loss distribution:

- First, the law of large numbers to derive a simple, conditional on the single factor, credit loss distribution that can be integrated explicitly
- Second, an approximation to the credit portfolio loss distribution using the central limit theorem and numerical integration
- Third, using the moment generating function

All these approaches rely on a conditional independence assumption such that conditional on the firms factors, $\{Z\}$, the firms are independent since we have assumed independence of the firms idiosyncratic factors, $\{\varepsilon\}$. See equation (4.23) for the conditional default probability of a firm.

While direct approximations to credit losses are also useful in practice we will focus here instead on an approximation approach based on the conditional law of large numbers that can be applied in a general simulation context. In particular, firms can still maintain idiosyncratic and general (stochastic) properties for exposure and recovery models. That is, we focus on the case when the law of large numbers approximation is only applied to a set of firms migration and default process. The approach is similar to Lucas et al. (1999) (see also Schönbucher, 2000) although we do not attempt an approximation for the final credit loss distribution and instead focus on the approximation of credit migration frequencies only.

In practice this approach may be more useful because homogeneity of firms credit migration and default model is much less restrictive than having to assume homogeneity also in exposure and recovery for the firms. It is also the case that many models that try to approximate credit portfolio loss models loss distributions cannot incorporate general idiosyncratic and stochastic models for exposure and recovery.

To introduce the firm pool approximation model we let there be $l = 1, \ldots, L$ firms in a pool. The L firms are assumed to have the same initial rating and a common multifactor model, such that their standardized returns are,

$$\widehat{Z}_1 = \phi_1 \left(\sum_{j=1}^{N} \beta_j Z_j \right) + \sqrt{1 - R^2} \varepsilon_1$$

$$\ldots$$

$$\widehat{Z}_L = \phi_1 \left(\sum_{j=1}^{N} \beta_j Z_j \right) + \sqrt{1 - R^2} \varepsilon_L.$$

Hence, the $l = 1, \ldots, L$ firms have common multifactor parameters, $\{\beta\}$ but different idiosyncratic factors, $\{\varepsilon_1, \ldots, \varepsilon_L\}$.

Let $B_{1t}, \ldots, B_{\widehat{K}t}$ be the indicator which takes the value 1 if the firm is in rating class $k = 1, \ldots, \widehat{K}$ at time $t, t = 1, \ldots, T$. For different classes of rating categories we have $\widehat{K}$ distinct transition probabilities to the $\widehat{K}$ classes; that is, if a firm belongs to class k, we have p_{k1}, $p_{k2}, \ldots, p_{k\widehat{K}}$ transition probabilities. As we have explained previously the $\widehat{K}$ thresholds are obtained from the transition probabilities and the realized rating is determined by the realized return from the standardized multifactor model and the thresholds. In the following we will assume rating thresholds are denoted by I_{kt} and that rating classes are ordered such that rating class 1 is the highest quality grade and class $\widehat{K}$ is the lowest quality grade. For example, we can think of grade 1 as being the AAA grade and the grade $\widehat{K}$ as being the default grade in the Standard and Poor's rating scale. The reader is referred to Figure 4.2 and Table 4.5, which illustrates the decomposition of the thresholds for a firm rated BBB using the Standard and Poor's rating grade scale.

We can now write for firm l, assuming that the threshold for firm l to migrate to above class 2 (hence to class 1) is $I_{2t} < \infty$,

$$P(B_{1t} = 1) = P(\widehat{Z}_l > I_{2t}) = 1 - P\left(\varepsilon_l \leq \frac{I_{2t} - \phi_1\left(\sum_{j=1}^{N} \beta_j Z_j\right)}{\sqrt{1 - R^2}}\right)$$

where the probability is conditional on $\{\mathbf{Z}\}$ and $\lambda = \sqrt{1 - R^2}$. Similarly, for firm l to migrate to any of the $k = 2, \ldots, \widehat{K} - 1$ rating classes we can write

$$P(B_{kt} = 1) = P(I_{k+1t} \leq \widehat{Z}_l \leq I_{kt}) \tag{4.26}$$

$$= P\left(\varepsilon_L \leq \frac{I_{kt} - \phi_1\left(\sum_{j=1}^{N} \beta_j Z_j\right)}{\sqrt{1 - R^2}}\right) - P\left(\varepsilon_L \leq \frac{I_{k+1t} - \phi_1\left(\sum_{j=1}^{N} \beta_j Z_j\right)}{\sqrt{1 - R^2}}\right).$$

Finally, for rating class $\widehat{K}$ we obtain

$$P(B_{\widehat{K}t} = 1) = P(\widehat{Z}_l < I_{\widehat{K}t}) = P\left(\varepsilon_l \leq \frac{I_{\widehat{K}t} - \phi_1\left(\sum_{j=1}^{N} \beta_j Z_j\right)}{\sqrt{1 - R^2}}\right).$$

We note that this corresponds to an ordered Probit model (see Amemiya, 1985, ch. 7) and that each transition probability is a marginal transition probability. Of course, the rating thresholds $\{I_{kt}\}_{k=1}^{\widehat{K}}$ are dependent on the current rating, k, and typically induced using the normal distribution transformation of the marginal transition probabilities to rating classes $k = 1, \ldots, \widehat{K}$.

If the number of firms $l = 1, \ldots, L$ in the pool is large we can apply a conditional law of large numbers such that the expected fraction of firms that belong to rating class $k = 1, \ldots, \widehat{K}$ at time $t = 1$ is

$$E[(B_{kt}|\mathbf{Z})] = N\left(\frac{I_{kt} - \phi_1\left(\sum_{j=1}^{N} \beta_j Z_j\right)}{\sqrt{1 - R^2}}\right) - N\left(\frac{I_{k+1t} - \phi_1\left(\sum_{j=1}^{N} \beta_j Z_j\right)}{\sqrt{1 - R^2}}\right) \tag{4.27}$$

conditional on a realization of $\{\mathbf{Z}\}$ where N is the cumulative normal distribution and $I_{1t} = +\infty$, $I_{\widehat{K}+1t} = -\infty$.

Essentially, for each realization of $\{\mathbf{Z}\}$ we obtain a vector $\{B_{kt}\}_{k=1}^{\widehat{K}}$ with the expected realized rating fractions $[0,1]$ for each of the possible $k = 1, \ldots, \widehat{K}$ classes. Clearly, $\sum_{k=1}^{\widehat{K}}$

$B_{kt} = 1$. Once this vector is obtained, we can of course value a set of exposures for, say, firm l by using the rating fractions, $\{B_{kt}\}_{k=1}^{\widehat{K}}$. Specifically, if $\mathbf{B}_t$ is such a realized vector and $\{V_t^l\}$ is a $\widehat{K}$-dimensional vector with market values for firm l for all the $k = 1,\ldots,\widehat{K}$ rating categories, then we can write total market value for firm l, say π_l, as

$$\pi_l = \sum_{k=1}^{\widehat{K}} B_{kt} \times V_{kt}^l.$$

In practice, the difference for different $\{V_{kt}^l\}_{k=1}^{\widehat{K}}$ will be due to credit spreads associated with the different ratings, $k = 1,\ldots,\widehat{K} - 1$. Of course, for rating class $\widehat{K}$, $V_{\widehat{K}t}^l$, represents the recovery value in the event of default.

Now, at time $t = 2$ our starting point is the vector $\{B_{k1}\}_{k=1}^{\widehat{K}}$. This vector will in general have $\widehat{K}$ non-zero elements. Hence, in order to compute migrations at $t = 2$ we need to calculate all the transition probabilities from the current rating fractions (at $t = 1$), $k = 1,\ldots,\widehat{K} - 1$, migrating to either of the ratings $k = 1,\ldots,\widehat{K}$ (at $t = 2$). Conditional on $\{\mathbf{Z}\}$ we therefore obtain a $\widehat{K} - 1 \times \widehat{K}$ dimensional transition matrix, $\mathbf{A}(t) = \{A_{k\widetilde{k}}(t)\}$ where $k = 1,\ldots,\widehat{K} - 1$ and $\widetilde{k} = 1,\ldots,\widehat{K}$.

Let $\widetilde{\mathbf{A}}(t)$ be the $\widehat{K} \times \widehat{K}$ matrix that is defined by adding a $\widehat{K}$:th row of zeros for the $\widehat{K} - 1$ columns and unity for the $\widehat{K}$:th column. That is,

$$\widetilde{\mathbf{A}}(t) = \begin{bmatrix} A_{11}(t) & \cdots & A_{1\widehat{K}}(t) \\ \vdots & \cdots & \vdots \\ A_{\widehat{K}-11}(t) & \cdots & A_{\widehat{K}-1\widehat{K}}(t) \\ 0 & \cdots & 1 \end{bmatrix}$$

with the transition probability from state k to state $\widetilde{k}$ being

$$A_{k\widetilde{k}}(t) = N\left(\frac{I_{k\widetilde{k}t} - \phi_1\left(\sum_{j=1}^N \beta_j Z_j\right)}{\sqrt{1 - R^2}}\right) - N\left(\frac{I_{k\widetilde{k}+1t} - \phi_1\left(\sum_{j=1}^N \beta_j Z_j\right)}{\sqrt{1 - R^2}}\right) \quad (4.28)$$

where we have explicitly indicated in equation (4.28) that the transition probability rating thresholds, $I_{k\widetilde{k}t}$, depends on both the from and to state with $I_{k\widetilde{k}t}$ being the normalized threshold for a firm currently in state k migrating to state $\widetilde{k}$. With this matrix defined we can now compute the expected rating fractions at $t = 2$ using a first-order Markov Chain. Specifically,

$$\mathbf{B}_2 = \left[\widetilde{\mathbf{A}}(2)\right]'\mathbf{B}_1$$

such that we, conditional on $\{\mathbf{Z}\}$, obtain the expected rating fractions at $t = 2$. It is now clear that with the above algorithm we can apply, in general for any $t = 1,\ldots,T$,

$$\mathbf{B}_{t+1} = \left[\widetilde{\mathbf{A}}(t+1)\right]'\mathbf{B}_t. \quad (4.29)$$

This gives us the $t + 1$ current expected rating fractions conditional on a realization of $\{\mathbf{Z}\}$.

It is important to understand that with this algorithm we have reduced the computational burden of credit migration for a pool of $l = 1, \ldots, L$ firms that are homogeneous with respect to current rating and the multifactor model to the computational burden of a single firm. Again, we have not assumed any homogeneity in either exposure or recovery models. In this setting a homogeneous pool can safely maintain specific exposure and recovery models for its members. But, of course, applying a homogeneity assumption of exposure has the potential to reduce calculation time further if the exposure valuation is time consuming. For example, we could decompose the $l = 1, \ldots, L$ firms into further subclasses with sub-homogeneous exposure valuation and recovery models.

A Note on the Pools Based Multifactor Model and Large Loan and Retail Portfolios When the multifactor model is applied to large firms, as we have focused on here, the credit index $\widetilde{Z}$ in equation (4.21) is often referred to as a latent variable. This is because it is in general unobserved but can be inferred from the multifactor model itself. In practice, the firm credit index $\widetilde{Z}$ can be approximated by equity or inferred asset values for calibration of multifactor models. Alternatively, expert calibration can be used.

In the large homogenous pool setting of the multifactor model, it is also applicable more generally to large loan and retail portfolios. The major reason for this is that with a large portfolio we can now identify the previously unobserved credit index with the (transformed) historical empirical default frequencies of the large homogenous portfolio. Specifically, we can transform the historical default frequencies, $p(t)$, to a normal distribution and use the transformed series, $N^{-1}(p(t))$, as our definition of the credit index, $\widetilde{Z}$. Clearly, the credit index is no longer unobserved and we can use the actual credit default index $\widetilde{Z}$ in direct calibration of equation (4.21). The economic factors, $\{Z\}$, can for example be macroeconomic factors such as unemployment rates and GDP deviations from trend.

As the reader realizes, in this large pool setting, the multifactor model is now similar to a traditional credit scoring model with macroeconomic factors calibrated on the basis of observed default frequencies. The only difference is that we have transformed the model into normal rather than using directly a credit score model defined on the range of default probabilities $[0, 1]$, such as a Probit model. However, as we have seen above, for pools, the conditional transition probabilities (on Z) are described by an ordered Probit model. The model is hence now transformed into a dynamic credit score model (or, more generally, a dynamic transition matrix model). Consequently, with a different calibration interpretation, the model is now equally applicable to retail portfolios. We will return to discussing appropriate credit models for large loan and retail portfolios in the section on credit models for the banking book.

Markov View and Stress Testing of Credit Migration The Markov iteration algorithm in equation (4.29) computes the expected transition probabilities (conditional on a single realization of $\{Z\}$) for each possible state $k = 1, \ldots, \widehat{K}$ for each time $t = 1, \ldots, T$. Clearly, this is not only useful for credit pools approximations. It is also useful for economic scenario stress testing at bond or loan level. This is because by using the iteration equation (4.29) we obtain the pathwise expected rating transitions of the firm, loan or bond for a given scenario of the firms factors, $\{Z\}_{t=1}^{T}$. Specifically, the random sampling of R state transition paths, for a given $\{Z(t)\}_{t=1}^{T}$ economic scenario, and the subsequent calculation of expected state frequencies at times $t = 1, \ldots, T$ converges to the Markov iteration state frequencies, $\{B_t\}_{t=1}^{T}$, in equation (4.29) as R grows large. Specifically, let there be R, $\widehat{K}$-dimensional state transition indicators, $\{\mathbf{d}^r(t)\}_{r=1}^R$, that records unity at the realized state position at $t = 1, \ldots, T$ for each of the $r = 1, \ldots, R$ simulated state transition paths. Then

$$\mathbf{x}^R(t) = \left(\frac{1}{R} \sum_{r=1}^{R} \mathbf{d}^r(t) \right)$$

represents the estimated fraction of the firm in state $k = 1, \ldots, \widehat{K}$ at time t using the R state transition samples conditional on the economic scenario, $\{\mathbf{Z}(t)\}_{t=1}^T$. The collection, $\{\mathbf{x}^R(t)\}_{t=1}^T$, hence records the estimated state transition fractions at each time $t = 1, \ldots, T$. The Markov iteration equation (4.29) can now be understood as giving the case of

$$\mathbf{B}_t = \lim_{R \to \infty} \mathbf{x}^R(t)$$

conditional on the scenario $\{\mathbf{Z}(t)\}_{t=1}^T$. Hence, we can obtain the expected loss in an economic stress scenario *without* sampling. The reason that we obtain this relatively simple representation of the Markov iteration in this case is due to the fact that the transition probabilities depend only on time, through the realization of $\{\mathbf{Z}\}$ as in equation (4.27), and not on past state transition history. This type of model is referred to as a time inhomogeneous (non-stationary) Markov state transition model and leads to the simple state occupancy probabilities in equation (4.29). See Lancaster (1990, p. 116). Another important feature of the Markov state transition model in equation (4.29) is that it is homogeneous for firms with the same multifactor model. That is, the $\widehat{K} \times \widehat{K}$ matrix $\widetilde{\mathbf{A}}(t)$ is common, which enabled the relatively simple Markov approximation for pools. We will apply the pool Markov iteration feature of the model below, and, later in this chapter when we perform multi-horizon credit risk stress testing for the multifactor model we will use the Markov iteration again, avoiding expensive sampling of expected state transitions conditional on a given macroeconomic scenario, $\{\mathbf{Z}(t)\}_{t=1}^T$.

Expanding the Multifactor Model Example to Pools   We now extend the dynamic multifactor model example above by introducing pools in the portfolio in addition to the 8 firms in Table 4.11.[18] Specifically, the portfolio is enriched with 10 pools for which their current rating and pool sizes are listed in Table 4.22. While a homogeneous zero-coupon bond exposure per pool is not necessary in this model, we still assume in this example that the pools are also homogeneous with respect to exposure and recovery. The pool zero-coupon bond exposures aggregate notional amounts and recovery rates in % are also displayed in Table 4.22. As for the original firm's portfolio, all zero coupon bond exposures have a maturity of 5 years. The assumptions about valuation of the exposures, for a given rating fraction of the pool, is the same as in the previous examples on the dynamic multifactor model. Hence, we re-use the zero rates and the credit spreads we had in the firms case for this example.

---

[18]Recall that for pools we can interpret the credit index $\widetilde{Z}$ as the pool (transformed) default rates. Hence, with this interpretation the multifactor model can be used for all the retail credit risk exposures as well. In fact, this is a quite common approach for banks to implement their firmwide portfolio credit risk model.

TABLE 4.22 Pool Ratings, Size, and Exposures

Pool	Rating	Pool size	Notional amount	Recovery rate (%)
1	A7	1738	50,000,000	68
2	A7	3258	40,000,000	74
3	A4	539	7,000,000	78
4	A7	1828	120,000,000	72
5	A6	652	90,000,000	70
6	A4	47	15,000,000	69
7	A7	62	39,000,000	54
8	A7	312	27,000,000	70
9	A1	122	15,000,000	89
10	A7	85	12,000,000	70

The monthly multifactor models for the 10 pools, $\{\tilde{Z}^p_i\}_{i=1}^{10}$, depends on the $\{Z_i\}_{i=1}^{18}$ normal credit factors already used for the firms. We keep the pool multifactor models simple and set for each pool $m = 1, \ldots, 10$ the multifactor model as

$$\tilde{Z}^p_{m,l} = 0.67 \times Z_1 + 0.33 \times Z_2 + 0.92 \times \varepsilon^p_{m,l}. \tag{4.30}$$

Here, $l = 1, \ldots, L_m$. Hence, the pools share a common two-factor model. With these multifactor model specifications for the $m = 1, \ldots, 10$ pools we can now compute risk measures for the mixed firms and pools portfolio—similar to Table 4.16—across the different horizons such as 3 months, 6 months, 9 months, and 12 months.

A specific firm's new rating at a certain horizon will be decided, as before, by comparing the implied normal thresholds of the transition matrix using the current rating with the normalized credit index from equation (4.22). For a pool the calculation of the expected fraction of a pool in a particular rating class at a certain horizon use equation (4.27) and equation (4.29).

As in the previous example for the 8 firms we compute results at the horizons of 3, 6, 9, and 12 months using 100,000 scenarios and a confidence level of 99%. However, here we only display the results for 6 and 12 months. This is done in Table 4.23. Figure 4.6 also displays graphically the VaR and CVaR at the 12-month horizon for the firms, pools and the portfolio.

The portfolio risk, as measured by VaR and CVaR at the 99% confidence level is of course dominated by the pools due to their large exposure sizes. As in the example when we only had individual firms in the portfolio we note that contribution VaR may not be intuitive for the individual firms. For example, at both horizons, contribution VaR is zero for many firms. In contrast, for the pools we observe a contribution VaR and incremental VaR close to the standalone VaR. That the risk contributions and incremental risk measures are close to the standalone risk is a general phenomenon for credit risk portfolios as the diversification effect is generally small. This is in contrast to market risk portfolios, which may contain natural hedge positions such as short positions. Of course, in a credit portfolio, negative risk contributions and incremental risk may arise naturally from credit hedges such as credit default swaps and guarantees.

TABLE 4.23 Mixed Firm and Pool Portfolio Risk Measures at Horizons 6 and 12 Months

	MtM	VaR	CVaR	Cont VaR	Cont CVaR	Inc VaR	Inc CVaR
				6 months horizon			
Firm							
1	652,796	34,758	365,515	0	44,530	32,362	41,300
2	661,783	54,708	152,673	18,734	23,272	17,303	22,433
3	214,729	3,608	37,130	1,817	2,889	201	2,889
4	88,055	7,221	11,429	2,473	2,721	2,473	2,721
5	75,324	4,258	25,564	4,258	2,440	201	2,440
6	530,736	9,063	32,939	0	6,382	4,803	6,129
7	93,311	7,714	11,587	0	2,289	0	2,289
8	284,017	12,206	26,618	0	5,025	4,803	4,969
Pool							
1	30,129,668	893,626	1,202,695	898,833	1,202,065	889,984	1,201,976
2	24,103,774	608,607	811,665	613,432	811,244	613,026	811,229
3	4,632,483	91,537	113,639	91,357	113,582	91,357	113,582
4	72,311,203	1,793,410	2,372,425	1,807,960	2,371,205	1,797,216	2,370,782
5	55,953,939	1,016,463	1,337,256	1,020,236	1,336,562	1,014,858	1,336,461
6	9,926,749	238,553	308,640	237,909	308,456	238,291	308,456
7	23,501,141	823,533	1,101,948	828,144	1,101,377	819,127	1,101,330
8	16,270,021	493,056	669,025	495,531	668,668	495,531	668,662
9	10,901,807	93,180	123,552	92,706	123,463	92,843	123,463
10	7,231,120	200,502	268,316	201,784	268,177	201,784	268,177
Portfolio	257,562,617	6,315,174	8,394,348	6,315,174	8,394,348	6,315,174	8,394,348
				12 months horizon			
Firm							
1	652,796	49,767	735,915	0	116,760	64,931	112,804
2	661,783	65,458	364,018	65,458	51,021	30,008	49,199
3	214,729	3,916	75,026	1,322	8,544	7,132	8,527
4	88,055	8,573	12,642	10,594	4,693	9,586	4,693
5	75,324	28,332	30,769	0	6,690	9,456	6,673
6	530,736	9,450	106,967	0	13,498	10,749	13,416
7	93,311	9,230	16,465	0	3,665	0	3,665
8	284,017	15,810	52,100	0	10,112	12,509	10,054
Pool							
1	30,129,668	2,189,991	2,880,202	2,196,330	2,879,304	2,183,165	2,879,112
2	24,103,774	1,470,570	1,921,328	1,473,109	1,920,702	1,461,628	1,920,616
3	4,632,483	158,785	197,941	159,623	197,835	159,623	197,835
4	72,311,203	4,344,741	5,469,338	4,362,244	5,467,573	4,332,626	5,646,629
5	55,953,939	2,274,678	3,045,512	2,287,088	3,044,273	2,273,153	3,043,970
6	9,926,749	433,499	573,524	434,144	573,150	427,104	573,140
7	23,501,141	2,056,589	2,695,891	2,071,223	2,694,957	2,058,433	2,694,760
8	16,270,021	1,205,109	1,592,726	1,206,332	1,592,208	1,195,856	1,592,134
9	10,901,807	170,026	223,727	170,438	223,552	170,438	223,552
10	7,231,120	488,606	640,641	490,310	640,442	481,846	640,438
Portfolio	257,562,617	14,928,216	19,628,980	14,928,216	19,628,980	14,928,216	19,628,980

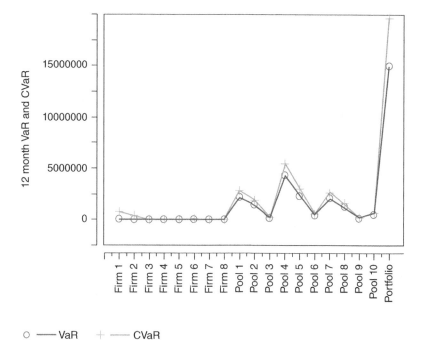

FIGURE 4.6 Mixed Firm and Pool Portfolio VaR and CVaR Risk Measures at the 12-Month Horizon

The observation of smooth risk contributions and incremental risk for the pools even using VaR as a risk measure is not surprising. This is because the conditional law of large numbers approximations used for the pools introduce a smoothness in empirical profit and loss. Hence, working with pools instead of individual firms also creates advantages in terms of the resulting loss distribution.

When creating the pools a natural question to ask is the number of pool members needed in order for the approximation in equation (4.27) to be good. Clearly, we assume the pool to be large enough such that for a pool with members $l = 1, \ldots, L$ we can average out the idiosyncratic components $\{\varepsilon_l^p\}_{l=1}^L$ rendering the expectation in equation (4.27) valid as approximation. Assuming this approximation is valid we have hence, conditional on $\{Z\}$, a simple multinomial distribution for the pools credit rating. In practice, a simulation comparison analysis can be conducted comparing the risk horizon obtained multinomial rating class distributions from the case of pooled firms $l = 1, \ldots, L$ versus idiosyncratic firm models $l = 1, \ldots, L$. We will consider such an example later when we discuss the creation of pools in the context of banking book credit scoring based credit portfolio models.

Convergence of Credit Risk Measures Credit loss distributions, due to the relatively rare event of default and migration, typically display much fatter tails than the normal distribution. We refer to Lucas et al. (1999) for a theoretical analysis of the loss tail behavior induced by a multifactor model as having naturally polynomial decaying (fat tailed distribution) rather than exponentially decaying tails (as for the normal distribution). The loss tail index is shown to be closely related to the correlation between the firms multifactor models.

Because with credit risk we attempt to model rare events the number of scenarios required to obtain stability in the risk measures may be quite large. It is often not unreasonable to consider number of scenarios in the range of 100,000–1,000,000 for portfolio credit risk models. Intuitively, we should require more scenarios for a portfolio with higher quality rating since the default event is even more rare than for lower quality portfolios. Pooling should also help to reduce the number of scenarios as we employ a conditional expectation rather than relying on sampling of idiosyncratic components. In particular, with pooling, the scenario attribution of at least some proportion of the portfolio to the defaulted fraction happens in general even for high quality grade pool of firms (since they have generally have very small but still non-zero default probabilities). As we saw from the last example, pooling also helps with obtaining a smooth loss distribution.

Another important component for the stability of credit risk measures is the choice of confidence level, and, the choice of risk measure (e.g., VaR or CVaR). For example, we have seen that VaR as a risk measure and in particular empirical risk contributions using VaR may not be straightforward to interpret for the case of subportfolios with one or just a few firms.

While the concern about having to use a large number of scenarios for portfolio credit risk portfolio analysis is easing over time thanks to the advance of computer technology and computational techniques, there are still researches on faster approximation techniques that avoids time consuming simulation. We have already mentioned Lucas et al. (1999) and Finger (1999). Analytical approximation techniques for one-factor models have been explored in Vasicek (2002) and Gordy (2003, 2004). Pykthin (2004) extends the analytical approximation techniques to multifactor models by using a corresponding one-factor model that has similar loss distribution properties to the multifactor model. See also Glasserman and Li (2005) on using importance sampling in the credit risk context.

For a given credit portfolio model one can investigate the number of scenarios required to, with a given confidence level, reach a certain desired maximum risk measure sampling error of say 3%. Finding an answer to that question in general requires experimentation with different simulation sample sizes and simulation seeds. For a given simulation seed we can investigate the VaR confidence levels, for different simulation sizes, using the order statistics based nonparametric probability bounds on VaR.[19]

Convergence Analysis Example for the Dynamic Multifactor Model with Both Pools and Individual Firms Table 4.24 displays 99% (α_1), 99.9% (α_2), and 99.99% (α_3) VaR, at the 12-month horizon level. The VaR risk measures are computed separately for the sub-portfolios of firms and pools, for different simulation sizes, together with the corresponding 95% coverage level VaR confidence intervals for VaR at the 99%, 99.9%, and 99.99% confidence level. In the table the lower and upper confidence intervals for the VaR(α_1) is denoted VaR$_L(\alpha_1)$ and VaR$_U(\alpha_1)$ respectively. A similar notation is used for VaR(α_2) and VaR(α_3) confidence levels.[20] In the table the notation N/A indicates that an empirical VaR is not available (or available only as the end point of the loss sample) for that particular simulation size and VaR confidence level.

Table 4.24 shows that even using 100,000 simulations for the credit risk portfolios yields a relatively large confidence interval for the VaR risk measure for very high confidence levels such as 99.99%. It is interesting to note that for the firms portfolio there is a very large

---

[19]See the advanced market risk chapter for a discussion of how to compute the probability bounds on VaR.

[20]The firms portfolio VaR at the 99% confidence level in Table 4.24 differs slightly from the corresponding VaR in Table 4.16 due to using different seeds for the simulation of systematic and idiosyncratic components.

TABLE 4.24 VaR and VaR Confidence Intervals for the Subportfolios of Firms and Pools for Different Simulation Sizes

Subport-folio	VaR(α_1)	VaR$_L$(α_1)	VaR$_U$(α_1)	VaR(α_2)	VaR$_L$(α_2)	VaR$_U$(α_2)	VaR(α_3)	VaR$_L$(α_3)	VaR$_U$(α_3)
				Simulation size = 10,000					
Firms	297,131	261,063	738,303	799,127	777,307	831,945	950,320	N/A	N/A
Pools	14,082,271	13,394,490	14,916,215	23,319,414	21,403,539	28,396,896	49,978,377	N/A	N/A
				Simulation size = 50,000					
Firms	270,436	232,911	731,267	824,686	814,576	835,102	1,005,958	937,640	1,552,903
Pools	14,636,145	14,295,319	15,030,642	24,999,344	23,820,670	26,240,716	42,947,529	32,488,772	49,978,377
				Simulation size = 100,000					
Firms	278,463	247,667	731,159	822,464	816,517	828,611	1,494,242	1,045,132	1,509,306
Pools	14,777,266	14,544,863	15,010,003	25,195,873	24,643,010	26,274,591	39,456,415	33,626,358	46,475,327

VaR confidence interval at the 99% level even using 100,000 simulations. Especially the upper bound VaR order statistic is very large compared to 99% VaR. This behavior can be explained by Figure 4.5 which shows that normal copula VaR for the firms portfolio jumps discretely at confidence levels slightly above 99%, which is where the upper VaR bound order statistic resides.

Figure 4.7 displays graphically the 99.9% VaR for the firms together with the 95% lower and upper confidence levels for the different simulation sizes. The VaR and the confidence intervals are expressed in percentage of the firms mark to market value of 2,600,752.

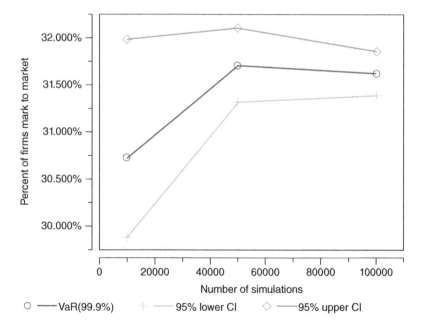

FIGURE 4.7 99.9% VaR (Expressed in Percentage of Current Mark to Market) for the Firms Together with the 95% Lower and Upper Confidence Levels for the Different Simulation Sizes

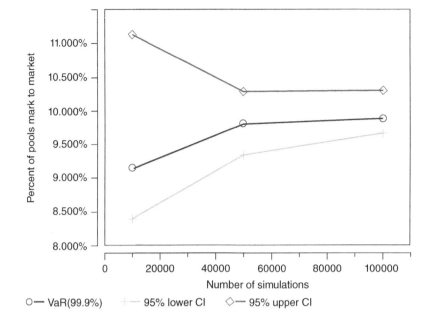

FIGURE 4.8 99.9% VaR (Expressed in Percentage of Current Mark to Market) for the Pools Together with the 95% Lower and Upper Confidence Levels for the Different Simulation Sizes

Figure 4.8 displays graphically the same information for the pools with the mark to market value for the pools being 254,961,865.

Calculation and Stability of Risk Contributions Oftentimes the stand-alone risk of an exposure is of less interest than its risk contribution to the portfolio. Hence, while the stability of the portfolio risk measure is a concern in credit risk portfolios there is also a concern about the stability of the risk contributions that are used for capital allocations. We have previously seen in our examples that pooling helps as does using CVaR contributions instead of VaR contributions. Alternatively, one can consider smoothed VaR contributions to reduce variance as we discussed in the advanced market risk chapter. A practical concern for large portfolios where one needs to calculate risk contributions at exposure level is that, in principle, all the exposure-level scenario profit-and-loss data that has to be kept in memory or stored to disk together with the portfolio-level loss information. This is to enable the subsequent exposure risk contribution calculations that depends on the portfolio-level tail scenarios. There are however several practical ways to avoid an exposure level storage for all the simulation scenarios. One approach that trades speed for reduced disk or memory requirements is to first calculate the portfolio-level results only and then identify the portfolio-level scenarios that are necessary for the exposure-level risk contributions, and, in a second-run calculate and store exposure-level loss for only these scenarios. A second approach is to produce results for the portfolio and the exposures at the same run but define a portfolio-level loss threshold where, most likely, losses below that threshold will not be part of the portfolio-loss tail and only store exposure-level loss information if the portfolio loss exceeds the threshold for that scenario. Since the exact threshold is not known with certainty a priory the threshold can be taken as a conservative low threshold. Hence, the method may store much more exposure-level losses than needed in the first method. On the other hand, it only requires one run.

Modeling Default Times In the multivariate Merton model—using a plain equity representation or the multifactor models representation—we have focused on the simulation of discrete migration and default events on a set of future time points, $t = 1, \ldots, T$. If we are only interested in the default time of an issuer it is of course more efficient to focus directly on estimating the default time rather than simulating discrete credit events until a default occurs. In the Li (2000) model, the modeling focus is on the survivor function, which gives the probability of survival up to t and is defined by

$$1 - F(t) = \overline{F}(t), \quad F(t) = P(\tau \leq t)$$

where $\tau > 0$ is a continuous random variable modeling the stochastic default time of an issuer. We also introduce the hazard rate

$$h(t) = \frac{f(t)}{\overline{F}(t)} = -\frac{d \ln \overline{F}(t)}{dt} \tag{4.31}$$

where $f(t)$ is the density of the distribution $F(t)$. Since $f(t) = -\frac{d\overline{F}(t)}{dt}$ the equation $h(t) = -\frac{d \ln \overline{F}(t)}{dt}$ corresponds to a differential equation in t, with solution, subject to the initial condition $\overline{F}(0) = 1$,

$$\overline{F}(t) = \exp\left(-\int_0^t h(u)du\right). \tag{4.32}$$

We can now define the default time of an issuer as the first time $\overline{F}(t)$ breaches the level of some variable $u \in [0, 1]$. Specifically, the default time is registered as[21]

$$\tau = \inf\{t : \overline{F}(t) \leq u\}.$$

Note that the probability of default over a fixed interval $[0, s]$ is equal to $F(s)$ yielding, for constant h, $\mathrm{PD} = 1 - \exp^{(-hs)}$ and hence we can solve for h that is consistent with the static version of the model over the horizon $[0, s]$. This feature is often used in calibration of the models default intensities, especially for the implied default intensities derived from the market spreads.

In the model formulation proposed by Li (2000), one makes use of a normal copula for the N-vector $\{u_i\}_{i=1}^N$ with $(u_1, \ldots, u_N) \sim C_u^N$ where C_u^N is the normal copula, implying also a normal copula for the N−vector of asset (equity) returns since the copula is invariant under strictly increasing componentwise transformations.[22] A straightforward generalization of the above model is to consider other copulas than the normal (e.g., the t-copula). Another alternative is to consider the Archimedean family of copula functions for u_i. See Rogge and Schönbucher (2003).

The Impact on the Joint Default Probability in the Model Using Different Copulas We consider the default time of 2 firms using the default time model by Li (2000). Each firm i is

---

[21] $\overline{F}(t)$ is often termed the (default) countdown process as $\overline{F}(0) = 1$ and $\overline{F}(t)$ is decreasing in t with $\lim_{t \to \infty} \overline{F}(t) = 0$.

[22] This is in contrast to correlation which is invariant only under strictly increasing *linear* transformations.

assumed to have a deterministic and constant hazard rate, h_i. To generate default times for the 2 firms, we first simulate uniforms, u_1, u_2 from a copula. Having obtained the uniforms, we can now calculate the default time for firm i, τ_i, as

$$\tau_i = \inf\{t : \exp(-h_i \times t) \leq u_i\} \equiv \inf\{t : 1 - \exp(-h_i \times t) \geq u_i\}. \tag{4.33}$$

Equivalently, we can also invert $u_i \sim U[0, 1]$ using the exponential distribution with parameter h_i as $\tau_i = \frac{-\ln(u_i)}{h_i}$. Hence, obtaining firm i:s default time. Clearly, correlated default times comes from the correlation in the u_i:s.

Figure 4.9 displays the simulation scatterplot of default times τ_1, τ_2 (expressed in years) from a normal copula with correlation parameter $\rho = 0$ using 100,000 simulations and $h_i = 0.05$ for both firms.[23] Figure 4.10 displays the corresponding simulation scatterplot of default times τ_1, τ_2 from the normal copula using the correlation parameter $\rho = 0.99$. Comparing the cases we notice a strong default dependence when the correlation is 0.99. Most defaults are joint as the default times for the 2 firms are concentrated on the diagonal in Figure 4.10.

Table 4.25 displays the obtained empirical probability of joint firm default before 2 years, $P(\tau_1 \leq 2, \tau_2 \leq 2)$, and before 10 years, $P(\tau_1 \leq 10, \tau_2 \leq 10)$, when $h_i = 0.05$ for both firms and

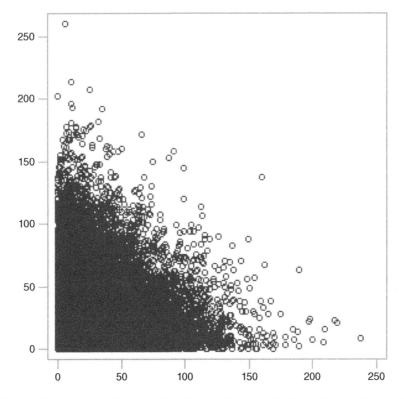

FIGURE 4.9 Simulation Scatterplot of Default Times (Expressed in Years) from a Normal Copula with Correlation Parameter 0 Using 100,000 Simulations

---

[23]That is a survival probability of $\exp(-0.05 \times t)$ for year t. Or, equivalently, a default probability for year t as $1 - \exp(-0.05 \times t)$.

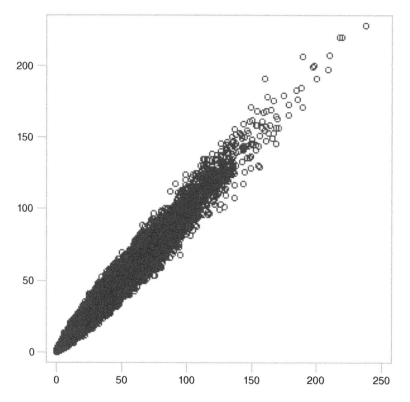

FIGURE 4.10 Simulation Scatterplot of Default Times (Expressed in Years) from a Normal Copula with Correlation Parameter 0.99 Using 100,000 Simulations

TABLE 4.25 Empirical Probability of Joint Firm Default Before 2 Years and 10 Years for Both Firms and Using Different Copulas

Copula	$P(\tau_1 \leq 3, \tau_2 \leq 3)$	$P(\tau_1 \leq 10, \tau_2 \leq 10)$
Normal ($\rho = 0$)	0.90%	15.50%
Normal ($\rho = 0.5$)	3.02%	23.33%
Normal ($\rho = 0.99$)	8.56%	37.17%
Normal ($\rho = 0.99999$)	9.48%	39.29%
t(3) ($\rho = 0.5$)	3.80%	23.50%
t(3) ($\rho = 0.99$)	8.71%	37.20%
t(3) ($\rho = 0.99999$)	9.49%	39.29%
Clayton ($\theta = 3$)	7.53%	31.57%
Clayton ($\theta = 10$)	8.87%	36.73%
Clayton ($\theta = 30$)	9.29%	38.44%

using different copulas for u_1 and u_2. Specifically, we use the normal copula, the t-copula and the Clayton copula. The joint default probabilities in Table 4.25 should be interpreted in the context of the marginal default probabilities, $P(\tau_i \leq 2)$ and $P(\tau_i \leq 10)$ which are approximately 9.51% and 39.36% respectively for both firm 1 and 2. From Table 4.25 we note, for example, that for the normal copula and $t(3)$ copula with correlation parameter $\rho = 0.99999$ the joint default probabilities are very close to the marginal default probabilities. This means that for this case almost all marginal defaults are also joint defaults. The joint defaults obtained with the Clayton copula in Table 4.25 seems to suggest that the Clayton copula is a useful alternative to the normal and t-copulas in parametrizing joint defaults.[24] However, it is important to remember that the Clayton copula only has lower tail dependence. Hence, when modeling long-term survival and conditional default over long term it may result in unwanted behavior in conditional default probabilities. To illustrate this Figure 4.11 displays the simulation scatterplot of default times τ_1, τ_2 (expressed in years) from the Clayton copula with $\theta = 30$ using 100,000 simulations and $h_i = 0.05$ for both firms. It is clear that there is only default dependence in the left tail (compare to Figure 4.10, which displays simulated default times from a normal copula with correlation parameter $\rho = 0.99$). Another drawback of the

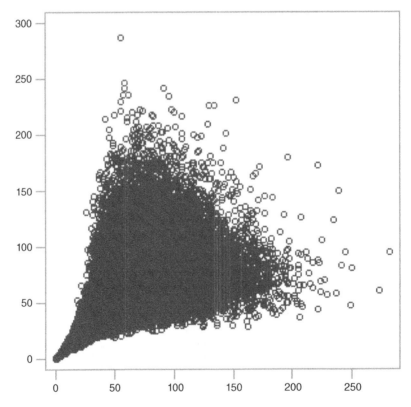

FIGURE 4.11 Simulation Scatterplot of Default Times (Expressed in Years) from a Clayton Copula with Copula Parameter 30 Using 100,000 Simulations

[24]Recall that for the Clayton copula as θ approaches 0 we obtain the independence copula, whereas as θ approaches ∞ we obtain the perfect dependence copula.

Clayton copula is that it only has a single parameter to specify the strength of codependency when many firms default times are to be modeled.

Default Times and Multifactor Models In our example above, we directly simulated correlated uniforms u_1, u_2 from a copula. However, we could also have used a multifactor model approach. Specifically, each firm i can have a standard normal factor model as in (4.22) such that for a firm i,

$$\widehat{Z}_i = \phi_i \left(\sum_{j=1}^{N} \beta_{ij} Z_j \right) + \sqrt{1 - R_i^2} \, \varepsilon_i$$

and we can now set

$$u_i = N(\widehat{Z}_i)$$

as the correlated uniforms that we use to calculate firm default times, τ_i. In this multifactor model the copula is applied to the credit factors $(Z_1, \ldots, Z_N)$ as in equation (4.24). A model that is often used in practice due to its simplicity is the one-factor model where

$$\widehat{Z}_i = RZ + \sqrt{1 - R^2} \, \varepsilon_i \tag{4.34}$$

with $\varepsilon_i \sim N(0, 1)$, $Z \sim N(0, 1)$ for all firms i. In this model there is only a single correlation parameter $\rho = R$ for each pair of firms.

Pricing Using the Default Time Model Once we have obtained the default times we can properly value the firms exposures. Specifically, if a firm has issued an instrument that has cash flows at times $t_1, \ldots, t_N$ and firm default time, τ, is $t_n < \tau < t_{n-1}$ we can calculate the value of obtaining cash flows up to t_{n-1} plus any recoveries. The default time model is also frequently used to value credit correlation products such as n:th to default basket credit default swaps and tranches of collateralized debt obligations. The standard basket credit default swap product is an insurance contract on the n:th default in a basket of large international corporate credits. For example, a basket credit default swap that pays off 1 unit of currency if at least 3 out of 10 firms defaults before 2 years can be easily valued using the simulation of firm default times and then calculating the probability of minimum 3 firm defaults before 2 years.

Before the 2007 crisis the market standard model for basket credit derivatives was the one-factor normal copula model with a single correlation parameter, $\rho = R$, between firms (see equation (4.34)) and constant default probabilities for each firm. For tranche-based products such as collateralized debt obligations the market participants calculated implied correlations for each tranche. As a result, an implied correlation curve referred to as "correlation smile" was observed in the market.[25] Several attempts were made by the practitioners to fix the smile. See for example Amato and Gyntelberg (2005). However, after the credit crisis, the use of the simple one-factor model and in particular the normal copula have been heavily criticized. However, our examples in Table 4.25 have shown that the normal copula with high values for the correlation parameter, ρ, is capable of producing strongly correlated defaults. The main critique should hence be targeted toward the use of too-low (optimistic) correlations by market participants. See Hediorn and Kahlert (2010) on the sharply increasing implied correlations during the 2007 financial crisis.

---

[25]The term "correlation smile" follows from similar results seen from option implied volatilities.

Economic Capital for a Portfolio of Traded Bonds

Considering the calculation of economic capital for issuer credit risk in the trading book one must recognize that trading books in banks mainly consist of positions held with intent to trade or hedge other positions. This is in contrast to banking books that are usually made of held to maturity items. When considering issuer credit exposure and economic capital in the trading book it is therefore natural to consider a trading horizon or liquidity horizon of credits. The trading or liquidity horizon should reflect the intended holding period and market depth of the credits.

When trading credits liquidity horizons are shorter than the risk measurement horizon one needs to consider a trading intent model at the liquidity horizons. A trading intent model captures, at the liquidity horizons, the portfolio strategy. An example of such a portfolio strategy is to maintain the credit quality and risk of the portfolio. With this strategy, when trading credits at their liquidity horizon, the requirement is that the credit, assuming credit migration has happened, is replaced by a credit with the same risk profile such that the initial risk level of the portfolio is maintained. In practice this means that the newly traded credit should have the same initial rating as the original credit but also that the new credit should not change the portfolio features such as concentration or the maturities of the investments. Therefore, in order to preserve the initial risk level from both an exposure and portfolio perspective the newly traded credit should have the same stand-alone characteristics as well as correlation with the rest of the portfolio.

This specific trading intent model for economic capital is used in the Basel (Basel Committee, 2009b) internal model for trading book credit risk, termed the Incremental Risk Charge (IRC). The incremental risk charge includes positions that are subject to risk charges for specific interest rate risk such as corporate bonds. However, the incremental risk charge captures the credit migration and default risk holding fixed any market variations such as interest rate risk and spread risk within a rating class. The incremental risk charge is not allowed to capture any diversification effects between market and credit risk. This means that the incremental risk charge is added to the total market risk charge.

When we consider economic capital calculations of a traded bond portfolio we will use the regulatory IRC framework as the definition of the economic capital trading intent model. In the economic capital model the trading horizon is of course specified by the bank while in the regulatory IRC case restrictions on the specification is given. Specifically, the trading horizon or liquidity horizon is subject to a floor of 3 months. Moreover, investment grade credits are expected to be more liquid than non-investment-grade and hence have a shorter liquidity horizon. In this setting the liquidity horizon represents the time required to sell the position or to hedge all material risks covered by the incremental risk charge model in a stressed market.

The regulatory IRC is assessed by banks on weekly basis at a 99.9% VaR confidence level using a risk horizon of 1 year. No specific model, approach or method is prescribed for banks in terms of the IRC estimation. This is in contrast to Basel II models for banking book, where the risk weight calculation is set to a one-factor model that every bank uses.

In the calculation of bond loss with the IRC trading model the profit and loss made at the liquidity horizon, by trading back into a bond with the same start rating, is aggregated to the final horizon. That is, for a bond with a 3-month liquidity horizon the loss is aggregated at the 3, 6, 9, and 12 month horizon to obtain the 12-month horizon trading loss. As a general rule for investment grade credits, for example, bonds belonging to rating class Aaa, Aa, or A in the Moody's rating categories, the incremental risk charge (as measured by 99.9% VaR at the 12 month horizon) is smallest when the shortest liquidity horizon of 3 months is used.

For medium-quality bonds the incremental risk charge level is generally constant and does not depend on choosing either of the 3, 6, 9, or 12 month liquidity horizons. For the speculative grade rating classes, for example, bonds in rating classes B and Caa using the Moody's rating categories, it is typically always beneficial to assume a long liquidity horizon if one wants to minimize the level of IRC.

These risk impacts due to choosing different trading liquidity horizons for bonds with different credit qualities come from two competing effects.

- First, for bonds with short liquidity horizons there is a mitigation effect of preventing the bond from further downgrades by trading it frequently.
- Second, there is the effect of the possibility of multiple defaults.

Of these two effects the multiple default effect will generally be more pronounced for speculative grade credits as the probability of default is severe even for short liquidity periods and hence incremental risk charges will generally increase the shorter the liquidity horizon. For medium investment grade credits these two effects will in general offset and the incremental risk charge will be approximately the same across liquidity horizons. For investment grade credits the effect of the multiple defaults is low for short liquidity horizons as the frequent trading effectively prevents severe downgrades.

Not surprisingly this behavior coincides with results in the credit spread term structure modeling literature. For example, Merton (1974), Sarig and Warga (1989), Fons (1994), Longstaff and Schwartz (1995) and especially Jarrow et al. (1997). That is, that the investment grade credits have increasing credit spreads and the non-investment grades or speculative grades have downward sloping spreads reflecting the survival contingent effects. It also shows that the market and regulatory rationale for assigning stressed liquidity horizons to credits is aligned with banks preferred choice of liquidity horizons to minimize the IRC add-on to the total capital charge for the trading book. See Skoglund and Chen (2011) for further discussions on the IRC and a numerical analysis illustrating the competing effects of multiple defaults and mitigation by trading. However, we will also analyze some of the IRC portfolio risk effects below in a numerical example.

To analyze the impact on the IRC charge for banks the Basel committee performed a quantitative impact study on the portfolio effects of IRC. The findings of the Basel quantitative impact study (Basel Committee, 2009d) is, not surprisingly, that the IRC capital will on average increase the total risk capital charge. However, more related to the findings in Skoglund and Chen (2011) on the competing effects is the Basel quantitative impact results obtained from the 25 sample banks when different uniform choices of liquidity horizons are made for the bank portfolios. The Basel results show an increase in the IRC capital when liquidity horizons increase. Specifically, increasing the liquidity horizon from 1 month to 6 months on average increases the capital charge with 20%. In addition, for sample banks that provided estimates for both 1-month and 3-month uniform liquidity horizons the average increase in the capital charge is 3%. These results are therefore consistent with the Basel sample banks having, on average, investment quality bond portfolios.

Below we will consider an empirical example of economic IRC portfolio risk effects. Our application example will use a 1-year horizon with 3-month trading intervals. An issue one faces in the construction of a 3-month matrix is that the shortest time interval in which transition matrices are estimated is often a year. Hence, we usually need to derive a shorter horizon transition matrix from a given 1-year transition matrix. For this purpose it is convenient to use a generator matrix and we derive this generator matrix before we proceed with the IRC example.

Generator Matrix and Short-Term Transition Matrices Introducing the concept of a generator matrix that accompanies a transition matrix we let for any pair of states j and k, q_{jk}, be defined by,

$$q_{jk} = v_j p_{jk}$$

where v_j is the rate at which the process makes a transition when in state j and p_{jk} is the probability that the transition is into state k. Then we have defined the rate q_{jk} to be the rate, when in state j, that the process makes a transition into state k. It follows that for $\widehat{K}$ states,

$$v_j = \sum_{k=1}^{\widehat{K}} v_j p_{jk} = \sum_{k=1}^{\widehat{K}} q_{jk}$$

which leads to $p_{jk} = \sum_{k=1}^{\widehat{K}} \frac{q_{jk}}{v_j} = 1$. Mathematically

$$\mathbf{Q} = \begin{bmatrix} -v_1 & q_{12} & \cdots & q_{1\widehat{K}} \\ q_{21} & -v_2 & \cdots & q_{2\widehat{K}} \\ \cdots & \cdots & \cdots & \cdots \\ q_{\widehat{K}1} & \cdots & q_{\widehat{K}\widehat{K}-1} & -v_{\widehat{K}} \end{bmatrix}$$

is the generator matrix for a continuous time Markov chain. For any time period r, the transition probability matrix from time 0 to time r is

$$\mathbf{A}(r) = \exp(\mathbf{Q}r). \tag{4.35}$$

Specifically, the one-year transition matrix $\mathbf{A}$ is simply $\mathbf{A}(1) = \exp(\mathbf{Q})$ and for a three-month transition matrix, $\mathbf{A}\left(\frac{3}{12}\right)$, we have that $\mathbf{A}\left(\frac{3}{12}\right) = \exp(\frac{1}{4}\mathbf{Q})$.

In a credit risk Markov chain model the default state, $\widehat{K}$, is assumed to be absorbing. That is once in default an exposure or firm cannot recover from it. Correspondingly the transition matrix has $p_{\widehat{K}\widehat{K}} = 1$ and $p_{\widehat{K}j} = 0$ for all $j = 1, 2, \ldots, \widehat{K} - 1$. Similarly the corresponding generator matrix in this case has $q_{\widehat{K}1} = \ldots = q_{\widehat{K}\widehat{K}-1} = v_{\widehat{K}} = 0$.

Now the question remains how a generator matrix can be derived from a one-year transition matrix, $\mathbf{A}$. There are several approaches in the literature; however, Israel, Rosenthal, and Wei (2001) propose an effective method as follows:

$$\mathbf{Q} = \sum_{i=0}^{n} (-1)^i \frac{\mathbf{D}^{i+1}}{i+1} \tag{4.36}$$

where $\mathbf{D} = \mathbf{A} - \mathbf{I}$, with $\mathbf{I}$ the identity matrix. The required power, r, of the initial transition matrix $\mathbf{A}$ is then calculated as $\mathbf{B} = \exp(r\mathbf{Q})$ using the Taylor expansion approximation

$$\mathbf{B} = \mathbf{I} + \sum_{i=1}^{n} \frac{(r\mathbf{Q})^i}{i!}.$$

In this way we can obtain transition probabilities for the 3-months horizon as well as longer horizons such as 6 months and 9 months from the generator matrix $\mathbf{Q}$.

TABLE 4.26 Moody's 1920–1996 Average One-Year Transition Matrix for the Non-Default Rating Grades Aaa, Aa, A, Baa, Ba, B, and Caa, and the Default State, D

Rating	Aaa	Aa	A	Baa	Ba	B	Caa	D
Aaa	0.9218	0.0651	0.0104	0.0025	0.0002	0	0	0
Aa	0.0129	0.9162	0.0611	0.007	0.0018	0.0003	0	0.0007
A	0.0008	0.025	0.9135	0.0511	0.0069	0.0011	0.0002	0.00014
Baa	0.0004	0.0027	0.0422	0.8916	0.0525	0.0068	0.0007	0.0031
Ba	0.0002	0.0007	0.0044	0.0511	0.8708	0.0557	0.0046	0.0125
B	0	0.0004	0.0014	0.0069	0.0652	0.852	0.0354	0.0387
Caa	0	0.0003	0.0004	0.0037	0.0145	0.06	0.783	0.1381
D	0	0	0	0	0	0	0	1

Example Calculation of the Generator Matrix from a Moody's One-Year Transition Matrix
Our base transition matrix, **A**, is the Moody's long-run or TTC one-year transition matrix between 1920–1996 displayed in Table 4.26.

This transition matrix has empirical transition probabilities for the Moody's rating classes Aaa, Aa, A, Baa, Ba, B, and Caa, as well as the default state, D. The matrix has been estimated conditional on no withdrawal of rating and hence contains no category attributed to non-rated exposures as is usually the case. We refer to Moody's (1997) for details on how the transition matrix has been estimated.

We now construct a generator matrix from the Moody's transition matrix using equation (4.36). Table 4.27 displays the generator matrix, **Q**, obtained from the Moody's one-year average transition probability matrix for the Moody's rating classes Aaa, Aa, A, Baa, Ba, B, and Caa, as well as the default state, D.

Having available the generator matrix we can now generate a transition matrix at any frequency as $\mathbf{B} = \exp(r\mathbf{Q})$. We will make use of the generator matrix in Table 4.27 when we calculate bond portfolio economic capital using different, short-term, trading liquidity horizons for bonds.

Example IRC Portfolio Risk Effects We consider the analysis of portfolio level economic capital using a simple portfolio with 1 bond in each of the Moody's rating categories Aaa, Aa, A, Baa, Ba, B, and Caa. All the bonds notional are 100 units of currency with a recovery rate of 25%. Each of the bonds are zero coupon bonds with 4 years to maturity. For an analysis

TABLE 4.27 The Transition Generator Matrix Obtained from Moody's 1920–1996 Average One-Year Transition Matrix for the Non-Default Rating Grades Aaa, Aa, A, Baa, Ba, B, and Caa, and the Default State, D

Rating	Aaa	Aa	A	Baa	Ba	B	Caa	D
Aaa	−0.078426	0.0655632	0.0101495	0.0025099	0.0001981	0.000003425	0.0000010726	0.00000033363
Aa	0.0129921	−0.084197	0.0616064	0.0067839	0.0018027	0.0003031	0	0.000709
A	0.0007784	0.0252062	−0.085778	0.0516558	0.006706	0.0010851	0.0002033	0.0001437
Baa	0.000402	0.0026288	0.042664	−0.109352	0.053329	0.0065479	0.0006829	0.0030973
Ba	0.0002012	0.0007008	0.0042233	0.0519202	−0.130752	0.056879	0.0044131	0.0124147
B	0	0.0004024	0.0014054	0.0065817	0.0665542	−0.149997	0.0366668	0.0383868
Caa	0	0.0003049	0.0003881	0.003705	0.014297	0.0620952	−0.220949	0.1401583
D	0	0	0	0	0	0	0	0

TABLE 4.28 Bond Discount Rates for the 7 Non-Default Moody's Rating Classes, Aaa, Aa, A, Baa, Ba, B, and Caa Respectively, for Maturity Terms 3 and 4 Years

Rating category	Interest rate (3 years)	Interest rate (4 years)
Aaa	0.02651775	0.02934361
Aa	0.02687823	0.02990976
A	0.02784931	0.03124889
Baa	0.02933442	0.03306486
Ba	0.03176641	0.03581472
B	0.05451719	0.05929989
Caa	0.12388839	0.12019516

horizon of 1 year we therefore require the 3- and 4-year bond discount rates for a bond rated in one of the rating classes Aaa, Aa, A, Baa, Ba, B, and Caa. The bond discount rates are displayed in Table 4.28.

Each of the bonds have a common multifactor model,

$$\tilde{Z} = 0.6231 \times Z_1 + 0.33 \times Z_2 + 0.0268 \times Z_3 + 0.0201 \times Z_4 + 0.89 \times \varepsilon_1$$

where the standard deviation and correlation between credit factors, Z_1, Z_2, Z_3, and Z_4 are already given in Tables 4.12 and 4.13, respectively.

To model rating transitions at the liquidity horizons we will use the generator transition matrix we obtained above in Table 4.27. Using the generator transition matrix and the multifactor models we can now compute the economic capital required to support the portfolio using the IRC trading intent model.

Table 4.29 displays the portfolio economic capital, as measured by VaR and CVaR at the 99.9% level using 100,000 simulations, required over a 12-month horizon to support the portfolio with different trading intervals assumed for all the bonds. The portfolio mark to market is 529 units of currency.

We notice from Table 4.29 that economic capital increases with an increased trading frequency. This is because the lower-rated bonds contribute more to losses then through the multiple default effect. The case of 12 months trading interval is of course the economic capital with no trading and is consistent with the 12-month risk measure for our previous examples on the dynamic multifactor model.

TABLE 4.29 Economic Capital Required Over a 12-Month Horizon to Support the Portfolio with Different Trading Frequencies Assumed for all the Bonds

Trading interval	Economic capital	
	VaR(0.999)	CVaR(0.999)
3 months	297	337
6 months	269	298
9 months	229	257
12 months	184	210

The minimal VaR based economic capital measure for the portfolio is obtained when the bonds in rating categories Aaa, Aa, A have a short trading interval and the bonds in rating categories B and Caa have a long trading interval. For example, when bonds rated in the category Aaa, Aa, A, and Baa have a trading interval of 3 months, bonds rated in category Ba, B, and Caa have trading interval of 12 months we obtain VaR-based economic capital as 164 units of currency (not shown in Table 4.29). If we instead assign a 12-month trading interval to Aaa, Aa, A, and Baa rated bonds and a 3-month interval to Ba, B, and Caa rated bonds we obtain the VaR-based economic capital as 309 units of currency (also not shown in Table 4.29). Hence, the banks preferred choice of liquidity horizons to minimize the economic capital (IRC capital) is aligned with regulatory required choice of liquidity horizons—allowing short liquidity horizons for higher rated bonds and requiring long liquidity horizons for low quality bonds.

As we have seen in the above example the choice of trading intervals (liquidity horizons) of banks credit portfolios can have a significant impact on the 1-year horizon economic capital. While the regulatory IRC specification of trading intervals is prescribed the economic capital model can have any choice of trading intervals for credits. However, the regulatory specification tends to yield the lowest portfolio risk. Compared to a model with no trading intent over the 1-year horizon, the regulatory specification yields also in general a lower portfolio risk, as it benefits from a mitigation effect of preventing high-quality bonds from further downgrades by trading them frequently.

CREDIT MODELS FOR THE BANKING BOOK

Banking book credit exposures typically include loans, leases, and facilities. For commercial business with large and to some extent medium-sized firms, the Merton style models discussed above are widely used in the industry. In this section we will focus on the exposures mainly in the form of consumer and small firms loans, mortgages, credit cards and leases. In contrast to large corporates, consumers and small firms do not have publicly traded equity. Nor do they have publicly traded debt.

Banking book portfolios are generally large with a relatively small contribution for each loan. While relatively little is known about each loan, the behavior of large pools of loans can be inferred with a high degree of statistical certainty.

Traditionally, financial institutions employ credit score models—estimated on pools of loans—to retrieve credit scores for an individual loan. Credit score models include borrower-specific (idiosyncratic) factors such as, for example, age, income, previous delinquency history and yields a probability of default prediction based on the values of the specific factors at a given point in time. Credit score models used in portfolio credit models also include a macroeconomic view of the key factors that can drive default risk over time. Default dependence is hence introduced through the common macroeconomic factors.

In credit models with multiple states, such as when tracking delinquency status, the credit score models must also estimate the transition probabilities to the non-default delinquency states. In a multiple-states credit model, the credit transition models can be estimated individually for each from and to state or use a multinomial model approach. In the latter case, the transition probabilities are automatically constrained to sum to unity as is required by a transition probability model.

This structure of estimating transition probabilities is not too different from the multifactor model we used in the context of wholesale exposures and bonds. However, the difference is that here we are explicitly regressing the factors that drive default and transition rates of loans on the historical rates, while in the multifactor model, default and transition rates were given exogenously (through the transition matrix) with a multifactor model for the random credit index. However, the reader may recall that when the multifactor model was given a pool interpretation the model was essentially reduced to an ordered Probit model regression for the transition rates with the economic factors and their regression coefficients describing the deviation of transition probabilities from long-run or unconditional on the business cycle.

Our exposition of credit models for the banking book first starts with the simple one-period binomial loss model for homogeneous and heterogeneous portfolios. This model is the foundation of many credit portfolio models and also leads to tractable solutions in some cases. The most important tractable solution case is the specific model used for credit risk capital requirements in Basel II. After our discussion of the simple binomial model we consider estimation and simulation of credit scores or credit transition probabilities which is the main model component in building a credit portfolio model. In a credit portfolio model the credit score or credit transition probabilities generally capture both idiosyncratic credit features as well as common economic factors impact. Having available the credit score or credit transition models one can sample empirical loan state transitions over time conditional on the economic scenario using a state transition matrix. However, in some cases, analogous to our pool approximations for the multifactor model one can employ simple Markov iterations to compute the expected state occupancy probabilities conditional on the state transition matrix.

Economic capital for loan portfolios is, due to the hold to maturity nature of loan portfolios, more focused on long planning horizons for capital than on short-term horizons as for traded credit portfolios. We therefore focus on estimating economic capital for loan portfolios with an approach founded in the classical insurance risk theory approach that considers an initial risk reserve to support the portfolio over its lifetime. We end this section with a discussion of a particular credit scoring model that can be solved numerically in some cases and hence avoid simulation. This is the actuarial model also known as the CreditRisk$^+$ model. While in practice simulation based models are frequently used to capture all the credit portfolio model characteristics such as state path-dependency and stochastic recovery in the event of default the CreditRisk$^+$ model is still important as a benchmark model.

The Binomial Loss Model

We consider loan portfolio representations in three cases. First, when the portfolio is large and homogeneous. Second, when the portfolio is large with homogeneous large subportfolios, and, finally when the portfolio is either small or heterogeneous. The case of large homogeneous portfolios have been extensively studied in the literature and is also the foundation for Basel II credit risk capital for the banking book.

Homogeneous Large Portfolio As the default indicator for the i:th credit in a portfolio we consider the Bernoulli loss indicator L_i where

$$L_i = \left\{ \begin{array}{l} 1 \text{ with probability } p_i \\ 0 \text{ with probability } 1 - p_i \end{array} \right\}$$

with $p_i \in [0, 1]$ the probability of default. As model for p_i we consider the case when

$$p_i = g_i(\mathbf{Z}, \mathbf{Y}_i),$$

g_i being the so-called score function, $\mathbf{Y}_i$ the parameter vector and $\mathbf{Z}$ the stochastic N-dimensional vector of score risk factors, having density $f_{\mathbf{Z}}(\mathbf{Z})$.

For a credit portfolio with $M \geq 1$ members the conditional (on $\mathbf{Z}$) Fourier-Laplace transform $\varphi_{f_L}(\cdot)$ of the conditional loss density, f_L, is now given by

$$\varphi_{f_L}(\xi) = \Pi_{i=1}^{M}[p_i \exp(i\xi) + (1 - p_i)].$$

Hence, the conditional portfolio loss is distributed as binomial. Using the properties of the binomial distribution the correlation between default events of loan i and j is

$$\text{corr}(L_i, L_j) = \frac{\text{cov}(L_i, L_j)}{\sqrt{\text{var}(L_i)}\sqrt{\text{var}(L_j)}} = \frac{\text{cov}(p_i, p_j)}{\sqrt{p_i(1 - p_i)}\sqrt{p_j(1 - p_j)}}. \tag{4.37}$$

The correlation between default events is therefore fully captured by the covariance of p_i and p_j.

A special case of the conditionally binomial portfolio distribution that we will consider is when the p_i:s are homogeneous. That is, $p = g(\mathbf{Z}, \mathbf{Y}_i)$ is the homogeneous score function for all $i = 1, \ldots, M$. Using that the portfolio is homogeneous (conditional on $\mathbf{Z}$) we have that

$$P\left(\sum_{i=1}^{M} L_i \leq m\right) = \sum_{\bar{m}=0}^{m} \binom{M}{m} (F_p(p))^{\bar{m}}(1 - F_p(p))^{M-\bar{m}},$$

for $m \leq M$, and with $F_p(p) = \int f_p(p)dp$. Note also that in this homogeneous portfolio setting the default correlation formula in equation (4.37) reduces trivially to

$$\text{corr}(L_i, L_j) = \frac{\text{var}(p)}{p(1 - p)}$$

and hence the default correlation increases by the variance of $f_p(p)$. The case of perfect default correlation, $\text{corr}(L_i, L_j) = 1$, happens here if p itself is a Bernoulli distributed random variable with probability p of being unity and probability $(1 - p)$ of being null since then $\text{var}(p) = p(1 - p)$.

Assuming that the portfolio is large, formally $M \to \infty$, and employing the conditional law of large numbers,

$$P\left(\frac{1}{M}\sum_{i=1}^{M} L_i = p|\mathbf{Z}\right) = 1$$

we can derive that (see Vasicek, 1991)

$$P\left(\frac{1}{M}\sum_{i=1}^{M} L_i \leq \frac{m}{M}\right) = \int_{[0,m/M]} dF_p(p). \tag{4.38}$$

Here, $dF_p(p) = f_p(p)dp$. Hence, for the infinitely large homogeneous portfolio with homogeneous score function $p = g(\mathbf{Z}, \mathbf{Y})$ and homogeneous recovery adjusted exposure E we can obtain the portfolio loss at the α confidence level as

$$\int_{[0,\alpha]} f_p(p)dp \times E$$

where f_p denotes the density of p.

Example Score Functions If $f_p(p)$ is the logistic density,

$$g(Z, Y) = \Lambda(\beta'Z) = \frac{\exp^{-\beta'Z}}{1 + \exp^{-\beta'Z}}$$

and $Z \sim N(\mu, \Sigma)$. Then, following Westin (1974),

$$f_p(p) = \frac{1}{\sqrt{2\pi(\beta'\Sigma\beta)}} \frac{1}{p(1-p)} \exp\left\{-\frac{1}{2(\beta'\Sigma\beta)}\left[\ln\left(\frac{p}{1-p}\right) - \mu'\beta\right]^2\right\}.$$

and $\int_{[0,m/M]} dF_p(p)$ can be solved by numerical integration.

As a second example consider the homogeneous one-factor model. That is, the special one-factor case of equation (4.22)

$$\hat{Z}_i = RZ + \sqrt{1 - R^2}\varepsilon_i, \quad \varepsilon_i \sim N(0,1) \quad \forall i, i = 1, \ldots, M, Z \sim N(0,1) \qquad (4.39)$$

triggering a default for loan i when $N(\hat{Z}_i) < p$ with N the cumulative normal distribution function and p the default probability. We have previously mentioned that this one factor model (see also equation (4.34)) was the foundation for pricing credit derivatives before the 2007 crisis. Note here that the one-factor model corresponds to a (standardized) CAPM model for systematic risk where R is homogeneous. Using that ε_i is a standardized normal variable,

$$P(L_i = 1) = P(\hat{Z}_i < N^{-1}(p)) = P\left(\varepsilon_i < \frac{N^{-1}(p) - RZ}{\sqrt{1 - R^2}}\right)$$

$$= N\left(\frac{N^{-1}(p) - RZ}{\sqrt{1 - R^2}}\right) = \Lambda_p(Z, \lambda)$$

where $\Lambda_p(Z, \lambda)$ corresponds to the specific score function $g(Z, Y)$. In this model, generally referred to as the Vasicek one-factor model, the homogeneous portfolio default rate density, $f_p(p)$, is being given by

$$f_p(p) = \phi(Z)\left|\frac{dp}{dZ}\right|^{-1} = \frac{\sigma}{R} \frac{\phi(Z)}{\phi\left(\frac{\Phi^{-1}(p) - RZ}{\sigma}\right)}$$

where $\sigma = \sqrt{1 - R^2}$ and with ϕ the density function of a standard normal variable. Integration using equation (4.38) then yields the distribution function of the loss fraction as

$$\overline{K}(p) = P\left(\frac{1}{M}\sum_{i=1}^{M} L_i \leq \frac{m}{M}\right) = N\left(\frac{1}{\sqrt{1 - R^2}}\left(\sqrt{R^2}N^{-1}\left(\frac{m}{M}\right) + N^{-1}(p)\right)\right).$$

It is practice to express this distribution using the equivalent formulation of equation (4.39)

$$\hat{Z}_i = \sqrt{\beta}Z + \sqrt{1 - \beta}\varepsilon_i.$$

The asset correlation, measuring the exposure of loan i to systematic risk, is then $\sqrt{\beta}$. This model formulation yields,

$$K(p) = P\left(\frac{1}{M}\sum_{i=1}^{M} L_i \leq \frac{m}{M}\right) = N\left(\frac{1}{\sqrt{1-\beta}}N^{-1}(p) + \sqrt{\frac{\beta}{1-\beta}}N^{-1}\left(\frac{m}{M}\right)\right). \qquad (4.40)$$

The calibration parameters here are the homogeneous CAPM $\beta{:}s$ common to all loans and the common, "normalized," default threshold, $N^{-1}(p)$.

As we discussed in the context of the Merton-based multifactor models—in this setting of a large homogeneous portfolio—the credit index, $\hat{Z}_i$, is not a latent (unobserved) variable anymore. We can observe, $\hat{Z}_i$, using the homogenous portfolios historical default rates, p. Specifically, applying the transformation, $N(\hat{Z}_i)$, we can convert the model, for example, in its single factor form in equation (4.39), to a classical regression analysis credit score model where we can estimate the impact of the systematic factors, Z, on the observed default rates.

The equation (4.40) is also recognized as the model in the Basel II regulation to compute advanced internal model based credit risk capital requirements for financial institutions banking book exposures at the 99.9% confidence level (i.e., $\frac{m}{M} = 0.999$). Note here that since equation (4.40) is concave in the most relevant range for p we have that

$$M \times K\left(\frac{1}{M}\sum_{i=1}^{M} p_i\right) \geq \sum_{i=1}^{M} K(p_i)$$

so that from the perspective of the regulated institution applying equation (4.40) on an individual level is desirable.

In the Basel II setting capital is adjusted by the loss given default (LGD) rate. Furthermore, capital is only held for the unexpected losses, consistent with banks making provisions for expected losses. There is also a regulatory maturity adjustment, yielding the actual Basel II capital requirement, $\tilde{K}(p)$, as

$$\tilde{K}(p) = \text{EAD} \times [\text{LGD} \times K(p) - \text{PD} \times \text{LGD}] \times \tilde{M} \qquad (4.41)$$

where $\tilde{M}$ is the Basel II maturity adjustment and with EAD the exposure at default. The Basel II (Basel Committee, 2005c) explanatory note on the risk weight functions explains the rationale for each of the terms in equation (4.41). The regulatory assigned asset correlation parameter, β, depends on asset class. For large corporate exposures the correlation also depends on PD and the firm size with asset correlations increasing with firm size and decreasing with PD increases.

The large homogeneous portfolio approximation in equation (4.40) is appropriate in case of large homogeneous consumer portfolios. However, if the portfolio is not sufficiently large, such as a smaller commercial portfolio, it may be appropriate to consider a risk add-on for the remaining idiosyncratic risk. See Vasicek (2002), Gordy (2003), and Martin and Wilde (2002) on granularity adjustments to the assumption of infinitely large portfolios. Gordy and Lütkebohmert (2007) apply the granularity adjustment to the Basel II formula to real portfolios. The granularity adjustment is shown to be strongly correlated to the Herfindahl index, which, in this credit risk context, measures the size of firm exposures in relation to total exposures.[26] See also Pykthin (2004) on extensions to multifactor models.

Homogeneous Large Subportfolios Suppose instead of a single large portfolio we have $s = 1, \ldots, S$ infinitely large homogeneous subportfolios. That is, we have $s = 1, \ldots, S$ instances of

$$\int_{[0,\alpha]} dF_{p^s}(p^s) \times E^s$$

with $p^s = g^s(\mathbf{Z}, \mathbf{Y}^s)$, $s = 1, \ldots, S$. We are hence concerned with the composite default distribution

$$\sum_{s=1}^{S} Y^s \tag{4.42}$$

where $Y^s \sim f_{p^s}(p^s)$ (we assume unit loss amount in Y). Since each of the $s = 1, \ldots, S$ subportfolios are large we can apply a conditional law of large numbers such that

$$P\left(\frac{1}{M^s} \sum_{i=1}^{M^s} L_i^s = p^s \mid \mathbf{Z} \right) = 1.$$

Hence, in this model we can evaluate the defaulted fraction, conditional on $\mathbf{Z}$, using the expected loss obtained from the score functions, $\{p^s = g^s(\mathbf{Z}, \mathbf{Y}^s)\}_{s=1}^{S}$. Hence, even if we use simulation to calculate the portfolio loss the computational burden is minimal.

Here we can have a different average expected default frequency for each subportfolio $s = 1, \ldots, S$, corresponding to a rating categorization of the portfolio. In addition, we can allow for different $\mathbf{Y}^s$ vectors, that is, differences in the volatility of default rates over time across rating classes and/or loan segments. We can therefore conclude that if we are able to decompose a credit portfolio in the manner of equation (4.42), still reasonably maintaining the assumption that M^s, the number of loans in class s for $s = 1, \ldots, S$ is large, we have the potential to reduce a very large portfolio of size $\sum_{s=1}^{S} M^s$ to just a few categories S for the purpose of computations.

Example Portfolio with Homogeneous Large Subportfolios[27]   Table 4.30 displays the characteristics of a loan portfolio containing 200,000 loans that have been classified in $S = 8$ homogeneous groups. Each of the homogeneous groups has M^s loans with scoring function

$$p^s = N(N^{-1}(\overline{p}^s) - \beta_1^s Z_1 - \beta_2^s Z_2) \tag{4.43}$$

---

[26]Specifically, the Herfindahl index, H, is given by

$$H = \sum_{i=1}^{n} s_i^2$$

where n is the number of firms and s_i the exposure share of firm i. Since the firm exposure shares, s_i, are squared a relatively large Herfindahl index is obtained if there are few firms with a large exposure share. The Herfindahl index can hence be seen as a measure of exposure concentration in a portfolio.
[27]The example is taken from Nyström and Skoglund (2003a).

with specific scoring model parameters $\overline{p}^s$, (β_1^s, β_2^s). Here $\overline{p}^s$ is interpreted as the parameter that sets homogeneous group s model expected default frequency at the empirical default rate. The parameters β_1^s and β_2^s correspond to elements of the parameter vector Υ^s in the scoring equation $p^s = g^s(\mathbf{Z}, \Upsilon^s)$ where, in this example, g is the normal cumulative density function and the common factors, Z_1 and Z_2, are independent standard normal. That is, $Z_1, Z_2 \sim N(0, 1)$. The choice of β:s for the homogeneous loan groups (see Table 4.30) implicitly defines the strength of default correlation within as well as between groups. Table 4.30 also displays the individual loans in group $s = 1, \ldots, S$ recovery-adjusted exposure in unit of currency, E^s.

Table 4.31 displays simulated expected losses (EL), VaR and contribution VaR (Cont VaR) for the homogeneous groups as well as for the aggregate portfolio at the 99.9% confidence level. In the table Cont VaR is the simulated VaR risk contribution for the homogeneous subportfolios. Hence, Cont VaR/M^s is the risk contribution of a single loan in homogeneous group $s = 1, \ldots, S$. The number of simulations used is 10,000 and since the subportfolios are large we can simulate the score from the model in equation (4.43) using a representative member of each class $s = 1, \ldots, 8$. Subsequently, we multiply by the number of loans in the class, M^s, and the recovery-adjusted exposure, E^s, for one subportfolio member to obtain the scenario (expected) loss. Hence, while the portfolios size is 200,000 loans the computational burden is reduced to analyzing 8 representative loans.

We now move on to focus on the case when the portfolio is either heterogeneous, or the homogeneous portfolios are too small for a conditional law of large numbers.

Heterogeneous Portfolios or Homogeneous Small Portfolios   In the homogeneous large subportfolios example above we could employ the conditional law of large numbers as a dimension reduction technique for every subportfolio $s = 1, \ldots, S$. In practice, only one or just a few exposures may be considered to belong to a homogeneous group themselves. That is, the portfolio may be heterogeneous, or may only have small subportfolios that are homogeneous. For subportfolios $s = 1, \ldots, S$ with small number of loans M^s, the conditional law

TABLE 4.30   Portfolio Homogeneous Group Characteristics

Parameters	Subportfolio							
	1	2	3	4	5	6	7	8
M^s	25,000	12,500	10,000	25,000	40,000	50,000	25,000	12,500
$\overline{p}^s \times 100$	0.71	0.36	0.40	1.22	0.71	0.40	0.34	0.29
β_1^s	−0.09	0.02	0.01	−0.05	−0.02	−0.07	0.02	0.05
β_2^s	0.01	−0.05	−0.03	0.01	−0.03	−0.01	0.07	0.02
E^s	0.25	0.075	0.4	0.04	0.525	0.3	0.05	0.38

TABLE 4.31   Portfolio Homogeneous Groups Risk Measures

	Subportfolio								
	1	2	3	4	5	6	7	8	Aggregate
EL	45.8	3.49	16.1	12.3	150	61.5	4.41	14.3	309
VaR	93.7	5.6	21.4	18.2	203	112.6	8.31	23.18	442
Cont VaR	50.5	5.7	24.3	18.5	215.5	67.5	15	45	442

of large numbers may not be a good approximation. Of course, the most extreme case is a loan portfolio where each homogeneous subportfolio $s = 1, \ldots, S$ only has one member such that $M^s = 1$ for $s = 1, \ldots, S$. In this case S is usually of the order of millions of loans.

Taking the small subportfolio size into account we now need to consider a random sampling method for subportfolios s. Specifically, for each $s = 1, \ldots, S$ we proceed as follows:

1. Define M^s independent uniform, $u_i \sim U[0, 1]$, random variables. Loan i in subportfolio s is found to be in default if $p^s > u_i$. Here p^s is the realized score function, $p^s = g^s(\mathbf{Z}, \mathbf{Y}^s)$, conditional on a realization of $\mathbf{Z}$.
2. Define the default indicator, $\chi_{(p^s > u_i)}$, and compute the sum $\sum_{i=1}^{M^s} \chi_{(p^s > u_i)} \times E^s$ and record the loss in the scenario.

We note that in this context of small homogeneous portfolios we may as well have individual score functions for each loan in the portfolio. Hence, the portfolio is completely heterogeneous such that each homogeneous subportfolio $s = 1, \ldots, S$ only has one member. Of course, in practice we may also have a combined situation with some subportfolios being homogeneous and large enough for a conditional law of large numbers approximation and some heterogeneous (or small homogeneous). We can then employ the conditional law of large numbers simulation method for the large homogeneous subportfolios, whereas the uniform sampling method steps above are used for the heterogeneous (or small homogeneous) subportfolios.

For a large heterogenous portfolio (e.g., a mortgage portfolio) with loan-specific scoring models the uniform sampling method is of course computational heavy. However, loan-level models are being used in practice in portfolio credit risk analysis.

Applying a heterogeneous portfolio interpretation to the example portfolio in Table 4.30 we can consider the portfolio as having only 8 loans—each having a very large exposures taken to be $M^s \times E^s$. In that case VaR may not be the appropriate choice of risk measure. In particular the VaR for any of the 8 loans jumps discretely from zero to $M^s \times E$ as a function of the risk confidence level and since the portfolio is small its aggregate portfolio distribution characteristics are similar. Accordingly, this also makes it difficult to interpret VaR risk contributions. With this portfolio interpretation it is therefore desirable to consider risk measures that take into account all the tail losses such as CVaR.

Credit Transition Score Models

We are now concerned with the more general modeling of the transition probability of a loan or a borrower to a certain state $k = 1, \ldots, \widehat{K}$ at time $t = 1, \ldots, T$ and we define this transition probability as $P_i^{l,r}(t)$ as the probability of moving from state l to r for loan i. If we have that $P_i^{l,r}(t) = P_i^{l,r}$ for all $l = 1, 2, \ldots, \widehat{K}$ and $r = 1, 2, \ldots, \widehat{K}$, then the transition probability is said to be time homogeneous. However, in credit risk applications it is common that $P_i^{l,r}(t)$ depends on t through both macroeconomic variables as well as idiosyncratic variables such as age-indexed variables. The transition probabilities, $P_i^{l,r}(t)$, are then referred to as non-stationary or time inhomogeneous. This is the typical model case and the reader may recall that in the Merton inspired multifactor credit migration models we obtained, conditional on $\mathbf{Z}$, the expected state occupancy probabilities through a simple Markov iteration (see equation (4.29)). A key assumption to obtaining the simple, computationally efficient Markov iteration approximation was that the multifactor model transition rates did not depend on past transition history so that we could condition the state transition probabilities on the macroeconomic time variables, **Z**, and any other idiosyncratic time varying variable such as age. However, while for the trading book and wholesale credit exposures one generally does not include past transition history in the state transition probabilities this is more likely for the retail banking book.[28] In practice, for retail portfolios the dependence of the future transition probabilities on past state transitions comes from the modeling of transitions to delinquency states, which likely depend on delinquency history. Such historical events are usually modeled through indicators such as time since last delinquency, number of past delinquencies, spell of last delinquency. While this kind of path-dependence in state transition probabilities is not hard to capture in a simulation-based approach the corresponding Markov iterations for models with path-dependence in state transition probabilities can be more complex. The complexity comes from the fast expansion of the behavioral event space over time.

When modeling the joint credit quality of, for example, loans, consumers, and small firms, there are in general two distinct model approaches that can be used for the inclusion of the common macroeconomic variables, {**Z**}, that are important as drivers of the portfolio default and migration risk correlation. The first approach focuses on scoring consumers and firms, at a particular point in time, using a model with only idiosyncratic factors such as borrower income, age, past credit behavior, and delinquency history indicators.[29] Having point in time score models one therefore relies on an ex-post inclusion of the common macroeconomic time-variables, **Z**, when considering their use in a credit portfolio loss model. The second approach is focused on dynamic score models where one models explicitly the time dimension of the default indicator using both idiosyncratic factors and common credit factors.

Below we will first focus on the time inhomogeneous Markov case and introduce a dynamic scorecard model that depends on the macroeconomic factors; after that we will consider the point in time scorecard model and consider a special, multinomial logit approach to ex-post inclusion of the macroeconomic factors. After this we will return to the discussion of more general credit score or credit transition models that depend on past transition history as well as macroeconomic factors for their future transition probabilities.

Dynamic Markov Scoring Models Assuming $B_i(t)_{i=1}^M$ is a 0-1 binary default indicator for the M loans at time $t = 0, 1, \ldots, T$ and focusing on first-order Markov models, we have the Markov transition probabilities for loan or consumer i as

$$P_i(t) = \begin{bmatrix} 1 - P_i^{0,1}(t) & P_i^{0,1}(t) \\ 0 & 1 \end{bmatrix} \tag{4.44}$$

where $P_i^{0,1}(t)$ is the one-period default probability and $1 - P_i^{0,1}(t)$ is the one-period survival probability at time t conditional on survival up to time $t - 1$. That is,

$$P_i^{0,1}(t) = P(B_i(t) = 1 \mid B_i(t - 1) = 0).$$

---

[28]However, see Cantor and Hamilton (2004) on the failure of the assumption of a first-order Markov for the Moodys transition matrices. In practice however one still often employs the first-order markov assumption in the credit portfolio models.
[29]See Thomas, Edelmann, and Crook (2002) for a textbook account on models and performance measures used in credit scoring.

The last row of the transition matrix in (4.44) derives its behavior from the fact that the default state is absorbing.[30] The likelihood, L_Q, for the two-state first-order Markov model, is now given by

$$L_Q = \Pi_{i=1}^M \Pi_{t=1}^T \left[g_{it}^{B_i(t)} (1 - g_{it})^{(1-B_i(t))} \right]^{(1-B_i(t-1))},$$

where $g_{it} = g_{it}(\mathbf{Z}_t, \mathbf{X}_i, \boldsymbol{\beta}_i)$ is the score function, for example, the logistic function

$$g(v) = \frac{\exp(v)}{1 + \exp(v)}$$

with idiosyncratic score variables $\mathbf{X}_i$, systematic score variables, $\mathbf{Z}_t$, and parameter vector $\boldsymbol{\beta}_i$. This likelihood arises due to the fact that if $B_i(t-1) = 1$, then loan i is in default. Hence, the terms involving period t are raised to the power $B_i(t-1)$ because they are only observed when loan i does not go bankrupt in period $t-1$.

In practice, the dynamic score model may also need to handle the fact that some loans exit the portfolio at times without defaulting on their obligations (e.g., by prepayments). This feature of the Markov model is referred to as *right censoring*. Taking right censoring into account we have that

$$L_Q = \Pi_{i=1}^M \Pi_{t=1}^T \left[g_{it}^{B_i(t)} (1 - g_{it})^{(1-B_i(t))} \right]^{(1-B_i(t-1))d_i(t)} \tag{4.45}$$

where

$$d_i(t) = \left\{ \begin{array}{ll} 1 & \text{if no censoring occurs} \\ 0 & \text{if censoring occurs} \end{array} \right\},$$

and if $d_i(t-1) = 0$, then $d_i(t) = 0$. That is, if a loan exits, it does not come back.

Note that once we have calibrated the scoring model using the likelihood in equation (4.45), we can now simulate correlated loan credit scores by simulating the common credit factors, $\mathbf{Z}$, and evaluating the dynamic score model, $g_{it} = g_{it}(\mathbf{Z}_t, \mathbf{X}_i, \boldsymbol{\beta}_i)$. Loan i is found to be in default if $g_{it} > u_i$ where $u_i \sim U[0, 1]$ and $\{u_i\}_{i=1}^M$ are independent. Hence, in this model credit correlation derives from the correlated credit scores, $\{g_{it}\}_{i=1}^M$.

For examples of successful applications taking a direct dynamic approach to score model estimation using variants of the likelihood in equation (4.45) we refer to Shumway (2001) and Carling et al. (2002). In addition Carling et al. (2002) employ their dynamic scorecards directly in simulation of credit portfolio loss.

Stein et al. (2010) use a Cox proportional hazard model with time-varying covariates to represent the systematic factors for mortgage portfolios and model survival times. The Cox proportional hazard model (Cox, 1972) is a continuous time survival model. It models the duration to an event instead of the occurrence of the event as in the discrete Markov model. As in the discrete Markov model it can be used to model multiple types of events (competing states; e.g., time to migration in addition to time to default). It provides an alternative model approach to the discrete time Markov chain model we have considered. Essentially, this is the same relation as between an exponential distribution and a Poisson distribution. However, the discrete Markov model can also generate expected default (survival) times as well as the

---

[30] $B_i(0) = 0$ for all loans $i = 1, \ldots, M$ (or consumers or whatever the measurement objects may be) as they are not already in default at the start of the sampling period.

continuous time duration models can generate a default probability. Hence, in practice the exact choice of model may not be that important.

The modeling of survival times rather than discrete default events is frequently used for retail portfolios with default mode only models over longer horizons for computational efficiency reasons. The Cox proportional hazard model has a hazard rate, for loan i, as in equation (4.31) of the form

$$h^i(t) = \overline{h}(t) \exp(\boldsymbol{\beta}_i' \mathbf{Z}_t)$$

where $\boldsymbol{\beta}_i$ are the loan i specific factor loadings and the proportional term, $\overline{h}(t)$, introduces the non-stationarity baseline of the hazard rate over time—independent of the systematic factors.

Example of a Cox Proportional Hazard Model As a concrete numerical example, we consider the model

$$h^i(t) = 0.002 \exp(4.1 \times Z_1 + 50 \times Z_2 + 100 \times Z_3).$$

This model specifies an increasing hazard rate when any of the systematic factors, Z_1, Z_2, Z_3, increase with a baseline hazard rate of 0.002. To use the model in default sampling at times t_1, t_2, and t_3 or to calculate the survival time we need to define scenarios for the systematic factors. Using two different multi-horizon scenarios for the systematic factors, Z_1, Z_2, Z_3, over times t_1, t_2, and t_3 we now compute the hazard rate, h, the survival rate, S in %, the cumulative default probability, CP in %, and the incremental default probability, IP in %. The results are displayed in Table 4.32 together with the assumed scenarios for the systematic factors. Here the systematic factors, Z_1, Z_2, Z_3, are interpreted as respectively the debt-to-income ratio, the unemployment rate, and the interest rate. The two scenarios share the same time t_1 values for the systematic factors. At times t_2 and t_3 scenario 1 has a worsening debt-to-income ratio, an increasing unemployment rate (expressed in %), and increasing interest rates (expressed in %) while scenario 2 has the reverse scenario evolution. Because of the different evolution of the scenarios for the systematic factors, we find that scenario 1 has increasing incremental default probabilities at times t_2 and t_3 while scenario 2 has decreasing incremental default probabilities at times t_2 and t_3. Using a random sampling model we could now sample a uniform variable u for each t_1, t_2, and t_3 to determine whether the loan is in default at that time conditional on the scenario for the systematic factors.

TABLE 4.32 Cox Model Example with Two Different Scenarios for the Systematic Factors

Time	Z_1	Z_2	Z_3	h	S	CP	IP
				Scenario 1			
t_1	0.2	4%	2%	0.0248	97.55%	2.45%	2.45%
t_2	0.25	4.5%	2.3%	0.0775	92.54%	7.46%	5.01%
t_3	0.28	4.7%	2.5%	0.1581	85.38%	14.62%	7.16%
				Scenario 2			
t_1	0.2	4%	2%	0.0248	97.55%	2.45%	2.45%
t_2	0.15	3.5%	1.7%	0.0364	96.42%	3.58%	1.13%
t_3	0.12	3.3%	1.5%	0.0441	95.69%	4.31%	0.73%

We can also directly determine the default time of the loan, τ_i, using the survival function as in equation (4.33), although here we have a time-varying hazard rate such that the equivalent of equation (4.33) becomes

$$\tau_i = \inf \left\{ t \colon \exp \left(- \int_0^t h_i(s)\, ds \right) \le u_i \right\}.$$

The reader interested in further analysis of duration models is referred to Amemiya (1985, ch. 11) for an excellent account on Markov chain and duration (survival) models and the duration model as the continuous time limit of the discrete time Markov chain model. Lancaster (1990) also contains many examples of econometric models for duration analysis.

When prepayments is included in the duration model there are competing risks of prepayment and default. Prepayment increases the inflow of the capital but can reduce the future revenue. Different models of the prepayment can affect how the actual revenue evolves. The competing risk model is frequently used for mortgages as a homeowner may default or prepay at any point in time. The incentive for prepayment also depends on the costs. For example, in case there are significant prepayment penalties that can be charged by banks for homeowners the prepayment risk may be reduced significantly. It is important to recognize prepayment and default as truly competing risk effects. For example, during the 2007 financial crisis in the United States, because of low interest rates, one could expect to see high prepayment rates. However, because of significant declines in property prices high loan-to-value ratios made it difficult for borrowers to refinance and high prepayment rates were not realized. See An and Qi (2012) on the competing risk model using proportional hazard models. At each payment period, the model recognizes that the borrower faces the choice of either: (a) make the next scheduled mortgage payment, (b) refinance the mortgage and prepay the debt, or (c) default on the mortgage obligation.

With a statistical model approach to competing risks the competing risk effects can be modeled by the so-called multinomial logit models, which are used to model relationships between a polytomous response variable and a set of regressor variables. This model class has a wide application in the study of consumer choice behaviors. However, the borrower options can also be viewed from the financial engineering point of view.[31] We refer the reader to Chapter 7 on funds transfer pricing and profitability of cash flows and the discussion in that chapter on modeling consumer embedded optionality using either financial engineering approaches or statistical behavior models.

As we have mentioned, during the 2007 financial crisis, prepayments rates were very low in spite of a low interest rate environment. This low level of prepayments could not be predicted with the classical prepayment models focusing on prepayment incentive based on interest rate levels alone. To be able to predict accurately the low level of prepayments during the financial stress several other prepayment incentive factors have to be taken into account. Examples include the declining home property prices mentioned above as well as worsening credit scores in stress, tightening lending standards by banks and a more risk-averse behavior of consumers making them less prone to changing their contractual obligations. See Krainer and Laderman (2011) for an analysis of the prepayment and delinquency behavior in US mortgage portfolios during the crisis. The fact that prepayment rates tended to decline significantly during the 2007 financial crisis suggests that in many cases it is more prudent to

---

[31]Recall from the Merton pricing model that default can be viewed as a put option. Similarly, prepayment can be viewed as a call option.

assume very low or even zero prepayments under stress. However, zero prepayments may not be the most prudent assumption in all cases. It depends, for example, on how the contractual interest income loss is booked and the analysis horizon.

Building the Credit Transition Matrix When the credit risk model only has default and no default states, the corresponding transition matrix is simple as in (4.44) and only requires the estimation of a single transition probability, $P_i^{0,1}(t)$, to define the complete transition matrix. When the credit risk model has multiple competing states, which is the case we will mainly focus on, one has to consider models for each of the non-absorbing states transition probabilities, $\{P^{l,r}(t)\}_{l=1,r=1}^{\hat{K}-1,\hat{K}}$. Of course, since for each row $l = 1,\ldots,\hat{K}$ the transition probabilities must sum to unity we can choose one of the $r = 1,\ldots,\hat{K}$ as the "residual" probability for each $l = 1,\ldots,\hat{K} - 1$. Hence, we only need to estimate a maximum of $\hat{K} - 1$ transition probabilities for each row.

Once we have estimated all the necessary dynamic Markov scoring models for the different possible state transitions we can build the transition matrix by inserting the transition models. For this reason we assume that at $t = 0$ each of the non-defaulted loans are located in one of the classes $1, 2, \ldots, \hat{K} - 1$. To the classes we assign a $\hat{K} \times \hat{K}$ matrix of transition probabilities, $\mathbf{A} = \{A_{lr}\}$, with the last row of $\mathbf{A}$ defined as $[0\ 0\ \cdots\ 0\ 1]$ being the absorbing default state. That is,

$$\mathbf{A} = \begin{bmatrix} A_{11} & \cdots & A_{1\hat{K}} \\ \vdots & \cdots & \vdots \\ A_{\hat{K}-11} & \cdots & A_{\hat{K}-1\hat{K}} \\ 0 & \cdots & 1 \end{bmatrix}. \tag{4.46}$$

The transition matrix is hence a matrix valued stochastic process such that element $A_{lr}(t) = P^{l,r}(t)$ describes the probability, at t, that a loan in class l will make a transition to class r during the interval $(t, t + 1]$. If the transition probabilities and hence the transition matrix is loan specific for loan i, we can index it such that loan i has transition matrix $\mathbf{A}^i$ with transition probabilities, $\{P_i^{l,r}(t)\}_{l=1,r=1}^{\hat{K}-1,\hat{K}}$. While the transition matrix (4.46) only has one explicit absorbing state, there can in practice be more than one absorbing state in the credit transition matrix, for example, if prepayment is a competing risk. Other examples of competing risks include loan modification or restructuring. However, in that case the loan usually goes back to being in a non-defaulted state immediately after the modification.

Since by definition we have that,

$$\sum_{r=1}^{\hat{K}} A_{lr}(t) = 1, \tag{4.47}$$

$$A_{lr}(t) \geq 0$$

it means that individual transition models that are used to estimate the transition probabilities in a particular row of the transition matrix are constrained to sum to unity as required by a transition matrix. This is the case with the multinomial logit model that we will discuss below in the context of ex-post inclusion of macroeconomic factors to static Markov scoring models. However, in many cases the models for each transition rate in a row of the transition matrix can be estimated individually with no explicit multinomial model constraint, for example, using individual hazard models or binomial logistic regressions for the transition probabilities. In that case, one needs to normalize the row transition probabilities to sum to unity. A frequently used normalization formula in this context is the so-called log-odds ratio normalization that appears in the multinomial logistic model (see Begg and Gray, 1984 and equation (4.52)).

Point in Time Markov Scoring Models Returning to our discrete time Markov model, we can investigate the case when the default indicators $\{B_i(t)\}_{i=1}^M$ are assumed independent over time, $t = 1, \ldots, T$. In this case we have the extremely simple transition matrix

$$P_i(t) = \begin{bmatrix} 1 - P_i^{0,1}(t) & P_i^{0,1}(t) \\ 1 - P_i^{0,1}(t) & P_i^{0,1}(t) \end{bmatrix}$$

with associated likelihood,

$$L_Q = \Pi_{t=1}^T \Pi_{i=1}^M \left[g_{it}^{B_i(t)d_i(t)} (1 - g_{it})^{(1-B_i(t))} \right].$$

Such one-period scoring models are however only interesting in the case of a pure cross-section sample at a particular time point $t - 1$ of idiosyncratic factors with realized indicators $\{B_i(t)\}_{i=1}^M$. This is due to the assumption of exchangeability of default and non-default states. Due to this simplification, we may also drop the time-dimension and write

$$L_Q = \Pi_{i=1}^M \left(g_i^{B_i} (1 - g_i)^{(1-B_i)} \right) \tag{4.48}$$

which is the likelihood of the well-known qualitative response models such as the Probit model and logistic regression being frequently used for behavioral scoring.

We now focus on approaches to ex-post inclusion of the common credit factors. This is because in practice many scoring models are calibrated using behavioral scores at specific points in time, say monthly or quarterly, that is, the approach using the likelihood equation (4.48). While this creates a history of credit scores or, more generally, a realized migration over credit quality states obtained from the credit scores (which may be influenced by economic state) we require an ex-post inclusion of the common credit factors, $\{Z\}$, to understand their impact over time.[32] Our analysis is targeted toward discrete time Markov models rather than duration models as we will focus on models that can capture different credit quality transitions over time and not just time to an event such as default or transition.

Point in Time Markov Scoring Models and Ex-post Inclusion of Macroeconomic Factors Here we consider general, multinomial, score transition models, suggested by Nyström and Skoglund (2006), that are designed for an aggregate of loans and in particular the observed empirical time series of transition frequencies of loans. We focus on a multinomial logistic model because it is tractable for estimation and simulation and also automatically restricts transition probabilities for a state to sum to unity as is required by a transition matrix.

---

[32]The terminology "ex-post inclusion of the common credit factors" refers to the way the model is built before it is applied. It uses a two-step process that is often convenient in practice. The first step calculates the credit scores without macroeconomic variables. The second step then adaps the credit scores with macroeconomic models for the purpose of portfolio risk modeling and stress testing.

In addition, the log-odds ratios of the logistic model are linear, which simplifies the estimation considerably.

We should mention that similar approaches to dynamic transition matrix analysis are available in the literature and are usually based on the ordered Probit model. For example, Nickell et al. (2000) consider estimation of transition matrices that depend on macroeconomic variables. They consider an ordered probit model that allows a transition matrix to be conditioned on the business cycle and other factors such as industry. Belkin et al. (1998) use a default/no-default mode macroeconomic credit transition model based on the ordered Probit that is generalized by Wei (2003) to multiple credit states. Wei (2003) models the deviation of the conditional transition matrix from the long-term unconditional transition matrix. The deviation model is referred to as a Z-score model that is a standard normal regression depending on the common macroeconomic factor and rating grade specific factors. The term *Z-score* relates back to the famous Altman (1968) Z-score model for bankruptcy prediction. The reader may also recall that we obtained an ordered Probit formulation, for each row of the transition matrix transition rates conditional on Z, for the multifactor model inspired from the Merton structural approach. Hence, in this loan portfolio setting the model becomes a dynamic transition matrix model. Again, the main benefit of the multinomial logit approach is that the log-odds ratios of the model are linear equations.

Considering the representation of the empirical transition matrix we assume that a collection of $i = 1, \ldots, M$ loans have been scored at past times using the likelihood in equation (4.48). At each time t a loan i has also been classified into one of $k = 1, \ldots, \widehat{K}$ states based on the score or simply its current status (e.g., delinquent 60 days). Hence, we assume the existence of an empirical transition matrix of dimension $\widehat{K} \times \widehat{K}$. Such an empirical transition matrix can be obtained in several ways. The historical time series of empirical transition frequencies may come from internally calculated empirical transition matrices, obtained through a $(\widehat{K} - 1)$-dimensional grade decomposition of the interval $[0, 1]$ to generate rating grades from the idiosyncratic credit scoring model(s). This would typically be the case for retail segments as well as small and medium-sized corporates that do not have external ratings.

Before introducing the multinomial transition model for general $\widehat{K}$ we consider the modeling of default/no-default in the simple aggregate binary logistic model appearing in the well-known CreditPortfolioView scorecard simulation model due to Wilson (1997). In this two-state model for aggregate credit risk migration $p(t) = A_{12}(t)$ is the only cell in the migration matrix that we have to model. We will refer to $p(t)$ as the default rate for the interval $(t, t + 1]$. The aggregate scorecard simulation approach to portfolio credit risk of Wilson (1997) is then defined as

$$p(t) = \frac{\exp(\mu + Z(t)'\beta + v(t))}{1 + \exp(\mu + Z(t)'\beta + v(t))}. \tag{4.49}$$

Here $\{Z(t)\}$ is the vector of systematic factors, μ and β are constants. Just as in the multifactor model for bonds and wholesale exposures the systematic variables should be thought of as variables describing the evolution of economically relevant variables like interest rates and unemployment levels for the loans. The innovations $v(t)$ are assumed to be $N(0, \sigma)$ variables. The main idea in the approach of Wilson (1997) is that loans are supposed to satisfy a certain homogeneity with respect to default risk in the sense that all loans that belong to a specific industry sector, loan type, or geographical region as well as a specific rating class within share the same aggregate scoring model in equation (4.49). For a credit portfolio with $s = 1, \ldots, S$

homogeneous subportfolios we can introduce an index on all variables and parameters in equation (4.49) such that,

$$p_s(t) = \frac{\exp(\mu_s + Z_s(t)'\beta_s + v_s(t))}{1 + \exp(\mu_s + Z_s(t)'\beta_s + v_s(t))}$$

where each element of β_s is assumed non-zero. Collecting the $s = 1, \ldots, S$ models for the total portfolio either all $v_s(t) \sim N(0, \sigma_j)$ are assumed independent or $(v_1, \ldots, v_s) \sim N(\mathbf{0}, \mathbf{\Sigma})$ where $\mathbf{\Sigma}$ is a constant matrix. A useful property of the logistic model specifying $p(t)$ is that the logarithm of the ratio of the default rate and the survival rate is a linear model. That is,

$$\ln\left(\frac{p(t)}{1 - p(t)}\right) = \mu + Z(t)'\beta + v(t).$$

Let $\tilde{p}(t)$ be an empirical time-series of default frequencies. Then, assuming that at all times t there are sufficiently many defaulted loans, we can apply a frequency interpretation to $\tilde{p}(t)$. That is, we can assume that there is no measurement error in $\tilde{p}(t)$ and we can write the equation to be estimated as[33]

$$\ln\left(\frac{\tilde{p}(t)}{1 - \tilde{p}(t)}\right) = \mu + Z(t)'\beta + v(t).$$

Of course, in the case of a portfolio with $s = 1, \ldots, S$ homogeneous segments we similarly have

$$\ln\left(\frac{\tilde{p}_s(t)}{1 - \tilde{p}_s(t)}\right) = \mu_s + Z_s(t)'\beta_s + v_s(t). \tag{4.50}$$

This defines a multivariate linear regression model for the S segments for which the seemingly unrelated estimation technique, as proposed by Zellner (1962), is efficient. With this estimation technique consistent parameter estimates are obtained by applying least squares equation by equation and in the second step an estimate of the covariance matrix of the least squares residuals is used to improve on the efficiency of the least squares estimator using the generalized least squares estimator. In the special case that $Z_s(t)$ are common for all $s = 1, \ldots, S$ seemingly unrelated regression reduces to least squares equation by equation. See Amemiya (1985, p. 197). In applications, this is quite likely to be satisfied across loan classes within a specific sector, loan type, or geographical region.

The basic idea for the more general modeling of state migration risk in Nyström and Skoglund (2006), as opposed to just default risk, is to consider the multinomial logistic model introduced by Theil (1969) for each row of the transition matrix,

$$\mathbf{A} = \begin{bmatrix} A_{11} & \cdots & A_{1\hat{K}} \\ \vdots & \cdots & \vdots \\ A_{\hat{K}-11} & \cdots & A_{\hat{K}-1\hat{K}} \\ 0 & \cdots & 1 \end{bmatrix}$$

---

[33]From an econometric perspective measurement error in $\tilde{p}(t)$ need not induce inconsistency of the parameter estimates. Specifically we could assume that the empirically computed $\tilde{p}(t)$ measures the true default frequency $p(t)$ with a measurement error $d(t) \sim N(0, \tilde{\sigma})$ independent of $\tilde{p}(t)$. In this case we could subsume the measurement error in the residual term $v(t)$.

as in (4.46). Note that since for each $l = 1, 2, \ldots, \hat{K}$, we have the restriction that $\sum_{r=1}^{\hat{K}} A_{lr}(t) = 1$ the choice of functional form is somewhat limited. The multinomial logit formulation expresses the log of a ratio of probabilities as a function of variables. More specifically for $l = 1, 2, \ldots, \hat{K} - 1$ and $r = 1, 2, \ldots, \hat{K} - 1$ we have that

$$\ln \left(\frac{A_{lr}(\mathbf{Z}(t))}{A_{l\hat{K}}(\mathbf{Z}(t))} \right) = \bar{f}_{lr}(\mathbf{Z}(t)). \tag{4.51}$$

This can also be rephrased as

$$A_{lr}(\mathbf{Z}(t)) = \frac{\exp(\bar{f}_{lr}(\mathbf{Z}(t)))}{1 + \sum_{r=1}^{\hat{K}-1} \exp(\bar{f}_{lr}(\mathbf{Z}(t)))}, \tag{4.52}$$

$$A_{lK}(\mathbf{Z}(t)) = \frac{1}{1 + \sum_{r=1}^{\hat{K}-1} \exp(\bar{f}_{lr}(\mathbf{Z}(t)))}.$$

In the following we let $\overline{A} = \{\overline{A}_{lr}\} = \{\bar{f}_{lr}\}$ denote the $(\hat{K} - 1) \times (\hat{K} - 1)$ matrix of log ratios of probabilities. One relevant choice for the function $\bar{f}_{lr}(\mathbf{Z}(t))$ is

$$\bar{f}_{lr}(\mathbf{Z}(t)) = \mu_{lr} + \mathbf{Z}(t)' \boldsymbol{\beta}_{lr} + v_{lr}(t) \tag{4.53}$$

where μ_{lr} and $\boldsymbol{\beta}_{lr}$ are constants and either all $v_{lr} \sim N(0, \sigma_{ls})$ are assumed independent or $(v_{11}, \ldots, v_{\hat{K}-1\hat{K}-1}) \sim N(\mathbf{0}, \boldsymbol{\Sigma})$ with $\boldsymbol{\Sigma}$ a constant matrix. Hence, we now have a straightforward generalization of the two-state model of Wilson (1997) to a multistate setting. The set of equations can be calibrated to empirical transition frequencies using seemingly unrelated regression in the same manner as the aggregate logit model.[34] This is because the model in equation (4.53) is linear.

General Scoring Models that Depend on Past Transition Behavior In the dynamic Markov scoring model the score function, $g_{it} = g_{it}(\mathbf{Z}_t, \mathbf{X}_i, \boldsymbol{\beta}_i)$, depends on the idiosyncratic score variables $\mathbf{X}_i$, the systematic (macroeconomic) score variables, $\mathbf{Z}_t$, and the parameter vector $\boldsymbol{\beta}_i$. Let now $\mathbf{q}_{it}$ be the vector holding the past states we track. For example, $\mathbf{q}_{it}$ could track the monthly state occupancy from the last 2 years by assigning each of the past state numbers or labels from the last 24 months in the vector. The length of the past history we need to track is of course related to how fast the past state information "dies out" in predicting current state transitions. From the past state vector $\mathbf{q}_{it}$ we can create summary indicator variables such as time since last occupancy of a certain state, number of occupancies, and the spells of the occupancies. Let these indicators be denoted by $\mathbf{I}_{it}$ and subsume their parameters in the extended $\boldsymbol{\beta}_i$ parameter vector, $\tilde{\boldsymbol{\beta}}_i$. This gives the credit score or transition function

$$g_{it} = g_{it}(\mathbf{Z}_t, \mathbf{X}_i, \mathbf{I}_{it}, \tilde{\boldsymbol{\beta}}_i). \tag{4.54}$$

---

[34]Specifically, the model is calibrated to the empirical transitions over time transformed to log-odds ratios.

We can now characterize the score variables as being (i) idiosyncratic variables such as bureau credit score, region etc. such as $\mathbf{X}_i$,[35] (ii) common economic variables such as $\mathbf{Z}_t$, or (iii) dynamically updated based on past state transitions such as $\mathbf{I}_{it}$.

With transition models such as equation (4.54) for each transition probability we still build the state transition probability matrix $\mathbf{A}(t) = \{A_{lr}(t)\}$ as in (4.46). The only difference is that the future state transition probabilities in the transition matrix depend on the previous state occupancies through the indicators, $\mathbf{I}_{it}$. As we have mentioned previously, state dependence in the transition probabilities can easily happen in practice when modeling loan delinquency. The delinquency loan transition matrix with default and prepayment as competing absorbing states in Table 4.33 serves as an example.

In Table 4.33 we have the loan current state, delinquency states for the loan being 30, 60, 90, 120, and 150 days past due, as well as the absorbing default and prepayment state. Here, the default state is assumed equivalent to delinquent 180 days and is in practice a technical default definition rather than a "true" default definition. Each row of the transition matrix has competing risks such as when the loan is current this month at the next month there is competing risks of delinquent 30 days and prepayment. Because the loan cannot migrate to, for example, delinquent 60 days in a month from current the transition rate from current to delinquent 60 days is zero.

Considering now a transition probability model for a particular transition probability in the matrix, say $A_{12}(t)$, being the transition probability from current to delinquent 30 days, it is reasonable to assume that this transition probability is not only influenced by the economic state through $\mathbf{Z}_t$ but also by the idiosyncratic past loan states. A simple example are the delinquency indicator functions that are unity if the loan has previously been delinquent in one of the delinquency states and null otherwise. Because this indicator function tracks occupancy of all delinquency states it also represents knowledge of the severity of any previous delinquencies. In practice, the exact timing of any previous delinquencies matter as well as frequency of past delinquencies. For example, some borrowers are frequently delinquent, and delinquency may not be a sign of ultimate default or even increases in transition rates to more severe delinquency states, while for some borrowers that have never previously been delinquent their first delinquency may be a strong sign that they will continue their delinquency spell to more severe delinquencies with ultimate default.

TABLE 4.33 Example Loan Delinquency Transition Matrix

	Current	D30	D60	D90	D120	D150	Prepay	Default
Current	$A_{11}(t)$	$A_{12}(t)$	0	0	0	0	$A_{17}(t)$	0
D30	$A_{21}(t)$	$A_{22}(t)$	$A_{23}(t)$	0	0	0	$A_{27}(t)$	0
D60	$A_{31}(t)$	$A_{32}(t)$	$A_{33}(t)$	$A_{34}(t)$	0	0	$A_{37}(t)$	0
D90	$A_{41}(t)$	$A_{42}(t)$	$A_{43}(t)$	$A_{44}(t)$	$A_{45}(t)$	0	$A_{47}(t)$	0
D120	$A_{51}(t)$	$A_{52}(t)$	$A_{53}(t)$	$A_{54}(t)$	$A_{55}(t)$	$A_{56}(t)$	$A_{57}(t)$	0
D150	$A_{61}(t)$	$A_{62}(t)$	$A_{63}(t)$	$A_{64}(t)$	$A_{65}(t)$	$A_{66}(t)$	$A_{67}(t)$	$A_{68}(t)$
Prepay	0	0	0	0	0	0	1	0
Default	0	0	0	0	0	0	0	1

---

[35]We also count the age-indexed variables such as loan age here. The age-indexed variable values at $t = 1, \ldots, T$ are known at $t = 0$. For simplicity we do not index $\mathbf{X}_i = \mathbf{X}_i(t)$.

When delinquency behavior is included in the transition probability model we must in general track the delinquency behavior for a particular loan simulated state transition path across, $t = 1, \ldots, T$. That is, we need to dynamically update the vector $\mathbf{I}_{it}$ that holds information about past transition states. When delinquency behavior is included in the model it is also important to understand the interaction between macroeconomic variables and the delinquency behavior. For example, a particular borrower's past delinquencies may be driven by past bad economic states that saw the borrower in difficulty meeting payments. It may also be driven by borrower idiosyncratic factors as well as behavior that is largely independent of economic state. The explicit modeling of loan delinquencies may hence mask the effect of macroeconomic variables in determining future delinquencies. This should be taken into consideration when the main model objective is to capture the changes in the credit quality of the portfolio over a business cycle or a worst-case economic scenario for $\mathbf{Z}(t)$, that is, to capture the variation of the credit losses due to systematic effects. In practice, currently delinquent accounts are likely to contribute significantly to portfolio losses in the short run, while current accounts are likely to contribute to portfolio losses over a longer time horizon. The impact of the macroeconomic variables on delinquency and default behavior also depends strongly on the choice of calibration period as well as the credit quality of the borrower. If the model is calibrated on a period with small changes in the macroeconomic environment (as opposed to the 2007 financial crisis period), it is likely that the model will not be able to capture correctly the different credit quality segments' sensitivity to the economic cycle. It will therefore also not be able to predict correctly the amount of losses in severe economic scenarios. See Canals-Cerdá and Kerr (2015), who employ credit score models with macroeconomic factors to credit card portfolios calibrated on data including the 2007 financial crisis. They find that the impact of macroeconomic factors is significant but heterogeneous across portfolio risk segments with the prime (better quality) borrowers being more sensitive to the economic cycle.

Comparing the delinquency model approach with the point in time credit score model with ex-post inclusion of macroeconomic factors in equation (4.53) we note that in the credit score model we first create, at different times, credit quality grades based on the idiosyncratic loan behavior.[36] Such idiosyncratic loan behavior may of course include past delinquency behavior. However, given many loan grade classifications over time, we use macroeconomic variables to indicate likely common future delinquency and default behavior in the portfolio for a grade. Hence, the loan grade, at each time, is determined by its idiosyncratic behavior while the future portfolio behavior over time is driven by the common economic state variables. The sensitivity of future delinquencies and default to the economic state depends on the loan grades historical sensitivity, obtained when calibrating the model equations (4.53) to the historical behavior.

The modeling of delinquency behavior also depends on the measurement frequency. For example, with a quarterly time horizon we can reduce the monthly delinquency states in the transition matrix in Table 4.33 to D90 (delinquent 90 days) and the default state (delinquent 180 days). This gives the reduced transition matrix in Table 4.34. A quarterly delinquency transition matrix specification was used by the Federal Reserve in the United States for the 2012 CCAR supervisory projected loss estimates for residential mortgages. The idiosyncratic score factors included the original interest rate margin or spread relative to a reference

---

[36] As we have discussed, different credit quality grades have in general different sensitivities to the economic factors. Hence, it is usually not sufficient to consider current loans as a homogeneous group when estimating its sensitivity to the economic factors.

TABLE 4.34 Example Loan Delinquency Transition
Matrix—Reduced Delinquency States with a Quarterly
Measurement Horizon

	Current	D90	Prepay	Default
Current	$A_{11}(t)$	$A_{12}(t)$	$A_{13}(t)$	0
D90	$A_{21}(t)$	$A_{22}(t)$	$A_{23}(t)$	$A_{24}(t)$
Prepay	0	0	1	0
Default	0	0	0	1

rate (e.g., 30-year Treasury yield), borrower original credit score, current loan to value, and delinquency history. Key macroeconomic drivers included the state level unemployment rate, national property price index, and market interest rates. See Federal Reserve (2012) CCAR frequently asked questions. A specific bank can of course choose to use a monthly transition model (as in Table 4.33) for their CCAR quarterly stress test projections.[37] However, the projected monthly losses then need to be aggregated to the CCAR required quarterly horizons.

Models that include delinquency states have in general a more complex cash flow calculation due to the tracking of the past delinquency. This means that cash flows depend on the past state and not only the current state. Consider a monthly measurement horizon with a monthly payment loan that is currently past due 30 days (one month). If in the previous state the loan was past due 120 days (four months), the loan cash flows in the current state include the past 3 months' accruals as well as the required current monthly payment.

Different ways to solve the delinquency model as well as the other credit transition models we have discussed in this section will be discussed in detail below.

Simulation of State Transitions and Markov Iteration

Simulation of State Transitions To simulate a credit state for a loan i we take as given a state transition matrix, $\mathbf{A} = \mathbf{A}(t)$, at a particular time t. Here we assume that each row of the transition probability is normalized to sum to unity, for example, using a log-odds ratio normalization or an explicit multinomial model specification. However, we do not assume a specific model for the transition rates in the transition matrix such that the transition models can contain past transition information such as past delinquency behavior.

Sampling a uniform random variable $u_i \in [0,1]$ we have that the transition state of loan i, previously in state l at t, is determined by the $k = 1,\ldots,\widehat{K}$-dimensional transition indicator $\mathbf{d}_i(t)$ where element k of $\mathbf{d}_i(t)$ is unity if and only if

$$u_i \in \left(\sum_{r=1}^{k-1} A_{lr}(t+1), \sum_{r=1}^{k} A_{lr}(t+1) \right). \qquad (4.55)$$

The sampling at $t = 1,\ldots,T$ creates a state transition path determined by the $\widehat{K}$-dimensional transition indicators $\{\mathbf{d}_i(t)\}_{t=1}^{T}$. We again note that the transition matrix $\mathbf{A} = A(t)$ can depend on time, be specific for loan i, and be based on loan i's past state transitions. Still, once the

---

[37]CCAR considers the scenario analysis over the next nine quarters.

dynamic transition matrix transition probabilities have been obtained the evaluation of the new loan grade is trivial. Note also from equation (4.55) that we only need to update the time $t + 1$ transition probabilities for row l of the transition matrix, $A(t + 1)$, and not all the transition probabilities. This saves computational time since the transition probabilities obtained from the models generally have to be recomputed for each t and loan i.

For a portfolio of $i = 1, \ldots, M$ loans this sampling is done independently. Hence, credit correlation results from the correlated transition intensities driven by the systematic factors, $\{Z\}$. As for the Merton-based multifactor model, we can of course consider various distributions and copulas for the systematic factors, $\{Z\}$.[38] When transition rates depend on past loan behavior the past loan behavior also drives the credit correlation. Consider a loan portfolio, now current, but with loans that have recently been delinquent and thus, in general, having higher transition probabilities of the loans moving from current to delinquent state.

Markov Iteration: Pools, Stress Testing and the Conditional Law of Large Numbers When the loan transition models are time inhomogeneous (non-stationary) Markov and homogeneous across loans we can use a relatively simple pool approximation based on the expected state transitions for a loan. That is, for a large pool of loans that are homogeneous with respect to rating grade (state) at $t = 0$ and the score transition model we can make use of the conditional law of large numbers to understand the frequency of transition from rating class l at $t = 0$ to rating class $k = 1, \ldots, \hat{K}$ at any time t by iterating the relation

$$y(t) = [A(t)]'y(t - 1). \tag{4.56}$$

Here $y(t)$ is a $\hat{K} \times 1$ vector of frequencies and $y(0)$ contains zeros in all positions except at position l. Note that we used the same Markov iteration equation in the context of portfolio credit risk for bonds and the multifactor model (see equation (4.29)). This iteration equation is of course of particular use in applications to large-scale homogeneous portfolios as it has the potential to reduce the computational burden considerably. As for the multifactor model case we do not have to assume homogeneity in recovery or exposures, which makes the method especially appealing. All that is required is that the pool shares a common current rating and homogeneous transition models. This is the case with the multinomial logit transition models in equation (4.53) yielding a homogeneous state transition matrix for each t.

As for the Markov iteration equation for bonds in the multifactor model the algorithm in equation (4.56) is not only useful for credit pools approximations. It is also useful for stress testing at loan level. By using the iteration equation (4.56) for a specific loan i we obtain the expected state transition fractions of the loan for a given multi-horizon scenario of the credit factors, $\{Z\}$. That is, the random sampling of R state transition paths for a given $\{Z(t)\}_{t=1}^{T}$ scenario and the subsequent calculation of expected state frequencies at times $t = 1, \ldots, T$

---

[38]Note here the differences between model approches to assign credit correlation in credit portfolio models. In the Merton-based credit portfolio models dependence is derived from the dependence of the uniform random variables $u_i \in [0, 1]$ where $u_i = N(\hat{Z}_i)$ for the multifactor model case. The transition probabilities are exogenously given as constant, long-run, transition probabilities. In contrast, in this reduced form correlated credit score model approach to credit portfolio risk the uniform variables $u_i \in [0, 1]$ are independent between loans while the transition probabilities are stochastic and dependent.

converge to the Markov iteration state frequencies, $\{\mathbf{y}(t)\}_{t=1}^{T}$, in equation (4.56) as R grows large. Specifically, for a loan i we have that

$$\mathbf{y}^{i}(t) = \lim_{R\to\infty} \mathbf{x}_{i}^{R}(t) = \lim_{R\to\infty} \left(\frac{1}{R} \sum_{r=1}^{R} \mathbf{d}_{i}^{r}(t) \right)$$

where $\{\mathbf{d}_{i}^{r}(t)\}_{r=1}^{R}$ are the $r = 1, \ldots, R$, $\hat{K}$-dimensional transition indicators for loan i obtained from the state transition sampling conditional on the economic scenario, $\{\mathbf{Z}(t)\}_{t=1}^{T}$. Hence, as in the multifactor model, we can obtain the loan expected loss in a stress scenario *without* sampling.

The computational advantage of equation (4.56) for a pool of loans relies on the assumption of homogeneity in the state transition matrix, $\mathbf{A}(t)$, in the pool. Similarly, the simplicity of the Markov iteration to compute expected state fractions of a loan or a pool of loans relies on the assumption that the transition rates do not depend on past state transitions.

When the loan transition models depend on past transition behavior, such as past delinquency history, the corresponding pool iteration as in equation (4.56) can be very complex. A simple example serves as illustration. We assume that at $t = 0$ there is a pool of loans, with the same past transition behavior, that have future homogeneous state transition probabilities conditional on the experienced state transition behavior, that is, the state transition matrix, $\mathbf{A}(t)$, is common for any of the loans in the pool that take a common future state transition path. Given the same past behavior, such homogeneity can be obtained by classifying loans in approximately homogeneous groups based on their transition probabilities—similar to what we did for the multinomial logit model. The added complexity here is of course that we need to allow a specific loan's future experienced state transition history to influence its state transition probabilities in the future. Consider now a loan in state k that migrates to the vector of state fractions $\mathbf{y}(1)$ at time step 1—determined by the k:th row of the transition matrix $\mathbf{A}(1)$. That is,

$$\mathbf{y}(1) = [\mathbf{A}(1)]'\mathbf{y}(0).$$

Now, at time step 2 we need to incorporate the fact that the state history influences the transition probabilities and hence we obtain at time step 2,

$$\mathbf{y}(2) = \sum_{k_1=1}^{\hat{K}} [\mathbf{A}_{k_1}(2)]'\mathbf{y}_{k_1}(1)$$

where $\mathbf{A}_{k_1}(2)$ is the $t = 2$ state transition probability matrix for loans previously (i.e., at $t = 1$) in state k_1 and $\mathbf{y}_{k_1}(1)$ is a $\hat{K}$-dimensional vector that has the state fractions of loans in state k_1 at time 1 and zeroes elsewhere. At time step 3 we now obtain,

$$\mathbf{y}(3) = \sum_{k_1=1}^{\hat{K}} \sum_{k_2=1}^{\hat{K}} [\mathbf{A}_{k_1 k_2}(3)]'\mathbf{y}_{k_1 k_2}(2)$$

where $\mathbf{A}_{k_1 k_2}(3)$ is the $t = 3$ state transition probability matrix for loans previously in state k_1 at time 1 and k_2 at time 2, and, $\mathbf{y}_{k_1 k_2}(2)$ is the state vector that has the state fractions of loans in state k_1 at time 1 and k_2 at time 2 and zeroes elsewhere.[39] For $t = 4$,

$$\mathbf{y}(4) = \sum_{k_1=1}^{\hat{K}} \sum_{k_2=1}^{\hat{K}} \sum_{k_3=1}^{\hat{K}} [\mathbf{A}_{k_1 k_2 k_3}(4)]' \mathbf{y}_{k_1 k_2 k_3}(3)$$

where past state transition history is k_1, k_2, k_3 and $\mathbf{y}_{k_1 k_2 k_3}(3)$ has the time 3 state fraction of loans that has passed through states k_1, k_2, k_3 and zeroes elsewhere. For general $t = 1, \ldots, T$ we have by induction that

$$\mathbf{y}(t) = \sum_{k_1=1}^{\hat{K}} \cdots \sum_{k_{t-1}=1}^{\hat{K}} [\mathbf{A}_{k_1 \ldots k_{t-1}}(t)]' \mathbf{y}_{k_1 \ldots k_{t-1}}(t-1). \tag{4.57}$$

The iteration equation (4.57) looks like a branching tree version of the simple iteration equation (4.56) with branching by past state history. There is also a subsequent sum over all the branch iterations to find the total cumulative fraction of the ways the loan could enter a certain state k from a certain state history at time t. This means that with no absorbing states we have in general $\hat{K}^{t-1}$ evaluations of the equivalent of the iteration equation (4.56) at time step t. In practice, however, some states are absorbing (like default state) or impossible to reach from other states, which reduces the computational burden. Hence, albeit with a bit more complexity the Markov iteration approximation can still be used for pools when the transition probabilities depend on past state transition history. Note that in this iteration $\{\mathbf{y}(t)\}_{t=1}^{T}$ holds the state occupancy stock at $t = 1, \ldots, T$. Besides, in this algorithm, the exact state flow history is fully retained because of the branching of the Markov iteration by state history. This means that subsequent cash flow calculations can also depend on past state transitions. We give an explicit example as well as discussion of the iteration in equation (4.57) for the sample quarterly delinquency matrix in Table 4.34 in the appendix to this chapter.

If we relax the assumption that the state transition probabilities for loans in the pool are homogeneous—conditional on past state transition experienced—we have to index the state transition for loan i. This gives

$$\mathbf{y}^i(t) = \sum_{k_1=1}^{\hat{K}} \cdots \sum_{k_{t-1}=1}^{\hat{K}} [\mathbf{A}^i_{k_1 \ldots k_{t-1}}(t)]' \mathbf{y}^i_{k_1 \ldots k_{t-1}}(t-1) \tag{4.58}$$

and the Markov iteration is not pool based anymore. That is, we need to execute the iteration per loan i. However, the iteration equation (4.58) can still be valuable for stress testing because an evaluation of equation (4.58) can still be faster than simulating a large number R of loan i state transitions conditional on an economic scenario, $\{\mathbf{Z}(t)\}_{t=1}^{T}$. Since in the case of stress testing the analysis interest is usually centered at the expectation level (loss or cash flow) for the given scenario, equation (4.58) is a valid alternative to a full simulation.

Skoglund and Chen (2015) consider stress testing applications using the exact Markov iteration in equation (4.58) for the quarterly delinquency transition matrix in Table 4.34

---

[39]That is $\mathbf{y}_{k_1 k_2}(2)$ element k_2 has the product of the state transition probability of loans migrating to state k_1 at $t = 1$, and the state transition probability of loans in state k_1 at $t = 1$ migrating to state k_2 at $t = 2$.

(see also the appendix specific Markov iteration for the quarterly model). They compare state transition sampling using 1,000, 10,000, 100,000, and 1000,000 simulations to the exact Markov iteration for a quarterly model that uses the specific delinquency indicators; quarters since last delinquent and ever delinquent 90 days, with proportional hazard model specifications for the transition intensities. Predicting loan future state occupancies as well as loan-ending balances, default and prepayment amounts for the next 8 quarters—conditional on a macroeconomic scenario—they find that the loan level prediction can be quite poor with simulation compared to the exact Markov iteration. Compared to simulation the exact Markov iteration also has the advantage of giving the same (exact) results every time. This is in contrast to simulation-based approaches where a user needs to manage the seeds (typically on loan level) for reproducibility. Hence, while a simulation based approach can be quicker to implement initially due to its simplicity it is hard to argue for its use in this quarterly model since the exact Markov iteration method is feasible. The same paper by Skoglund and Chen (2015) also analyze Markov iteration versus state transition sampling for stress testing with the monthly delinquency transition matrix model in Table 4.33. State transition sampling is used for a monthly model which tracks months since last delinquent. However, for a monthly model with delinquency state indicator functions (for example ever delinquent 30 days and ever delinquent 60 days) the exact Markov iteration is simple. This is because we can condition on the state occupancy indicator being set or not to reduce the exact Markov iteration, at each $t = 1, \ldots, T$, to a bounded sum that is only marginally more complex than the simple Markov iteration in equation (4.56).

Clearly, in practice, when the transition probabilities depend on past state history, one must weigh the computational complexity and burden of performing many state transition samplings of the path for each member of a large homogeneous pool of loans using equation (4.55) versus a potentially more complex Markov iteration for the pool. In practice the number of state transition samples, R, required to converge to the Markov state frequencies can be very large for a particular loan (since most transition frequencies like default and prepayment are usually very small). Accuracy on a large portfolio of homogeneous loans may not require the same amount of state transition samples for each loan. This is because we benefit from the law of large numbers across the portfolio size dimension when sampling. The same reasoning applies to stress scenarios where the Markov iteration represents the expected state transition fractions conditional on the economic scenario. The convergence of a particular loan with state sampling may require a very large number of state sampling paths. However, if we are only interested in portfolio-level expected losses in a stress scenario, we can benefit from the averaging of expected losses across the large portfolio. Convergence is of course not a concern for the Markov iteration because it always provides the true expected fraction of the loan in each state at any point of time as does the expected loan loss and cash flow values these fractions lead to.

Mortgage Portfolio Risk Analysis: An Illustration

We now consider an extensive example that illustrates the main components of banking book portfolio credit risk models. Our example uses the multinomial logit model with ex-post inclusion of common macroeconomic factors. Our focus is on a mortgage portfolio as in general mortgage portfolios are more complex due to the recovery being tied to the property value, which may likely be low at the exact time of significant amounts of defaults in the portfolio. Other loan portfolios such as leasing portfolios also need to model the correlation between default and recovery explicitly using the underlying collateral while credit card portfolios may use simpler models of uncollateralized recovery. However, the uncollateralized recovery rate may still follow the business cycle and be correlated with the default rate. The focus is on the modeling of the macroeconomic factors that drive both credit state migration and recovery. Our modeling example does not consider prepayment as a competing risk such that default is the only absorbing state.

In our example we focus on credit state and default migration over multiple, path-dependent, yearly horizons for the mortgage portfolio. Because of the yearly horizons of the model we do not model delinquency states until default. We assume that the credit scoring models used for the mortgage portfolio have classified the loans in multiple non-default internal rating (grade) categories based on the actual credit quality (such as default probability) over time, yielding empirical credit grade transitions for $k = 1, \ldots, 9$ states. Clearly, idiosyncratic borrower factors such as past delinquency behavior are important in determining the default probability at a point in time and hence the borrower credit grade at a particular point in time. These internal rating categories and their empirical migration frequencies are reused in the credit portfolio model calibration to macroeconomic variables and subsequent analysis of the credit portfolio risk.

The construction of multiple credit grades occurs naturally based on the loan credit scores. Even if default only happens in the default state, the use of a ratings (credit state) based approach is important to capture the specific loan grades' sensitivity to the economic state. Clearly, poor credit quality borrowers may be more sensitive to the economic state and more likely to become delinquent or default in bad economic states. It is also important to model multiple credit grades since we are concerned with the portfolio behavior over longer term and one may otherwise underestimate the long-term credit losses as defaults may happen subsequently as a consequence of period credit (quality) grade migrations. It is also the case that economic value models of the banking book may consider the migration to credit grades as the basis for fair economic values.

In our application of the loan transition model to a mortgage portfolio, we consider 14 sample subportfolios. The subportfolios contain both individual and pooled exposures, and for the purpose of this example we assume that mortgages in a subportfolio are homogeneous with respect to both credit transition model as well as exposure and recovery characteristics. However, this is not necessary in practice, and different levels of homogeneity can be used for credit transition model, collateral (recovery), and exposure characteristics. The portfolio characteristics are displayed in Table 4.35.

The rating grade[40] scale for the loans is assumed to be a 9-grade scale labeled $1, \ldots, 9$ where the 9th grade is the default grade. Each mortgage subportfolio is hence assigned a non-default rating grade between $1, \ldots, 8$. In Table 4.35, each subportfolio has also a pool size, a loan to value, a current loan specific and total subportfolio notional in units of currency, a credit margin, and a link to a property price index, that we will subsequently use to revalue the property collateral for the mortgages. For the purpose of this example, to retain the current portfolio structure over a longer period of time (including to the end of our analysis horizon of 10 years) we assume no amortization of the notionals for the mortgages and that the mortgages are fixed rate mortgages—which will hence resemble coupon bonds with a very long maturity. The fixed credit margin of a mortgage in Table 4.35 is defined as the customer rate in excess of the funding rate. The funding rate is here defined as the matched

---

[40]We use the term *rating grade* here for the loans' different credit state classes although the term is less appropriate for loans than for large corporate exposures that have an external rating.

TABLE 4.35 Mortgage Portfolio Characteristics

Subportfolio	Rating	Pool size	Loan to value	Notional	Total notional	Credit margin (%)	Property index
1	5	3	0.85	1,000,000	300,000	1.5	1
2	4	1	0.95	1,000,000	100,000	1.3	1
3	7	1	0.95	1,000,000	100,000	2.0	1
4	3	2	0.85	1,000,000	200,000	1.1	2
5	4	4	0.80	1,000,000	400,000	1.2	3
6	1	1	0.90	1,000,000	100,000	1.0	1
7	2	1	0.85	1,000,000	100,000	1.1	1
8	4	65	0.95	1,000,000	6,500,000	1.3	3
9	3	1,623	0.85	1,000,000	162,300,000	1.0	3
10	8	8,003	0.95	1,000,000	800,300,000	1.1	4
11	2	9,012	0.90	1,000,000	901,200,000	1.2	5
12	4	11,013	0.95	1,000,000	1,101,300,000	1.0	5
13	5	14,390	0.90	1,000,000	1,439,000,000	1.0	1
14	6	27,803	1	1,000,000	2,780,300,000	0.90	4

maturity funds transfer rate at which a loan branch would synthetically receive funds from the Treasury. For now we don't have to be explicit about exactly how this funds rate is defined and just take the credit margin for given. We will come back to the issue of funds rates in Chapter 7 on funds transfer pricing and profitability of cash flows.

An important component in a credit portfolio model for mortgages is the modeling of property values. In Table 4.35 we assigned property indices to the subportfolios, which will allow us to consider correlation between default and recovery rates for the mortgage portfolio. The loan to value of a mortgage in Table 4.35 is defined as the current notional divided by the current value of the property. The loan-to-value ratio is frequently used as a risk statistic for first-lien mortgages, which we also assume to be the case here. For example, from Table 4.35 we note that subportfolio 1 has a loan to value of 0.85, indicating that the current mortgage notional is 85% of the current property value for the 3 mortgages in this subportfolio. Specifically, for the mortgages in subportfolio 1 the current property value can be inferred from the current notional and the loan to value of 0.85 as 850,000 units of currency. With first-lien mortgages, we can use the current loan to value and property index to calculate the recovery once a mortgage is in default, or a fraction of a homogeneous pool is in default. Specifically, the loss given default, $LGD(t, d)$, at a particular time, t, and scenario, d, is given by

$$LGD(t, d) = \max[E - R(t, d); 0] \tag{4.59}$$

$$R(t, d) = \max\left[\min\left[\frac{(1-\gamma)}{LTV} \times \left[\frac{S(t, d)}{S}\right] \times E; E\right]; 0\right].$$

Here, E is the outstanding notional of the loan, LTV is the current loan to value, and $S(t, d)$ is the property index value at time t in scenario d with S the current property index value, and, γ the haircut rate.[41] Hence, $\frac{S(t,d)}{S}$ represents a normalized growth rate for the property value.

---

[41]The haircut notation here is slightly different than the usual Basel convention of haircut, which is $1 - \gamma$ in our terminology.

The haircut rate, γ, is here capturing the fact that the value of a property in default may not sell at the market price, for example, due to auction. We set $\gamma = 0.4$ for all mortgages, that is, a default value haircut of the property value of 40%. Effectively, this haircut rate increases significantly the effective loan-to-value ratios for the mortgages when in default.

Models and Model Calibration In order to calculate credit losses and net credit returns (that is, credit margins minus credit losses) for the mortgage portfolio in Table 4.35 we need to calibrate

- The model for credit migration
- The models for the property indices

Starting with the calibration of the loan credit migration model we assume a common linear log-odds ratio transition model for all subportfolios and a single systematic factor, Z. Hence, we use the model in equation (4.53). Note that since the model is calibrated on log-odds ratios it is linear. To calibrate the model we need sample historical transition frequencies for the grades $1, \ldots, 9$ transformed to log-odds ratios using equation (4.51) as well as sample historical data for the systematic factor.[42] Table 4.36 displays the history, over

TABLE 4.36 Historical Data for the Systematic Factor

Time period	Systematic
t_1	−2.97907
t_2	−3.20206
t_3	−3.10497
t_4	−1.86945
t_5	0.38718
t_6	2.73456
t_7	2.55742
t_8	2.3365
t_9	2.11298
t_{10}	2.34202
t_{11}	0.94814
t_{12}	−0.24386
t_{13}	−1.05581
t_{14}	−1.33316
t_{15}	−0.73623
t_{16}	0.55308
t_{17}	0.55275

---

[42] We use a single systematic factor in our calibration of mortgage portfolio transition probabilities. This is for illustration only as the model can easily handle many macroeconomic factors. For example, the property prices in addition to macroeconomic variables such as unemployment rates are often important to explain defaults and rating transitions. A drop in property price leads to a loss of home equity and some consumers may see less economic value in continuing to meet their mortgage payments. Apart from macroeconomic variables rating grade transition and default may also depend on idiosyncratic time variables such as loan age.

TABLE 4.37 Sample Historical Log-Odds Ratios for Rating Grade 5

Time period	log51	log52	log53	log54	log55	log56	log57	log58
$t1$	0.79226	1.083	2.23154	1.4886	2.61322	1.81285	0.66787	0.48998
t_2	0.78626	1.077	2.22554	1.4826	2.60922	1.81485	0.66987	0.49198
t_3	0.78626	1.077	2.22554	1.4826	2.60922	1.81485	0.66987	0.49198
t_4	0.86426	1.155	2.30354	1.5606	2.66122	1.78885	0.64387	0.46598
t_5	0.98426	1.275	2.42354	1.6806	2.74122	1.74885	0.60387	0.42598
t_6	1.12826	1.419	2.56754	1.8246	2.83722	1.70085	0.55587	0.37798
t_7	1.11626	1.407	2.55554	1.8126	2.82922	1.70485	0.55987	0.38198
t_8	1.10426	1.395	2.54354	1.8006	2.82122	1.70885	0.56387	0.38598
t_9	1.09286	1.3836	2.53214	1.7892	2.81362	1.71265	0.56767	0.38978
t_{10}	1.10426	1.395	2.54354	1.8006	2.82122	1.70885	0.56387	0.38598
t_{11}	1.02026	1.311	2.45954	1.7166	2.76522	1.73685	0.59187	0.41398
t_{12}	0.95426	1.245	2.39354	1.6506	2.72122	1.75885	0.61387	0.43598
t_{13}	0.90326	1.194	2.34254	1.5996	2.68722	1.77585	0.63087	0.45298
t_{14}	0.88826	1.179	2.32754	1.5846	2.67722	1.78085	0.63587	0.45798
t_{15}	0.92426	1.215	2.36354	1.6206	2.70122	1.76885	0.62387	0.44598
t_{16}	0.99626	1.287	2.43554	1.6926	2.74922	1.74485	0.59987	0.42198
t_{17}	0.99026	1.281	2.42954	1.6866	2.74522	1.74685	0.60187	0.42398

17 yearly time periods, $t_1, \ldots, t_{17}$, of the single systematic factor and Table 4.37 displays, for current rating grade 5, a sample of the historical log-odds transition probabilities used. The log-odds transition probabilities are denoted $\log 51, \ldots, \log 58$ for transition to the non-default rating grades $1, \ldots, 8$ in Table 4.37. Note that we only need the historical log-odds transition probabilities for the non-default grades as with the multinomial logit model the residual probability is attributed to the default probability.

In Table 4.38 we have explicitly converted the sample log-odds ratios $\log 51, \ldots, \log 58$ to their corresponding transition probabilities. In the table the transition probabilities are

TABLE 4.38 Sample Historical Transition and Default Probabilities for Rating Grade 5 in Percent

Time period	p51	p52	p53	p54	p55	p56	p57	p58	p59
t_1	5.105%	6.827%	21.531%	10.242%	31.537%	14.165%	4.508%	3.773%	2.312%
t_2	5.092%	6.810%	21.475%	10.216%	31.519%	14.242%	4.532%	3.794%	2.320%
t_3	5.092%	6.810%	21.475%	10.216%	31.519%	14.242%	4.532%	3.794%	2.320%
t_4	5.261%	7.036%	22.188%	10.555%	31.729%	13.262%	4.220%	3.532%	2.217%
t_5	5.515%	7.375%	23.258%	11.064%	31.956%	11.846%	3.770%	3.155%	2.061%
t_6	5.808%	7.768%	24.496%	11.653%	32.079%	10.297%	3.277%	2.743%	1.879%
t_7	5.784%	7.736%	24.395%	11.605%	32.075%	10.420%	3.316%	2.775%	1.894%
t_8	5.760%	7.704%	24.294%	11.557%	32.069%	10.544%	3.355%	2.809%	1.909%
t_9	5.737%	7.673%	24.197%	11.511%	32.063%	10.663%	3.393%	2.840%	1.923%
t_{10}	5.760%	7.704%	24.294%	11.557%	32.069%	10.544%	3.355%	2.809%	1.909%
t_{11}	5.589%	7.475%	23.573%	11.214%	32.001%	11.443%	3.642%	3.048%	2.015%
t_{12}	5.452%	7.291%	22.994%	10.939%	31.910%	12.189%	3.879%	3.247%	2.099%
t_{13}	5.344%	7.147%	22.540%	10.722%	31.816%	12.789%	4.070%	3.407%	2.166%
t_{14}	5.312%	7.105%	22.405%	10.658%	31.784%	12.969%	4.127%	3.455%	2.185%
t_{15}	5.389%	7.207%	22.727%	10.812%	31.857%	12.539%	3.990%	3.340%	2.138%
t_{16}	5.539%	7.409%	23.364%	11.114%	31.972%	11.711%	3.727%	3.119%	2.045%
t_{17}	5.527%	7.392%	23.311%	11.089%	31.964%	11.778%	3.748%	3.137%	2.053%

denoted p51,...,p58. However, the table also displays the residual default probability, denoted p59. The transition probabilities and the default probability are expressed in %. To convert the log-odds ratios log51,...,log58 to transition probabilities we use equation (4.52). For example, to convert the log-odds ratio log51 into a transition probability, p51, we calculate

$$p51 = \frac{\exp(\log 51)}{1 + \sum_{r=51}^{58} \exp(\log r)}.$$

We can see from Tables 4.36 and 4.38 that there is a general tendency for transition probabilities to better grades to increase when the systematic factor is above its mean of zero. Hence the model is structured so that negative values of the systematic factor represent bad states, that is, a recession compared to the normal equilibrium case. This of course means that positive values imply better states than usual. Hence, we observe that the transition probabilities to worse grades and default decrease when the systematic factor is positive.

The current 1 year, implied from log-odds ratios at $t = t_{17}$, empirical transition matrix is displayed in Table 4.39 for the non-default grades 1,...,8. The probability of default for a grade is obtained as 1 minus the sum of all the non-default transition probabilities for the grade. The obtained percentage default probabilities from Table 4.39 for the grades 1,...,8 are hence approximately, 0.0126%, 0.0411%, 0.1321%, 0.6932%, 2.0532%, 5.3692%, 10.712%, and 20.652%, respectively.

Using the sample historical log-odds ratios and the sample systematic factor historical time series we can now calibrate the loan transition model parameters in equation (4.53) for our mortgage portfolio. We denote the calibrated parameters by μ_{lr} and β_{lr} for $l = 1, 2, \ldots, 8$ and $r = 1, 2, \ldots, 8$. The actual parameter values obtained are displayed in Table 4.40.

Having calibrated the loan transition model we can now simulate transition probabilities using a model for the systematic variable. We calibrate the historical data of the systematic variable to a Vasicek equilibrium model such that

$$dZ(t) = a[b - Z(t)]dt + \sigma dW(t)$$

where $W(t)$ is the Wiener process, and the parameter b is the mean reversion level around which all future trajectories will evolve in the long run. The parameter a characterizes the speed at which trajectories will regroup around the mean reversion rate and σ is the instantaneous volatility. Using standard regression analysis we calibrate the discretized version of the Vasicek model. We obtain the calibrated parameters as $a = 0.203$, $\sigma = 0.99$. The Vasicek model mean reversion level, b, is set to null since Z represents business cycle swings. We also assume that $Z(0) = 0$ such that we start with a neutral business cycle.

TABLE 4.39 The Current 1-Year Empirical Transition Matrix for the Grades 1,...,9

Grade	1	2	3	4	5	6	7	8
1	0.8204359	0.0676553	0.0479158	0.0238038	0.0139341	0.0114370	0.0084761	0.0062159
2	0.1536897	0.6716423	0.1478260	0.0092357	0.0072619	0.0052881	0.0033143	0.0013307
3	0.0736036	0.1790445	0.5026551	0.1747898	0.0392729	0.0176572	0.0078266	0.0038296
4	0.0773778	0.1058910	0.1523119	0.3543873	0.1475829	0.1025561	0.0381307	0.0148297
5	0.0552702	0.0739192	0.2331106	0.1108938	0.3196393	0.1177806	0.0374813	0.0313732
6	0.0284548	0.0473742	0.0584621	0.0856876	0.1361664	0.3662104	0.1528394	0.0711128
7	0.0105512	0.0315219	0.0407653	0.0521379	0.0832237	0.2109122	0.2539283	0.2098393
8	0	0.0022836	0.1134881	0	0.0378495	0.1115249	0.1930884	0.3352371

TABLE 4.40 Calibrated Parameters for the Loan Transition Model

	$s=1$	$s=2$	$s=3$	$s=4$	$s=5$	$s=6$	$s=7$	$s=8$
μ_{ls}								
$l=1$	8.77	6.29	5.94	5.24	4.71	4.51	4.21	3.90
$l=2$	5.91	7.39	5.89	3.11	2.87	2.56	2.09	1.18
$l=3$	4.00	4.89	5.92	4.89	3.40	2.60	1.78	1.07
$l=4$	2.38	2.70	3.06	3.91	3.06	2.70	1.71	0.76
$l=5$	0.96	1.27	2.40	1.66	2.72	1.75	0.60	0.43
$l=6$	−0.66	−0.15	0.05	0.43	0.89	1.88	1.05	0.28
$l=7$	−2.35	−1.26	−1.00	−0.75	−0.29	0.63	0.84	0.65
$l=8$	−19.53	−4.54	−0.63	−19.55	−1.73	−0.65	−0.11	0.43
β_{ls}								
$l=1$	0.019	−0.019	−0.019	−0.019	−0.019	−0.019	−0.019	−0.19
$l=2$	0.019	0.019	−0.019	−0.019	−0.019	−0.019	−0.019	−0.019
$l=3$	0.038	0.038	0.038	−0.019	−0.019	−0.019	−0.019	−0.019
$l=4$	0.05	0.05	0.05	0.05	−0.019	−0.019	−0.019	−0.019
$l=5$	0.05	0.05	0.05	0.05	0.038	−0.019	−0.019	−0.019
$l=6$	0.07	0.07	0.07	0.07	0.07	0.09	−0.019	−0.019
$l=7$	0.09	0.09	0.09	0.09	0.09	0.09	0.057	0.038
$l=8$	0.09	0.09	0.09	0.09	0.09	0.09	0.11	0.13

In order to complete the models we also need to model the evolution of the property indices, $S_1(t,w),\ldots,S_5(t,w)$. We recall from Table 4.35 that the subportfolios were allocated to one of five different property indexes, which we need to model in order to be able to calculate the mortgage loss given default in equation (4.59) once a mortgage has defaulted. We assume that the property price indices follow geometric Brownian motion models such that for each $v=1,\ldots,5$ we have that

$$dS_v(t) = \mu_v S(t)dt + \sigma_v S(t)dW_v(t)$$

with

$$\sigma = (0.05, 0.056, 0.049, 0.062, 0.063)$$

the vector of calibrated volatilities to the sample yearly historical indices in Table 4.41. While the sample historical average growth rates of the property indices in Table 4.41 are positive, for prudence, we assume that the future average growth rates of property values are zero and restrict $\mu_v = 0$ for all $v = 1,\ldots,5$. Hence, the calibrated volatilities are constrained estimates.

Figure 4.12 displays graphically the historical price indices in Table 4.41 (left scale) and the historical data for the systematic factor (right scale) in Table 4.36.

We note again here that our mortgage credit portfolio loss model not only captures default correlation over time, through the systematic factor Z, but also incorporates correlation between property prices and default rates. Historical property prices in general decayed at the same time as there was a recession cycle (negative values of the systematic factor). Hence, the model incorporates the historically observed positive correlation between increasing default rates and increasing loss given default rates. The empirical correlations between the systematic factor and the $1,\ldots,5$ different logarithmic returns to the price indices are respectively $0.51, 0.82, 0.58, 0.73$, and 0.63. The correlations are positive as expected because

TABLE 4.41 Historical Property Price Indices

Time period	S_1	S_2	S_3	S_4	S_5
t_1	154	187	147	133	145
t_2	150	186	144	127	140
t_3	149	182	140	125	139
t_4	152	186	146	129	142
t_5	159	191	150	134	150
t_6	176	201	156	139	159
t_7	184	223	169	149	170
t_8	198	238	178	162	187
t_9	210	258	189	179	199
t_{10}	223	278	199	199	221
t_{11}	234	299	212	222	239
t_{12}	241	321	227	234	259
t_{13}	225	346	213	220	240
t_{14}	235	344	207	219	245
t_{15}	241	350	220	215	260
t_{16}	246	348	221	214	279
t_{17}	249	351	223	212	278

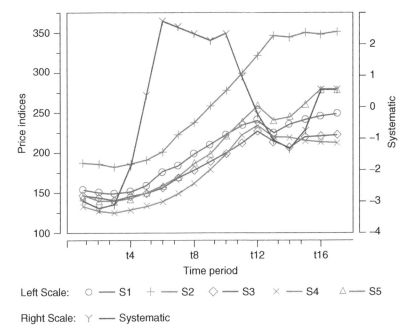

FIGURE 4.12 Historical Data for the Systematic Factor and the Price Indices

high values of the systematic factor are associated with a strong economy and high property growth values.

We also have a very strong empirical correlation within the price indices' logarithmic returns. It is important to note that these correlations are also used when we simulate future values of the systematic factor, Z, and the property prices, $S_1, \ldots, S_5$. In our analysis, we assume a multivariate normal distribution for the systematic factor and the property price indices. Hence, we assume a normal copula.

Analysis of Credit Portfolio Losses Having defined all the models and the model parameters we can simulate the portfolio credit losses due to defaults using the models. We analyze the mortgage portfolio risk over the horizons of $1, \ldots, 10$ years using 100,000 simulations and using a risk confidence level of 99.9%. In the calculation of credit migrations, we apply the conditional law of large numbers approximation in equation (4.56) to the subportfolios $8, \ldots, 14$ in Table 4.35. Here subportfolio 8 is the smallest subportfolio that we apply the conditional law of large numbers to with 65 mortgages while subportfolio 14 has 27,803 mortgages. The other subportfolios, that is, subportfolios $1, \ldots, 7$, use a multinomial state sampling approach for *each* member of the subportfolio.

The credit migration and default analysis for the portfolio uses a path-dependent model for mortgage rating grades $1, \ldots, 9$ over time with calculation of marginal default losses at each yearly horizon. Hence, a mortgage that is in default at a particular scenario and time remains in default for all the remaining time steps of the particular scenario.

We first focus on analyzing the portfolio level marginal credit losses displayed in Table 4.42 and Figure 4.13. The table and figure display the aggregate portfolio expected losses, EL, and the 99.9% confidence level risk measures, VaR and CVaR, for the horizons of $1, \ldots, 10$ years. We note that both marginal expected losses and risk, as measured by VaR and CVaR at the 99.9% confidence level, are decreasing over time. This is a characteristic of a portfolio that is dominated by loans in low credit quality grades. This is because the relatively high probability of default causes a large short-term loss rate. At longer horizons, the low credit quality loans either have already defaulted or have migrated to a better grade. We observe from Table 4.35 that indeed some of the large pools have a low credit grade for the loans in the pool, specifically subportfolios 10, 13, and 14, which also have substantial total notionals.

TABLE 4.42 Aggregate Portfolio Marginal Risk and Expected Loss at Horizons of $1, \ldots, 10$ Years

| Horizon (years) | Marginal credit default losses | | |
	VaR(0.999)	CVaR(0.999)	EL
1	200,538,078	207,074,919	133,692,343
2	190,137,788	199,775,375	110,216,346
3	169,303,797	178,704,241	90,521,334
4	145,741,162	154,254,603	73,536,377
5	126,548,043	134,249,430	60,767,243
6	111,386,805	118,013,278	51,541,187
7	101,552,469	108,065,916	45,015,925
8	93,056,927	99,174,650	40,296,470
9	87,447,331	93,181,494	36,902,797
10	83,109,774	88,816,171	34,405,284

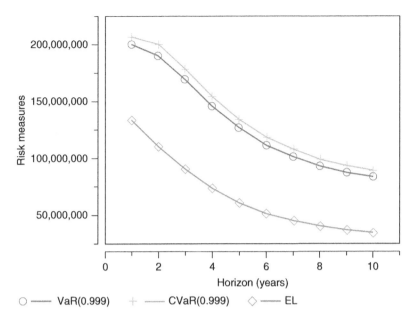

FIGURE 4.13 Aggregate Portfolio Marginal Risk and Expected Loss at Horizons of 1, ... , 10 Years

Table 4.43 displays the 99.9% VaR for the credit losses for the large pool subportfolios 10, 11, and 14 (see also Figure 4.14). The current grade for subportfolios 10 is 8 and for subportfolios 11 and 14 the current grade is 2 and 6, respectively. We notice that subportfolio 10, with loans rated in grade 8, displays a significant reduction in the risk of marginal losses over time due to the initial low quality rating grade. Of course, this is an important consideration when one considers a capital buffer to support the portfolio as, for subportfolio 10, the buffer would have to be large up front, that is, at the beginning of the planning horizon of 1, ... , 10 years. In contrast, subportfolio 11, which has current grade 2 for its loans, has an increasing risk profile. This is because for good-quality loans, the short-term risk is small.

TABLE 4.43 99.9% VaR for the Credit Losses for the Large Pool Subportfolios 10, 11, and 14

	Marginal credit default losses		
Horizon (years)	Subportfolio 10	Subportfolio 11	Subportfolio 14
1	97,282,375	177,243	85,097,385
2	49,120,226	892,977	105,533,772
3	30,202,493	2,201,052	95,381,564
4	20,969,151	3,945,399	77,932,818
5	15,591,528	5,692,897	63,289,681
6	12,332,963	7,278,345	52,363,804
7	10,231,951	8,554,459	44,897,419
8	8,782,051	9,482,992	39,767,520
9	7,752,477	10,134,061	35,499,537
10	7,100,282	10,558,647	33,040,395

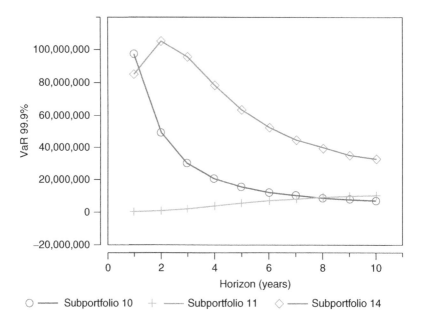

FIGURE 4.14 99.9% VaR for the Credit Losses for the Large Pool Subportfolios 10, 11, and 14

However, over time the risk increases due to credit migration. Clearly, for an initial very high quality portfolio there is a limited scope for improvement, but as time progresses the probability of significant downgrades increases. Subportfolio 14, starting out in rating grade 6, displays an initial increase in marginal risk and then a decrease.

Table 4.44 and Figure 4.15 display the same information as Table 4.43 for the subportfolios 1, 3, and 6, being in rating grades 5, 7, and 1, respectively. Similar to Table 4.43, we observe a hump-shaped marginal credit loss VaR profile for subportfolio 1 in grade 5, a stable marginal credit loss VaR profile for subportfolio 3 in grade 7, and an increasing marginal credit loss VaR profile for subportfolio 6 in grade 1.

TABLE 4.44 99.9% VaR for the Credit Losses for the Large Pool Subportfolios 1, 3, and 6

	Marginal credit default losses		
Horizon (years)	Subportfolio 1	Subportfolio 3	Subportfolio 6
1	52,843	44,971	0
2	61,369	47,387	36,453
3	60,042	48,900	40,116
4	57,738	49,433	41,316
5	51,012	49,826	43,849
6	50,089	49,887	45,290
7	51,492	50,653	46,009
8	51,483	51,438	47,306
9	51,556	50,715	47,792
10	52,236	51,289	48,219

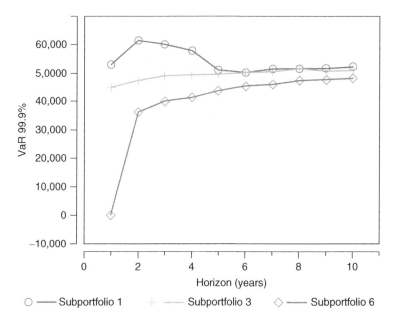

FIGURE 4.15 99.9% VaR for the Credit Losses for the Large Pool Subportfolios 1, 3, and 6

We can also consider risk contributions of the subportfolios to the aggregate portfolio.[43] Since the risk horizon is 10 years with marginal credit losses we can consider the aggregate default risk contribution over the years $1, \ldots, 10$ for the aggregate loss up to 10 years. Table 4.45 displays the VaR and CVaR summed risk contributions for the subportfolios, $1, \ldots, 14$ and the aggregate portfolio. Once again, but now in the context of retail portfolios, we notice that VaR contributions are not a particular good choice for risk and capital allocation when using random sampling of a few credits in a subportfolio. A zero VaR contribution is obtained for many of the subportfolios that do not use a conditional law of large numbers. In this case CVaR provides a much better approach to risk allocation as it considers the full tail of conditional losses—introducing smoothness. Indeed, the CVaR contributions in Table 4.45 are non-zero for every subportfolio and seem to reflect fairly the individual subportfolio's risk, taking into account the subportfolio rating, size, exposure, and loan to value. On the other hand, we can observe from Table 4.45 that VaR contributions work well when subportfolios are using the conditional law of large numbers. This is because the losses are then already smooth.

Using Table 4.45 we could, for example, use the aggregate risk VaR or CVaR summed over years $1, \ldots, 10$ as our definition of capital buffer—typically adjusting for the expected losses as they are treated as a reserve and should already be priced into credit margins. Here the aggregated expected default loss over the years $1, \ldots, 10$ is 676,895,310 in units of currency. However, such a measure cumulates worst-case marginal losses year by year rather than focusing on the path of cumulative loss that can happen up to the risk horizon of 10 years. We will return to this issue in the section on economic capital for loan portfolios below.

---

[43]For large retail portfolios the risk contributions are in general more interesting than incremental risk measures due to the relatively small size of each loan. A benefit of working with homogeneous subportfolios is that the risk contributions are better estimated on subportfolios than on individual loans.

TABLE 4.45 VaR and CVaR Summed Risk Contributions for the Subportfolios

Subportfolio	Summed contributions	
	Cont VaR	Cont CVaR
1	0	43,675.15
2	0	13,667.71
3	0	28,853.62
4	39,525.53	19,264.79
5	0	50,019.47
6	0	8,415.72
7	0	5,879.85
8	796,235.62	869,572.84
9	12,313,741.83	13,851,761.69
10	253,144,275.34	264,679,495.79
11	58,305,988.09	62,414,884.35
12	152,357,304.26	162,042,910.99
13	204,707,242.55	213,253,975.25
14	627,157,866.04	664,027,704.41
Aggregate	1,308,822,179.27	1,381,310,081.64

Net Credit Portfolio Losses Taking into Account Credit Margins In practice, it is common to calculate capital buffers with respect to unexpected loss, that is, a worst-case loss less expected losses. However, adjustments may be needed in practice to account for the fact that credit margins do not cover expected losses. While it is generally the case that credit margins for good credit grade portfolios are in excess of expected losses the credit margin for poor credit grade portfolios may not be sufficient to cover even expected losses.

Using the mortgage credit portfolio model, we now focus also on the loan's credit margin (see Table 4.35 for the loans credit margins) as a positive inflow as long as the mortgage is not in default. The credit margin minus the losses is here referred to as the net credit loss of the portfolio. Table 4.46 and Figure 4.16 display the 99.9% VaR of the net credit loss versus

TABLE 4.46 99.9% VaR for the Net Credit Losses, Credit Losses, and the Expected Loss Adjusted Credit Losses for the Aggregate Portfolio

Horizon (years)	Marginal credit default losses		
	Net credit loss	Credit Loss	EL adjusted credit loss
1	139,737,024	200,538,078	66,845,735
2	132,578,257	190,137,788	79,921,442
3	114,204,488	169,303,797	78,782,463
4	92,934,718	145,741,162	72,204,785
5	74,906,284	126,548,043	65,780,800
6	61,355,506	111,386,805	59,845,618
7	52,598,020	101,552,469	56,536,544
8	45,255,156	93,056,927	52,760,457
9	40,524,100	87,447,331	50,544,535
10	37,129,571	83,109,774	48,704,490

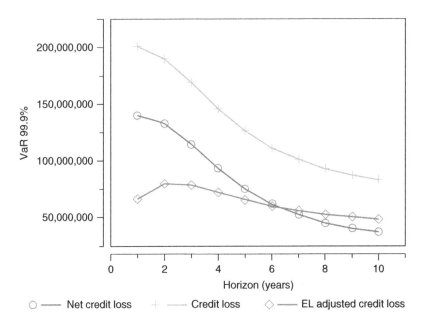

FIGURE 4.16 99.9% VaR for the Net Credit Losses, Credit Losses, and the Expected Loss Adjusted Credit Losses for the Aggregate Portfolio

the (raw) credit loss, and the expected loss adjusted credit loss for the aggregate portfolio over the years $1, \ldots, 10$. The (raw) credit loss and the expected-loss adjusted credit loss we can of course obtain directly from Table 4.42. Notice that with the credit margins assumed in Table 4.35, the marginal net credit loss may exceed the marginal credit loss adjusted by expected losses at longer horizons. That is, the credit margins are not sufficient to cover the marginal expected credit loss for the longer horizons. Hence, using information about the credit margins and analyzing the net loss as well is called for in this case.

Basel Regulatory Capital Another interesting question in the context of a loan credit portfolio model is to analyze the implied portfolio Basel regulatory capital when we use the formula in equation (4.41) to calculate minimum required capital. That is, for each scenario realized probability of default (using the loan transition model) and loss given default (using the mortgage loss given default in equation (4.59)) we can use equation (4.41).[44] In case of the subportfolios $8, \ldots, 14$ where the conditional law of large numbers is applied, the regulatory formula is, of course, used for each of the different pool fractions, probability of default. The regulatory capital required for the defaulted mortgages or mortgage pool fractions are the greater of zero and the difference between the loss given default and the bank's best estimate of expected loss. This is because the bank's reserve allocated based on the best estimate of the expected loss already covers the loss due to the default. The excess actual loss is still going to be covered by the capital.

Performing this analysis for the mortgage portfolio yields a distribution of capital values implied by the regulatory formula for which measures such as worst-case capital requirement

---

[44]In the calculation we set the Basel maturity adjustment to unity. That is, $\widetilde{M} = 1$ in equation (4.41). The correlation level, β, is set to 0.15. We also impose a probability of default floor at 0.03%.

can be calculated using risk measures. Our approach here to worst-case capital requirements is different from the regulatory approach. The regulators require financial institutions to use long-run or stressed PD and LGD values as inputs to the capital requirement calculations. That is, the regulatory capital requirements adjust the inputs rather than analyzing the risk of the output under different economic scenarios for PD and LGD. It is however still of interest to consider a risk-based view on regulatory capital requirements in the context of the portfolio credit risk model. We will also return to the issues on whether risk levels should be based on the point in time versus through the cycle ratings, and whether risk is better measured by stabilizing inputs or outputs in credit risk models.

Table 4.47 and Figure 4.17 display the non-defaulted loans' regulatory capital worst-case 99.9% VaR and expected value over the risk horizon of $1, \ldots, 10$ years for the aggregate portfolio.[45] Due to the average credit portfolio quality we observe a decaying worst-case and expected regulatory capital over time as there are significant defaults in the portfolio. On the other hand, this means that the required loss reserve is increasing and that the institution needs a larger relative expected loss reserve than if the portfolio credit quality was initially good. Indeed, a good credit quality portfolio should have increasing worst-case and expected capital requirements due to downgrades for the non-defaulted loans. This is evidenced by Table 4.48 (see also Figure 4.18), which shows the same as Table 4.47 for the grade 2 rated subportfolio 11. Finally, we note that the worst-case marginal 10-year regulatory capital is approximately a factor 3.3 times larger than the worst-case 10-year marginal credit loss for the aggregate portfolio (see Table 4.42, 99.9% VaR at the 10-year horizon being 83,109,774). We will come back to the issue of reconciling internal credit portfolio model capital requirements with regulatory capital requirements when we discuss economic capital for retail portfolios.

Investigating the Appropriateness of the Conditional Law of Large Numbers Approximation Until now we have worked under the implicit assumption that subportfolio $8, \ldots, 14$ losses are well approximated using the conditional law of large numbers approximation. While in general

TABLE 4.47 Regulatory Capital 99.9% VaR and Expected Value Over the Risk Horizon of $1, \ldots, 10$ Years for the Aggregate Portfolio

Horizon (years)	Marginal regulatory capital	
	Worst-case	Expected
1	592,036,602	432,508,149
2	521,253,033	345,455,085
3	447,698,751	282,155,559
4	396,799,507	237,236,914
5	357,966,981	205,572,599
6	327,586,768	182,881,307
7	309,127,388	166,579,545
8	294,819,807	154,443,344
9	282,538,031	145,416,040
10	274,724,729	138,542,858

---

[45]The confidence level used in the regulatory capital formula is 99.9%.

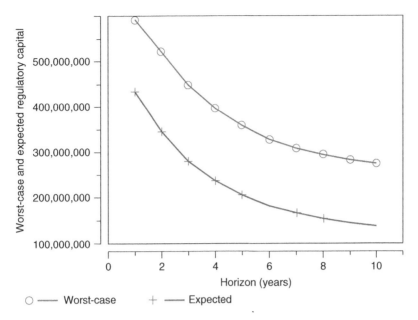

FIGURE 4.17 Regulatory Capital 99.9% VaR and Expected Value over the Risk Horizon of 1, ..., 10 Years for the Aggregate Portfolio

TABLE 4.48 Regulatory Capital 99.9% VaR and Expected Value over the Risk Horizon of 1, ..., 10 Years for Subportfolio 11 in Grade 2

Horizon (years)	Marginal regulatory capital	
	Worst-case	Expected
1	7,173,699	4,852,891
2	12,783,034	7,489,363
3	18,738,875	10,131,264
4	24,444,653	12,369,657
5	28,888,832	14,093,157
6	32,505,716	15,320,978
7	35,148,379	16,159,566
8	37,045,743	16,676,412
9	38,052,449	16,977,009
10	38,800,194	17,123,135

we would expect the expected loss to be well approximated using the conditional law of large numbers even for a small pool the interesting question is whether the approximation is valid for the high quantiles at, for example, confidence level 99.9% that we are using here.

Starting with the aggregate portfolio and using random sampling for all members of the pools 8, ..., 14 that we previously approximated with the conditional law of large numbers in Table 4.42, we can now compare the 99.9% VaR and CVaR. This is done in Table 4.49 where the new marginal credit loss sampling VaR and CVaR are displayed together with their % increase compared to Table 4.42. Using sampling we observe a yearly average 0.47%

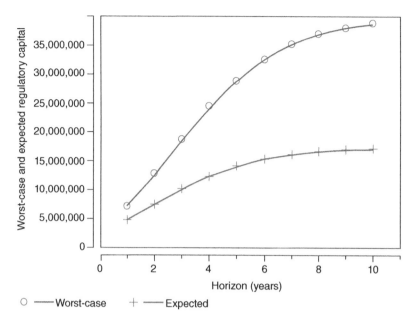

FIGURE 4.18 Regulatory Capital 99.9% VaR and Expected Value over the Risk Horizon of 1,..., 10 Years for Subportfolio 11 in Grade 2

TABLE 4.49 Aggregate Portfolio Marginal Risk and Percent Increase of Marginal Risk for 1,..., 10 Years Using Sampling for all the Portfolio Loans

Horizon (years)	Marginal credit default losses			
	VaR	VaR % increase	CVaR	CVaR % increase
1	200,899,863	0.18%	207,776,288	0.34%
2	190,540,994	0.21%	200,459,600	0.34%
3	170,100,100	0.47%	178,906,181	0.11%
4	146,734,039	0.68%	154,618,499	0.24%
5	126,328,963	−0.17%	134,482,533	0.17%
6	111,965,452	0.51%	118,570,048	0.47%
7	102,218,593	0.65%	109,463,275	1.29%
8	93,937,971	0.94%	99,872,805	0.70%
9	87,602,508	0.17%	93,273,234	0.10%
10	83,972,018	1.03%	89,404,321	0.66%

increase in risk with VaR and a yearly average increase of 0.44% with CVaR. Hence, at the aggregate portfolio level it seems that the conditional law of large numbers approximation for the subportfolios 8,..., 14 is a fair approximation. Figure 4.19 displays graphically the portfolio VaR and CVaR % increase.

However, we are also interested in subportfolio contributions to aggregate portfolio risk as well as their standalone risk being approximated well with the conditional law of large numbers. Therefore, we also need to validate the specific subportfolios for the conditional law of large numbers approximation. Starting with subportfolio 8 we compare the sampling

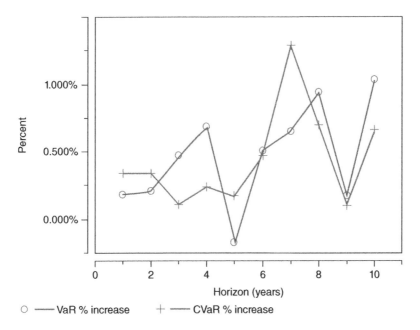

FIGURE 4.19 Aggregate Portfolio Percent Increase of Marginal Risk for 1, ..., 10 Years Using Sampling for all the Portfolio Loans

TABLE 4.50 Marginal 99.9% VaR Credit Losses at Horizons of 1, ..., 10 Years for Random Sampling and the Percent Increase vs. Using Conditional Law of Large Numbers for Subportfolio 8

	Subportfolio 8	
Horizon (years)	VaR	VaR % increase
1	134,707	503%
2	226,142	196%
3	263,669	157%
4	265,350	149%
5	257,957	152%
6	255,584	165%
7	239,594	166%
8	236,839	180%
9	230,003	187%
10	224,454	189%

credit loss marginal VaR 99.9% with the conditional law of large numbers approximation in Table 4.50 and Figure 4.20. We note that there is a significant difference attributed to idiosyncratic risk and hence the conditional law of large numbers approximation for subportfolio 8 significantly underestimates risk. However, in the context of the aggregate portfolio the loss contribution for subportfolio 8 is small. For example, the subportfolio 8 summed credit loss VaR contribution in Table 4.45 as % of aggregate portfolio credit loss is about 0.06%.

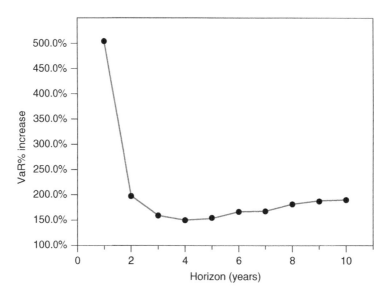

FIGURE 4.20 Subportfolio 8 Percent Increase of Marginal Risk for $1, \ldots, 10$ Years Using Sampling for all the Portfolio Loans

Hence, from an aggregate portfolio risk perspective the poor approximation of subportfolio 8 with the conditional law of large numbers is not a major concern. On the other hand, if we are interested in subportfolio 8 risk contributions and standalone risk, we should use the sampling method for subportfolio 8.

Now, doing the same comparison for subportfolio 10 (with 8,003 members) and subportfolio 14 (with 27,803 members) we find much smaller differences in 99.9% marginal VaR profiles over the years $1, \ldots, 10$. See Table 4.51 and Figure 4.21. We can conclude that while, in general, using the conditional law of large numbers for a subportfolio has significant benefits—including reduction of calculation time and the introduction of smooth tail

TABLE 4.51 Marginal 99.9% VaR Credit Lossses at Horizons of $1, \ldots, 10$ Years for Random Sampling and the Percent Increase vs. Using Conditional Law of Large Numbers for Subportfolio 10 and 14

Horizon (years)	Subportfolio 10		Subportfolio 14	
	VaR	VaR % increase	VaR	VaR % increase
1	97,243,751	−0.04%	86,273,882	1.38%
2	49,626,979	1.03%	106,011,978	0.45%
3	30,548,846	1.15%	95,710,514	0.34%
4	21,249,787	1.34%	78,408,160	0.61%
5	16,015,614	2.72%	63,545,759	0.40%
6	12,801,922	3.80%	52,741,548	0.72%
7	10,608,563	3.68%	45,560,930	1.48%
8	9,153,882	4.23%	39,861,247	0.24%
9	8,136,627	4.96%	36,057,736	1.57%
10	7,409,614	4.36%	33,640,221	1.82%

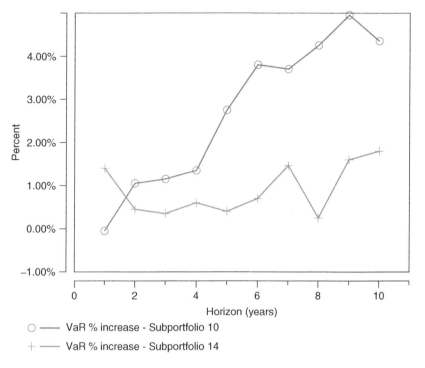

FIGURE 4.21 Subportfolio 10 and 14 Percent Increase of Marginal Risk for $1, \dots, 10$ Years Using Sampling for all the Portfolio Loans

losses—the use of the conditional law of large numbers needs to be carefully vetted to avoid underestimation of (idiosyncratic) risks. Of course, in all comparison cases of sampling and conditional law of large numbers approximation, the expected loss profiles over the horizons of $1, \dots, 10$ years are very close for both approaches and do not require a large pool. But, as we have shown here, the conditional law of large numbers approximation for high VaR quantiles, here 99.9%, may be very poor in practice for smaller subportfolios.

Point in Time and Through the Cycle Models—with Applications to Regulatory Stress Testing

While probabilities of default and transition probabilities for externally rated corporates and bond issues are in general based on long-run average rates published by the rating agencies, credit scoring models generally focus on a point in time assessment of the default probability. However, the long-term credit risk of a loan is based on both the current risk grade using the score at a certain time t and the sensitivity of the loan credit quality to the economic cycle. We may hence assign a relatively high long-term probability of default to a loan with a low time t scorecard probability of default. This is because the longer-term viability of the loan may be questionable, based on its sensitivity to the business cycle.

In the industry the concepts of Point in Time (PIT) and Through the Cycle (TTC) are generally used to distinguish between credit grades or probability of default rates that are experienced at time t versus adjusted for the economic cycle. The choice of exact measure for the default probability depends on the use case. For example, the Basel calculation of risk-weighted assets using equation (4.41) requires the use of long-run average probability of defaults or even downturn adjusted probability of defaults as well as loss given defaults. This can be seen as an attempt to stabilize banks' regulatory capital requirements over the years. Indeed, the stability is seen as a desirable attribute of a capital reserve. However, as argued by Aguais et al. (2006), it is preferable to stabilize the outputs of a model rather than stabilize the inputs, as in the latter case, the model will not measure current risk. The current risk is better measured by the PIT definition.

In portfolio credit risk models it is therefore desirable to focus on PIT estimates of credit scores and instead apply a long-term view when assigning capital requirements. Such a long-term view achieves the objective of ensuring a relatively stable capital reserve. We consider one example of such an approach, inspired by the classical insurance risk reserve methodology, when we discuss economic capital for loan portfolios. Still, a bank needs to maintain both a PIT and a TTC version of credit scoring models. In general, the TTC model is derived from the PIT model and a model for the systematic factors that describe the economic cycle. The key to converting a PIT estimate to a TTC estimate is to define the current economic cycle. Once this is defined the systematic factors model can be used to compute a credit's probability of default or, more generally, a credit's transition probability rates unconditional on the systematic variables and hence the economic cycle. For example, in our mortgage portfolio analysis the credit state transition probabilities, hence the transition matrix, depend on the economic cycle such that different values of the economic factor Z yield different transition rates for credits in states $k = 1, \ldots, \hat{K}$. Carlehed and Petrov (2012) use a one-factor version of the Merton-inspired model as in equation (4.39) and an autoregressive, Vasicek equilibrium model type, formulation for the single economic cycle indicator to convert PIT probability of default estimates to TTC. As Carlehed and Petrov (2012) also argue, the probability of default definition used in long-term profitability assessment should be carefully made to avoid countercyclical behavior. For example, long-term loans with profitability assessed with PIT probability of default during an economic downturn will appear less valuable than when assessed using a TTC probability of default. At the same time, in economic upswings, the TTC probability of default will lower the value compared to using a PIT probability of default. This is being prudent.

Regulatory Stress Testing with Point in Time Probability of Default Point in time default probability or rating transition models, connected to macroeconomic variables, are an important component to translate the macroeconomic regulatory credit book stresses required in both CCAR and EBA to credit loss and projected risk weighted assets impact. Later in this chapter, we will consider explicit examples of credit portfolio macroeconomic stress testing for both the Merton-inspired multifactor models, discussed in the previous section of this chapter, as well as the credit score models with macroeconomic variables, discussed in this section. However, already here we will review some of the specific EBA credit book stress methodologies (EBA, 2014) for computing the flow of defaulted assets and connect the calculation to our Markov iteration approaches for credit models with some simple numerical examples to illustrate. We refer to Skoglund and Chen (2015) for stress testing applications with the monthly and quarterly dynamic delinquency models using both state transition simulation and Markov iteration. The dynamic delinquency models are frequently used in CCAR stress testing.

In the methodological notes of the EBA stress the flow of defaulted assets should be counted using PIT probability of default. Specifically, having available the time t PIT probability of default (PD) for a credit grade conditional on the economic scenario at time t one multiplies PD with the remaining non-defaulted exposure (E) at $t - 1$. This gives the flow of defaulted assets (FD) as

$$FD(t) = PD(t) \times E(t - 1) \tag{4.60}$$

with E(0) the current exposure, and with remaining exposure at t as

$$E(t) = (1 - PD(t))E(t - 1).$$

When there are multiple credit grades or credit qualities available for a loan in a transition matrix, which is the situation we have considered in this chapter, we can employ the Markov iteration conditional on the stress scenario (such as in equation (4.56) for the credit score model and in equation (4.29) for the multifactor Merton inspired model) to define $\{FD(t)\}_t^T$ in equation (4.60) as the $t = 1, \ldots, T$ defaulted fraction of the loan. This defaulted loan fraction is obtained from the $t = 1, \ldots, T$ state transition vector. Specifically, we have the usual Markov iteration equation,

$$\mathbf{y}(t) = [\mathbf{A}(t)]'\mathbf{y}(t - 1) \tag{4.61}$$

where as before $\mathbf{y}(t)$ is a $\hat{K} \times 1$ vector of state frequencies and $\mathbf{y}(0)$ contains zeros in all positions except at the current loan position l. The transition matrix $\mathbf{A}(t)$ exact transition rates are of course determined by the specific choice of model with the PIT transition rates at $t = 1, \ldots, T$ depending on the economic factors, $\mathbf{Z}(t)$. This now gives for $E(0) = 1$

$$FD(t) = y_{\hat{K}}(t) - y_{\hat{K}}(t - 1)$$

such that

$$\sum_{s=1}^{t} FD(s) = y_{\hat{K}}(t)$$

where $y_{\hat{K}}(t)$ is the $\hat{K}$:th element of $\mathbf{y}(t)$ having the defaulted fractions of the loan until t and $y_{\hat{K}}(0)$ is null as we start out with no defaulted fractions of the loan.[46] Alternatively, if the loan Markov iteration is more complex such as for credit score models with delinquency tracking, using the Markov iteration equation (4.58), one can resort to state transition sampling to define $\{FD(t)\}_t^T$. However, see also our example Markov iteration for a quarterly delinquency model in the appendix to this chapter and Skoglund and Chen (2015).

Once the flow of defaulted assets, FD(t), is available for each time $t = 1, \ldots, T$ we can adjust the default flow for recoveries using the PIT loss given default model, LGD(t), and compute the impairment flow of losses, I(t), on the time t newly defaulted portion of the

---

[46]Note that from equation (4.60) a forward-looking one-period probability of default is

$$PD(t) = \frac{FD(t)}{E(t - 1)} = \frac{[y_{\hat{K}}(t) - y_{\hat{K}}(t - 1)]}{E(t - 1)}E(0) = \frac{[y_{\hat{K}}(t) - y_{\hat{K}}(t - 1)]}{[1 - y_{\hat{K}}(t - 1)]}$$

since $E(t - 1) = [1 - y_{\hat{K}}(t - 1)]E(0)$. Here, $\{PD(t)\}_{t=1}^{T}$ constitutes a forward PD curve, and since $y_{\hat{K}}(t) - y_{\hat{K}}(t - 1)$ represents the additional portion of default that happens during the period $(t - 1, t]$ and $1 - y_{\hat{K}}(t - 1)$ is the survival probability (portion) up to time $t - 1$, PD(t) is indeed a conditional default probability.

loan, adjusting for the already made provisions. The EBA-specific impairment flow formula for assets defaulted at t is

$$I(t) = \max[\mathrm{FD}(t)\mathrm{LGD}(t) - \alpha\mathrm{P}(t-1), 0]$$

where $\alpha \leq \mathrm{PD}(t)$ and $\mathrm{P}(t-1)$ is the stock of provisions made against non-defaulted assets at $t-1$. Here α is the share of $\mathrm{P}(t-1)$ that is linked to initially non-defaulted assets at $t-1$ that enter into default status at t.

To account for the fact that collateral asset quality can worsen over the stress scenario (hence PIT loss given default increase over $t = 1, \ldots, T$), additional EBA impairments must be made on old defaulted assets at t. The specific formula for the impairment loss on old defaulted exposures, $\widetilde{\mathrm{I}}(t)$, is given by

$$\widetilde{\mathrm{I}}(t) = \widetilde{\mathrm{P}}(t-1)\max\left[\frac{\mathrm{LGD}(t)}{\mathrm{LGD}(t-1)}\mathrm{D}(t) - 1, 0\right]$$

where $\mathrm{LGD}(t)$ is the loss given default at t for the stock of defaulted assets, $\widetilde{\mathrm{P}}(t-1)$ is the stock of impairments for old defaulted assets, and $\mathrm{D}(t)$ is a default portfolio characteristic parameter that may not be in effect if the bank's loss given default model already takes the impairment dynamics of old defaulted assets into account. We refer to the EBA (2014) methodological notes for further details on the impairment flow formulas.

While the defaulted flow of assets calculation under the stress scenario uses the PIT probability of default and the PIT loss given default models, the EBA projected risk weighted assets calculation should use the regulatory, downturn adjusted version of the models. However, it is expected that the regulatory version of the models is also influenced by the macroeconomic scenario. Given stressed regulatory probability of default and loss given default at t the projected risk weighted asset is calculated with the usual risk weighted asset formula in equation (4.41) for the non-defaulted loan fraction. However, there can also be a contribution from the defaulted flow at t if the (non-stressed) regulatory loss given default parameter exceeds the PIT loss given default at t.

While EBA considers a static balance sheet, we can also easily extend the iteration in equation (4.61) to handle loan growth or decay rates (or portfolio level growth and decay rates if the model is applied on portfolio level) over the stressed times $t = 1, \ldots, T$. Let $\mathbf{G}(t)$ and $\mathbf{D}(t)$ be diagonal matrices with diagonal elements $(1 + g_k(t))$ and $(1 + d_k(t))$, respectively, for $k = 1, \ldots, \widehat{K} - 1$ and unity at the diagonal element for default grade $\widehat{K}$ (since there is no growth or decay for the defaulted fraction of the loan). We now have $\{g_k(t)\}_{k=1}^{\widehat{K}-1}$ credit grade specific growth rates and $\{d_k(t)\}_{k=1}^{\widehat{K}-1}$ credit grade specific decay rates for the loan (or portfolio of loans) such that we can extend equation (4.61) to

$$\mathbf{y}(t) = [\mathbf{A}(t)]'\mathbf{G}(t)\mathbf{D}(t)\mathbf{y}(t-1). \tag{4.62}$$

Hence, we are capturing loan or portfolio growth or decay rates per grade (that is, state $k = 1, \ldots, \widehat{K} - 1$). A good example in practice of what the decay rates can be used for is to capture (state dependent) amortization profiles. Since both the multifactor Merton inspired model and the macroeconomic credit score model economic stress testing are based on the Markov iteration (4.61) for stressed expected losses, conditional on a scenario for $\{\mathbf{Z}(t)\}_{t=1}^{T}$, they can be directly deployed in the above EBA specific stress testing approach, either at granular loan level or homogeneous subportfolio level as desired. They can also be used to analyze portfolio growth and decay effects using the extended Markov iteration (4.62). A prerequisite is of course that the regulatory prescribed scenarios have been converted into corresponding scenarios for the bank's actual economic factors, $\mathbf{Z}$, being used in the models.

We now illustrate the computation of the flow of defaulted assets, FD(t), with two simple numerical examples using first the multifactor Merton-inspired model and second the credit score model.

Multifactor Model Numerical Example In order to compute explicit numerical default rates from the multifactor model we assume a specific model is given as in equation (4.21),

$$\tilde{Z}_i = 0.5Z_1 + 0.4Z_2 + 0.1Z_3 + 0.9\varepsilon_i \tag{4.63}$$

which hence has three economic factors, $\mathbf{Z} = (Z_1, Z_2, Z_3)$. The covariance matrix of $\mathbf{Z}$ is specified by

$$\Sigma = \begin{bmatrix} 1 & 0.5 & 0.4 \\ 0.5 & 1 & 0.6 \\ 0.4 & 0.6 & 1 \end{bmatrix}.$$

We also have a given, long-run, transition probability matrix with eight states as in Table 4.52. Here the transition matrix probabilities are expressed in percentages.

Normalizing the model in equation (4.63) with

$$\phi_i = \sqrt{\frac{R_i^2}{\beta_i \Sigma \beta_i'}} = \sqrt{\frac{1 - \lambda_i^2}{\beta_i \Sigma \beta_i'}} = 0.518\,04$$

we obtain the standardized model as

$$\hat{Z}_i = 0.518\,04(0.5Z_1 + 0.4Z_2 + 0.1Z_3) + 0.9\varepsilon_i.$$

This gives the standardized model R_i^2 as

$$R_i^2 = 1 - \lambda_i^2 = 0.19.$$

TABLE 4.52 Sample Long-Run Transition Matrix

State	1	2	3	4	5	6	7	8
1	91	7	1	0.8	0.2	0	0	0
2	1.1	91	6	0.9	0.6	0.4	0	0
3	0.17	3	91	5	0.5	0.2	0.09	0.04
4	0.05	0.15	6	87	5	1	0.6	0.2
5	0.09	0.4	0.81	7.7	81	7.8	1.2	1
6	0	0.5	0.7	0.8	7	80	6	5
7	0	0	0.8	1.2	3	12	60	23
8	0	0	0	0	0	0	0	1

TABLE 4.53 State Thresholds from the Sample Transition Matrix

State	1	2	3	4	5	6	7	8
1	+inf	−1.34	−2.05	−2.32	−2.87	−inf	−inf	−inf
2	+inf	2.29	−1.41	−2.07	−2.32	−2.65	−inf	−inf
3	+inf	2.92	1.85	−1.56	−2.39	−2.71	−3.01	−3.35
4	+inf	3.29	2.87	1.53	−1.49	−2.09	−2.40	−2.87
5	+inf	3.12	2.58	2.22	1.34	−1.28	−2.01	−2.32
6	+inf	+inf	2.47	2.25	2.05	1.34	−1.22	−1.64
7	+inf	+inf	+inf	2.40	2.05	1.64	0.95	−0.73

To apply the model we convert the transition probabilities in Table 4.52 to corresponding transition matrix thresholds. This is done in Table 4.53 where +inf and −inf refers to the largest positive and negative value respectively.

With this threshold matrix we can now obtain conditional transition probabilities using equation (4.27) and a specific scenario for $\{Z(t)\}_{t=1}^{T}$. For example, if $Z_1(t) = Z_2(t) = Z_3(t) = -2$, we have that

$$A_{lr}(t) = N\left(\frac{I_{lr} + 1.036}{0.9}\right) - N\left(\frac{I_{lr+1} + 1.036}{0.9}\right)$$

which increases the threshold values and hence puts larger probabilities on migration to lower quality states. Similarly, if $Z_1(t) = Z_2(t) = Z_3(t) = 2$, we have that

$$A_{lr}(t) = N\left(\frac{I_{lr} - 1.036}{0.9}\right) - N\left(\frac{I_{lr+1} - 1.036}{0.9}\right)$$

which reduces the thresholds, giving larger probabilities to migration to higher quality states. For each scenario $\{Z(t)\}_{t=1}^{T}$ we can hence construct a conditional transition matrix, $A(t)$, for each $t = 1, \ldots, T$ where negative values for $Z = (Z_1, Z_2, Z_3)$ indicate a downturn economic cycle, which can be seen as a stress scenario if the $Z = (Z_1, Z_2, Z_3)$ shifts are severe enough. As we have discussed, in practice the economic factors represent variables that are important in describing the credit quality of the loan issuer.

Consider now an explicit economic scenario for $\{Z(t)\}_{t=1}^{5}$ as in Table 4.54. Using this scenario and the Markov iteration (4.61) for a loan in state $k = 3$ at $t = 0$ we can obtain the $t = 1, \ldots, 5$ state occupancy probabilities. Table 4.55 displays the obtained conditional state occupancy probabilities as percentages.[47]

Hence, from Table 4.55, we know how the loan balances are distributed in states $k = 1, \ldots, 8$ at each time $t = 1, \ldots, 5$ under the economic scenario in Table 4.54. For example, at $t = 4$ the cumulative defaulted portion of the loan is approximately 9%. Since we are concerned with the flow of defaulted assets, FD(t), we create the equation

$$\Delta y_{\hat{R}}(t) = y_{\hat{R}}(t) - y_{\hat{R}}(t-1) = \text{FD}(t) \tag{4.64}$$

---

[47]In the table we have expressed the state occupancy probabilities as percentages rather than fractions and truncated the decimals of the state occupancy percentages. Hence, a particular column's state occupancy percentages may not sum exactly to 100%.

TABLE 4.54 Sample Scenario for the
Economic Factors in the Multifactor Model

Factor/Time	1	2	3	4	5
Z_1	−1	−1.5	−2	−2.5	−3
Z_2	−1	−1.5	−2	−2.5	−3
Z_3	−1	−1.5	−2	−2.5	−3

TABLE 4.55 Conditional State Occupancy Percentages Under the Economic
Scenario for the Multifactor Model

State/Time	1	2	3	4	5
1	0.0067	0.0068	0.0048	0.0026	0.0011
2	0.4188	0.4708	0.3601	0.2118	0.0957
3	87.225	70.434	50.797	31.384	15.841
4	10.472	21.773	30.153	31.511	24.950
5	1.1329	4.1003	9.0033	14.002	15.717
6	0.4623	1.7528	4.5159	8.6566	12.177
7	0.1987	0.8578	2.4526	5.2074	8.1742
8	0.0826	0.6035	2.7116	9.0229	23.042

where $y_{\hat{K}}(t)$ is the $\hat{K}$:th element of $y_{\hat{K}}(t)$.[48] The defaulted flow can be adjusted for recoveries of course. We can also assign a cash flow vector to each state $k = 1,\ldots,\hat{K}-1$ and time t,

$$c(t) = \begin{bmatrix} c^1(t) \\ \vdots \\ c^{\hat{K}-1}(t) \\ 0 \end{bmatrix}$$

to compute the $t = 1,\ldots,5$ non-default state-dependent stressed expected cash flows, $e(t)$, as

$$e(t) = [y(t)]'c(t).$$

Here we have set the cash flow from the default state to null since the recovery cash flow is usually calculated from adjusting the default flow at t, $FD(t)$, with a PIT loss given default model. We will see an example of this later with the credit score model.

Finally, we can also add assumed growth and decay rates (for example amortization) in the iteration equation (4.62) to the model. Either way, the application of the Markov iteration is trivial and requires minimal computation time.

Credit Score Model Numerical Example To make the credit score model explicit for our numerical stress testing example we assume, as in our mortgage portfolio example above

---

[48]Note here that the sum of the elements of $\Delta y(t)$ is null since the net migration between two time periods must sum to zero.

TABLE 4.56 Sample Mu Parameter Matrix for the Multinomial Logit Model

	$\mu_{1.}$	$\mu_{2.}$	$\mu_{3.}$	$\mu_{4.}$	$\mu_{5.}$	$\mu_{6.}$	$\mu_{7.}$	$\mu_{8.}$
$\mu_{1.}$	8.773	6.294	5.949	5.249	4.713	4.516	4.216	3.906
$\mu_{2.}$	5.915	7.390	5.892	3.119	2.879	2.561	2.094	1.182
$\mu_{3.}$	4.004	4.893	5.925	4.893	3.400	2.601	1.787	1.072
$\mu_{4.}$	2.388	2.702	3.065	3.910	3.066	2.702	1.712	0.768
$\mu_{5.}$	0.966	1.256	2.405	1.662	2.729	1.754	0.609	0.431
$\mu_{6.}$	−0.666	−0.157	0.053	0.435	0.898	1.879	1.054	0.288
$\mu_{7.}$	−2.357	−1.263	−1.006	−0.760	−0.292	0.637	0.839	0.656
$\mu_{8.}$	−19.539	−4.544	−2.737	−1.231	−1.036	−0.656	−0.115	0.428

TABLE 4.57 Sample Beta Parameter Matrix for the Multinomial Logit Model

	$\beta_{1.}$	$\beta_{2.}$	$\beta_{3.}$	$\beta_{4.}$	$\beta_{5.}$	$\beta_{6.}$	$\beta_{7.}$	$\beta_{8.}$
$\beta_{1.}$	0.020	−0.020	−0.020	−0.020	−0.020	−0.020	−0.020	−0.020
$\beta_{2.}$	0.020	0.020	−0.020	−0.020	−0.020	−0.020	−0.020	−0.020
$\beta_{3.}$	0.040	0.040	0.040	−0.020	−0.020	−0.020	−0.020	−0.020
$\beta_{4.}$	0.060	0.060	0.060	0.060	−0.020	−0.020	−0.020	−0.020
$\beta_{5.}$	0.060	0.060	0.060	0.060	0.040	−0.020	−0.020	−0.020
$\beta_{6.}$	0.080	0.080	0.080	0.080	0.080	0.10	−0.020	−0.020
$\beta_{7.}$	0.100	0.100	0.100	0.100	0.100	0.100	0.060	0.040
$\beta_{8.}$	0.100	0.100	0.100	0.100	0.100	0.100	0.120	0.140

with this model, that there is a single economic factor Z_1 that drives the transition rates. Later we will also consider a loss model that will depend on a second economic factor Z_2 that drives the loss given default through its interpretation as a collateral value index. We assume a transition model with $\hat{K} = 9$ states has been calibrated such that we have the calibrated model parameters $\{\mu_{lr}\}$ and $\{\beta_{lr}\}$ in Tables 4.56 and 4.57, respectively.[49]

With the model parameters set we can use equation (4.52) to compute the conditional transition probabilities. Using the same explicit economic scenario for $\{Z_1(t)\}_{t=1}^{5}$ as in Table 4.55, we obtain the $t = 1,\ldots,5$ state occupancy probabilities in Table 4.58 for a loan initially in state 4. As in Table 4.55, we display in Table 4.58 the obtained conditional state occupancy probabilities as percentages.

In this case, because the transition matrix retains quite high movement to better quality grades even under stress we have directions of migration both to the default state as well as to better states. For this sample loan we also assume there is a simple PIT LGD(t) model, similar to equation (4.59), based on collateralized recovery at a particular time t and defined by

$$\text{LGD}(t) = 1 - \left[\frac{Z_2(t)}{Z_2(0)\text{LTV}} \right]. \tag{4.65}$$

---

[49]Note here the similarity with the multifactor model where the model parameters $\{\mu_{lr}\}$ in this context are assumed to be estimated on past transitions while in the multifactor model the equivalent $\{\mu_{lr}\}$ parameters are obtained from the long-run transition matrix.

TABLE 4.58 Conditional State Occupancy Percentages Under the Economic Scenario for the Credit Score Model

State/Time	1	2	3	4	5
1	7.46	12.34	15.85	18.39	20.12
2	10.22	15.06	17.38	18.30	18.47
3	14.69	18.47	18.31	17.31	16.31
4	34.19	17.52	12.68	10.78	9.73
5	15.93	13.36	10.42	8.66	7.62
6	11.07	11.14	9.61	8.31	7.36
7	4.11	5.65	5.81	5.49	5.08
8	1.60	3.55	4.23	4.22	3.97
9	0.73	2.91	5.69	8.56	11.34

Here, as before, LTV is the current loan-to-value relationship between the exposure level and the collateral for the exposure. Hence, we interpret $Z_2(t)$ as a property index value at time t with $Z_2(0)$ the current property index value such that $\frac{Z_2(t)}{Z_2(0)}$ represents a normalized growth rate for the property index value. We set $Z_2(0) = 1$ for convenience. Clearly, the PIT LGD model in equation (4.65) does not constrain LGD(t) between zero and unity. For simplicity, this constraint is not needed for our numerical example.

Using the PIT LGD model in equation (4.65) we can adjust the default flow, FD(t), to expected loss rates, EL(t) = FD(t)LGD(t), using Table 4.58 and a scenario for $\{Z_2(t)\}_{t=1}^{T}$. Assuming that the current loan to value is unity and that property index values decay in the scenario with a factor of 0.1 for each time $t = 1, \ldots, 5$ we get the percent expected loss rates displayed in Table 4.59.

An Economic Capital Model for Loan Portfolios

While point in time estimates for probability of default are generally used in internal credit portfolio models, financial institutions are searching for a stable, non-cyclical answer to the appropriate level of economic capital. Here, we consider an insurance approach discussed in Nyström and Skoglund (2006) that achieves stable capital levels due to a long-term view. The approach is inspired by the classical risk theory. In classical risk theory (see Mikosh, 2006; Grandell, 1991) an insurance firm collects premiums, P, and suffers losses, L. Hence, with initial capital level u of the insurance company we have that, for a given scenario d,

$$R(u, T, d) = u + \sum_{t=1}^{T} C(t)$$

$$C(t) = [P(t, d) - P(t - 1, d)] - [L(t, d) - L(t - 1, d)].$$

TABLE 4.59 Expected Loss Rates Using the PIT LGD Model

Time	1	2	3	4	5
Loss	0.073	0.436	0.834	1.148	1.390

Here, $R(u, T, d)$ is the remaining risk reserve at T given an initial amount of capital, u. $C(t)$ is the net difference between premiums collected and liability payouts in the interval $(t - 1, T]$. The insurance analogy is relevant because in the simplest classical insurance model

$$X(t) = u + ct - \sum_{k=1}^{N(t)} L_k$$

the insurance premiums flow at rate c and the number of claims are Poisson distributed, $N(t)$, with claim sizes, L_k. Transferred to the credit portfolio the premiums, c, can be thought of as the loan credit margins (over the funding rate) and the Poisson process, $N(t)$, as the number of credit events with loss given default, L_k.

We now define

$$\tau = \tau(u, d) = \inf_T (R(u, T, d) \le 0)$$

as the first time the remaining risk reserve is negative. If $R(u, T, d) > 0$ for all T, then $\tau = \infty$. We also have that

$$S(T') = P(\tau > T') = P\left[\inf_{T \le T'} R(u, T, d) > 0 \right]$$

which is referred to as the survival probability to time T'. Here,

$$\inf_{T \le T'} R(u, T, d) > 0$$

is the lowest amount recorded in the risk reserve process during $t = 1, \dots, T'$. We can also define the ruin probability as $R(T') = 1 - S(T')$, and the insurance company can now define u such that with confidence level α it is solvent.

Our approach to loan portfolio credit risk economic capital will be similar to the insurance risk reserve approach. However, we choose a slightly different way to extract negative contributions to the initial capital, u. Specifically, we set

$$\widetilde{R}(u, T, d) = u + \sum_{t=1}^{T} \min[C(t), 0]. \tag{4.66}$$

In this case we add to the initial capital all the negative contributions. The reason we choose this formulation is because by construction the bank will experience periods of positive contribution to the total cash flows as well as periods of negative contribution to the total cash flows. It is prudent to assume that the bank will not save positive contributions from one period to another to neutralize negative contributions at subsequent periods. Due to the obligations, for instance, to shareholders, in good times, the bank may use that profit. With this formulation the bank should make sure to be guarded against periods that give a negative contribution to the total cash flows.

The above formulation is also consistent with the fact that financial institutions do not raise capital once a year. Banks rather focus on capital planning periods that may be very long (e.g., 5–10 years) and include a full business cycle. The length of the planning horizon determines the choice of T, and in general the longer the planning period the more stable is the capital obtained. This is because the capital contributions, calculated using equation (4.66), will then cover both good and bad times for the economic cycle such that the actual credit quality of the portfolio at the exact starting point will make a smaller and smaller contribution.

Based on equation (4.66) we can now define a stable, planning-based economic capital measure for the loan portfolio. We have

$$EC(T, \rho) = \min \left\{ u; \rho \left(\widetilde{R}(u, T, d) \right) \geq 0 \right\} \tag{4.67}$$

where ρ denotes the risk measure. Hence, for every scenario, d, we cumulate all the negative contributions over times $t = 1, \ldots, T$ and create a distribution. The distribution will be truncated upward by zero and downward by the maximum cumulative negative contribution over time. We can now, using the bank's preferred survival probability, calculate the VaR(α) or CVaR(α) of the left tail of this distribution. The number obtained is the α confidence level economic capital needed to support the portfolio over the planning period, that is, to within α confidence level, prevent the aggregate negative contributions from the portfolio to be larger than the capital base.

When calculating economic capital using equation (4.67), one may either include loan credit margins over the funding rate as a positive source of cash flows or not. That is, there is also a source of returns analogous to the premiums in the insurance risk model. Future assumptions of the credit margins are then also needed in the model. An important special case is when one assumes that the credit margins are, currently and in the future, set such that they equal to the expected losses. In this case, one can focus on the modeling of losses and we then retrieve the "usual" definition of capital, that is, risk measure loss, EC(T, ρ), minus expected loss being defined as unexpected loss (and capital).

Example Economic Capital and Capital Allocation for the Mortgage Portfolio Continuing our example with the mortgage portfolio, we use equation (4.67) to calculate VaR- and CVaR-based EC at the 99.9% confidence level using the net credit loss (credit margins less credit losses) for the mortgage credit portfolio model example. Hence, we cumulate the negative marginal net losses across $1, \ldots, 10$ years for all simulations and calculate the EC measures from the distribution. Table 4.60 displays the aggregate portfolio EC measures.

We notice that with this path-based and conservative measure for economic capital, the economic capital level is close to and a bit above the 1-year required worst-case regulatory capital, based on 99.9% VaR, for the portfolio in Table 4.47 of 592,036,602 units of currency. Hence, in this case, the economic capital level using the insurance approach is reconciled with the worst-case regulatory capital level.

Once the economic capital using, for example, VaR or CVaR is obtained, one can use the traditional Euler allocation of VaR and CVaR. This is because all the conditional subportfolio losses sum by definition to the aggregate portfolio loss, year by year and scenario by scenario, using equation (4.67). Table 4.61 displays the VaR EC contributions for the subportfolios.

In the table negative values for the economic capital VaR contributions represent negative contributions, that is, net credit hedges. For example, subportfolio 11 with rating grade 2 and

TABLE 4.60 Aggregate Portfolio Economic Capital Using the Insurance Approach

VaR EC	654,577,618
CVaR EC	700,544,204

TABLE 4.61 VaR-Based Economic Capital Risk
Contributions for the Subportfolios

| | Contributions |
Subportfolio	VaR EC
1	−40,500
2	−11,700
3	46,862
4	−19,800
5	−43,200
6	−9,000
7	37,361
8	79,431
9	−1,553,920
10	177,613,573
11	−34,547,791
12	55,037,601
13	73,812,495
14	384,176,204
Aggregate	654,577,618

a credit margin of 1.2% has sufficient marginals and small enough losses to yield a negative economic capital contribution to the aggregate portfolio. This is also the case for subportfolio 9 with rating grade 3 and credit margin 1%. Some of the subportfolio contributions for the small sampling subportfolios $1, \ldots, 7$ may seem counterintuitive. For example, subportfolio 1 with rating grade 5 and a 1.5% credit margin has a negative economic capital contribution, while subportfolio 7 with rating grade 2 and credit margin 1.1% has a positive net loss contribution. Indeed, as we have noticed before, VaR is not in general a good measure for contributions of small subportfolios and the calculation of CVaR contributions or smoothed VaR contributions is required to avoid conditioning on a single realized loss path with typically large volatility in contributions as we change the confidence level slightly.

We finally emphasize that with this path-based definition of economic capital reserve, the economic capital depends on

■ The risk (planning) time horizon, T, and potentially the timing of losses
■ The size of credit margins (or size of expected losses if expected loss is used to create unexpected loss)
■ The size of the losses suffered

If the planning horizon, T, is sufficiently long to cover a business cycle, the economic capital reserve should be stable, and in addition, largely independent of the starting point (good or bad current state). Of course, the longest planning horizon is the planning horizon, T, where T is set equal to the longest maturity in the portfolio.

While we have used a fixed portfolio in the calculation of economic capital, in practice, one must also take into account the additional economic capital required for the planned portfolio growth. The portfolio growth can come in the form of extended loans to existing customers as well as new customers' loans. Taking into account extended loans to existing customers can simply use loan size scaling on the subportfolio losses over the years consistent with the yearly extension rate assumed. New customer loans enter the portfolio at a certain rate over the years and must in general be separately accounted for as a flow. Unless the bank has a strategy to grow in a particular segment, it is often realistic to assume that the new customer growth portfolio has the same composition as the existing portfolio, which can simplify calculations.

The Poisson Mixture Model and CreditRisk⁺

Now we will revisit the binomial loss model discussed previously, through considering a specifically simple linear form of the score function $p = g(\mathbf{Z}, \mathbf{Y})$ and employing the Poisson approximation to the binomial. As we will see, this will enable us to obtain an (almost) analytical solution to the portfolio loss distribution. With this configuration the binomial loss model is referred to as the CreditRisk⁺ model and is widely employed in the industry. In the CreditRisk⁺ model we have the linear form scoring model,

$$p_i = \bar{p}_i \sum_{j=1}^{J} w_{ij} Z_j \tag{4.68}$$

for loans $i = 1, \ldots, N$ where

$$Z_j \sim \text{independent Gamma}(\alpha_j, \beta_j)$$

and $w_{ij} \geq 0$, $\forall ij$ with $\sum_{j=1}^{J} w_{ij} = 1$ for all i. The factor loadings for a loan i, $\{w_{ij}\}_{j=1}^{J}$, measure the sensitivity of loan i's default probability to the factors $\{Z_j\}_{j=1}^{J}$. In this setup the $\bar{p}_i$:s can be taken to be the unconditional default probabilities and the existence of positive correlation between obligor i and i' is determined by $w_{ij} > 0$ and $w_{i'j} > 0$ for at least one j. We can now consider a characterization of the distribution of

$$\sum_{i=1}^{N} L_i | \mathbf{Z} \tag{4.69}$$

where L_i is a Bernoulli default indicator and $\mathbf{Z} = (Z_1, \ldots, Z_J)'$. Since conditional on $\mathbf{Z}$ the default indicators, L_i, are independent we have that the (conditional) probability generating function is given by

$$G_{L_i|\mathbf{Z}}(t) = 1 + p_i(t-1)$$

for $i = 1, \ldots, N$. Using the common approximation $\log(1+x) \approx x$ we can write

$$G_{L_i|\mathbf{Z}}(t) = 1 + p_i(t-1)$$
$$= \exp(\log(1 + p_i(t-1)))$$
$$\approx \exp(p_i(t-1))$$

for small p_i and t close to 1. In fact, $\exp(p_i(t-1))$ is the probability generating function of the Poisson distribution and hence this approximation is equivalent to saying that the default indicators are Poisson(p_i) distributed. The idea is that as long as p_i is small, we can ignore the constraint that a single obligor or loan can default only once (seeing the probability of defaulting more times being very small for small p_i). Since $L_i|Z$ is independent, we can use the multiplicative property of probability generating functions under independence such that

$$G_{\sum_{i=1}^N L_i | Z}(t) = \Pi_{i=1}^N \exp(p_i(t-1))$$

$$= \exp(\pi(t-1))$$

where $\pi = \sum_{i=1}^N p_i$. To derive the unconditional probability generating function of $\sum_{i=1}^N L_i$ we need to integrate out the systematic factors, Z. We omit the derivation here. However, it is a standard result in statistics that a Poisson-Gamma mixture distribution (with J independent Gamma factors) is distributed as the convolution of J independent negative binomial variables. See Casella and Berger (1990). Performing the integration hence results in the probability generating function of the resulting negative binomial distribution being

$$G_{\sum_{i=1}^N L_i}(t) = \Pi_{j=1}^J \left(\frac{1-\delta_j}{1-\delta_j t} \right)^{\alpha_j}. \tag{4.70}$$

Here,

$$\delta_j = \frac{\beta_j \pi_j}{1 + \beta_j \pi_j} = \frac{\overline{\beta}_j}{1 + \overline{\beta}_j}$$

and

$$\pi_j = \sum_{i=1}^N \overline{p}_i w_{ij}.$$

Using the properties of the gamma distribution we can also write

$$\alpha_j = \mu_j^2 / \sigma_j^2 = \frac{\left(\alpha_j \overline{\beta}_j \right)^2}{\alpha_j \overline{\beta}_j^2} = \alpha_j$$

where μ_j, σ_j^2 are respectively the mean and variance of the gamma distribution j. Similarly,

$$\overline{\beta}_j = \sigma_j^2 / \mu_j = \frac{\alpha_j \overline{\beta}_j^2}{\alpha_j \overline{\beta}_j} = \overline{\beta}_j.$$

Now, let's assume we have defined the key parameters of the model. That is,

- The average default rate for an obligor, $\overline{p}_i$
- The sector j loadings for obligor i, w_{ij}
- The volatility of default rate for obligor i, σ_i

Then, α_j, β_j are calibrated, using that $\mu_j = \alpha_j\beta_j$ and $\sigma_j = \sqrt{\alpha_j\beta_j^2}$, such that $\alpha_j = \mu_j/\beta_j$, $\beta_j = \sqrt{\frac{\sigma_j^2}{\alpha_j}}$, and hence, finally, $\alpha_j = \mu_j/\sqrt{\frac{\sigma_j^2}{\alpha_j}} = (\mu_j\sigma_j)^2$ and $\beta_j = \mu_j$. It now only remains to devise estimators of the sector average default rate and default rate volatilities. That is,

$$\mu_j = \sum_{i=1}^{N} \overline{p}_i w_{ij}$$

$$\sigma_j = \sum_{i=1}^{N} \sigma_i w_{ij}$$

and using these estimates we can now calibrate the Gamma-distribution of sector j by using the relations between μ_j, σ_j and α_j, β_j detailed above.

In case there is only one sector, that is, $J = 1$, we of course obtain a negative binomial distribution for losses such that

$$P\left(\sum_{i=1}^{N} L_i = n\right) = (-1)^n \binom{\alpha}{n} \left(\frac{1}{1+\overline{\beta}}\right)^{\alpha} \left(1 - \frac{1}{1+\overline{\beta}}\right)^n$$

for $n = 0, 1, \ldots, N$. However, in general the default event distribution is not negative binomial but an independent sum of negative binomial distributions.

In practice, we are interested in the loss distribution and not just the distribution of default indicators, requiring the introduction of N adjusted exposures $\{E_i\}_{i=1}^{N}$. Define therefore $\overline{E}_i$ as the loan size of obligor i and l_i as the percentage loss given default. Then,

$$E_i = l_i\overline{E}_i$$

represents the loss given default of obligor $i, \ldots, N$. Since adjusted exposure, E_i, is exogenously given, we obtain a simple adjustment to the probability generating function in equation (4.70) as

$$\Pi_{j=1}^{K} \left(\frac{1 - \delta_j}{1 - \delta_j P_j(t)}\right) \tag{4.71}$$

where δ_j was defined previously, and

$$P_j(t) = \frac{1}{\pi_j} \sum_{i=1}^{N} \overline{p}_i w_{ij} t^{E_i}.$$

The equation (4.71) defines an analytic generating function for the CreditRisk$^+$ model. The loss can be computed by the Panjer recursion originally suggested in the CreditRisk$^+$ (1997) manual. However, for a large portfolio containing many exposure bands, the Panjer recursion may be numerically instable due to summation of very small positive and negative numbers. Haaf, Reiss, and Schoenmaker (2004) therefore suggested a stability treatment of the Panjer recursion (see also Giese, 2004). Gordy (2002) focused on the saddle point method.

The saddle point method uses the cumulants of the distribution and the Lugannani-Rice tail probability formula. See equation (4.27). It hence approximates the tail density using a normal distribution. Since the saddle point method is a continuous approximation we also gain another advantage from the point of view of risk management. Specifically, the VaR produced by the saddle point method is smooth and differentiable, hence allowing for a consistent interpretation and calculation of risk contributions. In an example below we will focus on these computational methods for CreditRisk$^+$. However, see also Grundlach and Lehrbass (2004) on other computational methods for CreditRisk$^+$.

Example CreditRisk$^+$ Portfolio Analysis   We consider a sample CreditRisk$^+$ portfolio analysis using a sample portfolio from the original CreditRisk$^+$ (1997) manual.[50] The sample portfolio has 25 loans that are displayed in Table 4.62. The CreditRisk$^+$ portfolio model is calibrated through assigning for each loan i,

- $\bar{p}_i$, the average default probability over time,
- the factor loadings, w_{ij} for $j = 1, 2, 3$ factors,

TABLE 4.62   CreditRisk$^+$ Portfolio Parameters

Loan	$\bar{p}_i$	w_{i1}	w_{i2}	w_{i3}	γ_i	σ_i	E_i
			CreditRisk$^+$ parameters				
1	30%	30%	10%	10%	50%	15%	358,475
2	30%	25%	25%	25%	25%	15%	1,089,819
3	10%	25%	20%	30%	25%	5%	1,799,710
4	15%	5%	10%	10%	75%	8%	1,933,116
5	15%	10%	10%	30%	50%	8%	2,317,327
6	15%	20%	10%	20%	50%	8%	2,410,929
7	30%	10%	10%	55%	25%	15%	2,652,184
8	15%	25%	20%	30%	25%	8%	2,957,685
9	5%	25%	25%	25%	25%	3%	3,137,989
10	5%	10%	5%	10%	75%	3%	3,204,044
11	2%	10%	10%	30%	50%	1%	4,727,724
12	5%	20%	10%	20%	50%	3%	4,830,517
13	5%	25%	25%	25%	25%	3%	4,912,097
14	30%	10%	10%	55%	25%	15%	4,928,989
15	10%	25%	30%	20%	25%	5%	5,042,312
16	8%	10%	5%	10%	75%	4%	5,320,364
17	5%	20%	10%	20%	50%	3%	5,435,457
18	3%	10%	10%	30%	50%	2%	5,517,586
19	8%	25%	20%	30%	25%	4%	5,764,596
20	3%	10%	10%	55%	25%	2%	5,847,845
21	30%	25%	20%	30%	25%	15%	6,466,533
22	30%	10%	5%	10%	75%	15%	6,480,322
23	2%	25%	20%	30%	25%	1%	7,727,651
24	10%	20%	10%	20%	50%	5%	15,410,906
25	8%	10%	10%	5%	75%	4%	20,238,895

---

[50]Specifically, we consider the sample portfolio in the example 3 accompanying spreadsheet of the CreditRisk$^+$ manual. This portfolio has a total of 4 Gamma factors assigned to 25 loans. See appendix B of the CreditRisk$^+$ manual for information on the spreadsheet.

- the probability of default volatility over time, σ_i, and
- the exposure, E_i.

We also assign weight to a loan idiosyncratic Gamma factor, $\gamma_i = 1 - \sum_{j=1}^{3} w_{ij}$, that is also used in the original CreditRisk$^+$ model. Hence, in total the portfolio loans in Table 4.62 depend on 4 Gamma factors. The assumed loan portfolio CreditRisk$^+$ model parameters are also displayed in the table.

Using the CreditRisk$^+$ sample portfolio of loan exposures we calculate the portfolio credit VaR using an adjusted Panjer recursion and the saddle point method by Gordy (2002). The adjusted Panjer recursion uses the Haaf, Reiss, and Schoenmaker (2004) suggested stability treatment. The portfolio 95%, 97.5%, 99%, 99.9%, and 99.99% confidence level VaR is displayed in Table 4.63. The original CreditRisk$^+$ manual accompanying spreadsheet calculates VaR up to the 99.9% confidence level using the regular Panjer recursion and is also displayed in Table 4.63 for reference. The adjusted Panjer and the saddle point method yield similar results for the sample portfolio. The results are also close to the Panjer VaR obtained from the CreditRisk$^+$ manual spreadsheet. The portfolio expected loss is 14,221,863 units of currency with a total portfolio exposure of 130,513,072 units of currency. Hence, credit VaR ranges between approximately 26% and 60% of the portfolio exposure for the different confidence levels. The relatively large VaR values are not surprising given the high average default rates for the loans in Table 4.62. The unexpected portfolio loss can now be constructed as the VaR minus expected loss. For example, at the 99% confidence level, unexpected loss capital is about 37% of the portfolio exposure while the loss reserve is about 10% of the portfolio exposure.

While the Panjer recursions and the saddle point VaR are close for the sample portfolio for all the confidence levels, we can also consider adjustments to the portfolio in Table 4.62. Specifically, if we let the average default probability, $\overline{p}_i$, of each loan be reduced by a factor of 10, yielding a loan portfolio with relatively low default rates, we obtain adjusted Panjer and saddle point VaR at the 99% confidence level as 20,180,634 and 10,362,146, respectively, the portfolio expected loss being 1,422,186. Hence, there are now significant differences between the methods. Such large differences for a small portfolio can be attributed to the continuous approximation of the saddle point method. Figure 4.22 displays the CreditRisk$^+$ model loss probability distributions with adjusted default rates (see panel a) and for unadjusted default rates (see panel b). The loss probability distributions are obtained from the adjusted Panjer recursion. In case of adjusted default rates we obtain a highly erratic loss probability density. This can be compared to the loss probability density using the unadjusted loan average default rates, which is much more smooth for tail losses, that is, in the VaR region. However, for large

TABLE 4.63 Portfolio VaR for the CreditRisk$^+$ Portfolio Using the Adjusted Panjer Method, the Saddle Point Method, and the Original Panjer Method in the CreditRisk$^+$ Manual

Confidence level	Method		
	Adjusted Panjer	Saddle point	Panjer (CreditRisk$^+$ manual)
95%	34,771,682	34,929,811	34,771,678
97.5%	40,396,993	40,515,015	40,396,985
99%	47,368,254	47,472,259	47,368,235
99.9%	63,422,244	63,536,395	63,422,062
99.99%	78,191,784	78,297,809	N/A

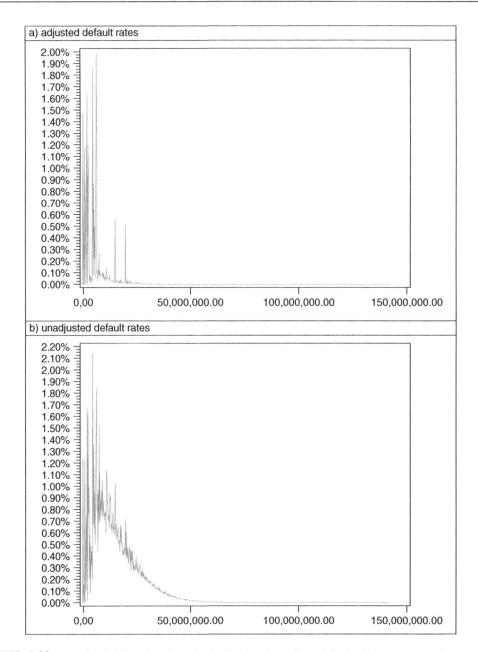

FIGURE 4.22 Loss Probability Density Obtained from the Adjusted Panjer Recursion When Average Loan Default Rates Are Reduced by a Factor of 10 and When the Average Deafult Rates Are Unadjusted

portfolios Gordy (2002, 2004) reports that the saddle point approximation works better than the Panjer method. Since large portfolios in general introduce more smoothness to the losses, this is not surprising.

While we have focused on VaR as a risk measure in the CreditRisk⁺ model one can also consider risk measures such as CVaR. The Panjer recursion methods produce the full loss

TABLE 4.64 Loan Level Volatility Contributions for the Case of 99.99% VaR with Volatility Contributions Scaled to Sum to VaR

Loan	Volatility contributions
1	155,003.41
2	665,344.89
3	411,890.31
4	653,439.94
5	906,027.46
6	913,753.68
7	2,391,297.75
8	1,326,014.15
9	486,595.76
10	462,190.95
11	279,421.75
12	932,336.08
13	1,012,891.29
14	2,032,673.29
15	6,177,055.34
16	1,139,703.30
17	1,662,665.49
18	727,345.91
19	798,439.01
20	1,967,742.01
21	9,362,354.00
22	9,453,161.10
23	703,994.02
24	15,120,161.13
25	18,450,282.27
Portfolio	78,191,784.29

density as in Figure 4.22 from which an empirical CVaR can be obtained. Similarly, we can obtain risk distortion and spectral measures since they are based on weighted VaR points of the loss distribution. Gordy (2002, 2004) obtains CVaR using the saddle point method.

The CreditRisk$^+$ manual also gives relatively simple formulas for how to compute volatility contributions of a loan to the portfolio volatility. Once calculated we can of course scale such volatility contributions using, for example, VaR to obtain VaR summable contributions. Table 4.64 displays the loan-level scaled volatility contributions using the 99.99% adjusted Panjer VaR. The scaled volatility contribution at the portfolio level of course equals the portfolio VaR at the 99.99% confidence level. We refer to Haaf and Tasche (2002) for simple computation of VaR and CVaR risk contributions in the CreditRisk$^+$ model using multiple runs of the model.

Notes on Calibration of the CreditRisk$^+$ Model When calibrating the CreditRisk$^+$ model one can take a similar approach as in equation (4.50) for $s = 1, \ldots, S$ homogeneous segments to calibrate the factor loadings, $\{w_{ij}\}_{j=1}^{J}$, for a loan i belonging to segment s. As we noted for equation (4.50), in the case that the factors are common for all $s = 1, \ldots, S$, seemingly unrelated regression reduces to least squares equation by equation. However, a complicating factor for the Credit Risk$^+$ model is that factors are assumed Gamma distributed, and in particular independent. A natural approach to achieve independent risk factors in the normal distribution case is principal component analysis. See Lesko et al. (2004) on this approach. Alternatively, one can extend the CreditRisk$^+$ model to include correlated factors. This is done by Burgisser et al. (1999).

When the CreditRisk$^+$ model is used as a one-factor model, it is especially easy to calibrate. Specifically, from the properties of a Poisson mixture model we obtain the default correlation in the CreditRisk$^+$ model as

$$\text{corr}\left(L_i, L_j\right) = \frac{\text{cov}\left(L_i, L_j\right)}{\sqrt{\text{var}\left(L_i\right)}\sqrt{\text{var}\left(L_j\right)}} = \frac{\text{cov}\left(p_i, p_j\right)}{\sqrt{\text{var}\left(p_i\right) + \text{E}\left(p_i\right)}\sqrt{\text{var}\left(p_i\right) + \text{E}\left(p_i\right)}}$$

which, in case of a homogeneous portfolio, with $p = p_i = p_j \ \forall ij$ reduces to

$$\text{corr}\left(L_i, L_j\right) = \frac{\text{var}(p)}{\text{var}(p) + \text{E}(p)} = \frac{D}{D+1}$$

where D is the variance-to-mean ratio, often called the dispersion ratio. For a one-factor $Z \sim \text{Gamma}(\alpha, \beta)$ homogeneous Poisson gamma mixture model, we hence have

$$\text{corr}\left(L_i, L_j\right) = \frac{\beta}{\beta + 1}$$

which yields

$$\beta = \frac{\text{corr}\left(L_i, L_j\right)}{1 - \text{corr}\left(L_i, L_j\right)}$$

and hence can be calibrated based on observed default correlations.

The Role of the CreditRisk$^+$ Model Compared to Simulation-Based Models In practice, many banks use a simulation-based approach to portfolio credit risk. This enables the inclusion of important features such as stochastic loss given default models and stochastic exposure models. However, with its simplicity, the Credit Risk$^+$ model is a benchmark model for the more complicated simulation-based approaches to portfolio credit risk. It can be used for validation and reconciliation of risk levels in more complex models. Because the computational time for the Credit Risk$^+$ model is usually measured in seconds or minutes even for large portfolios it is also useful for a quick analysis of portfolio risks, for example, when adding new, significant corporate loans.

Both due to its calibration approach as well as being a default mode model CreditRisk$^+$ is more suited to loan portfolios. It is also termed the *actuarial approach*. However, a few attempts have been made to extend the model to rating migrations and the associated mark to market. See Bröker and Schweizer (2004).

FIRMWIDE PORTFOLIO CREDIT RISK AND CREDIT RISK DEPENDENCE

Since we have used apparently different models for the trading book and the banking book portfolio credit risk, a natural question is how to integrate and reconcile the different models for firmwide portfolio credit risk. Another question is how one can capture explicit credit contagion in the portfolio credit risk model such that a firm's default can almost surely induce other firms to default due to their business relationships.

Joint Codependency with Different Models

To explain how to join the apparently different structural and reduced form models we have discussed, we let $B_{1t}, \ldots, B_{\widehat{K}t}$ be the indicator that takes the value 1 if a firm or loan is in rating class $k = 1, \ldots, \widehat{K}$ at time t, $t = 1, \ldots, T$. For different classes of rating categories, we have $\widehat{K}$ distinct transition probabilities to the $\widehat{K}$ classes. That is, if a firm or loan belongs to class k, we have $p_{k1}, p_{k2}, \ldots, p_{k\widehat{K}}$ transition probabilities.

Consider first how we can put the structural model (Merton-based approaches) in the reduced form (credit scoring model) setting. As in equation (4.26) we have rating thresholds denoted by I_{kt} and rating classes are ordered such that rating class 1 is the highest quality grade and class $\widehat{K}$ is the lowest quality grade. Then, we can write for a firm i,

$$P(B_{kt} = 1) = P(I_{k+1t} \leq \widehat{Z}_i \leq I_{kt})$$

where the probability is conditional on the systematic credit factors $\{\mathbf{Z}\}$ with $I_{1t} = +\infty$ and $I_{\widehat{K}+1t} = -\infty$, or, equivalently,

$$P(B_{kt} = 1) = P(\pi_{k+1t} \leq u \leq \pi_{kt}) \tag{4.72}$$

for $u = N\left(\widehat{Z}_i\right)$ with $\widehat{Z}_i$ being, for example, the normalized multifactor model as in equation (4.22). Here, $\pi_{kt} = N(I_{kt})$ is the transition probability and u is a uniform random variable.

We can now introduce dependence as follows:

- A copula on u, $C(u)$ for the different issuers.
- A dependence between π_{kt} for different obligors and loans. That is, introduce dependence between the transition probabilities.

The case of a copula on the uniforms for the different issuers, $C(u)$, is effectively the Merton style model with equity as proxy. In case of the multifactor model we instead modeled $\widehat{Z}_i$ as a standard normal, correlated credit index. The dependence was specified between the driving factors, $\mathbf{Z}$. However, since the copula is invariant to monotonic transformations such as the probability transformation, $u = N\left(\widehat{Z}_i\right)$, we have that $C(u)$ is an equivalent representation of the dependence.

The case of specifying dependence in π_{kt} is what we used in the reduced form credit scoring models. Such models are termed *conditional independence* models in Yu (2003). We can think of the stochastic transition probabilities, π_{kt}, as stochastic barriers for a given realization of u. The model with independence copula for u and stochastic, correlated, transition probabilities is then recognized as the reduced form credit scoring models we have studied. The model where the transition probabilities are non-stochastic (fixed barriers) but the copula of u, $C(u)$, is not the independence copula is the Merton style portfolio models case.

Using equation (4.72), it is also easy to see that it is straightforward to combine the different models. Within a specific model all the default correlation arises from the driving factors $\mathbf{Z}$ and their dependence. However, this is also true between models. The exact model for evaluating the rating conditional on $\mathbf{Z}$ is of course different. In the structural case we use $u = N\left(\widehat{Z}_i\right)$ and the fixed barriers π_{kt}. In the reduced form case we use the transition probability, π_{kt} conditional on $\mathbf{Z}$, and independent uniform u across loans. Hence, only the scoring rating transition method is used differently for the two models. Default correlation and codependency between models still arises in the same way as for different obligors or loans in a single model, that is, through the systematic factors, $\mathbf{Z}$.

One can of course also consider a model with both dependence structures. We can term this model a structural model that has the added uncertainty of stochastic transition probabilities, π_{kt}, that is stochastic barriers, I_{kt}. This is referred to as a doubly stochastic or incomplete information model. For example, we have previously mentioned that Saa-Requejo and Santa-Clara (1987) introduced unobserved default barriers in Merton model. They modeled jointly the default barrier and firm value as correlated Geometric Brownian motions. Duffie and Lando (2000) and Giesecke (2001, 2004) interpret the model as modeling uncertainty about firms' values. There are also industry models, such as Moody's hybrid model for public firms (2000), that combine information from reduced form scorecard modeling with structural information such as equity for firm rating assessments.

Indirect and Direct Codependency in Credit Risk Models

In both our Merton style and credit scoring–based credit portfolio models there is interaction between firms and loans default and transition probabilities due to common factors, $\mathbf{Z}$. Hence, the general tendency for default probabilities to be high at the same time is driven by the correlations between the common factors. However, in these models there is no explicit connection between the default probabilities of surviving firms and default events that have happened. For example, information about the default history of a large firm may very well have a direct impact on the default probability of a set of smaller surviving firms that depend on the large firm as buyer of their products.

Structurally, we can make a distinction between indirect and direct dependence in credit risk models. In the credit risk management the concept of key risk driver is usually used for a driving macroeconomic variable that drives the credit index in a multifactor model or the transition probability in the reduced form scoring model. It is essentially an observable process, like GDP, unemployment, or equity index, that influences the default and transition frequency. The key risk drivers introduce an indirect codependency between default risk processes. This latent variable approach is a useful way of introducing default codependency that is not directly observed or easily measured. Another form of codependency is a direct codependency between firms or loans default and transition indicators. A simple example is when a firm default causes another firm to default almost surely due to their relationships.

We have used the notion of copula to model the codependency between the latent variables. However, we could also employ a copula approach to model direct codependency. One simple example is to use the upper Frechet copula (perfect codependency) on default indicators to capture the fact that if a firm defaults, then almost surely other firms default as well due to their strong business relationships. Instead of having a dependence in the default indicator itself, conditional on a firm's default we can consider a default event triggering a direct jump in the default probability or the credit index of another firm.

Models with a direct codependency are also referred to as default contagion models. Usually, default contagion models are used in a setting where structural relationships can be established between firms such that a specific primary firm's default can cause a jump of the default probability of secondary firms that are dependent on the primary firm. The initial analysis of such structural relationships between firms can use network analysis. The connectedness between different firms can be due to common exposures, default protection selling, or buyer and seller relationships.

In the Merton-based multifactor model, default contagion to a secondary firm once a primary firm has defaulted can be parameterized as a sudden downward jump in the credit index, $\hat{Z}$, of the secondary firm. This extends the multifactor model in equation (4.22) to also track default indicators for the portfolio. In reduced form models, modeling the default intensities (probabilities) for firms, a jump in the default intensity for a secondary firm can be triggered based on including a default indicator for a primary firm in the secondary firm's credit scoring model. See Jarrow and Yu (2001) for concrete examples of modeling interacting default intensities in a primary–secondary framework. More recently, Errais, Giesecke, and Goldberg (2010) use the so-called Hawkes process to naturally capture default event feedback in transition probabilities of surviving firms.

While a certain bank may use network analysis and default contagion in their portfolio credit risk model regulators also tend to use such models. However, now the perspective is financial system stability and the fact that large losses or the failure of some banks can potentially give rise to negative contagion effects on other banks in the system, either through direct bilateral linkages or more indirectly through financial system confidence effects. See the Financial Stability Institute 2012 paper (Jo, 2012), which considers a network model for financial systems where initial default losses (or funding losses) may see a bank in default with subsequent financial network contagion. Financial network analysis is also a part of the European central bank macroeconomic stress testing framework for the systemic risks (ECB, 2013).

CREDIT RISK STRESS TESTING

Credit risk stress testing is a core activity in banks. As we noted already in the context of market risk, stress testing it is also becoming more and more important with the development of stress test–based regulations such as CCAR and EBA that focus on firmwide stress testing. For many banks the earnings from the credit books is a major contributor to the firmwide earnings. Hence, the credit books stressed earnings and loss calculation play a significant role in the firmwide stress. The systematic portfolio credit risk stress testing usually focuses on a few major outputs.[51] They are,

- The impairments resulting from expected losses and provisions as well as the associated earnings impact that can happen in the future in a given scenario
- The potential future capital requirements in a given scenario

This is because the stress tests by both CCAR and EBA focus on putting limits on the projected future capital ratios under macroeconomic stress scenarios as we discuss in detail in Chapter 9 on firmwide scenario analysis and stress testing. The capital ratio is here actual capital divided by required capital with excess losses consuming actual capital and excess earnings being a potential contributor to increasing actual capital. We emphasize again that in the firmwide CCAR and EBA stress tests the (issuer) credit risk contribution to projected

---

[51]See the advanced market risk analysis chapter for a general discussion of the different approaches to stress testing such as portfolio sensitivity analysis, systematic stress testing, hypothetical stress scenario, and integration of stress and model analysis. The integration of model-based views and multi-horizon stress tests dicussed in the context of market risk provides an opportunity to integrate the EBA and CCAR stress tests with the bank's model-based approach to credit risk capital charges.

earnings, losses, and capital is generally the most significant for most banks due to the size of credit portfolios and their income contribution.

When stressing expected loss and the capital requirement using the credit risk model one faces three key issues:

- First, the fact that the stress scenarios are usually defined in terms of high-level macroeconomic indices that need to be transformed to the actual credit portfolio risk factors, Z
- Second, the fact that even if the scenario for macroeconomic factors is given as a single scenario there can still be a significant variation in the conditional distribution for the actual credit portfolio risk factors, Z
- Third, the fact that credit risk models usually have a systematic risk component as well as an idiosyncratic risk component

We have already discussed how to resolve the first issue in practice in the context of systematic portfolio stress tests in the chapter on advanced market risk analysis, that is, either by using equivalent historical shifts of the actual credit portfolio risk factors, Z, or by using models to transfer stress scenarios such as the conditional normal distribution in equation (3.21) or the factor model approach in equation (3.22). Note that both these model approaches not only yield a stress scenario in terms of Z that we can apply to our credit portfolio model. They are also essentially equivalent approaches. That is, they are both based on correlation specifications because the linear regression coefficient in the factor model is essentially interpreted as covariance divided by variance.

The second issue is related to the fact that there can be a large dispersion in the conditional stress distribution for Z. Using a model to transfer stress with only the expected stress value for Z conditional on macroeconomic factors does not provide adequate information about the possible dispersion of the conditional loss and conditional capital requirement. This can however be resolved by using the full distribution of Z in the stress transfer models in equation (3.21) and equation (3.22). The stressed results can then use prudent measures of conditional stress in terms of the usual risk measures such as VaR. The only difference is that the VaR is now a conditional and not an unconditional risk measure.

The third issue is more subtle but related to the second issue of dispersion for a given stress scenario. For a single Z stress scenario the credit portfolio model realized loss depends on the idiosyncratic risk. We can hence decide to include idiosyncratic risk or not. If we include idiosyncratic risk, we obtain a distribution of loss conditional on the single Z stress scenario. From this distribution we can take an expectation. Another approach is to use a conditional law of large numbers to average out the idiosyncratic risk for any firm or loan in the stress scenario. Specifically, using the conditional law of large numbers (Markov iteration approach) a given Z scenario yields a single realized loss profile and realized capital requirement profile over time.

Stress tests on losses and (regulatory) capital requirements based on Z scenarios can be seen as a special case of all the simulation-based portfolio credit risk examples in this chapter. In the simulation-based examples we have used a model for Z, and in the context of both multifactor models and credit score models, we have used (sub)portfolios with and without a conditional law of large numbers assumption. The stress testing can be viewed as just shifting the model used to generate the D Z realizations, or providing just a single scenario for Z. Depending on the idiosyncratic risk specification for the portfolio the output for a single Z scenario can be many potential losses or just one realized loss. In case the model has idiosyncratic risk, yielding many potential losses, a measure is needed to retrieve a single loss profile, for example, an expectation or a more prudent tail loss scenario. If a conditional law of large numbers assumption is used for the portfolio, the output is a single realized loss conditional on the single Z scenario.

As a preliminary example of using portfolio credit risk simulation models for stress testing consider our credit score mortgage portfolio example. In this model we applied risk and summary measures such as expected loss to the $1, \ldots, 10$ year marginal loss and also calculated minimum regulatory capital scenarios. For each Z scenario the subportfolios that used a conditional law of large numbers had a single realized marginal loss and capital requirement profile. Hence, the Z scenario could in this case have been a stress scenario rather than a model-simulated scenario—generating a single projected loss and capital under the scenario. Because we had many Z scenarios (and because some subportfolios did have idiosyncratic risk remaining) we created distributions of losses and capital requirements from which subsequent measures such as worst-case loss and capital requirement could be obtained.

Stress Testing with Multifactor Model

In the specific setting of the multifactor model we can consider stress testing both the key model parameters and the factors driving the firm's credit index, $\tilde{Z}_i$, that is, stress testing the systematic and idiosyncratic components of $\tilde{Z}_i$ (see equation (4.21)). Consider first stress testing the assumptions about the multifactor model's core parameters, including:

- The assumptions about firm credit migration and default probabilities (the transition matrix used).
- The firm- or pool-specific model for the credit index, $\tilde{Z}_i$, that drives credit migration and default with a given transition matrix. This includes the factor loadings, β, as well as the parameter λ for the idiosyncratic factor in equation (4.21) or its standardized version in equation (4.22).
- The correlations between factors, Z, and more specifically the copula used for the factors.

When model parameters such as transition matrix, factor loadings, and correlations are stressed it is usually performed for the purpose of model validation and model sensitivity analysis to the assumptions rather than for the purpose of analyzing the impact of credit market stress on credit portfolio loss. The use of stressed model parameters can also be preferred in practice because of prudence. The reason why credit migration and default probabilities are not stressed directly in macroeconomic scenarios is because of the implicit model assumption. That is, the transition matrix is a long-run average transition matrix with credit factors and firm-specific effects driving changes in firm transition probabilities. Hence, one can think of the transition probabilities as exogenously given long-run probabilities while the macroeconomic (credit) factors represent the systematic variation in credit quality for a firm over time.

Systematic macroeconomic stress for a given credit model includes macroeconomically induced or specific systematic stress tests on Z—either through economically relevant scenarios or using hypothetical stress such as reverse stress tests. It can also include idiosyncratic firm effects. Focusing on systematic stress our objective now is to analyze the credit loss in different scenarios for the credit index, $\tilde{Z}_i$, through stressing its systematic and, possibly, its idiosyncratic component. In systematic macroeconomic stress testing we hence focus our analysis on the multifactor model,

$$\tilde{Z}_i = \sum_{j=1}^{N} \beta_{ij} Z_j + \lambda_i \varepsilon_i$$

for firm i or pool i. Here, we note that stress can arise from either or both of the following:

- The systematic component (macroeconomic shock), $\{Z_j\}_{j=1}^{N}$
- The idiosyncratic component (firm specific shock), ε_i

Any firm or pool multifactor model can hence be stressed by a suitable choice of stress scenario for the components $\{Z\}, \{\varepsilon\}$. The resulting scenario credit index for firm i or pool i, $\widetilde{Z}_i^S$, is hence obtained as

$$\widetilde{Z}_i^S = \sum_{j=1}^{N} \beta_{ij} Z_j^S + \lambda_i \varepsilon_i^S$$

where $\left\{Z_j^S\right\}_{j=1}^{N}, \{\varepsilon_i^S\}_{i=1}^{M}$ are the predefined scenario values.

Given $\widetilde{Z}_i^S$ for all the portfolios firms and pools we can now calculate the portfolio credit transitions and hence profit and loss in the scenario as we were using a regular simulation scenario. Hence, as we mentioned, systematic credit portfolio scenario analysis fits within the general multifactor model simulation framework. It is just a scenario instead of many scenarios.

In practice it can be quite difficult to explicitly specify all the firm's idiosyncratic shocks, $\{\varepsilon_i^S\}_{i=1}^{M}$, explicitly. Stress testing then focuses only on specifying shifts for the systematic components, $\left\{Z_j^S\right\}_{j=1}^{N}$. This is the case in EBA and CCAR credit stress tests. For economic scenarios on the systematic components, the expected firm credit transition to a credit state, conditional on $\left\{Z_j^S\right\}_{j=1}^{N}$, can be calculated analytically using the conditional law of large numbers approach that we used in equation (4.27) and the Markov iteration for time inhomogeneous Markov state transition models in equation (4.29). Hence, in systematic stress testing of $\left\{Z_j^S\right\}_{j=1}^{N}$ we can apply the "pool case" to all individual firms in the portfolio as well. By doing this we obtain a single estimate of the portfolio expected loss in the systematic scenario, $\left\{Z_j^S\right\}_{j=1}^{N}$. Another approach is of course to sample the idiosyncratic component many times for a given Z scenario yielding several credit state paths. However, as we discussed in the context of the pool case for multifactor models, if one is interested in the expected state transition behavior conditional on the macroeconomic scenario, there is no need to use sampling of state transition paths. This is because the sampling of transition paths for a firm and the subsequent calculation of firm expected state transition frequencies will converge to the Markov state frequencies in equation (4.29). For this reason our systematic stress testing example below uses the conditional law of large numbers.

Example Stress Scenarios As an example of systematic stress testing in the multifactor model we consider four stylized, multi-horizon systematic scenarios for our sample pools' subportfolio in Table 4.22. The pools' share the systematic factors Z_1, Z_2 across the horizons of 3, 6, 9, and 12 months. See equation (4.30) for the pools' multifactor models. The scenarios we use are (i) one extremely distressed scenario, (ii) one extremely strong economy scenario, (iii) one moderate economic distress scenario, and (iv) one moderately stronger economy scenario. The extremely distressed scenario has Z_1, Z_2 increasing negatively over the horizons such that

$$Z_1 = Z_2 = (-1, -2, -3, -4)$$

while the scenario for the extremely strong economy is given by

$$Z_1 = Z_2 = (1, 2, 3, 4).$$

The moderate economic distress and moderately stronger economic scenarios include perturbation of a 3, 4, 5, and 6 (monthly) standard deviation downward and upward shock of Z_1, Z_2 respectively (see Table 4.12 for the monthly standard deviation of the Z_1, Z_2 factors). For the horizon of 3 months this implies a 1.73 standard deviation shock on the 3-month volatility. For the 6-month horizon this implies a 1.63 standard deviation shock on the 6-month volatility. For the 9-month horizon this implies a 1.66 standard deviation shock on the 9-month volatility. Finally, for the 12-month horizon this implies a 1.73 standard deviation shock on the 12-month volatility. This is because the n-month volatility is obtained from the 1-month volatility scaled by $\sqrt{n}$. The resulting moderate economic distress shock scenario is then given by

$$Z_1 = (-0.235, -0.314, -0.3925, -0.471)$$
$$Z_2 = (-0.2544, -0.3392, -0.424, -0.5088)$$

with corresponding positive shocks for the moderately stronger economy scenario.

The pools' subportfolio expected loss, calculated using the conditional law of large numbers, in each scenario, is displayed in Table 4.65 and Figure 4.23. In the extreme economic distress scenarios, the loss is never above 40% of the pool's portfolio current mark to market of 254,961,865. This is because the upper bound on loss is the recovery of the pools (see Table 4.22 for the pools' recovery rates ranging between 68% and 89%). The extremely strong economy scenario has negative losses (profits) as expected. Even though the average credit quality of the pools' portfolio is quite low (see the pools' current ratings in Table 4.22) the potential upside of the portfolio (i.e., the profits) when the portfolio migrates to better credit grades is less than the potential loss that can happen. Note that both these scenarios are extreme. Compared to the Z_1, Z_2 factors standard deviation the economic shocks have been very large. This has led to the two scenarios (extreme economic distress and extremely strong economy) yielding almost maximum loss and maximum profit respectively over the horizons. In the moderate economic distress and moderately stronger economy scenarios, we obtain lower expected credit losses/gains for the horizons of 3, 6, 9, and 12 months.

Stress Testing with Macroeconomic Credit Score Model

In the credit score model approach to portfolio credit risk, the loan default or transition probability is driven by the score equation. The score equation model parameters indicates the sensitivity of the default or transition rate to **Z** for a loan. One example of a score equation is the log-odds ratio formulation of the multinomial transition matrix model in equation (4.53). Another example is the linear score equation of the CreditRisk$^+$ model in equation (4.68).

TABLE 4.65 The Pools' Portfolio Loss in Each Scenario

Scenario	Horizon loss			
	3 months	6 months	9 months	12 months
Extreme economic distress	49,602.141	83,788.112	92,565.720	101,010.398
Extremely stronger economy	−20,867.046	−38,271.245	−40,593.821	-38,622.250
Moderate economic distress	2,155.822	4,694.470	7,874.905	11,823.497
Moderately stronger economy	−1,570.031	−2,809.385	−3,894.454	−4,853.395

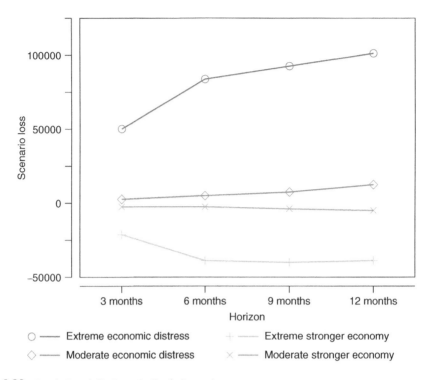

FIGURE 4.23 Pools Portfolio Loss in Each Scenario

The credit portfolio loss distribution is of course also driven by the assumed multivariate distribution for Z as in the multifactor model case. A difference with the multifactor model is that the idiosyncratic risk is not captured explicitly in the score equation itself but rather in the random sampling of a uniform that is compared to the scenario realized transition or default rate to determine the new rating state.[52]

As for the multifactor model, the score model parameters may be stressed for the purpose of model validation and model sensitivity analysis but are usually taken as given for systematic stress tests on Z. Another similarity with the multifactor model is that the conditional law of large numbers approach using the Markov iteration yields the expected state frequencies conditional on a single Z scenario. In case the state transition probabilities only depend on macroeconomic factors and not past state transitions, this Markov iteration is simple as in equation (4.56), while it can be more complex when past state transitions matter, as we have discussed previously. In practice, one therefore does not have to simulate state transitions for a given Z scenario if one is only interested in the conditionally expected loan behavior under a stress scenario.[53] This is because for a given systematic stress scenario we can retrieve the

---

[52]Although we can also think of the regression error in the score equation as a source of idiosyncratic risk for the fitted score model. However, this error is rarely accounted for in practice.

[53]Specifically, one does not have to simulate in the macroeconomic credit score model we apply here. See Skoglund and Chen (2015) for stress test applications of the dynamic delinquency models using both state transition sampling and expanded Markov iteration approaches to capture past state dependence. The dynamic delinquency models are an extension of the macroeconomic credit score model to include past state dependency through delinquency state indicators.

conditional scenario expected loss or other scenario measures such as Basel capital requirements that depend on scenario realized PD and LGD analytically. Hence, for systematic stress testing using the scoring model approach, all the individual loans as well as pools in the portfolio can use the conditional law of large numbers and Markov iteration. This is in contrast to the VaR model case where only the sufficiently large pools use a conditional law of large numbers—retaining the idiosyncratic risk for smaller portfolios and specific loans.

Example Stress Scenarios As an example stress testing of the credit score model approach, we analyze the portfolio losses, net earnings (net interest income), and Basel regulatory capital for the non-defaulted stock under three scenarios using again our example mortgage portfolio in Table 4.35.[54] The models used are the same as in our previous example applications of the mortgage portfolio analysis.[55] We consider one baseline scenario and two stress scenarios over the portfolio horizon of 10 years. The two stress scenarios are an extreme economic distress and a moderate economic distress scenario. The portfolio risk factors are the systematic risk factor and the five property indices previously displayed in Figure 4.12. The systematic risk factor here represents swings in the business cycle and drives the period transition rates through the multinomial logit dynamic transition matrix model.

To calculate the stressed losses, the associated net earnings, and regulatory capital for the portfolio we use the conditional law of large numbers for all the 14 subportfolios regardless of their portfolio size, even for the single loan subportfolios. The baseline scenario has a neutral business cycle for the systematic factor for all time periods and no growth or decay for the price indices. In the extreme economic distress scenario there is a strong negative growth of the systematic business cycle factor and the price indices decline with 5 % per year. In the moderate economic distress, the systematic factor has less negative growth and the price indices decline with only 1% per year. Figure 4.24 displays the systematic risk factor scenarios in the extreme and moderate economic distress cases and the portfolio stress results are displayed in Table 4.66. Figure 4.25 also shows graphically the evolution of portfolio net earnings and regulatory capital for the scenarios. Due to the low initial quality of the sample mortgage portfolio, all the scenarios—including the baseline—display initial negative net earnings. In the baseline and moderate economic distress scenarios, net earnings eventually become positive. Clearly, the expected loss reserve consumption for the portfolio is large during the 10-year stress period. In addition to a large loss reserve consumption, there can be capital consumption in adverse scenarios. The exact capital consumption of course depends on both stress scenario and portfolio quality. Due to the poor initial portfolio quality, the contribution from stress scenario to capital consumption is typically less significant than would happen for a good-quality portfolio. In all the scenarios the portfolio has a decaying regulatory capital due to significant portfolio defaults being covered by loss reserve and potentially capital.

---

[54] Stress test regulations like EBA can also have a risk weighted asset contribution from the defaulted flow if the regulatory LGD parameter exceeds the stressed PIT LGD. However, for the purpose of illustration of the behavior of the regulatory capital for the non-defaulted stock over time we set regulatory capital for the defaulted flow to zero exactly as we did in the mortgage portfolio risk analysis example. Another difference with the EBA stress test regulation in this example is that we use the stress test PIT PD and PIT LGD to compute the regulatory capital while EBA requires that "regulatory risk parameters worsen."

[55] Recall that in our previous applications of the mortgage portfolio we analyzed the credit losses, the credit margin minus the losses, referred to as the net credit loss of the portfolio, as well as the Basel II regulatory capital. The credit margin minus credit losses is what we refer to as the net earnings of the portfolio in this scenario analysis.

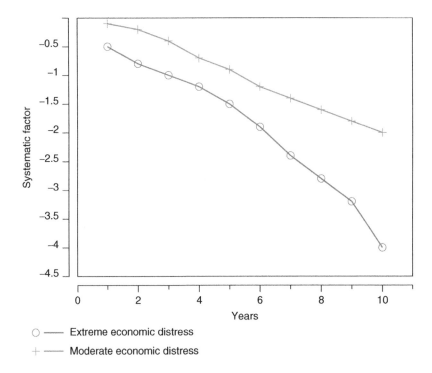

FIGURE 4.24 Systematic Risk Factor Scenarios in the Extreme and Moderate Economic Distress Cases

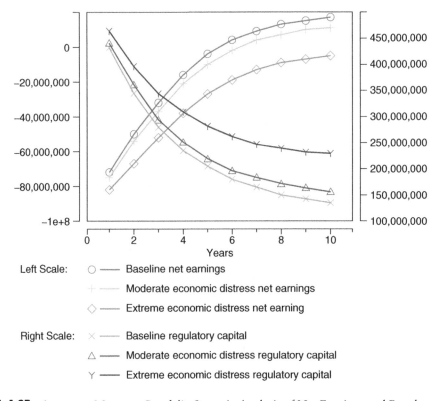

FIGURE 4.25 Aggregate Mortgage Portfolio Scenario Analysis of Net Earnings and Regulatory Capital

TABLE 4.66 Mortgage Portfolio Scenario Analysis of Losses, Net Earnings, and Regulatory Capital

Scenario	1 year	2 years	3 years	4 years	5 years	6 years	7 years	8 years	9 years	10 years
Horizon loss										
Baseline	133,508,890	108,878,057	88,449,118	71,252,680	58,425,374	49,252,609	42,745,936	38,102,898	34,748,719	32,286,885
Moderate economic distress	136,547,773	112,949,472	93,194,539	76,142,019	63,450,235	54,309,015	47,789,584	43,294,942	40,071,857	37,722,912
Extreme economic distress	143,836,829	125,364 825	108,514,537	93,413,504	80,516,899	71,394,671	64,658,240	60,100,785	56,905,015	54,715,465
Horizon net earnings										
Baseline	−72,104,756	−49,986,898	−31,590,637	−16,041,910	−4,578,810	3,431,992	8,920,396	12,648,084	15,161,643	16,838,049
Moderate economic distress	−75,143,639	−54,058,312	−36,336,057	−20,931,249	−9,603,671	−1,624,414	3,876,749	7,456,041	9,838,505	11, 402,022
Extreme economic distress	−82,432,695	−66,473,666	−51,656,055	−38,202,734	−26,670,335	−18,710,070	−12,991,907	−9,349,802	−6,994,653	−5,590,532
Horizon regulatory capital										
Baseline	432,638,449	344,558,237	280,528,709	235,154,573	203,055,604	180,151,698	163,595,153	151,440,285	142,358,369	135,436,485
Moderate economic distress	442,135,212	357,425,793	295,803,325	251,478,133	220,763,127	198,887,893	183,078,239	172,245,068	164,310,582	158,343,917
Extreme economic distress	463,021,937	396,151,965	344,420,039	309,529,195	281,058,163	262,166,757	248,376,439	239,604,707	233,714,943	229,974,903

The extreme economic distress scenario regulatory capital requirement is seen to decrease at a much slower rate than the moderate economic distress or baseline scenario. Hence, in the economic distress scenario we have not only more consumption of the capital due to larger losses and negative net earnings but also a significantly higher regulatory capital requirement for the stock of non-defaulted mortgages. This of course means that capital ratios such as actual capital divided by capital requirements will tend to be very low unless initial capital is very large, or capital can somehow be raised during the stress period.

Our mortgage portfolio stress testing example has been focused on the aggregate, portfolio which has a low initial quality. It is also interesting to see the effect of the stress scenarios when the portfolio quality is good. We therefore focus on the scenario net earnings and regulatory capital for subportfolio 11, which has an initial rating in class 2 and a large credit margin of 1.2% (see Table 4.35). This case is also more realistic in terms of subportfolio 11 being closer in credit quality to many banks' actual mortgage portfolios. Figure 4.26 displays the scenario results for subportfolio 11. We notice from the figure that net earnings is positive for all scenarios although the net earnings decrease fast in the extreme economic distress scenario. Because of the good initial portfolio quality we observe for all scenarios an increase in the regulatory capital over time since there is migration to lower quality grades but not necessarily defaults. In the extreme economic distress case the increase in regulatory capital is significant, suggesting that it is vital that the initial large earnings are retained and used to build up the capital base in order to meet the significant increase in required regulatory capital.

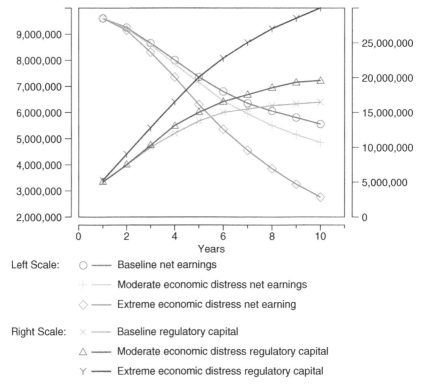

FIGURE 4.26 Mortgage Portfolio Subportfolio 11 in Rating Class 2 Scenario Analysis of Net Earnings and Regulatory Capital

We finally note that this scenario analysis example has focused on the scenario projected portfolio losses, earnings, and regulatory capital, which are also some of the main stress test measures needed for the portfolio credit risk regulatory CCAR and EBA stress testing exercises. Of course, in practice regulation may dictate specific calculation approaches and the scenario horizons. We have previously discussed the specific EBA methodology with stress tests over 3 years while CCAR considers the scenario analysis over the next nine quarters. A distinct difference in practice is also that while our sample mortgage portfolio was stressed directly in terms of the systematic factor and the five property indices banks have to first convert the prescribed regulatory macroeconomic scenarios into the actual portfolio risk factor shifts. For example, regulatory national home property price index scenarios need to be converted to regional property price index scenarios.

FEATURES OF NEW GENERATION PORTFOLIO CREDIT RISK MODELS

For many banks the portfolio credit risk models that are in use today were largely developed about 10 years ago with the introduction of Basel II risk weighted assets. Back then, one of the main drivers for developing internal credit economic capital models was to capture portfolio concentration risk and the subsequent risk allocation for budgeting and planning.[56] One-year-horizon bank capital allocations to credit exposures with the economic capital model were contrasted with the summable risk weighted asset of the exposure. The (relative) difference of the allocation was partly attributed to concentration risk. Now, with the introduction of the firmwide stress testing in (for example) CCAR, credit models are required to predict both earnings and loss over multiple horizons with path-dependence to capture more granular the timing of loss. Consequently, banks are currently revisiting their credit risk economic capital models. In this section we review some of the core developments that are currently underway in banks' portfolio credit risk models.

Multi-Horizon Models for Banking Book

Traditionally, many banks' portfolio credit risk economic capital models have focused on a single one-year horizon for the risk analysis consistently with the Basel credit risk regulation. The single one-year risk horizon was also driven by the rating agencies' risk analysis. This single one-year time horizon was largely applied to both the banking book and trading book exposures. However, as we have discussed in this chapter, for trading book exposures, the modeling of liquidity trading horizons during the one-year risk horizon has made its way through the incremental risk charge. The majority of the portfolio credit risk examples in this chapter have used multi-horizon models that capture the path-dependent nature of credit losses over time. We have argued that it is an important feature of the credit portfolio model to capture the timing and the materialization of credit risk losses over time as this enhances understanding of the potential evolution of reserve and capital requirements. Regulators are nowadays also interested in how different scenarios' credit loss can unfold over time requiring multi-horizon path-dependent credit models. For example, in CCAR the scenarios are implemented in credit models as the path-dependent evolution over nine quarters with capturing of the marginal credit loss at each quarter.

---

[56]Recall that in both the market and credit risk context we have used the Euler risk contribution divided by the standalone risk to obtain a position or subportfolio diversification index in the context of the portfolio.

Modeling the Recovery Process for Banking Book Portfolios

In the incremental risk charge model for the trading book the loss is realized instantaneously at the trading horizon. This assumption is justified by the existence of quoted defaultable bond prices. That is, the bank does not have to wait for the ultimate legal recovery. However, this is not the case in practice for banking book exposures such as loans and mortgages. The recovery process can be quite long in practice. Moreover, it has workout costs that need to be integrated into the total loss.

In our banking book mortgage portfolio risk analysis example above we analyzed a mortgage portfolio with a specific model for recovery that captured the recovery in terms of the property value and the loan to value. The model assumed instantaneous recovery. Clearly, this is an approximation to reality as recovery is not instantaneous in practice, and in addition may not match model default events. For example, if default probability is measured on the basis of 90 days past due, then a fair portion of loans never go to ultimate recovery stages. In practice, recovery can therefore be measured on "multi-tier" levels using different default definitions. To distinguish recovery in model (technical) default we can introduce additional events and hence rating states where a certain probability that a loan in model default actually becomes in true default is assessed with probability π. We can think of such states as non-absorbing default states in the context of the transition matrix. Hence, default dynamics can be handled with an expanded multistate probability transition matrix. For example, using a monthly horizon credit model as the transition matrix in Table 4.33, a 30 days past due credit can only migrate to current, 60 days past due or prepay. See also Peura and Soininen (2005) on the loss measurements on multitier levels and the close connections between such loss measurements in Basel II and the loss measurement in accounting standards such as IAS 39.[57]

While one can measure additional default states such as capturing past due at different levels as well as "actual" default, one can also segment different types of recoveries. Default and actual sale of collateral is usually the last resort and, for example, for many corporate exposures restructuring may be the first option as the legal recovery of both the collateralized and uncollateralized portion of the exposure can be a timely process with large legal costs. Retail books recovery, such as mortgages, can also take time and is linked to the ability of the bank to sell the property timely.

Figure 4.27 displays a simplified potential recovery process that includes settlement or going back to healthy with probabilities α and $1 - \alpha$ respectively when the credit is in "technical" default. At the second step, even if there is a settlement, it may result in either recovery workout with associated sale of collateral (if any), or a restructuring. In Figure 4.27 these two events occur with probabilities β and $1 - \beta$, respectively. In this recovery process the probabilities α and β can of course be conditional on macroeconomic and borrower characteristics. At each step of the process it is also important to capture the typical delay in the timing of the cash flows. For example, even if a credit goes back to healthy it has usually been past due for a while with no cash inflow during the time. The recovery workout and restructuring phases can also take considerable time, delaying any cash inflows from the recovery or the restructured credit.

The requirements on the modeling of the exact recovery process and the timing of the recovery inflow of course get more important as banks consider multi-horizon credit models. This is both internally for better capturing portfolio credit risk economic capital required over

---

[57]IAS 39 is now replaced by IFRS 9.

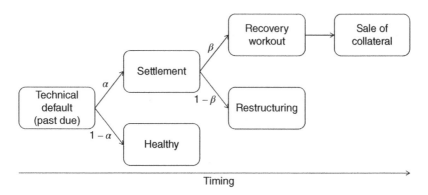

FIGURE 4.27 Potential Recovery Process

TABLE 4.67 Example Transition Matrix with Default, Prepayment, and Restructuring States as Competing Risks

	Current	Restructuring	Prepayment	Default
Current	$A_{11}(t)$	$A_{12}(t)$	$A_{13}(t)$	$A_{14}(t)$
Restructuring	1	0	0	0
Prepayment	0	0	1	0
Default	0	0	0	1

time as well as using the model in the firmwide regulatory stress testing. In practice we can capture the different types of recoveries as competing risks to actual default in the credit migration matrix. An example is a transition matrix that has competing states of default, restructuring, and prepayment. While the default and prepayment states are absorbing, the restructuring state is not and the loan returns to current after the restructuring with an adjusted loan. This is illustrated in the transition matrix in Table 4.67 where $\{A_{1r}(t)\}_{r=1}^{4}$ denotes the required transition probability models in the transition matrix. Of course, if there are multiple types of restructuring, these types can be represented as their own competing states in the transition matrix in Table 4.67.

Earnings and Loss Rather than Just Loss

The early portfolio credit risk models focused on the unexpected loss as the true capital charge with the expected loss being covered by the existing reserves. The idea was largely founded on the fact that pricing covered expected losses and prudence in the sense that pricing in excess of expected losses could not be counted as risk reducing. However, many books of business are run with margins well in excess of expected losses, and although the future achievable margins may be to some extent uncertain, such excess earnings do carry risk reducing value. Most people would not like to go as far as to argue that excess earnings can itself be a substitute for capital. Our mortgage portfolio example in this chapter has shown that excess margins can indeed be risk reducing. The mortgage example also showed that for portfolios with low margins the unexpected loss concept may not be appropriate either as the margins may not even cover expected losses.

Apart from recognizing earnings as potentially risk reducing it is of significant value to model earnings as part of the portfolio credit loss model.[58] Knowing when a particular credit exposure is healthy versus past due we can consistently accrue cash flows and capture the accrual if the credit exposure goes into a recovery workout process. Hence, we can consistently estimate cash flows, accrual, and recovery over multiple path-dependent horizons. However, traditionally for banks, the interest income earnings and loss projection have been separated. The asset and liability management system is generating the healthy cash flow projection and the credit system the loss projection. The two estimates are subsequently joined at the aggregate level. With the multi-horizon firmwide stress testing requirements in CCAR and EBA a best practice is emerging to model the asset interest income earnings and losses correctly at the most granular level. This is because regulatory and internal validation of the model logical correctness in calculating earnings cash flows, accrual, and recovery loss is more easily done at the most granular level. For example, in the EBA cost of funding and asset interest income projection under the macroeconomic scenarios, the asset side projection of interest income is assumed to incorporate the loss of cash flows due to non-performing assets. This integration of loss and interest income projection is especially important since the firmwide stress test regulations focus on the timing of earnings and loss over multiple horizons as opposed to loss at a single horizon of one year. Another complexity with a separate earnings and loss projection is that consistency between future balance projections and hence new originations needs to be managed between the systems.

Figure 4.28 displays the main components of credit models with cash flows. There are input data, credit models, cash inflows, and other cash amounts such as losses, cash outflows (funding expenses), and final model outputs. The input data include the current credit book as well as any assumed new originations and stock balance extensions during the analysis horizon. The input data also include the credit factors such as macroeconomic and collateral data and market (interest and funding) data to generate the cash flows from the credit book. The market data need to be complemented with the bank's reset rate (repricing) policies for different credit types when the customer rate is administered rather than market set. With the input data, especially the credit book and macroeconomic factors, the credit models calculate the credit state transition, the loss severity (recovery), and the exposure. Conditional on a realized state transitions a credit can, for example, (i) generate interest and principal income according to schedule, (ii) be past due with accrual of interest and principal, or (iii) be in default state with associated credit loss, recovery timing, and recovery value calculated by the recovery model.

In the third stage we therefore obtain the interest and principal income as well as loss given default and exposure at default.[59] If credit facilities are part of the analyzed credit book, then the assumed credit facility usage from the exposure model determines the facility balance and hence exposure at default. We also obtain a balance projection due to amortization as well as balance impacts from new originations and stock extensions. At this stage we can also optionally compute the projected risk weighted assets (regulatory required capital) under

---

[58]This enhances the portfolio credit risk model with cash flows. Another way to achieve the joint earnings and loss model is to enhance the asset and liability management system with the credit models. However, in this chapter we take the credit portfolio model expansion view.

[59]Note that although we have not explicitly considered prepayment in Figure 4.28, prepayment can induce a significant loss of contractual interest income. In contrast, default can induce a significant loss of principal as well as contractual interest income.

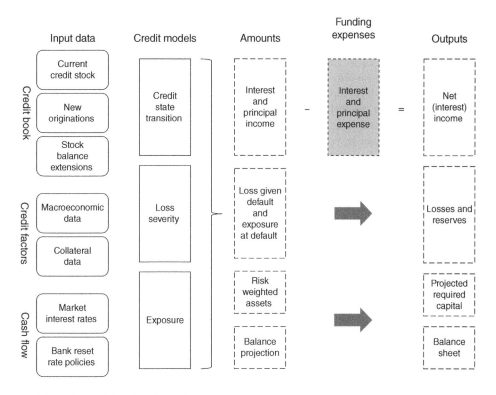

FIGURE 4.28 Credit Model with Cash Flows

stress as we did for the mortgage portfolio example in this chapter because we have available the scenario probability of default, the loss given default, and the remaining healthy balances as inputs to the risk weighted assets equation (4.41).

While the third stage has generated income and recovery flows (from loss given default) we are ultimately interested in the net (interest) income. The interest and principal expense needed to construct net (interest) income from the interest and principal income is coming mainly from the funding and is the fourth step of subtracting funding expenses in Figure 4.28. In practice, the incorporation of funding expenses can be done in two ways. The first approach is to subtract the funding expenses at the portfolio level. Here the funding expenses can be calculated separately at an aggregated level and then used to adjust the credit book interest income. The second approach, which we have used in the mortgage portfolio example in this chapter, assigns a funding rate to each credit and generates the net (interest) income directly on credit level. This approach is feasible using the concept of funds transfer pricing as we will discuss in Chapter 7. Specifically, the funds transfer price creates a matched balance sheet for the credit book while the residual portfolio of actual funding versus matched funding is managed separately. As we will also discuss in Chapter 7 the cost of funding projection in, for example, EBA assumes a rollover of funding at higher rates (with higher funding market rates derived from the macroeconomic scenario) and that these higher rollover funding rates can only partially be passed on to the asset side interest income. Hence, in the scenario, the bank's reset rate policies for the loans are not allowed to pass on the full impact of the higher funding costs into customer rates.

Loan-Level Models

While it may be clear from our discussions in this section that the more detailed recovery process modeling as well as the earnings modeling calls for credit risk models at the most granular level, we also mention this progress to loan level models as a separate topic here. The benefit of the loan level models is the ability to validate the logic of the earnings and loss process at loan level for the different types of portfolios. Another benefit is that the projected risk weighted asset capital calculations for the CCAR and EBA firmwide stress testing operate on the loan level and can be reconciled with the existing loan-level regulatory calculations. The downside of loan-level granular models is of course that more computing power and storage capacity are in general required. However, the Markov iteration equations for the multifactor model and the macroeconomic credit score model discussed in this chapter alleviate the need for expensive state transition sampling to calculate stressed expected losses and cash flows since the sampling converges to the Markov state frequencies. The horizon state dependent expected cash flows can then simply be obtained by weighting the state cash flows with the correspondent Markov state transition probability at the horizon, obtained from the iterations in equation (4.29) or equation (4.56). Of course, as we discussed for the credit score models obtaining the Markov state frequencies and the required tracing of the past state occupancy of a loan is more complex when the state transition probabilities depend on past state history such as past delinquencies, especially if the number of non absorbing states in the transition matrix is large and the delinquency indicators track the exact state path. In those cases, state transition sampling may still be the preferred model approach although as shown in Skoglund and Chen (2015) exact Markov iteration approaches are feasible for quarterly delinquency models and monthly delinquency models with state occupancy indicators.

Granularity of Credit Factors

While the portfolio credit risk models are becoming more granular in terms of loan-level earnings, recovery, and loss measurement, it is reasonable to ask what should be the granularity of the systematic credit factors, Z. We can of course have a very granular portfolio evaluation but still just a few systematic credit factors driving the portfolio risk. For example, for the corporate portfolio we can consider just a few macroeconomic equity indices rather than very specific regional and branch indices. Similarly, we could consider a country-level unemployment and property price index for the mortgage portfolio rather than specific regional indices. The benefit of using just a few systematic credit factors is of course that the reduced set of risk factors is more easily interpreted and hence also modeled and stressed. The reduced set of risk factors may also be directly linked to regulatory macroeconomic scenarios specified by regulators—avoiding the need for models to transfer stress from just a few high-level macroeconomic factors to the actual portfolio risk factors, however, significantly reducing the risk factors in the portfolio credit risk model has negative consequences that usually overweigh its benefits. The main issue is that in order to be valuable for business in capital allocation and stress the risk model needs to capture the different volatility levels between regions and branches. Clearly, the portfolio manager expects to see a risk reduction in portfolios after moving exposure from a volatile branch or region to a less volatile branch or region. Capturing the portfolio diversity in exposure to systematic credit factors may be hard with just a few factors. Another issue with just a few factors is the loss of sensitivity analysis of the business impact to the risk factors for better business planning and reverse stress testing scenario construction. The current portfolio credit risk model development is therefore to consider more granular credit factors, still maintaining the connection to just a few (regulatory specified) macroeconomic factors in model risk and stress testing using models to transfer stress such as conditional distributions or factor models.

HEDGING CREDIT RISK

The rise in trading volumes of credit-risky assets and the need for financial institutions to hedge credit risk has triggered the creation of credit derivatives. Credit derivatives are securities whose payoff is conditioned on the occurrence of a credit event. The credit event can be bankruptcy or failure of a payment obligation and market standard definitions are developed by ISDA.

Single-name credit default swaps represent the bulk of traded credit derivatives and is similar to a traditional credit guarantee. It is usually an over-the-counter (OTC) type contract between the protection buyer and protection seller. The protection buyer makes fixed premium payments to the seller at fixed intervals such as a quarter until the covered credit event happens or the contract matures. In certain contracts, a lump-sum up-front payment instead of periodical payments are paid by the buyer. If a credit event does not occur until the maturity of the contract, the seller pays nothing to the buyer. If a credit event does occur before the maturity, the seller guarantees to pay the loss of the buyer as stipulated in the credit protection leg. Typical default payments include cash settlement or physical delivery of an equivalent non-defaulted reference credit. In case of physical delivery the protection seller hence has typically a cheapest-to-deliver option.

A basket credit default swap is an insurance contract on the k:th default in a basket of credits. It is hence a credit correlation product and can in principle be used for hedging a credit portfolio against multiple default losses. While the pricing of a single-name credit default swap depends on the survival of the referenced credit, the pricing of basket credit default swaps depends on the joint survival curve for the reference entities. Clearly, default correlations are a significant component of the fair value of basket products. As we have mentioned previously, before the 2007 crisis, the market standard model for basket credit derivatives was the one-factor normal copula model where

$$\hat{Z}_i = RZ + \sqrt{1 - R^2}\varepsilon_i$$

with $\varepsilon_i \sim N(0, 1)$, $Z \sim N(0, 1)$ for all firms i. In this model there is only a single correlation parameter between firms and constant default probabilities for each firm. For tranche-based credit correlation products such as collateralized debt obligations the market participants calculated implied correlations, ρ, for each tranche and obtained what was referred to as a correlation smile.

Single-Name Credit Default Swaps

Starting with a concrete example of a single-name credit default swap contract consider a 5-year maturity credit default swap where the protection buyer pays a premium of 90 basis points per quarter on a notional amount of 100 units of currency. The quarterly payments are hence $100 \times 0.009 \times 0.25 = 0.225$. If the reference credit defaults, the protection seller pays to the buyer a cash settlement of the notional minus the recovery value. Assuming recovery is 45% the cash settlement in default is hence 55 units of currency. It is also typical for the protection buyer to pay any accrued premiums to the protection seller if default happens between two premium payments. If the reference credit does not default during the 5 years, the total premiums paid by the protection buyer are $0.225 \times 20 = 4.5$. Based on this example we conclude that to value a single-name credit default swap contract we need several components. This includes:

- Contract payment details (e.g., frequency of payments and maturity date). We also need to know if there is an accrued payment of the buyer in case of default and if there is an up-front fee for the credit protection.
- We need market data such as an interest rate for discounting payments, a credit default probability curve, or equivalently a survival probability curve, and to know the expected recovery rate in cash settlement.

The Premium and Protection Leg of the Credit Default Swap   Having contract and market information we can value a given contract as the difference between the present value of the premium leg and the protection payment leg. Specifically, denoting the premium leg by P_s and the protection leg by P_d the credit default swap value is given by

$$V = P_s - P_d.$$

For a new contract we solve for the fair premium, s, that equates the two legs.

Consider first the premium payment leg. Assuming no accrued payments we can write this leg as

$$P_s(t_0, t_N) = S(t_0, t_N) \sum_{n=1}^{N} D(t_{n-1}, t_n) d(t_0, t_n) Q(t_0, t_n) = P_s^*(t_0, t_N) S(t_0, t_N) \qquad (4.73)$$

where $t_1, \ldots, t_N$ are the premium payment dates, $S(t_0, t_N)$ the contractual premium rate, $D(t_{n-1}, t_n)$ the daycount between $[t_{n-1}, t_n]$, $d(t_0, t_n)$ the discount factor, and $Q(t_0, t_n)$ the survival probability up to t_n. Hence, the premium leg is paid conditional on a positive survival probability. The survival probability, $Q(t_0, t_n)$, is given by

$$Q(t_0, t_n) = 1 - F(t_0, t_n) = \overline{F}(t_0, t_n) = P(\tau > t_n)$$

where $\tau > 0$ is a continuous random variable modeling the stochastic default time. As in equation (4.31) we also introduce the hazard rate

$$\overline{F}(t_0, t_n) = \exp\left(-\int_{t_0}^{t_n} h(u)\, du\right).$$

The protection leg, P_d, of the credit default swap contract has a payment conditional on default such that

$$P_d(t_0, t_N) = (1 - r) \int_{t_0}^{t_N} d(t_0, u) Q(t_0, u) h(u)\, du \qquad (4.74)$$

where r is the recovery rate. This is the expected present value of the payments since we compute the discounted probability of survival up to t and then default in the next small time interval. Specifically, we have that

$$h(t) = \lim_{dt \to 0} \frac{P(t \leq \tau < t + dt \,|\, \tau \geq t)}{dt}.$$

It is hence the probability of default in the short interval of length dt after t—conditional on survival at t. The fair swap value is now set as

$$S(t_0, t_N) = \frac{P_d(t_0, t_N)}{P_s^*(t_0, t_N)} \tag{4.75}$$

where if there are any accrual premium payments, they are added to the premium leg.

Default Probability Information   To price a given credit default swap contract the most important information is the default probability of the credit. Different levels of default probabilities will impact the fair swap premium. Default rates (and survival rates) can be derived from the hazard rate, $h(t)$. The hazard rate used for fair value may be extracted from one of the following:

- The market as market observed credit default swap premia
- Using historical default rates

If hazard rates are obtained from the market, then the fair swap value in equation (4.75) is usually referred to as a no-arbitrage price.

Assuming there are market-quoted credit default swap premiums, $S(t_0, t_N)$ for the maturities of t_1, t_2, and t_N we can solve for the implied hazard rate from equation (4.75) and obtain a piecewise hazard rate as $h(t_0, t_1)$, $h(t_1, t_2)$, and so on. This procedure is referred to as *bootstrapping the hazard rate* and is analogous to obtaining the market zero-coupon curve from traded instruments.[60]

In case of using historical default probabilities we can use the cumulative default probabilities, CP, to obtain the hazard rate. That is,

$$p(t_{n+1}|t_n) = \frac{\mathrm{CP}_{t_{n+1}} - \mathrm{CP}_{t_n}}{1 - \mathrm{CP}_{t_n}} = 1 - \exp(-\int_{t_n}^{t_{n+1}} h(u)\,du)$$

yielding

$$\bar{h}_{t_n} = \frac{1}{t_{n+1} - t_n} \int_{t_n}^{t_{n+1}} h(u)\,du$$

so that we can define a piecewise hazard as

$$\bar{h}_{t_n} = \frac{1}{t_{n+1} - t_n} \ln \left[\frac{1 - \mathrm{CP}_{t_{n+1}}}{1 - \mathrm{CP}_{t_n}} \right].$$

Example Pricing Single-Name Credit Default Swaps   We now consider an example of credit default swap pricing using the credit default swap pricing model introduced above.[61] In the example we assume that default is measured on a monthly time horizon and that accruals

---

[60]As an alternative to credit default swap premia one can consider the spread of floating rate notes in the market. This is because the portfolio of a floating rate note and a credit default swap should be risk-free and hence the floating rate note spread should equal the swap premia.

[61]See O'Kane and Turnbull (2003) for a detailed derivation of credit default swap pricing.

TABLE 4.68 Annualized Fair Premiums in Basis Points, Per Unit of
Swap Notional, for 5- and 10-Year Credit Default Swap Contracts
with Different Survival Curves

Maturity term	Survival curve	Annualized swap premium (bps)
5 year	A	38.22
5 year	B	125.72
5 year	C	316.08
5 year	A + 10 bps	36.38
5 year	B + 10 bps	123.74
5 year	C + 10 bps	313.76
5 year	A − 10 bps	40.06
5 year	B − 10 bps	127.71
5 year	C − 10 bps	318.40
10 year	A	103.10
10 year	B	132.28
10 year	C	215.79
10 year	A + 10 bps	102.01
10 year	B + 10 bps	131.11
10 year	C + 10 bps	214.86
10 year	A − 10 bps	104.19
10·year	B − 10 bps	133.45
10 year	C − 10 bps	217.18

are paid by the protection buyer. The interest rate used for discounting is assumed to be
flat at 2% and we use a recovery rate of 40%. Table 4.68 displays the annualized fair premiums in basis points, per unit of swap notional, for 5- and 10-year credit default swap
contracts with different survival curves, A, B, and C for the terms $1, 2, \ldots, 10$ years. We also
display the sensitivity of the swap premium to a + and −10 basis point parallel shift of the
survival curves.

The survival curves A, B, and C are displayed in Table 4.69 and Figure 4.29. The A
survival curve is typical for high-grade credits credit spreads with a low short-term default

TABLE 4.69 Sample Survival Curves A, B, and C

	Survival curve		
Maturity term	A	B	C
1 year	0.999	0.98	0.94
2 years	0.995	0.96	0.89
3 years	0.99	0.94	0.85
4 years	0.98	0.92	0.81
5 years	0.96	0.90	0.78
6 years	0.945	0.88	0.76
7 years	0.92	0.86	0.75
8 years	0.89	0.84	0.745
9 years	0.855	0.82	0.74
10 years	0.815	0.80	0.738

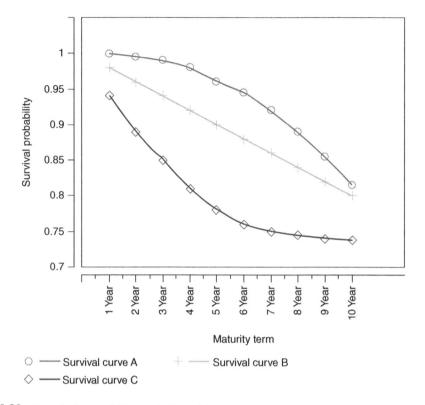

FIGURE 4.29 Sample Survival Curves A, B, and C

probability and an increasing default probability over time. The B survival curve is flat over the term and resembles a medium-grade credits credit spread. The C survival curve is typical of low-quality credits credit spread with a decreasing default probability. Because of the behavior of the survival curves we note from Table 4.68 that with the A survival curve the swap premium increases with maturity term since the incremental default probability increases over the years. For the B survival curve the swap premium is almost the same for the 5- and 10-year maturity swap, and for the C survival curve the annual swap premium is smaller for the longer maturity swap.

The better the credit quality and the shorter the maturity of the swap, the more sensitive is its fair market value to a parallel shift in the survival curve. For example, the impact on the swap price of a 10-basis-point parallel shift of the A survival curve for a 5-year swap is about 5% for both an upward and downward shift while for the corresponding 10-year maturity swap it is about 1%. Here, a 10-basis-point increase in the swap survival curve increases the credit quality while a 10-basis-point decrease decreases the credit quality.

While the single-name credit default swap example calculates the fair premium for a new swap protection we can also mark to market a swap with a given contracted premium. That is, we can calculate the market loss on this contract, Δ, as

$$\Delta = [S^* - S(t_0, t_N)]P_s(t_0, t_N)$$

where $S(t_0, t_N)$ is the contracted premium, S^* the current fair market premium. For example, assume we have contracted a 5-year maturity swap protection with a premium of 45 basis points and a notional of 1,000,000. Assuming the A survival curve is extracted from the current market priced swaps (with premium 38.22 as in Table 4.68) we now obtain the market loss as $\Delta = 3{,}230$ units of currency. On the other hand, if the original contract premium was 30 basis points, the market loss is $\Delta = -3{,}920$ units of currency, that is, a profit. Since the credit default swap profit increases when the fair market premium increases (because of market perceived increase in default risk) compared to the initial contract rate it provides a mark-to-market hedge of issuer default risk. The portfolio of a credit-risky bond and a credit default swap contract on the bond should hence be (close to) immunized against credit risk profit and loss.

Credit Default Swaps and Counterparty Risk   While credit derivatives such as credit default swaps serve the primary purpose of credit protection, they themselves induce credit risk from the protection seller default, known as counterparty credit risk. Specifically, a hedged credit exposure still has remaining double-default risk. In case of significant counterparty risk on the default protection leg of the credit default swap the payment leg price should be modified to reflect this default risk. Following Hull and White (2000), when facing counterparty credit risk, four events can happen:

1. The counterparty defaults with no default of protected reference credit.
2. The counterparty defaults with subsequent default of protected reference credit.
3. The counterparty does not default with no default of protected reference credit.
4. The counterparty does not default with default of protected reference credit.

In case of counterparty risk the protection buyer hence runs the risk of facing the double-default event 2 with no subsequent payoff from the default protection leg. Taking into account counterparty risk in the valuation of credit default swaps clearly lowers the value (and hence the fair premium). The most significant driver for the downward value adjustment is of course the correlation between the counterparty default and the protected reference credit default. Hence, the price adjustment depends on the specific model driving the issuer and guarantor counterparty double default. In the multifactor model this correlation derives from common systematic factors and potentially common idiosyncratic factors. The Basel double-default formula uses a one-factor model for the issuer and the guarantor counterparty with double default driven by both the common systematic factor and the common idiosyncratic factor.

Credit Default Swaps on Portfolio Indices

A credit default index swap is essentially a portfolio of single-name credit default swaps. When a portfolio member defaults the protection buyer receives a notional payment. At the same time the protection premium is reduced because of the reduction in notional. In the market standard contracts, such as iTraxx and CDX indices, the credit portfolio is homogeneous such that for K members in the credit portfolio the protection notional payment if default occurs is $1/K$ times the portfolio notional value. The valuation of a credit default index swap can use all the portfolio members' specific default probabilities and value the portfolio of the single-name contracts as the sum of the K contracts. However, market quotes of credit default index swaps also include creation of an index spread curve that is used to value the contract as if it is only one single-name credit default swap. See O'Kane (2008, ch. 10).

While the credit default index swap is not a credit correlation product per se—being a portfolio of single-name contracts—it is frequently used as an approximate macroeconomic hedge for a credit portfolio exposure. There are nowadays many different index portfolios traded in the market. For example, the iTraxx has large European indices, European sector indices, Asian indices, and sovereign indices. It hence allows a broad exposure or hedge to specific credit markets. As we will discuss in the next chapter on counterparty credit risk the credit default index swap is also recognized, to some extent, as a regulatory eligible hedge for a bank's counterparty credit risk portfolio.

Basket Credit Default Swaps

The standard basket credit default swap insures the k:th default in a basket of K large international corporate credits. Suppose therefore we have available a *joint* survival curve for $K - k + 1$ reference entities, $Q(K - k + 1, t_0, t_n)$. The premium payment leg of the basket credit default swap can now be calculated using the single-name credit default swap premium leg in equation (4.73), replacing the survival function, $Q(t_0, t_n)$ with the joint survival function, $Q(K - k + 1, t_0, t_n)$. Similarly, the protection payment leg in equation (4.74) can be calculated using the unconditional default probability of the k:th default, which, again, can be obtained from $Q(K - k + 1, t_0, t_n)$. We can therefore conclude that conditional on the joint survival, $Q(K - k + 1, t_0, t_n)$, the basket credit default swap contract can use exactly the single-name credit default swap price as in equation (4.75). The trick in practice is how to obtain the joint survival curve for a basket of credits. To obtain this we of course need a portfolio credit risk model.

We can write the general survival distribution for a portfolio with $k = 1, \ldots, K$ credits as

$$S(t_{n_1}, \ldots, t_{n_K}) = Q(\tau_1 < t_{n_1}, \ldots, \tau_K < t_{n_K})$$

with survival copula, C, such that

$$C = C(S(t_{n_1}), \ldots, S(t_{n_K})).$$

Previously in this chapter—in the discussion of the default time model of Li (2000)—we calculated the probability of joint firm default for $K = 2$ using different copulas including the normal, t, and Clayton copula in Table 4.25. That is, we calculated the joint survival function,

$$Q(\tau_1 < t_{n_1}, \tau_2 < t_{n_2}) = P(\tau_1 \leq t_{n_1}, \tau_2 \leq t_{n_2}).$$

We can therefore use a default time copula simulation to price basket credit derivatives. Our example in Table 4.25 also showed that the normal copula with high values for the correlation parameter, ρ, is perfectly capable of producing strongly correlated defaults. However, the normal copula model has been heavily criticized after the 2007 crisis for underestimating default risk. Partly, this can be assigned to the market using overoptimistic low asset correlations.

The One-Factor Copula Model for Correlated Default Times   In case of a one-factor asset model several researchers have developed approaches that avoid copula simulation. For example, Laurent and Gregory (2003) use the fast Fourier transform with the one-factor copula. Hull and White (2004) use numerical integration of a one-factor copula model to price basket credit derivatives and tranches of Collateralized Debt Obligations (CDOs). Andersen and Sidenius (2004) use a recursion approach and allow random factor loadings.

In the single-factor normal copula model we have that

$$\hat{Z}_k = RZ + \sqrt{1 - R^2}\varepsilon_k$$

with $\varepsilon_k \sim N(0,1)$, $Z \sim N(0,1)$ for all firms $k = 1, \ldots, K$. In this model there is only a single correlation parameter $\rho = R$ for each pair of firms and, conditionally on Z,

$$P(\tau = t_n | Z) = N\left(\frac{N^{-1}\left[P\left(\tau = t_n\right)\right] - \rho Z}{\sqrt{1 - \rho}}\right)$$

with the conditional cumulative probability of k defaults at t_n as

$$P(k, t_n | Z) = \frac{K!}{(K-k)!k!}[P(\tau = t_n | Z)]^k [1 - P(\tau = t_n | Z)]^{K-k} \tag{4.76}$$

and the marginal default probability

$$P(k, t_n, t_{n+1} | Z) = P(k, t_{n+1} | Z) - P(k, t_n | Z).$$

Following Hull and White (2004) equation (4.76) can be numerically integrated to obtain the joint, unconditional on Z, survival curve, $Q(K - k + 1, t_0, t_n)$, for example, using Simpson's one-third rule or Gauss-Hermite integration. Once the joint unconditional survival curve is obtained we proceed with valuation using the single-name credit default swap pricing formula.

Example Basket Credit Default Swap Premiums Using the One-Factor Copula Model We compute sample fair premiums for a few basket credit default swaps to illustrate the behavior of fair swap premiums for different correlation parameters and different number of basket defaults. As in the above single-credit default swap example, we assume a flat 2% discount rate, a 40 recovery rate, a monthly default interval, and that accruals are paid by the protection buyer. When integrating equation (4.76) we use Simpson's one-third rule. However, the exact choice of numerical integration method has minimal impact on the results. The maturity term for the basket credit default swaps is 10 years and the survival curve is homogeneous for all basket members as survival curve A in Table 4.69. The basket size is 10 members.

Table 4.70 displays the fair annualized swap premiums in basis points when we vary the normal copula correlation parameter, ρ, between 0 and 0.5 and the number of defaults in the basket between 1, 3, and 7. We note from Table 4.70 that for a low number of basket defaults the assumption of low correlation increases the fair premium as it is more likely to reach the low number of defaults in this case. For many basket defaults the fair premium with a zero correlation is close to null as such events are highly unlikely with zero correlation. In contrast, using a correlation of 0.5 yields still significant fair premiums for many basket defaults. Clearly, in the zero correlation case, as multiple defaults are highly unlikely, the fair premium decreases sharply as we increase the number of defaults. As the correlation increases most defaults are joint defaults and hence the fair premium does not reduce that much as we increase the number of defaults in the basket. Of course, in the special case of perfect positive correlation such that all defaults are joint defaults the fair premium is independent of the basket defaults number.

TABLE 4.70 Annualized Fair Premiums in Basis Points, Per Unit of Swap Notional, for 10-Year Basket Credit Default Swap Contracts with Different Number of Basket Defaults and Normal Copula Correlation Parameter

Correlation (ρ)	Basket defaults no.	Annualized swap premium (bps)
0	1	659.40
0	3	147.94
0	7	0.2044
0.5	1	256.25
0.5	3	84.521
0.5	7	20.772

A Note on Securitization and Basket Credit Default Swaps In addition to single-name and basket credit default swaps, banks also use vehicles generally known as securitization instruments to transfer credit risk. Although we should remark here that after the 2007 financial crisis investors' interest in securitization has been significantly reduced and hence there is in general much less market interest in these types of relatively complex credit constructions. Before the financial crisis securitizations were widely used as funding instruments and to reduce the regulatory capital. Shortly after the crisis the securitization market in the United States was largely nonexistent, while in Europe many banks still package and issue securitizations. However, the issues are retained on balance sheet rather than sold to investors. One of the main drivers for European banks to still issue securitizations and keep them on balance sheet is to create European central bank eligible collateral. Hence, the motivation for securitization has changed from achieving reduction in regulatory capital to creating collateral that can be pledged. See Scopelliti (2014) on the European bank incentives for securitizations.

While there are many variations of securitization instruments, the basic idea remains the same. In general, a securitization is a process of packaging assets into a pool that can be converted into securities that can be purchased by investors. These assets are typically managed or serviced by a Special Purpose Entity (SPE). The SPE packages these assets into several securities known as tranches. Of course, tranches of a pool can bear different levels of risks depending on the structure. Tranches are generally structured in orders with a priority in cash flow allocation and sold to investors in the form of notes.[62] The investors pay an up-front investment in exchange for the future cash flows from the tranche. In a cash securitization, investors basically take over all risks embedded in the cash flows, including credit risk, market risk, and prepayment risk.[63] As the cash flows are divided into tranches with different risk profiles, the notes are not equal—representing different levels of risks. The tranche with the highest credit risk is often called the equity tranche and the tranche with the lowest credit risk is called the super-senior tranche. The tranches in between the equity and super-senior tranches are referred to as mezzanine tranches. See Tavakoli (2003) for details on securitization and other structured finance products.

---

[62]The exact rule for allocation of cash flows to tranches is referred to as a waterfall.
[63]With the sophistication of credit derivatives, banks can choose to only transfer the credit risk to investors while retaining the rest of the risks and the actual cash flows of the underlying assets on the balance sheet. This type of program is often referred to as a synthetic securitization. In a synthetic structure the underlyings are usually credit derivatives of the assets where protection is provided by the SPE. Depending on the structure, an investor may or may not be required to provide upfront investment.

The fact that a tranche of a securitization has an attachment point and a detachment point as a proportion of the underlying pool means that we can represent the tranche fair risk spread as the fair premium of a tranche credit default swap. In case of a homogeneous portfolio the tranche credit default swap can in turn be represented by a set of basket credit default swaps on the underlying pool credits. To see this note that for a securitization tranche with attachment and detachment points relative to the underlying pool of 10% and 20% in a basket of 100 homogeneous credits we can represent the tranche as the sum of kth to default basket credit default swaps. Specifically, we can represent the tranche fair risk spread as the sum of the 10th to the 20th to default basket credit default swaps. This is because an investor holding both the securitization tranche and the 10th to the 20th default basket credit default swaps should earn the risk-free rate, as the tranche investment is now fully hedged. Hence, we can price the tranche using the one-factor normal copula model as in the basket credit default swap pricing example above.

The tranche implied correlations from a one-factor normal copula model often exhibits a so-called correlation smile for tranches on the same pool. Correlation tends to be the lowest for the mezzanine tranches and higher for the equity and super-senior tranches. Referring to the findings in our basket credit default swap example in Table 4.70, we can conclude that equity tranches value decreases with lower correlations (that is, a small basket defaults number) while super-senior tranche value decreases with higher correlations (that is, a large basket defaults number). Hence, in practice, using the simple one-factor model, there may not be a single correlation value that fits all tranches. McGinty et al. (2004) proposed the concept of base correlation. Using base correlation, instead of implying correlation on regular tranches, "first loss tranches" are created virtually so that they all have the same lower attachment point of 0% while keeping the detachment point of each of the regular tranches. The base correlations are the implied correlations from the first loss tranches. The base correlations turn out to be smoother and upward shaped with respect to the tranches' detachment points.

In the general securitization case, or in case of using more complex credit models, a full evaluation of a securitization deal may require simulation of the future losses from the underlying assets in the pool and a corresponding attribution of the losses to the tranches. One of the credit portfolio models we have discussed in this portfolio credit risk chapter can be used to compute the credit losses from the underlying pool. The additional feature needed to perform simulation valuation of a securitization tranche from a given credit portfolio model is to apply a post-process structure of loss (cash flow) allocation to the tranches. Moreover, in order to judge the credit quality of a particular tranche we also need to determine what threshold levels of losses are consistent with different credit ratings. We refer to Nyström (2007) as one example of using a simulation-based credit portfolio approach to allocate credit losses to tranches. Nyström (2007) also links the expected tranche losses to methods used by rating agencies to judge credit quality.

REGULATORY CAPITAL FOR CREDIT RISK

It is practice in credit risk to estimate both the expected loss and the unexpected (tail) loss. The expected loss of credit risk is in theory covered by the credit risk provision or by the credit spread. Compared to expected loss the tail loss that induces the capital requirement has been more emphasized by the regulators, partly because of the complexity in estimating tail loss and the need of ensuring business continuity. As we discussed in the introduction to this book, the first Basel accord in 1988 simply categorized credit exposures into gross tiers of risk weight and was criticized by many banks for failing to reflect risk sensitivity and recognize risk mitigations. The next generation of regulation known as Basel II significantly improved the credit risk capital requirement. First it brought necessary sophistication into the regulatory capital paradigm by introducing three pillars that set the minimal capital requirement (pillar 1), a supervisory review that encourages banks to improve their internal risk management practice in credit risk (pillar 2), and proper disclosure and market disclosure (pillar 3).

In the first pillar itself Basel II introduced risk sensitive risk weights that allowed banks to benefit from their internal models if these models better reflect the risk exposures of the bank. The regulatory credit risk capital requirement in Basel II can be summarized as the aggregation of the Risk Weighted Assets (RWA) for $i = 1, \ldots, N$ exposures:

$$RWA = \sum_{i=1}^{N} EAD_i \times RW_i. \tag{4.77}$$

Here, EAD_i stands for the exposure at default for exposure i and RW_i is the risk weight either from the risk weight tier that the asset is mapped to in the standardized approach or based on the Basel II formula in equation (4.40) in the internal ratings–based approach.

The majority of banks are allowed, or in some cases required, to adopt the internal ratings–based approaches that are based on their internal models. In the internal ratings–based approaches banks can use their own probability of default models in the foundation internal ratings–based approach. In the advanced internal ratings–based approach, banks can apply their own models to loss given default, credit conversion factors for the credit facility exposure, and the exposure effective maturity estimations as well.

One of the reasons that regulators could introduce risk sensitive capital requirements using banks' own probability of default models was because in most medium-sized and large banks, especially in the banking book business, the development of internal ratings and a scorecard system was a well-established practice. As part of the acceptance criteria for banks to employ their own models, model validation, and documentation requirements were also specified. Another eligibility requirement of using banks' own models is that the models reflect the banks' business operation and are not only developed for the regulatory capital purpose and actually used in business decisions. Therefore, thanks to Basel II there has been significant investment in the internal ratings systems in banks, which propagates the maturity of the risk infrastructure and banks' own economic capital practice as well. Basel II certainly had the most significant impact on banks' credit risk analysis methods and lending processes in general.

Even after the 2007 financial crisis and with the introduction of Basel III the credit risk weights introduced with Basel II are largely retained—which indicates the relative robustness of the Basel II rules.[64] The two major Basel III additions and revisions of the credit risk weight framework were focused on large exposure and securitization. The large exposure framework was finalized in 2014 for effective measurement and management of concentration risk.

Recently, a Basel consultation paper (Basel Committee, 2014c) is aiming at revising the gross standardized approach to credit risk by reducing exclusive reliance on external ratings

---

[64]However, there have certainly been voices raised about the suitability of the internal ratings–based approach as a basis for risk-based capital charges, for example, the speech by Governor Daniel K. Tarullo at the Federal Reserve Bank of Chicago Bank Structure Conference, Chicago, May 8, 2014. The view put forward is that defining risk-based capital charges with stress scenarios is more appropriate given the success of CCAR. We will return to a discussion about firmwide stress testing as basis for capital charges in Chapter 9.

and make the standardized approach more risk sensitive and hence more comparable to the internal ratings–based approaches. The assignment of risk weights to financial institutions and corporates will be assigned based on borrower's financial conditions rather than external ratings. For financial institutions this includes the capital ratio and for corporates their revenue and leverage. The standardized risk weight for residential and commercial mortgages is replaced by a risk weight that depends on the loan-to-value ratio and/or the debt service coverage ratio. There are also changes to credit mitigant eligibility criteria and how they can reduce the risk weight of the borrower.

For trading book positions an important update to regulatory capital requirements came with Basel 2.5 in 2009 when there was a new incremental risk capital charge for credit risk in the trading book. As we have discussed in this chapter the incremental risk charge is focused mainly on bonds in the trading book with liquidity trading horizons assigned to credits. There is no prescribed model although it is natural to consider portfolio credit risk models for large firms inspired by the Merton (1974) structural model. The incremental risk charge adds to the trading book capital for market risk. That is the current market risk charge discussed in the previous chapter. For some banks there are also additional trading book charges added for correlation trading portfolios and standardized charges for securitizations. The current regulatory proposal for a fundamental review of the market risk in the trading book (Basel Committee, 2012, 2014a) also proposes changes to the incremental risk charge. Specifically, the incremental risk charge is replaced by an incremental *default* risk charge that removes the requirement to model migration risk. The Committee is also considering a more prescriptive model approach by explicitly requiring two-factor models and calibration of correlation parameters on listed equity prices using a one-year observation period based on a period of stress. In the new proposal equity positions must also be included to capture their issuer default risk and the regulators specifically mention that sovereign exposures need to be part of the model. The main reason that regulators consider elimination of migration risk from the incremental risk charge is to remove the possible double count with spread risk in the market risk measure—especially since with the new proposed liquidity adjusted market risk measure based on CVaR (see equation (3.29)) the liquidity horizons for credit spreads are relatively long.

In addition to issuer default risk charges using the Basel risk-weighted assets formula in equation (4.40), there are also default-based counterparty credit risk charges using the formula. The counterparty credit risk exposures include derivatives such as swaps. The exposure at default is therefore more complicated for the counterparty credit risk. Basel allows three methods: current exposure, standardized, and internal model methods. Regulatory derivative counterparty risk capital charges will be covered in the next chapter on the same topic.

Regulatory Risk Components

For the banking book credit risk capital requirement the main building blocks of the internal ratings–based approaches are the well-known risk components:

- Probability of default
- Loss given default
- Exposure at default

as well as an effective maturity component. The risk components are inputs to the risk weight function with a regulatory credit risk horizon of one year. Therefore, all the risk components should be estimated based on a one-year horizon.

Probability of default modeling has a long history in the industry even before the introduction of Basel II. In contrast, loss given default and exposure modeling is a newer practice that was mainly driven by the Basel II requirements. In the loss given default estimation, one factor to consider is whether the loss is ex-ante or ex-post the effect of credit risk mitigation. Another complication in the loss given default estimation lies in the recovery data. Recovery usually takes time to fully work out, and it is important to get the actual losses net of all the workout costs into the data used for loss given default modeling. For the banking book the uncertainty in the exposure estimation mainly comes from the unutilized portion of the committed credit facilities for which a credit conversion factor (CCF) is either supplied by the regulator or estimated by the bank (in the advanced internal ratings–based approach). Engelmann and Rauhmeier (2006) collected contributions in probability of default, loss given default, and exposure estimation at the time many institutions were implementing Basel II.

When the risk components are estimated individually, the correlation among them is often neglected. However, there is clear evidence that in stressed cases, such correlation should not be neglected. All the risk components are therefore required to use stressed estimates and are subject to validation.

Since regulatory capital represents the minimal capital set by regulators, it is important to reconcile the capital with the economic capital models in practice. The Basel regulatory credit risk capital is primarily based on the single-factor model used to derive the Basel II formula in equation (4.40). The fundamental idea can in part be attributed to Michael Gordy. First, Gordy (2000) established the similarity between the Merton (1974) model approach and the actuarial model approach when only default loss is considered (see also Koylouglu and Hickman, 1998). Second, Gordy (2003) derived an asymptotic single risk factor model that he proved to be portfolio invariant. The portfolio invariance feature was a critical justification for the model to serve as a universal risk weight function. In most cases, especially in the retail asset class, the large homogeneous portfolio assumption is applied. Basel II, however, requires a regularity check to make sure the retail portfolio meets the assumption so that no exposure to one counterparty can be more than a small fraction of the total portfolio exposure. Further adjustment is used when the granularity is not met.

Risk Mitigation and Regulatory Capital

Basel II credit risk regulatory capital requirement opened up for banks to more effectively account for credit mitigations. Banks can employ various credit risk mitigation vehicles, including the traditional financial and physical collaterals and credit guarantees. In addition, Basel II was the first to recognize the benefit of credit transfer through credit derivatives. The risk weight of the exposure portion that is covered by the mitigation can be substituted by the risk weight of the risk mitigants that are supposed to be lower. For the credit protections the double-default treatment was applied, which we have previously discussed in this chapter.

Because of the opportunity cost of banks' capital, the recognition of the credit risk mitigation and transfer gives banks incentive to actively manage their credit risk. Optimally allocating the credit risk mitigants in order to minimize the total risk weighted asset creates an effective credit risk management decision.

When credit risk mitigants are present with an exposure, the exposure can be decomposed into an unsecured portion and several secured portions that take the adjusted value of the credit risk mitigant. The secured portions take the risk weights that correspond to the mitigants. With credit risk mitigants, the risk-weighted asset in equation (4.77) can now be written as:

$$RWA = \sum_{i=1}^{N} \left(\sum_{j_i=1}^{m_i} S_{j_i} \times RW_{j_i} + US_i \times RW_i \right)$$

where the secured portion S_{j_i} of exposure asset i is protected by mitigation j, and US_i is the unprotected portion. Each exposure can of course be secured by several credit risk mitigants, $j_i = 1, \ldots, m_i$ and multiple exposures can share credit risk mitigants. In practice, additional multipliers that represent the corresponding collateral haircuts or maturity mismatch adjustments are also introduced into the RWA formula. With this RWA formulation we can obtain an optimal credit risk mitigant allocation by allocating portions of total exposure to different protection, that is, the secured portion S_{j_i} and the remaining unprotected portion US_i, such that

$$RWA = \sum_{i=1}^{N} \left(\sum_{j_i=1}^{m_i} S_{j_i} \times RW_{j_i} \times M_{j_i} + US_i \times RW_i \right).$$

where the sum of all protected and unprotected portions corresponding to asset i should obviously be the original exposure at default for the asset. Here multiplier M_{j_i} is assigned according to the haircuts and maturity mismatch adjustment. Chen (2009) devised a network flow representation where the optimal allocation is achieved as a minimum cost network flow problem. Additional constraints can be introduced to restrict the valid amount of a credit protection. The network connection describes the applicability of a credit risk mitigant according to the protection agreements. Only when a mitigation can be contractually applied to an exposure a network arc between the two can be established. We refer to Chen (2009) for details and examples of the optimization.

APPENDIX

In this appendix we make the Markov iteration in equation (4.57) explicit for the transition matrix in Table 4.34, which is reproduced here in Table 4.71 for convenience.

Assuming the loan is current at $t = 0$ we have at $t = 1$ that

$$\mathbf{y}(1) = [\mathbf{A}(1)]'\mathbf{y}(0) = \begin{bmatrix} A_{11}(1) & A_{21}(1) & 0 & 0 \\ A_{12}(1) & A_{22}(1) & 0 & 0 \\ A_{13}(1) & A_{23}(1) & 1 & 0 \\ 0 & A_{24}(1) & 0 & 1 \end{bmatrix} \begin{bmatrix} 1 \\ 0 \\ 0 \\ 0 \end{bmatrix} = \begin{bmatrix} A_{11}(1) \\ A_{12}(1) \\ A_{13}(1) \\ 0 \end{bmatrix}.$$

TABLE 4.71 Example Loan Delinquency Transition Matrix—Reduced Delinquency States with a Quarterly Measurement Horizon

	Current	D90	Prepay	Default
Current	$A_{11}(t)$	$A_{12}(t)$	$A_{13}(t)$	0
D90	$A_{21}(t)$	$A_{22}(t)$	$A_{23}(t)$	$A_{24}(t)$
Prepay	0	0	1	0
Default	0	0	0	1

At $t = 2$, we split up the iteration in the two parts for the two non-absorbing states current and D90, yielding the subiterations,

$$\tilde{\mathbf{y}}_1(2) = [\mathbf{A}_1(2)]'\mathbf{y}_1(1) = \begin{bmatrix} A_{11}^1(2) & A_{21}^1(2) & 0 & 0 \\ A_{12}^1(2) & A_{22}^1(2) & 0 & 0 \\ A_{13}^1(2) & A_{23}^1(2) & 1 & 0 \\ 0 & A_{24}^1(2) & 0 & 1 \end{bmatrix} \begin{bmatrix} A_{11}(1) \\ 0 \\ 0 \\ 0 \end{bmatrix} = \begin{bmatrix} A_{11}(1)A_{11}^1(2) \\ A_{11}(1)A_{12}^1(2) \\ A_{11}(1)A_{13}^1(2) \\ 0 \end{bmatrix},$$

$$\tilde{\mathbf{y}}_2(2) = [\mathbf{A}_2(2)]'\mathbf{y}_2(1) = \begin{bmatrix} A_{11}^2(2) & A_{21}^2(2) & 0 & 0 \\ A_{12}^2(2) & A_{22}^2(2) & 0 & 0 \\ A_{13}^2(2) & A_{23}^2(2) & 1 & 0 \\ 0 & A_{24}^2(2) & 0 & 1 \end{bmatrix} \begin{bmatrix} 0 \\ A_{12}(1) \\ 0 \\ 0 \end{bmatrix} = \begin{bmatrix} A_{12}(1)A_{21}^2(2) \\ A_{12}(1)A_{22}^2(2) \\ A_{12}(1)A_{23}^2(2) \\ A_{12}(1)A_{24}^2(2) \end{bmatrix},$$

where $A_{lr}^k(2)$ indicates the transition probability at time $t = 2$ from state l to state r conditional on state at time $t = 1$ being state k. Of course, we know beforehand that the corresponding $\tilde{\mathbf{y}}_4(2)$ iteration vector is composed of zeroes since the default state is absorbing and cannot be reached directly from the current state. Hence, we do not need to compute that subiteration. We also know beforehand that the corresponding iteration vector $\tilde{\mathbf{y}}_3(2)$ would just reproduce the transition probability $A_{13}(1)$ from $\mathbf{y}(1)$ in state position 3 for migration from the current state to the prepayment state, with zeroes elsewhere. This is because the prepayment state is absorbing such that once a loan has entered the prepayment state it never goes back. Essentially, it exits the portfolio once the prepayment cash flow has been made.

We can now sum up all the possible ways the loan can be in a state k at time $t = 2$ using the equation,

$$\mathbf{y}(2) = \sum_{k_1=1}^{\hat{K}} [\mathbf{A}_{k_1}(2)]'\mathbf{y}_{k_1}(1).$$

Since

$$\tilde{\mathbf{y}}_{k_1}(2) = [\mathbf{A}_{k_1}(2)]'\mathbf{y}_{k_1}(1)$$

we obtain that,

$$\mathbf{y}(2) = \sum_{k_1=1}^{4} \tilde{\mathbf{y}}_{k_1}(2) = \begin{bmatrix} A_{11}(1)A_{11}^1(2) + A_{12}(1)A_{21}^2(2) \\ A_{11}(1)A_{12}^1(2) + A_{12}(1)A_{22}^2(2) \\ A_{11}(1)A_{13}^1(2) + A_{12}(1)A_{23}^2(2) + A_{13}(1) \\ A_{12}(1)A_{24}^2(2) \end{bmatrix}.$$

We can interpret these state occupancy probabilities as the sums of the products of probabilities of the different paths the loan can take to end up in a state $k = 1, \ldots, 4$. For example, at time step $t = 2$, the loan can end up in state current either through staying in current at both time step $t = 1$ and $t = 2$, or, by migrating to the D90 state in time step $t = 1$ and then back to current in time step $t = 2$. Similarly, the loan can end up in the default state if the loan migrates to the D90 state in time step $t = 1$ and then in time step $t = 2$ migrates to the default state. This is the only possible migration path to default at time step $t = 2$ as the default state is unreachable from other states than the D90 state.

At $t = 3$ we now have to split again the two non-absorbing states current and D90 into further subcases corresponding to the transition path the loan took. To indicate the transition probability at time $t = 3$ from state l to state r conditional on state at time $t = 1$ being state k and state at time $t = 2$ being s we will use the notation, $A_{lr}^{ks}(3)$. With this notation we obtain the $\widetilde{\mathbf{y}}_{11}(3)$ and $\widetilde{\mathbf{y}}_{12}(3)$ subcases as,

$$\widetilde{\mathbf{y}}_{11}(3) = [\mathbf{A}_{11}(3)]'\mathbf{y}_{11}(2) = \begin{bmatrix} A_{11}(1)A_{11}^{1}(2)A_{11}^{11}(3) \\ A_{11}(1)A_{11}^{1}(2)A_{12}^{11}(3) \\ A_{11}(1)A_{11}^{1}(2)A_{13}^{11}(3) \\ 0 \end{bmatrix},$$

$$\widetilde{\mathbf{y}}_{12}(3) = [\mathbf{A}_{12}(3)]'\mathbf{y}_{12}(2) = \begin{bmatrix} A_{11}(1)A_{12}^{1}(2)A_{21}^{12}(3) \\ A_{11}(1)A_{12}^{1}(2)A_{22}^{12}(3) \\ A_{11}(1)A_{12}^{1}(2)A_{23}^{12}(3) \\ A_{11}(1)A_{12}^{1}(2)A_{24}^{12}(3) \end{bmatrix}.$$

Of course, again we know beforehand that computing both $\widetilde{\mathbf{y}}_{13}(3)$ and $\widetilde{\mathbf{y}}_{14}(3)$ is unnecessary since there is no new contribution to the migration from time step $t = 3$ as both states are absorbing.

Doing the same calculation for the corresponding $\widetilde{\mathbf{y}}_{21}(3)$ and $\widetilde{\mathbf{y}}_{21}(3)$ subcases we have that,

$$\widetilde{\mathbf{y}}_{21}(3) = [\mathbf{A}_{21}(3)]'\mathbf{y}_{21}(2) = \begin{bmatrix} A_{12}(1)A_{21}^{2}(2)A_{11}^{21}(3) \\ A_{12}(1)A_{21}^{2}(2)A_{12}^{21}(3) \\ A_{12}(1)A_{21}^{2}(2)A_{13}^{21}(3) \\ 0 \end{bmatrix},$$

$$\widetilde{\mathbf{y}}_{22}(3) = [\mathbf{A}_{22}(3)]'\mathbf{y}_{22}(2) = \begin{bmatrix} A_{12}(1)A_{22}^{2}(2)A_{21}^{22}(3) \\ A_{12}(1)A_{22}^{2}(2)A_{22}^{22}(3) \\ A_{12}(1)A_{22}^{2}(2)A_{23}^{22}(3) \\ A_{12}(1)A_{22}^{2}(2)A_{24}^{22}(3) \end{bmatrix}.$$

Summing up our contributions at time step $t = 3$ we use the equation

$$\mathbf{y}(3) = \sum_{k_1=1}^{\hat{K}} \sum_{k_2=1}^{\hat{K}} [\mathbf{A}_{k_1 k_2}(3)]'\mathbf{y}_{k_1 k_2}(2),$$

where in our notation,

$$\widetilde{\mathbf{y}}_{k_1 k_2}(3) = [\mathbf{A}_{k_1 k_2}(2)]'\mathbf{y}_{k_1 k_2}(3).$$

Hence, we have, for example, the y(3) cumulative state occupancy probability for state current as

$$A_{11}(1)A_{11}^1(2)A_{11}^{11}(2) + A_{11}(1)A_{12}^1(2)A_{21}^{12}(2) + A_{12}(1)A_{21}^2(2)A_{11}^{21}(2) + A_{11}(1)A_{12}^1(2)A_{21}^{12}(2)$$

which again represents the different paths the loan can take at time steps $t = 1, 2$ and still be in current state at $t = 3$. Similarly, for the default state we have

$$A_{11}(1)A_{12}^1(2)A_{24}^{12}(2) + A_{12}(1)A_{24}^2(2).$$

Now, for example, to obtain y(9), being the state occupancy vector at time step $t = 9$ and corresponding to a 9-quarter horizon analysis of the credit migration, as required by, for example, CCAR credit stress tests, we only need 256 subiterations of equation (4.56). This is because the number of effective states that we need to calculate the iteration for is only 2 since both the prepayment and the default states are absorbing with no migration from these states. This is hence quite manageable in practice for computer implementation and allows model implementation without simulation for large pools of loans as well as in economic scenario stress testing applications. However, the practicality of the Markov iteration in equation (4.57) depends largely on the state dimension in the transition matrix when the analysis time horizon is reasonably large. For example, if the state transition matrix has 10 non-absorbing states, then the number of required subiterations of equation (4.56) at time step $t = 9$ would be 100 million. In such cases, we might be better off doing the state transition sampling in equation (4.55). However, deciding between simulation or using the Markov iteration for a specific model also calls for a detailed analysis of the specific model variables used. In practice, there are usually significant simplifications of the iteration that can be made for a specific model. For example, the delinquency indicator functions used in the state transition models may not track the complete history. See Skoglund and Chen (2015) on Markov iteration for monthly models with many delinquency states using state occupancy indicator functions.

Finally, we note that in this iteration, the flow of expected state occupancy probabilities is not captured in y(t). It only captures the cumulative state occupancy probabilities. However, due to the structure of the iteration, we can also track the history of the flow to a final particular state. This means that subsequent cash flow calculations can also depend on past state transitions. In practice, most cash flow calculations only depend on the from and to state rather than the whole state history, which simplifies matters. For example, in our quarterly delinquency matrix in Table 4.71 the cash flow typically only depends on from and to state since accruals happen in the D90 state, and when a loan migrates back to current it should have paid the accruals as well as any regular scheduled cash flows. A loan that migrates from D90 to D90 must have paid the previous time step accruals to remain in state D90. Otherwise, the loan would have migrated to default state.

CHAPTER 5

Counterparty Credit Risk

Counterparty credit risk measures the replacement cost of a derivative contract should the counterparty default anytime during the life term before honoring the contractual cash flows. In an over-the-counter (OTC) derivative transaction the mark-to-market value is not constant, and hence the credit exposure changes in response to market factors at each future date. Counterparty credit risk is therefore measured as an exposure profile over the remaining life of the transaction. The actual profile depends on the assumption of market factors and deal specifics, such as deal-aging. Since the exposure is from a bilateral contact, the mark to market of the exposure can be positive or negative. However, there is only counterparty credit risk if the exposure is positive.

Several exposure measures are used by banks in practice. For example, the expected exposure profile is frequently used for pricing counterparty credit risk and in Basel regulatory default risk charges. However, banks also calculate potential future exposures that represent a maximum amount of exposure at a high level of confidence, say 99%, at any future date. The collection of such exposure values across time is often referred to as potential future exposure profile or peak exposure profile at a given confidence level. The peak exposure is frequently used to manage counterparty limits in much the same way as market risk VaR limits are managed. In assessing the feasibility of a new trade with a counterparty (i.e., that the trade is within the peak exposure limits established by the bank), the incremental exposure from the new trade is used to assess the impact of the trade pre-deal. Similarly, the marginal (Euler) contribution of a deal to the exposure is calculated. The marginal contribution is used to assess marginal impact of trades post-deal. For a portfolio of derivatives counterparty exposure is often mitigated through netting agreements and collateral.

When pricing OTC derivatives, there is not only the risk-free value of the contract that needs to be marked to market. The valuation should also take into account the risk of counterparty default by adjusting the risk-free value by the expected losses due to counterparty default. The market value of an OTC derivative is hence broken down into a risk-free component and an expected loss term that reflects the credit valuation adjustment (CVA). CVA can here be seen as the cost of hedging the counterparty credit risk of a derivatives contract.

When calculating CVA, banks can either take into account only the counterparty default risk (unilateral CVA) or also their own default risk (bilateral CVA). In the first case the CVA adjustment reduces the mark-to-market value of the contract to the bank, while in the second case the effect depends on both the relative default probabilities of the counterparties and the specific exposure profiles. The bilateral CVA hence has two components. The first component is the positive unilateral CVA component (reduces mark-to-market value) based on the counterparty defaulting; the second component is negative (increases mark-to-market value) based on the bank defaulting. Bilateral CVA can be viewed as an attempt to establish a fair net price adjustment between the two counterparties for a derivative transaction.

Before the 2007 financial crisis, counterparty credit risk was in practice perceived as one-way with the largest institutions charging smaller institutions and corporate treasuries for counterparty credit risk in derivatives transactions. However, the 2007 financial crisis, with the failure or near-failure of large institutions, has shattered the perception that the larger institutions are "too big to fail." Counterparty credit risk is now considered two-way. Hence, both sides of the derivative transaction demand to be compensated for taking on the other party's counterparty credit risk. In addition, the pricing of counterparty credit risk has recently evolved from a passive insurance accounting practice to being actively priced and risk managed through a dedicated centralized CVA trading desk. The CVA desk performs two vital functions. First, it quotes CVA to traders and provides incremental CVA for trader pre-deal decision support. The desk also keeps records of historical CVA prices (premiums) in case of trade cancellations and subsequent reimbursements from the CVA desk to traders. Second, the CVA desk is a risk management desk that manages centrally the counterparty exposure transferred to the desk.

In this chapter we first introduce the CVA pricing of trades using a step-by-step exposure simulation framework that fits well within a bank's current exposure simulation process. Calculating CVA is computational intensive as it involves pricing of typically long dated trades at various points in the future at each market simulation path. Typically, the future time points at which trades are valued depends on the underlying characteristic of trades such as exact cash flow dates. It is especially complex to capture collateralized trades since the collateral calls and returns need to be calculated at the margin days. Due to the complexities in calculating CVA, market participants have searched for simple formulas for CVA. It is therefore practice to calculate CVA using the assumption of independence between exposure and default. This allows CVA calculation as a simple multiplication post-processing using the default probability from the credit system, the expected exposure profile from the exposure system, and the discount curve from the market system. However, market correlations between counterparty default probability and the exposure can induce wrong-way risk that needs to be accounted for, and we consider a correlation model that allows CVA computation in case of wrong-way risk. The drawback is that CVA must now be computed by jointly integrating default probability and market exposure path by path. In practice the exposure calculation must also take into account the collateral margining process with frequent margin call and posting rules.

After a discussion on pricing counterparty credit risk we move on to consider the CVA distribution and CVA tail risk. This is important, both for calculating the Basel III CVA capital charge and for the need to understand CVA tail risks in general. While wrong-way risk may have a significant impact on CVA itself, it is natural to expect that the effect on the risk of CVA as measured, for example, by VaR is even greater. This is an important consideration for the CVA desk as tail risks typically remain unhedged in practice and need to bear capital.

While our discussions in this chapter initially focus on specific trades' exposure profiles and CVA, the third section of the chapter takes a portfolio view and analyzes the effect of netting on the portfolio exposure and CVA. In a portfolio-setting exposure, measures and CVA can also be decomposed to trade contributions using the Euler allocation approach.

The next topic in the chapter is focused on some of the recent developments in the industry for pricing derivatives and CVA calculations. This is the deviation from Interbank rates in risk-free discounting, the use of advanced approaches to calculate CVA and CVA Greeks, as well as funding cost adjustments for derivatives.

We end the chapter with a review of the regulatory capital for counterparty credit risk. With the introduction of Basel III there are both counterparty default charges and mark-to-market charges for counterparty exposures. The counterparty default risk charges were introduced already with Basel II while the mark-to-market charges are relatively recent with Basel III. However, Basel III has also been focused on strengthening the Basel II default risk capital charge in that regulators now require calibration on stressed periods and that banks must use backtesting techniques to validate their models.

In our analysis in this chapter we illustrate the concepts using sample exposures of plain interest rate swaps and cross-currency swaps. Swaps represent the bulk of bilateral derivatives notional and the interest rate swaps exemplify a hump-shaped exposure profile while the cross-currency swaps exemplify an increasing exposure profile. The hump-shaped exposure profile for the interest rate swap is due to the fact that as time evolves there are fewer cash flow exchanges left between the parties. For the cross-currency swap the final foreign exchange of notional amounts in currency drives the majority of the risks.

COUNTERPARTY PRICING AND EXPOSURE

Market Standard Pricing Metrics

A loan granted by a financial institution to a corporate carries the risk of corporate default and loss of the principal notional outstanding on the loan. For a loan the future exposure at default is often predictable and known with a high degree of certainty. In contrast, for a simple fixed-for-floating interest rate swap agreement, the future exposure is largely unknown. The financial institution's future exposure in the simple interest rate swap depends on the future realized interest rates. If the financial institution is a payer of the fixed leg and the counterparty is the payer of the floating leg in the swap, the financial institution's future exposure increases with future high rates and decreases with future low rates. Hence, for a derivative such as a swap the future exposure is a random variable. Different paths of future interest rates yield different exposure levels for the financial institution.

If we let $V(t, T)$ denote the trade mark-to-market value at time t for a contract maturing at T, we can write the exposure as

$$\max[V(t, T), 0] \tag{5.1}$$

if default occurs. We recognize equation (5.1) as essentially the payoff of a call option on the underlying market value, $V(t, T)$, with strike 0, conditioned on default. We are hence essentially trying to price a derivative. The pricing of this derivative and hence the counterparty credit risk is known as the CVA.

Recall that in the classical Black and Scholes (1973) derivative pricing the no-arbitrage market price is obtained if the expectation of the derivative payoff is taken under the risk-neutral measure.[1] One approach to price the counterparty credit risk is therefore to discount the (risk-neutral) expected credit losses to today. The standard pricing formula is given by

$$\text{CVA}(t, T) = (1 - R)E[I_{(\tau < T)} \max[V(\tau, T), 0]]$$

where $I_{(\tau < T)}$ is an indicator function that is 1 if the default time is $\tau < T$ and null otherwise and R represents the recovery rate expected to be received on the outstanding derivative claims at default.

---

[1] See Björk (1998, Theorem 6.8).

Setting $R = 0$ for convenience we can now write

$$\text{CVA}(t, T) = E\left[\int_t^T \max\left[V(t, v), 0\right] dS(t, v)\right]$$

where $S(t, v)$ is the survival function of the counterparty. Discretization of the time steps into $[t_i]_{n=1}^N$ where $t_0 = t$ and $t_N = T$ and taking an expectation inside the summation we have

$$\text{CVA}(t, T) = \sum_{n=1}^N E[\max[V(t, t_n), 0][S(t, t_{n-1}) - S(t, t_n)]]$$

$$= \sum_{n=1}^N E[V(t, t_n)^+ p(t_{n-1}, t_n)]$$

where $p(t_{n-1}, t_n)$ is the default probability between times (t_{n-1}, t_n), conditional on the survival up to time t_{n-1}, and $z^+ = \max(z, 0)$.

Assuming the default probability, $p(t_{n-1}, t_n)$, is deterministic and given, we can further write

$$\text{CVA}(t, T) = \sum_{n=1}^N \text{EE}(t_n) p(t_{n-1}, t_n). \tag{5.2}$$

Here, $\text{EE}(t_n)$, denotes the expected exposure at time t_n and, again, $\{t_n\}_{n=1}^N$ is a set of discrete time points in the future with t_N being the maturity date of the derivative.[2] Clearly, equation (5.2) calculates the counterparty default risk price as an expected credit loss as it weights the future default probabilities with the future expected exposure profile. A natural question to ask here is what makes equation (5.2) a price of counterparty credit risk as opposed to an expected loss reserve. One preliminary answer to that question is that we can view the counterparty default risk adjustment in equation (5.2) to the risk-free derivative price as a market price if we can somehow extract it from market prices. For example, for a simple interest rate swap agreement with a counterparty, we could:

- Extract the counterparty default probability, $p(t_{n-1}, t_n)$, from traded credit default swaps or counterparty-issued bond spreads.
- Calculate the swap contract expected exposure, $\text{EE}(t_n)$, using an interest rate model that is calibrated to the current market. For example, we could use the well-known Hull-White (1990) no-arbitrage model calibrated to the current market rates and traded instruments in the market such as swaptions.

Based on the fact that we can view CVA as a derivative price, it is clear that pricing CVA is more difficult than pricing the swap. While the risk-free pricing of a swap depends only on current market interest rates the CVA value adjustment of a swap also depends on market

---

[2]In the above equations we have suppressed the discounting of future credit default losses to today to ease notation.

volatility.[3] Market practitioners therefore fit the volatility component of market models of interest rates such as the Hull-White model to traded instruments such as swaptions. Calibrating the CVA inputs to the market is referred to as risk-neutral calibration and is the main argument behind referring to equation (5.2) as a market price. However, in practice it does not necessarily mean that the bank can trade the CVA in the market or hedge CVA completely using market hedge instruments at the cost of CVA. The main reason is that the CVA in equation (5.2) depends on an unknown exposure profile and a perfect hedge requires the CDS notional to be linked to the specific trade exposure.[4] Such a CDS contract is referred to as a *contingent* CDS and has of course to be negotiated specifically with a counterparty. A CVA hedge based on a fixed notional market quoted CDS can be very costly when it is based on some worst-case exposure level. See Gregory (2010, ch. 9) on the hedging of CVA with CDS contracts.

Example of Swap CVA   To illustrate the calculation of CVA using equation (5.2), we consider an example of a simple 5-year maturity swap with current mark-to-market value of zero. Table 5.1 displays the swap expected exposure profile, $EE(t_n)$, the survival probability of the counterparty, $S(t, t_n)$, and the corresponding incremental default probability, $p(t_{n-1}, t_n)$, of the counterparty at discrete times $\{t_n\}_{n=1}^{15}$. These discrete times correspond to a time grid interval of 4 months during the 5-year term of the swap. The default probability, $p(t_{n-1}, t_n)$, in Table 5.1 is simply defined as

$$p(t_{n-1}, t_n) = S(t_0, t_{n-1}) - S(t_0, t_n).$$

The swap notional is assumed to be 1,000,000 units of currency. Since our example is a swap, the expected exposure profile in Table 5.1 displays the well-known hump-shaped profile. This is due to the time trade-off between increasing interest rate risk over time and decreasing number of swap payments left.

Using the expected exposure, $EE(t_n)$, and the default probability, $p(t_{n-1}, t_n)$, we now calculate CVA using equation (5.2). We obtain the CVA in units of currency as 4,625.82, or, expressed in % of swap notional, approximately 0.462%. This is hence the up-front fee the trader is charged by the CVA desk. Alternatively, the CVA charge can be converted to a running spread charge on the receiving leg if the CVA costs are passed on to the counterparty.[5]

In our example, we already have a survival probability for the counterparty. However, as we discussed above, the survival probability may be inferred from market-traded credit default swaps. Recall from equation (4.32) that we can write the survival probability as

$$S(t) = \exp\left(-\int_0^t h(u)\, du\right)$$

---

[3]The risk-free value of a swap is the net value of the fixed and the floating leg. The floating rate leg future cash flows (and hence price) only depends on the current market rates using the implied forward rates to derive expected future cash flows. Hence, the swap price itself is independent of market volatility of interest rates.

[4]In the previous chapter, specifically in the section on hedging credit risk, we discussed the pricing and hedging of credit risk using credit default swap (CDS) instruments.

[5]It is practice by dealers to refer to CVA as a negative value since CVA reduces the risk-free market value. However, we will refer to CVA as a positive value in our discussions.

where h is the hazard rate. If the hazard rate is constant over time, we have that

$$S(t) = \exp\left(-\int_0^t h(u)du\right) \approx \exp\left(-\int_0^t \frac{c}{1-r}du\right) \qquad (5.3)$$

since the credit default swap premia and bond spread, c, is approximately $h(1-r)$. See equation (4.1). Hence, assuming there exists a market quoted 5-year credit default swap premia at 500 basis points and a recovery rate of 40% we have the annualized hazard rate, h, as

$$h = \frac{500/10000}{1 - 0.4} \approx 0.0833.$$

With this hazard rate we can now obtain counterparty survival probabilities using equation (5.3). We obtain that

$$S(t_0, t_1) \approx \exp(-0.0833 \times d(t_0, t_1)) \approx 0.9730$$

with $d(t_0, t_1) = \frac{4}{12}$ the daycount function between dates (t_0, t_1). This is actually the method we used to derive the survival probabilities in Table 5.1. That is, we started with a counterparty quoted 5-year credit default swap premia at 500 basis points and a recovery rate of 40% to derive each survival probability, $S(t, t_n)$, in Table 5.1.

We can also analyze the sensitivity of the CVA to changes in the counterparty default risk. This is easy since we have assumed that the counterparty default probability is deterministic and hence independent of exposure. We can hence hold expected exposure constant and only shift the hazard rate. For example, a 1-basis-point upward shift of the counterparty is applied to the hazard rate such that $\tilde{h} = h + 0.00001$. We can then use equation (5.3) to derive the new survival probabilities for the counterparty and subsequently the new CVA. Table 5.2 displays the CVA obtained and the credit CVA delta compared to base when perturbing

TABLE 5.1 Sample CVA for a Swap

Time	Expected exposure	Survival probability	Default probability
t_0	0	1.0000	0
t_1	8,782	0.9730	0.0270
t_2	11,968	0.9467	0.0263
t_3	14,083	0.9211	0.0256
t_4	15,569	0.8963	0.0249
t_5	16,597	0.8721	0.0242
t_6	17,248	0.8485	0.0236
t_7	17,565	0.8256	0.0229
t_8	17,565	0.8033	0.0223
t_9	17,248	0.7816	0.0217
t_{10}	16,597	0.7605	0.0211
t_{11}	15,569	0.7400	0.0205
t_{12}	14,083	0.7200	0.0200
t_{13}	11,968	0.7005	0.0194
t_{14}	8,782	0.6816	0.0189
t_{15}	0	0.6632	0.0184

TABLE 5.2 Sample CVA Swap Sensitivity to Counterparty Default Risk

Credit sensitivity	CVA	CVA credit delta
+100 basis points	5,354.04	728.22
+10 basis points	4,701.24	75.42
+1 basis point	4,633.39	7.57
0 basis points	4,625.82	0
−1 basis point	4,618.25	−7.57
−10 basis points	4,549.81	−76.01
−100 basis points	3,838.32	−787.5

the current counterparty credit default swap premia of 500 basis points with 1, 10, and 100-basis-points upward and downward shifts. The table shows, for example, that the CVA impact of a 100-basis point increase of the counterparty CDS premia is approximately a 16% higher CVA.

In our example we have assumed a constant hazard rate and the existence of a single 5-year CDS contract traded for the counterparty. However, in practice the exact term structure of credit risk and the CVA credit deltas (and possibly second-order gammas) for the different CDS tenors are key in the CVA desk's dynamic hedging of the CVA credit risk component. Still, in case of assuming independence between the exposure and credit component in CVA, such credit deltas are trivial to compute by simply bumping the market CDS premias and then recomputing the survival and default probabilities using equation (5.3).

Analytical CVA for Swaps The swap expected exposure, $EE(t_n)$, in Table 5.1 was given in our example. However, in principle it can be derived analytically in terms of swaption prices. Sorensen and Bollier (1994) show that the expected swap exposure at time points $\{t_n\}_{n=1}^{N}$ can be expressed as $\{t_n\}_{n=1}^{N}$ maturity European swaptions on the underlying swap with maturity $t_N = T$. This is because at each $\{t_n\}_{n=1}^{N}$ the counterparty has the option to default—hence canceling the swap contract with a swaption. Of course, for a fixed rate payer counterparty the swaptions are receiver swaptions as this cancels the fixed rate leg of the swap. Similarly, for a counterparty receiving the fixed leg the canceling swaption is a payer swaption. Using the Sorensen and Bollier expected swap exposure we can therefore write swap CVA as

$$\text{CVA}(t, T) = \sum_{n=1}^{N} \widetilde{V}(t, t_n, T) \, p(t_{n-1}, t_n) \tag{5.4}$$

where $\widetilde{V}(t, t_n, T)$ is the value of a reverse swap position European swaption with option maturity at t_n and swap maturity at T. We can hence think of equation (5.4) as the value of a credit default swap where the protection leg of the credit default swap contract has a payment conditional on default that varies over time. Specifically, the payment leg notional is the market value of the swaptions. As we have mentioned before such a credit default swap contract is referred to as a contingent credit default swap. Equation (5.4) also makes clear again that to price CVA we cannot use the simple credit risk discounting approach that we used to price the issuer credit risk in bonds in the previous chapter (see the pricing equation (4.1)).

Bilateral Credit Risk and Institution Default While CVA is recognized as the price of counterparty credit risk, practitioners usually also consider an institution's own default risk when pricing bilateral counterparty credit risk. The adjusted CVA (ACVA) considers an institution's own default risk in CVA such that

$$\text{ACVA}(t, T) = \sum_{n=1}^{N} E[V(t, t_n)^+ p(t_{n-1}, t_n)] S_I(t_{n-1}, t_n)$$

where $S_I(t_{n-1}, t_n)$ is the institution's survival probability. In general, the incorporation of the institution's survival rate can be seen as naturally hedging CVA profit-and-loss volatility in case of a general increase in default rates. This is because the institution's survival probability, $S_I(t_{n-1}, t_n)$, may be lower at the exact time when counterparty default rates, $p(t_{n-1}, t_n)$, are high. Although we have that $\text{ACVA}(t, T) \leq \text{CVA}(t, T)$, the natural risk mitigating effect relies on a scenario with common behavior in credit quality.

The so-called bilateral CVA (BCVA) is seen as a fair price agreement for the net counterparty credit risk between two parties,

$$\text{BCVA}(t, T) = \text{ACVA}(t, T) - \sum_{n=1}^{N} E[-V(t, t_n)^- p_I(t_{n-1}, t_n)] S(t_{n-1}, t_n) \qquad (5.5)$$

where $V(t, t_n)^- = \min(V(t, t_n), 0)$ is the negative exposure, that is, the counterparty view on the exposure, $p_I(t_{n-1}, t_n)$ is the institution's incremental default probability, and $S(t_{n-1}, t_n)$ is the counterparty survival function. The second component in equation (5.5) is referred to as debt value adjustment (DVA) and captures the counterparty view on ACVA. We therefore have that

$$\text{BCVA}(t, T) = \text{ACVA}(t, T) - \text{DVA}(t, T).$$

This introduces a second potential hedge component to CVA. In case of a general market default rate increase the institution default probability, $p_I(t_{n-1}, t_n)$, is high when the counterparty survival probability, $S((t_{n-1}, t_n))$, is low.

The use of DVA in practice has been severely criticized. One of the main concerns is that to monetize DVA an institution must practically default. See Gregory (2009) for an extensive discussion. On the other hand, DVA is needed for fair bilateral pricing. That is, it is the net fair price adjustment that counterparties can potentially agree on as it captures the net CVA.

After the recent credit crisis, with the failure or near-failure of large institutions counterparty credit risk is now considered two-way. Hence both sides of the derivative transaction demand to be compensated for taking on the other party's counterparty credit risk, which creates a need for BCVA. Even accountancy rules permit use of DVA (e.g., US GAAP) where some adjustment for own default is required. In Europe, IAS 39 is compatible with a DVA term but not a requirement. While BCVA is a fair net price adjustment to the risk-free value CVA is still to be considered the institution's measure of counterparty credit risk that needs to be hedged.

Example of Swap CVA Continued We now continue our swap example in Table 5.1 to also compute ACVA and BCVA. Table 5.3 displays the CVA, ACVA, and BCVA under different assumptions for the counterparty and institution's survival probability (CDS premia) using the expected exposure in Table 5.1 for both counterparties (i.e., we assume symmetry in expected exposure, $E[V(t, t_n)^+]$, and expected negative exposure, $E[-V(t, t_n)^-]$). The different CDS premia assumed for the counterparty and institution are 300, 500, 800, and 1,000 basis

TABLE 5.3 Sample CVA, ACVA, and BCVA for a Swap

Counterparty CDS (bps)	Institution CDS (bps)	CVA	ACVA	BCVA
500	500	4,625.82	3,823.73	0
300	500	2,987.02	2,459.34	−1,662.14
100	500	1,073.28	880.17	−3,569.27
800	500	6,649.09	5,528.62	2,101.66
1000	500	7,753.59	6,472.09	3,280.34
500	300	4,625.82	4,121.48	1,662.14
500	100	4,625.82	4,449.44	3,569.27
500	800	4,625.82	3,426.96	−2,101.66
500	1000	4,625.82	3,191.75	−3,280.34

points. As before we assume there is only one traded CDS instrument at the 5-year maturity and that the hazard rate is constant over time. Of course, in case of symmetric expected exposures, the BCVA when the institution and counterparty have the same credit default swap premia is null. This is because the ACVA of both the institution and the counterparty are equal. However, clearly, both parties are taking counterparty credit risk.

Table 5.3 also displays CVA, ACVA, and BCVA when there is asymmetry in the credit default swap premia between the counterparty and the institution. In the asymmetric cases the better credit quality counterparty is generally requiring the counterparty to cover for the asymmetry as measured through BCVA. Realistically, the better credit quality counterparty can ask the other counterparty to cover for this asymmetry in a negotiation of price. It is important to realize that even after a net BCVA transfer, typically the majority of the CVA component still remains. For example, in Table 5.3 when the counterparty credit default swap premia is 800 basis points and the institution credit default swap premia is 500 basis points, the swap CVA is 6,649.09 units of currency. This is while the fair net transfer (BCVA) is 2,101.66 units of currency. Hence, for the institution, a residual counterparty credit risk price (CVA) of 4,547.43 still remains. In case the institution is of lower credit quality than the counterparty it may end up as a net payer of BCVA. For example, from Table 5.3, if counterparty credit default swap premia is 500 basis points and the institution credit default swap premia is 1,000 basis points, then the institution is a net payer of 3,280.34 units of currency. Still, the institution faces a counterparty credit risk price (CVA) of 4,625.82 units of currency.

Using Table 5.3 we can also analyze the natural hedge effects of ACVA and BCVA. By construction we have of course that

$$BCVA \leq ACVA \leq CVA.$$

Focusing on ACVA initially, we can investigate the relative effect of a 100 bps upward shift of both the counterparty and institution credit default swap premias when they both have initially 500 bps credit default swap premias. In this case we obtain the ACVA as 4,275.39 units of currency. The corresponding CVA is now 5,354.04 units of currency. The percentage change in CVA is hence approximately 15.7% (see Table 5.3 for the base CVA and ACVA when both the counterparty and institution credit default swap premias are 500 basis points). For ACVA the corresponding change is 11.8%. Hence, the simultaneous increase in institution and counterparty credit default swap premias is hedged using ACVA. However, keeping the institution's credit default swap premia constant at 500 basis points when the counterparty credit default swap premia increases by 100 basis points we obtain ACVA as 4,434.40 units of currency, giving a 15.9% change in ACVA. Hence, the hedging effect of ACVA derives from common behavior of the counterparty and institution's credit default swap premias as we remarked above.

Focusing on BCVA it introduces a second hedge component in the DVA term due to the institution's default probability and the counterparty survival probability. Consider the case when initially the counterparty credit default swap premia is 500 bps and the institution's is 300 basis points. From Table 5.3 we obtain the BCVA as 1,662.14 units of currency. With a 100-basis-points upward shift of both the counterparty and institution's credit default swap premia we now obtain the BCVA as 1,550.53 units of currency. This is hence a reduction in BCVA of approximately 7%. On the other hand, with a 100 basis points downward shift we obtain BCVA as 1,784.61 units of currency which is an increase of approximately 7%. Compared to the corresponding percentage shifts of ACVA of 11.6% and −14% respectively the BCVA changes are smaller and hence further hedge changes in credit quality.

It is noticeable here that the direction of change is different with BCVA and ACVA. To understand this note that we can write BCVA as the ACVA from the institution point of view minus the ACVA from the counterparty point of view (i.e., DVA). The ACVA from the institution perspective goes from 4,121.48 to 4,601.11 with a 100-basis-point increase in credit default swap premias. The corresponding ACVA from the counterparty view goes from 2,459.34 to 3,050.58. Hence, the ACVA from the counterparty view increases relatively more than the increase in the ACVA from the institution's point of view. This is of course due to the relatively larger actual percentage increase in credit risk for the institution. In the case of the ACVA for the institution the survival hedge from the decrease in the survival probability of the institution is less than perfect and hence ACVA still increases. For the counterparty ACVA its survival hedge is much less (in percent change in credit quality) and hence the institution default (counterparty view on CVA) effect is much higher.

Pricing CVA in Practice   If one considers CVA the fair price of counterparty credit risk, then naturally traders' profit and loss should take into account the CVA to avoid selective trading with lower quality counterparties. However, in reality traders may find a challenge in actually pricing CVA into trades with counterparties that also want to be compensated for their counterparty credit risk. Trades between banks and with approximate symmetric positive and negative exposure profiles may yield a BCVA close to zero.[6] Still, the trader needs to pay the CVA. If this cost cannot be passed on to the counterparty, then it must come from the existing premiums, reducing profitability. In addition, there are other risk charges that need to be passed on to the traders' profit and loss. This includes capital costs and, potentially, funding costs. This raises the question of how CVA can be reduced significantly for trades—that is, reduce the counterparty credit risk. There are several possibilities including:

- One can hedge CVA. However, the hedging of CVA is not an easy task and also induces hedge costs that replace the CVA costs. The complexity inherent in hedging CVA is also the main reason for banks to centralize CVA hedging in a CVA desk.

---

[6]The profitability situation is worst for lower credit quality institution as the BCVA when trading with good quality counterparties is generally negative. That is, the institution has to make net payments. This is in addition to the CVA charge.

- One can reduce counterparty exposure significantly by entering into collateral agreements that require frequent counterparty posting of collateral by the counterparty, for example, in cash currency of the trade. However, this comes at the cost of operationalizing collateral management with monitoring of counterparty exposures, making collateral calls, and so on. However, even with perfect collateralization of the exposure there is still residual risk of exposure increases in the grace period between last collateral call and the ultimate counterparty default event. In addition, if the collateral agreement is a two-way agreement such that the institution also has to post, then the institution faces a funding liquidity risk—potentially having to fund large amounts of collateral when negative exposure increases significantly.
- One can move the trade through a central clearing counterparty. However, this can require frequent posting requirements analogous to collateralized trades. In addition, there may be additional responsibilities such as responsibility to provide general liquidity support to the central clearing entity if needed, introducing potentially even more funding liquidity risk than in bilateral collateralized trades.

Trades with different types of counterparties may also decide which of the above approaches are possible for the institution. For example, when the counterparty is a corporate treasury rather than another bank, then it is unlikely they will be able to support operationally collateral agreements with frequent margining. It is also unlikely that the corporate treasury will have the possibility to move the trade through a central clearing counterparty directly. Hence, in this case the institution can choose to hedge CVA. When the counterparty is another bank it is likely that the primary CVA reduction is based on netting and collateralization with frequent margining. The decision for the institution to move certain (supported) trades to a central clearing counterparty versus bilateral with collateralization can be quite complex. It is a function of both any current capital requirement reliefs as well as taking into account uncertainty in potential future liquidity support.

Assessment of Counterparty Default Probability

The counterparty default probability together with the exposure are the two central components of CVA in equation (5.2).[7] In practice the market implied default probability can be derived from:

1. Market quoted credit default swap premiums for the counterparty
2. Market quoted bond spreads for the counterparty

We recall from the portfolio credit risk chapter that there is a theoretical relationship between credit default swap premium and bond spreads. Specifically, a credit-risky bond with credit spread ξ should have a credit default swap premium approximately ξ as well. This is because the fully hedged portfolio of the credit-risky bond and the credit default swap should earn the risk-free rate.

If no counterparty-specific information on market implied default probability is available, one has to resort to approximations. This is usually referred to as a mapping procedure

---

[7]However, recall that in equation (5.2) we have suppressed the notation for discounting and have also assumed a zero recovery rate.

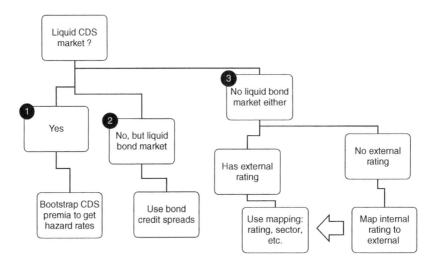

FIGURE 5.1 Obtaining Default Probabilities of Counterparties

where the counterparty characteristics such as external rating and specific industry are used to map the counterparty to similar counterparties with market implied default probabilities available. If no external rating is available, one can map an internal rating assignment to an approximately equivalent external rating. Figure 5.1 illustrates the typical process to obtain counterparty default probabilities.

Using market quoted credit default swap premias, at each term, the premia is converted to hazard rates, h, by bootstrapping of the credit default swap price. That is, by the inversion of hazard rates from quoted credit default swap premia. Such an inversion uses numerical procedures on the credit default swap pricing function (see equation (4.75)). We refer the reader to O'Kane (2008, ch. 7) and Castillaci (2008) on the numerical bootstrapping of credit default swap premiums.

Assuming we have assigned a time grid of $n = 1, \ldots, N$ discrete time points in equation (5.2) we can estimate the incremental default probability, $p(t_{n-1}, t_n)$, using piecewise linear interpolation of the bootstrapped hazard rate. Specifically, to estimate the incremental default probability, $p(t_n, t_{n+1})$, we use

$$p(t_n, t_{n+1}) = S(t_0, t_n) - S(t_0, t_{n+1})$$

$$= \exp\left(-\sum_{i=1}^{n} h\left(t_i\right) d(t_i, t_{i-1})\right) - \exp\left(-\sum_{i=1}^{n+1} h\left(t_i\right) d(t_i, t_{i-1})\right). \quad (5.6)$$

Here $S(t_0, t_n)$ is the survival function up to t_n, $h(t_i)$ is the hazard rate at t_i and $d(t_i, t_{i-1})$ is the daycount between times (t_i, t_{i-1}).

Example Calculation of Incremental Default Probabilities As a concrete numerical example of how incremental default probabilities are calculated assume the market implied hazard rate, h, is available at maturity points of 0.5 years, 1 year, 3 years, and 5 years and denoted $h_{0.5}$, h_1, h_3, and h_5, respectively. That is, we assume that traded CDS instruments on the counterparty exist at these maturity points. We also assume that a CVA calculation grid of

$n = 1, \ldots, 5$ yearly time points is used up to an assumed trade maturity point of 5 years. Using the hazard rates, for the first year we obtain

$$S(t_0, t_1) = \exp(-h_{1/2} \times d(t_0, t_{1/2}) - h_1 \times d(t_{1/2}, t_1))$$
$$p(t_0, t_1) = 1 - S(t_0, t_1)$$

such that we use the market implied hazard rate at 0.5 years and 1 year. This is because we have a yearly time grid for CVA default probabilities and a more granular observation of hazard rates. For the second year,

$$S(t_0, t_2) = S(t_0, t_1) \exp(-h_2 \times d(t_1, t_2))$$
$$p(t_1, t_2) = S(t_0, t_1) - S(t_0, t_2)$$

since we use right endpoint interpolation of the hazard rate to find the relevant hazard rate. Similarly, for year 3,

$$S(t_0, t_3) = S(t_0, t_2) \exp(-h_3 \times d(t_2, t_3))$$
$$p(t_2, t_3) = S(t_0, t_2) - S(t_0, t_3).$$

Finally, for years 4 and 5 we obtain, respectively,

$$S(t_0, t_4) = S(t_0, t_3) \exp(-h_4 \times d(t_3, t_4))$$
$$p(t_3, t_4) = S(t_0, t_3) - S(t_0, t_4)$$

and

$$S(t_0, t_5) = S(t_0, t_4) \exp(-h_5 \times d(t_4, t_5))$$
$$p(t_4, t_5) = S(t_0, t_4) - S(t_0, t_5).$$

Hence, again we use right endpoint interpolation of the hazard rate.

Market Default Rates or Historical Default Rates? It is natural to ask why the counterparty default probability necessarily should be extracted from market and not be a simple historical default probability. The simple answer is that regulators (and today most large banks) view CVA as a market price rather than a loss reserve. Hence, the relevant measure of default risk is market based. As we discussed in the context of portfolio credit risk and specifically market pricing of corporate bonds, in practice quoted bond credit spreads (and credit default swap premiums) are due to not only default risk but also other components such as liquidity risk. As one example study we quoted Manning (2004), who finds that only 8%–11% of the variability in default rates for the top investment grades can explain the variability in credit spreads. In addition market implied default risk can be quite volatile with significant jumps in quotes. Hence, using market implied default rates is a concern for institutions that do not want to take a mark-to-market approach to CVA as it essentially forces them to institute CVA hedging to reduce the market volatility. On the other hand, this is the objective of regulators with Basel III, that is, going forward, to create strong incentives for banks to mitigate the profit-and-loss volatility in counterparty default risk, avoiding the large market losses observed during the 2007 crisis. However, in times of stress many banks may face the need to hedge or re-hedge at exactly the same time potentially driving hedge costs significantly upward. Another concern with hedging CVA profit-and-loss volatility is that in practice, when the counterparty is a smaller institution or corporate, there is typically no direct hedge market available and the bank has to resort to proxy hedges such as iTraxx and CDX indices. Such proxy hedges are only given partial credit by regulators.

Exposure Simulation Framework for CVA

In practice, equation (5.2) is usually too complex to evaluate analytically. Exceptions include Sorensen and Bollier (1994), who express plain interest rate swap CVA analytically in terms of swaptions. However, analytical formulas typically rely on simple exposures with no further complications such as netting, wrong-way risk, and collateral while in practice these components are essential to understanding CVA.

   Looking at equation (5.2), an obvious method to calculate CVA is to simulate the possible mark-to-market values of the contract at time points, $\{t_n\}_{n=1}^N$, and then apply an exposure calculation to obtain expected exposure, $\{EE(t_n)\}_{n=1}^N$. Finally, we would multiply expected exposure by the counterparty default probability to obtain CVA. This approach also falls naturally into a bank's existing exposure system for Basel II counterparty exposure capital calculations as the work of calculating exposures has already been done in this context. Using this exposure simulation framework for CVA, the step-by-step process followed is:

1. Calibrate and simulate $d = 1, \ldots, D$ market scenarios, from relevant interest rate, foreign exchange models, and so on, at time points, $\{t_n\}_{n=1}^N$.
2. Price the trade under the $d = 1, \ldots, D$ market scenarios, taking into account the aging of the contract. This gives a pricing array for a contract as $\{v_{d,n}\}_{n=1,d=1}^{N,D}$.
3. Calculate the expected exposure, $EE(t_n)$, at each $\{t_n\}_{n=1}^N$ as the empirical average of $\{\max[v_{d,n}, 0]\}_{d=1}^D$ from the simulation.
4. Obtain the CVA by aggregating expected exposure, $EE(t_n)$, and the default probability, $p(t_{n-1}, t_n)$, over time as in equation (5.2),

$$CVA(t, T) = \sum_{n=1}^N EE(t_n)\, p(t_{n-1}, t_n).$$

   Note that in this framework computations are done along all simulated paths going forward in time. A number of Monte Carlo scenarios are generated for market risk factors that impact the trade valuation at discrete time steps. The contract is valued at every time step along each simulated path, from which the exposure profile is subsequently calculated. See also Canabarro and Duffie (2003) and Pykthin and Zhu (2007) on this exposure simulation framework for CVA. We also note here that when choosing the number of market scenarios $d = 1, \ldots, D$ for CVA in the above process it is useful to recall that we are actually estimating an expectation and not a tail risk. Therefore, simulation samples in the order of 5,000–10,000 are reasonable in practice for most deals.

DVA and Bilateral CVA   We can also enhance the above process slightly to also calculate DVA. Specifically, in step 3 we then also need to calculate the negative expected exposure, $EE^-(t_n)$, at each $\{t_n\}_{n=1}^N$ as the empirical average of $\{\min[v_{d,n}, 0]\}_{d=1}^D$. Subsequently, in step 4, we can now also obtain the DVA by aggregating the negative expected exposure, $EE^-(t_n)$, and the institution default probability, $p_I(t_{n-1}, t_n)$, and weighting by the counterparty survival probability, $S(t_{n-1}, t_n)$, over time. To obtain the bilateral CVA as ACVA minus DVA we of course also have to weight the CVA in step 4 above with the institution survival probability, $S_I(t_{n-1}, t_n)$.

Market Scenarios and Market Models   While the above process is simple in principle there are a few points worth noting. First, we established above that the default probabilities used, $p(t_{n-1}, t_n)$ and $p_I(t_{n-1}, t_n)$, should be market based. Does the same reasoning apply to the market scenarios? Again, this depends on the hedging view. For an interest rate swap the exposure depends on both the current term structure of interest rates and the volatility. Taking a market view it therefore seems natural to fit the volatility component of market models of interest rates to traded instruments such as swaptions. In practice the Hull-White model is often used, where

$$dr(t) = a_r[\delta(t) - a_r r(t)]dt + \sigma_r dW_r(t). \tag{5.7}$$

Here $W_r(t)$ is the Wiener process, the parameter a_r characterizes the mean reversion rate, σ_r is the instantaneous volatility of the short-rate model, and $\delta(t)$ is calibrated to the current term structure of interest rates. Specifically,

$$\delta(t) = f'(t) + a_r f(t) + \frac{\sigma_r^2}{2a_r}(1 - \exp(-2a_r t)) \tag{5.8}$$

with $f(t)$ the (instantaneous) forward curve and $f'(t)$ its derivative. Bond prices are analytic in the Hull-White model. See Hull (2006, ch. 28). Hence, from the short-rate, $r(t)$, in equation (5.7) we can derive the full term structure of interest rates. Specifically, we have the Hull-White zero-coupon bond price, $P(0, t, T)$, as

$$P(0, t, T) = A(0, t, T)\exp(-B(0, t, T)r(t))$$

with

$$B(0, t, T) = \frac{1 - \exp(-a_r(T - t))}{a_r}$$

$$A(0, t, T) = \frac{-[B(0, t, T)]^2 \sigma_r^2 \theta}{4a_r} - F(0, t, T)d(t, T) + B(t, T)f(t)$$

where $\theta = 1 - \exp(-2a_r d(0, t))$, $d(\cdot)$ is the daycount convention, and $F(0, t, T)$ is the implied forward rate from the spot zero curve. The complete zero-coupon rate term-structure, $r(0, t, T)$, for zero rate maturity T at time t can now be obtained from the simulated short-rate, $r(t)$, at t as

$$r(0, t, T) = \frac{B(0, t, T)r(t) - A(0, t, T)}{T - t}. \tag{5.9}$$

The simulation of the Hull-White short-rate from equation (5.7) requires the calculation of $\delta(t)$ from the instantaneous forward curve, $f(t)$, and its derivative, $f'(t)$, as in equation (5.8). It also requires parameters for the mean reversion rate, a_r, and the volatility, σ_r. When the model parameters are calibrated to market prices the focus is on finding parameters a_r, σ_r^2 that minimize the squared or absolute differences between observed market prices and Hull-White model prices. For example, European swaptions and caps may be used in the calibration. For both European swaptions and caps the market price is quoted using the analytical Black (1976) model. However, both caps and European swaption prices are analytical with the Hull-White model as well.[8]

For an interest rate swap contract the choice of calibrating instruments is naturally European swaptions. This is because of the Sorensen and Bollier (1994) swap CVA formula in equation (5.4), which expresses swap CVA as a function of $\{t_n\}_{n=1}^{N}$ option maturity reverse swap position European swaptions on the underlying swap with maturity $t_N = T$.

Example Hull-White Calibration and Simulation We calibrate the Hull-White model volatility, σ_r, using European receiver swaption market quotes for the purpose of calculating CVA for a 10-year maturity payer swap. In the calibration we hold fixed a_r at 0.03 and obtain a global best fit Hull-White volatility, σ_r. Table 5.4 displays the market available receiver swaptions option maturity, swap maturity, and market quotes of volatility and the market Black model price based on the market volatility quote. Clearly, to be consistent with the Sorensen and Bollier (1994) swap CVA, and the fact that we assume that the Hull-White model volatility, σ_r, is fixed over time, we should choose receiver swaptions where the sum of option maturity and swap maturity is 10 years. In our example there are three liquid swaption quotes in the market that we use to calibrate a global best fit volatility. They are the receiver swaptions with option maturity 3, 4, 5 years and corresponding swap maturity 7, 6, 5 years. The market quotes for the three European receiver swaptions are at the money with the forward swap rate as the strike. The swaptions strike rate is also displayed in Table 5.4 and the underlying swaps for the swaptions are assumed to have semiannual payments and principal unity.

To obtain the best fit Hull-White volatility, σ_r, we minimize the squared difference between the Black market price and the Hull-White price for our $i = 1, 2, 3$ market quotes. That is, we solve numerically for

$$\min_{\sigma_r} \sum_{i=1}^{3} [V^B - V^{HW}(\sigma_r)]^2$$

where V^B is the Black market value in Table 5.4 and $V^{HW}(\sigma_r)$ is the Hull-White market price as a function of the Hull-White volatility. Through the numerical solve we obtain a calibrated Hull-White volatility of $\sigma_r \approx 0.00989$.

Table 5.4 displays the corresponding best replicating Hull-White price using the solved volatility. Clearly, with a best global fit Hull-White volatility, σ_r, to the market prices

TABLE 5.4 Black Model Market Quotes for European Receiver Swaption and Hull-White Prices

Option maturity	Swap maturity	Market volatility	Market Black price	Strike	Hull-White price
5 years	5 years	0.332995	0.03557	0.027328	0.03467
4 years	6 years	0.34735	0.03745	0.025307	0.03687
3 years	7 years	0.36545	0.03681	0.023066	0.03820

---

[8]Again, see Hull (2006, ch. 18) and also Jamshidian (1989) on the analytic pricing of coupon bonds and European swaptions using the Hull–White model.

none of the replicating Hull-White prices match the market contracts exactly. A better contract-by-contract fit can of course be obtained if σ_r is allowed to be time dependent. We refer to Gurrieri, Nakabayashi, and Wong (2009) for more examples on calibrating the Hull-White model to market prices.

Once we have obtained the Hull-White model parameters a_r, σ_r^2 we can simulate the short-rate model using equation (5.7). The simulation of the short-rate requires that we also fit $\delta(t)$ in equation (5.8) to the current term-structure. This fit is based on the current zero curve. Table 5.5 and Figure 5.2 display the current market zero curve quotes and the instantaneous forward curve, $f(t)$, built from the zero quotes. The zero curve in Table 5.5 was also the zero curve we used for pricing swaptions in the Black model and the Hull-White model.

For illustration Figure 5.3 displays 10 sample simulation paths for our calibrated Hull-White model when we use a current short-rate quote of 0.156% as the initial short-rate. Each scenario is simulated over 10 years with a daily simulation for each of the assumed 260 business days in a year—giving 2,600 business days simulation time points for the 10-year horizon. The simulation uses the zero curve quotes in Table 5.5 to derive the $\delta(t)$ in equation (5.8). From Figure 5.3 we immediately note a drawback of the Hull-White model in that it does not restrict interest rates to nonnegative. This is especially apparent in

TABLE 5.5 Market Zero Rate and Instantaneous Forward Rate Term Structure

Curve tenor	Zero rate	Instantaneous forward rate
1 month	0.2080%	0.2392%
2 months	0.2638%	0.3743%
3 months	0.3186%	0.4014%
4 months	0.3211%	0.3313%
5 months	0.3237%	0.3364%
6 months	0.3262%	0.3415%
7 months	0.3288%	0.3466%
8 months	0.3313%	0.3517%
9 months	0.3339%	0.3568%
10 months	0.3364%	0.3619%
11 months	0.3390%	0.3686%
1 year	0.3418%	0.3744%
2 years	0.3730%	0.4985%
3 years	0.4670%	0.8292%
4 years	0.6144%	1.2977%
5 years	0.8085%	1.8377%
6 years	1.0260%	2.3232%
7 years	1.2410%	2.6533%
8 years	1.4295%	2.9060%
9 years	1.6101%	3.1384%
10 years	1.7691%	3.2932%
15 years	2.3356%	3.3964%
20 years	2.5709%	3.2700%
25 years	2.6853%	3.1585%
30 years	2.7602%	2.9961%
40 years	2.7676%	2.6672%
50 years	2.7100%	2.5660%

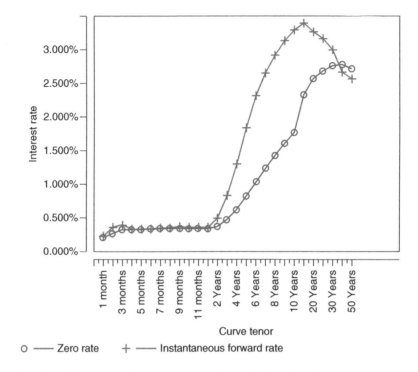

FIGURE 5.2 Market Zero Rate and Instantaneous Forward Rate Term Structure

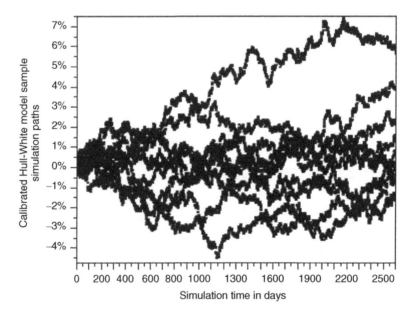

FIGURE 5.3 Sample Simulation Paths for the Calibrated Hull-White Model

a current low interest rate environment, as is the case for our market quotes. Once we have obtained the short-rate simulation paths from the Hull-White model we can also generate the complete term structure of future zero rates using equation (5.9). This future zero rate term structure is the input to the swap pricing with a subsequent swap exposure calculation.

Calculating Swap Exposure Profiles and CVA   We now consider a few stylized examples of interest rate and cross-currency swap exposure and CVA to gain intuition for the exposure profiles and the counterparty pricing metrics. In our example we will consider simple stylized equilibrium models and parameters that can capture the core aspects of the risk factors affecting the exposure and pricing metrics.

Market Models   Starting with the models for interest rates we assume that the current term structure of interest rates is flat at 5%. We model the future term structure at term points 1, 3, and 6 months as well as at 1, 3, 5, and 10 years. We use a Cox, Ingersoll, and Ross model (Cox, Ingersoll, and Ross, 1985) for each node. Specifically, we model the interest rate, $r(t)$, at term node m, denoted $r_m(t)$, as

$$dr_m(t) = a_r[b_r - r_m(t)]dt + \sigma_r \sqrt{r_m(t)}dW_m(t) \qquad (5.10)$$

where $W_m(t)$ is the Wiener process for term node m. Here the parameter b_r is the mean reversion level around which all future trajectories will evolve in the long run. The parameter a_r characterizes the speed at which trajectories will regroup around the mean reversion rate b_r over time, and σ_r is the instantaneous volatility of the short-rate model. The parameters for each term node m are set as

$$b_r = 0.05$$
$$a_r = 0.1$$
$$\sigma_r = 0.06.$$

Since our current term structure is flat at 5% each term node mean reversion level corresponds to the implied forward rate and hence the model future rates are by design consistent with the implied forward rate curve. An important feature of the Cox, Ingersoll, and Ross model is that interest rates are always nonnegative.

Figure 5.4 displays the paths from 1,000 sample simulated trajectories for the 1-year interest rate term node on a monthly time grid using 260 business days per year and 10 years into the future (i.e., 2,600 business days). Since the initial interest rate is set at 5%, as is the implied forward rate(s), the simulated interest rate trajectories are pulled back to the 5% level for b_r at the mean reversion speed, a_r. When interest rate models in different currencies are needed to price cross-currency swaps the interest rates in both currencies follow the same model above and have the same current term-structure of interest rates.

To value and calculate exposure and CVA for cross-currency swaps we also need a model for the forward foreign exchange rate term structure. For simplicity we assume that there is a singe forward foreign exchange rate. The simulation of the forward foreign exchange rate also uses a Cox, Ingersoll, and Ross model. Specifically, we have that

$$df(t) = a_f[b_f - f(t)]dt + \sigma_f \sqrt{f(t)}dV(t)$$

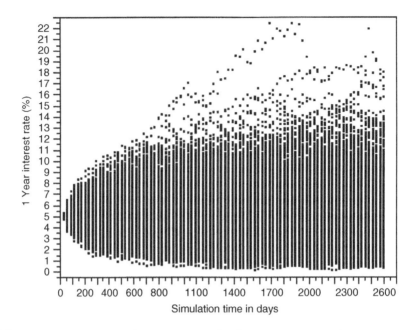

FIGURE 5.4 10,000 Simulated Market Trajectories for the 1-Year Term Node Interest Rate on Days $1, \ldots, 2600$

where $V(t)$ is a Wiener process, and $f(t)$ is the forward foreign exchange rate and the model parameters are set such that

$$b_f = 9$$
$$a_f = 0.001$$
$$\sigma_f = 0.2.$$

The long-term forward exchange rate is set to 9, which we also assume is the current market exchange rate. Note that the rate of mean reversion, a_f, and volatility, σ_f, are quite different from the interest rate model. In particular, the assumed rate of mean reversion is much lower and the volatility much higher compared to the interest rate model. While mean reversion in exchange rates is supported by the purchasing power parity, empirical evidence of mean reversion is a debated question. See, for example, Cheung and Lai (1994, 2000) and Sweeney (2000). Hence, in our model for forward foreign exchange rates, while we include mean reversion, the degree of mean reversion is low and volatility of the forward foreign exchange rate is significantly higher than the volatility of interest rates.

Figure 5.5 displays the paths from 1,000 sample simulated trajectories for the forward foreign exchange rate on a monthly time grid using 260 business days per year and 10 years into the future. Compared to the simulation of the 1-year interest rate in Figure 5.4, the simulation paths resemble more a standard geometric Brownian motion process due to the low degree of mean reversion.

Swap Exposure Profiles Using the interest rate and foreign exchange simulation models we can calculate the exposure profiles for plain swaps as well as cross-currency swaps. In the

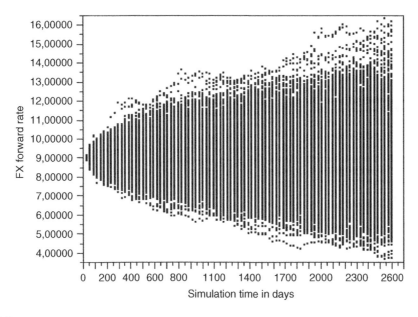

FIGURE 5.5 10,000 Simulated Market Trajectories for the FX Forward Rate on Days $1, \ldots, 2600$

example exposure profiles we assume a zero correlation *between* interest rates and the forward foreign exchange rate models while *within* interest rates there is a 60% correlation.

Figure 5.6 displays expected exposure (EE), the running mean of expected positive exposures (EPE), and the peak exposure (PE) profile for a 10-year at-the-money (ATM) fixed rate payer swap (i.e., the fixed rate swap leg is equal to the implied forward rate of 5%).[9] The deal notional is 1,000,000 units of currency and the confidence level used for peak exposures is 99%. The exposure profiles have been calculated using 10,000 simulations and a monthly time grid up to maturity to capture the assumed monthly payment flows in the swap. The number of business days in a year is assumed to be 260. Hence, 10 years is 2,600 business days.

The swap exposure profile in Figure 5.6 displays the well-known hump-shaped profile due to the time trade-off between increasing interest rate risk and decreasing number of swap payments left. The corresponding in-the-money (ITM) payer swap exposure profiles (i.e., fixed rate less than implied forward rate) have current exposure greater than zero and hence future exposure profiles would be tilted downwards. Similarly, out-of-the-money (OTM) payer swaps (i.e., fixed rate greater than implied forward rate) have negative current mark to market, and hence future exposure profiles would be tilted upwards. Figure 5.7 illustrates the ITM case for the payer swap when the fixed rate is set to 4.5%, that is, 50 basis points less than the current and implied forward rate at 5%. In Figure 5.8 we also display the corresponding OTM case when the fixed rate is set at 5.5%.

In payer swaps counterparty exposure arises when the receiving floating rate is higher than the fixed rate paid such that the counterparty has to pay net positive flows. The exposure

---

[9]The expected *positive* exposure is defined as the single expected exposure value that is obtained by averaging over the full expected exposure profile. In our example exposure profiles we present the expected *positive* exposure as the running mean on the expected exposure. This means that the single expected *positive* exposure value is the last point.

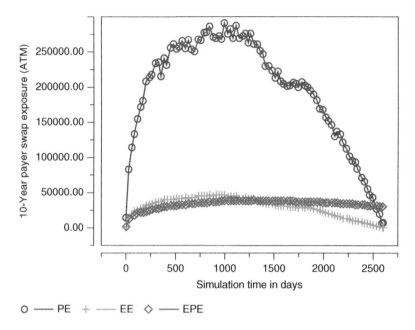

FIGURE 5.6 Expected Exposure, the Running Mean of Expected Positive Exposures, and the Peak Exposure Profile for a 10-Year at-the-Money Payer Swap

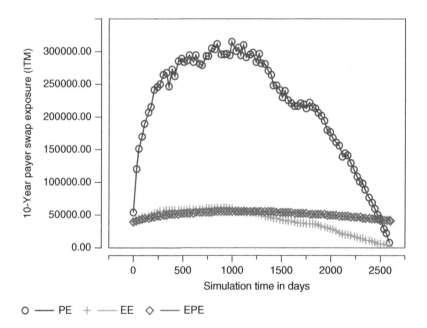

FIGURE 5.7 Expected Exposure, the Running Mean of Expected Positive Exposures, and the Peak Exposure Profile for a 10-Year In-the-Money Payer Swap

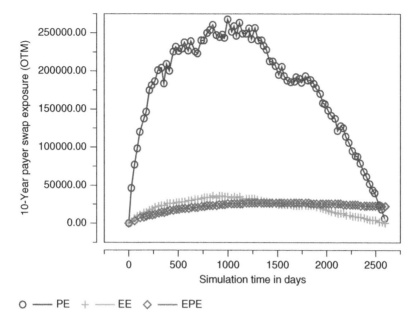

FIGURE 5.8 Expected Exposure, the Running Mean of Expected Positive Exposures, and the Peak Exposure Profile for a 10-Year Out-of-the-Money Payer Swap

can be very high as the receiving floating rate can be very high in the future. See Figure 5.4. For receiver swaps exposure arises when the floating rate paid is lower than the fixed rate. However, if interest rates are assumed bounded below by zero, then the exposure in the receiver swap is bounded. In our exposure analysis of the swaps we use a Cox-Ingersoll-Ross model for the interest rates that ensures that the rate is always nonnegative. Hence, in this case worst-case or peak exposure profiles for payer and receiver swaps are not symmetric and the counterparty that has the receiver swap position faces less worst-case counterparty exposure. This is illustrated in Figure 5.9, which displays the EE, EPE, and PE profiles for an ATM receiver swap. Compared to Figure 5.6 the PE profile is significantly lower. We emphasize again that this asymmetry of peak exposure profiles for payer and receiver swaps depends on the model chosen. Using a Hull-White model interest rates are not bounded below by zero and can become negative as in Figure 5.3. Hence, with the Hull-White model the peak exposure profiles of the payer and receiver swaps are very similar. While peak exposure profiles are higher for the payer swap the EE profiles are similar for payer and receiver swaps. This is illustrated in Figure 5.10. In Figure 5.10 the EE profile for the receiver swap is actually a bit above the EE profile for the payer swap. Hence, while the risk of the payer swap exposure is higher the counterparty price (which is based on EE) may be higher for the receiver swap.

In contrast to the hump-shaped profile for plain swaps, cross-currency swap exposure is strictly increasing in time. This is due to the large exchange of notional at maturity, which drives the majority of risk in cross-currency swaps. Figure 5.11 displays EE, the running mean of expected positive exposures, EPE, and the peak exposure, PE, profile for a 10-year ATM cross-currency payer swap. As for the plain swaps the notional is 1,000,000 units of currency. Payer cross-currency swaps that are ITM for the final foreign exchange (i.e., stipulated exchange rate in contract is less than the current and expected future foreign exchange rate)

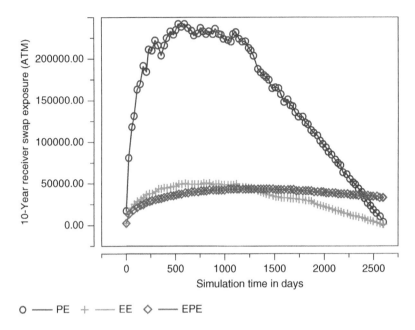

FIGURE 5.9 Expected Exposure, the Running Mean of Expected Positive Exposures, and the Peak Exposure Profile for a 10-Year at-the-Money Receiver Swap

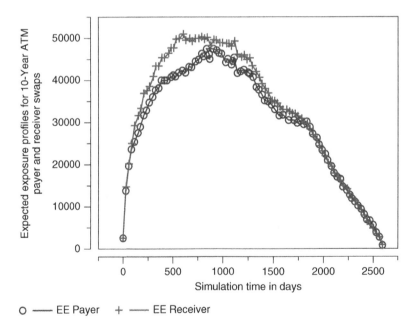

FIGURE 5.10 Comparison of Expected Exposure for 10-Year at-the-Money Receiver and Payer Swaps

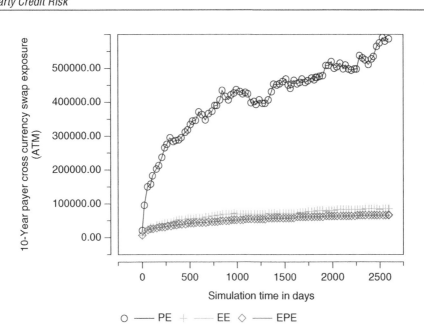

FIGURE 5.11 Expected Exposure, the Running Mean of Expected Positive Exposures, and the Peak Exposure Profile for a 10-Year at-the-Money Cross Currency Payer Swap

display a parallel shift upwards of the exposure profile. Similarly, OTM payer cross-currency swaps on the final foreign exchange display a parallel shift downward.

The exposure profiles for the plain and cross-currency swaps are smooth over time due to the fact that both payment legs pay at the same frequency (recall that monthly payments are assumed). However, if the payment frequencies of the legs are unequal, the swap exposure profiles display the well-known rolloff risk. Figure 5.12 displays EE, the running mean of expected positive exposures, EPE, and the 99% confidence level PE profile for a 10-year ATM payer swap when the payment leg frequency is quarterly and the receiving leg frequency is yearly. Clearly, this payer swap is more risky since the receiving leg exposure is built up over a longer time before the actual payment is received. The reverse case is illustrated in Figure 5.13 and is of course less risky. For deals with rolloff risk it is important that the simulation time points are set such that the exposure jumps due to rolloff risk are captured. That is, one should choose the CVA time grid, $\{t_n\}_{n=1}^N$, so that we capture major cash flows that affect the exposure profile materially.

While we have focused on exposure profiles for swaps and cross-currency swaps in our examples the well-known hump-shaped exposure profile for swaps and the increasing exposure profile for cross-currency swaps is typical for other products as well. For example, foreign exchange forwards and plain foreign exchange swaps display the increasing exposure profile of cross-currency swaps due to the final currency exchange. We refer to Cesari et al. (2009, ch. 9–11) and Gregory (2010, ch. 4) for further examples of derivative exposure profiles.

Swap CVA Having analyzed the swap exposure profiles for a few stylized swap examples we continue with pricing the counterparty risk in the exposures. For that purpose we also need the counterparty and institution default probabilities. We assume that both the counterparty and the institution have quoted CDS premiums at the term points 1, 3, and 6 months as well as 1, 5, and 10 years. The current quoted CDS premias for both the counterparty and the

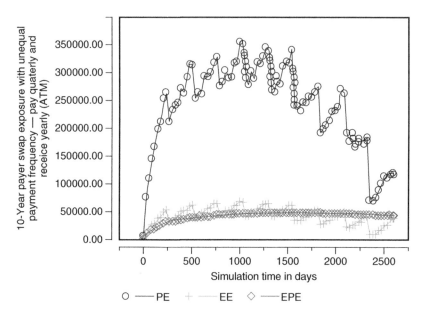

FIGURE 5.12 Expected Exposure, the Running Mean of Expected Positive Exposures, and the Peak Exposure Profile for a 10-Year at-the-Money Payer Swap with Unequal Payment Frequencies—Pay Quarterly and Receive Yearly

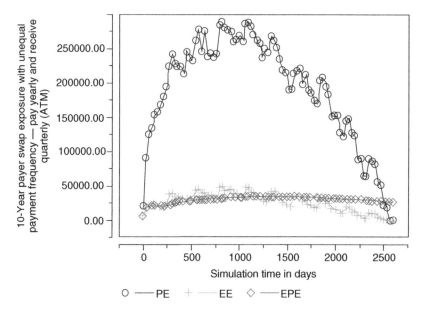

FIGURE 5.13 Expected Exposure, the Running Mean of Expected Positive Exposures, and the Peak Exposure Profile for a 10-Year at-the-Money Payer Swap with Unequal Payment Frequencies—Pay Yearly and Receive Quarterly

TABLE 5.6 Currency Amount Up-Front CVA, ACVA, DVA, and BCVA Charges for Swaps and Cross Currency Swaps. The Swap Notional Is 1,000,000 Units of Currency for All Deals

Deal	CVA	ACVA	DVA	BCVA
5 Year Payer swap (ATM)	1,752.31	1,642.97	1,766.22	−123.26
5 Year Payer swap (ITM)	2,503.30	2,354.90	1,115.34	1,239.56
5 Year Payer swap (OTM)	1,183.42	1,105.09	2,591.16	−1,486.07
5 Year Payer CCY swap (ATM fx)	6,143.84	5,610.07	6,102.90	−492.83
5 Year Payer CCY swap (ITM fx)	18,050.94	16,609.07	1,417.76	15,191.31
5 Year Payer CCY swap (OTM fx)	1,449.96	1,307.61	14,347.52	−13,039.91
10 Year Payer swap (ATM)	9,746.99	8,275.61	9,010.86	−735.25
10 Year Payer swap (ITM)	12,865.64	10,998.40	6,232.06	4,766.34
10 Year Payer swap (OTM)	7,265.14	6,120.97	12,357.80	−6,236.83
10 Year Payer CCY swap (ATM fx)	20,796.05	16,443.91	18,384.56	−1,940.65
10 Year Payer CCY swap (ITM fx)	45,812.14	36,686.80	7,436.84	29,249.95
10 Year Payer CCY swap (OTM fx)	8,470.39	6,595.55	33,488.23	−26,892.68
10 Year Receiver swap (ATM)	10,557.29	9,010.86	8,275.61	735.25

institution is 30, 50, 70, 100, 400, and 700 basis points, respectively. We also assume that the recovery rate for both the counterparty and institution is null such that to a high degree of approximation the observed CDS quotes are equivalent to hazard rates since the credit default swap premia and bond spread, c, is approximately $h(1 − R)$ with h the hazard rate and R the recovery rate.

Table 5.6 displays the up-front CVA, ACVA, DVA, and BCVA charges for different plain swap deals in units of currency when we also discount the charges using the current zero rates, which are assumed flat at the 5% level. In Table 5.6 the plain payer swaps that are ITM or OTM have fixed contract rates at 4.5% and 5.5% respectively. Hence, the OTM and ITM payer swaps have a contract difference of 50 basis points versus the current and implied forward interest rate of 5%. For the ATM case the fixed rate swap leg is equal to the current and implied forward rate of 5%. The cross-currency swaps in Table 5.6 are always ATM with respect to the interest rate. However, they can be ITM or OTM with respect to the final foreign exchange. The ITM payer cross-currency swap has a contract agreed exchange rate of 8 compared to the current and expected forward foreign exchange rate of 9. Similarly, the OTM payer cross-currency swap has an agreed exchange rate of 10 compared to the current and expected forward foreign exchange rate of 9. Starting with the 5- and 10-year maturity plain payer swaps we notice that the ACVA for the ATM swaps are slightly lower than the DVA, yielding a negative BCVA. This is because the EE of receiver swaps is slightly above the EE of payer swaps. See Figure 5.10. The ITM 5-year and 10-year maturity plain swaps display, as expected, a higher ACVA and lower DVA than the ATM case, yielding positive BCVA. That is, there is net bilateral positive credit risk. For the OTM plain swaps we observe the opposite situation of course. Turning to the cross-currency swaps, the 5- and 10-year maturity cross-currency swaps display significantly higher credit charges than the plain swaps. This is, of course, due to the large risk in the final exchange of currency. For example, the 10-year payer cross-currency swap that is ITM has a CVA charge of 45,812.14 units of currency, which is approximately 4.5% of the deal notional of 1,000,000 units of currency. Clearly, with such credit risk charges it is hard to make the deal profitable. Because the BCVA is positive in this case the deal counterparty may be willing to cover part of the CVA corresponding to approximately 3% of deal notional (29,249.95 units of currency). However, the remaining portion is a credit cost attributed to the deal.

Note finally that in our examples in Table 5.6 we have assumed that the institution and the counterparty have the same credit risk quality. This means that the driver of BCVA is the net EE profile, which is materially different only for ITM and OTM cases. The net EE profile is of course the difference between the institution's expected exposure view and the counterparty expected exposure view (i.e., expected negative exposure for institution). Changing the assumption of symmetry in credit quality can clearly introduce large asymmetries in bilateral credit risk charges for ATM deals as well. In particular, the lower quality counterparty will face a higher DVA than ACVA and hence a net negative bilateral risk.

Market Correlations, Wrong-Way Risk, and Counterparty Pricing

Market Correlations The specific assumptions about the correlations between market models is central to CVA. In a cross-currency payer swap positive correlation between the forward foreign exchange rate and the interest rates increases counterparty exposure as it is more likely that the final foreign exchange is in favor at the same time as the deal is ITM for the interest rates. The positive correlation also increases exposure for the cross-currency receiver swap. This is because the positive correlation also makes it more likely that interest rates are low at the same time as the forward foreign exchange rate.

Example Market Correlation Impact on CVA In Table 5.6 we assumed a zero market correlation *between* the forward foreign exchange rate and the interest rates when we calculated CVA, ACVA, and so on, for the cross-currency swaps. Table 5.7 displays the CVA, ACVA, DVA, and BCVA for the cross-currency swaps in Table 5.6 with a 60% market correlation *between* the forward foreign exchange rate and the interest rates. We note from Table 5.7 that with positive market correlation both ACVA and DVA increase similarly in currency amounts—yielding similar BCVA as in the case of zero market correlation between the foreign exchange rate and interest rate models. We note that the CVA increase is relatively larger for the OTM cross-currency swaps. For example, the 10-year OTM cross-currency swaps display a CVA increase of approximately 50% compared to the zero market correlation case.

TABLE 5.7 Currency Amount Up-Front CVA, ACVA, DVA, and BCVA Charges for Cross-Currency Swaps with 60% Market Correlation. The Swap Notional is 1,000,000 Units of Currency for All Deals

Deal	CVA	ACVA	DVA	BCVA
5 Year Payer CCY swap (ATM fx)	7,258.52	6,646.79	6,951.26	−304.47
5 Year Payer CCY swap (ITM fx)	18,906.34	17,398.31	1,995.02	15,403.28
5 Year Payer CCY swap (OTM fx)	2,198.03	1,998.93	14,869.38	−12,870.45
10 Year Payer CCY swap (ATM fx)	26,043.98	20,751.81	21,909.13	−1,157.31
10 Year Payer CCY swap (ITM fx)	50,826.60	40,766.44	10,634.70	30,131.74
10 Year Payer CCY swap (OTM fx)	12,637.86	10,006.67	36,194.77	−26,188.10

Correlation Symmetry The fact that both ACVA and DVA increase with an almost same BCVA compared to the independent case is due to the symmetry of correlation (normal copula) such that both payer and receiver risks increase. Using instead a *t*-copula we could increase the dependence and hence the unilateral exposure risk. However, the payer and receiver risk would still be symmetric with the *t*-copula. If we would like to capture a non-symmetric dependence between the forward foreign exchange rate and the interest rates, we could use a copula with either upper or lower tail dependence. The Gumbel copula displays only upper tail dependence and hence induces increased exposure only for cross-currency payer swaps with dependent forward foreign exchange rate and interest rates compared to the independent case. The Clayton copula displays only lower tail dependence and hence induces higher exposure for cross-currency receiver swaps only.

Wrong-Way Risk While market correlations such as correlations between equity, foreign exchange, and interest rates may increase exposure and hence CVA for given counterparty default probabilities, the CVA also depends on the correlation between exposure and the default probability. Wrong-way risk refers to the situation when exposure is in general high at the same time as the default probability is high. Right-way risk is when exposure is in general small when default probability is high. In other words, wrong-way risk reflects a positive correlation between exposures and default probabilities so on paths where exposures are high also corresponds to an increase in the default probability. Right-way risk exhibits the opposite behavior whereby increasing default probabilities correspond to lower exposures.

A simple approach often used in practice to adjust counterparty pricing metrics for wrong-way risk is to adjust exposures conservatively upwards while still using the independent CVA model in equation (5.2). Conservatively assuming that exposures will likely be high when default rate is high we can replace EE in equation (5.2) with a worst-case quantile of exposures, that is, a peak exposure, PE, such that

$$\mathrm{CVA}(t, T) = \sum_{n=1}^{N} \mathrm{PE}(t_n)\, p(t_{n-1}, t_n). \tag{5.11}$$

Essentially, with a roughly similar profile shape for expected and peak exposures, this amounts to scaling independent CVA such that

$$\mathrm{CVA}(t, T) = \beta \sum_{n=1}^{N} \mathrm{EE}(t, t_n)\, p(t_{n-1}, t_n) \tag{5.12}$$

where β is the wrong-way risk factor. However, a natural question is how we can know what the relevant β is without actually modeling the wrong-way risk explicitly. It may therefore be natural for the institution to actually validate the assumed $\beta:s$ using an explicit model of wrong-way risk. This is not so different from how banks currently validate internal alpha adjustments on expected positive exposures for the Basel II default risk capital charge. In practice, to minimize computational burden and complexity, daily and intraday calculations of CVA can be based on the independent CVA formula with β adjustment, that is, equation (5.12). One can then update β as exposures and/or default probability change significantly for a counterparty while still benefiting from the simple, relatively quick, independent CVA formula. As we have remarked before the independent CVA formula allows CVA calculation as a simple multiplication post-processing using the default probability from the credit system, the expected exposure profile from the exposure system, and the discount curve from the market system.

To model wrong-way risk explicitly we can use a model for codependency between default rates and market variables that drive exposures. Skoglund et al. (2013) analyze wrong-way risk through a correlation model dependence structure between exposure and default probability. Similarly, Hull and White (2012a) model the wrong-way risk in CVA. However, Hull and White (2012a) make use of non-stochastic models for codependency between default rate and exposure. Of course, a correlation model captures only general economic wrong-way risk and does not capture specific wrong-way risk such as a causal relationship whereby a sudden jump to default moves the market variables. This can be a concern with sovereign counterparties and currency exposures. See Levy and Levin (1999).

Using a model for "economic correlation" codependency between default rates and market variables that drive exposures means that we can no longer use the simple CVA formula in equation (5.2),

$$\text{CVA}(t, T) = \sum_{n=1}^{N} \text{EE}(t_n)\, p(t_{n-1}, t_n).$$

Instead, we require that CVA be calculated through jointly integrating default and exposure scenarios. That is, for scenarios, $d = 1, \ldots, D$ we have that

$$\text{CVA}(t, T) = \frac{1}{D} \sum_{n=1}^{N} \sum_{d=1}^{D} [V(t, t_n, d)^+ p(t_{n-1}, t_n, d)]. \tag{5.13}$$

This wrong-way risk CVA model still fits in the general exposure simulation framework for CVA. The only complication is that we cannot separately compute default probabilities and exposures anymore.

To specify the correlations between the counterparty default probability (CDS premiums) and the market variables driving exposure requires detailed knowledge of the counterparty business model and business sensitivities to assess the degree and even sign of codependency. For example, is the counterparty default risk higher in high or low interest rate environments? In the first case, payer swaps with the counterparty have wrong-way risk and receiver swaps have right-way risk. Or, is default more likely in both situations, for example, low interest rates signaling a general downturn with higher default rates while high interest rates might see the counterparty in trouble of meeting their liability payments? Cross-currency swaps can display double wrong-way risk in the sense that the second component of wrong-way risk for cross-currency swaps is the correlation between the foreign exchange forward rate and the default rate.

Example Wrong-Way Risk Analysis To analyze the impacts of wrong-way risk on CVA we model directly the term structure of CDS premias (hazard rates) using a Cox, Ingersoll, and Ross model. As before the counterparty CDS term structure has the term points, 1, 3, and 6 months as well as 1, 5, and 10 years and the current quoted CDS premias for the counterparty is 30, 50, 70, 100, 400, and 700 basis points, respectively. For the 10-year term point the simulated CDS premias follow the model,

$$dp(t) = a_p[b_p - p(t)]dt + \sigma_p \sqrt{p(t)}dZ(t) \tag{5.14}$$

where $p(t)$ is the 10-year CDS premia and the Cox, Ingersoll, and Ross model parameters are set such that

$$b_p = 0.07$$
$$a_p = 0.1$$
$$\sigma_p = 0.07.$$

This means that the 10-year CDS premia is mean reverting to its current level of 700 basis points and that the mean reversion speed is the same as for the interest rates (i.e., 0.1). The volatility of the 10-year CDS premia is 0.07 compared to 0.06 for the interest rates. Using this model we simulate paths of 10-year future CDS premia. Given the path of the simulated 10-year CDS premia we obtain CDS premia for the other term points by fixed parallel shifts of the simulated 10-year CDS premia. For example, the 5-year term simulated CDS premia is obtained as

$$dp_5(t) = dp(t) + (0.04 - b_p)$$

where 0.04 is the initial CDS premia for the 5-year term. This simple model ensures that the CDS premia term structure is non-decreasing over time as is required to maintain positive implied incremental default probabilities in equation (5.6).

Table 5.8 displays the wrong-way risk CVA for the interest rate and cross-currency swap deals in Table 5.6 with an 80% correlation between the counterparty CDS premias (hazard rates) and the interest rates and the foreign exchange forward rate. The 80% correlation induces a 60% market correlation between foreign exchange and interest rates market models, hence, the same market correlation we used for the cross-currency swaps in Table 5.7. Table 5.8 also displays the β adjustment for wrong-way risk CVA (CVA β WR) compared to the case of no wrong-way risk (but still a 60% market correlation between the forward exchange rate and the interest rates) as well as the β adjustment for wrong-way risk CVA

TABLE 5.8 Currency Amount Up-Front CVA Charges for Swaps with Wrong-Way Risk. The Swap Notional Is 1,000,000 Units of Currency for All Deals

Deal	CVA	CVA β WR	CVA β WR+MKT
5 Year Payer swap (ATM)	3,134.21	1.78	1.78
5 Year Payer swap (ITM)	4,197.77	1.67	1.67
5 Year Payer swap (OTM)	2,251.21	1.90	1.90
5 Year Payer CCY swap (ATM fx)	12,842.98	1.76	2.09
5 Year Payer CCY swap (ITM fx)	28,286.89	1.49	1.57
5 Year Payer CCY swap (OTM fx)	4,587.04	2.08	3.16
10 Year Payer swap (ATM)	15,680.85	1.60	1.60
10 Year Payer swap (ITM)	19,843.79	1.54	1.54
10 Year Payer swap (OTM)	12,148.52	1.67	1.67
10 Year Payer CCY swap (ATM fx)	40,407.46	1.55	1.94
10 Year Payer CCY swap (ITM fx)	72,070.00	1.41	1.57
10 Year Payer CCY swap (OTM fx)	21,287.05	1.68	2.51
10 Year Receiver swap (ATM)	5,112.37	0.48	0.48

(CVA β WR+MKT) when there is no market correlation or wrong-way risk. Of course, the plain interest rate swaps are not affected by market correlation between the foreign exchange forward rate and the interest rates and this β adjustment is only different for the cross-currency swaps. To obtain the β adjustment for only wrong-way risk we have used the CVA in Table 5.6 for plain interest rate swaps and the CVA in Table 5.7 for cross-currency swaps. To obtain the β adjustment for both market correlation and wrong-way risk for cross-currency swaps we have used the cross-currency swap CVA in Table 5.6.

Table 5.8 shows that the implied β adjustment for wrong-way risk on CVA itself is highest for OTM swaps and lowest for ITM swaps. This is because wrong-way risk introduces an higher likelihood of an OTM deal becoming ITM at the same time as default rates are high. Similarly, current ITM deals already have a significant likelihood of being ITM in the future. The combined wrong-way risk and market correlation effect on cross-currency swaps shows that the CVA can be significantly different under different model assumptions. The 5-year OTM cross-currency swap CVA has increased by a factor of 3.16 when both wrong-way risk and market correlation are taken into account. The 10-year receiver swap of course displays right-way risk and the CVA reduction compared to the case of no wrong-way risk is more than 50%. When both the counterparty and the institution share the same market and default correlation the 10-year receiver swap CVA can be seen as the CVA from the counterparty point of view (i.e., DVA) of the institution. Hence, in this case the CVA of the payer swap has increased significantly due to the wrong-way risk. However, the DVA has been significantly reduced due to right-way risk. Of course, there are still some risk mitigating effects in ACVA (and DVA) because, with common market and default correlations, the institution's survival probability, $S_I((t_{n-1}, t_n))$, is lower at the exact time when counterparty default rates, $p(t_{n-1}, t_n)$, are high.

Collateralized Exposures

In practice counterparty exposure rarely remains uncollateralized when trades are between banks. Most banks have the capacity to manage a collateral margining process with frequent margin call and posting rules using dedicated collateral management teams. The exposure margin call and posting rules are stipulated by a so-called credit support annex (CSA) agreement. The standard CSA agreement specifies collateral margin calls and collateral flows using agreed collateral parameters such as

- The independent amount that needs to be posted
- The margin threshold above which collateral is transferred
- The minimum collateral transfer amount
- The margin frequency

A non-zero threshold and minimum transfer amount avoids too much operational workload with frequent collateral calls for small changes in exposure. If the amount of collateral that needs to be posted or returned is less than the minimum collateral transfer amount, then no transfer of collateral occurs. That is, collateral is posted and returned in blocks. Effectively, for a post or return to happen on a margin day the absolute exposure change has to exceed the sum of the threshold and the minimum transfer amount.

The failure to post the required collateral by one side allows the other side to terminate outstanding transactions. CSA agreements are additions to an International Swaps and Derivatives Association (ISDA) master agreement, which specifies that all transactions between two parties are to be netted and considered as a single transaction in case there is an early termination event.

When a counterparty to the institution is not able to manage collateral calls such as a small pension fund the exposure may remain uncollateralized. Alternatively, the institution may require the counterparty to post an independent amount. This may also happen when the credit rating of the counterparty is significantly lower than the institution's.

Clearly, an effective collateral agreement with low threshold and minimum transfer amount and frequent posting can reduce counterparty credit risk and hence CVA significantly. Collateralization is therefore an important credit risk mitigant. Effectively, collateralized trades with a margin agreement replace a large portion of the counterparty credit risk at the cost of potential funding liquidity risk. There is also an operational cost for handling the margining process with a dedicated collateral management team. In some cases, collaterals are also held by a custodian.

While a collateral agreement with daily margin calls and zero threshold and minimum transfer can be viewed as a perfect collateralization, in practice, it is prudent to assume that collateral is not received instantaneously following a collateral call. That is, a period of time can elapse between the events that the counterparty ceases to post collateral and there is an early termination by the institution. Indeed, it is also a regulatory requirement to properly include collateral settlement risk—sometimes called margin period of risk or cure period—in the calculation of collateralized exposures. The margin period of risk captures the fact that even if collateral is not delivered exactly when called there is a grace period before the bank actually determines the counterparty is in default. The concept of margin period of risk can include multiple collateral settlement risks. It is generally defined as the time period from

1. The last exchange of collateral covering a netting set of transactions with a defaulting counterparty, until
2. That counterparty is closed out and the resulting market risk is rehedged

That is, when the counterparty defaults there is a grace period where exposure does not get offset by counterparty posts, or the counterparty does not return collateral as expected. It may also be the case that the collateral already posted, or that is being posted or returned by the counterparty, needs to be converted to currency cash in a potential illiquid market.

Currently, the ISDA CSA collateral agreements are transitioning into so-called standard CSAs (see ISDA press release, 2011) where daily collateral posts are in cash currency only with one netting set per trade currency and close to zero threshold and minimum transfer. This means that the majority of exposure risk remaining is due to the exposure rise in the grace period that may not get offset by (cash) collateral. Hence, the modeling of this collateral settlement risk is a key concern for the industry. Clearly, without collateral settlement risk and with a standard CSA agreement the institution exposure and CVA to the counterparty is practically null. It is therefore of significant importance to understand the impact on counterparty exposure and pricing with different assumptions on the collateral settlement risk.

As an illustration of collateral flows Figure 5.14 displays an example of collateral posts and returns when both the counterparty and the institution need to post collateral for a sample exposure profile. The example exposure profile is from a 1-year (260 business days) at-the-money plain interest rate swap with a principal notional of 1,000,000. The institution or bank posting leg has a margin threshold of 800 units of currency and a minimum collateral transfer amount of 200. The institution posts collateral every 10 days. However, from

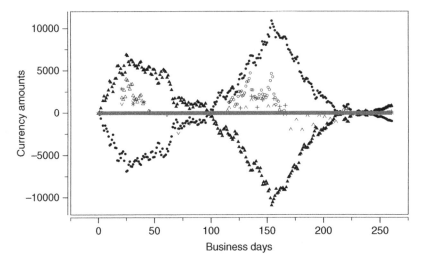

- ● Institution Uncollateralized Exposure
- ○ Institution Collateralized Exposure
- ▲ Counterparty Uncollateralized Exposure
- △ Counterparty Collateralized Exposure
- ∧ Institution Margin Call (+) and Actual Return (−)
- ∨ Counterparty Margin Call (+) and Actual Return (−)
- + Actual Collateral Delivered by Counterparty
- ∗ Actual Collateral Delivered by Institution

FIGURE 5.14   Sample Collateral Flows for a 1-Year at-the-Money Interest Rate Swap Exposure Path

the perspective of the counterparty there is a 10-day margin period of risk. The bank receiver leg (i.e., the counterparty posting leg) has a margin threshold of 500 and a minimum collateral transfer amount of 100. The counterparty posts collateral every 5 days and from the perspective of the bank there is a 10-day margin period of risk. In Figure 5.14 we first have an increasing exposure from the counterparty point of view. The counterparty then calls for collateral, which is indicated by the counterparty margin call spikes in Figure 5.14. Due to the non-daily posting of the institution and the margin period of risk the actual collateral delivered by the institution is delayed as indicated by the spikes of actual collateral delivered by the institution. This causes the counterparty uncollateralized and collateralized exposure to be equal in the beginning of the exposure rise. However, eventually exposure is offset and collateralized exposure decreases significantly. When the exposure later decays the counterparty returns collateral to the institution, which is displayed in Figure 5.14 as negative counterparty margin calls (i.e., returns). In this example, the return of collateral happens without delay. After 100 days the exposure profile from the counterparty perspective has declined to zero and there is now an increasing positive exposure from the institution point of view. The institution hence now needs to call for collateral from the counterparty, which we can see from the spikes of institution margin call in Figure 5.14. Since the counterparty posts at a higher frequency (every 5 days) the institution collateralized exposure is more quickly offset than the counterparty collateralized exposure was. As when the counterparty had a positive exposure to the institution the exposure decays after some time and the institution then returns collateral to the counterparty without delay.

In principle, the exact calculation of collateralized exposure is trivial as in Figure 5.14. However, in practice it can become quite complex to incorporate. Consider a 10-year payer swap with daily margin frequency. In order to calculate exactly collateralized exposure the simulation time point interval needs to be daily. This requirement can be excessive for the exposure and CVA system. To overcome the requirement on daily simulation horizons for exposures with daily collateral calls one can use an approximation model. A popular collateral approximation model is the so-called lagged collateral model. The lagged collateral model calculates the collateral calls only at the lookback points where the lookback points are equal to the time interval of the collateral settlement risk (e.g., 10 days). That is, for a given, uncollateralized, exposure simulation time grid, $\{t_n\}_{n=1}^N$, we also need to simulate at the lookback points. Hence, rather than requiring a daily simulation for a daily margin frequency we have simply doubled the requirements of simulation time points compared to the uncollateralized case. However, doubling the simulation time points for the collateralized case means in practice significantly more exposure calculation time.

In order to further reduce the number of time points for exposure simulation with collateral it is natural to try to avoid simulation on the lookback time points altogether and hence only use the "uncollateralized" exposure simulation time grid, $\{t_n\}_{n=1}^N$. This would put the calculation time for collateralized exposure on par with uncollateralized exposure. In this regard, Pykthin and Zhu (2006) propose a method that relies on an assumption that the portfolio value at time t_n is normally distributed. One can then obtain the conditional portfolio value distribution at the lookback time points using Brownian bridge.[10] Pykthin (2009) further extends the method to avoid the assumption that the portfolio value at time t_n is normally distributed—replacing it with the assumption that conditional on a scenario realization the portfolio value at time t_n is conditionally normal. Comparing with the lagged collateral model Pykthin (2009) reports that his approximation performs very well for a range of sample trades. See also Gibson (2005) and Gregory (2010, ch. 5) on collateralized exposure.

The lagged collateral model is a convenient approximation to exact collateral calls and is frequently used in practice by banks to calculate exposure for collateralized trades. The lookback time point approximation approaches by Pykthin and Zhu (2006) and Pykthin (2009) allow the computation time for collateralized trades to be practical and on par with uncollateralized trades. It is therefore not surprising that banks have adopted the lagged collateral model approaches. One must remember that the lagged collateral model only focuses on the collateral calls at the settlement period lookback points. The potential intervening time points of collateral returns by the institution are overlooked. Similarly, the potential delay in counterparty return of institution posted collateral is not captured. Therefore, the lagged collateral model itself can underestimate collateralized exposure. The lagged collateral model can also overestimate exposure. This is because it can ignore valid margin calls made previous to the lookback point that get received before the simulation time point. Essentially, the lagged collateral model coincides with an exact collateral calculation when exposure is monotonically increasing. In other cases it can either underestimate or overestimate exposure.

---

[10]The Brownian bridge is the term used for the process that has as its distribution the conditional distribution of a Wiener process. The distribution at the lookback time point is naturally a conditional distribution. Specifically, conditional on the simulation time grid, $\{t_n\}_{n=1}^N$, values.

Collateral Dynamics and the Lagged Collateral Model We now focus on the mechanics of collateral calls and posts for both unilateral and bilateral margin agreements. We compare an exact collateral approach with the lagged collateral model in order to enhance understanding about when the lagged collateral approximation is good versus not so good in practice. In our exposition we will focus mainly on simplified cases with daily margin, zero threshold, and zero minimum transfer amount. We do this purposely to ease notation and to focus on the most important aspects of the collateral settlement risk. Pykthin (2009) contains the formulas for the general collateralized exposure implied from the lagged collateral model. In our swap examples later we will also consider more general cases where margining can be for example weekly and with threshold and minimum transfer amounts non-zero. The collateral posted and returned by either the counterparty or the institution is, however, always assumed to be in cash currency, which is consistent with the industry move to standard CSAs and currency cash as the main source of collateral. In order to illustrate the dynamics of the collateral and its effect on the actual exposure we do not assume the appearance of a custodian agent in the process.

Unilateral Agreement The case where the counterparty posts collateral according to a margin agreement but the institution does not post is referred to as a unilateral margin agreement. The counterparty posts according to the posting frequency, λ, where λ is usually daily. Assuming no delay in collateral settlement the institution collateralized exposure, CE, at a time point t_n is

$$CE(t_n) = E(t_n) - CB(t_n)$$

where $E(t_n)$ is the uncollateralized exposure of the institution and $CB(t_n)$ is the value of collateral posted by the counterparty. We assume that the collateral posted is in the trade(s) cash currency. Assuming t_n is a margin call day and t_{n-1} is the previous margin call day a valid margin call is made at t_n if

$$E(t_n) - CB(t_{n-1}) > T + MTA$$

where T is the threshold and MTA is the minimum transfer amount of the CSA agreement. Of course, if

$$E(t_n) - CB(t_{n-1}) < -(T + MTA)$$

the institution returns collateral. Assuming that the threshold and minimum transfer amount is zero or negligible we have that a valid margin call is made at t_n if

$$E(t_n) - CB(t_{n-1}) > 0.$$

The institution margin call amount, MC, is hence

$$MC(t_n) = \max[E(t_n) - CB(t_{n-1}), 0]$$

and return amount, R,

$$R(t_n) = \min[E(t_n) - CB(t_{n-1}), 0].$$

Clearly, with no delay in settlement and daily margin the institution exposure, $E(t_n)$, remains offset at all times $t = t_1, \ldots, t_N$. Even if there is a non-zero threshold and minimum transfer the exposure is bounded by the effective threshold of T + MTA. However, the recent crisis has shown that settlement closeouts can amount to long risk horizons. That is, we cannot assume that collateral is delivered immediately by the counterparty or that the portfolio is closed out immediately if collateral is not delivered instantaneously. Hence, an institution that considers its collateralized exposure to a counterparty needs to include the settlement risk.

When considering settlement risk we assume there is a delay in receiving the daily collateral posts from the counterparty once a valid margin call has been made. Assuming a collateral settlement risk period of $t_n - t_1$ a positive call amount at t_1, $MC(t_1)$, is received by the institution at t_n. With settlement risk we therefore have that

$$CE(t_n) = \max[E(t_n) - MC(t_1) - CB(t_{n-1}), 0] \qquad (5.15)$$

where $CB(t_{n-1})$ is the cash balance of collateral at t_{n-1}. We take the maximum in equation (5.15) since we do not allow overcollateralization of the institution. This means that we assume that excess collateral is returned by the institution instantaneously (i.e., with no settlement delay). This assumption is prudent from a risk management perspective. The exact collateral cash balance, $CB(t_{n-1})$, depends in general on the exact exposure path at times $t_1, \ldots, t_n$.

While we have assumed that the institution returns collateral instantaneously one can also ask whether the actual instantaneous return is based on what has actually been received from the counterparty (with delay) versus what should have been posted (with no delay). In the latter case collateralized exposure can be higher than uncollateralized when mark to market is in favor of the institution since the institution returns collateral that has not been physically settled.

As mentioned previously the lagged collateral model has quickly become a standard market model to include the ISDA CSA effect on collateralized exposure in potential future exposure calculation as well as in counterparty pricing using CVA. Following Pykthin (2009), the lagged collateral model specification is such that at time t_1 we have portfolio value $V(t_1)$ and collateral balance $CB(t_1)$. Then, with settlement delay $t_n - t_1$, the posted amount at t_n, $P(t_n)$, is:

$$P(t_n) = MC(t_1) = \max[V(t_1) - CB(t_1), -CB(t_1)]$$

and the collateral balance, at t_n is:

$$CB(t_n) = CB(t_1) + P(t_n) = \max[V(t_1), 0].$$

Hence, the lagged collateral model implied collateralized exposure, CEL, at t_n is:

$$CEL(t_n) = \min\{\max[V(t_n), 0], \max[V(t_n) - V(t_1), 0]\}.$$

With this model specification for collateralized exposure we note that it ignores intervening returns of collateral between the time point t_n and the lookback time point t_1. It also ignores previous periods institution calls before the lookback time point t_1 that can be delivered before the time point t_n.

Example of Unilateral Exact Collateral Calls Versus the Lagged Collateral Model It is illustrative to consider an example of the key differences between an exact collateral calculation and the approximative lagged collateral model. Table 5.9 illustrates the calculation of collateralized exposure, CE, using exact collateral calls and returns as well as using the lagged

TABLE 5.9 Collateralized Exposure—All Margin Calls Get Delivered Regardless of Exposure Offset and Institution Returns Based on What Has Actually Been Received

	Exposure time points					
	t_1	t_2	t_3	t_4	t_5	t_6
E(t)	1,000	2,000	500	3,000	9,000	13,000
MC(t)	1,000	1,000	0	1,500	6,000	4,000
MD(t)	0	0	1,000	1,000	0	1,500
R(t)	0	0	500	0	0	0
CB(t)	0	0	500	1,500	1,500	3,000
CE(t)	1,000	2,000	0	1,500	7,500	10,000
CEL(t)	1,000	2,000	0	1,000	8,500	10,000

collateral model collateralized exposure, CEL. In our example, we assume a zero threshold and minimum transfer amount and the remargin frequency is daily with a settlement risk of 2 days during days $t_1, \ldots, t_6$. Day 0 exposure and collateral balance is zero.

In Table 5.9 we have used the notation MD(t) to represent the actual delivered collateral amount by the counterparty at t to the institution. All the intermediate collateral agreement calculation variables such as collateral balance, CB(t), used in Table 5.9 are using an exact calculation and we only present the final lagged collateral model exposure, CEL(t).

To understand the CE and CEL exposures obtained in Table 5.9 note that at time t_1 the institution makes a valid margin call of 1,000 units of currency based on the uncollateralized exposure at t_1, E(t_1), being 1,000 units of currency. Similarly, at t_2, the institution makes a valid margin call,

$$MC(t_2) = E(t_2) - E(t_1) = 2,000 - 1,000 = 1,000.$$

Because of settlement delay of the counterparty posts the collateral called for at t_1, MC(t_1), gets delivered at t_3. At t_3 the uncollateralized exposure is 500 units of currency, that is,

$$E(t_3) = 500.$$

The institution hence needs to return 500 units of currency instantaneously to avoid overcollateralization. The institution return amount is denoted R(t) in Table 5.9. For both an exact collateral calculation and the lagged collateral model the collateralized exposure at t_3 is null. That is,

$$CE(t_3) = CEL(t_3) = 0.$$

At time point t_4 the exposure, E(t_4), is 3,000 units of currency. Hence, the institution makes a valid residual margin call of 1,500 units of currency. This is because at the same time the institution receives the 1,000 units of collateral in currency called for at time t_2. At this point, the exact collateral calculation gives a different collateralized exposure, CE(t_4), than the lagged collateral model exposure. Specifically,

$$CE(t_4) = 1,500$$

while
$$CEL(t_4) = 1,000.$$

This is because the lagged collateral model ignores the institution instantaneous return of collateral at time t_3 to avoid overcollateralization of the institution. On the other hand, at time t_5, the lagged collateral model exposure is higher than the exact collateralized exposure. We have that
$$CE(t_5) = 7,500$$

while
$$CEL(t_5) = 8,500.$$

That is, the lagged collateral model overestimates collateralized exposure. In this case, the lookback point for the lagged collateral model is t_3, with no valid margin call for the institution. It ignores the previous periods call, at t_2, that gets posted with delay at t_4. Finally, at time point t_6 the lagged and exact collateral models again yield the same collateralized exposure. This is because uncollateralized exposure, $E(t)$, is non-decreasing across time points, t_4, t_5, t_6.

In our example above, we have assumed two important things:

1. The margin call made at t_2 by the institution is still delivered at t_4 by the counterparty even if the collateralized exposure is offset at t_3.

A more natural assumption is that the institution call made at t_2 never gets delivered because of the exposure offset at t_3. In this case, the collateralized exposure for t_4, $CE(t_4)$, increases to 2,500 units of currency. Similarly, the collateralized exposure at t_5, $CE(t_5) = 8,500$ (i.e., the same as for the lagged collateral model). Since the margin call made at t_4 is honored at t_6 we obtain the same time t_6 exposure. That is, $CE(t_6) = 10,000$. This case is displayed in Table 5.10.

2. The institution returns collateral only based on what has actually been received (i.e., it only returns actual posts, not what has been called for but not delivered yet).

This is a reasonable assumption in practice. However, if there is an operational process flaw such that the institution returns are based on what has been called for rather than actually

TABLE 5.10 Collateralized Exposure—Margin Calls That Are Later Offset Do Not Get Delivered and Institution Returns Based on What Has Actually Been Received

	Exposure time points					
	t_1	t_2	t_3	t_4	t_5	t_6
$E(t)$	1,000	2,000	500	3,000	9,000	13,000
$MC(t)$	1,000	1,000	0	2,500	6,000	4,000
$MD(t)$	0	0	1,000	0	0	2,500
$R(t)$	0	0	500	0	0	0
$CB(t)$	0	0	500	500	500	3,000
$CE(t)$	1,000	2,000	0	2,500	8,500	10,000
$CEL(t)$	1,000	2,000	0	1,000	8,500	10,000

TABLE 5.11 Collateralized Exposure—All Margin Calls Get Delivered Regardless of Exposure Offset and Institution Returns Based on What Should Have Been Received

	Exposure time points					
	t_1	t_2	t_3	t_4	t_5	t_6
E(t)	1,000	2,000	500	3,000	9,000	13,000
MC(t)	1,000	1,000	0	2,500	6,000	4,000
MD(t)	0	0	1,000	1,000	0	2,500
R(t)	0	0	1,500	0	0	0
CB(t)	0	0	−500	500	500	3,000
CE(t)	1,000	2,000	1,000	2,500	8,500	10,000
CEL(t)	1,000	2,000	0	1,000	8,500	10,000

delivered, then, clearly, at time t_3, the institution return, $R(t_3)$, is 1,500 units of currency instead of 500 units of currency. This would result in an exact collateralized exposure, CE(t), at t_3 of 1,000 units of currency instead of 0. Hence, at this time collateralized exposure is greater than uncollateralized exposure. Similarly, the exact collateralized exposure at t_4 now increases to at least 2,500 units of currency (3,500 units of currency if we assume that the institution call at t_2 never gets delivered). At t_5 the exact collateralized exposure is now 8,500 units of currency (9,500 units of currency if we assume that the institution call at t_2 never gets delivered).

Table 5.11 displays the collateral case when the margin call at t_2 still gets delivered while the institution returns collateral based on what should have been received. In Table 5.12 we also display the corresponding collateral case when the margin call at t_2 doesn't get delivered.

We note from above with case 1 that the underestimation of collateralized exposure in the lagged collateral model increases at t_4 and that collateralized exposure is no longer overestimated by the lagged collateral model at t_5. With case 2 the lagged collateral model underestimates exposure at both time points t_3 and t_4. Moreover, the lagged collateral model does not overestimate collateralized exposure anymore at time t_5. If we have both case 1

TABLE 5.12 Collateralized Exposure—Margin Calls That Are Later Offset Do Not Get Delivered and Institution Returns Based on What Should Have Been Received

	Exposure time points					
	t_1	t_2	t_3	t_4	t_5	t_6
E(t)	1,000	2,000	500	3,000	9,000	13,000
MC(t)	1,000	1,000	0	3,500	6,000	4,000
MD(t)	0	0	1,000	0	0	3,500
R(t)	0	0	1,500	0	0	0
CB(t)	0	0	−500	−500	−500	3,000
CE(t)	1,000	2,000	1,000	3,500	9,500	10,000
CEL(t)	1,000	2,000	0	1,000	8,500	10,000

and 2, then the lagged collateral model underestimates exposure significantly at time points, t_3, t_4, t_5. At other time points the exact and lagged collateral model exposures coincide.

Bilateral Agreement When both the counterparty and the institution are subject to collateralization the margin agreement is said to be a bilateral margin agreement. In the bilateral margin agreement case it is conservative to assume that the counterparty can delay both its post and returns but the institution posts and returns collateral without delay. In the unilateral margin agreement case we noted that collateralized exposure can exceed exposure if the institution returns collateral based on what should have been posted by the counterparty. In the bilateral case this case can happen because of the institution posting leg of the margin agreement. This is because now the counterparty can delay the returns of collateral posted by the institution, causing counterparty overcollateralization. Hence, both the poster and receiver leg of a bilateral margin agreement can cause counterparty overcollateralization. The contribution to counterparty overcollateralization from the poster and receiver legs can happen at the same time and hence for bilateral margin agreements one cannot in general separate the posting and receiving parts of the collateral calculation.

Assuming as before a zero threshold and minimum transfer amount the institution collateral balance under the approximative lagged collateral model is

$$CB(t_n) = \max[V(t_1), 0] + \min[V(t_1), 0] \qquad (5.16)$$

with $t_n - t_1$ the settlement risk period for the counterparty. The first term in equation (5.16) is the case when the institution receives collateral and the second term captures the case when the institution posts. The lagged collateral model collateralized exposure is then given by

$$CEL(t_n) = \max[V(t_n) - CB(t_n), 0]$$
$$= \max[V(t_n) - V(t_1), 0].$$

Clearly, as in the unilateral case, the lagged collateral model ignores the dynamics of intervening time points between $t_n - t_1$. Consider a mark to market in favor of the counterparty in t_{n-1}. Assuming daily margin, the institution posts the required collateral to the counterparty at t_{n-1}. If the mark to market is in favor of the institution at t_n, the counterparty does not return the institution posted amount in t_{n-1} at t_n due to settlement risk. This can clearly cause overcollateralization of the counterparty such that collateralized exposure exceeds exposure. In such cases the lagged collateral model can underestimate also exposure arising from the poster leg.

Example of Bilateral Exact Collateral Calls Versus the Lagged Collateral Model Table 5.13 displays sample collateral dynamics for the exact collateral model and the lagged collateral model in case of a bilateral agreement. As for the unilateral agreement case all the intermediate collateral agreement calculation variables such as collateral balance, $CB(t)$, used in Table 5.13 are using an exact calculation. We only present the final approximative lagged collateral model exposure, $CEL(t)$. In the example we have assumed that counterparty delayed posts are still delivered even if the exposure is later offset at the settlement delay. As in the unilateral cases, removing this assumption increases the counterparty exposure. However, the institution does not return collateral posted with delay if at that time point the institution is undercollateralized. The settlement risk period used is two days as in the unilateral case. In the table we use the notation $V(t)$ for the market value of the trade, $E(t)$ is the uncollateralized

TABLE 5.13 Bilateral Agreement Collateralized Exposure—All
Counterparty Margin Calls Get Delivered Regardless of Exposure
Offset and Institution Returns Based on What Has Actually Been
Received

| | \multicolumn{6}{c}{Exposure time points} |
	t_1	t_2	t_3	t_4	t_5	t_6
V(t)	100	200	−500	300	900	1,300
E(t)	100	200	0	300	900	1,300
NE(t)	0	0	500	0	0	0
MC(t)	100	100	0	300	600	400
MD(t)	0	0	100	100	0	300
R(t)	0	0	100	0	0	0
MP(t)	0	0	500			
RRC(t)	0	0	0	500	0	0
ARC(t)	0	0	0	0	0	500
CB(t)	0	0	−500	−400	−400	400
CE(t)	100	200	0	700	1,300	900
CEL(t)	100	200	0	100	1,400	1,000
COC(t)	0	0	0	400	400	0

exposure, and NE(t) is the uncollateralized exposure from the counterparty view, that is, the negative exposure from the institution point of view.

Dealing with a bilateral agreement we also need to introduce notation for the institution post of collateral, MP(t) as well as the counterparty required and actual return of collateral posts from the institution, RRC(t) and ARC(t), respectively. Again, our assumption is that the institution posts and returns collateral instantaneously but the counterparty delays both its posts and returns by the settlement risk period. Because the institution posts with no delay but the counterparty can delay returns we can clearly have a situation of counterparty over-collateralization. The notation we use for the counterparty overcollateralization is COC(t). The remaining notation in Table 5.13 is the same as the notation used in Table 5.9 for the unilateral agreement case.

In Table 5.13 we have a situation of increasing exposure, E(t), initially for the institution at t_1 and t_2, then a negative market value at t_3 such that the counterparty has an exposure to the institution. At t_4, t_5, and t_6 we have again an increasing exposure for the institution. At t_3 the counterparty actually delivers the 100 units of currency called by the institution at t_1,

$$MD(t_3) = 100.$$

This amount is however returned instantaneously by the institution since it has no exposure,

$$R(t_3) = 100.$$

At the same time the counterparty makes a valid margin call of 500 units of currency to cover their exposure. This margin post is delivered by the institution instantaneously,

$$MP(t_3) = 500.$$

At t_4 the exposure becomes positive again for the institution and they make a valid margin call for 300 units of currency. While 100 units of currency is received at t_4 due to the margin call at t_2 the counterparty delays both its return of collateral posted by the institution at t_3 as well as the margin call made at t_4. This results in a net collateral balance for the institution of -400 units of currency at t_4. As mentioned, we here assume that the institution does not return the delayed post of the 100 units of currency since it is undercollateralized. Since the exposure at t_4 is 300 units of currency the exact collateralized exposure is 700 units of currency and exceeds exposure. The counterparty overcollateralization is hence 400 units of currency.

In contrast the lagged collateral model exposure is 100 units of currency as the lookback point is t_2. It ignores the fact that at t_3 the institution posted an amount to cover the counterparty's exposure to the institution that does not get returned instantaneously. At t_5 the exposure has increased to 900 units of currency and the institution makes a valid margin call of 600 units of currency. However, due to settlement delay no collateral is delivered by the counterparty at t_5 such that collateralized exposure still exceeds uncollateralized exposure. This is because the counterparty is still overcollateralized at t_5. In this case the lagged collateral model collateralized exposure exceeds the exact collateralized exposure by 100 units of currency because it does not include the fact that the institution returns 100 units of currency to the counterparty at t_3. At t_6 the lagged collateral model again overestimates collateralized exposure by 100 units of currency compared to the exact case. This is because it does not capture the 100 units of currency posted with delay by the counterparty at t_4. However, if we assume the call at t_2 got canceled at t_3 (because at t_3 the institution has no exposure), we would have the same collateralized exposure at t_6 for the lagged collateral model and the exact case.

In this bilateral collateral agreement example there are two sources of collateralized counterparty exposure:

- First, the settlement delay in margin calls made by the institution
- Second, the fact that the counterparty has settlement delay in returns of collateral as well

This settlement delay in returns of collateral can clearly cause collateralized exposure to exceed exposure with counterparty overcollateralization as the result.

Our next and final example of bilateral margin agreements assumes that the institution returns based on what should have been received rather than what has actually been posted by the counterparty. Hence, we use the assumption in case 2 above for the unilateral agreements. Using the same trade value and exposure profiles as in Table 5.13, Table 5.14 displays this case. In this case the institution returns 200 units of currency to the counterparty at t_3. This is based on what should have been posted (with no delay) rather than what has been posted. This causes an overcollateralization of the counterparty already at t_3 with 100 units of currency such that collateralized exposure exceeds exposure.

As in Table 5.13, we still have counterparty overcollateralization at t_4 and t_5 such that collateralized exposure exceeds exposure. Due to the return in t_3 the collateralized exposure at t_4 and t_5 rises by 100 units of currency. The collateralized exposure levels in t_4 and t_5 are now a combination of settlement delay in counterparty returns and the excess returns at t_3. In this case the lagged collateral model exposure never exceeds the exact exposure. However, as before, the exact collateral exposure can exceed the lagged collateral model exposure. This happens at time points t_3 and t_4.

Collateralized Swap Exposure Having discussed the collateral dynamics for collateral agreements in simple stylized exposure cases we now analyze the impact of unilateral ISDA CSA

TABLE 5.14 Bilateral Agreement Collateralized Exposure—All Counterparty Margin Calls Get Delivered Regardless of Exposure Offset and Institution Returns Based on What Should Have Been Received

	Exposure time points					
	t_1	t_2	t_3	t_4	t_5	t_6
V(t)	100	200	−500	300	900	1,300
E(t)	100	200	0	300	900	1,300
NE(t)	0	0	500	0	0	0
MC(t)	100	100	0	300	600	400
MD(t)	0	0	100	100	0	300
R(t)	0	0	200	0	0	0
MP(t)	0	0	500			
RRC(t)	0	0	0	500	0	0
ARC(t)	0	0	0	0	0	500
CB(t)	0	0	−600	−500	−500	300
CE(t)	100	200	100	800	1,400	1,000
CEL(t)	100	200	0	100	1,400	1,000
COC(t)	0	0	100	500	500	0

agreements on the institution's 1-year maturity plain interest rate swap exposures using an exact collateral calculation. That is, we simulate exposure and the corresponding exact collateral calls on a daily frequency for each of the 260 business days assumed in a year. The interest rate model used for simulation of interest rate paths is the same model we have used before in our examples. Specifically, we use the model in equation (5.10) with the same parameters as before.

Since with frequent collateral posts a long-term exposure is effectively transformed into a short-term exposure (until the next margin call day with no settlement risk) it is sufficient to consider relatively short-term swap exposures as illustration of the collateral effects. In our exact collateral calculation we make the assumption that the institution returns collateral instantaneously based on what has actually been received. Moreover, in case of settlement risk the delayed collateral posts of the counterparty do not get canceled even if exposure has been reduced.

Figure 5.15 displays expected exposure (EE), the running mean of expected positive exposures (EPE), and the peak exposure (PE) profile for a 1-year ATM fixed rate payer swap (i.e., the fixed rate swap leg is equal to the implied forward rate of 5%). The deal notional is 1,000,000 units of currency and the confidence level used for peak exposures is 99%. The exposure profiles have been calculated using 10,000 simulations and a daily time grid up to maturity. As before the swap has monthly payment flows.

Figures 5.16, 5.17, and 5.18 display the same 1-year swap exposure but now collateralized with a daily margin frequency. In all cases the margin threshold and minimum transfer amount are set to 500 and 100 units of currency respectively. In Figure 5.16 we assume no settlement risk while in Figures 5.17 and 5.18 we have a 5- and 10-day settlement risk respectively. We note from Figure 5.16 that in the case of daily margining and no collateral settlement risk the exposure is bounded by the threshold plus the minimum transfer amount. Hence, with daily margining and zero threshold and minimum transfer the daily exposure

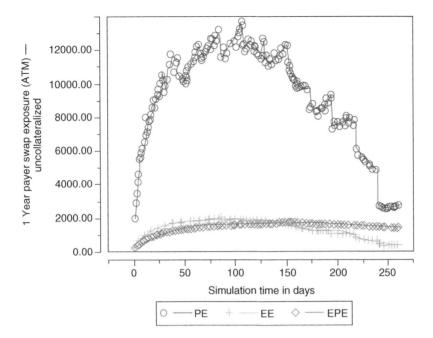

FIGURE 5.15 Expected Exposure, the Running Mean of Expected Positive Exposures, and the Peak Exposure Profile for a 1-Year at-the-Money Payer Swap With No Collateral

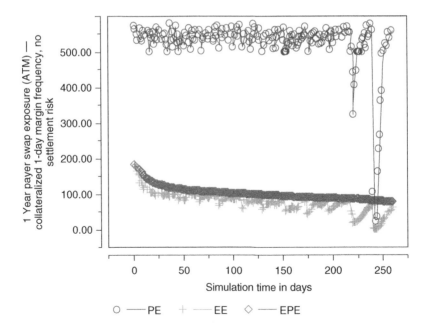

FIGURE 5.16 Expected Exposure, the Running Mean of Expected Positive Exposures, and the Peak Exposure Profile for a 1-Year at-the-Money Payer Swap with Daily Margin and No Settlement Risk

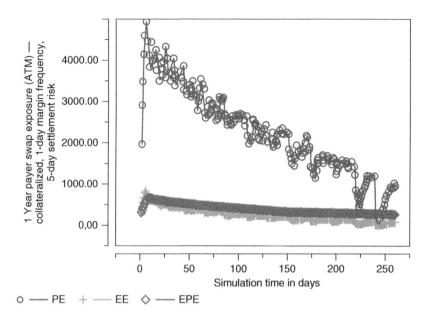

FIGURE 5.17 Expected Exposure, the Running Mean of Expected Positive Exposures, and the Peak Exposure Profile for a 1-Year at-the-Money Payer Swap with Daily Margin and 5-Day Settlement Risk

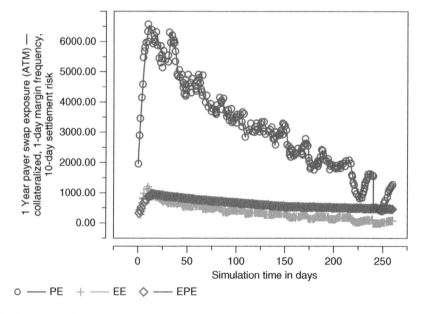

FIGURE 5.18 Expected Exposure, the Running Mean of Expected Positive Exposures, and the Peak Exposure Profile for a 1-Year at-the-Money Payer Swap with Daily Margin and 10-Day Settlement Risk

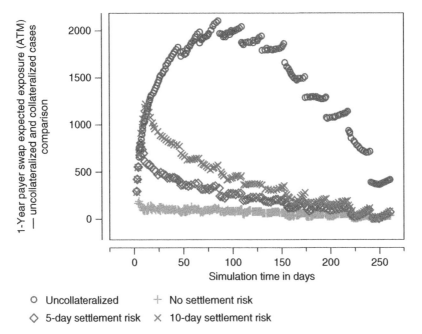

FIGURE 5.19 Expected Exposure for a 1-Year at-the-Money Payer Swap, Uncollateralized and with Different Settlement Risks

would be offset at all times. However, when there is a 5- or 10-day settlement risk as in Figures 5.17 and 5.18, then the sharply increasing (peak) exposures in the beginning of the swap are not fully mitigated due to the settlement delay. Eventually exposure is offset substantially after we have reached the peak of the exposure profile of the swap. This is because when the maximum swap exposure has been reached the swap exposure is decreasing again. The settlement delay impact is clearly not as severe when exposure is declining.

Figure 5.19 displays the expected exposure profiles for the uncollateralized and collateralized 1-year swaps for comparison. The different expected exposure profiles imply that we expect significant differences in CVA for the uncollateralized case and the collateralized cases. This is because swap CVA is essentially the integration of expected exposure times the incremental default probability over time. See equation (5.2). We can also calculate the EPE from the EE profiles in Figure 5.19. For the uncollateralized swap EPE is 1,948 units of currency. The EPE for the collateralized swaps is 77, 244, and 406 units of currency respectively for the case of no settlement risk, 5-day settlement risk, and 10-day settlement risk. This is a significant reduction compared to uncollateralized case.

We can also compare the case of settlement risk versus margin call frequency risk. Figure 5.20 displays expected exposure (EE), the running mean of expected positive exposures (EPE), and the peak exposure (PE) profile for the 1-year fixed rate payer swap with 10-day margining frequency with no settlement risk. As before the deal notional is 1,000,000 units of currency and the collateral agreement margin threshold and minimum transfer amount are set to 500 and 100 units of currency respectively. We notice from Figure 5.20 that at the 10-day margining frequency intervals the maximum exposure is pulled down to the threshold plus the minimum transfer. However, at non-margining days exposure can rise

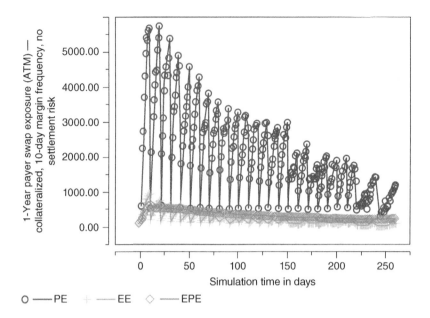

FIGURE 5.20 Expected Exposure, the Running Mean of Expected Positive Exposures, and the Peak Exposure Profile for a 1-Year at-the-Money Payer Swap with 10-Day Margin Frequency and No Settlement Risk

significantly. Comparing with Figure 5.18, which has daily margining but 10-day settlement risk, we find that 10-day settlement risk can be "worse" than 10-day margining frequency risk. This is because when there is no settlement risk the collateral called for at margin days can in principle perfectly offset exposure at the call day (assuming zero threshold and zero minimum transfer amount). However, in case of settlement risk the collateral called for may never offset exposure on the day collateral is received. The differences between the two situations are the largest when exposure is rising. We can therefore conclude that it is not prudent to use an increased margin frequency assumption to approximate settlement risk.

The combined risk of a non-daily margining frequency and settlement risk is displayed in Figures 5.21 and 5.22. Figure 5.21 displays the case of a 10-day margining frequency and 5 day settlement risk. Figure 5.22 displays the exposure for the same 10-day margining frequency but with a 10-day settlement risk. We can conclude from these figures and the figures that display exposure profiles with daily margining and settlement risk that exposure jump risk is the main risk for collateral agreements with settlement risk and/or non-daily margin frequency. Collateral agreements with settlement risk and/or non-daily margin frequency have limited value when exposure is very volatile. However, the collateral agreement has substantial value when exposure is fairly constant or decreasing.

Collateralized Swap CVA Having analyzed the swap exposure profiles with collateral agreements we now compute CVA for the 1-year swaps using different unilateral CSA collateral agreement assumptions. As before, the counterparty CDS term structure has the term points, 1, 3, and 6 months as well as 1, 5, and 10 years and the current quoted CDS premias for the counterparty is 30, 50, 70, 100, 400, and 700 basis points respectively. However, since we are in this case only considering short-term 1-year swaps, only the CDS term structure up to 1 year is used in the CVA calculation. The results are displayed in Table 5.15 for the

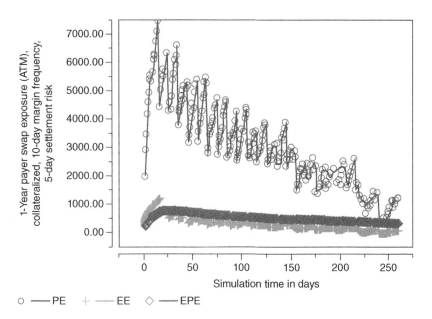

FIGURE 5.21 Expected Exposure, the Running Mean of Expected Positive Exposures, and the Peak Exposure Profile for a 1-Year at-the-Money Payer Swap with 10-Day Margin Frequency and 5-Day Settlement Risk

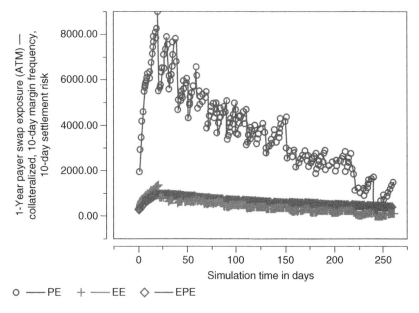

FIGURE 5.22 Expected Exposure, the Running Mean of Expected Positive Exposures, and the Peak Exposure Profile for a 1-Year at-the-Money Payer Swap with 10-Day Margin Frequency and 10-Day Settlement Risk

uncollateralized case as well as collateralized cases with 1, 5, or 10 days settlement risk and 1, 5, or 10 days margining interval. The margin threshold and the minimum transfer amount are 500 and 100 units of currency respectively for all collateral agreements. In the table we have also included the effect of swap wrong-way risk β adjustment factor for an 80% correlation between the counterparty CDS premias (hazard rates) and the interest rates, similar to Table 5.8 for the plain swaps but now focused on the 1-year swaps with different collateral agreements. The model used for CDS premia is the same model we have used previously for modeling wrong-way risk, that is, the model in equation (5.14).

We observe from Table 5.15 that the up-front CVA charges are quite small in currency amount compared to the 1,000,000 notional amount—even for the uncollateralized case. This is because of the short-term horizon of the swap deals. In the most ideal case of daily margining and no settlement risk the CVA is approximately a factor of 20 lower than the uncollateralized case. Even for the worst collateral case in Table 5.15 of 10-day margin interval and 10-day settlement risk the CVA is approximately a factor of 4 lower that the uncollateralized case. This shows that collateral can significantly reduce CVA and that collateral is a strong mitigant of both counterparty exposure and counterparty credit risk valuation adjustments.

As we have mentioned previously there is a strong incentive to reduce CVA in order to make deals profitable and also reduce hedging costs. On the other hand, with collateral the counterparty is now required to manage the collateral calls, which is an operational cost. Previously we discussed that settlement risk of an exposure is not being prudently approximated by using an increased margin frequency with no settlement risk. Table 5.15 shows indeed that the CVA for a swap with a 1-day margin interval and a 10-day settlement risk is higher than the case of the swap with no settlement risk (0 days) and a 10-day margining interval. The 10-day settlement risk case has a CVA of 2.41 units of currency while the 10-day margin interval case has a CVA of 1.35 units of currency.

Focusing on wrong-way risk β adjustments in Table 5.15 we find that the wrong-way risk β adjustment to CVA is slightly increasing for a fixed margin interval as the settlement risk period increases. The wrong-way risk adjustment is naturally largest for the uncollateralized case. Collateral can to some extent mitigate the wrong-way risk. This is because even with delay in settlement or infrequent margining the large exposure and default probability joint rise over a longer time is eventually mitigated.

CVA RISKS

The exposure simulation framework to calculating CVA yields a distribution for exposures as well as a distribution for counterparty default probabilities. Above we calculated the wrong-way risk CVA through jointly integrating default and exposure scenarios. That is, for scenarios, $d = 1, \ldots, D$ we have that

$$\text{CVA}(t, T) = \frac{1}{D} \sum_{n=1}^{N} \sum_{d=1}^{D} [V(t, t_n, d)^+ p(t_{n-1}, t_n, d)].$$

It is natural to also consider the full distribution of CVA, denoted dCVA(t, T, Ω), such that

$$\text{dCVA}(t, T) \sim \left\{ \sum_{n=1}^{N} \left[V(t, t_n, d)^+ p(t_{n-1}, t_n, d) \right] \right\}_{d=1}^{D}. \tag{5.17}$$

TABLE 5.15 Currency Amount Up-Front CVA Charges for 1-Year Uncollateralized and Collateralized Swaps with Different Collateral Parameters and with and Without Wrong-Way Risk. The Swap Notional is 1,000,000 Units of Currency

Collateral parameters		CVA	CVA β WR
Margin interval	Settlement risk		
1 day	0 days	0.53	2.26
1 day	5 days	1.51	2.38
1 day	10 days	2.48	2.41
5 days	0 days	0.98	2.29
5 days	5 days	1.67	2.32
5 days	10 days	2.31	2.41
10 days	0 days	1.35	2.31
10 days	5 days	1.93	2.38
10 days	10 days	2.44	2.42
Uncollateralized case		10.56	2.77

In the context of the CVA distribution in equation (5.17) we can consider several standard tail risk measures such as VaR and CVaR. The CVA distribution, dCVA(t, T, Ω), can also be conditional. For example, we can consider the conditional distribution of CVA conditioning on either default rate or exposure at their current values. We can denote these conditional distributions by dCVA$(t, T, \Omega)_p$ and dCVA$(t, T, \Omega)_V$ respectively. Of course, in case of independence between default rate and exposure the conditional distributions reduce to the marginal distributions.

The conditional distribution dCVA$(t, T, \Omega)_V$ is the distribution used in the Basel III VaR-based regulatory capital charge for CVA based. This is because in the regulatory CVA charge exposure is held constant and assumed independent of the default. Hence, the conditional distribution reduces to a marginal CVA default risk distribution.

Example of CVA Tail Risk Analysis Using the same models for interest rates and CDS premia as we have used before in our examples Table 5.16 displays the 99% CVA VaR for the 10-year ATM, ITM, and OTM payer swaps as well as the ATM 10-year receiver swap. In Table 5.16 we use different CVA distributions corresponding to the cases of

- Default risk only
- Market risk only
- Market and default risk with wrong-way risk.[11]

---

[11]Note that our examples in Table 5.16 focus on the CVA distributions over the life of the 10-year maturity swap trades. As we will discuss in the section on counterparty credit risk regulation in this chapter the advanced Basel III regulatory CVA charge for default risk is focused on calculating two 10-day 99% VaR charges using a calibration period of one-year. The first charge is based on the current one-year period and the second is based on a stressed one-year period.

TABLE 5.16 10-Year Swap Currency Amount Up-Front CVA 95% VaR for the Cases of Default Risk Only, Market Risk Only, and Both Market and Default Risk with Wrong-Way Risk. The Swap Notional is 1,000,000 Units of Currency for all Deals

	CVA distribution VaR 99%			CVA	
Deal	Default risk only	Market risk only	Both (WR)	Independent	Both (WR)
10 Year Payer swap (ATM)	19,277.57	48,004.60	94,813.60	9,746.99	15,680.85
10 Year Payer swap (ITM)	25,394.61	53,739.66	105,909.67	12,865.64	19,843.79
10 Year Payer swap (OTM)	14,342.74	42,368.49	83,87979	7,265.14	12,148.52
10 Year Receiver swap (ATM)	21,048.44	39,492.83	14,535.81	10,557.29	5,112.37

Here we have used the same wrong-way risk model as before in the joint market and default risk distribution with-wrong way risk, that is, 80% correlation between interest rates and market default rates.

Table 5.16 also displays the incurred CVA using the independent CVA assumption and the wrong-way risk model. The incurred CVA is simply the current CVA charge. We notice from the table that the default risk charge is approximately 2% of notional of the ATM 10-year payer swap. However, the current (incurred) CVA charge is about 1% of swap notional. The ITM 10-year payer swap has the largest 99% confidence level VaR default risk charge. On the other hand, the incurred CVA charge is also largest in this case.

The market risk only charge is higher for all the swaps than the default risk only charge. Of course, this observation in the context of our sample swaps and sample models is ultimately due to the volatilities used in default risk versus market models. However, it is not unreasonable in practice that the largest-tail risk contribution is due to exposure variation.

When there is both market and default risk (with wrong-way risk) we notice that the 99% VaR charges increase significantly compared to the default risk only or market risk only charge. This increase is only partially mitigated by the wrong-way risk incurred CVA.

The reader interested in more examples on the tail risk of CVA may consult Skoglund et al. (2013), who focus on the tail risk implied β adjustment for wrong-way risk for collateralized and uncollateralized swaps. The wrong-way risk implied β factor is naturally increasing with tail confidence level. In particular, wrong-way risk can introduce significantly larger (loss) tail risks adjustments than the implied β wrong-way risk adjustment on CVA itself. Since tail risks remain partially unhedged and need to bear capital the impact of wrong-way risk on the required CVA risk buffer can hence be very high, while Basel III only requires market participants to hold capital against credit spread volatility of CVA. That is, default risk only, market participants still need to understand the tail risk for both market-and credit-based tail risk.

PORTFOLIOS OF DERIVATIVES

Netting

Up until now our focus has been on exposure and CVA for specific trades. However, an institution usually has multiple trades with a counterparty and in practice some of these trades may be offsetting. That is, the trades' mark-to-market values have opposite signs. However, when there is no agreement to net the trades each trade is settled independently. The institutions exposure is hence the sum of all the individual exposures to the counterparty on a trade-per-trade basis. An ISDA netting agreement between two parties allows the trades covered under the agreement to be netted out in the portfolio aggregation. In case of a netting agreement for $m = 1, \ldots, M$ trades with a counterparty the aggregate exposure, at time t_n, is

$$E(t_n) = \max \left[\sum_{m=1}^{M} V_m(t_n), 0 \right].$$

We notice here that for a netting agreement to yield value there must be at least one trade in the netting set with a negative market value. Perfect netting of course occurs if there is always an exact canceling trade in the netting set. In practice there may be more than one netting set for trades with a counterparty, for example, trades of similar type or trades in the same currency. For $k = 1, \ldots, K$ netting sets the counterparty exposure, at time t_n, is hence obtained in two steps. First, we aggregate exposure in the $k = 1, \ldots, K$ netting sets

$$E_k(t_n) = \max \left[\sum_{m=1}^{M_k} V_m(t_n), 0 \right] \tag{5.18}$$

and second, we obtain the counterparty level exposure by aggregating the netted exposures across the netting sets. That is,

$$E(t_n) = \sum_{k=1}^{K} E_k(t_n).$$

If an ISDA CSA collateral agreement is in place for the kth netting set, it is applied to the netting set exposure in equation (5.18), after the netting of the subportfolio. The institution's collateralized exposure to the counterparty, for netting set k, is then given by

$$CE_k(t_n) = \max \left\{ \max \left[\sum_{m=1}^{M_k} V_m(t_n), 0 \right] - CB_k(t_n), 0 \right\}$$

where $CB_k(t_n)$ is the collateral balance for netting set k. If all the K netting sets have ISDA CSA agreements, the aggregate counterparty exposure is hence

$$CE(t_n) = \sum_{k=1}^{K} CE_k(t_n).$$

Example Swap Portfolio Netting Effects To illustrate the effect of trade netting Table 5.17 displays an example of the impact of netting on the CVA with a portfolio of 4 trades. The trades include ATM 5-year and 10-year payer swaps as well as ATM 7-year and 10-year receiver swaps using the same models as in our previous exposure examples. Because of the offsetting nature of the trades we should in this case expect netting to yield a significant reduction of exposure and CVA. This is indeed what we find in Table 5.17. Netting reduces the portfolio CVA by a factor of approximately 8. Figure 5.23 displays the trade and netted portfolio EE profiles and Figure 5.24 displays the trade and netted portfolio 99% confidence level PE profiles. For this portfolio an important first level of risk mitigation is clearly netting. The second level of mitigation is potentially an ISDA CSA collateral agreement on the netting set.

TABLE 5.17 Currency Amount Up-Front CVA for a Portfolio of Swaps—With Netting and No Netting. The Swap Notional is 1,000,000 Units of Currency for all Deals

Deal	CVA
5 Year Payer swap (ATM)	1,752.31
7 Year Receiver swap (ATM)	4,392.80
10 Year Payer swap (ATM)	9,746.99
10 Year Receiver swap (ATM)	10,557.29
Portfolio (no netting-sum)	26,449.39
Portfolio (netting)	3,259.37

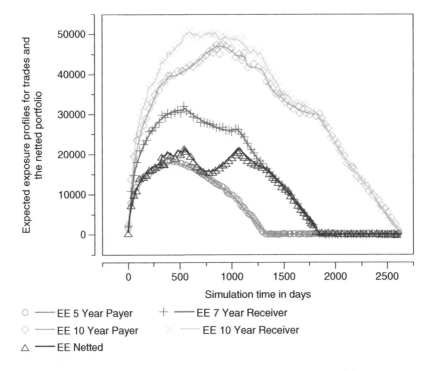

FIGURE 5.23 Expected Exposures for Portfolio Trades and the Netted Portfolio

Marginal and Incremental Portfolio Trades

Expected Exposure and CVA In the context of a netted portfolio of trades a natural question is how we can decompose the exposure and CVA into trade contributions. Previously, in the context of market risk and portfolio credit risk, we have used the Euler contributions in the simulation-based case to calculate risk contributions to VaR and CVaR. In the simulation-based setting the Euler contribution is essentially a conditional expectation. Focusing on Euler contributions to a netted portfolio EE we first note that to compute the

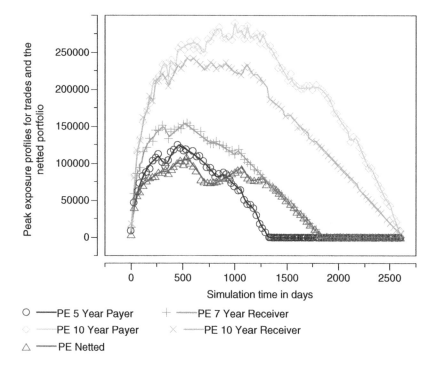

FIGURE 5.24 Peak Exposures for Portfolio Trades and the Netted Portfolio

portfolio netted EE, at time t_n, for netting set k, we take an empirical expectation across scenarios, $d = 1, \ldots, D$. That is,

$$EE_k(t_n) = \frac{1}{D} \sum_{d=1}^{D} \left[\max \left[\sum_{m=1}^{M_k} V_m^d(t_n), 0 \right] \right].$$

The Euler contribution of trade m to the portfolio EE_k at time t_n, $D_{EE_k(t_n)}(m)$, is hence

$$D_{EE_k(t_n)}(m) = \frac{1}{D} \sum_{d=1}^{D} [V_m^d(t_n) \mid E_k^d(t_n) > 0]. \tag{5.19}$$

This is because a marginal contribution to the netted portfolio EE_k at time t_n can only be made when $E_k^d(t_n) > 0$. That is, the portfolio netted value is positive for scenario d.

The fact that each trades marginal EE sums to portfolio netted EE also means that we can define a marginal CVA using the marginal EE. Specifically, for $m = 1, \ldots, M_k$ trades in the $k{:}th$ netting set we can decompose the netted portfolio CVA as

$$\mathrm{CVA}(t, T) = \sum_{n=1}^{N} EE_k(t_n) \, p(t_{n-1}, t_n)$$

$$= \sum_{n=1}^{N} \left[\sum_{m=1}^{M_k} D_{EE_k(t_n)}(m) \right] p(t_{n-1}, t_n). \tag{5.20}$$

We therefore have that

$$
\begin{aligned}
\text{CVA}(t, T) &= \sum_{m=1}^{M_k} \left[\sum_{n=1}^{N} D_{EE_k(t_n)}(m)\, p(t_{n-1}, t_n) \right] \\
&= \sum_{m=1}^{M_k} D_{\text{CVA}(t,T)}(m)
\end{aligned}
$$

where $D_{\text{CVA}(t,T)}(m)$ is the Euler contribution to CVA from trade m. Hence, from the Euler allocation of EE we automatically have an Euler allocation of CVA in terms of trade contributions to CVA. Note here that across the netting sets of a counterparty the EE and CVA contribution to the $k = 1, \ldots, K$ netting sets is trivial since we have that the counterparty EE is just a sum of EE across the netting sets. That is,

$$
E(t_n) = \sum_{k=1}^{K} E_k(t_n).
$$

This means that within each netting set we can obtain the Euler contributions of EE and CVA as in equation (5.19) and equation (5.20). However, across netting sets the corresponding contributions reduce to the simple sum of EE and CVA.

Numerical Example of Marginal EE for Trades In Table 5.18 we display three scenarios for the sample netting set portfolio used in Table 5.17. For each of the trades in the portfolio—which includes a 5-year payer swap, a 7-year receiver swap, a 10-year payer swap, and a 10-year receiver swap—we compute trade and portfolio aggregate mark to market for the three scenarios across an exposure simulation time grid, $\{t_n\}_{n=1}^{11}$. The 11 time points in the time grid correspond to the day 1 exposure and a time point for every year until the final maturity of the portfolio at 10 years. Clearly, after a trade has matured it will have zero mark-to-market value for all three scenarios in Table 5.18. Table 5.18 also displays the portfolio and trade EE as well as the marginal EE, $D_{EE_k(t_n)}(m)$, of each trade to the portfolio netted EE. The trade marginal EE are computed using equation (5.19).

To see how equation (5.19) is used to derive the marginal EE for trades in Table 5.18 consider the 5-year payer swap marginal EE at time t_1 (i.e., the 1-day exposure). In scenario 1 the 5-year payer swap mark to market is–2,811.59 units of currency. In scenario 2 the mark to market is 2,663.94 units of currency, and in scenario 3, $-3,820.18$ units of currency. The marginal $EE(t_1)$, $D_{EE_k(t_1)}(m)$, is hence

$$
\frac{1}{3} \sum_{d=1}^{3} [V_m^d(t_1) \mid E_k^d(t_1) > 0] = \frac{1}{3}[V_m^1(t_n) + V_m^3(t_n)] = \frac{-2,811.59 - 3,820.18}{3} = -2,210.59.
$$

(5.21)

Note here that the average of market values in equation (5.21) does not use scenario 2. This is because in scenario 2 the portfolio market value at time t_1 is negative and hence the netted portfolio exposure does not satisfy the condition, $E_k^d(t_1) > 0$.

Figure 5.25 displays graphically the trades marginal EE and the portfolio netted EE in Table 5.18. By definition the marginal EE of all the trades in Table 5.18 sum to the portfolio EE.

TABLE 5.18 Trade and Netted Portfolio Mark to Market, Expected Exposure, and Marginal Exposure for 3 Scenarios

Simulation time	5 Year Payer swap (ATM)				
	Scenario 1	Scenario 2	Scenario 3	Marginal EE	Trade EE
1 day	−2,811.59	2,663.94	−3,820.18	−2,210.59	887.98
1 year	8,102.22	−30,471.66	−42,540.19	−24,337.28	2,700.74
2 years	12,628.30	−10,879.55	−62,154.78	−24,344.78	4,209.43
3 years	−15,119.55	−15,038.48	−50,351.79	−21,823.78	0
4 years	1,557.03	−12,335.43	−16,237.10	−5,412.37	519.01
5 years	−2,105.74	−608.90	−1,570.75	−1,225.50	0
6 years	0	0	0	0	0
7 years	0	0	0	0	0
8 years	0	0	0	0	0
9 years	0	0	0	0	0
10 years	0	0	0	0	0

	7 Year Receiver swap (ATM)				
	Scenario 1	Scenario 2	Scenario 3	Marginal EE	Trade EE
1 day	3826,08	−3727,28	5173,13	2999,74	2999,74
1 year	−27810,76	56120,01	54957,01	37025,67	37025,67
2 years	−14757,44	72513,44	74467,42	48993,62	48993,62
3 years	29832,35	−47425,14	116663,73	48832,03	48832,03
4 years	−6526,14	8586,75	116009,61	38669,87	41532,12
5 years	15566,45	−22403,79	67697,74	27754,73	27754,73
6 years	9415,06	−22217,78	18724,41	9379,82	9379,82
7 years	955,81	1490,68	2297,50	1581,33	1581,33
8 years	0	0	0	0	0
9 years	0	0	0	0	0
10 years	0	0	0	0	0

	10 Year Payer swap (ATM)				
	Scenario 1	Scenario 2	Scenario 3	Marginal EE	Trade EE
1 day	−5,173.11	5,134.27	−6,970.60	−4,047.90	1,711.42
1 year	38,928.21	−80,038.62	−77,549.72	−52,529.45	12,976.07
2 years	22,589.59	−118,588.74	−114,065.36	−77,551.37	7,529.86
3 years	−82,608.48	−57,333.04	−170,954.54	−84,521.01	0
4 years	−24,548.52	7,250.35	−188,617.80	−62,872.60	2,416.78
5 years	−70,832.58	85,336.31	−190,364.08	−87,065.55	28,445.44
6 years	−46,481.47	70,899.07	−72,682.01	−39,721.16	23,633.02
7 years	−2,011.84	35,583.99	−118,283.63	−28,237.16	11,861.33
8 years	35,949.01	23,062.21	−49,491.32	0	19,670.41
9 years	44,258.10	−7,690.89	−1,314.66	0	14,752.70
10 years	2,885.95	−697.88	−2,194.85	0	961.98

(continued)

TABLE 5.18   (*continued*)

	10 Year Receiver swap (ATM)				
	Scenario 1	Scenario 2	Scenario 3	Marginal EE	Trade EE
1 day	5,173.11	−5,134.27	6,970.60	4,047.90	4,047.90
1 year	−38,928.21	80,038.62	77,549.72	52,529.45	52,529.45
2 years	−22,589.59	118,588.74	114,065.36	77,551.37	77,551.37
3 years	82,608.48	57,333.04	170,954.54	84,521.01	103,632.02
4 years	24,548.52	−7,250.35	188,617.80	62,872.60	71,055.44
5 years	70,832.58	−85,336.31	190,364.08	87,065.55	87,065.55
6 years	46,481.47	−70,899.07	72,682.01	39,721.16	39,721.16
7 years	2,011.84	−35,583.99	118,283.63	28,237.16	40,098.49
8 years	−35,949.01	−23,062.21	49,491.32	0	16,497.11
9 years	−44,258.10	7,690.89	1,314.66	0	3,001.85
10 years	−2,885.95	697.88	2,194.85	0	964.25

	Portfolio			
	Scenario 1	Scenario 2	Scenario 3	Portfolio EE
1 day	1,014.49	−1,063.34	1,352.95	789.15
1 year	−19,708.53	25,648.35	12,416.82	12,688.39
2 years	−2,129.13	61,633.89	12,312.64	24,648.84
3 years	14,712.80	−62,463.62	66,311.94	27,008.25
4 years	−4,969.11	−3,748.68	99,772.51	33,257.50
5 years	13,460.71	−23,012.69	66,126.99	26,529.23
6 years	9,415.06	−22,217.78	18,724.41	9,379.82
7 years	955.81	1,490.68	2,297.50	1,581.33
8 years	0	0	0	0
9 years	0	0	0	0
10 years	0	0	0	0

Peak Exposures and Wrong-Way Risk CVA   The Euler decomposition of *EE* can be extended straightforwardly to *PE* and other tail risk measures on the exposures. The Euler decomposition of tail-based exposure risk measures uses the same principles as for market risk measures. Let the *PE* (VaR) exposure at time t_1 be given. Then the *PE* contribution of the trades is just the mark to market of the trades for this VaR scenario at time t_1 (assuming VaR is identified with a specific scenario). By linearity we can apply the same approach to linear combinations of scenarios, for example, *PE* measures based on CVaR or risk distortion measures, that we discussed in the advanced market risk chapter, that weights scenarios. For illustration Figure 5.26 displays the Table 5.18 worst-case scenario exposure decomposition into trade contributions.

That we can decompose *PE* measures as well as *EE* means that wrong-way risk CVA models using a worst-case exposure profile as a proxy for the correlation between default probability and exposures, such as in equation (5.11), can be decomposed into trade CVA contributions. However, when wrong-way risk is modeled explicitly with correlation between default probability and exposure we must of course integrate the exposure and default probability path by path as in equation (5.13). The basis for the CVA contributions is then the product of default probability and market value.

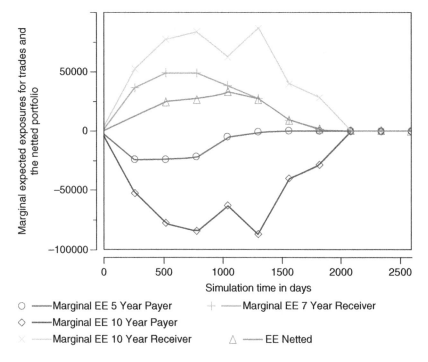

FIGURE 5.25   Marginal Expected Exposures for Portfolio Trades and the Netted Portfolio

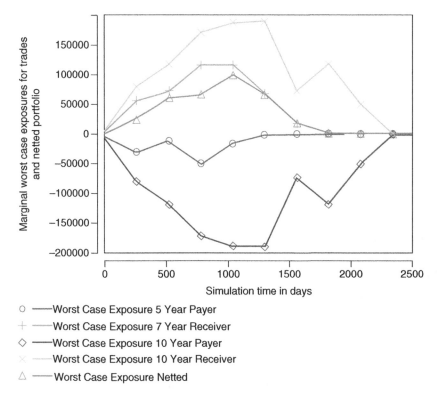

FIGURE 5.26   Marginal Worst-Case Exposures for Portfolio Trades and the Netted Portfolio

Decomposition with Collateral   A complication in practice is when the netting set has a collateral agreement. That is, how can we decompose *EE*, *PE*, and CVA contribution of trades to netting set when there is an ISDA CSA agreement? In that case we of course have to decide for a model of distributing netting set collateral back to trades. Specifically, for netting set k we have that collateralized exposure, $CE_k(t_n)$, at time point t_n can be written as

$$CE_k(t_n) = \max\{\max\left[\sum_{m=1}^{M_k} V_m(t_n), 0\right] - CB_k(t_n), 0\}$$
$$= \max[E_k(t_n) - CB_k(t_n), 0]$$

where $E_k(t_n)$ is the uncollateralized exposure and $CB_k(t_n)$ is the collateral balance. Once we have obtained the uncollateralized Euler allocation of *EE*, $D_{EE_k(t_n)}(m)$, for trade $m = 1, \ldots, M_k$ we now need to allocate $CB_k(t_n)$. In principle there are multiple ways to allocate the netting set trades common collateral balance, $CB_k(t_n)$, back to the trades and theoretical arguments have to be given for one way or another. Naturally, one would try and distribute the collateral back to the trades consuming collateral in fair allocations. We refer to Pykthin and Rosen (2010) for a discussion of Euler allocations with collateral agreements.[12]

New Trade Impact on CVA   While exposure and CVA contributions are used to decompose an existing portfolio of trades one can also ask what is the exposure and CVA impact of a new trade or a set of new trades. Assuming that the new trade does not change the counterparty default probability we have that the change in CVA, ΔCVA, due to the new trade(s) is

$$\Delta CVA(t, T) = \left[\sum_{n=1}^{N} \widetilde{EE}_k(t_n) - \sum_{n=1}^{N} EE_k(t_n)\right] p(t_{n-1}, t_n)$$
$$= \sum_{n=1}^{N} \Delta EE_k(t_n) p(t_{n-1}, t_n).$$

Here, we have used the notation $\widetilde{EE}_k(t_n)$ for the netting set *EE* with the new trade(s) and $EE_k(t_n)$ is the original portfolio *EE*. Clearly, $\Delta EE_k(t_n)$ can be negative if the new trade(s) is offsetting and hence incremental CVA can be negative. As for CVA contributions this simple formula of incremental CVA in terms of incremental *EE* only works in case of no wrong-way risk. In case of wrong-way risk we of course have to integrate the incremental trade(s) exposure and the default probability path by path using equation (5.13).

RECENT COUNTERPARTY CREDIT RISK DEVELOPMENTS

OIS Discounting for Derivatives

During the 2007 financial crisis the spread between market rates like LIBOR (London Interbank Offered Rate) and OIS (Overnight Index Swap) increased significantly, suggesting that

---

[12]Of course, if the collateral is on trade level rather than on netting set level, then taking into account collateral in the Euler allocation of netting set exposure to trades is trivial as we just use the trades' collateralized exposure as basis for the netting and hence the allocation.

LIBOR is no longer a good approximation to risk-free rates. With the collateralization of the derivatives market to significantly reduce counterparty credit risk—either through bilateral agreements or central clearing—it is harder to argue for using LIBOR to discount derivative cash flows. The OIS rates are now preferred by dealers to value, for example, collateralized interest rate swaps because it removes the bank credit risk that is being priced into LIBOR. However, as Hull and White (2013) argue, OIS should be used to discount all derivatives—whether collateralized or not—as the credit risk adjustment is made through CVA to the risk-free market value. When OIS discounting is used the payment curve of the floating rate leg (LIBOR) must be bootstrapped relative to the OIS discount curve to ensure swap prices to par. See Bianchetti (2012). Smith (2012) also provides simple numerical examples of the calculation.

Advanced CVA Calculations and CVA Greeks

Our examples of CVA have focused on simple swap products and an intuitive exposure simulation framework for CVA. The exposure simulation framework used here can be referred to as a forward simulation framework. This is because the portfolio trades are valued under scenarios for the market risk factors at future discrete time steps, $\{t_n\}_{n=1}^{N}$. Obtaining CVA is then a post-process calculation on the exposure. The forward simulation approach to CVA works well for simple interest rate and cross-currency swaps. This is because the forward swap pricing is analytical with minimal pricing time for the $d = 1, \ldots, D$ market scenarios across the time steps, $\{t_n\}_{n=1}^{N}$. This is also true for many other deals, including foreign exchange swaps and foreign exchange forwards, caps and floors, equity forwards, swaps, and vanilla equity and foreign exchange options as well as European swaptions. However, products such as Bermudan and American swaptions do not have an analytic pricing and the exact pricing typically requires either simulation or a lattice approach. Hence, using the forward simulation framework we require time-consuming nested simulation valuation for each market scenario path $d = 1, \ldots, D$ and time step, $\{t_n\}_{n=1}^{N}$. To reduce the pricing time in the exposure simulation framework nested simulation can be avoided. One simple approach is to approximate the complex deal with a simpler deal that can be priced analytically. That is, use an approximate analytic pricing model. For example, we can represent a Bermudan swaption as a European swaption. Another approach is to use LSMC as the foundation for pricing. We have previously discussed LSMC in the context of reducing pricing time in the first market risk chapter. A core feature of LSMC is that it uses only the $d = 1, \ldots, D$ market scenarios and the specification of the regression function for calculating continuation value of the option at time points, $\{t_n\}_{n=1}^{N}$. By its valuation approach LSMC also gives a complete price distribution from which exposure measures and CVA can be computed. We refer to Cesari et al. (2009) for details on a computationally attractive CVA process that has as its foundation LSMC for pricing.

Another complexity in practice is that the efficient hedging of CVA requires the calculation of CVA Greeks with respect to model parameters such as counterparty CDS premia and market models for exposure. When there is no wrong-way risk such that CVA can be calculated as in equation (5.2),

$$\text{CVA}(t, T) = \sum_{n=1}^{N} \text{EE}(t_n)\, p(t_{n-1}, t_n)$$

the CVA finite difference sensitivity to counterparty CDS premia is easily obtained by perturbing the CDS premia of the counterparty, and using the implied shifts of the counterparty default probability, $p(t_{n-1}, t_n)$, to compute the CVA sensitivity. No simulation is required. However, even under an independent market and default probability assumption for CVA, the CVA sensitivity to market parameters such as initial yield curve in general requires a re-computation of expected exposures, EE, that is, a re-simulation of exposure. The usual finite difference approximation to sensitivities traditionally employed in market risk use an upward and downward shift (bump) for each point on the yield curve to arrive at the perturbed market value. However, consider applying the traditional finite difference approximation to CVA for a plain interest rate swap with a market model for the yield curve. If the yield curve has 20 points, we require 40 re-simulations (to include both +/–bumps) of exposure to compute CVA first-order finite difference sensitivities to the yield curve. Clearly, this approach is not feasible in practice as the institution may have hundreds or even thousands of market parameters in the CVA calculation for which sensitivities are needed. Moreover, we have not yet considered calculation of second-order sensitivities to the market parameters. To avoid finite difference approximations Capriotti et al. (2011) propose using adjoint algorithmic differentiation in the context of CVA to approximate first-order sensitivities efficiently. The method applies the chain rule of differentiation to obtain first-order Greeks at the same time as CVA itself is obtained. The computational cost of obtaining CVA sensitivities in addition to CVA is at most a factor 4 regardless of dimension and complexity of the portfolio. See also Homescu (2011a, 2011b) on methods for efficient sensitivities computation. Cesari et al. (2009) use perturbation in the LSMC regression function to obtain price sensitivities to the CVA market parameters at the same time as the price is computed. It is a two-step method where first the total price derivative with respect to the market parameters is obtained. Second, the total derivative is orthogonalized—removing the correlation in the total derivative.

Funding Value Adjustments

A trader that needs to fund collateral posts can fund at the bank's funding rate. However, posted collateral may earn a lower rate than the bank's funding rate, for example, if the funding rate is LIBOR and the rate paid on collateral is OIS. Funding value adjustments (FVA) take into account future funding requirements (to fund collateral posts) and funding benefits (received collateral from counterparty). As long as neither the institution nor the counterparty has defaulted the bank can gain the funding spread for borrowing when the counterparty posts (i.e., positive exposure) and lose the lending funding spread when posting (i.e., negative exposure). For a fixed (over time) funding spread for borrowing, f_B, and fixed funding lending spread, f_L, we can therefore write the FVA as

$$\text{FVA}(t, T) = \sum_{n=1}^{N} \text{EE}(t_n) S^*(t_{n-1}, t_n) f_B - \sum_{n=1}^{N} \text{NEE}(t_n) S^*(t_{n-1}, t_n) f_L$$

where EE is the expected exposure, NEE the negative expected exposure, and

$$S^*(t_{n-1}, t_n) = S_I(t_{n-1}, t_n) S(t_{n-1}, t_n)$$

with $S_I(t_{n-1}, t_n)$ the institution's survival probability and $S(t_{n-1}, t_n)$ the counterparty survival probability. We refer to Piterbarg (2010) and Burgard and Kjaer (2011) for details on FVA. However, whether to include FVA in the valuation is a debatable issue. See Hull and White (2012b) and the response by Burgard and Kjaer (2012) and Castagna (2012). Clearly, if a bank chooses to pass the FVA cost to clients, it can hold client costs down with low funding spreads. Hence, this creates a competitive advantage for banks with lower than average spreads.

COUNTERPARTY CREDIT RISK REGULATION

The first regulation for counterparty credit risk appeared in the Basel 1988 Capital Accord. It introduced the concept of current exposure method being based on the replacement cost (mark to market) and a specific add-on that should reflect potential future exposure. In a 1995 Basel amendment (Basel Committee, 1995), the current exposure method was updated with an enhanced add-on matrix and allowance for netting of add-ons in case of bilateral netting agreements. Counterparty risk is also part of the CCAR and EBA stress testing exercises. For example, CCAR requires bank holding companies with significant trading operations to consider a counterparty default scenario for the largest counterparty exposure. The resulting loss is an add-on component to CCAR firmwide stress similar as the market risk shock. EBA also considers a CVA stress from market-based loss contribution.

Basel Counterparty Default Risk Charges

In July 2005, with Basel II, the counterparty credit risk regulation was significantly updated to allow banks to use an internal model for exposure measurement (Basel Committee, 2005b). In total, three methods were now available to banks for exposure measurement:

1. The internal models method based on the bank's own exposure simulation models
2. The standardized method
3. The already existing current exposure method

In the internal models method the trades are marked to market at a significant number of time steps across several thousands of market states. In the second step the valuations are netted, and, finally, the dynamics of collateral agreements are taken into account to yield a distribution of exposure from which exposure measures are calculated.

In contrast to market risk where the time horizon for model evaluation is short (for example, one day), the simulation horizon for models for counterparty exposure is longer-term (for example, 10 years). This means that the model specifications should capture key characteristics of long-term observed behavior in the markets such as mean-reversion. On the other hand, model features such as stochastic volatility that is important for short-term market risk is typically less important.

The average counterparty exposure profile over time is a measure of the expected exposure to the counterparty. The expected *positive* exposure is subsequently defined as the single expected exposure value that is obtained by averaging over the expected exposure profile. The expected positive exposure measure is therefore often referred to as a "loan equivalent" exposure as it is a single value of counterparty exposure. The expected positive exposure is also the exposure measure used by regulators to calculate regulatory capital for default-based counterparty credit risk. Specifically, the regulators require the use of the *effective* expected positive exposure. This is simply the expected positive exposure based on a non-decreasing expected exposure profile to capture that maturing trades will likely be rolled over.

The Basel II counterparty credit risk charge requires banks to calculate regulatory capital based on a one-year horizon. The regulatory definition of exposure at default also depends on a so-called alpha factor. The alpha factor is supposed to capture effects not covered by the exposure model and can be regulatory prescribed or use an internal model. Using the regulatory exposure at default the capital requirement is based on the well-known Basel II risk weighted assets formula in equation (4.41). The Basel II counterparty credit risk regulatory capital hence depends on both the exposure and the default probability of the counterparty. It also depends on a maturity adjustment. This is because for netting sets with exposures longer than a year, the maturity adjustment is based on the ratio of discounted expected exposure past one year to discounted effective expected exposure of the first year. This means that while effective expected positive exposure—used as exposure at default in the risk weighted assets formula—is only based on a year, the exposure simulation time horizon must take into account the longest-dated contract in the netting set to calculate the maturity adjustment needed for risk weighted assets.

Enhanced Requirements on Counterparty Default Risk Charges

General Wrong-Way Risk and Alpha With the Basel III regulation (Basel Committee, 2011a) there is an increased focus on identifying and accounting for wrong-way risk. For example, to capture general wrong-way risk in the default risk charge, exposure is calibrated using a period of stressed market data. This is similar to the market risk framework with stressed VaR. Regulators also place additional constraints on firm's own estimates of the Basel II alpha factor.

Backtesting Requirements The Basel committee has also, with the introduction of Basel III, announced that backtesting of counterparty exposure models will be a requirement for internal models compliant banks. This means that the model specification and calibration will have to be validated carefully. However, backtesting counterparty credit risk is more complicated than backtesting market risk due to the potentially long exposure horizons to test. To expand the number of forecasts that can be tested one can consider using overlapping time intervals. This clearly leads to a larger amount of samples. However, at the same time autocorrelation is introduced. We refer to Richardson and Smith (1991) for a discussion on the use of overlapping time intervals in statistical tests. See also Epperlein et al. (2010) and Basel Committee (2010a) on counterparty credit risk backtesting.

For backtesting the counterparty exposure model can be decomposed in the model components of

1. Market risk factor models
2. Exposure valuation models
3. Collateral models
4. The netting and aggregation process

Assuming no model risk or model error in valuation, collateral calculation, or aggregation, the simulated risk factor distributions (and the assumed correlations between risk factors) drive the exposure distribution from which exposure measures are obtained. Hence, in counterparty credit risk the main driver of exposure is the risk factor models for interest rates, foreign exchange, equity, and so forth. Backtests on the risk factor distributions such as quantiles and density tests can use the backtesting methods we have discussed in the advanced market risk chapter, albeit with the added complexity of dealing with longer time horizons than in market risk. However, exposure level backtesting is also needed as the portfolio exposure not only depends on the univariate risk factor distributions but also on the assumed correlations.

Anfuso et al. (2014) discuss a credit exposure model backtesting framework that has the components of:

- Univariate risk factor models backtesting, using the empirical density probability integral transformation to uniform and standard density tests
- Model correlation backtesting
- Portfolio-level backtesting, again using the probability integral transformation but now on the simulated market values

They also propose an adjusted capital buffer calculation that takes into account how well the counterparty exposure profile performs in backtesting.

New Basel III Capital Requirements for Counterparty Credit Risk

Motivated by the recent crisis the Basel III regulation also sets forth two new capital requirements for counterparty credit risk. The new requirements are:

- Measuring counterparty market-based losses that are not due to default using a VaR model for CVA
- A charge for exposures that have specific wrong-way risk

This is in addition to the existing Basel II default capital charge for counterparty credit risk based on the risk weighted asset formula. The new CVA capital requirement is consistent with the fact that the majority of losses during the recent crisis were attributable to mark-to-market devaluation of OTC derivatives due to downgrades of derivative counterparties, as opposed to just outright defaults and realized losses. The new CVA charge can use an advanced internal model or a standardized approach depending on whether the bank's internal model for market risk is approved for interest rate specific risk.

Advanced CVA Charge   The advanced CVA capital charge uses the counterparty market default risk volatility (credit spreads or CDS premiums) as the basis for CVA VaR. The CVA model used is essentially equation (5.2),

$$\text{CVA}(t, T) = \sum_{n=1}^{N} \text{EE}(t_n)\, p(t_{n-1}, t_n)$$

and is explicitly specified as

$$\overline{\text{CVA}}(t, T) = \text{LGD} \sum_{n=1}^{N} \frac{\overline{\text{EE}}(t_n) + \overline{\text{EE}}(t_{n-1})}{2} \varphi(t_{n-1}, t_t) \tag{5.22}$$

where LGD is the market loss given default rate, $\overline{\text{EE}}(t_n)$ is the discounted expected exposure at t_n. That is, the discounted version of $\text{EE}(t_n)$, and

$$\varphi(t_{n-1}, t_t) = \max\left[0, \exp\left(\frac{-s\left(t_{n-1}\right) \times t_{n-1}}{\text{LGD}}\right) - \exp\left(\frac{-s\left(t_n\right) \times t_n}{\text{LGD}}\right)\right]$$

is the incremental default probability, $p(t_{n-1}, t_n)$, with $s(t_n)$ the counterparty credit spread at t_n. See equation (5.6). Dividing the counterparty credit spread by the LGD we obtain the counterparty default rate (hazard rate). If counterparty credit spreads are not available in the market, a proxy spread is used based on external rating and so on (see Figure 5.1).

The specific requirement is that banks must hold capital for mark-to-market losses in counterparty exposure equal to a 10-day horizon 99% confidence level VaR for CVA risks. Similar to the market risk VaR charge the capital charge is the sum of both current one-year calibration period CVA charges and stressed one-year calibration period CVA charges with a prescribed regulatory multiplier of 3 on the total charge. Credit hedges such as single-name CDS contracts and index CDS are allowed to be counted in the CVA charge.

The fact that the advanced CVA charge is based on a 10-day horizon as in market risk and a fixed exposure profile means that banks can, with little modification, use their existing market risk bond VaR model to compute the charge. The fixed exposure profile is in this context simply viewed as a bond notional profile.

Standardized CVA Charge The standardized CVA capital charge is based on a first-order approximation to the variation of CVA in equation (5.22) and a log-normal distribution assumption for credit spreads that uses one-factor models. See Pykthin (2012) for the derivation. The standardized CVA formula is based on a one-year 99% VaR with the prescribed capital charge formula, K_S, as

$$
K_S = \gamma \sqrt{\left(\sum_{k=1}^{K} 0.5 w_k \left(M_k EAD_k - M_k^h B_k \right) - \sum_{l=1}^{L} w_l M_l B_l \right)^2 + \sum_{k=1}^{K} 0.75 w_k^2 (M_k EAD_k - M_k^h B_k)^2 }
$$

(5.23)

where $k = 1, \ldots, K$ are the counterparty netting sets. The standardized CVA formula inputs include:

- w_k, which is a regulatory prescribed credit spread volatility per rating class.
- M_k and EAD_k, which are essentially the Basel II effective maturity and exposure at default for the netting set.
- B_k, which is the notional of a single-name CDS hedge for counterparty k and M_k^h the hedge effective maturity.
- Finally, w_l, M_l and B_l are used to reflect index CDS hedges with B_l the index CDS notional and w_l is assigned to the regulatory credit spread volatility rating class based on the index average.

The multiplying factor $\gamma = 2.33$ in equation (5.23) is here coming from the choice of the 99% level confidence VaR and the normal distribution assumption.

Criticism of the CVA Charge The new CVA capital component put forward by Basel III has been criticized by the industry. See Pengelley (2011). A key issue is that the CVA capital charge is restricted to changes in the credit spread of the counterparty and does not model the sensitivity of CVA to changes in market factors. This means that the CVA desk market risk hedges are not recognized within the regulatory CVA model and could potentially be adding to the bank's market risk capital requirement. Recently, however, the Basel Committee is considering to review the CVA framework allowing banks to count market risk hedges and advanced CVA banks to have fully internal models.

Mitigating Regulatory Costs

The new CVA capital charge and the strengthened Basel default risk charges for counter-party exposure means that banks will face significantly larger regulatory costs associated with bilateral derivative trading. On one hand, these costs can be mitigated by the CVA desk actively hedging the counterparty credit risk. However, hedging comes at a cost, and regula-tory eligible hedges only include certain credit hedges while market hedges are not recognized. In addition, many derivative counterparties don't have liquidly traded CDS so a CVA desk typically hedges the illiquid names using a combination of single-name proxies and/or indices.

An alternative for banks is to move trades through central clearing. While historically OTC derivatives have mainly remained as a bilaterally netted contract market regulators have encouraged establishment of financial market infrastructures with central clearing. Essen-tially, centralized clearing is a process with a legally obligated central counterparty (CCP) that stands between parties with respect to contracts traded between them. This structure permits multilateral netting of contracts that are entered into by any counterparty in the CCP. The CCP has a layer of capital structures to protect the CCP. This typically includes an initial mar-gin posted by the members as well as a variation margin that is used to cover daily exposure changes up to a certain confidence level. In addition the CCP members have to contribute to a guarantee fund, which is a shared insurance fund for uncollateralized loss. However, if the guarantee fund turns out to be insufficient, CCP members have the obligation (up to some level) to bail out the CCP.[13] While moving trades through a CCP can reduce counterparty credit risk—as does of course collateral agreements with bilateral trades as well—it is clear that counterparty credit risk has to some extent been replaced by potential funding liquidity risk. This is the risk that the bank has to fund collateral or bail out the CCP exactly at a time when the bank may find it hard to attract funds.

---

[13]Basel III (Basel Committee (2013)) has included a charge for a bank's exposure to a CCP default fund as a function of risk sensitivity of CCP default fund.

Three

Asset and Liability Management

CHAPTER **6**

Liquidity Risk Management with Cash Flow Models

Classical asset and liability management focuses on a balance sheet view of the firm and the control of two key balance sheet risks: interest rate risk and liquidity risk. Banking book interest rate risk impact on profit and loss is often measured through the net interest margin of assets and liabilities. The net interest margin impact of interest rate changes is a cash flow view on the asset and liabilities interest flows. However, one can also assess the impact of the present value of all cash flows. This is a long-term solvency view referred to as an economic value view of the balance sheet.

The analysis of net interest margin and economic value of balance sheet is focused on short- and long-term profitability of the balance sheet. Profitability of a balance sheet is of course also connected to liquidity. However, profitability is no guarantee for liquidity. A financial institution that is long-term solvent (economic value view) can be short-term illiquid. We can define liquidity risk management broadly as the management of the bank's ability to meet its obligations as they come due, without incurring losses. In contrast to risk-based capital for other forms of risks, such as market and credit risk, the cushion for liquidity risk is not created through additional capital. This is because the hedge for liquidity risk is ultimately cash to offset the negative flows and restore liquidity.

Traditionally, liquidity risk exposure of a financial institution is measured as the funding gap of assets and liabilities. This is constructed from the cash inflows and outflows of the balance sheet. Both normal and stressed funding gaps are created and the liquid assets that can hedge out the funding gap are applied to the funding gap to test adequacy of the liquidity cushion. It is also practice for financial institutions to monitor structural balance sheet liquidity ratios such as market value of liquid hedge assets over amount of non-maturing or non-sticky deposits. Here, the amount of non-sticky deposits includes the deposits that can likely be withdrawn at any point in time in a liquidity crisis. The amount of liquid hedge assets should be able to cover such a scenario.[1]

Lately, funding liquidity risk has received serious attention from the regulators, banks, and investors. A brief retrospective on the 2007 financial crisis serves as a good illustration of the significance of liquidity risk, and how it resulted from a subprime (credit) risk. The beginning of 21st century saw a low mortgage rate environment thanks to the global interest

---

[1]See Dermine and Bissada (2002) or Choudry (2007) for an introduction to classical liquidity and interest rate risk asset and liability management tools. In this chapter we cover extensively the behavioral modeling of cash flow and interest income in the context of liquidity risk. We have also discussed the credit risk impact on interest and principal income in Chapter 4 in this book. We will also return to the issue of bank profitability analysis in the next chapter on funds transfer pricing and profitability of cash flows as well as in Chapter 9 on firmwide scenario analysis and stress testing.

in US mortgage–backed securities (securitization). As a result, the boom of the US housing market led to a surge of low-quality subprime mortgage loans. After peaking in mid-2006, US house prices started to decline accompanied by increasing mortgage rates. Borrowers' ability to refinance their variable rate loans decreased. As adjustable-rate mortgages began to reset at higher interest rates (causing higher monthly payments), mortgage delinquencies increased. Over 100 mortgage lending companies went bankrupt as subprime mortgage–backed securities could no longer be sold to investors to acquire funds during late 2007. Starting in the fourth quarter of 2007, the higher delinquency rate caused investors to suffer increasing credit losses even for premium rated mortgage backed securities. The values of these securities deteriorated very quickly. Financial institutions that invested in mortgage backed securities recognized massive losses as they adjusted the value of their holdings to a fraction of the purchase prices. Even the fair value of the mortgage loans retained by many lending institutions had to be adjusted downwards.

Because of a lack of confidence (in other institutions profitability and liquidity) the interbank lending and capital markets funding dried up. Hence, the credit crisis triggered a systemic liquidity risk. This of course caused significant funding problems for many banks that relied on rollover of short-term funding to sustain their business. For traditional banks a major funding source comes from consumer and small business deposits. However, in the period preceding the subprime crisis, some banks shifted part of their funding base to capital markets. One example is Northern Rock in UK, which was one of the top five mortgage lenders in UK. Its business model was to borrow from money market, issue mortgage loans, and then resell the loans to the capital markets through securitization. When the global interest in mortgage backed securities dried up in late 2007, the bank was unable to repay the short-term funding from the money market.

Not only capital markets funding was impacted by the crisis. For banks that had a healthy, stable funding from deposits, the governments around the world still had to take measures to enhance depositors' confidence. For example, in the United States, Congress approved a temporary increase in the deposit insurance limit from \$100,000 to \$250,000, which was effective from October 3, 2008, through December 31, 2010, and subsequently made to be permanent. Even with stabilized deposit market, short-term funding during the crisis was still far short from what banks needed to fulfill their liquidity intermediation mission. The capital markets funding in the form of asset backed commercial paper, for which a majority of the underlying assets are mortgage loans, dried up because of the devaluation of the mortgage backed securities. Another short-term funding source for banks is the interbank loans—loans that banks make to each other. The systematic liquidity shortage significantly increased the lending rates.

Kwan (2009) found that LIBOR to OIS rate spread increased from about 5 to 7 basis points for one-month and 7 to 9 basis points for three-month before the crisis to a 350 basis points peak in the fourth quarter of 2008.[2] Clearly, bank liquidity became very costly. On September 14, 2007, Northern Rock sought and received a liquidity support facility from the Bank of England, to replace funds it was unable to raise from the money market. This event had significant cost to the bank in terms of its reputation to its depositors. A bank run took place. On February 22, 2008, the bank was nationalized. In January 2008, Countrywide Financial, once the largest mortgage banker in the United States, was bought by Bank

---

[2] As we discussed in the counterparty credit risk chapter the increasing spread between LIBOR and OIS caused the industry to move to use OIS discounting rather than LIBOR discounting in the risk-free valuation of derivatives.

of America. Six months later, Fannie Mae and Freddie Mac, representing $5 trillion in mortgage obligations, were nationalized by the US government as mortgage losses increased. In addition, two large US banks, Washington Mutual and Wachovia, became insolvent and were aquired by JP Morgan Chase and Wells Fargo, respectively.

Not only banks and lending institutions suffered the liquidity crunch; investment and insurance institutions that invested heavily in the mortgage related instruments suffered, too. When the market lost the trust of the creditworthiness and the value of mortgage backed securities, these institutions that held the related investment and obligations posted significant risk to their counterparties. As a result they faced significantly increased margin requirements in their trades. All these increased funding requirements came in the midst of a funding crunch already in the system. In March 2008, investment bank Bear Stearns, although it still had significant book asset values, was hastily merged with bank JP Morgan with $30 billion in government guarantees, after it was unable to continue borrowing to finance its operations. Shortly after, investment bank Lehman Brothers filed for bankruptcy. The world's largest insurer, AIG, was 80% nationalized by the US government, due to concerns regarding its ability to honor its credit default swap obligations. The liquidity crisis in the financial system quickly spread. Corporates, municipalities, and countries found themselves in great liquidity need.

Because of the liquidity intermediation role of banks, measurement and management of liquidity risk has always been a concern for regulators. The first Basel Committee document on sound practices in liquidity risk management was issued in 1992 (Basel Committee, 1992). In year 2000, this document was superseded by the Basel committee paper, "Sound Practices for Managing Liquidity in Banking Organizations" (Basel Committee, 2000). The paper focused on 14 guiding principles for measuring and managing liquidity risk. The principles are especially focused around developing a structure for managing liquidity, measuring net funding requirements, managing market access, contingency planning, and internal controls for risk management. In the wake of the 2007 financial crisis, the regulatory focus on liquidity risk was further strengthened, emphasizing the importance of managing liquidity risk due to its possible system-wide repercussions effects. In response to the liquidity crisis, in 2008 the Basel committee issued a new guiding document, "Principles for Sound Liquidity Risk Management and Supervision" (Basel Committee, 2008). That document replaced the consultative document from 2000 and now contains 17 guiding principles for liquidity risk management. In December 2009, the Basel committee approved for the Basel III consultation a package of proposals to strengthen further global capital and liquidity regulations. The consultation paper, "Strengthening the Resilience of the Banking Sector," enforces the importance of a global liquidity framework with minimum reporting standards to complement the 2008 paper's focus on guiding principles. The key minimum reporting standards in the new liquidity risk framework are a short-term 30-day Liquidity Coverage Ratio (LCR) and a longer-term structural funding stability measure known as the Net Stable Funding Ratio (NSFR). In addition, there are also monitoring liquidity metrics such as maturity mismatch, funding concentration, and unencumbered (available for sale) assets available. The new liquidity risk regulation forms an integral part of the Basel III (Basel Committee, 2013a) regulation that is supposed to strengthen the regulation, supervision, and risk management based on the lessons learned from the 2007 financial crisis.

The objective of regulators is to equip banks with adequate liquidity going forward as well as to create a liquidity buffer comprising highly liquid assets that can be used to counterbalance a period of liquidity stress. Since the main purpose of the cushion for liquidity risk is to mitigate the net cumulative cash outflows, it is done by using a pool of high-quality liquid assets that can be sold immediately or used as collateral (pledged) for short-term loan (repo) transactions to raise funds. A difference between liquidity risk and other risks such as credit and market risk is that in general liquidity risk is not the direct cause of bank failure. Indeed, liquidity risk is usually a consequential risk experienced due to significant losses due to other risks (e.g., credit losses, market events, operational risk events, etc.) that are triggers for liquidity problems for a financial institution. Liquidity risk of an institution is also significantly affected by other market participants and the public perception of the bank. In particular the bank's reputation is instrumental in its ability to raise and retain funds.

If liquidity risk is not managed properly, it can in turn lead to a solvency issue as the institution may take a big loss in fire-sale of valuable assets in order to raise funds. Since liquidity risk is a consequential risk one can argue that effectively mitigating liquidity risk is as much about holding sufficient capital buffers for the traditional market, credit, and operational risks as it is about holding a pool of unencumbered highly liquid assets to mitigate net cash outflows. By mitigating other risks via sufficient capital an institution effectively guards against subsequent reputational and liquidity crisis. However, this conventional thought was proven not adequate in the recent crisis. The market devaluation of the mortgages and mortgage backed financial products shook market confidence in a large range of assets on many institutions' banking book as well as many standard collaterals in the capital markets. Liquidity risk is also different across institutions as the liquidity risk is largely a reputational risk and, in a crisis situation, the available funding sources may differ significantly across institutions. For example, a bank that has access to the repo market may be considered, ceteris paribus, to be in a better position than a bank that has no access to the repo market. The bank with an established position in the repo market may still have access to secured funding while the bank with no access to the repo market can only rely on unsecured funding and selling liquid assets to generate cash. The potential drawback of being forced to sell liquid assets in a stress situation is that they may have to be sold at significant discounts, especially if counterparties to the bank are aware of the liquidity crisis situation the bank is in.

In this chapter on liquidity risk we focus mainly on the core quantitative aspects of a bank's liquidity risk management.[3]

First, we consider the measurement of liquidity risk. In general, the measurement of liquidity risk is path-dependent and complex. This is because funding liquidity is generally defined as the ability to settle obligations with immediacy and is concerned with mitigating flows. A firm is able to satisfy the demand for cash, and hence is liquid, as long as at each point in time outflows of cash are smaller or equal to inflows and the hedging flows that can be generated.

Second, we consider scenario analysis of the bank's potential cash inflows and outflows in a liquidity crisis. In the liquidity risk analysis of the net cash outflows from the assets and liabilities there are key market and behavioral uncertainties that need to be addressed, for example, the behavior of depositors in the stickiness of funding and the behavior of the committed facility counterparties. All of these potential sources affect the reduced expected inflow and increased expected outflow of cash to the bank and must be analyzed in order to define a suitable level of highly liquid assets that can be used in counterbalancing the net outflow.

---

[3]The liquidity risk measurement and management book by Matz (2011) is a good complement to our more quantitative, method focused liquidity risk discussion. In particular Matz focuses more on the qualitative aspects of liquidity risk management and what can be learned from history by liquidity risk managers.

Third, we consider how a bank can test the sufficiency and optimize the liquidity execution of its dedicated liquidity buffer. Such analysis and tests of the bank's current endowment hedge portfolio is a core part of the bank's contingency funding plan.

Fourth, we consider the bank's planning of the optimal choice of endowment hedging portfolio and structure of the balance sheet to mitigate vulnerability to liquidity risk. The focus is on maintaining a high-quality liquidity portfolio that can efficiently hedge liquidity outflows under stress scenarios, to generate sufficient counterbalancing capacity. Since holding standby counterbalancing capacity has an opportunity cost the firm would like to hold the minimum cost portfolio that suffices for hedging out the negative flows. Minimal cost can here be measured both as an opportunity cost (forgone return relative to investing in business) and as an up-front cost of acquiring the portfolio. We focus on minimizing up-front cost in our optimization analysis examples but the optimization can be easily recast to minimize opportunity costs if the pool of earmarked hedging assets is to be selected from existing investment assets.

In the fifth section we consider a special case of liquidity risk measurement when the hedging portfolio is composed of cash or cash equivalent assets. In general, liquidity insolvency happens the first time the firm cannot generate sufficient counterbalancing capacity from the liquidity hedging portfolio to cover the funding gap. The complexity arises from the fact that there is uncertainty in the creation of counterbalancing capacity from the firm's liquidity hedging portfolio. This means that liquidity solvency at $T > t$ does not guarantee solvency at t. With a cash hedging capacity we can consistently measure the firm's liquidity insolvency probability as monotonic and we can therefore consider relatively simple liquidity risk measures.

We end this chapter with a discussion of the key components of the Basel III (Basel Committee, 2013a) liquidity regulation.

MEASUREMENT OF LIQUIDITY RISK

The measurement of market and credit risk is typically based on VaR or other risk measures such as CVaR for a certain time horizon, T. For market and credit risk the required solvency capital is generally monotone across time such that for a given amount of capital, solvency at $T > t$, implies solvency at t. However, the definition of a liquidity risk measure can be more complex. For a given funding gap, constructed at time buckets, $t = 1, \ldots, T$, liquidity insolvency happens the first time, t, a net outflow occurs for which the financial institution cannot raise sufficient funds. In particular, the capability of executing the liquidity hedging portfolio to generate sufficient counterbalancing capacity across times, $t = 1, \ldots, T$, results in a term structure of liquidity risk across $t = 1, \ldots, T$ and a path-dependency of liquidity risk. The financial institution may be able to generate liquid funds at $t + 1$ to cover the gap at t. However, this still results in insolvency at t. Because of this general path-dependent nature of liquidity solvency it is more difficult to devise an appropriate liquidity risk measure than in the case of market and credit risk. Below we follow Skoglund and Chen (2012) and Chen and Skoglund (2014) and define liquidity risk insolvency using an analogy based on the classical insurance ruin theory approach to insolvency. With this approach, insolvency occurs the first time a risk reserve process, composed of cash inflows and outflows and the hedging capacity, turns non-positive. See also Drehmann, Elliot, and Kapadia (2007) and Drehmann and Nikolau (2009) on the definition of funding liquidity risk.

If we assume that the liquidity hedging portfolio is available to convert to cash at any time $t = 1, \ldots, T$, then we obtain a relatively simple measure of liquidity exposure that is monotone across time. Such an assumption is appropriate if the hedging portfolio is composed of cash or cash equivalents. As we shall see later, this is also consistent with the Basel III definition of a liquidity buffer where eligible hedging assets are converted to cash equivalents using haircuts on accounting or market values.

Liquidity Exposure with General Liquidity Hedging Capacity

Because liquidity risk is a consequential risk in general we assume that cash inflows and outflows are occurring under a perceived market stress and/or an institution specific stress. We therefore assume a comprehensive market and/or bank-specific scenario d is given. Having net cash outflows in scenario d for all $t = 1, \ldots, T$, $\{cf(d, t)\}_{t=1}^{T}$, we can construct a cumulative net cash flow, $F(d, T)$, with $cf(d, t)$ the t:th net cash flow under scenario d at time $t = 1, \ldots, T$, as

$$F(d, T) = \sum_{t=1}^{T} cf(\omega, t).$$

Here, $F(d, T)$, can also be referred to as a forward liquidity need under scenario d. See Fiedler (2007). We cumulate the positive and negative outflows as a positive flow at time t is assumed to be rolled over to $t + 1$ and cover any negative outflows at $t + 1$. This can happen if cash at t is put in an overnight account to $t + 1$. The interest rate raised on the overnight account is, however, assumed immaterial and not included in our analysis.

The forward liquidity need at t is composed of the negative and positive cash flows at t, that is, $cf^{-}(d, t)$ and $cf^{+}(d, t)$ plus the rolled over positive flow from $t - 1$. This gives

$$F(d, T) = \sum_{t=1}^{T-1} cf(d, t) + cf^{-}(d, T) + cf^{+}(d, T).$$

If the bank has no liquidity supplying assets to hedge negative outflows, then $\{F(d, t)\}_{t=1}^{T}$ must be positive for all $t = 1, \ldots, T$ for survival. Clearly, a positive $F(d, t + 1)$ does not help if $F(d, t) < 0$. This means that liquidity insolvency occurs the first time the process $\{F(d, t)\}_{t=1}^{T}$ is negative.

A financial institution holds a portfolio of high-quality liquidity supplying assets to cover negative cash outflows from $\{F(d, t)\}_{t=1}^{T}$ at all $t = 1, \ldots, T$. The cash counterbalancing capacity is generated from selling or collateralized borrowing of the hedge portfolio. A specific liquidity execution strategy results in a specific set of cash counterbalancing flows. We denote these flows at times $t = 1, \ldots, T$ by $\{C(d, t)\}_{t=1}^{T}$ where we have used the notation $C(d, t)$ to indicate that the flows and hence the specific liquidity execution strategy depend on the scenario d. Hence, it depends on the specific forward liquidity need, $\{F(d, t)\}_{t=1}^{T}$. Clearly, any liquidity execution strategy of the hedge portfolio will try to ensure that

$$\sum_{t=1}^{T} [C(d, t) + cf(d, t)] > 0 \tag{6.1}$$

for all $t = 1, \ldots, T$.[4] The first time t equation (6.1) turns negative liquidity insolvency occurs. This condition is important as sufficient counterbalancing capacity flows may not be available at t, and hence, the exact possible timing of the counterbalancing capacity flows is essential.

---

[4]Note that we cumulate any excess cash counterbalancing capacity at t to $t + 1$ in analogy with the net cash flows, which are assumed to be rolled over in overnight accounts.

In analogy with ruin probability in classical risk theory we now define the risk process, $R(C, T, d)$, such that[5]

$$R(C, T, d) = \sum_{t=1}^{T} [C(d, t) + cf(d, t)]. \tag{6.2}$$

The first stochastic time, τ, the risk process, $R(C, T, d)$, becomes negative is

$$\tau(T, C, d) = \inf_{T}(R(C, T, d) < 0). \tag{6.3}$$

In particular if $R(C, T, d) \geq 0$ for all T, then $\tau(T, C, d) = +\infty$. We note that

$$S(T, C, d) = P(\tau > T) = P\left[\inf_{t \leq T} R(C, T, d) \geq 0\right] \tag{6.4}$$

such that $1 - S(T, C, d)$ is the liquidity insolvency probability of the financial institution.

Example Liquidity Cash Flows, Counterbalancing Capacity, and Risk Reserve Process Table 6.1 and Figures 6.1 and 6.2 display sample net cash flows, $cf(d, t)$, the resulting forward liquidity exposure, $F(d, T)$, sample cash counterbalancing flows, $C(d, t)$, and the obtained risk reserve process, $R(C, T, d)$, for $t = 1, \ldots, 7$ time buckets. This is done for two liquidity scenarios, d_1 and d_2. In scenario 1, d_1, the counterbalancing flows are sufficient such that $R(C, T, d_1) > 0$ for all T. In scenario 2, d_2, the counterbalancing flows are not sufficient at $T = 6$ since $R(C, 6, d_2) = -1$. Using equation (6.3) we can refer to $T = 6$ as the scenario 2 time to insolvency. Also, using an equal probability for the two scenarios, $d_1, d_2 \in D$, we can calculate the joint scenario liquidity insolvency probability as a function of T. Specifically, we have that $S(T, C, D) = 1$ if $T \leq 5$ and $S(T, C, D) = 1 - S(T, C, D) = 0.5$ if $T \geq 6$.

Risk Reserve Process and Limits In this setting for liquidity risk it is clear that the firm must put limits on $\{R(C, t, d)\}_{t=1}^{T}$. That is, the process cannot be allowed to be negative under a plausible liquidity stress d for any $t = 1, \ldots, T$. Fiedler (2007) refers to a liquidity limit on $R(C, t, d)$ for all $t = 1, \ldots, T$ as an adjusted maximum cash outflow limit. It is natural for a

TABLE 6.1 Sample Cash Flows, Forward Liquidity Exposures, and Risk Reserve Process for 2 Liquidity Scenarios

Time	Scenario 1				Scenario 2			
	$cf(d_1, t)$	$F(d_1, T)$	$C(d_1, t)$	$R(C, T, d_1)$	$cf(d_2, t)$	$F(d_2, T)$	$C(d_2, t)$	$R(C, T, d_2)$
$t = 1$	3	3	1	4	−1	−1	2	1
$t = 2$	−4	−1	0	0	−2	−3	1	0
$t = 3$	2	1	2	4	−1	−4	2	1
$t = 4$	−3	−2	0	1	2	−2	0	3
$t = 5$	−1	−3	0	0	2	0	0	5
$t = 6$	3	0	0	3	−6	−6	0	−1
$t = 7$	3	−3	3	3	2	−4	1	2

---

[5]The reader may recall that we also used classical risk theory in the context of portfolio credit risk economic capital for loan portfolios in the portfolio credit risk chapter. We refer to that chapter for a brief background on classical risk theory and literature references.

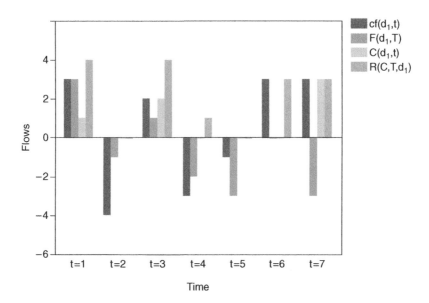

FIGURE 6.1 Sample Cash Flows, Forward Liquidity Exposures, and Risk Reserve Process for Liquidity Scenario 1

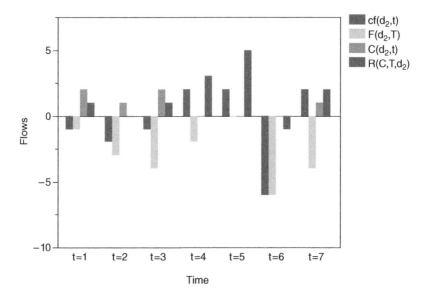

FIGURE 6.2 Sample Cash Flows, Forward Liquidity Exposures, and Risk Reserve Process for Liquidity Scenario 2

liquidity steering committee to monitor $\{R(C, t, d)\}_{t=1}^{T}$ over time and identify a limit breach if $R(C, t, d) < a_t$ where $a_t \geq 0$. Clearly, for shorter time horizons t the limit, a_t, should be stricter as there is less time (headroom) for the financial institution to adjust the situation, for example, by acquiring more hedging assets. In order to calculate $\{R(C, t, d)\}_{t=1}^{T}$ the financial institution must choose a particular approach to generate the cash counterbalancing flows from the liquidity hedge portfolio, that is, choose a particular liquidity execution strategy.

Liquidity Exposure with Cash Hedging Capacity

As we have seen, the management of liquidity risk is complex due to its general path-dependent nature of liquidity solvency. This complex path-dependent nature arises from the fact that the counterbalancing capacity realization of the liquidity hedging portfolio is also uncertain and path dependent such that counterbalancing capacity flows that can be realized in $t + 1$ may not be available in t. This can potentially cause a liquidity insolvency at t even if funds could eventually be raised at $t + 1$. Assume now instead that the liquidity hedging portfolio consists entirely of cash. This means that there is no uncertainty in the creation of cash counterbalancing capacity from the liquidity hedging portfolio and the cash is available for use in any $t = 1, \ldots, T$. Under a cash liquidity hedging capacity assumption we can simplify equation (6.1) to

$$\sum_{t=1}^{T} \min \left[\tilde{F}(d, t), 0 \right] > -M \tag{6.5}$$

with M the cash amount and where for $t > 2$

$$\tilde{F}(d, t) = cf(d, t) + \max \left[\tilde{F}(d, t - 1), 0 \right] \tag{6.6}$$

with $\tilde{F}(d, 1) = cf(d, 1)$. This is because the counterbalancing capacity has already been determined as the cash balance available at $t = 0$ and there is no uncertainty on flows. Effectively, we are now asking the question: How much initial cash, at $t = 0$, is needed to cover all the negative outflows for the scenario d? That is,

- We first observe the net cash outflow, $\{F(d, t)\}_{t=1}^{T}$, convert this net cash outflow into an effective cash exposure, $\tilde{F}(d, t)$, at each $t = 1, \ldots, T$.
- Finally, only the negative effective cash exposures need cash hedging capacity to be neutralized, and hence $\sum_{t=1}^{T} \min \left[\tilde{F}(d, t), 0 \right]$ cumulates the negative cash exposures into an effective minimum cash need for liquidity solvency.

Equation (6.5) expresses that the amount of cash, M, cannot be less than the effective cumulated cash need. The equation can also be used to check whether a cash hedging portfolio is sufficient for liquidity solvency, or used to define the minimum amount of cash liquidity needed to remain liquidity solvent.

It is important to recognize that with this simplifying assumption of a cash liquidity hedging portfolio liquidity solvency is no longer path dependent. In particular, $\sum_{t=1}^{T} \min \left[\tilde{F}(d, t), 0 \right]$, defines the smallest amount of cash liquidity needed for the firm to remain liquidity solvent at $t = 1, \ldots, T$. Liquidity solvency at T guarantees solvency at $t = 1, \ldots, T - 1$. Effectively, we can now simplify the risk process, $R(.)$, in equation (6.2) such that

$$R(M, T, d) = \sum_{t=1}^{T} \min \left[\tilde{F}(d, t), 0 \right] + M > 0 \tag{6.7}$$

guarantees solvency at T as well as at all $t < T$. The corresponding liquidity solvency probability, $S(T, C, d)$, for liquidity solvency up to T is now

$$S(T, M, d) = P[R(M, T, d) > 0]. \tag{6.8}$$

In particular, $S(T, M, d)$ is monotonic in T, which is an important property for the measure.

TABLE 6.2 Sample Cash Flows, Liquidity Exposures, and Required Cash Balance for 3 Liquidity Scenarios

Time	Liquidity scenario 1			Liquidity scenario 2			Liquidity scenario 3		
	$cf(d_1,t)$	$F(d_1,t)$	$\widetilde{F}(d_1,t)$	$cf(d_2,t)$	$F(d_2,t)$	$\widetilde{F}(d_2,t)$	$cf(d_3,t)$	$F(d_3,t)$	$\widetilde{F}(d_3,t)$
$t=1$	−5	−5	−5	−3	−3	−3	2	2	2
$t=2$	5	0	5	2	−1	2	−2	0	0
$t=3$	3	3	8	1	0	3	−1	−1	−1
$t=4$	−7	−4	1	−3	−3	0	3	2	3
$t=5$	−4	−8	−3	2	−1	2	−2	0	1
$t=6$	8	0	8	−4	−5	−2	−1	−1	0
$t=7$	−3	−3	5	2	−3	2	2	1	2
		$M^*=8$			$M^*=5$			$M^*=1$	

Example Cash Liquidity Need Table 6.2 displays sample net cash flows, $cf(d,t)$, the forward liquidity exposure, $F(d,t)$, and the $\widetilde{F}(d,t)$ component of the cash liquidity exposure for $t = 1,\dots,7$ time buckets and 3 different liquidity scenarios d_1, d_2, and d_3. The table also displays the required cash balance, M^*, where

$$M^* = P(d,T) = -\sum_{t=1}^{T} \min\left[\widetilde{F}(d,t),0\right] \tag{6.9}$$

is the definition of the required cash balance at $t = 0$. For liquidity scenario 1 the required cash balance is 8 units of currency. This required cash balance originates from a net funding requirement at $t = 1$ and $t = 5$. In liquidity scenario 2 the required cash balance is 5 units of currency, which derives from the $t = 1$ and $t = 6$ net funding gaps. Finally, for scenario 3 there is only a net funding gap at time $t = 3$ yielding a 1 unit of currency required cash balance. The cash liquidity need at the different times for the liquidity scenarios is also illustrated in Figure 6.3.

To see that the computed cash balances are indeed sufficient consider liquidity scenario 1. Having a cash balance at $t = 0$ of 8 units of currency we can use 5 units of the cash balance at $t = 1$ to neutralize the funding gap. At $t = 2$ and $t = 3$ we accumulate net positive inflows of 8 units of currency. The 8 units of currency have been put in overnight accounts and are available at $t = 4$ to neutralize the negative funding gap of −7. The remaining 1 unit of currency is put in the overnight account and used at $t = 5$ to reduce the net funding gap from −4 to −3. We now also use the remaining cash balance of 3 units of currency yielding a net funding requirement of 0 at $t = 5$. Finally, at $t = 6$ we have a positive inflow that can cover by itself the $t = 7$ outflow. Hence, we have net positive cash inflows at $t = 6$ and $t = 7$.

Components of the Liquidity Measure

We have seen that the measurement of liquidity risk is based on two major components:

1. The net cash flows, $\{cf(d,t)\}_{t=1}^{T}$, which are derived from scenario d cash inflows, $\{cf^+(d,t)\}_{t=1}^{T}$, and scenario d cash outflows, $\{cf^-(d,t)\}_{t=1}^{T}$
2. The realized scenario d cash counterbalancing capacity flows, $\{C(d,t)\}_{t=1}^{T}$, or in case of a cash or cash equivalent hedging portfolio the cash balance, M

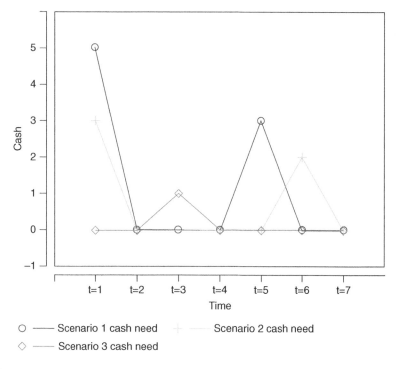

FIGURE 6.3 Cash Liquidity Needs for the 3 Liquidity Scenarios

For a given forward liquidity exposure, $\{F(d,t)\}_{t=1}^{T}$, derived from the net cash flows, $\{cf(d,t)\}_{t=1}^{T}$, it is useful to make a distinction between an expected cash liquidity need and the stress scenario d liquidity need. We can refer to the forward liquidity need in the expected situation, that is, the normal course of business as the structural liquidity mismatch in the balance sheet and the stress scenario d forward liquidity need as the contingency liquidity need.

The liquidity hedging portfolio is maintained specifically to cover the contingency liquidity needs. The daily normal business of managing the structural liquidity mismatches through short-term borrowing and lending is referred to as cash management. The contribution from contractual cash flows, such as loans and deposits with contractual maturity, to the forward liquidity need is limited since contractual cash flows in scenario d may not deviate that much from the expected situation. Of course, floating rate contractual cash flows can have some variability due to changing interest rates in the scenario d and defaults may increase, yielding less immediate cash inflows (assuming a delay between default and the actual recovery). Typically, however, the major contribution to the forward liquidity need is from potential cash flows and the embedded optionality in the balance sheet such as withdrawal of non-maturity deposits and increasing usage of committed facilities. This is because in a severe market distress scenario liquidity constraints may occur for many institutions such that they draw as much as possible from contingent credit lines and withdraw their deposits. At the time of a liquidity distress a bank run behavior of consumer deposits may also become a concern.

We now focus on the two components of the liquidity measure: first, the modeling of cash inflows and outflows, and second, the hedging of the liquidity exposure through generation of counterbalancing capacity. The concept of counterbalancing capacity refers to a bank's capacity of generating cash from its unencumbered assets. An unencumbered asset is an asset that the bank have full control over so that it can either sell it to generate a cash flow or use it in collateralized borrowing such as repo. In addition, a bank may also have lifelines with its central bank or other banks. However, these funding sources have a limit and the availability of credit lines committed to the bank by other financial institutions may be questionable in a market-wide liquidity distress scenario. The potential counterbalancing capacity of the institution is determined by its endowment hedging portfolio and the scenario d. The specific scenario d may impact the cash creation capability of the hedging portfolio due to market liquidity constraints in the scenario. Clearly, for a given scenario d and a given hedging portfolio endowment the strategy is to choose the least-cost, yet sufficient, cash conversion of the hedging portfolio.

LIQUIDITY EXPOSURE

While regulation for the purpose of risk management often divides the balance sheet of a bank into trading book and banking book (e.g., for credit risk) liquidity risk management involves the full balance sheet. The relevant distinction for the liquidity risk manager is between the assets that have been acquired for the purpose to hedge liquidity risk and the assets and liabilities that have been acquired as part of ordinary business. The first category of assets is the liquidity manager's cushion to hedge any negative cash outflows occurring from the bank's acquired assets and liabilities. In the liquidity manager analysis of the net cash outflows from the assets and liabilities there are key market and behavioral uncertainties that need to be addressed, for example,

- Behavior of depositors in the stickiness of funding
- Behavior of the committed facility counterparties
- Reduced early amortization incentives for mortgages and loans
- Potential drain of liquidity to margin requirements in OTC derivatives
- Extended call for collateral due to rating downgrade triggers

All of these potential sources can contribute to a reduced inflow and increased outflow of cash to the bank and must be analyzed in order to define a suitable level of highly liquid assets that can be used in counterbalancing the net outflow.

As we have mentioned previously, liquidity risk is a consequential risk from an effect of either market or bank-specific events. Hence, it is of importance that the potential sources that can drain cash inflow and increase cash outflow are analyzed under such events. For example, deposit volumes and the financial institution's committed lines of credit to other institutions might show remarkable stability under ordinary times. However, under a serious liquidity stress situation depositors may start to withdraw the deposits at a fast rate and institutions might draw significant amounts from their facilities. This is at the same time as the bank's counterparties may attempt to close previously committed lines of credit to the bank. The key principle in the analysis of liquidity is therefore that one should assume that the market and/or the bank is already exposed to significant stress. Capital markets funding should be assessed, recognizing that under stress markets are volatile so that refinancing (e.g., using commercial paper) may require much higher paid rates on the funding or, even worse, no willingness of market participants to roll over funding. We can broadly categorize the main sources of cash inflows and outflows as:

- Inflows
  The cash inflows of a bank's business typically come from cash from performing loans and accounts receivable payments, fees, investment income. The cash inflows can be classified as contractual, which are mostly predictable, and contingent, which are uncertain.

The uncertain cash inflows may include unscheduled payments (e.g., prepayment), delinquency, and recovered amount from the loans that are already written off. Rollover of funding sources is another important source of uncertain inflows. The uncertainty of the contingent inflows lies in both amount and timing. In a normal economic environment and business operation the uncertain cash inflows can still be predictable. However, for liquidity risk measurement and management, attention should be paid to stress scenarios where the inflows are largely unknown.

■ Outflows

A bank's cash outflows are due to accounts payable, deposit runoffs, matured and non-renewable obligations, credit facility drawdown, investment payoffs, and collateral (margin) requirements. The outflows may impose more uncertainty in terms of liquidity risk. In order to remain solvent, a bank cannot miss any contractual outflows, but it must also sustain committed, nonrevocable facilities offered to its customers, who will likely draw more in stress market and at the time when the customer's credit quality deteriorates. When the bank's investment mark-to-market values are on the downside, or bank's reputation, including credit rating, is damaged, the outflows due to collateral (margin) requirements can increase quickly as well as funding costs.

Before we enter a more detailed discussion on the creation of the financial institutions liquidity exposure, $\{F(d,t)\}_{t=1}^{T}$, derived from the net cash flows, $\{cf(d,t)\}_{t=1}^{T}$, it is useful to have a high-level view of the types of cash flows of a financial institution. While liquidity analysis proceeds by generating the cash flows of assets and liabilities under specified assumptions of market rates, credit risk, prepayment rates, customer behavior on deposit volumes, credit line utilization, and so on, some types of cash flows are more important to consider than others. A general categorization of inflows and outflows are contractual and uncertain flows. However, we can also decompose the balance sheet in more granular types of cash flow uncertainty:

1. The cash flow amount and timing are known, such as fixed rate bonds, fixed rate mortgages, term deposits.
2. The cash flow amount is stochastic but timing is known, such as floating rate notes, variable rate mortgages, swaps, equity dividends, variation margins for futures, payouts from European options.
3. The cash flow amount is known but timing is stochastic, such as loans with prepayment, callable bonds.
4. The cash flow amount and timing are stochastic such as demand deposits, savings account, commitments and credit lines, payouts from American and Bermudan options, margin (collateral) requirements.

Clearly, item 4 can be a major contributor to liquidity outflows. It is also there the financial institution needs to focus its analysis of liquidity outflow under the stress. As we have seen, given a forward liquidity exposure, $\{F(d,t)\}_{t=1}^{T}$, the bank is deemed to survive the scenario d if the counterbalancing capacity of the unencumbered assets can be used to cover the net cash outflows.

Basel Committee (2008) discussed three important components in a liquidity scenario specification:

(a) *The choice of time horizons.* As liquidity risk is path dependent the ability of surviving a liquidity event in a future horizon depends on the business and liquidity planning strategy in the earlier stages. When an institution is in a difficult situation of raising funds significant cash inflows in a later stage cannot really help. A bank's liquidity scenario must specify a set of cash flow horizons, $t = 1, \ldots, T$, that agrees with the survival plan.

(b) *Severity of the liquidity stress*. Because many cash flows have uncertain timing and amount the properness of the severity of a scenario requires the severity of the event itself that can trigger a reasonable net outflow amount and shortage of the funding as well as the appropriate modeling of the cash flows in the scenario.

(c) *Consistency with business*. The cash flow and funding modeling should be consistent with the business model of the institution. At the same time, the scenario should be applicable to the business nature of the institution. For example, for an institution that relies heavily on capital markets funding it is important to focus the scenario on capital market funding events.

Liquidity risk is less focused on models (e.g., compared to market and credit risk) and more focused on scenarios. This is because liquidity risk is already conditioned on extreme events. Models that are used for other asset and liability management analysis, such as a model for interest rate sensitivity of deposit volumes, typically do not apply in extreme liquidity stress events. We can still learn from the past when designing liquidity stress. See Matz (2011, ch. 5) for an analysis of past liquidity events.

In addition to bank's own stress testing scenarios Basel III prescribes scenarios for liquidity risk for use in regulatory reporting. These scenarios include:

- The runoff of a proportion of retail deposits.
- A partial loss of unsecured wholesale funding capacity.
- A partial loss of secured, short-term financing with certain collateral and counterparties.
- Additional contractual outflows that would arise from a downgrade in the bank's public credit rating by up to and including three notches, including collateral posting requirements.
- Increases in market volatilities that impact the quality of collateral or potential future exposure of derivative positions and thus require larger collateral haircuts or additional collateral, or lead to other liquidity needs.
- Unscheduled draws on committed but unused credit and liquidity facilities that the bank has provided to its clients.
- The potential need for the bank to buy back debt or honor noncontractual obligations in the interest of mitigating reputational risk. Hence, the bank needs to continue to act as in a regular going-concern situation, for example, continue to extend loans that will consume funds.

We now consider concrete examples of generating liquidity cash inflows and outflows. This includes the banking book inflows and outflows as well as market funding sources and derivative flows such as net flows from derivatives and repos and derivative margin requirements.

We can think of a simple balance sheet representation of the bank as loans, mortgages, and so on (consumer, small business, corporate) on the asset side together with investment assets such as government bonds and central bank reserves.[6] The liability side of the balance

---

[6]The part of the investment assets that are allocated to the liquidity hedge portfolio are not used in the creation of the forward liquidity exposure of the financial institution. Central bank reserves are usually also counted toward the liquidity hedge portfolio.

TABLE 6.3 Sample Balance Sheet

Assets	Liabilities
Consumer and small business loans	Consumer and small business deposits
Corporate loans	Wholesale deposits
Investment assets	Interbank funding
Central bank reserves	Issued bonds (debt)
Fixed assets	Equity

sheet has deposits (consumer, small business, wholesale) that are either demand deposits that can be withdrawn at any time or term deposits with a fixed maturity. The liability side also has money market funding items such as short-term Interbank deposits and issued bonds funding. The simple balance sheet is displayed in Table 6.3.

In addition to on-balance items the financial institution also has, off-balance, facilities extended to the bank and issued facilities by the bank. It also has off–balance sheet derivative positions with net cash flows such as swaps, forwards, and options. In addition, collateral agreements may be in place that stipulate the posting and receiving of collateral for a given market exposure of the derivatives (e.g., per netting set), and may also include rating triggers that require additional posting from the bank in case of a rating downgrade.

Balance Sheet Cash Flows and Facilities

As mentioned above for many assets and liabilities the future cash flows are not known with certainty in terms of when they might occur and at what amount. For example, demand deposits have no assigned maturity, loans may have prepayment options, bonds in a similar fashion may be issuer callable and/or holder putable. In these situations the cash flows of assets and liabilities need to incorporate the uncertainty due to these unknown cash flow streams. This inclusion is important in order to capture a realistic scenario for liquidity risk.

Asset Inflows from Loans and Investment Assets For contractual loan cash flows we calculate the interest income and any amortization as a contribution to the cash inflows, $\{cf^+(d,t)\}_{t=1}^T$. Similarly, investment assets that are not allocated to the liquidity hedge portfolio make positive cash inflow contributions. While interest rates and bond coupons can be interest rate sensitive and hence depend on the specific scenario d we must also take into account the portfolio delinquency, default rates, and prepayment rates that might alter the cash inflows substantially.

Traditional prepayment models specify the prepayment rate of a pool of loans conditional on pool characteristics such as loan age, product type, and the refinancing incentive. In the model it is beneficial to prepay if it is cheaper to refinance a new loan. Hence, prepayment should be expected when offered loan rates drop below the paying rate. However, all borrowers don't refinance even if it would be beneficial for them and hence the prepayment rate is not discrete 0% or 100% but rather increases smoothly with the spread between the paying rate and the current refinancing rate. Penalty to prepayment and loan age are also important factors. When there is a penalty to prepayment, a consumer will have to bring the penalty into the decision process. The benefit of prepaying must outweigh the penalty. On the other hand, when a loan gets closer to its maturity, the incentive for refinancing tends to drop. We will discuss two common approaches to model customer behavior such as prepayment in the context of pricing embedded optionality in the balance sheet in the next chapter on funds transfer pricing and profitability of cash flows. The two approaches are the financial engineering approach and the statistical model approach. As we have mentioned previously liquidity risk is less focused on models and more focused on specific expert scenarios when assessing the liquidity exposure.

In the case of a liquidity risk scenario, it is prudent to assume that consumer prepayment rates are relatively low and hence additional funds generated by the prepayments decrease. The rationale is that in a crisis the price of funding increases and hence the prepayment incentive should decrease. With this rationale the consumer's request for additional funding, for example, through extensions of granted loans, should be expected to increase. At a minimum, the loan stock should be expected to increase with historical rates and thereby continue to consume funds for the bank. In addition, in a market-induced liquidity stress scenario the bank should expect consumer default rates to increase and hence some borrowers will be unable to meet their scheduled loan repayments. When a consumer is about to default, the ability to refinance will also diminish because it may be harder for the borrower to find a competitive refinancing rate due to the deterioration of the credit grade. Models for the modeling of default have been discussed previously in the chapter on portfolio credit risk. See also Schwartz and Torous (1992, 1993), who model prepayment and delinquency states jointly using the proportional hazard regression. The model allows time-dependent covariates that can represent macroeconomic environment condition during a liquidity stress. More recently, Dunsky and Ho (2007) consider a competing risk model framework (using the multinomial logit model) to capture the prepayment call option and default put option as truly competing risks.

As we mentioned above, liquidity risk analysis and planning should also take into account the change of business volume for the liquidity horizon. Clearly, an estimated amount of new target lending under a going-concern view introduces a need for additional funding at the same time as the new lending contributes with additional interest and amortization cash inflows. There are several ways that we can consider a going-concern business growth over the liquidity horizon. Specifically:

1. Specifying a target-ending balance at the end of each period, $t = 1, \ldots, T$
    This approach allows the business units to provide target ending balance at the end of each planning period. The liquidity risk manager can then apply the appropriate liquidity scenario d contingency assumptions (e.g., delinquency, default, prepayment, and recovery rates) in order to project the final cash flows for liquidity analysis purposes.
2. Specifying a target business growth rate
    Here, the ending amounts of the line items on the balance sheet are adjusted by the growth rate from the original model-based ending balance amount. The ending amount should have already reflected the contingent cash flows.
3. Forward-start positions and accounts
    New business can be modeled through positions and accounts that have a future start date. These positions and accounts can synthetically represent growth in any business unit or business line. These forward start positions and accounts can then be modeled similarly as the existing business.

Example of Cash Inflows with Behavioral and Business Growth Assumptions We now focus on an extended example using the target ending balances approach together with behavioral assumptions. Target ending balances are usually assigned by a bank's management or projected by business units for different segments of the portfolio, such as on the mortgage book.

TABLE 6.4 Delinquency Rates, Default Rates, Overdue Recovery Rates, and Prepayment Rates

Time	Delinquency rate $(\bar{d}_t)$	Default rate $(\bar{D}_t)$	Overdue recovery rate (r_t)	Prepayment rate (p_t)
$t = 1$	2%	2%	60%	5%
$t = 2$	2.1%	2.1%	55%	4.5%
$t = 3$	2.3%	2.3%	50%	4%

TABLE 6.5 Base Cash Flows

Time	Base cash flows $(cf(t))$
$t = 1$	984,485
$t = 2$	691,600
$t = 3$	402,367
$t = 4$	189,110
$t = 5$	142,712
$t = 6$	122,793
Overdue	127,574
Default	51,029

For each scenario d cash flows from existing business are first projected. With the target ending balance for each period new business cash flows necessary to meet the target ending balance for the future period are calculated. In our example we apply specific delinquency rates, $\bar{d}_t$, default rates, $\bar{D}_t$, and prepayment rates, p_t, on the portfolio.

The specific scenario d rates for $t = 1, 2, 3$ are displayed in Table 6.4. We also display in Table 6.4 the current overdue recovery rate, r_t. The recovery rate for defaults is assumed to be 0 as there is in general a long time lag between a default and the ultimate recovery for loans and mortgages. Table 6.5 displays the time $t = 1, \ldots, 6$ base contractual cash flows generated for the loans and the current amount of overdue and defaulted loans in the portfolio. In our example we have $t = 1, \ldots, 6$ cash flows that represent the aggregated cash flows from a book on which planning assumptions are made. Our analysis hence uses $t = 1, \ldots, 6$ time buckets. The last time bucket should then in actual applications contain all the residual maturity cash flows above the last time bucket.

For simplicity we assume no interest rate is paid on the cash flows such that they are only principal flows. This simplifies the example as we do not have to adjust the corresponding interest flows and can calculate target ending balances directly as a sum of the principal flows. However, the corresponding adjustments needed with interest flows should be clear from the example.

Using Table 6.4 we can adjust the base cash flows, $cf(t)$, in Table 6.5. First we adjust the base cash flow for $t = 1$; denoting the adjusted cash flows in the scenario d by $cf(d, t)$, we get that

$$cf(d, 1) = cf(1) \times (1 - \bar{d}_1 - \bar{D}_1) + r_1 \times O + \sum_{t=2}^{6} cf(t) \times p_1 = 1,099,079. \qquad (6.10)$$

Here O is the amount of already overdue loans of 127,574 from Table 6.5 with recovery rate, r_1. The $t = 1$ cash flow is hence adjusted by the default rate, $\bar{D}_t$, assumed at $t = 1$ and the delinquency rate, $\overline{d}_t$, assumption for $t = 1$. We also recover from the pool of already overdue loans using the $t = 1$ overdue recovery rate assumption, r_t. Finally, we adjust the $t = 1$ cash flow by the $t = 1$ assumed cash flow prepayment rates of future cash flows at $t = 2, \ldots, 6$. The cash flow, $cf(d, 1)$, is now referred to as a behavioral adjusted liquidity cash flow under scenario d. We now also need to adjust the base contractual cash flows, $\{cf(t)\}_{t=2}^{6}$, in Table 6.5 and obtain the new amount of overdue and defaulted loans at $t = 1$. We get, for example, that

$$cf^*(2) = cf(2) \times (1 - \overline{D}_1) - cf(2) \times p_1 = 643{,}188$$

such that the $t = 2$ cash flow is preliminary adjusted using the $t = 1$ assumptions for default rate and prepayment rate. This adjustment is made because we have already allocated the prepayment portion of base contractual cash flow $cf(2)$ to $cf(d, 1)$ in (6.10). The defaulted $t = 1$ time portion needs similarly to be removed from the $t = 2$ cash flow as it is written off.

Using the same calculation principle for the contractual cash flows at $t = 3, \ldots, 6$ we have that

$$cf^*(3) = 374{,}201,$$

$$cf^*(4) = 175{,}872,$$

$$cf^*(5) = 132{,}722,$$

$$cf^*(6) = 114{,}197.$$

We now also need an adjusted overdue and default rate at $t = 1$ as[7]

$$O_1(d) = O - O \times r_1 + cf(1) \times \overline{d}_1 - O \times \overline{D}_1 = 68{,}168.$$

$$A_1(d) = A + \sum_{t=1}^{6} cf(t) \times \overline{D}_1 + O \times \overline{D}_1 = 104{,}242.$$

Here, $A = 51{,}029$ is current amount of already defaulted loans. The scenario d overdue amount, $O_t(d)$, at $t = 1$ is adjusted by the overdue recovered portion, new delinquent cash flows, and the portion of overdue going in default. The scenario d defaults at $t = 1$ are adjusted by the $t = 1$ default rate on the cash flows and the overdue amount.

The remaining balance, at the end of $t = 1$, is now the sum of all the adjusted cash flows and the already overdue and defaulted amount. That is, denoting the ending balance at time t by B_t we have that

$$B_1 = cf(d, 1) + \sum_{t=2}^{6} cf^*(t) + O_1(d) + A_1(d) = 2{,}711{,}67.$$

The remaining balance, after $t = 1$, is hence $B_1 - cf(d, 1) = 1{,}612{,}591$. Now, in order to reach a target ending balance of say $1{,}800{,}000$ at $t = 1$ an $187{,}409$ of currency units of new business has to be introduced and funded and is hence a contribution to the negative cash flows, $cf^-(d, 1)$. Assuming the new business balance is issued at end of $t = 1$ and results in equally amortized cash flows at $t = 2, \ldots, 6$, each time needs to introduce a new cash flow of approximately $37{,}482$ currency units. Taking into account the defaults, delinquency, and prepayments

---

[7]In this example we assume for simplicity the overdue default rate to be the same as the default rate. In practice the overdue default rate may be higher.

we then have that the adjusted, new business $t = 2$, cash flow is

$$f_2(d, t) = 37{,}482 \times (1 - \overline{d}_2 - \overline{D}_2) + \sum_{t=3}^{6} 37{,}482 \times p_2 = 42{,}654.$$

Being at $t = 2$, we now perform the same adjustment on the $t = 2$ cash flow as in (6.10) based on $t = 2$ rates. That is,

$$cf(d, 2) = cf^*(2) \times (1 - \overline{d}_2 - \overline{D}_2) + r_2 \times O_1(d) + \sum_{t=3}^{6} cf^*(t) \times p_2 = 689{,}531.$$

This is hence our $t = 2$ behavioral adjusted cash flow. As above, we also adjust the other cash flows based on the $t = 2$ rates such that

$$cf^{**}(3) = cf^*(3) \times (1 - \overline{D}_2) - cf^*(3) \times p_2 = 349{,}504$$

and we also obtain that

$$cf^{**}(4) = 164{,}265,$$
$$cf^{**}(5) = 123{,}962,$$
$$cf^{**}(6) = 106{,}660.$$

We can also adjust the overdue and default rate at $t = 2$ as

$$O_2(d) = O_1(d) - O_1(d) \times r_2 + cf^*(2) \times \overline{d}_2 - O_1(d) \times \overline{D}_2 = 42{,}751.$$

$$A_2(d) = A_1(d) + \sum_{t=2}^{6} cf^*(t) \times \overline{D}_1 + O_1(d) \times \overline{D}_1 = 135{,}917.$$

The ending balance at $t = 2$ is now

$$B_1 - cf(d, 1) - cf(d, 2) = 923{,}060.$$

At $t = 2$ we had a new business cash flow, $f_2(d, t)$, of forward starting business issued in $t = 1$. This new business cash flow was equal to 42,654 units of currency. The $t = 1$ new business ending balance at $t = 2$ is hence $187{,}409 - f_2(d, t) = 144{,}755$. Assuming that the target ending balance at $t = 2$ is 1,200,000 units of currency we need to introduce forward starting business, at $t = 2$, of an amount of

$$1{,}200{,}000 - 923{,}060 - 144{,}755 = 132{,}185. \tag{6.11}$$

As before, this amount needs to be funded and contributes to the negative cash flows, $cf^-(d, 2)$. Distributing the $t = 2$ new business cash flow evenly, a new business cash flow of 33,046 currency units occurs at $t = 3, \ldots, 6$. Adjusting the $t = 3$ new business cash flow with the $t = 3$ rates assumptions,

$$f_3(d, t) = 33{,}046 \times (1 - \overline{d}_3 - \overline{D}_3) + \sum_{t=4}^{6} 33{,}046 \times p_3 = 35{,}492.$$

TABLE 6.6   Target Balance and Behavioral Adjusted Cash Flow Projection

Time	Target balance	CF ($t = 1$)	CF ($t = 2$)	CF ($t = 3$)	CF ($t = 4$)	CF ($t = 5$)	CF ($t = 6$)	Overdue	Default
0	.	984,485	691,600	402,367	189,110	142,712	122,793	127,574	51,029
1	1,800,000	**1,099,079**	643,188	374,201	175,872	132,722	114,197	68,168	104,242
2	1,200,000	**1,099,079**	**689,531**	349,504	164,265	123,962	106,660	42,751	135,917
3	1,000,000	**1,099,079**	**689,531**	**370,598**	153,916	116,153	99,941	28,431	154,021

We can of course now continue the behavioral adjustment for cash flows, obtaining the final behavioral scenario cash flow $cf(d, 3)$ as well as adjustments to $\{cf(d,t)^{**}\}_{t=4}^{6}$ and new scenario overdue and default rates, $O_3(d)$ and $A_3(d)$. The results of these calculations as well as our previous results are displayed in Table 6.6. In the table CF represents the cash flow and the final behavioral adjusted cash flows for $t = 1, 2$, and 3 are indicated in bold. Of course, expanding the Table 6.4 behavioral assumptions to $t = 4, 5$, and 6 we could repeat the same calculations as above to obtain final behavioral adjusted scenario cash flows, $cf(d,t)$, for all $t = 1, \ldots, 6$ periods.

While Table 6.6 provides us with the behavioral adjusted cash flows for $t = 1, 2$, and 3, in order to construct a liquidity gap with cash inflows and outflows for $t = 1, 2, 3$, we also need to know the funding need for new balances. Above we calculated the funding need at $t = 1$ as $187,409$ currency units and the funding need at $t = 2$ as $132,185$ currency units. We also calculated the new business cash flow at $t = 2$ of the $t = 1$ new business to be $42,654$ units of currency. To complete the scenario d liquidity gap for $t = 1, 2, 3$ for this book it remains to calculate the $t = 3$ new business to be funded and the $t = 3$ new business cash flows. Starting with the new business that needs to be funded—using the $t = 3$ target ending balance of $1,000,000$ from Table 6.6—we can first conclude that with no new business at either $t = 1$ or $t = 2$ the ending balance is

$$B_1 - cf(d, 1) - cf(d, 2) - cf(d, 3) = 923,060 - cf(d, 3) = 552,462.$$

Having a $t = 3$ target ending balance of $1,000,000$ units of currency we can calculate the forward starting business at $t = 3$ as $1,000,000 - 552,462 = 447,538$. However, we also need to adjust this for the new balances introduced already at $t = 1$ and $t = 2$. The $t = 1$ introduced new business ending balance at $t = 2$ is $144,755$. This is because

$$T_1 - (B_1 - cf(d, 1)) - f_2(d, t) = 187,409 - 42,654 = 144,755$$

where T_1 denotes the target ending balance at $t = 1$. We now adjust this balance for the $t = 3$ cash flow. The $t = 1$ new business nominal cash flow was equally distributed as a cash flow of 37482 units of currency at $t = 2, \ldots, 6$. At $t = 2$ we now adjust this rate, for $t = 3$, by the $t = 2$ default and prepayment rates. That is, denoting the initial nominal new business scenario cash flow by $g^*(3)$ we have that

$$g^*(3) = 37{,}482 \times (1 - \overline{D}_2) - 37{,}482 \times p_2 = 35{,}008.$$

We now finally adjust this nominal new business cash flow as

$$g(d, 3) = g^*(3) \times (1 - \overline{d}_3 - \overline{D}_3) + r_3 \times O_g(d, 2) + \sum_{t=4}^{6} g^*(t) \times p_3 = 37{,}992.$$

Here, $g^*(t) = 35,008$ for $t = 4, 5$, and 6 and $O_g(d, 2)$ is the amount of overdue at $t = 2$ of the new business. This amount is obtained using the $t = 1$ delinquent new business and the nominal $t = 2$ new business cash flow. Specifically,

$$O_g(d, 2) = O_g(d, 1) - O_g(d, 1) \times r_2 + 37,482 \times \overline{d}_2 - O_g(d, 1) \times \overline{D}_2$$
$$= 37,482 \times \overline{d}_2 \approx 787$$

since $O_g(d, 1) = 0$ as none of the new business has cash flows in $t = 1$ and hence cannot be overdue at $t = 1$. The $t = 1$ introduced new business balance is hence, $144,755 - 37,992 = 106,762$. We also need the $t = 2$ introduced new balance to obtain the $t = 3$ funding requirement for the new business target. This is given by $132,185 - f_3(d, t) = 96,694$ (see equation (6.11)). Hence, we can now obtain the $t = 3$ new business required forward starting exposure and associated funding requirement at $t = 3$ as

$$447,538 - 106,762 - 96,694 = 244,082.$$

Note that the total new business cash flow at $t = 3$ is the sum of the new business cash flows from new business introduced at $t = 1$ and $t = 2$. That is, $37,992 + f_3(d, t) = 73,484$. Since we now have behavioral adjusted cash flows for $t = 1, 2, 3$ as well as the funding requirement and new business cash flows we can construct a scenario d liquidity gap profile for $t = 1, 2, 3$. This is done in Table 6.7. Compared to the original cash flows in Table 6.5 for $t = 1, 2, 3$ we have reduced the cash inflows, especially at $t = 3$. Of course, in this model higher default probabilities yield less cash inflows, $\{cf^+(d, t)\}_{t=1}^T$, compared to base contractual cash flows, $\{cf(t)\}_{t=1}^T$. One can also reduce scenario d cash inflows by using higher delinquency rates and lower overdue recovery rates. High prepayment rates contribute to additional cash inflows in the short-term but reduce longer term cash flows. Funding requirements stem from business growth assumptions, here specified as target ending balances. We finally note that the adjusted liquidity inflow (gap) for $t = 1, 2, 3$ in Table 6.7 only represents the contribution of our specific book (to which we applied the planning and behavioral assumptions) to the firmwide liquidity gap. The firmwide liquidity gap contains the already existing rollover funding need as well as the liquidity inflows for all the other assets.

Different Models of Business Growth   From the example above it is obvious that the target ending balance approach is typically applied on subportfolios' aggregated balances rather than on the individual positions and account. This is true for the target growth rate approach

TABLE 6.7 Liquidity Gap with Inflows and Outflows

	Liquidity gap		
	$t = 1$	$t = 2$	$t = 3$
Cash inflow ($cf^+(d, t)$)			
Adjusted behavioral	1,099,079	689,531	370,598
New business	0	42,654	73,484
Cash outflow ($cf^-(d, t)$)			
Funding requirement	187,409	132,815	244,082
Net cash flow ($cf(d, t)$)	911,670	599,370	200,000

as well and the two approaches are essentially identical as we can always recast a target growth rate of new business volumes on the balance into an equivalent target ending balance amount. The fact that the target ending balance approach and the growth rate approach apply on aggregated portfolios (e.g., by product class) is seen as an advantage by the treasury analyst as this is the level of management views on growth rates. The forward-start approach has much better flexibility on one hand. It can be applied to any specific account as well as pool maintaining granular-level assumptions on behavior. On the other hand, it makes it more difficult to reconcile back with aggregate target ending balance or growth views of the balance sheet. In practice, it is common in liquidity risk analysis to use an aggregated approach such as target ending balance or target growth for loan portfolios but specify more granular position level behavior for large, important funding sources. This includes, for example, the rollover assumptions with significant funding counterparties, and we now turn our attention to the behavioral cash flow modeling of the bank's funding and liability outflows.

Funding and Liability Outflows

Deposits Similar to prepayment models deposit volume models aim to capture the consumer's decisions to withdraw and place funds in the bank account. The willingness to withdraw funds is expected to decrease with the increased relative performance of other funds (e.g., equity and other bank accounts). As for prepayment all consumers typically do not withdraw all funds and place in alternative fund sources even if it would be beneficial to them. Common models used to describe deposit volume are regression models with logarithmic volume change being explained by key variables, for example, interest rates, GDP, and seasonal terms as explanatory factors. Another type of model used frequently in practice is the core and non-core deposit model, which specifies a portfolio runoff amortization scenario for the core part. See Dev and Rao (2006, ch. 8). We will return to deposit models in the next chapter on funds transfer pricing and profitability of cash flows. As for prepayment models the deposit models used to analyze profitability in "normal" times are less valuable for analyzing potential liquidity outflows in extreme situations.

In a liquidity crisis situation one should expect an increased withdrawal rate of consumer's deposits. In particular, consumers may withdraw because of the need of additional funds in a crisis. Moreover, there may be a run at the bank. The actual deposit withdrawal rate assumed as a cash outflow, $cf^-(d,t)$, at $t = 1, \ldots, T$ is dependent on the specific liquidity scenario, d. Important parameters in determining withdrawal rates in a liquidity scenario include:

- If the deposit is a term deposit or a demand deposit. Term deposits may still be considered as immediately withdrawable if there is a relatively small penalty fee for early withdrawal.
- If the deposit is insured or not. A government insured deposit amount is of course less likely to be withdrawn and create a bank run because of depositor concerns about the credit quality of the bank.
- The type of depositor and the scope of the liquidity crisis scenario, d. For example, corporates are in general faster to withdraw than consumers. If the scope of the liquidity crisis is a general crisis for all financial institutions, then deposits posted by financial institutions should be assumed to be withdrawn at a very high rate. In case there is not a bank run yet insured consumer deposits may be viewed as more sticky.

When modeling deposit withdrawal rates at $t = 1, \ldots, T$ the exact liquidity scenario is important not only for the immediate withdrawal rate at $t = 1$ but also how withdrawal rates unfold as time progresses. For example, the beginning of the liquidity crisis may show large withdrawal rates only for some corporates with low withdrawal rates for consumers and small business. However, as the liquidity crisis unfolds it may induce more consumers to withdraw faster. The exact term structure of the liquidity crisis is hence of importance when analyzing liquidity scenarios. Of course, the exact term structure of the forward liquidity exposure is also important for measuring liquidity, the sufficiency of the liquidity hedge portfolio, and hence ultimately determining solvency. The same initial liquidity crisis may unfold very differently and the bank needs to analyze different ways a liquidity crisis can unfold to determine the best hedging portfolio. Once the bank has grouped deposits into different behavioral categories under the liquidity stress scenario d a deposit category withdrawal rate is applied for each $t = 1, \ldots, T$.

Example of Deposit Withdrawal Scenario Table 6.8 displays an example deposit withdrawal scenario where the deposit withdrawal rate is 10% initially for $t = 1$ and then increases. The deposit withdrawal rate at time t is here applied to the time $t - 1$ balance. The current balance is 100 units of currency. The resulting deposit balance and the cash outflows, $cf^-(d, t)$, are also displayed in Table 6.8.

Of course, while consumer and small business deposits are usually grouped in categories for the purpose of analyzing deposit withdrawal the bank's largest deposit counterparties are analyzed individually due to their size and importance in determining aggregate liquidity outflow.

Facilities Issued Facilities extended by the bank to its counterparties can be analyzed similarly to deposits. That is, consumer and small business facilities are grouped by expected behavior in the liquidity crisis scenario d and certain large facilities extended to corporates are analyzed individually. Key factors in analyzing the increased usage rate of a facility include:

- If the facility is committed or not. Some facilities are revocable, which can prevent further usage. In case the facility is revocable but with a time notice from the bank the revocability may not reduce the immediate usage.
- The type of counterparty for the facility. The exact liquidity distress scenario d should determine the expected increased usage rates for different types of counterparties.

Example of Facility Drawdown Scenario Table 6.9 displays a sample facility cash outflow where the current facility usage rate is 30%. In the liquidity distress scenario the usage rates increase for $t = 1, \ldots, 4$. The current facility limit is 100 units of currency. The resulting facility undrawn balance and the cash outflows, $cf^-(d, t)$, are also displayed in Table 6.9. Another way to express the increased facility usage rates in a scenario is to model the drawdown of the undrawn amount. For example, if the current undrawn amount is 70 units of currency, then

TABLE 6.8 Deposit Outflow Scenario

Time	Deposit withdrawal rate	Balance	outflow $(cf^-(d, t))$
$t = 1$	10%	90	10
$t = 2$	15%	76.5	13.5
$t = 3$	25%	57.375	19.125
$t = 4$	55%	25.825	31.55

TABLE 6.9 Facility Outflow Scenario

Time	Facility usage rate	Undrawn balance	Cash outflow $(cf^-(d,t))$
$t=0$	30%	70	.
$t=1$	45%	55	15
$t=2$	85%	15	40
$t=3$	95%	5	10
$t=4$	100%	0	5

a drawdown of 50% produces a cash outflow of 35 and also reduces the remaining balance to draw further on to 35.

Market Funding and Funding Facilities Extended to the Bank For universal banks a key trend observed in banks' funding profile is an upsurge in reliance on wholesale market funding that is both more volatile and costly compared to traditional sources of demand deposits. This trend has developed over a few years due to alternative sources of investments being available to consumers that provide better return compared to bank deposits. It is an issue for banks how to attract new stable core deposits. This is because if a bank raises its deposit rates in response to changes in market rates, while it should attract more consumer deposit inflows, the incremental depositors may display a rate opportunistic behavior. That is, the newly attracted deposit volume may not be attributed to the core stable funding.

While consumer behavior—and, in particular, its effect on deposit funding—is key to analyzing liquidity risk, the increasing trend of market-based funding calls for more understanding of the market-based funding behavior in a plausible liquidity scenario. In general, a bank should not rely on only unsecured interbank funding, committed liquidity lines from other banks, and long-term bond funding. Important lessons learned in the recent crisis are that diversity of funding is needed and that secured funding, such as repo funding, as well as the establishment of long-term relationships is of major importance to maintain a sufficient level of funding in a crisis.

In a liquidity crisis situation, it is prudent to assume that previously committed lines of credit are not available (or significantly reduced) and that unsecured funding will dry up. Plausible specific scenarios that may be considered by the bank are as follows:

- Wholesale funding rollover with a reduced rollover term and only with counterparties that have a strong relation with the bank. One should also account for an increased cost of funding contributing to the cash outflows, $cf^-(d,t)$, for the funding that is rolled over.
- Difficulty maintaining secured funding. Repos are rolled over only if there is a strong relation to the counterparty.

Clearly, repos that mature before the liquidity analysis horizon and are not rolled over will have a cash outflow at repo maturity date, $cf^-(d,t)$. On the other hand, the bank will receive back the pledged repo collateral and can potentially sell the asset to generate offsetting liquidity inflows. Reverse repos that mature before the liquidity analysis horizon and are not rolled over have a cash inflow, $cf^+(d,t)$. However, the counterparty pledged collateral asset is returned and not available anymore.

- Committed lines of credit are not available or significantly reduced. Hence, one should be cautious in counting on potential cash inflows, $cf^+(d,t)$, from funding facilities, especially from other banks as they likely face liquidity constraints at the same time and hence will try to close the bank's use of its credit lines.

Market Effects A specific market assumption can also affect the cash inflows and outflows. We have previously noted that floating rate cash flows that reprice during the term of the liquidity scenario are affected, for example, short-term money market funding. Currency risk is also an important factor to be included in the analysis of the institution's funding capability and the resulting forward liquidity exposure, $\{F(d,t)\}_{t=1}^{T}$, in the numeraire currency. A foreign exchange market shock can distress the actual amount of funding in a different currency.

Off–Balance-Sheet Derivative Flows

Negative cash outflows may not only occur due to the bank's consumer and market funding behavior. The net cash flows from derivatives such as swaps may be adversely affected depending on the market conditions assumed in the scenario d. Deals that move unfavorably to the bank can also cause a requirement to post additional collateral. For example:

- Exchange-traded positions usually have a variation margin that may increase at the discretion of the exchange.
- Bilateral OTC derivatives usually have collateral agreements (CSA agreements) as we have discussed previously in the context of counterparty credit risk.

The CSA agreement for a net portfolio of derivatives is usually associated with frequent margining requirements to close out counterparty risk should markets change rapidly and adversely for the bank. CSA agreements may also contain explicit rating triggers that force the bank to post additional margins in case of downgrade. Note that posting additional margin due to rating downgrade, market exposure, or both raises a funding requirement for the bank. Therefore, a bank-specific liquidity crisis—initiated by rating downgrade—can create a spiral of negative effects, ultimately causing further downgrades of the bank's rating.

As we have discussed in the context of counterparty credit risk, after the financial crisis, in order to enhance the counterparty risk mitigation, ISDA published Standard Credit Support Annex (SCSA). It is the annex to the ISDA Master Agreement and covers terms of the collateral arrangement between two counterparties. Notably, under the new standard CSA, one collateral requirement is called daily per currency each day, delivered in each currency or converted to a single currency with an interest adjustment overlay. The margin threshold and minimum collateral transfer amounts are set to zero or at low values. Only cash is eligible as variation margin collateral. The more stringent collateral requirements reduce counterparty credit risk but call for more careful management of the liquidity risk due to margining requirements.

Analyzing the potential liquidity outflow for bilateral OTC derivative agreements and margined positions held by a custodian is quite simple. To calculate the posting requirement and hence the cash outflow, $cf^-(d,t)$, due to bilateral CSA margin requirements we first need to calculate the exposure under the scenario d; we can then use the parameters of the CSA margin agreement to calculate the posting requirement as well as the effect of downgrade triggers. In case the collateral agreement allows non-cash assets to be posted, it is also prudent to assume, as part of the scenario d, that their value may depreciate and hence generate additional posting requirements. We refer to the chapter on counterparty credit risk for examples of calculating required CSA collateral posts. For margined positions with custodian the potential future exposure is a good indicator of future variation margin requirements.

However, the analysis of the perceived liquidity outflow due to margin requirements may not be that straightforward when positions are moved through central counterparty clearing. This is because the bank does not have full insight on the aggregated exposure from the members. Nor may they know the exact posting rule in advance that may be at discretion of the central counterparty. Hence, the funding (posting) requirement may come as a surprise. The bank may also have to provide liquidity support to a central counterparty if a member fails. Arnsdorff (2012) uses a model to estimate the potential exposure to a central counterparty in distress. The risk includes both the risk of losing already posted collateral as well as having to post more in order to bail out the central counterparty.

Combining the Risk and Finance View

Liquidity risk scenarios are focused on modeling expected behavior conditional on liquidity crisis and hence severe events. The behavioral modeling can be pool based, such as deposit withdrawal behavior of consumers and small business, and position or counterparty based, such as expected behavior of a financial institution counterparty in drawdowns on banks' granted credit lines and the counterparty's willingness to roll over funding with the bank. Different behavioral assumptions result in different cash inflows and outflows. Other behaviors such as default, delinquency, and prepayment in the liquidity crisis are usually analyzed on pool level for consumers and small business but can also be applied on detailed level. Regardless whether behavioral assumptions are applied on pool or detailed level, detailed level cash flows are in general produced. Detailed level cash flows are then aggregated to a higher level view where going-concern business growth is usually applied on aggregated balances (cash flows) for a product class as in the target ending balance example above. This structure of liquidity analysis fits well with using a bank's risk and cash flow system for detailed account- and position-level cash flows, and subsequently the finance view as post-processing incorporating planning. Hence, in this approach,

- First, detailed level cash flows are generated with base behavioral assumptions.
- Second, balance sheet cash flows are aggregated to a traditional financial balance sheet (cash flow) view.
- Third, target growth and ending balances are applied to the aggregated view of cash flows to generate adjusted cash inflow and outflows for business growth, and increase in default, delinquency, and so forth, compared to base.

HEDGING THE LIQUIDITY EXPOSURE

Once the institution's aggregate forward liquidity exposure, $\{F(d, t)\}_{t=1}^{T}$, has been obtained under a scenario d the next step is to strategize the execution of the liquidity hedging portfolio. Recall that the objective is to ensure that the liquidity reserve process, $R(C, T, d)$, is nonnegative for all T considered as liquidity horizons.[8] The first step in our analysis of counterbalancing capacity of the liquidity hedge portfolio is to define the assets available for use.

---

[8]In principle other restrictions or target goals of the liquidity reserve process can also be considered. For example, if the liquidity hedging portfolio does not include available central bank funding as last resort, there may be a maximum funding requirement restriction for each liquidity horizon, T.

The Basel III liquidity risk regulation underscores the importance of managing a liquidity contingency buffer in much the same way as capital. The focus is on maintaining a high-quality liquidity portfolio that can hedge liquidity outflows under stress scenarios. This is formalized in the new regulation by requiring banks to report so-called liquidity coverage ratios that test the sufficiency of the liquidity hedging portfolio under behavioral, market, and bank-specific stresses. Under these stresses the bank's liquidity portfolio needs to hedge the stressed funding outflow over the time horizon of 30 days under a going-concern assumption. This test becomes the regulatory test whether a bank has a sufficient short-term liquidity buffer.

The Basel III eligible buffer of liquidity hedging assets includes so-called level 1 and level 2A and 2B assets. Level 1 assets include cash, central bank reserves, and premium government and municipal bonds. Level 2A assets include high-quality corporate and covered bonds, and level 2B assets include lower quality corporate bonds and common shares. Haircuts on the hedge value of assets are prescribed by the regulation.

In our liquidity hedging analysis we will not impose the regulatory eligibility restriction explicitly. While in a regulatory context there are constraints on the liquidity buffers that can be used for testing an institution's liquidity coverage, in practice, in a liquidity stress the institution will consider all assets eligible for sale. This means that assets such as facilities, core assets may be part of a liquidity execution analysis even though the assets are not regulatory eligible in defining the size of the liquidity buffer. If the model is instead used to test the sufficiency of the regulatory counterbalancing capacity portfolio, then, naturally, only regulatory eligible assets are included in the model.

When there is no other funding source available, a firm has to resort to a certain asset and trade it for as good value as possible. Because selling an asset at an unfavorable time often incurs a big loss to the firm (i.e., a fire-sale situation), it is certainly not a preferred funding activity. The empirical literature has shown that institutions in general do not sell assets in a falling market (Boyson et al., 2010). Instead, institutions try to find other funding alternatives first. However, in extreme situations institutions do react to liquidity shocks by selling assets (Adrian and Shin, 2010). During the recent financial crisis Citi group sold off its profitable Smith Barney division to raise $11.1 billion in cash in March 2009. In August 2011, in the midst of other funding efforts, Bank of America sold about half of its shares in China Construction Bank one month after it sold its Canadian credit card division.

In general, a financial institution has the following types of funding sources:

- Contingent credit line

A contingent credit line is a commitment from a lender to extend a maximum amount of credit that the borrower can borrow at any time until the line matures. The drawdown on the credit line is usually up to the borrower as long as the limit is not breached. A contingent credit line is a very popular and relatively safe liquidity source next to cash. It can also function as a liquidity insurance (Thakor, 2005). Several empirical studies have found that contingent credit lines have a preset maximum amount, and usually impose a commitment fee up front, a use fee and interest rate for the used portion, and an unused fee for the undrawn portion. The fee for the unused portion is consistent with the fact that institutions price the opportunity cost of contingency liquidity as a liquidity buffer needs to be held should the institution use the facility extensively.

Contingent credit lines are used heavily by firms as a funding source. For example, Morgan (1998) finds drawdown on existing credit lines increases after a policy tightening.

Saidenber and Strahan (1999) find that firms drew extensively upon their bank lines when access to the commercial paper market was limited in 1998. Lenders tend to extend contingent credit lines to less liquidity constrained firms.

There is also an opportunity cost for a firm to draw down extensively from contingent credit lines in order to keep lenders willing to extend more credit lines in the future. Ivashina and Scharfstein (2010) and Campello et al. (2012) find that at the time of liquidity distress institutions tend to use the undrawn portion of their credit line as much as possible in the early stage of the distress, before the lender detects their liquidity difficulty. The more financially constrained a firm is, the more it draws down the credit line. This borrowing behavior typically leads to a tighter scrutinization from lenders in a later stage of a distress. Tirole (2005) has noted that lenders often prefer to keep discretion over the credit line by making the line revocable. In general, lenders have ways for limiting the extent of liquidity insurance nature of contingent credit lines in advance of a line drawdown. Both Sufi (2009) and Campello et al. (2011) find that illiquid firms have less access to credit lines than liquid firms.

In Basel III the base regulatory assumption in assessing cash inflows from credit lines is that the bank cannot use any of its contingent credit lines to raise funds. Banks therefore need to consider only the regulatory eligible level 1 and level 2 assets for the purpose of hedge sufficiency testing. However, this does not mean that at the time of liquidity distress contingent credit lines are not available to the bank. It only means that when a priori determining the size of the liquidity hedging, portfolio banks should not count on facilities being available.

- Short-term collateralized loans

Short-term secured borrowing facilities are effective for financial institutions. There are primarily two types of short-term secured borrowing facilities: asset-backed commercial paper and repurchase agreement. Both types use the assets that a firm owns as collateral. Once an asset is pledged as collateral, the asset is encumbered and is not up to free disposal of the firm. Such collateralized borrowing facilities are especially effective funding sources for banks in liquidity distress. See Gatev and Strahan (2006).

- Customer deposit

Accessibility to stable deposit funds is an advantage for retail and commercial banks. The deposit is considered as a countercyclical source of funding (Gatev, Schuermann, and Strahan, 2009) and is a preferred funding source for banks at normal economic situations. However, establishing additional deposit channels takes time, and at the time of a liquidity distress banks find it difficult to attract new deposits.

- Other borrowing facilities

Financial institutions, especially banks, have interbank borrowing facilities among themselves. This is an important uncollateralized borrowing capacity that is subject to the interbank interest rate. Interbank borrowing is usually a safe and effective funding source for banks. Chari et al. (2008) argue that the interbank lending market was active and well-functioning even as late as October 2008 during the financial crisis. Banks also have access to central bank funds. However, banks try to stay away from borrowing extensively from the central bank to avoid creating a reputation of being in liquidity distress.

When the financial institution's funding sources have been exhausted, the next step is to consider a sale of assets to raise cash. Holding cash is clearly a valuable and unsurpassed liquidity supplier. Bates et al. (2009) find that American firms hold more cash as a liquidity insurance now than ever due to the riskier business models in the modern economy. Cash and cash equivalents usually have low liquidity execution cost and limitation. However, because too much cash holding diminishes the growth opportunity of the firm due to the large opportunity cost of cash, cash and cash equivalents do not make up the entire liquidity hedge source. Furthermore, some cash equivalents, especially deposits with other banks, can still be subject to withdrawal limits.

To hedge liquidity exposures, the financial institutions also hold a dedicated asset portfolio. The asset portfolio can include government and corporate bonds, covered bonds, as well as equity. When an asset holding has been partially pledged as collateral (e.g., in a margin agreement), only the unencumbered portion is available. Note that the unencumbered portion of assets included in the liquidity hedge portfolio do not contribute cash flows to the forward liquidity exposure, $\{F(d, t)\}_{t=1}^{T}$. They are instead counted toward the counterbalancing flows of the liquidity reserve process, $R(C, T, d)$.

The treatment of repo and reverse repo agreements where an asset has been pledged versus received as collateral depends on the liquidity analysis horizon and the assumptions of rollover. When the repo agreement matures within the liquidity horizon the pledged asset is returned and there is an outflow, $cf^-(d, t)$, of the repo amount. However, the returned asset can now be used to raise offsetting liquidity—either with a new repo agreement or by selling the asset. For a reverse repo that matures within the liquidity horizon there is an inflow, $cf^+(d, t)$, of the repo amount. On the other hand, the asset received as collateral is returned and not available to raise cash. If the maturity of the reverse repo is longer than the liquidity horizon, then the collateral asset can potentially be used and counted toward available hedging assets to be used in a repo or sale. Of course, this is true for many of the received collaterals on the bank's balance sheet.

Given a sufficient liquidity hedging portfolio banks can strategize their response to a liquidity crisis, d, in advance through contingency funding plans. Such a contingency funding plan includes having a strategy for liquidity execution. Liquidity execution is therefore one of the core functions in the bank. In a liquidity execution, apart from the financial cost of the execution itself, a firm must also take into account reputational and opportunity cost. When multiple liquidity distress stages are anticipated banks can be more willing to hold onto the most liquid assets and not risk a fire-sale of the illiquid assets in later, more severe stages of the distress. This is clearly a decision-making process based on a long-term survival strategy. Therefore, an important aspect of liquidity management and in particular liquidity execution is to recognize the fact that a liquidity distress period usually evolves in multiple stages, and when the funding liquidity shortage evolves so does the borrowing cost and market liquidity as well. An institution's liquidity execution plan should therefore incorporate this multistage nature of the liquidity distress and the fact that execution costs, liquidity depth, and other market factors such as haircuts vary across stages. If the bank finds that the liquidity hedge portfolio has insufficient counterbalancing capacity under the liquidity scenario, d, it may have to acquire further liquid funds.

We consider next two different types of models of liquidity hedging. The first model is only based on a simple ranking preference of liquidity execution of assets. The second model uses optimization to find the best possible execution strategy for a given liquidity hedge portfolio. The optimization model for liquidity execution we use here is from Chen, Skoglund, and Cai (2012). Both the ranking and the optimization model for liquidity execution find a plausible survival liquidity execution if this is feasible with the assets at hand and for the given market situation. Hence, they ensure survival if possible. Deterministic methods of liquidity hedging—which essentially predefine the counterbalancing capacity cash generation from assets—do not have this feature. They generally require trial and error with different asset sale and repo strategies to determine if the liquidity hedge portfolio is sufficient for survival. See Fiedler and Kustner (2011) for a detailed example of a deterministic liquidity hedging approach that prescribes hypothetical asset sales, repo amounts, and inventory changes at $t = 1, \ldots, T$ from which counterbalancing flows are generated.

Using an optimal liquidity execution model, it is in general optimal for firms to rank liquidity facilities based on their anticipated execution costs and haircuts across the expected stages of a liquidity crisis and, should it be expected that all of the firm's liquidity capacity needs to be used to raise the funds, execute the lower quality assets first, saving the liquid assets for later execution as they do not have a significant decrease in value as liquidity distress worsens. However, when the firm does not expect to use all of its liquidity to raise the needed funds during the liquidity distress stages, then it can refrain from executing the least-quality assets to keep execution costs to a minimum. This behavior of optimal liquidity execution models leads to the discussion about two general liquidity hedge strategies referred to as "cash first" or "cash last" execution strategies. See Duffie and Ziegler (2003) in this regard.

Ranking-Based Liquidity Hedging Strategy

In a simple ranking-based model for liquidity hedging we assign to the liquidity hedge assets a rank of whichever asset we have a preference to sell first. Since there are no explicit market liquidity execution costs in this simple model, when the asset is sold we can incorporate liquidity costs by using fixed haircuts. The assigned haircuts of course depend on the asset quality as well as the market behavior in the liquidity scenario, d. For a given liquidity gap, $\{cf(d, t)\}_{t=1}^{T}$, we liquidate the assets in the ranking order to close the gap. For example, if the needed liquidity support at time $t = 1$ is an amount θ, we will first liquidate the assets ranked as priority 1 up to their available amount. Assuming the available amount is less than θ we will next continue to liquidate assets ranked second priority, and so on.

In case there are restrictions on how much of an asset can be sold at a particular time, the ranking is of secondary importance as the survival of the institution is of first priority. This means that assets ranked numerically higher may need to be executed before numerically lower ranked (higher priority) assets in case of sale restrictions at $t = 1, \ldots, T$.

Example of Ranking-Based Liquidity Hedging Consider a $t = 1, \ldots, 6$ period-by-period funding gap of 10. Having available 3 assets, asset 1, 2, and 3, ranked as 1, 2, and 3 respectively with liquidity adjusted market value of 100 each we would only use asset 1 to generate counterbalancing capacity in case there are no sale constraints on asset 1 that would prevent its use and we would liquidate 10% of asset 1 at each period to raise the needed funding for $t = 1, \ldots, 6$. Equivalently, since haircuts do not vary over time we could liquidate 60% of asset 1 at $t = 1$ and put it in a cash account to use at $t = 1, \ldots, 6$. We will refer to this liquidity hedge case as liquidity hedge scenario 1.

However, if there are constraints on the amount of assets that can be sold or utilized to raise cash, the liquidity execution may not follow the ranking. For example, if asset 1 can only be sold at $t = 6$ and asset 2 can only be sold after $t = 4$ while asset 3 has no sale restrictions, we obtain the ranked liquidity execution as a 10% sale of asset 3 in $t = 1, 2, 3$, a 10% sale of asset 2 in $t = 4, 5$, and a 10% sale of asset 1 in $t = 6$. This is because survival and a closing of the funding gap is the main goal. We refer to this hedge scenario as hedge scenario 2.

As a third liquidity hedging scenario consider asset execution limits such that asset 1 cannot be executed at $t = 2, \ldots, 6$ and only up to 20% in $t = 1$. Asset 2 can only be liquidated

TABLE 6.10 Ranking-Based Liquidity Hedging Scenarios with Asset 1, 2, and 3 Liquidation Percentages in the Scenarios

	Liquidity gap		Hedge scenario 1			Hedge scenario 2			Hedge scenario 3		
Time	$cf(d,t)$	$F(d,T)$	Asset 1	Asset 2	Asset 3	Asset 1	Asset 2	Asset 3	Asset 1	Asset 2	Asset 3
$t = 1$	-10	-10	10%	0%	0%	0%	0%	10%	20%	0%	30%
$t = 2$	-10	-20	10%	0%	0%	0%	0%	10%	0%	0%	0%
$t = 3$	-10	-30	10%	0%	0%	0%	0%	10%	0%	0%	0%
$t = 4$	-10	-40	10%	0%	0%	0%	10%	0%	0%	0%	0%
$t = 5$	-10	-50	10%	0%	0%	0%	10%	0%	0%	0%	0%
$t = 6$	-10	-60	10%	0%	0%	10%	0%	0%	0%	10%	0%

at $t = 6$ and asset 3 has no liquidation constraints at $t = 1$ but cannot be liquidated after. The ranking liquidation then sells 20% of asset 1 and 30% of asset 3 in $t = 1$ to cover the funding liquidity gap at $t = 1, \ldots, 5$. Finally, at $t = 6$ asset 2 is sold to cover the funding gap at $t = 6$.

Table 6.10 displays the ranked liquidity execution percentages of asset 1, 2, and 3 in our three liquidity hedge scenarios. It also displays the liquidity gap and the forward liquidity exposure obtained from the cash flows under scenario d.

The ranking-based liquidity execution model gives a simple approach to analyzing sufficiency of the liquidity hedging portfolio. Its main inputs are the current market value of assets as well as liquidity haircuts and market execution constraints for the asset. Insufficiency of the assets to guarantee liquidity solvency under scenario d, either because of non-sufficient liquidity adjusted market values to execute or because of market execution constraints, leads to a consideration whether some hedging assets can be substituted and/or if new assets need to be considered as part of the liquidity hedging portfolio. A drawback of the model is its simplicity. It does not capture the typical time costs of execution in a liquidity crisis since fixed haircuts are used. As a liquidity crisis unfolds the liquidity execution costs may increase leading to a trade-off between which types of assets should be executed first versus last. We therefore now turn our attention to liquidity execution models with time-varying execution costs that optimize the liquidity execution behavior.

Optimal Liquidity Hedging Strategy

In reality, among a firm's liquidity inventory, not all the available instruments are created equal. Various costs and constraints exist to deploy these instruments into cash, to create counterbalancing capacity. The costs can be due to interest rate charge in borrowing, bid–ask spread in trading as a result of the market impact of a security, or simply opportunity cost assessed by the management. Other than costs, constraints may also exist due either to the material limit attached to borrowing (e.g. letter of credit), trading limit, or internal limit.

To consider an optimal liquidity execution plan we start with a simple model where, in order to deploy an inventory of liquidity supplying instruments, only time constraints are imposed. This scenario indicates that as long as the cash conversion process follows a stable plan (not a fire-sale case), execution can be done on a fixed cost base. The model accommodates a multistage liquidity need where the liquidity gap and execution cost can be different across stages. In our model setting there are therefore K consecutive liquidity distress stages that a firm faces. This multistage nature is an important aspect for a liquidity management decision-making process, because in reality, when funding liquidity starts to show distress, firms' borrowing capacity and cost will worsen across stages. The second model extends the first model for tradable assets by assuming a linear price dependency on the volume.

Throughout we use the terms "instrument" or "facility" to represent a homogeneous class of liquidity suppliers subject to the same execution (transaction) cost and haircuts. It is hence not necessarily a single asset. Since the models consider the evolution of liquidity at K distress stages we also assume, for convenience, that these K stages are consecutive. The total liquidity gap across all distress stages is divided into stage $k = 1, \ldots, K$ specific gaps. Any fund raised during any transaction period in a stage is immediately applied to reduce the gap. Effectively, this means we make no distinction between cash raised at the beginning or end of a distress period. What matters is how cash is raised across distress stages, $k = 1, \ldots, K$, to fill the distress stage gap. However, within a distress period k naturally execution limits may differ since the limit is not necessarily triggered by the distress stage but could be exogenous. For example, cash withdrawal may be subject to deposit institution cash availability on a certain day and credit line drawdown may be subject to a daily limit

Liquidity Hedging with Fixed Execution Costs   In the first model with execution limits and fixed execution costs there are K consecutive liquidity distress stages that a firm faces. Each distress stage k has M_k execution periods when the firm can raise funds. A new liquidity gap G_k is incurred at each stage k. The firm has a portfolio of N_i, $i = 1, \ldots, N$, instruments available to deploy. Each instrument i has a market value or principal A_i with execution cost c_i and an execution limit l_{ij_k} at a given execution period, $j_k = 1, \ldots, M_k$, within a stage k. The firm's objective is to minimize the execution cost while raising the needed cash for the liquidity gap, G_k, for all $k = 1, \ldots, K$ from the given portfolio of liquidity supplying instruments. We define the cost function for each stage as

$$f_k = \sum_{i=1}^{N} \sum_{j_k=1}^{M_k} c_{i,k} x_{ij_k}. \tag{6.12}$$

The minimal cost portfolio optimization is

$$\min \sum_{k=1}^{K} f_k \tag{6.13}$$

where x_{ij_k} is the executed amount of asset i in period j_k within liquidity distress stage k and $c_{i,k}$ is the execution cost of asset i in distress stage k. Here $j_k = 1, \ldots, M_k$, $k = 1, \ldots, K$. The minimal cost optimization is subject to the following constraints for $i = 1, \ldots, N$, $j_k = 1, \ldots, M_k$, $k = 1, \ldots, K$,

$$x_{ij_k} \geq 0 \tag{6.14}$$

$$x_{ij_k} \leq l_{ij_k} \tag{6.15}$$

$$\sum_{k=1}^{k=K} \sum_{j_k=1}^{M_k} x_{ij_k} \leq A_i \tag{6.16}$$

$$\sum_{i=1}^{N} \sum_{j_k=1}^{M_k} x_{ij_k} - f_k \geq G_k \forall k \tag{6.17}$$

where constraint (6.15) is the execution limit for each instrument at period j_k within liquidity distress stage k. This limit can be due to either a cash withdrawal limit allowed for the period imposed by the deposit institution or a trading limit imposed by a security exchange authority to prevent market crash. Constraint (6.16) indicates the total executed amount cannot be more than what is available. Finally, constraint (6.14) is the liquidity gap to be met in each distress stage, $k = 1, \ldots, K$. The execution cost (6.12) is added to the gap in each stage.

Example of Liquidity Model with Fixed Execution Costs Using this liquidity execution model consider a firm that is expecting two liquidity distress stages, $k = 1$ and $k = 2$ respectively, where distress stage $k = 1$ has a duration of three days and distress stage $k = 2$ has a duration of two days. We assume that the cash that needs to be raised in each of the distress stages is 2,000,000 units of currency. Each liquidity facility can be executed up to a certain limit within a distress stage (in this case a day). When a liquidity facility is not available to convert to cash the limit is set to zero.

Table 6.11 displays the available liquidity sources together with their available amounts and liquidity type. The portfolio of liquidity supplying facilities includes cash or cash equivalents, bonds, a facility, and equities. Table 6.12 displays the available liquidity facilities with their fixed execution constraints in each of the days in the liquidity distress stage of $k = 1$ and $k = 2$. Table 6.12 also shows the fixed execution costs expressed in basis points of the liquidity facilities for each of the liquidity distress periods. For most of the liquidity facilities execution costs are higher in the second stage—reflecting a more severe liquidity distress in the second stage. In practice, one can interpret the execution cost as including an asset

TABLE 6.11 Liquidity Sources and Their Available Liquidity Amounts

Liquidity	Available amount	Liquidity type
Cash 1	500,000	small cost
Cash 2	1,000,000	small cost—not available immediately
Bond 1	700,000	small cost
Bond 2	800,000	medium to large cost
Facility	500,000	small to medium cost—may be constrained
Equity 1	600,000	medium cost
Equity 2	300,000	large cost

TABLE 6.12 Available Liquidity at Fixed Costs for each of the Days in Distress Stage 1 and 2

Liquidity	Liquidity stage, $k = 1$				Liquidity stage, $k = 2$		
	Cost	$j_1 = 1$	$j_1 = 2$	$j_1 = 3$	Cost	$j_2 = 1$	$j_2 = 2$
Cash 1	0 bp	500,000	500,000	500,000	0 bp	500,000	500,000
Cash 2	10 bp	0	0	1,000,000	10 bp	1,000,000	1,000,000
Bond 1	20 bp	500,000	500,000	500,000	40 bp	350,000	350,000
Bond 2	100 bp	300,000	300,000	300,000	200 bp	200,000	150,000
Facility	10 bp	0	250,000	250,000	20 bp	100,000	50,000
Equity 1	80 bp	200,000	200,000	200,000	180 bp	200,000	200,000
Equity 2	180 bp	0	150,000	150,000	300 bp	50,000	20,000

haircut—capturing the fact that the firm's liquidity execution will most likely have to be performed under a combination of general market stress and the firm-specific liquidity stress. The market stress will cause significant haircuts on non-cash equivalent liquidity due to a general flight-to-quality market behavior. In addition, the bank-specific stress will most likely cause other banks to try and constrain the bank's usage of outstanding facilities and other committed lines of credit.

Note that in this model known future cash flows (e.g., coupons) may be considered as part of a cash account. The execution limits may be used to constrain usage of coupon until it is received. For example, the liquidity facility "Cash 2" in Table 6.12 is not available during the first two days of liquidity distress stage $k = 1$ while it is available subsequently in the last day of distress stage $k = 1$ and in distress stage $k = 2$.[9]

Liquidity Hedging with Tiered Execution Costs For tradable assets our second liquidity hedge optimization model assumes a market liquidity cost dependent on volume. Following Jorion (2009) we assume an asset can be traded within a trading period up to a certain trading threshold v known as "market depth" at a market bid–ask spread c_0. In order to execute the trading in a bigger volume, market price moves unfavorably at a cost rate c_1 where $c_1 \geq c_0$ in excess to the market trading cost due to the big–ask spread. The cost of sale execution of the security is then

$$c(x) = \begin{cases} c_1(x - v) + c_0 v & \text{if } x > v \\ c_0 x & \text{otherwise.} \end{cases} \tag{6.18}$$

The cost function (6.18) can be equivalently written as

$$c(x) = (c_1 - c_0)(x - v)_+ + c_0 x$$

where

$$(x - v)_+ = \begin{cases} x - v & \text{if } x > v \\ 0 & \text{otherwise} \end{cases}$$

which can be further be expressed as

$$c(x) = (c_1 - c_0)y + c_0 x \tag{6.19}$$

with constraints $y \geq 0$ and $y \geq x - v$, where y is an auxiliary variable.

In each trading period of a liquidity distress stage k, an instrument i can be converted to cash at the cost of $c(x_i)$ as defined by (6.18) and (6.19), subject to a limit constraint l_i or a market trading threshold v_i. The funding gap that the liquidity plan must satisfy for each period is G_k. Each period has M_k trading periods when cash conversion can take place. The cost function in each stage is thus extended to

$$f_k = \sum_{i=1}^{N} \sum_{j_k=1}^{M_k} \left[(c_{1,i,k} - c_{0,i,k}) y_{ij_k} + c_{0,i,k} x_{ij_k} \right]. \tag{6.20}$$

---

[9]Note here that asset flows that depend on trades are assumed immaterial and are not considered. This is realistic in most cases because the time period of liquidity distress is assumed relatively short.

A minimal cost optimization problem can hence be defined as

$$\min \sum_{k=1}^{K} f_k \tag{6.21}$$

subject to the following constraints for $i = 1, \ldots, N$, $j_k = 1, \ldots, M_k$, $k = 1, \ldots, K$

$$x_{ij_k} \geq 0$$
$$x_{ij_k} \leq l_{ij_k}$$
$$y_{ij_k} \geq 0 \tag{6.22}$$
$$y_{ij_k} \geq x_{ij_k} - v_{ij_k} \tag{6.23}$$

$$\sum_{k=1}^{k=K} \sum_{j_k=1}^{M_k} x_{ij_k} \leq A_i$$

$$\sum_{i=1}^{N} \sum_{j_k=1}^{M_k} x_{ij_k} - f_k \geq G_k \forall k$$

plus any other linear business constraints. Note the newly introduced constraints (6.22) and (6.23) in this model compared to the first model. Here y is an auxiliary variable that helps create a linear representation of the trading cost as explained in (6.19).

Example of Liquidity Execution with Tiered Costs Adapting the numerical example of the first model to this second model with tiered execution cost we allow a quicker execution of traded assets, that is, less restrictive trading limits. However, the firm must pay a fire-sale cost when the "normal" market depth of an asset is breached. Table 6.13 displays the total available liquidity facilities in each of the days in the liquidity distress stage of $k = 1$ and $k = 2$. It also displays the tiered execution constraints, c_0 and c_1 respectively, for the liquidity facilities. Table 6.14 displays the tradable limits for liquidity facilities for the tiered execution cost c_0. After this limit and up to the total available limits in Table 6.13 the execution cost is c_1. As in the numerical example for the first model, for most of the liquidity facilities

TABLE 6.13 Available Liquidity at Tiered Costs for each of the Days in Distress Stage 1 and 2

	Liquidity stage, $k=1$					Liquidity stage, $k=2$			
Liquidity	Cost (c_0)	Cost (c_1)	$j_1=1$	$j_1=2$	$j_1=3$	Cost (C_0)	Cost (C_1)	$j_2=1$	$j_2=2$
Cash 1	0 bp	0 bp	500,000	500,000	500,000	0 bp	0 bp	500,000	500,000
Cash 2	10 bp	10 bp	0	0	1,000,000	10 bp	10 bp	1,000,000	1,000,000
Bond 1	20 bp	250 bp	700,000	700,000	700,000	40 bp	450 bp	700,000	700,000
Bond 2	100 bp	400 bp	800,000	800,000	800,000	200 bp	1000 bp	500,000	500,000
Facility	10 bp	200 bp	0	500,000	500,000	20 bp	400 bp	150,000	50,000
Equity 1	80 bp	300 bp	600,000	600,000	600,000	180 bp	500 bp	600,000	600,000
Equity 2	180 bp	550 bp	0	300,000	300,000	300 bp	1250 bp	100,000	100,000

TABLE 6.14 Available Liquidity at First-Tier Cost

Liquidity	Liquidity stage, $k = 1$ Market depth (c_0)	Liquidity stage, $k = 2$ Market depth (c_0)
Cash 1	500,000	500,000
Cash 2	1,000,000	1,000,000
Bond 1	500,000	300,000
Bond 2	300,000	100,000
Facility	250,000	50,000
Equity 1	200,000	100,000
Equity 2	150,000	20,000

execution costs are higher in the second stage—reflecting a more severe liquidity distress in the second stage.

Using a linear program we now solve the model with tiered execution cost using the sample data in Tables 6.11, 6.13, and 6.14 assuming that the cash that needs to be raised in each of the distress stages is 2,000,000 units of currency.[10] The optimal execution amounts are shown in Table 6.15. The optimal execution cost across stages 1 and 2 is 15,763 units of currency and the execution cost paid in each of stages 1 and 2 respectively is 12,952 and 2,811 units of currency. For example, the stage 2 execution cost is neutralized by executing an additional 2,811 units of currency of the liquidity facility bond 1. From Table 6.15 we note that the liquid cash position cash 1 is sold at stage 2 in full to raise the needed funds of the stage 2 liquidity distress. This behavior of not using the cash position cash 1 in distress period 1 is expected as the cost of executing the cash position is null in all stages while other assets typically have an increasing execution cost in stage 2. That is, since the cash position does not come with an increasing execution cost as the liquidity tightens up across stages, it is natural to hold the cash positions and liquidate first the positions that have an increasing execution cost as the liquidity distress becomes worse. We also observe the same behavior

TABLE 6.15 Optimal Liquidity Plan for Model with Tiered Execution Cost

Liquidity	Available amount	Optimal execution amount, $k = 1$ $j_1 = 1$	$j_1 = 2$	$j_1 = 3$	Optimal execution amount, $k = 2$ $j_2 = 1$	$j_2 = 2$
Cash 1	500,000	0	0	0	500,000	0
Cash 2	1,000,000	0	0	0	0	1,000,000
Bond 1	700,000	0	0	297,189	102,811	300,000
Bond 2	800,000	115,763	300,000	300,000	0	0
Facility	500,000	0	250,000	150,000	50,000	50,000
Equity 1	600,000	200,000	200,000	200,000	0	0
Equity 2	300,000	0	0	0	0	0
		Total raised amount = 2,000,000			Total raised amount = 2,000,000	

---

[10]An added value of a linear programming model as applied here is to leverage the sensitivity analysis from the duality theory of linear programming to study how the range of parameter change affects the optimal solution. See Chen, Skoglund, and Cai (2012) for examples.

for the cash position cash 2 as for cash 1. That is, the cash 2 position is executed in full in stage 2. Next, observing the liquidation behavior of the bond positions, that is, bond 1 and bond 2, we note that for bond 1 position, liquidation is spread out over the liquidity distress stages 1 and 2. The bond 1 position is sold in chunks, day by day, below the first-tier market depth limit of 300,000. Since there is not a significant difference in first-tier execution cost between stages 1 and 2, going from 20 bp to 40 bp, the bond 1 position is used to obtain liquidity also in distress stage 2 together with the cash positions. The stage 2 distress gap of 2,000,000 is almost fully covered by the 2 cash positions and bond 1 as their second-stage execution raises about 1,900,000. Note also that slightly less than 300,000 is sold of bond 1 in distress stage 1 to allow the use of the remaining bond 1 funds to cover both the gap and the execution cost in stage 2. The bond 2 has significantly higher first and second-tier execution costs than bond 1 and can be thought of as a lower quality bond with higher haircuts. Bond 2 has a first-tier execution limit in stage 1 of 300,00 and a stage 2 first-tier limit of 100,00. The increasing execution cost across stages as well as the significantly reduced first-tier execution limit makes it optimal to sell an amount of 715,763 of the bond (total amount is 800,000) in the days of liquidity distress stage 1. Nothing is sold of the bond 2 position in stage 2. This is because the firm can sell off significant amounts of bond 2 at low first-tier market costs only in stage 1. In addition, bond 2 has a significant increase in execution costs in stage 2 and hence liquidating the position in stage 1 rather than later is a better option to escape higher execution costs. This trade-off can be made for execution of bond 2 because there are other liquidity facilities in the portfolio such as the cash positions and bond 1 that do not have a significant diminishing value as the liquidity distress becomes more severe, and hence, can be used in stage 2 to cover the gap with very low execution cost. It is therefore cheaper to hold onto the low execution cost items of the cash positions and the high-quality bond 1 and instead execute bond 2 to raise funds initially. The facility liquidity source has a relatively low execution cost at first-tier market depth of 250,000 in stage 1 and a total of 350,000 is used of the facility in stage 1. The facility still has relatively low execution costs in stage 2 but the usage limit is getting much more constrained. However, the usage limit is still enough to cover using the limit at 50,000 per day, raising the final needed 100,000 to cover the liquidity gap in stage 2. The equity position equity 1 has a first-tier market depth in stage 1 of 200,000 while the first-tier market depth in stage 2 is reduced to 100,000 together with increased execution costs. This makes it optimal to use the equity 1 position fully up to the first-tier market depth of the days in stage 1 (200,000 per day) to get a relatively low execution cost to cover the remaining gap in liquidity distress stage 1. Finally, the equity position equity 2 is not used to cover the gap in either of the stages. This is because there are liquidity facilities with lower execution amounts that can cover the gap in both stage 1 and stage 2.

Analyzing this optimal execution behavior, we note that highly liquid sources, such as cash and cash equivalents, which remain liquid with low execution cost and haircut even in further distress, are optimal to hold until further distress stages and then execute at a still low cost. This is because their values do not diminish as stress increases across stages. High-quality instruments with low and not significantly increasing execution costs and haircuts across stages, such as bond 1, are spread evenly in sales across liquidity stages as the market impact across liquidity stages is low for premium quality assets. Hence, the cost of waiting to deploy such an asset is feasible from a cost perspective and the asset's use to obtain funds can be spread out over liquidity distresses. The facility—which has low first-tier market depth costs but a significant constraint in the usage limit across the days in the stages—resembles bond 1 in that it is used across liquidity stages up to the first-tier market depth limit, which has low execution cost. In the case of the facility, however, the stage 2 significant usage constraint causes small amounts to be drawn in each day of stage 2 (i.e., 50,000). The fact that liquidity facilities have relatively low execution costs across distress stages, and are a preferred way to raise funds, means that the counterparty offering the facility will try to close or significantly limit committed lines of credit as soon as possible in a liquidity distress to prevent this drawing behavior from the stressed firm. Considering instead liquidity raising assets with an execution cost, and haircut that is significantly worsening across stages we note that those are sold in the beginning of distress. This is because their liquidity values are higher in the initial phases of the distress when execution costs and haircuts are not as severe. The assets bond 2 and equity 1 are examples of such assets. In our case, the position with the highest execution cost, equity 2, was not used at all since cheaper liquidity execution can be done by the other assets. In our model, setting this means that a firm planning for the 2 stage liquidity distress—but ending up realizing a longer distress—will find itself holding only the lowest quality assets in the unanticipated continuation of the liquidity distress.

In Table 6.15 enough funds could be raised from other assets than equity 2. However, it is interesting to observe the liquidity behavior when we increase the first stage gap to 2,300,000 units of currency as this will force at least part of equity 2 to be used to raise funds. Table 6.16 displays the result when an additional cash of 300,000 needs to be raised in distress stage 1. The total execution cost in this case is 20,575 units of currency with cost in distress stage 1 of 17,764 and distress stage 2 has the same execution cost as before, that is, 2,811 units of currency. In this case the bond 2 is used in an additional approximately 75,000 in day 1 of distress stage 1. This uses all available liquidity facility of bond 2. We also note that now the firm has to use the liquidity facility equity 2 to raise all the funds needed across stages—selling it in the first liquidity distress stage at the last 2 days of the stress. The asset is executed at or below the first-tier market depth at 150,000 to raise the additional needed funds in stage 1. Due to the significant increase in execution cost and the significant decrease in the first-tier market depth for equity 2 in stage 2 it is better for the firm to sell equity 2 in the first stage rather than using any other asset that has a lower time cost of holding onto and deploying in stage 2 to generate liquidity.

In summary, we can therefore conclude that if the firm thinks it has to use all its liquidity facilities to survive the liquidity distresses, then it will sell the lower quality assets first because their value will deteriorate over time as the liquidity distress worsens and their maximum value in raising funds is likely at the beginning of distress. On the contrary, high-quality assets with low haircuts and execution costs, even in later and more severe stages of a liquidity distress, do not diminish in value significantly and are held to raise funds in later, more severe

TABLE 6.16 Optimal Liquidity Plan for Model with Tiered Execution Cost—Increased Gap Amount in Stage 1

Liquidity	Available amount	Optimal execution amount, $k = 1$			Optimal execution amount, $k = 2$	
		$j_1 = 1$	$j_1 = 2$	$j_1 = 3$	$j_2 = 1$	$j_2 = 2$
Cash 1	500,000	0	0	0	500,000	0
Cash 2	1,000,000	0	0	0	0	1,000,000
Bond 1	700,000	0	0	297,189	102,811	300,000
Bond 2	800,000	200,000	300,000	300,000	0	0
Facility	500,000	0	250,000	150,000	50,000	50,000
Equity 1	600,000	200,000	200,000	200,000	0	0
Equity 2	300,000	0	70,576	150,000	0	0
		Total raised amount = 2,300,000			Total raised amount = 2,000,000	

stages. Therefore, not surprisingly, Acharya et al. (2013) find that banks anticipating an intensified liquidity risk tend to raise cash reserve despite its high opportunity cost.

We can summarize the optimal behavior of liquidity executions as follows:

- If the firm expects a severe and relatively long liquidity distress period, consuming all of the firm's liquidity capacity needed to be used to raise the funds, it is optimal to rank liquidity facilities based on their anticipated execution costs and haircuts across the expected stages of a liquidity crisis and execute the lower quality assets first, saving the liquid assets for later execution.
- If the firm expects a relatively minor and short liquidity distress period, such that the firm does not expect to use all of its liquidity to raise the needed funds during the liquidity distress stages, then the firm can refrain from executing the lower quality assets to keep execution costs to a minimum.

However, this last strategy runs the risk that if the firm misjudges the length and the severity of the liquidity distress, it may end up holding only the lower quality assets exactly when those assets have their smallest value in raising funds. Put simply, the firm should use a "cash first" liquidation strategy if it thinks the liquidity distress will not be that severe and sufficient cash is available. If the firm suspects the liquidity distress will be severe—and likely require use of lower quality assets—it should use a "cash last" liquidation strategy.

Liquidity Hedging with Repo Possibility The optimal liquidity execution models considered here can be extended to accommodate collateralized borrowing. Instead of selling an asset, a firm can pledge it as collateral to borrow money. This form of liquidity creation is important because a firm may want to or sometimes even have to retain the ownership of an asset while the asset is useful to obtain liquidity. Once a portion of the repo asset is pledged as collateral, the portion is deemed as "encumbered" and cannot be traded until the pledge expires. By definition the troubled firm prefers to roll over repo agreements in a distress stage. However, across distress stages repos can be canceled partially or in full, affecting the encumbered portion, and moreover market variables such as repo haircut and repo rate may change across distress stages. We refer to Chen, Skoglund, and Cai (2012) for a model using optimal liquidity hedging with repo possibility.

STRUCTURAL LIQUIDITY PLANNING

Although liquidity risk is a consequential risk, with proper measurement and understanding of the cause and possible severity of the risk, enough liquidity buffer can be prepared in advance to provide sufficient counterbalancing capacity in liquidity distress. The focus is on maintaining a high-quality liquidity portfolio that can efficiently hedge liquidity outflows under stress scenarios. Since holding standby counterbalancing capacity has an opportunity cost the firm would like to hold the minimum cost portfolio that suffices for hedging out the negative flows. While the simplest way to build a liquidity portfolio is to hold affluent cash at hand this is not optimal for a profit-seeking institution. In general, high liquidity assets, such as cash, are most costly to hold but are less costly in terms of execution cost when needed to create liquidity. While our liquidity execution models discussed above focused on the best execution strategy for a given endowment liquidity hedge portfolio, we now ask the question of how we should define such a liquidity hedging portfolio in advance of liquidity crisis, that is, structurally plan and choose an optimal liquidity hedging portfolio.

When we consider a structural planning approach to liquidity hedging, we may also include the possibility of acquiring more assets and liabilities with naturally complementing flows—hence reducing the inherent structural liquidity risk in the balance sheet. The approach of acquiring more assets that can generate future cash flows that can complement the potential net cash outflows has been studied in both theoretical and empirical literature, including Diamond and Dybvig (1983), Kashyap, Rajan, and Stein (2002), and Cai and Thakor (2008), especially in the context of deposit and loan commitment. As liquidity intermediation agents banks have competitive advantage in structuring such natural liquidity hedging. However, with the complexity of embedded optionality in the banking products such as deposits and facilities, it is hard to be fully balanced through the traditional funding sources. It is especially complex to find natural complementing flows that can work even under liquidity stress. Hence, in general, banks also need to hold liquidity hedging portfolios to mitigate unexpected liquidity gaps that cannot be mitigated through acquiring naturally complementing cash flows.

These two different methods of optimal liquidity hedging portfolio are in general complementary. Acquiring more assets that can generate future cash flows that can complement the potential net cash outflows is a structural ongoing balance sheet management. Contractual cash flow–based liquidity hedging can also be viewed as an optimal portfolio allocation with liquidity constraint. An alternative to minimizing the hedging cost is to maximize bank's profit with liquidity and other business constraints. The leverage of dynamic counterbalancing capacity through use of credit facilities, asset sales, and repo agreements in order to generate liquidity at the exact time when net contractual cash flows cannot balance by itself is conditional on the current balance sheet structure.

Mitigating Balance Sheet Vulnerability with Contractual Cash Flows

The liquidity hedging with contractual cash flows reduces the inherent risks in the forward liquidity exposure, $F(d, t)$, from the current portfolio. This approach is closely related to the classical portfolio immunization in the asset and liability management. See Elton and Gruber (1995) for a textbook account on bond portfolio immunization through replicating the bond portfolio's duration and convexity. For liquidity risk, immunization is achieved by matching cash flows directly through finding the minimum cost portfolio such that the liquidity hedging asset portfolio matches the negative cash flows of $F(d, t)$. Kocherlakota et al. (1988) discuss expected cash flow matching optimization algorithms in the context of bond portfolio immunization. More recently, Chen and Skoglund (2012) develop a linear programming model to find a minimal cost replicating portfolio that generates enough cash flow to constrain the mismatched cash flows over a given planning horizon to meet a set of risk measure–based criteria such as CVaR constraints. We discussed briefly this model of cash flow replication optimization in the context of portfolio optimization in the advanced market risk analysis chapter.

In this setting, our objective is to choose the cheapest (up-front cost) portfolio that satisfies a given risk constraint.[11] Specifically, the risk constraint is that

$$\rho[R(0, t, D)] \geq \lambda_t \quad t = 1, \dots, T \tag{6.24}$$

[11]Instead of or in addition to minimal up-front cost an optimal objective is to choose the maximum return portfolio (i.e., the minimal opportunity cost portfolio). However, we focus on the minimal cost objective here.

where ρ is the CVaR risk measure and D is the set of all scenarios. Note here that we do not assume any counterbalancing capacity available as $C = 0$ in equation (6.24). The hedging capacity is coming from the choice of cash flows, $\{cf(d,t)\}_{t=1}^{T}$, through the choice of optimal asset holdings. In this model it can hence be natural to set $\lambda_t < 0$ since we have not yet taken into account the counterbalancing capacity of the liquidity hedge portfolio.

The contractual cash flow matching approach assumes that the assets in the portfolio generate contractual cash flows that naturally complement the liquidity term structure. No active intervention is required at any future horizons. In other words, we are searching for a portfolio of assets with the lowest present value cost that have a predetermined hedging capacity such that the expected net cash outflow is within the tolerance of the bank while the CVaR is controlled, for each $t = 1, \ldots, T$ at certain levels, $\{\lambda_t\}_{t=1}^{T}$. This liquidity cash flow optimization model is developed in Chen and Skoglund (2012, 2014), who derive a linear program for cash flow optimization where each asset has a cash flow stream under a set of scenarios $d = 1, \ldots, D$ and a market value that depends on the scenarios. We refer to those papers for details about the model but will consider an example from Chen and Skoglund (2014) here.[12]

Example Optimal Contractual Cash Flow Matching Table 6.17 displays distribution characteristics for a simulated liquidity gap for the horizons $t = 1, \ldots, 5$ using $D = 100,000$ scenarios. The distribution used to generate the scenarios is a tilted (to the negative side) lognormal distribution with distribution parameters that scale by horizon to increase the expected and worst-case liquidity gap severity across horizon. This choice of skewed negative distribution for the liquidity gap is because liquidity risk is analyzed conditional on a market or firm-specific stress, and under a stress a liquidity outflow is generally more likely than an inflow. We also simulate normal cash flows for four cash flow instruments with mean $\mu = 100$ units of currency and corresponding standard deviations $\sigma_1 = 20$, $\sigma_2 = 25$, $\sigma_3 = 30$ and $\sigma_4 = 35$ for the $i = 1, \ldots, 4$ assets. The cash flows are valued using present value with a fixed discount interest rate, r, set equal to 2%. The present value in a scenario d for instrument i is used as the market value, V_i^d, in the optimization. Since the cash flows are normally distributed the market values for the assets, $\{V_i\}_{i=1}^{4}$, are normally distributed as well. The expected market

TABLE 6.17 Distribution Characteristics of the Realized Liquidity Gap for $k = 100,000$ Simulations and $t = 1, \ldots, 5$ Horizons for the Model with Liquidity Hedging with Contractual Cash Flows

Liquidity horizon	Liquidity gap distribution characteristics					
	5% percentile	95% percentile	Mean	Standard deviation	Max	Min
1	−13,202	9,136	−2,605	9,730	9,960	−450,484
2	−22,470	8,775	−394	13,576	9,935	−640,433
3	−30,153	8,506	−2,751	16,670	9,930	−923,005
4	−36,483	8,271	−4,781	19,416	9,922	−981,155
5	−41,841	8,072	−6,503	21,606	9,913	−1,368,506

---

[12]Of course, the model may not only be used to find the optimal liquidity hedging cash flows versus the firm's current situation for forward liquidity exposure. The model can also be used to optimize the firm's strategic liquidity balance sheet more generally by experimenting with the selection of cash flows in the forward liquidity exposure.

value of an asset i, $E[V_i]$, is approximately 492.5 units of currency and the standard deviation, σ_i, is approximately $\sigma_1 = 44$, $\sigma_2 = 55$, $\sigma_3 = 66$, and $\sigma_4 = 77$ for the four assets. In the optimization we set the CVaR constraint, $\{\lambda_t\}_{t=1}^5$, to zero for all $t = 1, \ldots, 5$. This choice means that for a given choice of confidence level, α, conditional on exceeding that quantile, the firm is still expected to survive, that is, generate nonnegative liquidity flows for all horizons, $t = 1, \ldots, 5$.

Table 6.18 displays the obtained optimal portfolio holdings for the four normal cash flow instruments using a CVaR confidence level of $\alpha = 5\%$. The table also displays the normal assets mean and standard deviation for the cash flows and the corresponding values for reference. The minimum cost optimal liquidity hedging portfolio holds relatively more of the stable cash flows (the cash flows with a lower standard deviation). Such stable cash flows provide a base insurance and also come at a stable cost across scenarios. Highly volatile cash flows may be an insurance in case of severe distress but may also come at a significantly higher price when additional insurance is not needed. For this example, the application of the four cash flows succeeds in meeting the CVaR constraints. That is, the problem is feasible. However, as emphasized previously the existence of naturally complementing cash flows in practice for stressed liquidity outflows may be questionable. Hence, for practical situations tight zero constraints on CVaR may not be feasible. In those cases, the choice of constraints needs to be determined appropriately such that the problem is feasible with the cash flows at hand.

Table 6.19 displays the distribution characteristics of the realized liquidity flow, R_t^d, for the $t = 1, \ldots, 5$ horizons under the optimal choice of asset holdings in Table 6.18. While the realized liquidity outflow may be negative for some scenarios (e.g., the minimums are negative in Table 6.19 for all the horizons), the CVaR optimization constraints ensure that the tail average, beyond the confidence level α, is nonnegative for the optimal asset holdings.

TABLE 6.18 Optimal Liquidity Holdings and Distribution Characteristics for Cash Flows and Present Value for the 4 Liquidity Instruments in the Model with Liquidity Hedging with Contractual Cash Flows

Cash flow instrument	Optimal holding	Distribution—Cash flows		Distribution—Value	
		Mean (μ)	Std deviation (σ)	Mean (μ)	Std deviation (σ)
1	1,390	100	20	492.5	44
2	713	100	25	492.5	55
3	599	100	30	492.5	66
4	420	100	35	492.5	77

TABLE 6.19 Distribution Characteristics of the Realized Liquidity Flow under the Optimal Asset Holdings for $k = 100,000$ Simulations and $t = 1, \ldots, 5$ Horizons for the Model with Liquidity Hedging with Contractual Cash Flows

Liquidity flow	Distribution Characteristics					
	5% percentile	95% percentile	Mean	Standard deviation	Max	Min
R_1	232,300	399,546	322,789	54,849	500,939	−356,750
R_2	199,423	394,978	309,901	67,321	480,043	−657,099
R_3	178,664	390,866	301,622	80,185	500,748	−2,229,328
R_4	156,306	387,962	293,385	85,084	492,724	−1,504,905
R_5	140,871	385,103	285,933	95,549	492,666	−1,600,782

The next optimal liquidity hedging model assumes active management during the horizon, $t = 1, \ldots, T$, to mitigate the net cash outflows. The approach is more complex but incorporates the decision process the bank will follow, in a liquidity distress, for converting the dedicated liquidity hedging portfolio into counterbalancing capacity.

Choosing the Optimal Liquidity Hedging Portfolio

To define the dynamic counterbalancing-based model of optimal liquidity hedging we first review the two major types of dynamic liquidity facilities used to generate counterbalancing capacity as well as their costs, balances, and liquidity contribution, that is contingent credit facilities and assets.

1. Contingent credit facilities, including borrowing rights from the central bank

   A credit facility may explicitly or implicitly require an up-front fee. We assume this fee is relative to the facility limit L, that is, βL. The choice of facility limit L is subject to a cap l that is set by the facility creditor. Here, l is the maximum limit the counterparty offer and L is the limit applied for by the firm. This means that $L \leq l$ as the firm may choose not to use all the available facility as there is a fee associated with the limit. Most facilities are revolving at the preset limit L and the facility balance is between 0 and L. The drawn portion of a credit facility is subject to an interest rate charge, r, that is also included in the outstanding balance of the facility at the time. At any time t, a cash flow b_t can result from the credit facility. It can be either a drawn amount (positive contribution) or a payback amount (negative contribution). The cash contribution at time t is b_t, while the balance of the facility is $B_{i,t} + B_{i,t-1}r_{t-1}$, which is between 0 and L where $B_t = \sum_{s=1}^{t} b_s$. A negative balance is not possible at any time, that is $B_t \geq 0$.

2. Assets, including cash

   A firm can acquire x shares of a tradable, unencumbered security at time t for liquidity hedging purpose. The price of acquisition is xS_t with S_t the asset price, which includes the trading cost, and x the number of shares. In this model, we disallow short sale of any security, that is, $x \geq 0$. A limit, X_j, can also be imposed on the position on a security j such that $x_j \leq X_j$. Cash can be viewed as a special security with constant value through the entire planning period. Usually, only high-quality securities are considered to bear stable liquidity supplying capacity in liquidity stress. A security can meet the liquidity need in two ways.

   (a) First, it can be sold at the prevailing market price, assuming the volume of the sales is within market depth, v, to avoid excessive loss.

   Clearly, cost of acquiring the counterbalancing capacity is not the only measure of cost. When the liquidity supplying assets are needed to convert to cash to hedge negative outflows the firm pays liquidity execution costs. Such liquidity execution costs can be very high in the midst of a financial turbulence and hence the actual cash value of liquidity assets as well as the best execution strategy must be taken into account when selecting assets. At planning time, the objective is to construct a strategy such that a fire-sale can be avoided in any future horizon. This can be done by setting ex ante projected sales to be bounded under the projected market depth of the asset in a scenario.

   (b) The second way of obtaining cash from an asset is to use it for a collateralized borrowing, typically through a repurchase agreement (repo) contract.

   At any time t, δx_t shares of a security can be traded. When liquidity is needed, a portion of an asset can be sold. Similarly when the underlying portfolio has a cash surplus, a portion of the asset can be bought back. The total cash flow from the trading is $\delta x_t S_t$, which includes trading cost. To avoid short selling of an asset, we introduce two legs of trading: y_- is sale (positive cash contribution) and y_+ is purchase (negative cash contribution). The cash flow from trading can be expressed as $(y_{-,t} - y_{+,t})S_t$. Both $y_{-,t}$ and $y_{+,t}$ must be nonnegative (i.e., $y_{-,s} \geq 0$ and $y_{+,s} \geq 0$). We also constrain the sales according to the market depth such that $y_{-,t} \leq v_t$, where v_t is the market depth proxy at time t. The separation of the two trading legs also makes the trading cost incorporation an easy extension to the model. If a security is repo'ed, we denote the repo'ed share of a security as q. The shares to be used as collateral in repo contracts can be controlled by setting a limit Q. For example, Q is set to zero for a cash asset as it is not a repo instrument, The actual contribution to the cash flow from repo at time t is $q_t S_t h_t$ where h_t is a haircut to the collateral. We assume that all securities can be accepted for repo at any time. However, there may be a significant haircut. We also assume an existing repo can be rolled over. Hence, $q_t \geq 0$.

Except for an initial endowment to acquire certain assets, the entire hedging strategy is self-financing without further cash flow injection. Any liquidity providing asset can be sold, repo'ed, and replenished at any time; however, no short sale of the asset can be allowed. Therefore, at any time t, the total traded and repo'ed shares of the asset by the time cannot be more than the initial endowment of the asset, that is,

$$x - \sum_{s=1}^{t}(y_{-,s} - y_{+,s} + q_s) \geq 0.$$

A security can also generate coupon or dividend income based on the number of shares held at that time. We assume the encumbered portion also contributes to this income as the firm still owns the portion. Assuming coupon or dividend rate is e this cash income is thus the current holding of the asset multiplied by the income rate, e. That is, at time t,

$$\left[\sum_{s=1}^{t}(y_{+,s} - y_{-,s}) + x\right] e_s.$$

The optimal dynamic counterbalancing-based hedging portfolio is a minimal cost liquidity supply portfolio that has an active counterbalancing capacity to meet liquidity need. Because of the dynamic counterbalancing activity in this model the point-in-time liquidity cash flow gap is used as direct input. When there is a positive cash flow gap, the optimized rebalancing activity should always use it to refresh the liquidity inventory by either paying back a borrowing or buying additional assets, depending on what is optimal for that specific scenario, d, and path, $t = 1,\ldots,T$. In this model the firm minimizes the cost of obtaining the liquid funds subject to balance and cash flow conditions, holding constraints (such as short-selling), buy and sell constraints (for example, market depths), repo limits, and CVaR constraints on the liquidity reserve process. The model finds an optimal initial endowment for a liquidity hedging portfolio that can cover liquidity risk on target horizons. In addition, it details the counterbalancing trading strategy on each simulated path by the optimal selection of the cash flow from a credit facility, b, asset buys, y_+, asset sales, y_-, and repo portion q at each scenario $d = 1,\ldots,D$ and horizon $t = 1,\ldots,T$. The model provides the liquidity hedging decision maker with the complete hedging strategy for realized scenarios $d = 1, \ldots, D$ across horizons, $t = 1, \ldots, T$.

Example Optimal Dynamic Counterbalancing Capacity In this model there is an optimal initial endowment portfolio that can be traded or repo'ed through the liquidity horizons. We consider an example from Chen and Skoglund (2014) using three types of assets. First, for credit facilities that have an offered limit of l and an asked limit of L where $L \leq l$, the firm may ask for a smaller limit than the cap offered in order to avoid paying usage fee at rate β, which is paid for the requested limit, L. Second, for bonds that can be traded and repo'ed with haircut, h_t, for $t = 1, \ldots, T$, the bonds can also pay coupon, e_t, for $t = 1, \ldots, T$. Finally, we have cash. As in the first model we simulate liquidity gaps. In this case the simulation of the liquidity gap uses a tilted negative lognormal distribution as for the first model but we have now additional Poisson jumps with a Gamma distribution severity that adds significantly to the standard deviation and the severity of the negative tail of the liquidity gap. Table 6.20 displays the simulated liquidity gap distribution characteristics using 100,000 scenarios for horizons, $t = 1, \ldots, 5$. As in the previous model example the liquidity gap severity increases across horizons.

In the first analysis of this model we consider a portfolio of two credit facilities, a bond and cash. The first credit facility has limit capped at 10,000 and a usage fee of 0.1%. The second credit facility has limit capped at 1,000 and a usage fee of 0.01%. The interest rate cost for using either of the credit facilities is 2%. The bond price is assumed to follow a geometric Brownian motion process with mean 1% and a standard deviation of 0.1%. The current bond price is 100 units of currency. This choice of model for the bond price implies that the bond price has a stable, slightly increasing price over horizons as is generally expected of high-quality bonds in distress. That is, the flight-to-quality behavior under market uncertainty tends to increase price of high-quality bonds. The bond also pays a coupon, e_t, which is simulated as a uniform distribution times the bond price and a scale factor of 10%. The average annual coupon is hence close to 5%. However, during the liquidity crisis time $t = 1, \ldots, T$ the coupon is small and there is no significant impact on the results as the time is generally short. However, relative cash flow contributions from bonds can be important in normal times as there is in general a trade-off between the quality (value) of the bond in distress and its coupon level in normal times. The haircut for the bond is simulated as uniform ranging between a haircut rate of 70% and 100%. We also have a cash position in the portfolio. As in the first model we set the CVaR constraint, $\{\sigma_t\}_{t=1}^5$, to zero for all $t = 1, \ldots, 5$.

TABLE 6.20 Distribution Characteristics of the Realized Liquidity Gap for $k = 100,000$ Simulations and $t = 1, \ldots, 5$ Horizons for the Model with Optimal Liquidity Hedging with Counterbalancing Capacity

Liquidity horizon	Liquidity gap distribution characteristics					
	5% percentile	95% percentile	Mean	Standard deviation	Max	Min
1	−565,725	−51,630	−247,308	166,299	9,838	−2,275,780
2	−568,626	−54,082	−250,417	166,461	9,792	−2,004,916
3	−572,832	−55,882	−252,866	166,688	9,800	−1,980,572
4	−572,619	−57,340	−254,735	166,583	9,831	−2,287,871
5	−576,098	−58,556	−256,426	167,106	9,749	−2,357,170

TABLE 6.21 Optimal Initial Endowment for the Case of a Stable or Increasing Bond Price and the Case of a Declining Bond Price for the Model with Optimal Liquidity Hedging with Counterbalancing Capacity

	Optimal endowment	
Asset	Case: Stable/Increasing bond price	Case: Declining bond price
Credit Facility 1	10,000	10,000
Credit Facility 2	1,000	1,000
Bond	17,751	0
Cash	0	1,882,965

Table 6.21 displays the optimal initial endowment obtained from the optimization model for this portfolio with stable bond price. The optimization results are found in Table 6.21 under the case: Stable/increasing bond price. The initial endowment chooses first to secure the credit facilities up to the available limit. That is, the firm applies for the maximum credit limits. This is because the up-front usage fees for the credit facilities are relatively small compared to asset or cash acquisition. Note here that in the initial endowment for the credit facilities the firm simply applies for the credit facility at limit $L \le l$. There is no usage of the limit for the initial endowment, just a securing of the facilities. Second, the firm buys 17,751 positions in the bond. There is no initial cash endowment in the optimal counterbalancing capacity for this portfolio. This is because cash is more costly to acquire than the bond, which has stable, slightly increasing price over the horizons.

It is also interesting to observe the self-financing optimal trade behavior for two sample simulated paths in Table 6.22. In sample optimal trading path 1, the bond position is sold across horizons (negative sign is a sell) to raise additional cash. In the last horizon, the credit facilities are also used to raise cash (positive sign is a use of the facility). In sample optimal trading path 2 the facilities are used to maximum in the first horizon but then paid back in horizon 2 and 3 (paid back facility is negative sign). The facilities are drawn again in horizon 4 to generate the cash needed to cover the gap and finally a portion is paid back in the last horizon. This activity of using and paying back the facilities across horizons occurs because should cash raised through a facility not be needed in a horizon it is cost optimal to pay back, avoiding the interest rate on excessive facility usage. The first horizon also buys more bonds and then sells the bond over horizons 2, 3, and 4 to generate cash. Note that these strategies are self-financing and the obtained surplus liquidity gap at a horizon can also be used to buy additional instruments such as the bond. Moreover, for each sample path the strategy implemented is the minimum cost strategy consistent with the optimization model.

TABLE 6.22 Sample Optimal Trading Paths for the Case of Stable or Increasing Bond Price for the Model with Optimal Liquidity Hedging with Counterbalancing Capacity

	Sample trading path 1					Sample trading path 2				
Asset	$t=1$	$t=2$	$t=3$	$t=4$	$t=5$	$t=1$	$t=2$	$t=3$	$t=4$	$t=5$
Credit Facility 1	0	0	0	0	9,066	10,000	−200	−9,800	10,000	−200
Credit Facility 2	0	0	0	0	1,000	1000	−20	−980	1000	−20
Bond	−209	−409	−162	−733	−771	31	−465	−647	−1204	0
Cash	0	0	0	0	0	0	0	0	0	0

If the firm cannot include facilities in the liquidity hedging portfolio for reasons such as disbelief of availability in distress or forbidden by certain corporate policy, then both facility limits can be set to 0; the optimization will then allocate all the initial endowment to the bond. This case of no facilities available is consistent with Basel III as Basel does not allow firms to account for credit facilities when defining the size of the counterbalancing capacity portfolio. However, a firm may still want to include credit facilities in their internal model for analyzing optimal liquidity hedging portfolio and optimal trading strategy.

In the above liquidity optimization, the bond was preferred to cash because it has generally a stable price or increasing price in distress. This is generally true for high-quality bonds such as high-quality government bonds that qualify for the Basel-eligible counterbalancing capacity portfolio. However, if we now let the bond have a negative drift such as mean of −2%, is the bond still preferred to cash? Table 6.21 displays the optimal initial endowment when the bond price has a trend downwards across liquidity horizons as would generally be expected of low-quality bonds where the price is lowest in the severest distress. This corresponds to the case declining bond price in Table 6.21. Table 6.21 shows that in this case, even if the bond pays out coupons, the preferred allocation between bonds and cash is now instead only cash and nothing of the bond at the beginning. This shows that there is consistency between firm's optimal liquidity portfolio and the Basel III requirements of eligible initial endowments in the firm's counterbalancing capacity portfolio. That is, from an optimal liquidity hedging perspective, a firm would prefer holding cash over low-quality bonds with an expected price decay in liquidity distress. In essence, only stable high-quality bonds are preferred to cash in the firm's optimal liquidity hedging portfolio produced by the model. Clearly, in this case cash is safest and may not be the most costly anymore if the bond price is expected to decline in liquidity distress. As in the optimal initial endowment in Table 6.21 for the case of stable/increasing bond price removing the reliance on credit facilities all the initial endowment allocation is to cash.

COMPONENTS OF THE LIQUIDITY HEDGING PROGRAM

A firm's approach to liquidity hedging involves first and foremost a structural balance sheet optimization of avoiding taking on too much balances that can create a significant structural funding gap and hence a significant forward liquidity exposure that can only be covered with excessive uncertain rollover of funding. Secondly, it involves a structural planning of holding a sufficient liquidity hedge portfolio under a range of scenarios, $d = 1, \ldots, D$. Given a choice of liquidity hedging portfolio the portfolio must be tested under various assumptions on market execution costs and execution limits under plausible liquidity stress scenarios.[13] The above activities are also key components of a bank's broader liquidity contingency funding plan that helps banks strategize their response to liquidity crises. While creating a contingency funding plan banks take into consideration how a funding crisis evolves in different stages. This is due to the fact that while a liquidity crisis unfolds, the initial stage presents liquidity managers with a unique opportunity to take remedial action that may not be available in the later stages of the crises. Therefore, a contingency funding plan should incorporate preparedness

---

[13]Note that a bank's liquidity hedging and planning program may be defined per bank entity such that an entity is viewed as a self-sufficient funding unit from a liquidity perspective and hence needs to carry its own sufficient liquidity hedging portfolio.

of a bank to deal quickly at the first signs (early warning indicator) of an increased potential funding need. Contingency funding plans are developed to fulfill two important objectives:

1. To increase going forward cash generation
2. To maintain the market goodwill of the bank

   In fulfillment of the second objective, some banks might even take liquidity reducing actions in the initial stage in order to signal market confidence in their viability. A good practice is to form a plan that manifests actions during the early warning indication stage itself (no current funding problem yet increased level of liquidity risk) and includes low-cost steps to improve liquidity, for example, increasing standby liquidity reserves. An example is to attempt to alter the mix and maturity of assets and liabilities to decrease net cash outflow from sight to the liquidity horizon. Another example is to intensify building liquidity reserves constituted by certain predefined securities that are highly liquid in all kinds of stress situations.

   Other than the contingency funding plan spanning different stages of a potential liquidity crisis (i.e., actions involved during the early warning stage to mild crisis stage to a severe crisis unfolding), it also needs to consider administrative policies and procedures during the span of a liquidity crisis—for example, what is the responsibility of the senior management during a funding crisis, what are the contact details of members of the crisis team, which team would be responsible for identifying assets that should be sold, which team would be mobilized to talk to significant investors in the bank, and so on. See Matz (2011, ch. 10) on best practices for liquidity crisis contingency planning for banks.

CASH LIQUIDITY RISK AND LIQUIDITY RISK MEASURES

While in general liquidity risk and in particular liquidity solvency are path-dependent we also introduced in equation (6.5) a relatively simple measure of liquidity risk solvency expressed in terms of the amount of cash needed to survive a given liquidity scenario, d. We now expand on this simple cash hedging approach to liquidity solvency to derive a relatively simple risk measure of liquidity risk.

Cash Liquidity at Risk

Note that the liquidity solvency probability in equation (6.8) is, with the assumption of cash liquidity hedging capacity, simply measured as a standard VaR measure. This represents a significant simplification compared to the general case in equation (6.4) and allows liquidity risk to be measured using classical market and credit risk measures. In particular, the monotonic definition of liquidity solvency in equation (6.8) allows us to define a meaningful single risk measure on a time horizon, T. A natural risk measure in this context of liquidity solvency is the VaR measure on the distribution of $R(M, T, d)$ in equation (6.7) for all $d = 1, \ldots, D$. This is because such a risk measure allows the explicit expression of a firm's liquidity risk appetite by choosing a liquidity solvency probability, α, at risk horizon T. We will denote this risk measure cash liquidity at risk (CLaR), where

$$\text{CLaR}(\alpha, T) = -\text{VaR}[R(0, T, D)].$$

Here, $\text{CLaR}(\alpha, T)$ defines the amount of cash liquidity needed for the firm to be liquidity solvent at risk horizon T with probability α. It is worth noting here again that under the assumption of a cash portfolio, CLaR is not a complex path-dependent measure of liquidity solvency. It is a single, monotonic risk measure for a given horizon, T. It is also consistent with the regulatory LCR liquidity risk measure as we will discuss below. Therefore, it provides a valid base for a firm's liquidity risk cost and benefit allocation. Of course, other risk measures such as CVaR can also be used on the distribution of $R(0, T, D)$.

Portfolio Cash Liquidity Exposure

The calculation of the portfolio minimum cash liquidity need, $P(d, T)$, to remain solvent for scenario d and time horizon T was defined in equation (6.9) as

$$M^* = P(d, T) = -\sum_{t=1}^{T} \min\left[\widetilde{F}(d, t), 0\right].$$

For a portfolio of $i = 1, \ldots, N$ liquidity instruments we obtain $P(d, T)$ from the aggregation of the N liquidity instruments cash flows. That is,

$$\widetilde{F}(d, t) = \sum_{i=1}^{N} cf_i(d, t) + \max\left[\widetilde{F}(d, t-1), 0\right]$$

for $t > 2$, and $\widetilde{F}(d, 1) = \sum_{i=1}^{N} cf_i(d, 1)$. Clearly, with this portfolio aggregation, a positive cash flow from liquidity i can cover a liquidity need from liquidity j. Therefore, the realized portfolio cash liquidity need, $P(d, T)$, is less than or equal to summing the corresponding scenario realizations, d, for the liquidities $i = 1, \ldots, N$. That is, $P(d, T) \leq \sum_{i=1}^{N} P_i(d, T)$ where

$$M^* = P(d, T) = -\sum_{t=1}^{T} \min\left[\widetilde{F}(d, t), 0\right] \leq -\sum_{i=1}^{N}\sum_{t=1}^{T} \min\left[\widetilde{F}_i(d, t), 0\right] = \sum_{i=1}^{N} P_i(d, T) = M_i^*.$$

$$(6.25)$$

If we now let the realized scenario d be defined as the CLaR(α, T), that is, let discrete scenarios $d = 1, \ldots, D$ comprise the sample space for discrete realizations $\{P(d, T)\}_{d=1}^{D}$, then for $\alpha \times D$ an integer we can uniquely identify, from the distribution of $\{P(d, T)\}_{d=1}^{D}$, the CLaR(α, T) as a particular scenario $\widetilde{d}$. This is the realized CLaR(α, T) scenario. Of course, in practice a firm may choose any plausible scenario d for which it might like to decompose liquidity risk. We focus here on the CLaR(α, T) realized scenario simply for analogy with VaR Euler allocations for market and credit risk. Having identified that scenario as scenario $\widetilde{d}$ we can write

$$\mathrm{CLaR}(\alpha, T) = P(\widetilde{d}, T) \leq \sum_{i=1}^{N} P_i(\widetilde{d}, T).$$

This inequality will be useful for devising a method of allocating CLaR(α, T), as we will see later.

Example Calculation of Portfolio Cash Liquidity Need Table 6.23 illustrates the calculation of the portfolio cash liquidity need, M^*, as well as the corresponding cash liquidity need for subportfolios or liquidity instruments, M_i^*. Specifically, Table 6.23 illustrates standalone liquidity instruments' calculation of cash liquidity exposure for the specific scenario realization, d, for $i = 1, 2, 3$ liquidity instruments and $t = 1, \ldots, 7$. It displays the liquidity instrument $i = 1, 2, 3$ standalone liquidity gaps, $cf_i(d, t)$ for $t = 1, \ldots, 7$, as well as

TABLE 6.23 Calculation of Standalone and Portfolio Minimum Liquid Cash Need for the 3
Liquidity Instruments

	Liquidity 1		Liquidity 2		Liquidity 3		Portfolio	
Time	$cf_1(d,t)$	$\widetilde{F}_1(d,t)$	$cf_2(d,t)$	$\widetilde{F}_2(d,t)$	$cf_3(d,t)$	$\widetilde{F}_3(d,t)$	$cf(d,t)$	$\widetilde{F}(d,t)$
$t=1$	−5	−5	−3	−3	2	2	−6	−6
$t=2$	5	5	2	2	−2	0	5	5
$t=3$	3	8	1	3	−1	−1	3	8
$t=4$	−7	1	−3	0	3	3	−7	1
$t=5$	−4	−3	2	2	−2	1	−4	−3
$t=6$	8	8	−4	−2	−1	0	3	3
$t=7$	−3	5	2	2	2	2	1	4
	$M_1^*=8$		$M_2^*=5$		$M_3^*=1$		$M^*=9$	

the intermediate calculations of $\widetilde{F}_i(d,t)$ for $t=1,\dots,7$ to obtain the final liquidity instrument i minimum cash liquidity need, A_i^*. Table 6.23 also contains the corresponding calculations for the portfolio consisting of the $i=1,2,3$ liquidity instruments. In Figure 6.4 we also illustrate the cash liquidity need at the different times for the three liquidities and the portfolio as well as the summed liquidity need from the three liquidities.

From Table 6.23 we observe that liquidity 1 has a standalone liquidity cash exposure of 8. That is, $M_1^*=8$. This standalone liquid cash exposure is obtained by first converting the liquidity gap into an effective cash liquidity exposure using equation (6.6). Finally, we

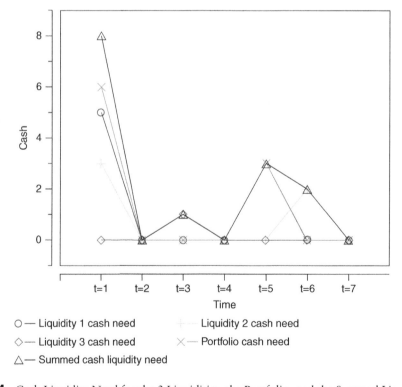

FIGURE 6.4 Cash Liquidity Need for the 3 Liquidities, the Portfolio, and the Summed Liquidity Need

calculate the summed liquidity cash need. Liquidity instruments 2 and 3 have corresponding cash liquidity needs of 5 and 1, respectively. That is, $M_2^* = 5$ and $M_3^* = 1$ when cash liquidity need is measured standalone for the realized scenario d. The reader may notice that we have used the same sample numbers in Table 6.23 as in Table 6.2. Albeit here the individual liquidity gaps are assumed to come from the same scenario applied to different liquidity instruments rather than the same liquidity instrument liquidity gap under different scenarios. In Table 6.23 the corresponding cash liquidity measure for the portfolio of liquidity instruments $i = 1, 2, 3$ is $M^* = 9$. The portfolio minimum cash liquidity need is hence nine units of cash. Consistent with equation 6.25, this is less than the sum of standalone liquidity cash needs from the liquidity instruments $i = 1, 2, 3$ since $\sum_{i=1}^{N} M_i^* = 14$. Note that as above if $d = \tilde{d}$ is the realized portfolio cash liquidity exposure scenario that corresponds to CLaR(α, T), we can set $P(\tilde{d}, T) = \text{CLaR}(\alpha, T)$.

Allocating Cash Liquidity Risk

Having a single, monotonic measure of liquidity risk, such as CLaR, the next natural step seems to be to allocate the opportunity cost of holding the standby cash liquidity needed to the contributing risk components, that is, to allocate the contributions to CLaR. As we have discussed in previous chapters it is practice in market and credit risk to use risk and capital allocations based on the Euler allocations. Such allocations are in general trivial to compute for market and credit risk. However, the relative complexity of the CLaR measure makes such allocations of the aggregate contingency liquidity need more difficult in the context of liquidity risk. While the allocation process is more complex we can still attempt a decomposition for liquidity risk. Specifically, from equation (6.25) we can find that the total, in the portfolio context, positive cash contribution, $\varphi \geq 0$, for the cash liquidity need in scenario d is

$$\varphi = \sum_{i=1}^{N} M_i^* - M^*$$

where if $d = \tilde{d}$ and $D \times \alpha$ is an integer, this is the CLaR(α, T) realized scenario from the distribution of $\{P(d, T)\}_{d=1}^{D}$ and we can write

$$\varphi = \sum_{i=1}^{N} M_i^* - \text{CLaR}(\alpha, T).$$

This total positive contribution can be distributed across liquidity instruments $i = 1, \ldots, N$ in many ways and we consider one example of such a distribution here.

First note that for a given liquidity instrument i we can observe (i) the standalone liquidity need as defined by M_i^*; (ii) when liquidity instrument i is covering the liquidity need from another liquidity instrument j or a subset of liquidity instruments.

Of course, liquidity instrument i may not be the only liquidity instrument covering a liquidity need for other liquidity instruments, and in that case we have to decide on a model for how to distribute the positive contributions to the set of liquidity instruments.

Example Allocation of Cash Liquidity Need In Table 6.23 we found that the realized portfolio (CLaR) scenario requires a minimum amount of 9 units of currency in cash for survival. In contrast, from Table 6.23, summing the liquidity need, liquidity instrument by liquidity instrument, we find that the required cash is 14 units of currency. That is,

$\sum_{i=1}^{N} M_i^* = 14$. Hence, the portfolio positive contribution is $\varphi = 5$. We can now allocate this positive contribution across $t = 1, \ldots, T$ as follows. First, for $t = 1$ liquidity 3 reduces the portfolio liquidity need from 8 to 6. This is because, for $t = 1$,

$$6 = \left| \min \left[\tilde{F}(d,t), 0 \right] \right| < \left| \sum_{i=1}^{3} \min \left[\tilde{F}_i(d,t), 0 \right] \right| = 8$$

which attributes an initial 2 units of positive contribution to liquidity instrument 3. Next, for $t = 3$,

$$0 = \left| \min \left[\tilde{F}(d,t), 0 \right] \right| < \left| \sum_{i=1}^{3} \min \left[\tilde{F}_i(d,t), 0 \right] \right| = 1$$

and a positive contribution of 1 unit of currency is needed to neutralize the negative outflow from liquidity 3. Both liquidity instruments 1 and 2 have sufficient liquidity to cover this outflow. In this case, a model is needed for a fair allocation of the positive contribution of 1 unit of currency to the liquidities. One simple alternative is to make an even split allocating a positive 0.5 units of cash to liquidity instruments 1 and 2. A more complex allocation model may be called for in cases where the contributing liquidity instruments can only cover partially or a liquidity instrument can cover in full but another can only cover partially. In our particular case we could have weighted the relative positive inflows of liquidity instruments 1 and 2, which are 8 and 3 units of cash, respectively. With such a distribution of the positive contribution liquidity instrument 1 would be allocated $\frac{8}{11}$ units of currency and liquidity instrument 2 $\frac{3}{11}$ units of currency. The final positive portfolio contribution occurs at $t = 6$,

$$0 = \left| \min \left[\tilde{F}(d,t), 0 \right] \right| < \left| \sum_{i=1}^{3} \min \left[\tilde{F}_i(d,t), 0 \right] \right| = 2$$

and is allocated only to liquidity instrument 1 as only this liquidity instrument covers the negative outflow. This means that we have now allocated the total positive contribution, $\varphi = 5$, such that we can summarize the liquidity instruments' contribution, denoted $\text{CLaR}^D(\alpha, T)$, to the needed $\text{CLaR}(\alpha, T)$ cash liquidity. Specifically, we obtain $\text{CLaR}_i^D(\alpha, T)$ for liquidity instrument i as $\text{CLaR}_i^D(\alpha, T) = M_i^* - \varphi_i$. This allocation is done in Table 6.24 based on the liquidity instruments and the portfolio in Table 6.23. In Table 6.24 we have used the simple alternative of an even split when allocating the positive contributions to liquidity instruments 1 and 2 in

TABLE 6.24 Portfolio Allocated
Cash Liquidity Contributions

Liquidity	Measure		
	M_i^*	φ_i	CLaR_i^D
1	8	2.5	5.5
2	5	0.5	4.5
3	1	2	−1
Portfolio	.	5	9

$t = 3$. We note that $\sum_{i=1}^{3} \mathrm{CLaR}_i^D(\alpha, T)$ by definition sums to $\mathrm{CLaR}(\alpha, T)$. Interestingly, liquidity 3 is contributing negatively to the minimum cash liquidity need as defined by $\mathrm{CLaR}(\alpha, T)$. It is hence in the context of the portfolio, reducing the need for contingency cash by 1 unit of currency. It is, in the context of the portfolio, an aggregate, over $t = 1, \ldots, T$, cash liquidity supplier rather than a cash liquidity consumer.

In our allocation of the cash liquidity need we have not made a distinction between allocating cash liquidity held for contingency liquidity risk versus cash held for expected liquidity mismatch. In an aggregate portfolio context, the expected cash liquidity need is derived from the firm's structural liquidity mismatch, that is, the liquidity needed to cover mismatches under the expected environment. The risk management portion of the liquidity need, and in our CLaR context, is the unexpected contingency liquidity need that may arise in a stress scenario. It is important to recognize that a firm that does not separate the unexpected contingency liquidity need from the expected liquidity need when allocating liquidity risk will inevitably find themselves allocating positive liquidity contributions to assets such as loans with steady positive flows. However, this allocated positive flow does not contribute to reducing the need for cash contingency liquidity. Indeed, it is only if the loan tends to generate more positive flows than expected (e.g., through increased prepayments) under liquidity distress that it should be allocated a positive contribution to the unexpected cash liquidity need.

REGULATION FOR LIQUIDITY RISK

The Basel III strengthened liquidity regulation is the regulators' response to the lessons learned in the 2007 financial crisis. Two key reporting measures are put forward as the standard for supervisors of liquidity risk. This is the liquidity coverage ratio (LCR) and the net stable funding ratio (NSFR). In the application of these measures the bank must consider behavioral scenarios. We now focus briefly on the regulatory required reporting LCR and NSFR measures as well as monitoring measures put forward by the regulators.

Liquidity Coverage Ratio

The regulatory LCR measures the ratio of high-quality unencumbered assets that are available to hedge the cash outflow from assets and liabilities. In the regulatory context the liquidity hedge portfolio is referred to as the stock of high-quality liquid assets (HQLA). The stress is measured under a short-term horizon of up to 30 days and the stress scenario(s) examined should contain both institution-specific shocks (e.g., downgrade) as well as systemic liquidity crisis. This includes a loss of deposits, a loss of unsecured funding, as well as increases in margin calls for derivatives and calls on the bank's committed credit lines. Under the horizon of 30 days the LCR of the bank should always exceed 100%. That is, the counterbalancing capacity of the unencumbered assets should neutralize any negative outflows from the encumbered assets and liabilities under the stress scenario. The stock of counterbalancing capacity assets should be assets that retain liquidity even under severe stress conditions.

If a bank fails the test of achieving an LCR of 100% for the time horizon of 30 days under the stress scenarios, then the bank must adjust their pool of unencumbered assets accordingly. The focus is hence on maintaining a high-quality liquidity portfolio that can hedge liquidity outflows under stress scenarios. This conditioning of liquidity scenarios on a stress is, as we remarked above when considering our representative scenario, d, because liquidity is in general a consequential risk. Under these stresses the bank's liquidity portfolio needs to hedge the stressed funding outflow over the time horizon of 30 days under a going-concern assumption. This test becomes the regulatory test of whether a bank has a sufficient short-term liquidity buffer.

The Basel III eligible buffer of liquidity hedging assets include so-called level 1, level 2A, and 2B assets. Depending on the asset classification different regulatory haircuts are applied.[14] The formal regulatory test computes the liquidity coverage ratio, denoted LCR, as

$$\text{LCR} = \frac{\text{Cash value of liquidity buffer}}{\text{Net cash outflows}} > 100\% \tag{6.26}$$

where the denominator has the net cash flows under the regulatory prescribed scenario. The net cash outflows are constructed as the total expected cash outflows minus total expected inflows. The net cash outflow in equation (6.26) is specifically decomposed as

$$\text{Net cash outflows} = \text{Cash outflows} - \text{Cash inflows} \times 0.75$$

so that cash inflows are capped at 75% of inflows. The cash inflows may have to be adjusted by prescribed regulatory parameters. For example, we have that:

- Inflows from performing loans, deposits with other banks, and maturing reverse repos on noneligible buffer assets have a regulatory allowed inflow of 100%.
- However, potential inflows from operational accounts with other banks and backup lines are regulatory prescribed to 0% and hence have no inflow.

The cash outflows also have regulatory prescribed parameters. For example:

- Small business and consumer deposits have prescribed runoff factors that depend on deposit features resulting in cash outflows.
- Corporate deposits also have prescribed runoff factors. Corporate deposits have in general a higher prescribed runoff rate than consumer and small business deposits. The financial institution's runoff deposit rate is conservatively set to 100%.
- Potential cash outflows also include maturing repos where the regulatory prescribed outflow rate depends on the underlying repo asset quality. When eligible buffer assets are used as collateral there is in general a small runoff factor while repos using non–buffer eligible assets may have a 100% outflow.
- Credit facilities have a drawdown factor that depends on the counterparty. For example, the regulatory drawdown rate for credit facilities to financial institutions or liquidity facilities is 40%.

The numerator of the LCR equation (6.26) is the cash value (haircut-adjusted value) of the stock of eligible high-quality assets. As with cash outflows the regulation prescribes eligibility and the asset haircuts based on, for example, issuer characteristics. Naturally, only unencumbered portions of assets can be counted toward the stock. Assets pledged to the bank as collateral can potentially also be counted toward the stock, for example, assets received as collateral in reverse repo agreements that mature after the regulatory liquidity horizon of

---

[14]The regulation also prescribes the maximum holdings of level 2A assets to 40% and level 2B assets to 15%.

30 days. For an asset to be eligible the asset must also be in direct control of the treasury. Hence, the specific entity and internal organization structure of the firm may be important in determining regulatory eligibility of an asset.

In principle the regulatory LCR measure in equation (6.26) does not consider a term-structure of cash flows on $t = 1, \ldots, 30$ days. Cash inflows and cash outflows as well as the cash value of the numerator are considered on a single horizon of 30 days with no analysis of the exact flow date. Specifically, runoff and drawdown factors are used to generate cash outflows under the liquidity horizon. This can be seen as a weakness of the regulatory LCR measure, because, as we have discussed, liquidity risk solvency is path-dependent and the availability of funds at the end of the 30-day period may not be useful to mitigate insolvency in the beginning of the period. Also, the specific unfolding of a liquidity crisis may be important for determining solvency. The LCR measure is hence a special case of our general liquidity risk measure with a cash hedging portfolio and a single 30-day time bucket t for the liquidity cash flows. Using our cash liquidity risk measure we can generalize the denominator of the LCR measure to be measured at time buckets $t = 1, \ldots, T$ as we will discuss next.

Generalized Liquidity Coverage Ratio To put the regulatory LCR measure in the context of our cash measure of liquidity exposure and liquidity solvency—and hence reconcile with internal liquidity models—we let d denote the specific regulatory scenario and set $T = 30$ days. The numerator of the LCR measure does not have a term-structure, similar to our cash liquidity risk measure. Implicitly, the regulatory LCR measure assumes that the liquidity buffer can generate cash liquidity at any point in time during the 30-day period, albeit with a predetermined haircut. This is equivalent to assuming an amount of cash, M, is available during the 30-day period, the cash amount being the current value of the liquidity buffer adjusted by the regulatory haircuts. Turning to the definition of the denominator it is consistent with the forward liquidity need, with cash counterbalancing capacity, under scenario d. This means that we can express the regulatory LCR measure using a term structure $t = 1, \ldots, T$ for cash inflows and outflows, in our notation, as

$$\text{LCR} = \frac{M}{-\sum_{t=1}^{30} \min\left[\widetilde{F}(d,t), 0\right]} > 100\% \tag{6.27}$$

or, equivalently, the firm passes the regulatory LCR test if

$$\sum_{t=1}^{30} \min\left[\widetilde{F}(d,t), 0\right] > -M. \tag{6.28}$$

This last equation (6.28) makes clear that when cumulating the denominator liquidity exposure over time, $t = 1, \ldots, T$, the LCR measure in equation (6.27) is not defined with respect to the regular net cumulative cash outflows in the denominator. It should be properly defined with the correct cumulative measure of net cash outflow under a cash equivalent portfolio.

We can also further generalize the regulatory LCR measure to allow non-cash or non-cash equivalent hedging capacity. However, we are then back in our general, pathdependent liquidity risk measure with the risk process, $R(C, T, d)$, in equation (6.2). In this case a liquidity hedging model is needed to convert the hedge portfolio into cash counterbalancing capacity and ultimately determine solvency at the path, $t = 1, \ldots, T$.

Managing the Liquidity Coverage Ratio   A firm can always adjust its liquidity hedge portfolio to improve its LCR ratio. This adjustment of the liquidity hedge portfolio can come from either:

- The acquiring of new hedge assets (i.e., increase the size of the buffer),[15]
- or replacing existing hedge assets of lower quality (higher regulatory haircut) with higher quality assets (e.g., cash carries no regulatory haircut).

Of course this means in general more costs for the banks, either indirectly through higher opportunity cost (high-quality assets in general carry a higher opportunity cost) or directly through fees in a collateral swap.

This management of the firm's LCR ratio focuses on managing the numerator. A firm can also, on a longer term basis, try and improve its LCR ratio by adjusting the denominator of LCR. It can decrease cash outflows by acquiring longer duration liabilities (e.g., deposits) and try to increase the stability of deposits. However, longer funding in general means higher funding costs for bank. Hence, there is in practice a trade-off between increased funding costs versus regulatory LCR costs by requiring more regulatory eligible hedge assets. A bank can also reduce the amount of offered liquidity and credit facilities. Again, there is a trade-off between, on one hand, less returns for the firm versus regulatory LCR costs of the liquid buffer. We can therefore conclude that the management of the firm's LCR ratio cost is the management of the trade-off between acquiring more liquid buffer costs, or accepting reduced earnings or increased funding costs. However, naturally, firms may try to offload the liquidity cost onto the consumers of liquidity to mitigate reduced earnings or funding costs, for example, by pricing the contingency liquidity cost of holding the buffer into credit and liquidity facilities and nonstable deposits. The costs are then passed onto the consumers rather than the firm. We will return to the issue of liquidity pricing in the next chapter on funds transfer pricing and profitability of cash flows.

It is important for a financial institution to forecast the potential future LCR ratio at a future time, T, applying the future contractual cash flows between the current time t and the future time T. This is to enable actions today, at t, for predictable plausible LCR effects in the future. For example, known maturing funding of the buffer produces new buffer funding requirements that need to be planned for as early as possible. In projecting future LCR one can also experiment with different business rollover assumptions and plan ahead for actions to improve LCR should those rollover assumptions impact the bank's LCR negatively.

Net Stable Funding Ratio

While the LCR measures the short-term impact of a liquidity stress and in particular the survival of the bank during a 30-day term it does not measure structural funding liquidity. Effectively, a bank can have structural problems with stability of their funding channels (e.g., only unsecured short-term channels) over a longer term and still satisfy the LCR regulatory requirements with a sufficient buffer of liquid assets. On a longer-term crisis, however, eventually, the counterbalancing capacity of the hedging assets is reduced and the bank must resort,

---

[15]When aquiring new hedge assets that need to be funded we assume the funding matures after the regulatory liquidity horizon of 30 days such that the aquiring of the new hedge asset only makes a positive contribution in the numerator of LCR.

at least partially, to stable funding channels that work even in stress. The regulators' proposed NSFR measures this stability of funding channels by considering a one-year horizon. The general idea is that long-term assets should be funded by long-term liabilities to avoid potential liquidity problems when funding rolls over. Long-term funding includes bond funding, core deposits, and equity. The short-term funding includes non-core deposits and money market funding that, in principle, should be hedged by unencumbered assets.

The regulatory NSFR ratio is constructed by the ratio of available stable funding to the required stable funding (Basel Committee, 2014d). The required stable funding is a weighted sum of the balance amounts of assets with regulatory prescribed multipliers that are close to 1 for long-term nontradable assets. The available stable funding is obtained by summing up the funding with, again, regulatory prescribed multipliers close to 1 for long-term funding. As for the LCR ratio the NSFR ratio should exceed 100%. That is, long-term assets should be funded by at least as much long-term liabilities. This is to ensure the firm does not run into potential liquidity issues in refunding long-term assets.

Traditionally, banks have computed structural liquidity ratios like the NSFR ratio for a long time. Rating agencies also use such structural liquidity ratios to assess liquidity of banks. Most well known is probably Moody's Cash Capital Position (CCP). Moody's uses this measure to analyze the liquidity structure of a bank's balance sheet as part of its external rating assignment. The CCP simply compares the amount of unsecured short-term funding (e.g., < 1 year) as well as the level of non-core deposits to the hedging capacity of the unencumbered assets. The CCP is the difference between the amounts and a bank with a positive CCP is deemed to have a stable liquidity structure. Clearly, the CCP measure is consistent with the regulatory incentive behind the NSFR, to promote long-term funding.

Regulatory Liquidity Monitoring Tools

The liquidity measurement, cash flow modeling, and liquidity hedge analysis discussed in this chapter help banks to establish forward-looking monitoring capability of their liquidity situation. The monitoring practice should serve the purpose of effective reporting as well as decision making. Bank should set a target liquidity survival horizon and monitor current and future liquidity demand and supply that is consistent with the survival horizon. Liquidity limits are often the targets the monitoring is compared against. Liquidity risk modeling and monitoring should not be isolated from the macroeconomic environment or micro-behavior of the bank. Liquidity risk is a consequential risk that is closely tied to the other risks a bank faces. The growing globalization of the economic and increasing market-based funding necessitate the closer monitoring of the market behavior. At the same time, liquidity distress can rise from a bank's own business practice as well. Any news about a bank's business or operational loss can trigger a reputation crisis and lead to widening of funding spread or even close of funding sources. For example, JP Morgan's multibillion-dollar trading loss at the beginning of 2012 caused a downgrade of its credit rating by Fitch Ratings in worrying about the bank's risk management system and internal control process.

Apart from market monitoring, regulators require banks to monitor:

- Cash flow gaps under a contractual maturity mismatch of the firm
- The funding concentration
- The stock of eligible regulatory hedging assets used in the numerator of LCR

Cash Flow Gaps   The maturity mismatch monitoring in the classical asset and liability management usually focuses on the projection of the cash flows based on a static view of balance sheet. The Financial Services Authority[16] of United Kingdom published "Strengthening Liquidity Standards" in 2009. In that policy statement, several report templates are widely adopted by many jurisdictions. This includes traditional ratio-based reports and cash flows based on stress scenarios.

Basel III also requires banks to conduct cash flow maturity mismatch analyses based on going-concern behavioral assumptions of the inflows and outflows of funds in both normal situations and under stress. The cash flow gap monitoring serves several objectives to the management:

- *To get an overview of the liquidity healthiness and liquidity need.* The liquidity gap should not be only at the bank level, but needs to be sliced into branches, regions, lines of business, and cash flow currencies.
- *To check the validity of the liquidity funding plan.* The cash flow gaps must be monitored together with bank's funding plans to make sure the funding availability can sustain the liquidity need.
- *To aid the decision process of bank's business strategy.* A timely view of the cash flow performance provides insight into the extent to which the bank relies on maturity transformation under its current contracts and adjusts the loan or deposit acquisition strategy to get a contractual hedge.
- *To plan for liquidity emergent execution plan.* When an emergent large net cash outflow is in sight, the bank can get sufficient time to prepare for a liquidity execution plan based on the current counterbalancing capacity.

Clearly, with a contractual maturity mismatch, since many banks fund relatively short and lend long, the survival time can be quite short with no rollover of funding. The contractual maturity mismatch monitoring can be seen as complementary to the liquidity coverage ratio, which is based on going-concern assumptions with regulatory prescribed rundown (rollover) rates.

Funding Concentration   One lesson learned from the recent financial crisis is the danger of over-reliance on specific funding source. When banks draw significant funds from a few specific counterparties, the contagion in the financial system can introduce increased liquidity risk not only to the bank itself but also into the entire system. When significant funding counterparties are identified, banks should also study the possibility of wrong-way funding risk, that is, whether the counterparty can be a stable funding source at the time the bank increases its funding demand.

The concentration is limited not only to a particular wholesale funding counterparty but also to the type of source and currency. For example, when a bank relies heavily on the asset backed commercial paper market for the short-term funding, the close-down of the market due to any reason can lead to a significant liquidity crisis of the bank. Similarly, when a bank's majority funding is dominated by a particular currency, a tightening control of the currency

---

[16]UK FSA is now split into the Financial Conduct Authority and the Prudential Regulation Authority.

or turbulence in the foreign exchange market can cause liquidity difficulty of the bank. For this reason, Basel III requires monitoring of three funding concentration items:

1. Funding liabilities sourced from each significant counterparty as a percentage of total liabilities
2. Funding liabilities sourced from each significant product/instrument as a percentage of total liabilities
3. List of asset and liability amounts by significant currency

Funding concentration monitoring can be seen as complementary to the NSFR reporting. The NSFR ratio promotes banks to steer part of their funding toward long-term stable funding. However, the funding is not necessarily diversified.

Counterbalancing Capacity A bank must closely monitor its counterbalancing capacity available in the form of the liquidity hedging portfolio. The bank should model the characteristics of the unencumbered assets and borrowing capacity in the inventory, especially at the time of economic and market turbulence. For example, when the market crashes, the flight-to-quality effect can lead to significant loss of value of the low-quality assets. Basel III requires banks to monitor

- Available unencumbered assets that are marketable as collateral in secondary markets
- Available unencumbered assets that are eligible for central banks' standing facilities

Business Concentration Although diversification is a general principle of the banking business, it is sometimes hard to implement in practice. Every bank has its business sweet-spot in terms of business sector, region, and currency. The concentration of the business can increase the liquidity risk to the bank. The bank must be able to understand the timing and severity of surge of funding demand including drawdown, prepayment, and default risk in the business and plan funding accordingly.

As discussed in the cash flow modeling among the most difficult to analyze yet important to understand is the potential behavior of the bank's counterparties in using committed facilities and guarantees offered by the bank. The bank must monitor several aspects of the facilities. The first is its concentration. Because the facilities are typically drawn down at the time of need, if a bank has over-concentrated credit facilities offered in a certain business sector and region, the contagion effect in the sector and region can quickly deplete the bank's funding, ultimately dragging the bank into a liquidity distress if the bank is not prepared for the surge of such demand. The bank must also monitor the total limit of the open facilities and their utilization rate, both current and projected.

Funds Transfer Pricing and Profitability of Cash Flows

Funds transfer pricing creates a shadow of assets and liabilities. Real assets are funded by synthetic liabilities to produce a matched balance sheet for the asset. Similarly, real liabilities receive income from synthetic assets for the same purpose. Through fund transfer pricing a bank can analyze more efficiently its net interest margin and its expected profitability. Specifically, the net interest margin profitability and risk analysis can, with funds transfer pricing, be broken down to loan and position level. The same applies to a traditional economic value (solvency) view, which now also can be broken down to the most granular level.[1]

Breaking down balance sheet profitability and solvency to the most granular level is important for segmenting the portfolio supplier versus consumers of portfolio profitability and solvency.

Traditionally, funds transfer pricing is used by financial institutions to:

1. Achieve centralization of risks, that is, clear branches' risks that are most efficiently managed centrally such as interest rate risk.
2. Measure ex-ante performance of traditional banking book items such as loans, mortgages, and deposits.

A loan or deposit clearing of interest rate risk is achieved through the funds transfer price, defined as the matched maturity funding rate plus a markup for business costs. In effect this is an interest rate swap agreement between the branch and the clearing center and the price of the swap is usually null. For ex-ante performance evaluation of branches the assigned funds transfer rate is used to measure an interest margin to the transfer rate of the synthetic instrument. Funds transfer pricing can be seen as creating a portfolio split such that:

- Branches manage the actual asset minus the synthetic funding, that is, the customer leg of the transaction versus the synthetic funds transfer instrument.
- Treasury manages the residual portfolio of the actual funding leg minus the synthetic asset.

We can write this portfolio split, P, as

$$P = (A1 - B) + (B - A2) \tag{7.1}$$

---

[1]As in the liquidity risk chapter we assume the reader is familiar with classical asset and liability management, specifically, the classical interest rate risk and profitability measures. See Dermine and Bissada (2002) or Choudhry (2007) for an introduction.

where $A1$ is an asset such as a loan, B is the synthetic funds transfer instrument and $A2$ is the actual treasury funding. Hence, the first term creates a balanced balance sheet for the loan while the second term includes the pool of all treasury funding assets, $A2$, with no further breakdown. The residual, $B - A2$, is hence managed by treasury on an aggregate portfolio profit-and-loss basis. This assignment of a matching funding asset or liability to a corresponding branch liability or asset achieves balanced balance sheets for branches so that each branch becomes a consistent performance measurement unit.

Many traditional banking products face credit risk and liquidity risk in addition to the interest rate risk. It is also the case that many traditional banking products carry embedded optionality features such as prepayment and withdrawal options. As funds transfer pricing is concerned with ex-ante profitability and incentive creation it is important that the bank's funds transfer pricing program includes all the risk costs faced by the bank. For example, in clearing branch credit risk the size of the risk spread added in the funds transfer price could be related to the cost of clearing the risk for traded assets that have liquid credit default swap markets. While such hedge risk costs may be available for traded assets the risk spread for non-traded traditional balance sheet items has to be defined internally using expected loss projections and hence be based on a reserve methodology. The clearing of credit risk from branches and centralization to treasury may seem a natural step as the efficient hedging of credit risk requires a portfolio perspective. However, there are also drawbacks to clearing branch's credit risks. Most notably the clearing of the credit risk can remove the branch's incentive to actually manage the credit issued by the branch locally.

A complex issue in funds transfer pricing is how to measure funds transfer prices when future cash flows are uncertain. This is the case for most deposits where consumers can withdraw their funds at any point in time and hence the branch has in effect issued a withdrawal option on the account. Other examples include loans with prepayment and associated caps and floors. Since the funds transfer rate should represent the actual cost of matched maturity funds a bank cannot ignore incorporating the additional cost for embedded options in branch products. If they do, then incentives to issue embedded products that can raise the interest rate willingly paid by consumers, such as caps and floors and embedded call options, increase. Moreover, since the funds transfer price is not adjusted accordingly there is no indication on what spread on the consumer rate is needed for the branch to achieve profitability.

Recently, due partly to the Basel III regulation for liquidity risk, the pricing of liquidity risk cost and benefits onto firm's assets and liabilities through funds transfer pricing has become a widespread practice. Just like a firm is pricing expected credit losses and the opportunity cost of capital, liquidity pricing should be instituted in a way that rewards providers of liquidity and charges its users. Inclusion of liquidity risk in bank's (funds transfer) pricing is also a regulatory requirement. In particular, Basel Committee (2008) specifies that banks should incorporate liquidity costs, benefits, and risks in the product pricing, performance measurement, and new product approval process for all significant business activities. CEBS (2010) also focuses on the need for firms to develop a sound practice of pricing liquidity risk. The CEBS guidelines target a liquidity cost concept that includes not only direct, structural liquidity mismatch funding costs, but also associated indirect costs such as opportunity cost of holding contingency liquidity buffer, the cost of holding the liquidity hedging portfolio to mitigate funds outflow in liquidity stress. See also Grant (2011). Neu et al. (2007) similarly decompose the pricing of funding liquidity risk into two distinct components:

1. Mismatch or funding liquidity cost
2. Contingency liquidity costs, that is, the cost of holding stand-by liquidity

It is important to recognize that the opportunity cost of the standby liquidity portfolio can be managed by a firm. As we discussed in the liquidity risk chapter, a priori, a firm would like to hold the minimum (opportunity) cost liquidity hedging portfolio that with high probability can generate the counterbalancing capacity needed. A cost-efficient program for liquidity hedging immediately translates into a competitive price adjustment for liquidity consuming assets and liabilities in the firm's funds transfer pricing. For example, the bank's issued facilities carry a liquidity contingency cost for the unused part that will likely be drawn under liquidity stress. This cost needs to be passed on to the consumer to remain profitable.

In ex-ante performance measurement the spread between the consumer rate and the funds transfer price is an indication of the prospective future economic value generated. For an account with a positive economic value banks rank the economic value based on risk adjustment.[2] The general idea is that for two accounts with the same economic value one would prefer the one with the least risk. Of course, a customer can be profitable even if some accounts with the customer carry negative expected economic value. Similarly a subportfolio with certain types of credits may have negative expected economic value but still be a necessary bank offer in order to retain customers and gain profits on other products with the customer. Hence, when measuring ex-ante profitability using funds transfer pricing it is important to have a holistic customer perspective. It is also important to recognize that risk-based funds transfer pricing provides an economic value pricing but not necessary a traditional profitability-based pricing. It measures the ex-ante fair value performance. This ex-ante fair value performance may or may not be realized.

In this chapter we first introduce the basic matched maturity funding concept to create synthetic funds transfer instruments for interest rate risk. Second, we consider risk-based funds transfer pricing that takes into account credit risk and capital, embedded optionality, as well as liquidity risk. After having discussed how to introduce all the risk costs in the funds transfer rates we discuss the decomposition of profitability, as measured by net interest income and solvency measures, using funds transfer pricing. Funds transfer rates are also core in the calculation of economic fair value of banking book assets and liabilities. The funds transfer rate(s) are used in discounting uncertain, non-traded cash flows, including all costs and risk spreads. After a discussion on the scope of funds transfer pricing we end the chapter with a review of regulation areas where profitability analysis is a core requirement. Parts of our exposition in this chapter draw from Skoglund (2013).

BASIC FUNDS TRANSFER PRICING CONCEPT

Basic funds transfer pricing focuses on assigning a clearing rate that is consistent with the asset or liability maturity. For example, the Interbank cost of funding curve is used to generate a fixed term deposit funds transfer rate that is consistent with the maturity of the funds.[3] The net interest margin for the branch is obtained as the difference between the funds transfer rate and the consumer funds rate. As consumer deposit rates are in general lower than market funding rates the net interest margin tends to be positive. Another example is the calculation of the

---

[2]The bank's equity holders' expected return on equity gives an indication of the threshold that needs to be satisfied in order for the account to contribute to improving the bank's expected return.

[3]The Interbank curve is the bank cost of funding with other banks using short-term money market instruments, forward rate agreements, etc. On a longer term the funding curve is usually composed of the cost of the bank's long-term bond funding.

funds transfer rate and the net interest margin for a bullet payment loan. While the duration of the actual funding base may be significantly shorter than the duration of the bullet loan the loan is attributed to the interbank rate consistent with the loan duration as the funds transfer rate. This yields an interest margin between the bullet loan paying rate and the interbank rate.

In the above two simple cases there was only one payment, which allowed us to define the funds transfer rate as the funding rate that is applicable at maturity of the cash flow. In case we have a loan with several payments until maturity it is clear that the funds transfer rate cannot be the funding rate at maturity. In particular, all the cash flows from the loan must be accounted for as they need to be funded accordingly. Taking into account all cash flows, weighting by the relevant funding rate, we get the funds transfer price (FTP) as

$$\text{FTP} = \frac{\sum_{t=1}^{T} \text{CF}(t) \times f(t)}{\sum_{t=1}^{T} \text{CF}(t)} \tag{7.2}$$

where $\text{CF}(t)$ is the cash flow at time t, $t = 1, \ldots, T$, and $f(t)$ is the bank funding rate at t.

This method of assigning funds transfer (prices) rates to a contract is usually referred to as the "exact" method as it computes the funding using an exact match of all cash flows of the contract. Another method is to calculate the duration of the contract and then assign the contract the funding rate corresponding to the duration. However, the duration approach is only an approximation and requires the same amount of computations as for the exact method as both approaches require cash flows of the contract to be computed.[4] The exact method is therefore often used in practice.

Example of FTP for a Mortgage and a Loan

In Table 7.1 we provide an example of calculating funds transfer rates for a mortgage and a loan using the exact method in equation (7.2). The mortgage example is an annuity with semiannual payment frequency, a notional of 100,000 units of currency, and 5.5 years until maturity.[5] The loan example pays interest quarterly with a fixed amortization of 30,000 units of currency on a notional of 1,900,000 units of currency. The loan maturity term is 12.5 years. The funding curve, $f(t)$, used in the calculation is displayed in Table 7.2 and Figure 7.1.

Table 7.1 displays the calculated FTP in % with an approximate 2.6% FTP for the mortgage and an approximate 3.9% FTP for the loan. The higher FTP for the loan is of course due to its longer maturity cash flows and the increasing term-structure of funds rates in Table 7.2.

Having calculated the funds transfer price for a particular asset or liability the actual transfer amount is then simply the funds transfer price times the notional amount. We also note that while in this example we applied the FTP calculation to the individual instruments FTP can in principle also be applied to pools of instruments. For example, we could apply FTP to a portfolio aggregate of mortgage cash flows. However, our focus in this chapter will be on individual instruments FTP as this allows the most granular breakdown of profitability analysis.

---

[4]In addition, duration-based measures require a numerical root-finding with respect to the yield rate.
[5]An annuity can pay a fixed total amount at all the payment times or pay an adjusted total annuity amount at the payment times to ensure the debt is fully paid at the maturity. The first case is a fixed annuity and the second case is a variable annuity. Our example is a variable annuity.

TABLE 7.1 Calculation of Fund Transfer Rates for a Mortgage and a Loan

Contract type	Interest frequency	Amortization type/amount	Notional	Maturity term	FTP (%)
Mortgage	Semiannual	Annuity	100,000	5,5 Years	2.6307
Loan	Quarter	30,000	1,900,000	12,5 Years	3.9961

TABLE 7.2 Funding Curve Used in Calculation of Funds Transfer Rates

Maturity term	Interest rate (%)
1 Month	2.15
3 Months	2.22
9 Months	2.44
1 Year	2.54
3 Years	3.31
4 Years	3.62
5 Years	3.88
7 Years	4.24
9 Years	4.46
10 Years	4.55
15 Years	4.52

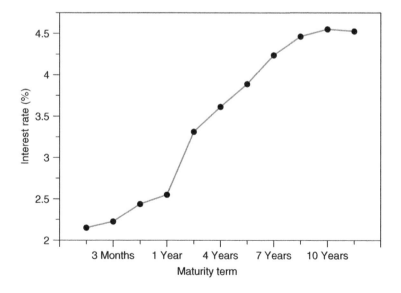

FIGURE 7.1 Funding Curve Used in Calculation of Funds Transfer Rates

RISK-BASED FUNDS TRANSFER PRICING

As we have mentioned previously the inclusion of risk costs is an important component in a bank's funds transfer program. Without considering the risks, in general, ex-ante profitability is not a fair measure of ex-post profitability. Since a bank's management planning of future growth areas of the bank is often based on ex-ante profitability projections all risks and embedded costs need to be taken into account.

Note that both risk spreads and matched maturity funding costs are assigned at origination. The assigned risk costs on top of the matched maturity funding costs are therefore usually based on long-term behavior rather than focused only on the current risk situation. If risk spreads are assigned based on the current situation in a downturn, the bank faces increased funding costs and needs to increase offered rates to be profitable—yielding a contraction in the loan market. Similarly, in good times, the current risk spreads are typically smaller than usual and loan offered rates can decrease—potentially leading to an expansion. The reader may recall that we have already had this discussion of using current versus long-term risk in the chapter on portfolio credit risk and, specifically, in the discussion of the TTC and PIT rating methodologies.

Even if long-term risk costs are used, the bank may still monitor future risk spreads as a basis for unexperienced profit and loss. For floating rate products both the funding cost and risk spreads can in principle be viewed as repricing. The adjustment of customer paying rates based on banks' changing funding costs at repricing is standard practice. However, it may be harder for banks to adjust risk spreads significantly upwards for certain customers even if contractually possible at repricing times. Risk spreads for floating rate products may hence follow a long-term, product maturity, risk assessment approach as for fixed rate products.

Credit Risk and Capital

For traded assets with credit risk the cost of clearing default risk is the corresponding credit default swap premium and hence the markup on the transfer price is determined by the market in which the credit trades. Clearing credit risk, the interest margin obtained is now classified as:

1. Treasury residual margin (using actual duration of funding)
2. Total branch interest margin on funds transfer price
3. Branch risk adjusted margin for credit risk

When clearing credit risk using the credit default swap curve the credit default swap curve is added to the interbank funding curve to obtain a new funding rate that includes the effect of clearing the default risk. The branch economic value added spread is now taken as the loan paying rate minus the funding cost—inclusive of credit risk. Clearing traded credit risk the total transactions between the branch and the treasury are

(a) The interest rate swap
(b) The treasury-issued credit default swap to the branch

While the above clearing works for traded credits and credits that can at least approximately be mapped to traded credits, a large part of the banking book items with credit risk do not have a market. That is, there is no given market price of credit. While securitization on banking book items may provide some information on the price of default risk, it is generally difficult to extract such information from the underlying pools.

In the case of non-traded credits, the cost of funds for credit must therefore be generated internally. Ideally, one has available estimates of expected credit losses as well as allocated risk or capital. In the cost of capital approach to funding costs, one splits the funding into two parts. The first part is the risk-free funding and the second part is the risky funding. Specifically, denoting the base transfer rate by FTP, expected credit loss in percent of notional by EL, required return on equity capital in percent by E, and allocated credit risk capital, in percent of notional, by w, we have that

$$\overline{\text{FTP}} = \text{FTP} \times (1 - w) + \text{E} \times w + \text{EL}. \tag{7.3}$$

Here, $\overline{\text{FTP}}$ is the total risky funds transfer price that is allocated to the credit. The funding is effectively split up in two parts:

1. Risk-free interbank funding
2. Risky equity funding

The split between the two is decided by the allocated credit risk capital for the contract, and since equity funding is usually much more expensive than interbank funding, $\overline{\text{FTP}}$ is increasing in allocated credit risk capital (risk).[6]

Example FTP for a Mortgage Continued Table 7.3 displays the calculation of $\overline{\text{FTP}}$ for the sample mortgage in Table 7.1. The calculation is also split up in the effect from only credit risk capital,

$$\overline{\text{FTP}}_C = \text{FTP} \times (1 - w) + \text{E} \times w$$

and only expected losses. That is, spread,

$$\overline{\text{FTP}}_{EL} = \text{FTP} + \text{EL}.$$

The calculation uses the funding curve in Table 7.2 as well as an expected loss curve, an allocated capital curve, and a curve for projected cost of equity funding. These latter curves are displayed in Table 7.4. Our example uses a slightly increasing term-structure for expected losses of the mortgage as well as term-structures of allocated capital and cost of equity. The term-structure of capital rates can in practice be replaced by a single (average yearly)

TABLE 7.3 Funds Transfer Pricing for Credit Risk for the Mortgage in Table 7.2

FTP (%)	$\overline{\text{FTP}}_C$ (%)	$\overline{\text{FTP}}_{EL}$ (%)	$\overline{\text{FTP}}$ (%)
2.6307	2.8016	4.9122	4.929

[6]The equity funding cost is determined by the opportunity cost of equity, that is, by the investor's expected return on equity.

TABLE 7.4 Funds Transfer Pricing for Credit Risk for the Mortgage in Table 7.2

Maturity term (M)	EL(M) (%)	w(M) (%)	E(M) (%)
1 Year	2.081	0.1	8
3 Years	.	.	8.5
5 Years	2.150	0.5	9.3
10 Years	.	1	10
20 Years	2.219	.	11

capital rate. Similarly, the term-structure of equity capital rates in this example illustrates increasing expected returns over time from investors but may of course in practice be replaced by a single return rate.

Note that the calculation of the single implied $\overline{\text{FTP}}$ for expected losses, EL, and capital, w, uses a solve method. Specifically, we numerically solve for the single implied risky spread of the contract versus the case with zero EL or zero allocated capital, w, or both zero. From Table 7.3 we find that the expected loss has the largest impact on the $\overline{\text{FTP}}$ rate. That is, $\overline{\text{FTP}}_{EL}$ has the largest contribution to the credit-risky FTP rate, $\overline{\text{FTP}}$. The example also shows that incorporating the risk costs due to credit risk for this mortgage is required. The credit-risky FTP rate is significantly higher than the base FTP rate.

A key issue when using $\overline{\text{FTP}}$ as the vehicle for calculating funds transfer prices to branches is that the allocated capital, w, should be the Euler risk contribution. This is because the pricing incentives distributed to the branches will then be consistent with local portfolio optimization as we discussed in the context of economic justification of Euler risk contributions in the first market risk chapter.

Other Risk Charges and Expenses The process of adding other risk charges such as operational risk charges follows the same approach as for credit risk. That is, we can interpret w as the total economic capital allocated and EL as the total expected losses. Non-risky charges such as operations and business costs are in general treated as fixed additions to $\overline{\text{FTP}}$. See Dev and Rao (2006, ch. 4) for a discussion of different methods of expense allocations to funds transfer prices.

Embedded Optionality

For many assets and liabilities the future cash flows are not known. For example, demand deposits have no assigned maturity, loans may have prepayment options, bonds may be issuer callable and/or holder putable, and a loan may have a cap or floor on the rate. In these situations the funds transfer price needs to incorporate the uncertainty due to these unknown cash flow streams. This inclusion is important in order to distribute to the branches the right pricing and valuation incentives for these products.[7]

---

[7]Note that when a bank can charge penalties ex-post from the customer, then the embedded optionality may not be part of the funds transfer price. For example, in some countries, when a customer prepays, the bank can charge the customer a prepayment penalty at the time of prepayment that fully compensates the bank, that is, ex-post. If instead prepayment is free or the ex-post prepayment penalty is limited, then the bank should include a prepayment penalty charge ex-ante in the funds transfer price.

To price these embedded options one can in general consider two different approaches: They are the financial engineering approach and the statistical model approach. In the financial engineering approach the embedded option is formulated as a market priced embedded option. The option is valued using a market model for the short-rate such as the Hull-White and the implied model parameters are extracted from similar market instruments. Finally, the funds transfer price is adjusted with the embedded option value using a so-called option adjusted spread. In the statistical model approach a model of behavior is formulated, for example, a prepayment model or a model of deposit volume. The cash flows are evaluated under the model and the funds transfer spread needed for the uncertainty is calculated.

Financial Engineering Approach to Valuation of Embedded Options In the financial engineering approach the embedded options are American in nature, such as

- Early withdrawal of deposits
- Early prepayment features

Embedded options can be viewed as bond or loan and option packages. For example, in a callable bond the issuer has the right to repurchase the bond cash flows at prespecified price. This corresponds to:

1. Selling the option-free bond
2. Selling a call option on the bond

The value of the bond or loan is the traditional value minus the call option value.

For a putable bond the holder has right to sell back the bond at prespecified price. It corresponds to:

1. Buying the option free bond or loan
2. Buying an option to sell the bond (put option)

The value is the bond value plus the put option value.

The valuation of the American embedded call or put option relies on a model for the interest rate. The standard market model uses either the Hull and White model (Hull and White, 1994, 1996),

$$dr = (b(t) - ar)dt + \sigma dW(t)$$

or the Black-Karasinski model (Black and Karasinski, 1991),

$$d \ln r = (b(t) - a \ln r)dt + \sigma dW(t).$$

Here r is the short-rate of interest, σ is the volatility, a is the mean reversion rate, and $dW(t)$ is the increments of the Wiener process. The time-dependent parameter, $b(t)$, is chosen to fit the current term structure of interest rates.

Having specified the model for the interest rate, r, the next step is to value the embedded American option. Hull and White (1994, 1996) specify a trinomial tree approach to solving for the option value. In particular for the Hull-White model the first step is to initially consider a tree for the discretized process,

$$dr^* = -ar^* dt + \sigma dW(t)$$

and then convert the tree into a tree for the full model by translating

$$\alpha(t) = r - r^*.$$

Using this tree the bond prices consistent with the current term-structure can be calculated and the bond price lattice can be solved backwards to obtain the option price consistent with the term-structure.

For embedded cap and floor rates to a repricing bond or loan these are consistently valued using the classical Black commodity options model, Black (1976), for European options.[8] The cap and floor options for each repricing term are referred to as caplets and floorlets respectively and the option value is the sum of the value of all the caplets and floorlets

Having calculated the embedded option value the next step is to define the markup on the funds transfer price due to the embedded option. The concept of option adjusted spread (OAS) is used in this context. The OAS for a callable bond is defined as the fixed spread that when added to the set of spot (forward) rates used in valuation gives a callable bond value consistent with the non-callable bond value. In practice, this means we have to solve numerically for the OAS using the given value of the bond or loan without embedded options and the embedded option value(s). Having obtained the OAS we can now add this to the funds transfer price as

$$\overline{\text{FTP}} = \text{FTP} \times (1 - w) + \text{E} \times w + \text{EL} + \text{OAS}. \tag{7.4}$$

The obtained $\overline{\text{FTP}}$ now incorporates into the funds transfer price the effect of non-traded risk as well as any market priced embedded options.

Example OAS for a Floating Rate Note Table 7.5 displays the option adjusted spreads obtained from a 14-year maturity term floating rate note with embedded American call and cap and floor. The embedded call maturity term is 10 years. The table displays the obtained cap and floor OAS and embedded call OAS with different assumptions on the call strike level as percent of notional.[9] The cap and floor levels are set to 10% and 0.1%, respectively, and the cap and floor valuation is done using the Black model with volatility curves for the caplets and floorlets respectively. The American embedded call options are valued using the Hull-White trinomial tree with Hull-White model parameters set to

$$\sigma = 0.01,$$
$$a = 0.12.$$

TABLE 7.5 Option Adjusted Spreads for Caps and Floors and American Embedded Call Options Using Different Call Strikes

Interest frequency	Strike (%)	Call OAS (%)	Capfloor OAS (%)
Year	100	0.56	0.123
Year	89	1.334	0.123
Year	70	3.130	0.123

---

[8] Assuming forward rates are log-normal; see Hull (2006, pp. 619–622).
[9] The strike price is a quote strike price. That is, it includes accrued interest.

TABLE 7.6 Index Curve for Repricing of the Floating Rate Note and Volatility Curves for the Pricing of the Caplets and Floorlets Using the Black Model

Maturity term	Repricing index curve	Cap vol curve	Floor vol curve
0.5 Year	2.61	0.2	0.184
1 Year	4.24	0.23	0.19
2 Years	4.23	0.24	0.196
3 Years	4.23	0.245	0.223
5 Years	4.26	0.23	0.213
10 Years	4.35	0.223	0.196

The option adjusted spread is obtained by numerically solving for the fixed spread that would make an investor indifferent between the plain floating rate note and the floating rate note with the embedded optionality. For reference Table 7.6 displays the index curve for repricing of the floating rate note as well as the volatility curves used to price the caplets and floorlets.

Note that in our example the OAS adjustment to a fair market rate for the floating rate note is significant when the call strike is 70% of notional. For higher call strike rates the OAS adjustment is lower. The cap and floor OAS adjustment is quite small since the range of the floor and the cap is wide outside the range of market rates.

Applying the Financial Engineering Approach to Consumer Options Having derived a funds transfer pricing model incorporating the effect of market priced embedded options one may consider applying this model to consumer embedded options as well (e.g., prepayment options). However, when applying this model to non-traded risks there are several issues that need to be considered.

- First, consumers may not act as rational market players in the sense that embedded options are not exercised even when beneficial.

This is referred to as customer irrationality and a prime example is that all consumers who should rationally prepay at a certain time don't. Moreover, sometimes consumers prepay when they shouldn't. This phenomenon is observed in McConnell and Singh (1994), Stanton (1995), Levin (2001), and Levin and Davidson (2005).

- Second, when applying the OAS model to consumer options it is not clear what model parameters (e.g., implied volatility) should be used.

To solve the first problem of handling the apparent irrationality of consumers compared to market participants one may consider consumers as rational; however, they exercise their options subject to transaction costs. An example of a transaction cost is the effort it takes for a consumer to actually prepay the loan or withdraw the funds and place the funds in another account. Arguably, most consumers will not take action unless the cost of transactions is covered by the gain in exercising the embedded option. Also, one may argue that consumers don't follow markets continuously and the decision to exercise a prepayment option may happen only when the consumer realizes that there is considerable gain in doing so.

Van Deventer, Imai, and Mesler (2005, ch. 31–32) discuss the use of the transactions cost approach to irrational behavior in option exercise for consumers. The method is founded on the idea that consumers are rational but exercise their options subject to transactions costs. The transactions cost method to irrational consumer behavior was introduced in the context of analyzing prepayment behavior of collateralized mortgage transactions by McConnell and Singh (1994) and Stanton (1995). It attempts to estimate a cost of action or a cost of information.

We introduce a transaction cost tc such that the option is rationally exercised when in the money in terms of $Q = K + tc$ where K is the original strike price. Now, considering a large pool of consumers we may denote the density of Q by f_Q and set, for example,

$$f_Q(\alpha, \beta) = \frac{\frac{1}{\beta} \exp\left(-\frac{(Q-\alpha)}{\beta}\right)}{\left[1 + \exp\left(-\frac{(Q-\alpha)}{\beta}\right)\right]^2}, \quad -\infty < Q, \alpha < +\infty, \beta > 0$$

where $f_Q(\alpha, \beta)$ is the generalized logistic distribution. The parameters of $f_Q(\alpha, \beta)$ can be estimated by the method of maximum likelihood such that for representative consumer i the probability of exercise at $Q = q$ can be found. Of course for a fully rational consumer the cumulative density, F_Q, is degenerate with $F_Q = 0$ if $Q \le K$ and $F_Q = 1$ if $Q > K$.

To estimate the exercise probabilities for a pool of consumers we proceed on a basis similar to that used to assess credit risk with statistical scoring models. Here the risk factors include idiosyncratic behavioral variables as well as the common interest rates factors (market rates, loan rates, deposit rates) that trigger the action of the customers to, for example, prepay or renegotiate their mortgage or to reconsider the amount deposited as well as its allocation.

The approach taken above to model consumer embedded options in the financial engineering framework introduces a so-called subjective strike model—capturing the fact that consumers have transactions costs for exercising their options. In the subjective strike model the embedded option strike is adjusted by the consumer's transactions costs leading to a higher strike value and hence a larger gain in the value of refinancing or fund withdrawal is required for most consumers to act. In this consumer adjustment to the financial engineering model the transaction costs represent the sensitivity of consumers to exercise their options and these sensitivities are derived from historical data analysis on classifications of consumers based on, for example, product type, region, age, and income.[10]

For prepayments we can formulate the subjective strike model as borrowers refinance as soon as the present value of the loan is above the notional adjusted by the transactions cost. In this setting a loan has not been refinanced if the present value has not exceeded the notional adjusted by the transactions cost. Moreover, a refinancing occurs if and only if it is the first time that the present value of the loan exceeds the notional adjusted by the borrower's transactions cost. Note that this path dependency captures the phenomenon of burnout in prepayments, that is, that pools of loans that have already experienced large exposure to refinancing opportunities tend to have lower prepayment rates, other things being equal. This is because borrowers that are sensitive to refinancing opportunities prepay rapidly as soon as it is profitable. After a period of low refinancing rates, only the least sensitive borrowers still remain in the pool and prepayment rates decay. Formulated in terms of the transactions cost approach this means that after the borrowers with low transactions cost have already left the pool only the borrowers with high transactions costs remain.

---

[10] When estimating transactions costs on historical data there is generally a truncation effect in that for some consumers the gain in exercising was never high enough versus their transactions cost and hence their true transactions cost may not have been observed.

While the financial engineering approach to valuation of consumer embedded options has several drawbacks, such as the difficulty to estimate consumer transactions cost and option implied parameters such as volatility, it also has several advantages. Specifically, one of the main advantages with analyzing customer behavior in the context of rational no-arbitrage pricing is that the usual hedge techniques applied by fixed income traders are applicable. Indeed, a consequence of replacing the rational strike price with the estimated irrational strike price is that, from the perspective of the fixed income trader, the implicit option embedded bonds held by customers may be analyzed and hedged as any fixed income portfolio with embedded options. Also, the approach allows for an idiosyncratic valuation of customer optionality.

Statistical Model Approach to Valuation of Embedded Options In a statistical model or scenario-based approaches to valuation of consumer options the consumer behavior is described using the model and the cash flows of the contract are evaluated under the model. In contrast to the financial engineering approach, which may allow idiosyncratic valuation, these statistical models rely on large pools and the notion of the law of large numbers to derive behavioral statistics. Traditionally two types of statistical models have been used. These are prepayment models and volume models for deposits and facilities.

Prepayment models specify the prepayment rate of a pool of loans conditional on pool characteristics such as loan age, product type, and the refinancing incentive. In the model it is beneficial to prepay if it is cheaper to refinance a new loan. Hence, prepayment should be expected when offered loan rates drop below the paying rate. However, just as in the case of the financial engineering approach all borrowers don't refinance even if it would be beneficial for them and hence the prepayment rate is not discrete 0% or 100% but rather increases smoothly with the spread between the paying rate and the current refinancing rate. Sometimes the simple conditional prepayment rate (CPR) model is used. It specifies a deterministic rate of prepayment or a term-structure of deterministic prepayment rates. The term-structure of prepayment rates captures the burnout effect in prepayment. However, more complex stochastic models with explanatory variables such as current market rates driving prepayment decisions are needed to capture the prepayment incentive.

Similar to prepayment models, deposit volume models aim to capture the consumer's decisions to withdraw and place funds in the bank account. The willingness to withdraw funds is expected to increase with the increased relative performance of other funds (e.g., equity) and other bank accounts. As for prepayment all consumers typically don't withdraw all funds and place in alternative fund sources even if it would be beneficial to them.

As for prepayment models the models used to describe deposit volume can be stochastic or deterministic. Commonly used stochastic models include regression models with logarithmic volume change being explained by key variables, for example, interest rates, GDP, and seasonal terms as explanatory factors. A frequently used deterministic model is the core and con-core deposit model, which specifies a portfolio runoff amortization scenario for the core part. See Dev and Rao (2006, ch. 8).

Approaches to valuation and cash flow generation for deposits have been extensively studied in the literature. For example, see Selvaggio (1996) and Jarrow and Van Deventer (1998). In these approaches the value of the deposit funding increases with the spread between the funding rate, r_f, and the deposit rate, r_d, volume, V, and time, t. For example, Jarrow and Van Deventer (1998) specify the deposit present value, $PV(T)$, on a time interval $[0, T]$ as

$$PV(T, d) = \int_0^T V(t, d)[r_f(t, d) - r_d(t, d)]\widetilde{D}(t, d)$$

where $\tilde{D}$ is a discount factor and d is a particular scenario realization of the rates and the deposit volume. Taking an expectation over $d = 1, \ldots, D$ scenario realizations,

$$PV(T) = E\{PV(T, d)\}.$$

In this model, the value of the deposit increases with the spread, $r_f(t, d) - r_d(t, d)$, the deposit volume, V, and the deposit time, $[0, T]$.

Deposits traditionally represent a large part of the bank's liabilities. Small changes in volumes can give quite large changes in funding costs and interest income. Since the valuation of deposits is critically depending on the duration and many deposits are demand deposits with no assigned maturity, it is important to try and understand the effective duration of deposits. Moreover, to talk about the risk-adjusted returns for deposits we must understand their duration.

Having specified a model for the prepayment rate or the deposit volume, the next step is to evaluate the cash flows under the model. The funds transfer adjustment with a model is similar to an OAS approach using the present value without the model and the (expected) present value with the model.

For example, in a simple CPR model for prepayments there is a single accelerated loan cash flow assumption, while a stochastic model would produce many cash flow paths and hence many present value estimates from which an expectation can be taken. The prepayment OAS represents an adjustment for the expected contractual interest income loss which can be measured from the loss in present value due to the prepayment. Prepayment can also be viewed as a reinvestment risk in the sense that when prepayments tend to occur they can only be reinvested at the current lower market rates. When the prepayment model is used for products with quoted market prices such as mortgage backed securities one can solve (with a given prepayment model) for the internal rate of return that gives the quoted price. The OAS is the shift in discount rates that are needed to arrive at a specified price. Because prepayment rates generally rise when interest rates go down due to the prepayment incentive (which means market price increases) mortgage backed securities are in general negatively convex.

When the deposit model is deterministic, or equivalently, one uses only a single plausible scenario d for the volume, we can incorporate the adjustment in the base funds transfer rate. This is because of the associated deterministic cash flow adjustment. Specifically, in this approach the funds transfer rate under a specific scenario d is calculated as the usual FTP in equation (7.2) (but conditional on the scenario d for e.g., the deposit volume) and is denoted FTP(d). We can now extend the funds transfer price in equation (7.4) to also incorporate scenario or deterministic model adjustments, yielding

$$\overline{\text{FTP}}(d) = \text{FTP}(d) \times (1 - w) + \text{E} \times w + \text{EL} + \text{OAS}. \tag{7.5}$$

Example Non-Maturity Deposit Volume Scenario Table 7.7 calculates the funds transfer rate, FTP(d), for a non-maturity deposit with an associated scenario d volume schedule as well as a rule for the administered deposit rate. The administration rule for the deposit rate assigns a deposit rate for different market rate intervals. This rule reflects the fact that deposit rates are "sticky" and do not change with small changes in market rates. The deposit volume schedule, expressed as a factor on the current volume, and the administrative rule for the deposit rate are given in Tables 7.8 and 7.9, respectively. The deposit is repriced quarterly and interest is paid semiannually based on an underlying reference market rate and the administrative rules. We assume that the funding curve in Table 7.2 is used as the underlying market reference rate. Because of the deposit runoff scenario d in Table 7.8 the deposit is completely withdrawn after 11 years.

TABLE 7.7 Funds Transfer Rate for a Deposit with a Scenario for the Volume

Interest frequency	Current volume	FTP (d) (%)
Semiannual	85,432,890	2.615

TABLE 7.8 Deposit Volume Scenario Used to Calculate Deposit Funds Transfer Rate. The Deposit Volume Factor Acts as a Multiplier on the Current Volume

Term	Deposit volume factor
0,5 Year	1.1
1 Year	1.2
3 Years	1.2
5 Years	1.3
10 Years	1.3
11 Years	0

TABLE 7.9 Administrative Rate Rules for the Deposit

Market rate (%)	Administrative deposit rate (%)
<1	0
<3	1
<5	3
<7	4
<10	6
<15	9
Otherwise	9

Using the deposit volume schedule scenario d and the rule for the administered deposit rate, we can generate future deposit cash flows and subsequently use equation (7.2) to generate the scenario funds transfer price, FTP(d), in equation (7.5), which is displayed in Table 7.7.

Liquidity Risk

The pricing of liquidity risk cost and benefits onto firm's assets and liabilities through funds transfer pricing is not as widespread as the pricing of, for example, asset credit risk. However, just like firms are currently pricing expected credit losses and the opportunity cost of capital, liquidity pricing should be instituted in a way that rewards providers of liquidity and penalizes its users.

The liquidity pricing methodology can be decomposed into two distinct components:

1. Mismatch or funding liquidity cost
2. Contingency liquidity costs, that is, the cost of holding standby liquidity

We will consider each of these components next.

TABLE 7.10 Term Liquidity Spreads

Term	Term liquidity spread (bps)
1 Year	0
2 Years	13
3 Years	27
4 Years	35
5 Years	40

Pricing Mismatch Liquidity Risk The pricing of mismatch or funding liquidity cost, through a term liquidity charge applied to long-term illiquid loans as well as a liquidity credit applied for long-term stable funding such as core deposits, is relatively well developed. Such a term spread is used in firms' funds transfer pricing and provides relative incentives to business units to acquire shorter term loans and longer term stable funding. In the pricing of the expected structural liquidity mismatch costs and premiums there are two steps:

1. First, the firm measures its term structure of funding liquidity costs by swapping fixed funding costs into floating and observing the resultant spread for the given term.
2. Second, the liquidity spread is applied to the base rate in discounting of cash flows, either as consumer (adding spread to base rate) or supplier (subtracting spread from base rate).

Table 7.10 illustrates term liquidity spreads in basis points. For example, a 5-year loan with annual cash flows will, for valuation purposes, be charged with the term liquidity spread at each annual cash flow to account for the term liquidity locked in with the cash flow.

To convert the term liquidity spread assigned to cash flows such as in Table 7.10 to an FTP spread component we can use the OAS methodology. Denote therefore the value of an asset or liability, with cash flows discounted by the base funding rate, as V_0. Similarly, denote the value of the same asset or liability valued with cash flows discounted by the base funding rate and the mismatch term liquidity spread as V_1. We can now solve for the single implied liquidity mismatch spread by solving for the single implied spread, δ, that if added on top of the base funding rate in V_0 for all terms would yield value V_1. In the bank's funds transfer pricing system δ is added to the asset or liability matched maturity funds transfer price.

With credit, capital, embedded optionality, and term liquidity costs we can extend the FTP equation (7.5) as

$$\overline{\text{FTP}}(d) = \text{FTP}(d) \times (1 - w) + \text{E} \times w + \text{EL} + \text{OAS} + \delta.$$

This practice of including expected liquidity mismatch costs and benefits in firms (funds transfer) pricing is equivalent to the practice of including expected loss from, for example, credit risk. Since the liquidity mismatch spread is logically a charge or credit for expected mismatch we can also subsume δ into a new expected loss component, $\widetilde{\text{EL}}$, such that

$$\overline{\text{FTP}}(d) = \text{FTP}(d) \times (1 - w) + \text{E} \times w + \widetilde{\text{EL}} + \text{OAS}. \qquad (7.6)$$

Hence, the $\widetilde{\text{EL}}$ component can now consist of contributions from multiple risks such as:

- Expected credit loss adjustments
- Expected liquidity mismatch adjustments
- Expected operational risk costs

Again, the liquidity mismatch contribution can be both positive or negative depending on whether it is a charge or a credit for liquidity.

When pricing mismatch liquidity risk into products with unknown cash flows such as credit facilities and non-maturing deposits the expected future balance is frequently used to generate cash flows. This is because accounting for the costs of mismatch liquidity risk is concerned with the structural, expected mismatch of the balance sheet rather than the unexpected mismatch. As a fair approximation to the expected cash flow over all scenarios we can replace FTP by FTP(d) as in equation (7.5).

Example of Liquidity Mismatch for a Facility We consider a facility with a core (expected) usage of the facility being a constant drawdown of 25% until maturity. We can hence simply obtain FTP(d) as the funding rate at maturity since the facility behaves like a bullet loan in the scenario. Since there is only a single cash flow at maturity for the facility there is also no numerical solve routine needed to find the single implied liquidity mismatch spread rate. In particular, if the funding liquidity spread, at the maturity term of the facility, is 40 basis points, then $\delta = 40 \times 0.25 = 10$ basis points. That is, the facility is allocated an expected liquidity mismatch funding spread of 10 basis points.

Why Charge a Spread for Liquidity Mismatch? To understand the importance of a bank pricing mismatch liquidity risk into its liability products as well as into its asset products consider the choices a bank faces when funding in the market. A bank can get long-term funding in two ways:

1. Fund directly at long term maturity.
2. Take short-term funding (say overnight) and roll it over to the long term.

The market charges an implicit liquidity premium for funding through option 1. That is, long-term funding is, ceteris paribus, more expensive. This is because it has no rollover uncertainty (e.g., short-term funding may not roll over in a liquidity crisis). Clearly, on a cost basis banks then prefer to roll over short-term funding and not pay the inherent liquidity premium. Therefore, to create the correct incentives, FTP should reward long-term funding when we discount its value as it has less short-term liquidity risk.

Pricing Contingency Liquidity Risk While liabilities do not have to bear capital the uncertainty about the behavior of non-contractual liabilities such as deposits and the possibility to roll over short-term unsecured and secured market funding is the largest reason for a firm to hold a contingency liquidity buffer. The opportunity costs of holding contingency liquidity need to be priced accordingly.

For pricing contingency liquidity costs and benefits one expects to follow a similar approach to capital-based risks in the sense that the opportunity cost of maintaining the liquid hedging portfolio to cover unexpected contingency liquidity needs to be priced onto the consuming assets and liabilities. Moreover, assets and liabilities that have positive, unexpected contingency liquidity contributions should be rewarded.

We denote the contingency liquidity spread by

$$CLS = \Delta \times O$$

where Δ is the allocated unexpected contingency liquidity need and O is the opportunity cost of funding the liquidity need. This now extends the funds transfer price in equation (7.6) as

$$\overline{FTP}(d) = FTP(d) \times (1 - w) + E \times w + \widetilde{EL} + OAS + CLS.$$

As a concrete example, if a facility has an unused portion of 90%, and in the unexpected liquidity crisis situation there is a drawdown of 50% of the unused portion, then $\Delta = 45\%$ and $CLS = 45\% \times O$. Of course, the exact opportunity cost, O, depends on the bank's actual composition of the contingency liquidity portfolio and its associated execution cost to raise the funds in case of the drawdown. Cash equivalent assets in the liquidity hedging portfolio carry a high opportunity cost but have no or very low execution costs when needed to create liquidity.

It is important to understand that the concept of pricing the costs of holding liquidity contingency is based on severely stressed liquidity scenarios rather than expected structural liquidity mismatches. Indeed, the definition of the size and composition of the liquidity buffer is itself based on survival in extreme liquidity stress scenarios that generate stressed cash outflows. To define the stressed funding need of the liquidity buffer the bank can take a compliance regulatory scenario approach (i.e., use Basel III prescribed scenarios for liquidity coverage ratio). Alternatively, the bank can use (a set of) internal economic scenario(s) for the definition of the liquidity buffer. As we have discussed in the previous chapter on liquidity risk the regulatory LCR calculation for a bank has regulatory prescribed facility drawdown and deposit withdrawal rates under stress—based on features such as account characteristic and counterparty. Assuming there is no natural hedge for these stressed outflows the bank needs to hold a stock of high-quality liquid assets (adjusted for haircuts) to compensate for the stressed outflows. Holding the stock of assets carries an opportunity cost as the alternative would be investment in the business. Hence, the final liquidity contingency cost depends both on the bank's opportunity cost as well as specific balance sheet composition. The regulatory NSFR, which measures long-term liquidity stability of the balance sheet, is of course more connected to the liquidity mismatch spread, which rewards long-term stable liabilities.

In the calculation of the contingency liquidity risk spread, CLS, we can allocate contingency liquidity at the bottom-up facility level, or at a top-down portfolio level for a liquidity risk stress scenario. Specifically, Δ can be based on a standalone calculation per facility and deposit or its contribution. If the contingency liquidity need is allocated bottom-up, there is a potential inconsistency between bottom-up allocated contingency liquidity and firm-level estimated need for contingency liquidity. While natural hedges for contingency liquidity are harder to find than for market risk business units should, through the funds transfer pricing program, be allocated their contribution to the firm-level need for contingency liquidity. The Cash Liquidity at Risk measure, discussed in the liquidity risk chapter, with its allocation properties gives opportunity to allocate the liquidity contingency need top down, taking into account portfolio hedging effects, as is best practice for market and credit risk. Even if a regulatory definition is used to define the liquidity buffer, the bank still needs a model to distribute the liquidity buffer contributions to the assets and liabilities. Hence, in contrast to Basel banking book credit risk capital risk weighted assets as in equation (4.40) (which sum to total risk weighted assets), the bank needs its own model for distribution of liquidity contingency costs.

Note that since contingency liquidity costs stem from the opportunity cost of holding counterbalancing capacity a bank that holds a cost-efficient (optimal) counterbalancing capacity is capable of offering a more competitive market price on, for example, facilities and deposits. Clearly, holding excessive counterbalancing capacity buffers impacts the bank's profitability and the competitiveness of the bank. However, there is also complexity in measuring opportunity costs of the counterbalancing capacity. As we have discussed before there is a trade-off in the choice of counterbalancing capacity portfolio. Cash has high opportunity cost when not needed, but, when needed to create liquidity it has no liquidity execution costs. High-yield bonds may have low opportunity cost when not needed but may be very costly when needed to create liquidity. Liquidity hedging optimization, which we have discussed extensively in the liquidity risk chapter, should hence be a core function in banks. It is as important as managing capital.

Finally, a bit simplified, we can say that credit risk capital is held for on–balance-sheet asset items such as loans and facility drawn amounts. The capital cost is the opportunity cost of the capital base. Counterbalancing capacity is held for both assets and liabilities with a focus on potential future commitments such as a significant further draw on a facility in case of liquidity distress.

FUNDS TRANSFER RATE AND RISK ADJUSTED RETURNS

Focusing on the branch profitability measurement with FTP spreads—in evaluation of the ex-ante performance of an asset or liability—the funds transfer price serves as an estimate of the expected costs associated with the asset or liability. Hence, the funds transfer price is closely related to the contribution margin calculated in business economics. That is, the consumer paying rate minus the funds transfer price can be referred to as a contribution margin. In this context the contribution margin is often referred to as the economic value added. There is typically also one significant difference between the classical contribution margin concept as used in business economics and the economic value. Specifically, the economic value concept based on funds transfer price is an expected margin and is in general true only ex-ante. It is therefore important to consider the potential deviation of the economic value ex-post. As the ex-ante estimate is an expectation of risk losses it can often be more accurately assessed on large pools of assets or liabilities. One example is credit risk expected loss, which can be more accurately modeled on pools of similar loans.

The economic value added (EVA), for paying rate R,

$$EVA = R - \overline{FTP}$$

should generally be positive for an asset or liability to be expected to contribute to the bank's profitability. However, it is also the case that one wants to rank different EVAs based on their risk. In general, for two assets with the same EVA one prefers to acquire the asset with the less risk or capital (contribution). The concept of risk-adjusted return on capital (RAROC) compares the EVA to the capital (contribution) for a certain asset and ranks the assets accordingly. Specifically,

$$RAROC = \frac{EVA}{w} = \frac{R - \overline{FTP}}{w}$$

where w is the allocated capital. Noticeable is that many banks define a threshold for RAROC that every new asset's RAROC is expected to be above. The threshold is usually defined so that it is consistent with the equity holders' expected returns on the bank stock. In this case, any asset with a RAROC higher than the bank threshold contributes positively to meeting investor's expected returns.

Example of Mortgage Risk Adjusted Returns

Table 7.11 displays the economic value added and the 1-year RAROC of the credit-risky mortgage in Table 7.1. The 1-year RAROC is obtained by dividing the economic value by the capital allocated at 1-year horizon in Table 7.4. The average customer paying rate is assumed

TABLE 7.11   Economic Value and RAROC for the Credit-Risky Mortgage in Table 3

FTP (%)	Customer rate (%)	Economic value added (EVA)	RAROC
4.929	5.5	0.0057	5.707

to be 5.5%.[11] Based on the average customer paying rate and the funds transfer rate we can conclude that the mortgage is making a positive value contribution.

PROFITABILITY MEASURES AND DECOMPOSITIONS

With synthetic funds transfer instruments the bank's profit and loss is essentially split up in the branches net interest margin and the residual profit and loss portfolio of treasury. We represented this portfolio split in equation (7.1) as

$$P = (A1 - B) + (B - A2) \tag{7.7}$$

with $A1$ an asset, B the synthetic funds transfer liability, and $A2$ the actual treasury funding. Of course, if $A1$ is a liability such as a deposit, then the synthetic funds transfer instrument B is an asset.

For most banks there is structural interest rate risk and liquidity risk arising in the residual portfolio due to the fact that customers in general want both long-term loans and quick access to the deposits they made. The management of the interest-rate risk in the residual portfolio of long and short holdings is made more difficult than the management of a traditional bond portfolio due to embedded options on the customer side. As discussed previously, banking books contain numerous implicit options, such as early withdrawal options, options to transfer from less to more profitable accounts, prepayment options on mortgages, borrowing options, and so on. As any of these options are, to some extent, exercised in response to interest rate changes (market or administered rates), they induce nonlinear interest rate risk.

Balance Sheet Breakdown with Funds Transfer Instruments

The breakdown of the balance sheet that funds transfer instruments create with equation (7.7) is illustrated in Figure 7.2. Consistent with the notation in equation (7.7), Figure 7.2 denotes the branch customer leg of the transaction by $A1$ and the Treasury market funding leg by $A2$. Similarly, the synthetic FTP leg of the transaction is the B leg. Viewed standalone, both the branches and the Treasury funding have synthetic FTP B legs to create matched balance sheets on that level. Specifically, the matched balance sheet on the branches is the $A1 - B$ leg for assets and for the treasury the matched balance sheet is $B - A2$. In Figure 7.2 we also break down further the FTP B leg into its different risk-based components that we have discussed in this chapter. Specifically, this includes:

- Interest rate matched maturity funding costs
- Expected credit and (for example) operational costs

---

[11]Our example mortgage is an annuity and does not have a fixed interest rate. Based on the annuity payment calculations we can compute an average rate.

Actual assets vs. Actual liabilities

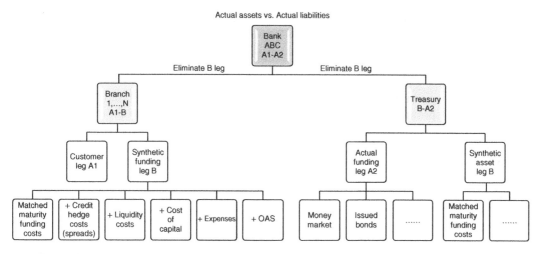

FIGURE 7.2 FTP Breakdown of the Balance Sheet

- Expenses
- Cost of capital
- Embedded optionality costs such as option adjusted spreads
- Mismatch and contingency liquidity costs

With this breakdown of the synthetic FTP *B* leg, branches' profitability and solvency can be measured on multitier levels using the components. For example, a loan or a whole branch may be profitable as long as credit cost components are not allocated while turning unprofitable if they are allocated. Note that profitability of the customer *A*1 legs minus the synthetic FTP *B* legs are summable across, for example, loans to branch or all branches in a region. In this structure the profitability of the treasury is also measured distinct from the branches profitability as the synthetic FTP assets minus the actual funding legs. That is, *B* − *A*2. We have hence created separate performance measurement units with the balance sheet breakdown in Figure 7.2 providing the foundation for the bank to analyze its profitability and solvency more granularly than on aggregate firmwide basis.

As we roll up the balance sheet to consider the profitability and solvency on the bank level, we eliminate the synthetic FTP *B* legs—obtaining actual assets versus actual liabilities at the aggregate level. This elimination is also illustrated in Figure 7.2.

Application to Net Interest Income and Economic Value View

On the aggregate bank level the net interest income analysis projects the interest income of the bank's assets and liabilities under various interest rate and other market scenarios to create a firmwide view of net interest income impact from the scenarios. Since most banks have significant amounts of short-term funding, there would be an artificial asymmetry in future interest flows from assets and liabilities if short-term funding is not rolled over. In addition to rollover assumptions to create a future matched balance sheet, it is also common to assume historical portfolio growth rates over the term of the net interest income projection.

A distinct difference between net interest margin profitability scenarios and liquidity scenarios is that profitability scenarios are in general focused on relatively modest market changes and that customers behave largely "as usual." This is in sharp contrast to liquidity risk, as we have discussed in the previous chapter, which focuses on already extreme events and the associated extreme customer behavior.

FTP is an important component in a bank's net interest margin profitability analysis. This is because when profitability is assessed on the branch level it is based on the customer leg $A1$ minus the FTP synthetic funding B issued. When profitability focuses on current rate spreads banks calculate economic values and risk adjusted returns as we did in Table 7.11 for the sample mortgage. When profitability focuses on the potential future stream of net interest income rather than current rate spreads the net interest income is measured as the interest income from the customer $A1$ leg minus the synthetic FTP B leg. The interest flow on the synthetic transfer instrument is the FTP rate where all relevant risk components and business expenses have been taken into account.

Example Net Interest Margin Profitability Analysis with FTP   To illustrate how FTP is used in practice for loan-level net interest margin profitability analysis we use a mortgage example. The mortgage example we use is similar to the example mortgage in Table 7.1 in that it has 5.5 years to maturity and a principal of 100,000 units of currency. We also use exactly the same FTP parameters for this mortgage, such as funding costs, credit spreads, and capital. That is, we use the expected loss curve, the allocated capital curve, and the curve for cost of equity funding in Table 7.4. These are the only FTP risk costs we use for the loan and hence we assume no business expenses and that the loan has no embedded optionality charge, that is, no prepayment features. In addition, the mismatch liquidity spread is assumed to be immaterial and as the loan has no prepayment feature that could potentially impact contingency liquidity risk positively its contribution to contingency liquidity risk is also null.

The current mortgage pays floating interest and fixed capital every 6 months with the next payment assumed to be immediate.[12] The mortgage floating rate payment uses the funding curve in Table 7.2. We also assume that the bank has put a fixed 1% spread on the floating rate at future repricing times and that the capital payments are fixed at 9,000 units of currency. This means that the last capital payment is a residual payment with the regular 9,000 in capital plus the 1,000 residual payment left.

Table 7.12 displays, similarly to Table 7.3 for the annuity mortgage, the fixed capital payment mortgage FTP rates. Table 7.13 displays the interest and capital flows as well as the net interest margin (NIM) versus the synthetic FTP instrument. The notation for the different NIM legs is following the same principle as for FTP in Table 7.12. We note from Table 7.13 that the mortgage $\underline{\text{NIM}}$ is positive, that is, profitable as long as we do not include the mortgage expected loss in $\overline{\text{NIM}}_{EL}$. Clearly, the 1% spread used by the bank on this mortgage is not sufficient given its expected loss. Consequently, the NIM with both expected loss and capital cost, $\overline{\text{NIM}}$, is also unprofitable for this mortgage. The contribution of this mortgage to the branch profitability is hence negative. In order to make the mortgage profitable the bank has to increase the current 1% spread policy on the mortgage. For illustration, Figure 7.3 also displays the different net interest income legs for the mortgage graphically.

---

[12]This is different from the previous mortgage example in Table 7.1, which is an annuity. We avoid using an annuity example in this context for simplicity because for annuities there can be differences in capital flows between the mortgage and its synthetic FTP instrument due to the different interest rates.

TABLE 7.12 Funds Transfer Pricing for the Mortgage Example with Fixed Capital Payments

FTP (%)	$\overline{FTP}_C$ (%)	$\overline{FTP}_{EL}$ (%)	$\overline{FTP}$ (%)
2.467	2.486	4.595	4.615

TABLE 7.13 Sample Mortgage Interest and Capital Flow as Well as Net Interest Margin Relative to Synthetic FTP Legs

Cash flow time	Interest	Capital	NIM	$\overline{NIM}_C$	$\overline{NIM}_{EL}$	$\overline{NIM}$
0 years	2,269.2	9,000	1,024.94	1,014.87	−60.89	−71.07
0.5 years	1,717.03	9,000	461.16	452.03	−523.02	−532.25
1 year	1,729.27	9,000	418.74	410.45	−474.93	−483.3
1.5 years	1,684.55	9,000	371.47	364.12	−421.3	−428.73
2 years	1,571.48	9,000	327.93	321.44	−371.93	−378.49
3 years	1,450.27	9,000	282.32	276.73	−320.2	−325.84
3.5 years	1,267.77	9,000	236.39	231.71	−268.11	−272.84
4 years	1,074.34	9,000	189.38	185.63	−214.78	−218.57
4.5 years	825.13	9,000	144.16	141.3	−163.5	−166.38
5 years	582.06	9,000	97.4	95.47	−110.46	−112.41
5.5 years	298.63	10,000	62.23	60.24	−73.71	−75.76

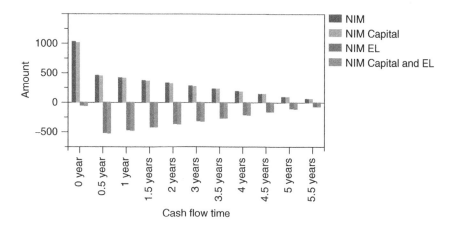

FIGURE 7.3 Sample Mortgage Net Interest Margin Relative to Synthetic FTP Legs

The net interest income measure holds the projected future profit and loss flows. These flows are also the basis for an economic value view that looks at the long-term solvency of the balance sheet. In this FTP context we can obtain a solvency view on account level. To obtain this for our example mortgage we just need to sum the discounted value of the different NIM legs in Table 7.13. Clearly, doing this the mortgage economic value contribution to the portfolio is negative when expected losses are taken into account as all the NIM components are negative for this case. We can interpret this as a negative equity situation for the mortgage as the value of equity is the residual value of the asset minus the liability.

BANKING BOOK FAIR VALUE WITH FUNDS TRANSFER RATES

Traded instruments like bonds have risk spreads embedded in the market quotes. The reader may recall from the portfolio credit risk chapter that we obtained the reduced form market credit spread in equation (4.1). Empirically, the market credit spread is significantly higher than empirical credit loss rates, suggesting that the market spread includes more than just credit risk, for example, liquidity risk and approximate capital costs associated with holding the position.

While the banking book items are not market traded, the FTP risk spreads are an attempt to capture all the risk costs associated with the position. Using the FTP rates in the fair discounting of account cash flows hence yields an internal model–based fair value for the banking book items. This approach to fair value is motivated since the FTP spreads represent the bank's best estimates of the risk spreads in absence of a market where spreads are embedded in the market quotes.

Example of Fair Values with FTP

Table 7.14 displays the fair values obtained, for the same sample mortgage we used for NIM and economic value above, using FTP discounting and the same breakdown of the fair value (FV) as in Table 7.12 for FTP. Using only the funding curve in discounting the fair value, FV, is above the principal value of 100,000 units of currency due to the 1% customer spread. However, when we add expected losses in discounting the fair value, $\overline{FV}_{EL}$, it is less than the principal value. This is also true when we have both expected losses and capital costs as in $\overline{FV}$.

To see how we can use the FTP fair value method for unearned profit and loss assignment in the banking book, we assume that at origination the fair value with all the risk costs for the mortgage, $\overline{FV}$, was exactly at principal value due to a lower expected lifetime credit loss and capital cost at origination. Since then, lifetime expected credit losses and capital costs, obtained from Table 7.4, have increased to much higher levels than at origination. This gives an unearned loss on the mortgage as $97,405 - 100,000 = -2,595$ units of currency. Assuming it is contractually and socially acceptable for the bank to increase the 1% customer spread at the next repricing they can increase the fair value and hence reduce the unearned loss.

A NOTE ON THE SCOPE OF FUNDS TRANSFER PRICING

The funds transfer price in general measures funding costs (assets) and funding benefits (liabilities). The matched maturity funding transfer price discussed here (and including risk spreads) is more amenable to banking book and buy-and-hold investment assets such as bonds. This is because their main source of profit and loss is net interest margins (over a funding cost).

TABLE 7.14   Fair Values for the Mortgage Example with Fixed Capital Payments

FV	$\overline{FV}_C$	$\overline{FV}_{EL}$	$\overline{FV}$
103,460	103,402	97,459	97,405

Many FTP risk spreads that are taken into account for banking book items such as cost of capital, expected loss, and so on are already priced by the market into investment assets such as bonds. This should be taken into consideration when FTP is used for (long-term) investments in market traded assets.

As a simple rule of thumb, one can consider the matched maturity funds transfer pricing discussed here as being appropriate for cases when net interest margin is the basis for profit and loss (buy-and-hold case). However, there are certainly portfolios where the profit-and-loss contributions are from both (short-term) net interest margin and mark to market. Hence, there is some ambiguity in reality.

The logical approach of FTP, to estimate funding costs and risk spreads, is used broadly for many financial instruments although the actual techniques may differ. For example, bilateral OTC derivatives such as floating rate agreements, swaps, and forwards estimate profit and loss using the net interest income from the legs as well as the discounted value of all net payments (mark to market). Adjustments for credit risk are through CVA as we have discussed in the chapter on counterparty credit risk. While in FTP up-front funding costs is the core many OTC derivatives such as swaps are unfunded. That is, they are entered into at zero cost with no funding needed. However, future funding requirements (to fund collateral posts) and funding benefits (received collateral from counterparty) are measured using FVA as we discussed in the counterparty credit risk chapter.

REGULATION AND PROFITABILITY ANALYSIS

In general, regulation is less prescriptive for profitability analysis and the core risks driving profitability in the banking book than regulation for market, credit, and liquidity risks. There are, however, areas where profitability analysis can be viewed, either directly or indirectly, as a core regulatory requirement. These include:

1. Funds transfer pricing requirements

    For example, Basel requirements instituted that developed credit risk models should be used in product approval and pricing as well as risk measurement. Consequently, banks use funds transfer pricing to price the credit risk explicitly onto credits as in equation (7.3). The credit risk capital is the available capital while the decomposition of capital to loan and customer levels can use an allocation scheme based on the regulatory risk weighted assets or the economic capital model. More recently, the Basel III liquidity risk requirements are instituting a necessary liquidity component in banks' funds transfer pricing as well. As we have already discussed in this chapter, Basel Committee (2008) specifies that banks should incorporate liquidity costs, benefits, and risks in the product pricing, performance measurement, and new product approval process for all significant business activities. CEBS (2010) also focuses on the need for firms to develop a sound practice of pricing liquidity risk.

2. Basel pillar 2 requirements

    Bank's profitability analysis and the interest rate risk assessment of the banking book is part of pillar 2 in Basel. Pillar 2 is based on four key principles:

    (i) Bank's own assessment of capital adequacy
    (ii) Supervisory review process
    (iii) Capital above regulatory minimum (established in pillar 1)
    (iv) Supervisory intervention

The principle of banks' own assessment of capital adequacy focuses on the need for banks to establish a sound internal capital adequacy assessment process (ICAAP). All material risks incurred by the bank should be part of the ICAAP process. Banking book interest rate risk is counted by regulators as a specific risk in pillar 2 that should bear capital and is hence part of the ICAAP process. The measure of interest rate risk in the banking book is traditionally referred to as the earnings at risk (EaR) and is a classical VaR measure. The EaR can be based on the net interest margin profit and loss under market interest rate scenarios or use a simplified repricing gap approach. Note that EaR can be more difficult to compute than market risk VaR. This is because the banking book contains numerous embedded optionalities that consumers may exercise at their discretion and the customer behavior may be impacted by the market scenarios. As we have discussed in this chapter there are two main model approaches to embedded optionality in the banking book. These are the (adjusted) financial engineering approach and the statistical model approach. Banks are also required to analyze the impact on profitability under standardized interest rate risk shocks.

While there are pillar 3 requirements on banks to disclose interest rate risk in banking book, the regulation is more principle based and there is no regulatory charge. Historically, there have been several bank failures due to interest rate risk, for example, the savings and loans crisis in the 1980s and 1990s in the United States, where banks' mismatch in the balance sheet created an exposure to sharply rising short-term funding rates. It is therefore surprising that regulators haven't yet instituted a specific charge for interest rate risk in the banking book. However, at the time of writing this book a Basel Committee Task Force on Interest Rate Risk (TFIR) is working on potential new regulatory measures for both interest rate risk in the banking book and the credit spread risk in the banking book using an economic fair value approach.

In this chapter we have discussed the importance of breaking down the net interest margin profitability analysis to granular levels. This is important for the bank's management to be able to take risk adjusted return–based decisions on where portfolio growth should be focused.

3. Firmwide stress testing

The relatively recent firmwide CCAR and EBA stress testing requires input from stressed net interest margin analysis. For example, CCAR focuses on the pre-provision net revenue (PPNR) stress testing. PPNR is the sum of three parts: net interest income, non-interest income, and non-interest expense. For most banks, PPNR is dominated by the net interest income from borrowing and lending. However, for banks with large trading operations there can be a significant contribution from net non-interest income. As we shall discuss in Chapter 9 on firmwide scenario analysis and stress testing one can use different approaches to obtain the banking book earnings and loss projections. One approach is to use the asset and liability management system for scenario-based interest income and expense projection, with no default risk component, and perform a separate credit loss projection from the credit system that is used to obtain a portfolio-level loss adjusted earnings. Alternatively, one can have an integrated model for interest income and default losses. This latter approach allows consistent loan-level estimation of cash flows, accruals, and losses as we have already discussed in the portfolio credit risk chapter in the context of the features of the new generation portfolio credit risk models (see Figure 4.28). The firmwide stress testing impact on the interest income and expense can come from:

(i) Higher general market funding rates and/or higher bank-specific funding spreads at the time of funding rollover, increasing interest expense
(ii) Reduced interest income due to non-performing assets (delinquencies and defaults)
(iii) Inability to roll over funding creating a cash liquidity need that must be emergency funded (likely at a loss)

In both CCAR and EBA the focus is on a stressed market impact (derived from the high-level regulatory macroeconomic scenario specification) on the net interest income, coming from (i) and (ii). It is assumed that the higher market funding rates can only partially be passed on to customers.[13] The potential liquidity impact from (iii) is currently not part of the scope.

We finally emphasize again that the breakdown of the net interest margin to granular levels discussed in this chapter may not be regulatory required but is key for risk-based decision making. Which customers and regions are more profitable? Where should portfolio growth be focused?

4. Fair values

Another regulatory application of funds transfer rates is fair value of banking book items using accounting standards. Since this book is about risk management rather than accounting we will not enter into a discussion about the accounting standards for financial reporting. However, the fair value based on funds transfer prices discussed in this chapter can be seen as an internal model approach to economic fair value and unearned profit and loss of the banking book.

---

[13] For example, when market rates go up the bank's rate policy for deposits (see example in Table 7.9) captures quickly the increase in market fund rates in the scenario while the corresponding rate policy for the loan's rates is more sluggish in the scenario, yielding an asymmetry in how fast (and by how much) market rate changes get passed on to asset versus liability side.

Firmwide Risk

Firmwide Risk Aggregation

Thus far we have developed risk management aspects into risk management at the individual (standalone) risk level, such as market risk, credit risk, and liquidity. While the individual silo risk management allows easy risk identification, measurement, and mitigation, recent global financial crises have proven the need for firmwide risk measurement, control, and decision making. Firmwide risk measurement requires ability to aggregate risk, identify risk concentrations and potential contagions among different risk sources, and accurately report and respond to the risk issues at the firmwide level.

Firmwide risk levels can be obtained in different ways. We will label two approaches according to Basel Committee (2010b):

1. Top-down approach
2. Bottom-up approach

The top-down approach to firmwide risk will be the focus in this chapter on firmwide risk aggregation while the next chapter on firmwide scenario analysis and stress testing will focus on the bottom-up approach to firmwide risk.

In the top-down approach we apply a correlated aggregation model to the results from the standalone risk analysis, for example, obtaining a firmwide risk measure like VaR. In the bottom-up approach we analyze standalone risk types based on the same scenarios from joint, correlated, market, and economic scenarios on financial risk factors. We then aggregate the results per scenario and subsequently obtain the firmwide risk measures from the joint distribution.

The key difference between the two approaches is where the risk aggregation takes place in the process. In the top-down approach, risk analyses within each silo risk system work independently to produce the risk measures based on the independent distributions resulting from the system. Risk aggregation is applied after the fact and the interaction between the risks is captured by a correlation or more advanced copula among the risk types. The benefit of this approach is of course that it uses existing risk systems for an independent end-to-end system.

Despite recent focus on firmwide risk analysis and stress testing using the bottom-up scenario approach, the top-down correlated aggregation approach to risk is still an important component in financial institutions enterprise risk measurement and management. This is because even if firmwide risk can be achieved for many risk types and lines of business using joint modeling (scenarios) of risk factors there may still be business lines and/or risk types that cannot be integrated bottom-up for many reasons, for example, a difficulty to specify granular risk factor–level dependence. Hence, in practice, firmwide risk measures are usually a combination of bottom-up risk approaches and a top-down risk aggregation approach. The risk types and lines of business that can be aggregated bottom-up become a marginal input source to the top-down risk aggregation approach. Aggregate enterprise risk can then be obtained at a second level—applying the top-down risk aggregation approach.

The combination of bottom-up and top-down approaches to enterprise risk measures is especially appealing for a mixed or hierarchical copula approach to risk aggregation that we will discuss below as an advancement of traditional copula approaches. This is because risks can be aggregated hierarchically, using different copulas, which gives more flexibility in designing the aggregation and using the best-fit models.

It is in principle also possible to include non-financial risks in a correlated aggregation approach to firmwide risk. For example, quantification of strategic and reputational risk is often modeled in a similar way to operational risk processes. That is, it is event and severity based. The events and their severity are usually assessed by expert views. The outcome is still a marginal loss distribution, and the assignment of event probabilities and correlations allows non-financial risks to be aggregated with other financial risks.

In this chapter we first discuss the traditional firmwide risk aggregation approaches including the linear and copula-based approaches as well as the more recent mixed copula approach. When the aggregated risk has been calculated the next step is to decompose the risks into contributing components, to perform a capital allocation taking into account diversification. Capital allocations are needed in risk adjusted returns analysis but also in measurement of concentration and diversification. We end the chapter with a discussion of regulation connected to firmwide risk aggregation.

CORRELATED AGGREGATION AND FIRMWIDE RISK LEVELS

Historically, institutions have implemented simple aggregation practices like aggregating risks by summation to achieve an overall risk measure. The simple summation of risks is also founded in the Basel II regulatory capital framework. Throughout the three generations of the Basel accord, the regulatory capital requirement is considered to be the sum of capital requirements calculated at the building block levels. However, the simple sum type aggregation has been challenged. Brockmann and Kalkbrener (2010) argue that the approach ignores the diversification effect across the portfolio, which was estimated to range from 10% to 30%. Basel Committee (2009e) also discussed the possibility of a compounding effect where summed up risk measurement actually underestimates the actual risk. This compounding effect can arise in practice, because, as we have discussed previously in the advanced market risk chapter, the sum of VaR for different risks is not necessarily an upper bound on the total risk.

To address the limitation of the simple sum method correlated aggregation methodologies can be used. For example, Kuritzkes, Schuermann, and Weiner (2002) consider a linear risk aggregation in financial conglomerates. Rosenberg and Schuermann (2004) study copula-based aggregation of bank-assurance market, credit, and operational risks using a comparison of the t- and normal copula. See also Dimakos and Aas (2004) and Cech (2006) for comparison of the properties of different copula models in risk aggregation. The main benefit of the copula approach to risk aggregation is that it provides a way of isolating the marginal behavior of individual risks from the description of their dependence structure.

Because of the long tradition of compartmentalized risk analysis the risk aggregation approach is practical for a quick implementation of firmwide risk measurement. The estimation of different sub-risk measures does not have to be based on an homogeneous methodology. The risk aggregation approach is convenient as it uses only high-level information about compartmentalized risks (e.g., empirical profit and losses or distribution specifications), and gross assumptions about dependence such as overall correlation between market and credit risks. Top-down risk aggregation is therefore also an important benchmark for bottom-up approaches that model the detailed interactions between different types of risk factors. Of course, the gross dependence assumption between risks is also a drawback of the method.

Linear Risk Aggregation

When the individual compartmental risks can be modeled by distributions in the elliptical family, tail risk measures such as VaR or CVaR can be modeled to take into account correlation effect when one aggregates the individual risks into total risk. For example, assuming the total risk is composed from n risk sources and can be modeled by an n-variate normal distribution with a correlation matrix, Σ, the standard deviation of the total risk, σ_p, can be written as

$$\sigma_p = \sqrt{\sum_{i=1}^{n} w_i^2 \sigma_i^2 + 2 \sum_{i=1}^{n} \sum_{j=1}^{n} w_i w_j \rho_{ij} \sigma_i \sigma_j}. \tag{8.1}$$

Here, ρ_{ij} denotes the correlation between risk type i and j, and σ_i is the standard deviation of risk type i.

The linear model for VaR risk aggregation takes the individual VaR risks as inputs and aggregates the risks using the standard formula for covariance. That is,

$$\text{VaR}(\alpha) = \sqrt{\sum_{i=1}^{n} [\text{VaR}(\alpha)_i]^2 + 2 \sum_{i=1}^{n} \sum_{j=1}^{n} \rho_{ij} [\text{VaR}(\alpha)_i][\text{VaR}(\alpha)_j]}$$

where α is the confidence level of the aggregate VaR. In this model there are two extreme cases. That is, the zero-correlation aggregate VaR,

$$\text{VaR}(\alpha) = \sqrt{\sum_{i=1}^{n} [\text{VaR}(\alpha)_i]^2}$$

and the perfect correlation VaR ($\rho_{ij} = 1$ for all i, j)

$$\text{VaR}(\alpha) = \sum_{i=1}^{n} [\text{VaR}(\alpha)_i].$$

More generally, the linear risk aggregation can be performed for economic capital measure, EC, such that for EC risks $\{EC_1, \ldots, EC_n\}$ we have

$$\text{EC}(\alpha) = \sqrt{\begin{pmatrix} \text{EC}_1(\alpha) \\ \cdots \\ \text{EC}_n(\alpha) \end{pmatrix}' \begin{pmatrix} 1 & \cdots & \rho_{n1} \\ \vdots & \ddots & \vdots \\ \rho_{n1} & \cdots & 1 \end{pmatrix} \begin{pmatrix} \text{EC}_1(\alpha) \\ \cdots \\ \text{EC}_n(\alpha) \end{pmatrix}}. \tag{8.2}$$

TABLE 8.1 Risk Aggregation Using the Linear Risk Aggregation Model

Sub-risks	Correlated risk	Independent risk	Additive risk	Contribution risk (%)
Market risk	250	250	250	11.89
Credit risk	312	312	312	12.37
Operational risk	119	119	119	3.03
Funding risk	345	345	345	11.31
Other risks	987	987	987	61.40
Aggregate risk	1,524.85	1,125.70	2,013	100

Example of Risk Aggregation with the Linear Model Table 8.1 displays an example risk aggregation using the linear aggregation model in equation (8.2). The example has 5 sub-risks:

1. Market risk
2. Credit risk
3. Operational risk
4. Funding risk
5. Other risks (e.g., business risks)

The sources for {EC...} in equation (8.2) are 250, 312, 119, 345, and 987 units of currency respectively.

The aggregate risk in Table 8.1 is obtained using the standalone sub-risks as well as a correlation matrix, Σ. The correlation matrix is given by

$$\Sigma = \begin{bmatrix} 1 & 0 & 0.25 & 0.25 & 0.75 \\ & 1 & 0.25 & 0.25 & 0.5 \\ & & 1 & 0.25 & 0.25 \\ & & & 1 & 0.25 \\ & & & & 1 \end{bmatrix}$$

where since correlation matrices are symmetric we only display the upper triangular part of the matrix.

Table 8.1 also displays the aggregate risk using independence and perfect correlation. The independent aggregate risk is obtained using zero correlations and the additive aggregate risk is obtained using correlations equal to unity. In the table we also calculate the actual contribution risk as a percentage of total risk. The contribution risk column is the actual Euler contribution from the sub-risks obtained in the context of the portfolio of total risks. As we have discussed previously in the context of market and credit risk this contribution risk is often compared with standalone risk to obtain a measure of the diversification level. For example, the market risk sub-risk has a standalone risk share of 16.3%, whereas the contribution risk share is 11.89%. We therefore obtain a diversification index for market risk in the context of firmwide risk as approximately 73%.

It is important to note that the above linear risk aggregation assumes elliptic distributions and that in general the additive risk measure using linear aggregation may not be an upper bound on the aggregate risk. Still, the linear risk aggregation model is widely used in practice. It is also used in regulation. In Basel II pillar 1 market risk, credit risk and operational risk are independently assessed and then simply summed up, using a perfect correlation assumption.

The European insurance solvency II regulation approach to an integrated solvency risk measure is first to decompose each exposure into different risk module estimations and then apply linear aggregation, using regulatory correlation matrices, into an overall risk measurement.

Copula Aggregation

The linear risk aggregation is a simple and convenient model to work with. The only data required are the estimates of the sub-risks' economic capital and the correlation between the sub-risks. It also brings in diversification effects that a simple summation approach does not capture. However, the model has some serious drawbacks as we have discussed. We therefore consider a risk aggregation model based on copulas that avoids several of the linear aggregation assumptions. Specifically, we avoid

1. The assumption that quantile of the enterprise risk and the quantiles of the individual risks come from the same elliptic density family
2. The assumption that the dependence structure relies on correlations and multivariate normal based dependence

While linear risk aggregation only requires a risk measure from the sub-risks copula methods of aggregation depend on the whole distribution of the sub-risks. One of the main benefits of a copula is that it allows the original shape of the sub-risk distributions to be retained. Furthermore, the copula also allows for the specification of more general dependence models than the normal dependence model. Essentially, the copula approach provides a way of isolating the marginal behavior of individual risks from the description of their dependence structure.

As mentioned above, when aggregating risk using copulas, the full loss density of the sub-risks, as well as the choice of copula and copula parameter(s), is required. This is only marginally more information than is required for the linear aggregation model. Using a copula model for aggregation, additional correlation parameters may also be required (e.g., for the student t-copula we also require a degree of freedom parameter).

Example of Copula Aggregation

In Table 8.2 we calculate VaR and CVaR copula aggregations using the normal, t-copula, and normal mixture copula for a 99% confidence level. The risk aggregation using the normal mixture copula is evaluated using a bivariate mixture with parameterization $NMIX(p_1, p_2, x_1, x_2)$. Here, p_1 and p_2 are the probabilities of normal states 1 and 2 respectively and x_1, x_2 are the mixing coefficients. The individual risks are the same as in Table 8.1 but the individual profit-and-loss densities are assumed to come from distribution rather than only have a standalone risk measure input such as $\{EC_1, \ldots, EC_5\}$ in Table 8.1. In our example we assume a standard normal distribution for the sub-risks. However, the normality assumption is just for illustration and we could of course have used other parametric distribution assumptions or used empirical profit-and-loss distributions as input to the aggregation. The use of the standard normal profit-and-loss distribution for the sub-risks implies that the 99% VaR for each sub-risk is approximately 2.32 units of currency. In the aggregation we use the same correlation matrix as in Table 8.1.

Table 8.2 shows that the copula risk aggregation VaR and CVaR increase when a non-normal copula model, such as the t-copula or the normal mixture copula, is used for

TABLE 8.2 Copula Value at Risk and Expected Shortfall Risk Aggregation Using the Normal Copula, t-Copula, and the Normal Mixture Copula

Copula model	Aggregate VaR(99%)	Aggregate CVaR(99%)
Normal	7.74	8.7
$t(10)$	7.93	9.28
$t(5)$	8.16	9.67
NMIX$(0.9, 0.1, 1, 10)$	8.06	9.94
NMIX$(0.9, 0.1, 1, 400)$	8.91	10.82

aggregations. For the t-copula the aggregate risk generally increases the lower the degrees of freedom parameter and for the normal mixture copula the aggregate risk generally increases with the mixing coefficient as expected.

MIXED COPULA AGGREGATION

A drawback of regular copula aggregation models is that they use a common copula for all aggregation nodes. While regular copula-based aggregation allows for a mix of univariate distributions at the leaf level many applications also require aggregations for complex cross-classification levels, and each level may have a different best-fit copula to aggregate the values. Practically, a single n-dimensional copula that would reflect the actual dependencies between all the different individual risks $i = 1, \ldots, n$ may not be available.

Fortunately, the copula approach can be quite easily extended to the case of different copulas between different risks and at different levels of the hierarchical aggregation. This is because copula aggregation uses a simulation framework and the empirical simulated copula aggregation on any sub-level can be used as input into the next level of aggregation using another copula. Essentially, once a sub-level copula has been determined, the application of a higher level copula deploys the usual copula techniques for that particular level of aggregation. Because of its simplicity, yet general usability, of mixed copula aggregation Skoglund et al. (2013) focus on its application and benefits over traditional copula aggregation. See also Arbenza et al. (2012) and Bruneton (2011) for a theoretical view of copula-based mixed risk aggregation.

The mixed copula aggregation is essentially a step-by-step aggregation where one first aggregates together risks within disjoint subsets of the set of all the n individual risks. This mixed approach to copula specification allows aggregate risk to be specified with partial sums that are more easily understood and use different best-fit copulas for a subset. The hierarchical nature of risk aggregation is also important for dimension reduction. Since large hierarchical risk aggregation trees can be broken down to subsets of aggregation, copulas that are only feasible in lower dimensions can be used for subsets of the aggregation tree.

While mixed copula risk aggregation is appealing, it also has some potential deficiencies compared to a single copula aggregation. Specifically, since the full dependence between all individual risks may not be explicitly specified, the induced dependence in a mixed copula tree between unconnected individual risks decreases with the number of copula aggregation steps. Hence, diversification increases with the number of copula aggregation layers between unconnected individual risks. See Bruneton (2011).

Example of Mixed Copula Aggregation

We now illustrate mixed copula aggregation with a concrete example from Skoglund et al. (2013). Figure 8.1 displays a sample hierarchical tree structure for risk aggregation. In this structure there are three business units. Business unit 1 has sub-risks in the category of market, credit, and operational risk. Business unit 2 has sub-risks in the category of credit and asset and liability management (ALM) risk. Finally, business unit 3 has sub-risks operational and insurance risk. In addition, each of these sub-risks are allocated to sub-types. For example, for business unit 1 the market risk sub-risk has sub-types equity and foreign exchange risk. Similarly, the business unit 1 sub-type credit risk sub-risks are split on retail and small and medium-sized enterprise (SME) segment, and corporates and bond credit risk. In this risk aggregation structure, risk is measured on the sub-type level and hence for each sub-type there is available either a parametric profit-and-loss distribution or a sample of simulated profit-and-losses.

With mixed copula aggregation the copulas used to aggregate each sub-hierarchy can be different. For example, we could aggregate the business unit 1 market risks (equity and foreign exchange risk) using a *t*-copula with 5 degrees of freedom. Subsequently we could aggregate the business unit 1 market, credit, and operational risks with a Clayton copula, and finally we could aggregate the risk of business units 1, 2, and 3 using a normal copula. Such a mixed approach to copula aggregation is natural to work with as the types of dependencies are expected to be different across the different layers of the hierarchy.

For convenience, we introduce the hierarchy notation H_j where $j \in \{1, 2, 3\}$ corresponds to business units 1, 2, and 3, respectively. For the sub-risks we have $H_{j,k}$ where $k \in \{1, 2, 3\}$ if $j = 1$ and $k \in \{1, 2\}$ otherwise, and finally for the sub-types $H_{j,k,l}$ where $l \in \{1, 2\}$ or is missing.

Table 8.3 displays four different mixed copula risk aggregation specifications for the hierarchical tree in Figure 8.1 on the levels of $H_j, H_{j,k}$, and $H_{j,k,l}$. In the table we have calculated VaR using a 99% confidence level for the four different mixed copula model specifications on the hierarchies and using $100,000$ copula and marginal simulations on each aggregation level. The sample copulas used are the *t*, Clayton, and Frank copulas on the hierarchies. Of course, the *t*-copula with a high degrees-of-freedom parameter is essentially the normal copula. Since both the Clayton and Frank copulas display lower tail dependence ($\theta < 0$ for the Frank copula), they are natural copulas for risk aggregation since our main interest is in aggregating tail loss. In the mixed copula aggregation we use the *t*-copula for aggregating risk on the business unit level, that is, on hierarchy level H_j with correlations set to 0.25, 0.5, and 0.3 between business unit 1,2, 1,3, and 2,3 respectively. We also use a *t*-copula to aggregate the insurance risks, life and non-life, for hierarchy $H_{3,2}$. The correlation is set to 0.5 between the two insurance risks. On the remaining hierarchies, we use either a Frank copula or a Clayton copula. On a specific hierarchy we denote use of the *t*-copula and its degrees of freedom v as t(v), the Clayton, and Frank copula, respectively, with parameter θ as c(θ) and f(θ), respectively. In the application, the leaf-level marginal distributions are assumed to be from a standard normal distribution. However, this assumption is for convenience without loss of generality as other specifications of the marginal distributions can easily be used. The use of the standard normal profit-and-loss distribution for the leaf levels implies that the 99% VaR on each leaf level is approximately 2.32 units of currency.

Table 8.3 shows that aggregate risk, as measured by 99% VaR, increases as the degrees of freedom, v, for the *t*-copula is lowered. Similarly, the aggregate risk increases for higher θ for the Clayton copula, and lower θ for the Frank copula. When risk is measured as the 99% VaR we note that the aggregated risk on the hierarchies for the Clayton copula has a limited

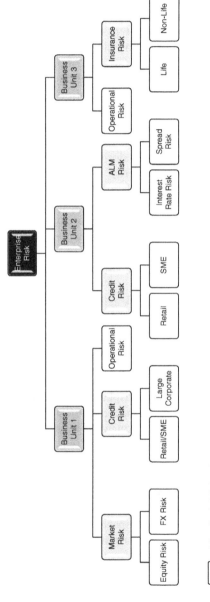

FIGURE 8.1 Sample Risk Aggregation Hierarchies

TABLE 8.3 Mixed Copula Value at Risk Using the *t*-Copula, the Frank Copula, or the Clayton Copula on the Different Hierarchies of the Sample Risk Aggregation

Model	H_j	$H_{1,k}$	$H_{1,1,l}$	$H_{1,2,l}$	$H_{2,k}$	$H_{2,1,l}$	$H_{2,2,l}$	$H_{3,k}$	$H_{3,2,l}$
				Copula aggregation model					
1	t(50)	c(1)	c(0.5)	c(0.3)	f(-1)	c(1)	c(0.5)	c(2)	t(50)
2	t(15)	c(3)	c(2)	c(1)	f(-3)	c(2)	c(1.5)	c(4)	t(10)
3	t(5)	c(8)	c(5)	c(4)	f(-8)	c(9)	c(7)	c(10)	t(3)
4	t(3)	c(15)	c(15)	c(15)	f(-15)	c(15)	c(15)	c(15)	t(3)
				Aggregation results VaR(99%)					
1	16.84	9.69	4.18	3.91	6.24	4.48	4.18	6.36	4.09
2	19.38	11.40	4.68	4.48	7.40	4.68	4.59	6.39	4.10
3	21.09	11.70	4.73	4.69	8.23	4.75	4.74	6.55	4.25
4	21.69	11.71	4.75	4.75	8.61	4.75	4.75	6.55	4.26

empirically relevant parameter range for the dependence parameter θ. In particular, as θ grows there is a rapidly decaying incremental dependence noted in the difference in the 99% VaR between models 3 and 4. We observe a similar situation for the Frank copula, although the empirically relevant range of θ for the Frank copula is greater than for the Clayton copula, as evidenced by the difference in aggregate risk on hierarchy $H_{2,k}$ for models 1–4.

Moving to a calculation of VaR at the 99.9% confidence level (not shown in Table 8.3) we obtain the aggregate risk at the top hierarchy, H_j, for mixed copula models 1–4, respectively, as 22.94, 26.78, 30.54, and 30.61. Even for this higher confidence level as the copula parameters θ and v increase (θ decrease for Frank copula), they have a diminishing effect on the risk. This trend continues when we further calculate VaR at the 99.99% confidence level.

CAPITAL ALLOCATION IN RISK AGGREGATION

One of the reasons why risk aggregation is useful at the enterprise level is for the management to understand the capital required by the entire bank. Answering the question how much capital is needed is of course a core requirement of the risk-based management. Having calculated aggregate risk using a method of risk aggregation, the next step is to allocate risks to the different sub-risks or business units. The risk allocation process helps the bank to understand the actual cost and measure the risk adjusted performance of the business.[1] This is the second important question about the capital, that is, if the capital is used efficiently.

In copula-based risk aggregation, the input for the sub-risks is the profits and losses or net income on the hierarchy. The calculation of risk contributions for top-down aggregation therefore follows the general methodology of calculation of Euler risk contributions that we have discussed in the advanced market risk chapter. However, when calculating risk contributions for multiple aggregation hierarchies in mixed copulas, the numerical additivity of the

[1] Recall that in the chapter on funds transfer pricing and profitability we used the allocated capital as the basis for risk adjusted profitability.

risk contributions only holds on the sub-risks to that hierarchy. This is because the mixed copula model decouples the aggregation into n partial sums and hence the numerical additivity of risk contributions from the copula simulations is only obtained for that partial copula. This is in contrast to a single copula approach where all leaf risks are joined together with a common copula yielding leaf-level risk contributions that by definition have risk contributions that numerically add up to total risk.

Within a mixed copula model we can still obtain a statistically consistent view on the decomposition of risk for each aggregation hierarchy. Specifically, using the sample aggregation hierarchy in Figure 8.1 we could calculate numerically additive risk contributions for equity risk and foreign exchange risk when aggregating market risk for business unit 1. We could subsequently calculate the numerically additive risk contribution of market risk, credit risk, and operational risk to business unit 1. While on the level of aggregating market, credit, and operational risk the copula marginal simulated risk for market risk may not be exactly retrieved as the aggregate market risk from the previous aggregation hierarchy—both measures should be statistically very close. The same reasoning holds when we calculate the numerically additive risk contributions to business units 1, 2, and 3 to the aggregate portfolio risk.

While not all risk contributions are numerically additive in a mixed copula simulation, the obtained hierarchical decomposition of risk contributions still contains all statistically relevant information on the contributions at all aggregation hierarchies. Hence, such numerical non-additivity is not of real concern in a mixed copula simulation and the lower level contributions can be simply rescaled to the risk contribution obtained from a copula simulation on a higher level of the hierarchy.

Example of Mixed Copula Capital Allocation

Table 8.4 displays the calculation of CVaR at a 95% confidence level using copula model 1 in Table 8.3 for the level of business unit aggregation to enterprise risk. The table also displays the CVaR 95% contributions of business units to enterprise risk. At this level of aggregation the risk contributions add up numerically; however, as mentioned above, lower level of aggregations risk contribution would have to be rescaled recursively based on the higher level to add up numerically.

TABLE 8.4 Calculation of ES Risk and Risk Contributions for Business Units 1, 2 and 3 to Enterprise Risk

| H_j | Aggregation level | | |
	$H_{1,k}$	$H_{2,k}$	$H_{3,k}$
Aggregation results CVaR (0.95)			
15.02	8.04	6.02	5.69
Contributions CVaR (0.95)			
15.02	6.71	4.2	4.11

Measuring Concentration and Diversification

Risk contributions are also key in a financial institutions approach to measuring and managing risk concentrations. The capital allocations—for a given risk measure—are based on the risk contributions. Once the capital allocation has been obtained one can also calculate capital diversification and concentration indices.[2] For example, from Table 8.4 we find that the diversification index for the copula aggregation hierarchies of business units to enterprise risk are 83,45%, 69,76%, and 72,23% respectively. This represents a capital diversification effect of about 20% to 30%. Hence, the business unit risk is diversified when aggregating to enterprise risk. A simple sum rule to obtain the business unit risk would not only overstate risk (using CVaR as risk measure) but also ignore the important information about the interrelationships between the business lines when analyzing their risk adjusted performances.

RISK AGGREGATION AND REGULATION

The growing practice of firmwide risk appetite and risk budgeting has called for a renewed focus on aggregated risk management at the firmwide level. According to the Financial Stability Board's "principles for an effective risk appetite framework" (FSB, 2013), risk appetite is defined as "the aggregate level and types of risk a financial institution is willing to assume within its risk capacity to achieve its strategic objectives and business plan."

Despite its importance, firmwide risk and risk aggregation to firmwide risk levels is still not a core risk analysis process in many financial institutions. For example, Basel Committee (2010b) found that risk aggregation models in financial institutions are not developed to support all the business functions and decisions for which the models are meant. As a result, the risk aggregation process does not cover all the risks financial institutions may face.

The ultimate goal of the regulatory capital is to set the minimum capital requirement for banks and help banks determine the appropriate capital level corresponding to the overall risk level that any specific bank is taking. Similar to the bank's internal economic capital, risk budgeting, and risk adjusted performance analysis, risk aggregation is also a key corporate exercise in the regulatory capital calculation.

The Basel II pillar 1 risk aggregation is straightforward in the sense that it assumes market risk, credit risk, and operational risk are independently assessed and then simply summed up. The general consensus is that the pillar 1 methodology fell short of adequate risk coverage, granularity, and interaction. In pillar 2, especially the Internal Capital Adequacy Assessment Process (ICAAP), regulators try to fix these issues. There are greater variations in the ICAAP implementation across jurisdictions. Some financial regulatory regimes take principles-based approaches to give banks more freedom toward the ICAAP exercise.

At the beginning of 2013, the Basel Committee issued a supervision paper on the "principles for effective risk data aggregation and risk reporting" (Basel Committee, 2013c). The paper recognizes the need for the global banking industry, especially the G-SIBs (Global Systematically Important Banks), to have a sound information system that can "help banks and supervisors anticipate problem ahead" and improve the "viability when the firm comes under severe stress." Under the principles, banks are required to have a firmwide risk aggregation system that can provide accurate and timely results that cover all material risks. Another key

---

[2] See the chapters on market risk analysis for how to compute concentration and diversification measures based on the Euler risk contributions.

principle for the risk aggregation is to be able to adapt to the fast changing risk reporting and decision-making need, especially in stress situations.

The theme of Basel Committee (2013c) is risk *data* aggregation and reporting. Its coverage is therefore broader than the firmwide risk aggregation models discussed in this chapter and also includes firmwide risk aggregation and reporting practices such as

- The aggregated credit exposure to a large corporate borrower or small retail exposures that has significant concentration
- Aggregation of counterparty credit risk exposures, including, for example, derivatives
- Trading exposures, positions, operating limits, and market concentrations by sector and region
- Liquidity risk indicators such as cash flows/settlements and funding
- Operational risk indicators that are time-critical (e.g., systems availability, unauthorized access)

Basel Committee (2013c) lays out 14 principles to warrant sound "overarching governance and infrastructure," "risk data aggregation capabilities," "risk reporting practices," and "supervisory review, tools, and cooperation." The principles cover from risk infrastructure to reporting and banks' internal governance as well as supervisory review and are displayed in Table 8.5.

At the end of 2013 Basel published a self-assessment-based report regarding the maturity of the banks' compliance to the first 11 of the 14 principles (Basel Committee (2013d)). From the report banks are weak in meeting principles connected to data architecture and IT infrastructure, accuracy, and integrity and adaptability.

TABLE 8.5 Basel Committee's Fourteen Principles for Effective Risk Data Aggregation and Risk Reporting

Overarching governance and infrastructure
  1. Governance
  2. Data architecture and IT infrastructure

Risk data aggregation capabilities
  3. Accuracy and integrity
  4. Completeness
  5. Timliness
  6. Adaptability

Risk reporting practices
  7. Accuracy
  8. Comprehensiveness
  9. Clarity and usefulness
  10. Frequency
  11. Distribution

Supervisory review, tools, and cooperation
  12. Review
  13. Remedial actions and supervisory measures
  14. Home/host cooperation

Pertaining to the theme of this chapter we will emphasize a little more on the 4 principles that are especially important for firmwide risk aggregation models. These 4 principles together with the governance also best summarize the 14 principles laid down by regulators in Basel Committee (2013c) and are:

1. Accuracy
2. Completeness
3. Timeliness
4. Adaptability

The principle of accuracy focuses on that risk aggregation should reach a level of accuracy that is appropriate to the risk management objective. Basel requires a robust control and governance of the data process, reconciling data from various data sources, and making sure data are consistent across all the risk systems that consume the data. Proper documentation is also required for the risk data. Completeness refers to the inclusion of all material risk in a bank. This requires the access to all required risk data in the bank. The timeliness principle requires banks to be prepared to aggregate and generate up-to-date risk data in a timely manner. Finally, adaptability means that the risk aggregation must be flexible enough to support on-demand risk aggregation requests. Such on-demand risk aggregation requests can include changes to the reporting hierarchies, the included risks, and so forth.

In general, a firmwide risk capital model is emerging in both regulatory and economic capital analyses. The top-down firmwide risk aggregation model discussed in this chapter of course plays an important role in banks' firmwide risk capital estimation. However, regulators have more recently also started to consider bottom-up approaches to firmwide risk that focus on capital or liquidity sufficiency under various firmwide scenarios. Examples include liquidity risk and the LCR measure discussed in the liquidity risk chapter, which is based on balance sheet scenarios, as well as the CCAR and EBA firmwide stress testing approaches.[3] The core idea is to consider the scenarios that trigger severe aggregated risk such as missing profit target or failing to meet minimum regulatory capital requirements. Consistent with a firmwide approach, the scenarios are applied to the entire balance sheet to capture the interactions among the risks.

---

[3]As we will see in the next chapter, CCAR and EBA do not test capital sufficiency per se but rather constrain the capital ratios (actual capital/required capital) under stress. This is of course in general a much tougher requirement.

Firmwide Scenario Analysis and Stress Testing

The concept and practice of stress testing has been around for many years in specific risk areas. In the previous chapters of this book we have introduced many methodologies for stress testing and scenario analysis as well as looked at several concrete stress testing examples. While these methodologies are still valid for firmwide scenario analysis and stress testing, special techniques and attentions are called for to successfully achieve the goal of firmwide capital adequacy in forward-looking stress scenarios. The 2007 financial crisis saw a lack of preparation for the liquidity crunch and capital drains in many financial institutions. Perhaps, if banks had worked through different economic scenarios prior to the crisis, they would have been in a better position. Inadequate preparation for crisis can led to systemic risk and severe economic and political turmoil. With the lessons learned from the 2007 financial crisis, regulators are now requiring both quantitative and qualitative methodologies for robust, forward-looking capital-planning processes that account for each bank's unique risks.

In the wake of the 2007 financial crisis, SCAP exercise started in the United States in 2009. Now its successor, CCAR, has become a major focus of the top 25 banks in the United States. CCAR requires bank holding companies with consolidated assets of $50 billion or more to submit annual capital plans to the Federal Reserve for review. However, smaller banks are also joining the group. The DFAST (Dodd-Frank Act Stress Testing) regulation requires US banking organizations with consolidated assets of $10 billion or more to conduct stress tests. The same evolution of the firmwide stress testing has been followed by other regulators over the world, for example, in Europe with the EBA stress testing. In Europe a specific country may also face a country-specific firmwide stress test regulation. An example is the Prudential Regulation Authority in UK (2013) where the prescribed macroeconomic scenarios are also to some extent overlapping with the EBA prescribed macroeconomic scenarios. Firmwide stress test regulations are also developing in the emerging markets. See, for example, the Reserve Bank of India guidelines (2013).

Initially, regulators emphasized credit losses and revenue by stressing a few macroeconomic risk factors—as was the focus of SCAP in the United States in 2009–10. Today, regulators are interested in not only the effect of stress scenarios on credit performance and revenue, but also the stressed results on a broader array of measures that include liquidity and full balance sheet projections. In other words, stress testing must now be an integral part of the bank's capital plan. The requirement to assess the influence of stress scenarios across these different measures has created many challenges for financial institutions. Stress testing has become a systematic way to examine/identify an institution's financial vulnerability.

The total balance sheet–based firmwide stress testing exercise certainly calls for adherence to sound data management principles. The need to integrate both risk and financial measures into stress scenarios when creating the capital plan is the other challenge in the firmwide stress testing. These common requirements come across most regulatory stress testing regimes and require banks to quantitatively project assets, liabilities, income, losses, and capital across a range of macroeconomic scenarios. Since these functions have thus far typically operated in independent silos the regulatory firmwide stress testing is obviously a change in practice for many financial institutions and has an impact on how banks manage risk beyond the stress testing itself. Building a solid firmwide stress testing process is done through several iterations that need constant improvement and investment. The firmwide stress testing process not only allows a bank to gauge its capacity to meet regulatory capital requirements such as CCAR and EBA, but also significantly improves an institution's ability to identify and prevent potential issues that may affect its revenue, liquidity, market growth, and earnings.

As we discussed above, the principle of scenario analysis and stress testing each of the bank's risks such as market and credit risks has a long history in risk management. However, firmwide stress testing with the aim of predicting the bank's complete income and balance sheet statements under stress has picked up relatively recently with the introduction of the CCAR and EBA stress tests. The firmwide stress testing approach also necessitates a collaboration between the bank's risk experts—responsible for generating earnings and loss impact under stress as specific income line statements—and the bank's financial balance sheet and capital management experts—responsible for analyzing the bank's available capital and planning future capital needs. In addition to analyzing sufficiency of bank capital under firmwide stress, one can also analyze the sufficiency of the liquidity buffer under the stress. This is the approach we took in the chapter on liquidity risk. Since liquidity risk is usually a consequential risk it is also natural to analyze bank capital sufficiency and liquidity sufficiency jointly under the stress scenarios.

In this chapter we first discuss two commonly used firmwide scenario model approaches. Both approaches are based on a bottom-up view of firmwide risk with scenarios for firmwide risk factors. Their differences stem from using silo risk systems to achieve a firmwide risk or using a firmwide risk model approach. Second, we discuss firmwide risk capital measures such as estimating firmwide risk capital need and firmwide scenario analysis with the focus on testing capital sufficiency. Such firmwide analysis extends the risk reserve approach to risk capital that we have used many times in this book to a firmwide capital setting. The approach focuses on the *risk capacity*, such as capital and earnings, versus the *risk exposure*. The risk exposure can be calculated using a statistical risk measure applied to many scenarios, for example, using VaR. The risk exposure can also be calculated from a single stress scenario. The approach is frequently used in the bank's ICAAP.

Our third topic in this chapter is the specific regulatory firmwide stress testing process in CCAR and EBA. The regulatory stress testing is different than the firmwide risk capital approach using a risk reserve analogy. In particular, it is focused on maintaining minimum capital ratios under stress and that banks remain financially viable even under stress. The risk exposure, coming from losses and earnings reductions, is estimated under regulatory prescribed macroeconomic scenarios. Since the regulatory stress scenario is focused on sufficient capital ratios under stress it also requires stressed estimation of required capital in addition to the stressed losses and earnings. Because the stress testing uses high-level macroeconomic scenarios, the use of models is critical to the materialization of the high-level macroeconomic scenario.

We end the chapter with a discussion of the future of firmwide stress testing and stress testing regulation.

FIRMWIDE SCENARIO MODEL APPROACHES

In practice, it may be impossible to isolate risk effects into categories like market and credit risk by creating artificial subportfolios that can allow compartmentalized risk analysis and then using a dependence model to integrate all the risks back together. Indeed, most risk types have complex interrelationships that stem from dependence on many of the core risk factors as well as behavior. More importantly, through a joint modeling of core risk factors for the risk types, institutions can better understand the consequences of each adverse scenario for risk factors across risk types and lines of business to proactively manage these scenarios.

In a bottom-up approach to firmwide scenario analysis, the risk system(s) carry out calculations on the scenarios that are generated from a joint distribution of the key risk factors. It is important to note that the bottom-up approach is useful not only for estimating firmwide risk levels but also for firmwide stress testing. This is because the method relies on aggregating risk values per scenario. Hence, this model approach is in practice used for the firmwide stress testing. In contrast, the firmwide risk aggregation models, discussed in Chapter 8, do not rely on joint correlated scenarios. They take a top-down approach to firmwide risk levels using a specified codependency between risk types. The risk aggregation is hence a process to aggregate compartmentalized risk measures into more comprehensive firmwide risk measures. In bottom-up firmwide scenario model approaches a bank can use either

- a silo approach per risk type and then aggregate the results, or
- a comprehensive firmwide risk model approach

Of course, the firmwide scenario model can also be a combination of the two. We will discuss these two firmwide scenario model approaches below.

Silo Approach

In the silo approach, each silo risk system is responsible for predicting a certain risk's profit and loss under the scenario(s). For example,

- The market risk system(s) generates the market risk profit and loss under the scenario(s).
- The asset and liability management system(s) generates the net interest income projection under the scenario(s).
- The credit risk system(s) generates credit loss under the scenario(s).

The portfolio-level net earnings for a given scenario are hence obtained as the sum of net interest income earnings less market and credit risk loss. Consequently, the specific market, credit, and profitability risk techniques discussed in this book are still important for the firmwide risk. In practice, one can of course add more of the bank's earnings and loss contributions to the income statement to obtain a more complete view—for example, non-interest income and expense such as fees and other risks than market and credit risks such as operational risk.

The core of the approach is that the scenario-by-scenario results are aggregated—across silo risk systems—so that one distribution or an aggregated scenario result is generated for firmwide risk analysis. In this approach the firmwide scenarios can be generated outside of the silo risk systems using a firmwide risk scenario generator. The subsequent risk aggregation is a separate process.

In practice, many of the firmwide risk scenarios are specified as high-level macroeconomic scenarios and hence in order to transform high-level macroeconomic stress scenarios to silo systems risk factors the bank uses models. As we have discussed, especially in the advanced market risk chapter but also in the portfolio credit risk chapter, models to transfer stress from macroeconomic risk factors to actual portfolio risk factors can be based on distribution models or factor models and the models themselves are sometimes referred to as satellite models.

Firmwide Risk Model Approach

The use of the existing silo risk systems for firmwide scenario analysis can in practice be quite complicated. Core challenges include maintaining consistency in scenarios applied across systems and in the subsequent aggregation of risk results across systems. A firmwide risk model approach has the benefit of a single independent financial risk analysis for firmwide stress. Using a firmwide model, it is clearly an advantage to not have to rely on silo systems for valuation and have to manage the subsequent aggregation from different systems. A clear advantage with a firmwide risk model approach is also that balance projections and management intervention can be more easily handled in a comprehensive single model approach, especially if management interventions at the next horizon depend on the projected risk results at the previous horizon, as this can create a complex feedback loop to silo risk systems that can be hard to manage consistently in practice.

Sometimes the separation of risks in the silo risk systems can also make it hard to consistently estimate key measures such as stressed earnings. For example, the asset and liability management system can certainly generate cash flows but typically does not incorporate the credit models to convert credit scenarios into scenario credit loss and the resulting loss of cash flows at delinquency and default. Hence, generating stressed credit losses in the credit risk system separately from the earnings cash flows in the asset and liability management system can easily create inconsistencies. It can also make it impossible to generate consistent loan-level scenarios on cash flows, accruals, and credit loss.[1]

Implementation by Books of Business   The core of the firmwide risk model approach is that it tries to integrate the earnings and loss predictions in a single model. In practice, it may be difficult to have a complete firmwide risk model for all books of business. The firmwide risk model is therefore often implemented per book of business. Similar to the silo approach, we then have a subsequent aggregation process to obtain firmwide risk. However, the aggregation is now distinct per book rather than by risk type for the same book of business. A gross decomposition is aggregation of trading book market risk and banking book earnings and loss. In practice, the banking book may be further decomposed into the different books of business such as mortgage, credit card, and so on that each have their own models for integrated earnings and loss prediction.

Approximative Firmwide Risk Model   In practice, each risk has its uniqueness in terms of risk factor sources and risk calculations. Because of the complexity of real portfolios and the need to analyze firmwide risk in the context of high-level macroeconomic scenarios, it is sometimes

---

[1]See also our discussion on features of the new generation portfolio credit risk models in Chapter 4 on portfolio credit risk.

a natural choice for the firmwide risk model to be implemented as an approximation to some of the granular risk models in the silo risk systems, that is, to use an approximative firmwide risk model. The approximation can be done in two ways:

1. Reduction in the number of risk factors
2. Portfolio approximation

A common technique used to achieve the reduced set of risk factors is the use of factor models, especially for expressing portfolio risk in core factors such as equity indices, exchange rates, interest rates, and macroeconomic factors such as property prices and unemployment rates. A classical example of a factor model is the CAPM where the universe of the equity returns risk can be reduced to a single market factor risk and equity betas. The CAPM model induces scenario values for the specific equities given scenario values for the market factor.

The portfolio approximation in firmwide risk models can use multiple techniques to approximate the detailed portfolios for the specific risks. The reader may recall that we discussed several portfolio and instrument pricing techniques in the first chapter on market risk (Chapter 2), including:

- Grid pricing and curve fitting
- Delta-Gamma approximations
- Least squares Monte Carlo and a proxy pricing technique using outer fitting scenarios and inaccurate valuations
- Replicating portfolios

All of these approaches are suitable for instruments as well as risk type (sub)portfolios. The best portfolio approximation to use is decided by the portfolio complexity and also the error acceptance in the approximation. For example, a natural approximation for a relatively simple market risk portfolio is to use the linear delta approach. The linear delta approach (risk position approach) is also used in CCAR and EBA market risk stress tests as we discussed in the advanced market risk chapter (Chapter 3) in the section on scenario analysis and stress testing. For the banking book earnings and loss projection the approximation can be based on pooling or a smaller replicating portfolio for a quick approximate stress analysis, although loan-level models are more frequently being used in practice as we discussed in the portfolio credit risk (Chapter 4). More elaborate approximation techniques may have to be used for complex portfolios that can have a large impact on stressed profit and loss, for example, Treasury interest rate risk hedges with optionality such as American and Bermudan swaptions.

Regulatory Benchmark Firmwide Risk Models Regulators also develop their own firmwide risk models for bank stress. For example, many central banks in Europe have developed high-level, macroeconomic bank risk models for stress testing. See, for example, the Bank of England RAMSI model (2012), the European central bank stress test model (2013), and the Czech national bank stress testing model (2013). These models rely mostly on balance sheet information from banks and macroeconomic risk models. Of course, banks themselves have more detailed information about the risk exposures, and hence a bank's own firmwide risk model can utilize more detailed portfolio information. It can therefore also be used to challenge regulatory views. Regulators may also develop their own more granular benchmark models for specific risks. For example, as we discussed in Chapter 4 on portfolio credit risk, the 2012

Federal Reserve CCAR supervisory credit stress tests used a specific quarterly delinquency transition matrix specification for the residential mortgages. Since then, the Federal Reserve has been building supervisory models for CCAR using the collected bank data.

Multiple Model Approaches

In practice, banks may of course use multiple model approaches in stress testing with both silo and firmwide risk model approaches. A central firmwide stress testing team may be responsible for maintaining macroeconomic scenarios, satellite models, and the firmwide risk model for the firmwide stress testing. At the same time the silo risk systems may be used to generate benchmark validations of stressed profits and losses under the same macroeconomic scenarios.

FIRMWIDE RISK CAPITAL MEASURES

Firmwide stress testing can provide significant values to bank management. One is for the management, including the regulator, to examine the capital planning and management decisions under different scenarios and ensure a satisfactory capital position for the bank under the scenarios. From a basic balance sheet point of view a bank's capital is defined as the total assets minus the total liabilities of the bank. At a specific point of time the value of capital can increase or decrease due to the change of the balance sheet. The key to the firmwide stress testing exercise is to apply the stress scenario to the projection of both the asset and liability side of the balance sheet. An incremental projection, period by period, starting from the current state at the time of the analysis means that the available capital can also be measured as the net earnings minus the losses adjusted by tax and capital actions. Capital actions include dividend plans and other accounting adjustments. Figure 9.1 presents a conceptual view of the steps involved in risk-based capital stress testing. The first step applies stress scenarios to obtain a stressed income statement, which is adjusted for taxes and other adjustments such as asset sale gains, such that we can obtain a final projected income statement under stress. In the first step a bank therefore calculates the stressed net revenue before loss provision and loss adjusted by recovery. The net revenue before loss provision, also known as pre-provision net revenue (PPNR) in CCAR, is composed of interest income, non-interest income, including fees and trading profit and loss, interest expense, and non-interest expense. Credit and operational losses will offset the net revenue for the same period. The second step calculates the available capital from the final projected income and the current available capital. This available capital is before management actions. Post-management action available capital is obtained in step 3. Adjustments to the available capital in step 2 include decisions on dividend payouts and capital preserving actions such as equity raises and balance sheet reductions.

Risk Measures and Stress Scenarios

When using a firmwide scenario approach to generate firmwide risk and capital measures, we can use two different approaches:

- First, we can generate a set of correlated firmwide risk factor scenarios that spans the different risks. We then calculate the profit and loss resulting from the scenarios and create a distribution to which we can apply the usual risk measures such as VaR and CVaR.

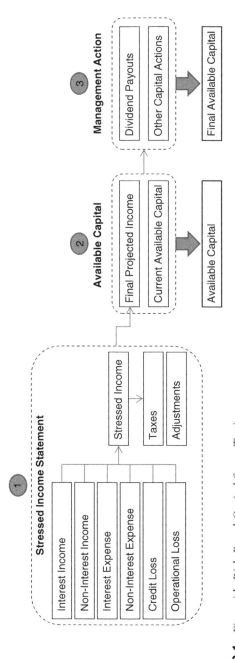

FIGURE 9.1 Firmwide Risk-Based Capital Stress Testing

In this risk measure approach we choose as our required firmwide capital essentially a worst-case scenario or weighted average set of scenarios decided by the risk confidence level used in the risk measure. If our current capital base is not sufficient to cover, for example, the calculated firmwide risk capital need, we can take capital preserving actions and plan for capital adjustments.

■ Second, instead of taking a worst-case risk measure approach to capital (and liquidity sufficiency) we can focus on sufficiency in a given predefined worst-case stress scenario.

Historically, regulatory risk capital for market and credit risks has followed the first approach, defining capital as a worst-case scenario from many scenarios using a risk measure. The liquidity regulation with Basel III instead focuses on the second approach, testing the sufficiency of the liquidity buffer using a given predefined worst-case stress scenario.

In both approaches to test capital and liquidity sufficiency the main steps followed are:

1. The firmwide scenario(s) are generated.
2. Satellite models are used to transfer the macroeconomic stress scenario(s) to actual portfolio risk factors if needed.
3. Scenario loss(es), earnings impact(s), and liquidity impact(s) are computed.
4. The available capital base and liquidity buffer are used to check sufficiency versus the risk measure (risk measure approach) or versus the loss and liquidity outflow in the scenario (stress scenario approach).
5. Depending on the outcome, management actions may be considered, for example, capital preserving or liquidity preserving actions.

Note that if the scenario(s) are multi-horizon, we may consider reasonable firm actions such as capital and liquidity preserving actions at the end of a scenario horizon before the next horizon of the scenario. In a multi-horizon scenario the depletion of the capital base or the liquidity buffer can also happen over time and the specific term-structure characteristics together with the severity of the scenario are important in deciding the exact outflows as well as the appropriate management response.

A Risk Reserve Approach—A Practical Illustration

In practice, the scenario(s) generated in step 1 above are high level. This is because we consider a firmwide stress and it is practical to start with a (set of) high-level macroeconomic scenario and then drill down to impact on portfolio-specific risk factors. The fundamental idea is for the bank to get a forward-looking understanding of the aggregated risk profile based on the scenario(s). The firmwide risk capital approach is here different from a risk capital approach per risk type as it focuses on a comprehensive, economically meaningful stress scenario. To capture reality the macroeconomic scenario is generally a multi-horizon scenario, specifying a path that macroeconomic variables can follow.

In the second step, when models are used, such as factor models or conditional distribution models, to transform the macroeconomic scenarios it is important to recognize that in practice the specific models used may have to be adapted to the severity of a scenario. For example, an extremely severe macroeconomic scenario may use a set of models that are different from a corresponding severe scenario. This is because the models need to capture the severity of the scenario and the potential breakdown of historical relationships such as correlations in extremely severe cases.

The third step of the process yields a per-scenario projected income statement with, for example, income statement line items earnings and loss contribution from:

- Earnings from the interest income projection from the assets and liabilities
- Losses from market risk
- Losses from issuer credit risk in banking book and trading book
- Losses from counterparty default and CVA
- Other losses, for example, from operational risk

The earnings from the interest income projection is a traditional net interest income projection. It can include a joint modeling of issuer credit risk and cash flows or use a post-adjustment of the net interest income with credit system projected losses. The interest income comes from, for example, loans, leases, deposits, and mortgages. The interest expense comes from deposits, issued bank debt, and other liabilities.

A bank also has earnings from non-interest income and non-interest expense. Recall that in CCAR the PPNR is the sum of three parts: net interest income, non-interest income, and non-interest expense. All three parts need to be stressed. Hence, this requires banks to develop models predicting non-interest income and non-interest expense such as bank fee income and administration and salary expenses under the macroeconomic stress. Due to the lack of granular historical data and previous model practice banks sometimes take a simplified "line item" approach for some of these non-interest income and non-interest expense earnings. The "line item" approach referred to here is different from the top-down approach used in Chapter 8. The line item approach still uses risk factors and scenarios to analyze risk impacts but operates on an aggregated level such as portfolio or income statement line item. Oftentimes regression models are fitted to the past line item behavior and the (macroeconomic) regressors are subsequently used to stress the line item behavior. We refer to Duane et al. (2014) on models and practices to predict non-interest income and non-interest expense.

Having obtained the stressed earnings we now obtain the scenario-based prediction of total losses using the profit-and-loss models for market risk, issuer credit risk, counterparty default risk, and CVA that have been discussed extensively in this book. Note that for CVA losses there is both a market risk effect on exposure as well as a credit component. A CVA increase can hence come from both market risk factors (exposure) and the credit component through counterparty CDS premia or bond spreads.

With scenario stressed earnings and losses available we can create an aggregate stressed income statement per scenario as in step 1 in Figure 9.1. We can also adjust the projected income statement with, for example, other projected incomes such as asset sale gains and earnings tax adjustments. This yields the bank's final projected net income in step 2 in Figure 9.1. Dividing the final projected income into earnings, E_d, and losses, L_d, contributions we can create the capital reserve, CR_d, for scenario d as

$$CR_d = C + E_d - L_d \qquad (9.1)$$

where C is the current available capital base. The capital reserve hence corresponds to the remaining available capital in step 2 in Figure 9.1 and is before consideration of management actions.

Having completed all the steps 1–4 to obtain a scenario d capital reserve, CR_d, we can now consider management actions, for example, to preserve capital. Of course, the best management intervention may be decided per scenario and hence may require a model of management intervention to be implemented if many scenarios $d = 1, \ldots, D$ are used in a risk measure approach to firmwide risk capital. In our capital risk reserve approach we assume, prudently, that there are no capital preserving actions by the bank. That is, the bank will not save positive contributions from the net earnings, NE_d,

$$NE_d = [E_d - L_d]$$

in one period to build up the current available capital base, C, in the next period.[2] This means that C is constant over time in this case (since there is no addition to the current available capital) and that we can calculate a required capital reserve over time, $t = 1, \ldots, T$, in the multi-horizon scenario d as

$$CR_d(T) = C + \sum_{t=1}^{T} \min[NE_d(t), 0].$$

If we use a stress scenario approach to analyze the sufficiency of the initial capital buffer, C, we clearly cannot allow $\{CR_d(t)\}_{t=1}^{T}$ negative at any $t = 1, \ldots, T$ in the stress scenario. In the risk measure approach we similarly sum all the negative contributions to $\{CR_d(t)\}_{t=1}^{T}$ over time for each scenario $d = 1, \ldots, D$ and apply a risk measure to the tail of summed negative contributions. If the chosen risk measure, at the specific confidence level and time, t, implies a loss, that is, that the risk reserve is exhausted, it is a sign we should increase the capital buffer, C, to ensure survival at that confidence level and time horizon.

The above approach to firmwide risk capital is based on *a risk reserve approach* and hence not depleting the capital buffer under a particular stress scenario or using a risk measure on many scenarios. This approach is founded in classical risk theory in insurance and is the approach to defining risk capital as well as defining the liquidity buffer that we have used in this book. This includes the market risk models as well as the portfolio credit risk models and the liquidity models. It is also the traditional approach for banks' ICAAP models. As we shall see next, the CCAR and EBA firmwide stress approach is different. That is, it is not used to define the capital buffer per se but rather to put limits on the minimum regulatory capital ratios.

REGULATORY STRESS SCENARIO APPROACH

While net profit and loss depend on the macroeconomic scenario, so does the required capital. Furthermore, there is a dependency of the required capital on the balance and loss projection. An obvious example is that the credit risk weighted assets change when the total balance and credit quality of the banks' asset changes due to either growth or loss. On the other side, if required capital increases too quickly to be sustained by the available capital business, growth and capital actions, such as dividend payouts and equity buy-back plans, must be adjusted. In this section we focus mainly on the bank-specific approach to regulatory firmwide stress

---

[2]In the portfolio credit risk chapter when we discussed the model for economic capital for loan portfolios we used a similar assumption. That is, it is prudent to assume that the bank will not save positive contributions from one period to another to neutralize negative contributions at subsequent periods. Due to the obligations for instance to shareholders the bank may distribute excess earnings.

testing. However, we also discuss briefly the second round of analysis performed by central banks to analyze the financial system stability, either using their own macroeconomic stress testing models, or by rolling up banks' own provided stress test results.

Bank-Specific Approach: A Total Balance Sheet View

Instead of focusing on stress scenarios to actually define the capital buffer both CCAR and EBA firmwide stress testing focus instead on banks maintaining *minimum capital ratios under stress*. The capital ratio is here actual capital divided by required capital. The compliance to regulatory stress scenarios is hence viewed as complementary to the already defined capital requirements. Here capital requirements are predominantly computed using risk models and a risk measure approach that is founded in a *risk reserve approach*. In general, maintaining a minimum capital ratio under stress is of course a much tougher requirement than meeting capital sufficiency.

Figure 9.2 presents a conceptual view of the elements involved in the regulatory stress scenario approach. Compared to Figure 9.1, we notice that stress scenarios are also applied to the required capital calculation and that the focus is the capital ratio rather than available capital per se. As part of the regulatory stress testing a bank may also face restrictions on what management actions can be assumed in step 3 to improve the capital ratio from step 2.

Both CCAR and EBA consider stress during multi-horizon macroeconomic stress scenarios. For example, the CCAR macroeconomic scenarios specify the evolution quarterly over the next 9 quarters. In EBA the macroeconomic scenarios are based on the evolution over 3 years. As we have discussed in the specific risk chapters, the scenarios include both macroeconomic scenarios and specific market risk scenarios with detailed risk factors, funding shock scenarios, as well as prescribed default of the largest exposure counterparty.

Creating the Balance Sheet Ratio   In both CCAR and EBA the current balance sheet is the basis for the first horizon projected income statement. The projected income statement is then the basis for the projected balance sheet statement at the end of the first horizon. The scenario realized capital ratios help to determine if the bank must take management action to increase capital to maintain the minimum capital ratio under stress.

For example, a bank can create the balance sheet ratio, R_d, for a scenario d such that

$$R_d = \frac{C + E_d - L_d}{\tilde{C}_d}$$

where, as in equation (9.1), C is the current available capital base, E_d is the projected earnings in the scenario, L_d is the projected losses in the scenario, and $\tilde{C}_d$ is now a measure of required capital under stress.

Using instead the retained earnings, RE_d, defined as the earnings minus losses and any additional loss provisions needed,[3] this results in

$$R_d = \frac{C + RE_d}{\tilde{C}_d}. \tag{9.2}$$

---

[3]For example, in Basel credit charges the deterioration of the credit quality of the portfolio induces an increase in the provisions and Basel expected loss. The requirement is that 50% of the difference between the two must be subtracted from the available capital. This is hence in addition to the scenario loss, L_d.

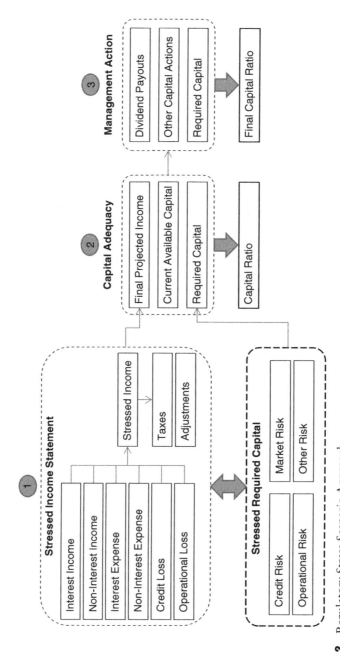

FIGURE 9.2 Regulatory Stress Scenario Approach

Hence, we now have a scenario capital ratio, R_d, that can be compared to a minimum required capital threshold. Because of the $t = 1, \ldots, T$ multi-horizon scenario the capital ratio of course has a scenario term structure as $\{R_d(t)\}_{t=1}^{T}$, which can be compared to time-based limits or a fixed limit over time.

Projecting Required Capital In the regulatory stress scenario approach the definition of required capital, $\widetilde{C}_d$, is the minimum regulatory capital and C is the capital base. Specifically, $\widetilde{C}_d$ is the sum of all the capital charges for the risks. However, we still need a specific definition of required capital for the different risks to calculate $\widetilde{C}_d$. This is in general based on the bank's approval for the specific risk models used in regulatory capital calculations. For example:

- Market risk regulatory capital impact can be based on the internal models approach with VaR and stressed VaR.

  In principle, a model-based charge can be based on a conditional distribution VaR, or use a simple replacement of VaR with stressed VaR as per EBA.[4] The conditional distribution VaR is the VaR obtained when we condition the portfolio risk factor distribution on the prespecified stressed macroeconomic factors. See our probabilistic stress testing example in Chapter 2 for an illustration of conditional stressed VaR.
- Issuer credit risk in banking book regulatory capital impact can use the Basel advanced internal models approach for the banking book, that is, the Basel risk weighted assets equation (4.40) found in Chapter 4 on portfolio credit risk.

  The regulatory macroeconomic stress scenarios ultimately impact the risk inputs to the risk-weighted assets such as probability of default and loss given default. We refer the reader to Chapter 4 on portfolio credit risk for an explicit example of stressing mortgage portfolio losses, net earnings, and Basel risk-weighted assets capital under macroeconomic scenarios.
- Issuer credit risk in trading book can use a stressed (parameters) or conditional distribution (on the macroeconomic factors) VaR for the incremental risk charge assuming the bank is currently using the model for the trading book credit risk.

  See Chapter 4 on portfolio credit risk for the incremental risk charge model as well as an example of stressed credit losses for a corporate credit portfolio that uses the multifactor model approach.
- Counterparty credit risk default charges are, as issuer default risk charges in banking book, also based on the risk-weighted assets in equation (4.40) using the estimated expected positive exposures as we discussed in Chapter 5 on counterparty credit risk. CVA charges can use a standardized formula-based approach or a VaR model capturing the variation in CDS premia or bond spreads for the counterparty.

Note here that while the regulatory definition of $\widetilde{C}_d$ is the sum of the minimum regulatory capital, in principle, internal stress testing could be based on other measures such as economic capital in the denominator of equation (9.2). This can involve using economic capital models for the specific risk types as well as overriding the simple risk sum approach using a correlated

---

[4]Recall from Chapter 3 (the advanced market risk chapter) that the current internal models based market risk charge is the sum of the regular and stressed VaR where the stressed VaR is the VaR calibrated on a stressed period. Replacing VaR by the stressed VaR hence leads to a stressed VaR charge that is two times the stressed VaR.

aggregation model of the different risks to obtain $\widetilde{C}_d$. We refer the reader to Chapter 8 for a discussion of correlated aggregation models.

Management Intervention and Balance Growth Assumptions Given a stress scenario realized balance sheet and capital ratio at a certain time t, $R_d(t)$, potential management intervention (capital preserving, dividend planning, and other capital actions) as well as balance sheet growth assumptions for the next horizon, $t + 1$, can potentially be considered. For example, in the Bank of England RAMSI model (2012), the bank decision rule followed is to expand the balance sheet at $t + 1$ only if both retained earnings, $RE_d(t)$, are positive and the capital ratio, $R_d(t)$, exceeds the minimum stress level. When the capital ratio is below the minimum stress level the retained earnings are used to build up the capital base. In case of negative retained earnings, the balance sheet is in runoff.

There are a few variations in the actual calculation details in practice between regulations. For example, when the European EBA stress testing exercise is performed by a specific bank, no management intervention is allowed. In contrast, in CCAR banks must incorporate both planned (baseline) and stress scenario specific capital actions. Another difference is the treatment of the growth of the balance sheet, which is static in EBA. In practice, the revenue projection should incorporate the change of the asset and liability balance, which, in turn, affects the income and expenses. The balance sheet change should also reflect the scenario instead of being static. For example, the increase of deposit volume and the high-quality assets is typically lower in adverse scenarios than a normal scenario. Likewise, the interest income and expense due to the additional business can vary according to the scenario.

Figure 9.3 illustrates the firmwide stress testing process for scenario horizons $t = 1, 2, 3$. The process in Figure 9.3 includes both liquidity ratios and capital ratios. However, currently both CCAR and EBA focus on the capital ratios under stress. In Figure 9.3, we have also included potential management intervention if allowed. If management intervention is not allowed, management projections such as balance forecasting are assumed to be made at the beginning of the process and remain for the duration of the stress test. Alternatively, balances are simply assumed constant. Of course, in principle, a management intervention of capital raising action can be an ex-post adjustment as all the scenario analysis horizons have run. However, this does not apply to the balance adjustments as balance adjustment will affect next horizon's balance sheet to be stressed for earnings, losses, and capital requirements.

In Chapter 6 on liquidity risk management, the reader can find an extensive example of modeling earnings and loss cash flows with behavioral and business growth assumptions. The example uses the concept of target ending balances for future balances together with prepayment and default assumptions. It also illustrates the importance of addressing liquidity and funding needs with balance growth. The target-ending balance case is an example of a portfolio-level top-down approach to balance growth. However, in practice behavioral models such as prepayment and default can be granular while business plan models such as the target-ending balance approach can be a (per horizon) post-process adjustment. That is, detailed-level cash flows are aggregated to a higher level view where going-concern business growth is applied on aggregated balances (cash flows) for a product class. We refer the reader back to our discussion in the liquidity risk chapter on combining the risk and finance view.

Bank-Specific Approach: More on Scenarios and Models

While we have already discussed the typical firmwide stress testing scenario model approaches the firmwide stress testing regulation calls for special attention on how banks manage the

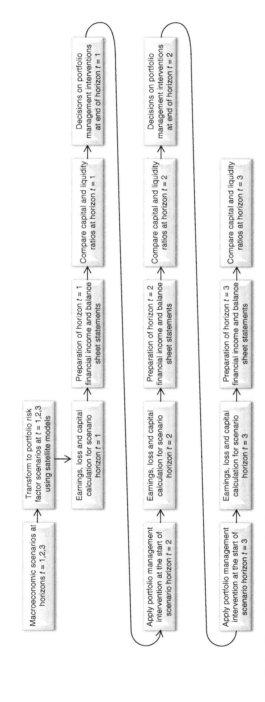

FIGURE 9.3 Firmwide Stress Testing Process

stress testing models and scenarios. This includes own scenario creation, the use of simplifed models in some cases, the role of management overlay in analytical stress testing models, and the need to recognize and manage the inherent model risk in the stress testing models.

Economic Scenario Generator—Own Developed Scenarios Since the regulatory scenarios are at very high level and only include major macroeconomic risk drivers affecting the entire economic system, banks are expected to extend the regulatory scenarios to better reflect the risks that materially affect the bank's business operations. For example, while regulatory scenarios usually include national real estate price indices, a bank that has residential or commercial mortgage exposures in certain regions must either derive the regional indices down to the granular level that corresponds to the exposure concentration from the regulatory national index scenario values or even further augment the scenario by creating new scenarios with these regional indices.

Regulators also expect banks to build the enterprise stress testing into their own risk management–based decision making, and thus demand banks to develop own macroeconomic scenarios that are relevant. Banks' own developed scenarios can be an extension of the regulatory scenarios by adding more macroeconomic variables, overriding certain regulatory specifications, or creating a completely new scenario. The own scenarios developed by banks should capture the key risk exposures and concentrations in bank portfolios.

Due to the complexity of bank portfolios it is in practice not easy for banks to realize the risk exposures that may traumatize the business. However, the task of finding severe impact scenarios conceptually amounts to considering reverse stress testing approaches. Reverse stress testing methodologies as well as associated dimension reduction methods for portfolios with many risk factors have been discussed at length in the advanced market risk chapter of this book. The concept of reverse stress testing is, however, universal and not specific to market risk. In general, it focuses on the outcomes that can hurt the bank significantly and then, through an appropriate method of reverse impact analysis, finds the stress scenarios that could generate such an outcome. We refer the reader back to the advanced market risk chapter for a detailed discussion and examples of reverse stress testing methodologies using both simulated market states and historical data as basis for reverse stress tests.

Long before the rise of the enterprise stress testing economic capital has existed as a common practice for bank capital management. Stress testing has been a supplement to the economic capital analysis often founded in model-based risk charges. This relation can clearly be seen in the traditional ICAAP "risk reserve" process described above. Of course the goal of stress tests is to provide a forward-looking view of banks' capital in addition to the economic capital models that are often drawn from historical data. This book has also covered a few other perspectives of the interplay between stress testing and models. The first is that a sound economic capital analysis can help identify the stress scenarios that can significantly impact a bank's capital adequacy. This is the practice of reverse stress testing discussed above. The second is the enhancement of the economic capital analysis with the forward-looking stress scenarios, which is a topic we covered as part of stress testing in the chapter on advanced market risk analysis under the heading of integration of stress and model analysis.

The Use of Simplified Time Series Forecasting Models for Line Items Due to the lack of granular historical data and appropriate models, banks are sometimes taking historical line item time series forecasting approaches for some components of the financial statements. A typical example is non-interest income and non-interest expense, which we have mentioned previously. There are many reasons why this approach is still acceptable to the regulators. Apart from the inherent data issues, in many cases the massive mergers and acquisitions that took place after the financial crisis have limited the ability of banks to present acceptable models for certain parts of the balance sheet. Banks may have introduced new business or changed the composition of the business.

In the United States, all the regulated banks are required to submit periodic financial and other information to their regulators. One of these reports is the quarterly consolidated report of condition and income, also known as the call report. Every national bank, state member bank, and insured bank is required by the Federal Financial Institutions Examination Council (FFIEC) to file a call report every quarter. The granularity of the call report also matches very well the regulatory stress testing requirement. Many banks that face the challenge of the granular data and models thus develop quarterly projection models to be able to respond to the regulatory scenarios by employing historical values of the risk factors in the scenarios as covariates to the historical line item numbers.

Management Overlay Although quantitative models by and large provide objective stress testing results management overlay is still investible at times. In most cases such overlay should be subject to management policies or managegment actions. In most cases management intervention and capital actions such as dividend plans are policy driven. Another decision-making-backed overlay example is the new business acquisition or write-off, which is hard to project by models. Such decisions can drive the new business projection and ending balance projections as input to the loss and revenue calculations. Again, the target ending balance example in Chapter 6 on liquidity risk management with behavioral and business growth assumptions is a concrete illustration of how to incorporate such assumptions. Other decision-based management overlay examples include the fee incomes that can depend on the fee structure policies.

The Role of Model Risk Management The enterprise stress testing exercise has put tremendous emphasis on the models for the entire balance sheet. Model risk management, including model governance, model validation, and documentation, has been given more attention. The model risk management issues reviewed in the first chapter of this book are all relevant to the firmwide stress testing. We emphasize here that the model assumption for the stress testing models is that these models can properly capture the tail behavior of the modeled subject. This includes the fact that market and consumer behavior can change significantly under stress situations. Such changes in behavior in stress typically impact correlations that can be far different from the correlations during normal times.

Systemic View: Financial System Analysis and Financial Contagion

The regulatory stress testing process described above focuses on the specific bank behavior under stress, specifically, the bank's performance of capital ratios under stress. At any point in time during the multi-horizon stress scenario capital ratios are examined and compared to limits. Management actions, if allowed during the path of the multi-horizon stress, take the form of remedial actions when limits are breached with an aim to improve the situation for the next horizon.

When central banks perform this stress testing exercise per bank, using their macroeconomic stress testing models, or by rolling up banks' own provided stress test results, they also need to add another step in the analysis to capture systemic risks, that is, that potential large losses or the failure of some banks can give rise to negative contagion effects on other banks in the system. If a systemically important bank fails to pass the test, it can have consequences on other banks through direct bilateral linkages or more indirectly through financial system confidence effects. We refer to the European Central Bank macroeconomic stress testing framework for the systemic risks (2013) for an example of how central banks' stress testing models that analyze the financial system as a whole include sophisticated financial network and contagion analysis models.

While regulators are increasingly using financial contagion models to analyze potential systemic risks in the banking system one would also expect that over time banks themselves will be required to analyze potential contagion effects in their own portfolios, and how microeconomic events, rather than only general macroeconomic situations, can create initial losses and subsequent contagion effects within a specific bank. A classical liquidity risk example is of course a loss of trust in the bank, due to some event such as an operational loss, and how the loss of trust can evolve to the different providers of funds to the bank, resulting in a liquidity crunch.

THE FUTURE OF FIRMWIDE STRESS TESTING

Firmwide stress testing is certainly here to stay. Regulatory mandated firmwide stress testing programs have also seen rapid expansion. The success of CCAR stress tests in the United States has inspired the development of the more recent stress tests by European EBA and other jurisdictions. See Schuermann (2013) for an interesting discussion on the CCAR and EBA stress test developments.

As we have discussed in this chapter, the EBA and CCAR stress tests focus on macroeconomic scenarios that can impact the bank's income statement (profit and loss impact) as well as the subsequent balance sheet (capital impact). When the regulatory stress scenario is hypothetical, models and/or expert judgment can be used to transfer stress. The use of models is critical to the materialization of the high-level macroeconomic scenario. Models are hence clearly central to both firmwide stress testing and the traditional risk-based model charges.

One could argue that the current focus of regulators on firmwide stress testing is a trend toward replacing risk-based model charges with stress scenarios, and ultimately a sign of distrust in models. The success of firmwide stress testing has also seen voices raised to replace risk-based model charges with stress testing charges. See, for example, the speech by Governor Daniel K. Tarullo, at the Federal Reserve Bank of Chicago Bank Structure Conference, Chicago, Illinois, May 8, 2014. Tarullo argues that the credit risk internal ratings-based approach is too complex, aids little in understanding the risks in the bank's balance sheets, and is backward looking. His view is that the supervisory stress tests developed by the Federal Reserve in the United States provide a much better risk-sensitive basis for setting minimum capital requirements—that is, to define risk-based capital charges using supervisory stress scenarios.

We would rather view the firmwide stress testing as complementary. Indeed, focusing only on a stress scenario approach to capital charges may put too much burden on supervisors and banks to come up with the right scenarios that anticipate future crisis events. An important step to overcome the deficiencies of risk-based model charges is to complement model-based views with forward-looking stress events, that is, integration of stress and model analysis.[5]

---

[5]Both the scenario-based analysis and risk-based model charges (economic capital based) certainly involve models to compute the loss for a given scenario. The distinction between the two approaches is

Even if regulators ultimately decide to abandon risk-based model charges for stress charges, the risk-based models will likely still play a vital role in the construction of banks' own scenarios via reverse stress testing. The requirement that banks need to develop own scenarios that can hurt the bank significantly is a necessary component in the stress testing. Especially if the regulatory stress testing is to replace or downplay the importance of risk-based model charges. The fact that each bank's unique risks needs to be accounted for when developing own scenarios also puts more pressure on the regulators to understand the relevance of each banks scenarios. It is also the case that the current firmwide stress testing approach for both CCAR and EBA do not focus directly on stress charges to define capital requirements but rather on putting constraints on the capital ratios—involving the traditional risk-based model charges as a core component.

In practice, the regulatory stress testing exercise has also developed into a test of the risk models in banks, and lately, increased regulatory scrutiny of the entire model life cycle—from model development to validation, implementation, and governance. Both CCAR and EBA put a huge emphasis on model risk. In CCAR the regulators view the stress testing process as a system of models and hence put emphasis on the need to measure model risk individually as well as across the network of models. Model sensitivity analysis is one of the tools to analyze the model impacts and to understand the models. Lack of adequate data, model insight, and modeling expertise have proven to be major challenges in many banks to carry out effective firmwide stress testing.

Many banks have of course had firmwide risk models in place for a long time as part of their ICAAP process. However, those models focus mainly on the risk capacity and the firmwide risk exposure of the bank rather than on putting limits on capital ratios under stress. More importantly, many banks' ICAAP processes were manual, usually involved simplified model approaches for assessing earnings and loss impacts, and were not part of a formal risk-based planning process that included both risk and finance.[6] As a consequence, the mandated firmwide stress testing has resulted in significant development of new firmwide risk models and firmwide risk processes. The current industry improvements in the firmwide stress testing of course also enable stronger risk-based capital planning processes in general for banks.

Firmwide stress testing is a complex yet important exercise to a bank. It requires a sound process that connects the macroeconomic scenarios, satellite models, the bank's portfolio, valuation, and risk systems as well as reporting into one end-to-end process. The regulators also anticipate that the process can be repeatable and sustainable. We again note that completing the stress testing process involves both the bank's risk experts—being responsible for scenario and satellite model management as well as projecting the earnings, losses, and capital under stress—as well as the bank's finance experts. The bank's finance experts construct the projected income and balance sheet statements from the risk information, at a certain scenario horizon t, and financial information such as tax rates and current available capital. The capital ratios and losses are then compared to regulatory or internally set limits. Based

---

therefore not on models to compute the loss for a portfolio but on the scenario set selection. Traditionally, risk-based model charges build a distribution from scenarios obtained from econometric models calibrated to the history and choose as the required capital a worst-case scenario according to the risk measure. The distinctive feature of the risk-based model is not how the scenarios are generated but that risk measures are applied to a set of scenarios.

[6] See the Basel Committee (2014b) paper on fundamental elements for a sound capital planning process.

on the performance of the bank in the scenario at a certain horizon t a decision on suitable management actions is taken, for example, on projected portfolio growth rates.

Hopefully banks will be inspired by the mandated CCAR and EBA firmwide stress testing and expand firmwide scenario analysis into a business practice to analyze different portfolios profitability under stress and use firmwide stress testing as a core component in forward-looking risk-based financial planning. The use of firmwide stress testing—both for regulation and business practice—puts pressure on the firmwide stress testing process to be formalized with proper controls, overall management of the process, transparency, and auditability. This is a challenge for many banks because, traditionally, many banks' business units, and consequently their risk systems, operate in silos. There is therefore a trend toward banks instituting central stress testing teams that have an overall responsibility for the firmwide stress testing and capital planning process.

In summary, the regulatory stress testing has motivated the risk management into a new era both qualitatively and quantitatively. Financial risk management expects more and more innovations and plays an ever more integral role in banks' business decisions.

References

Acerbi, C. (2002). Spectral Measures of Risk: A Coherent Representation of Subjective Risk Aversion, *Journal of Banking and Finance*, 26, pp. 1505–1518.

Acharya, V., Almeida, H., and Campello, M. (2010). Aggregate Risk and the Choice Between Cash and Credit Lines, Working Paper, New York University and University of Illinois.

Acharya, V., Almeida, H., and Campello, M. (2013). Aggregate Risk and the Choice Between Cash and Credit Lines, *Journal of Finance*, 68 (5), pp. 2059–2116.

Adrian, T. and Shin, H. S. (2010). Liquidity and Leverage, *Journal of Financial Intermediation*, 19, pp. 418–437.

Aguais, S. D., Forest, L. R., King, M., Lennon, M. C., and Lordkipanidze, B. (2006). Designing and Implementing a Basel II Compliant PIT-TTC Ratings Framework, in *The Basel II Handbook: A Guide for Financial Practitioners* (2nd Edition), Incisive Financial Publishing Ltd.

Alexander, S. T., Coleman, F., and Li, Y. (2004). Minimizing VaR and CVaR for a Portfolio of Derivatives, Working Paper, Cornell University, 2004.

Almgren, R. and Chriss, N. (2000). Optimal Execution of Portfolio Transactions, *Journal of Risk*, 3 (2), pp. 5–39.

Altman, E. I. (1968). Financial Ratios, Discriminant Analysis and the Prediction of Corporate Bankruptcy, *Journal of Finance*, September, pp. 189–209.

Altman, E. I. and Kishore, V. M. (1996). Almost Everything You Wanted to Know about Recoveries on Defaulted Bonds, *Financial Analysts Journal*, November/December, pp. 57–64.

Altman, E. I., Brady, B., Resti, A., and Sironi, A. (2005). The Link Between Default and Recovery Rates: Theory, *Empirical Evidence, and Implications, Journal of Business*, 78, pp. 2203–2227.

Altman, E. I., Resti, A., and Sironi, A. (2002). The Link Between Default and Recovery Rates: Effects on the Procyclicality of Regulatory Capital Ratios, BIS Working Paper No. 113.

Amato, J. D. and Gyntelberg, J. (2005). CDS Index Tranches and the Pricing of Credit Risk Correlations, *Basel Quarterly Review*, March, pp. 73–87.

Amemiya, T. (1985). *Advanced Econometrics*, Harvard University Press.

An, M. Y. and Qi, Z. (2012). Competing Risks Models Using Mortgage Duration Data under the Proportional Hazards Assumption, *Journal of Real Estate Research*, 34 (1).

Andersen, L. and Sidenius, J. (2004). Extensions to the Gaussian Copula: Random Recovery and Random Factor Loadings, Working Paper, Bank of America.

Anderson, T. W. (1958). *An Introduction to Multivariate Statistical Analysis*. New York: John Wiley & Sons.

Anfuso, F., Karyampas, D., and Nawroth, A. (2014). A Sound Basel III Compliant Framework for Backtesting Credit Exposure Models, available at http://papers.ssrn.com/sol3/papers.cfm?abstract_id=2264620.

Angelidis, T. and Benos, A. (2006). Liquidity Adjusted Value-at-Risk Based on the Components of the Bid–Ask Spread, *Applied Financial Economics*, 16 (11), pp. 835–851.

Arbenza, P., Hummel, C., and Mainik, G. (2012). Copula Based Hierarchical Risk Aggregation through Sample Reordering, *Insurance: Mathematics and Economics*, 51 (1), pp. 122–133.

Arnsdorf, M. (2012). Quantification of Central Counterparty Risk, *Journal of Risk Management in Financial Institutions*, 5 (3), pp. 273–287.

Artzner, P., Delbaen, F., Eber, J. M., and Heath, D. (1999). Coherent Measures of Risk, *Mathematical Finance*, 9 (3), pp. 203–228.

Bangia, A., Diebold, F. X., Schuermann, T., and Stroughair, J. D. (1999). *Modeling Liquidity Risk, with Implications for Traditional Market Risk Measurement and Management*. Wharton Financial Institutions Center.

Bank of England, (2012). RAMSI: A Top-Down Stress Testing Model, Stability Paper No. 17, September.

Bao, Y., Lee, T. H., and Saltoglu, B. (2004). A Test of Density Forecast Comparison with Application to Risk Management, Mimeo, University of California, Riverside, and Marmora University, Istanbul.

Barone-Adesi, G., Bourgoin, F., and Giannopoulos, K. (1998). Don't Look Back, *Risk,* 11, pp. 100–104.

Barone-Adesi, G., Giannopoulos, K., and Vosper, L. (1999). VaR without Correlations for Non-Linear Portfolios, *Journal of Futures Markets,* 19, pp. 583–602.

Barone-Adesi, G., Giannopoulos, K., and Vosper, L. (2000). Backtesting the Filtered Historical Simulation, unpublished manuscript.

Basel Committee (1988). International Convergence of Capital Measurement and Capital Standards, available at http://www.bis.org/publ/bcbs04a.pdf

Basel Committee (1992). A Framework for Measuring and Managing Liquidity, available at http://www.bis.org/publ/bcbs10b.pdf.

Basel Committee (1995). Treatment of Potential Exposure for Off-Balance-Sheet Items, available at http://www.bis.org/publ/bcbs18.pdf.

Basel Committee (1996). Amendment to the Capital Accord to Include Market Risks, available at: http://www.bis.org/publ/bcbs24.pdf.

Basel Committee (1999). Credit Risk Modelling: Current Practices and Applications, available at http://www.bis.org/publ/bcbs49.pdf.

Basel Committee (2000). Sound Practices for Managing Liquidity in Banking Organisations, available at http://www.bis.org/publ/bcbs69.pdf.

Basel Committee (2002). Quantitative Impact Study 3: Technical Guidance, available at http://www.bis.org/bcbs/qis/qis3tech.pdf.

Basel Committee (2005a). Basel II: International Convergence of Capital Measurement and Capital Standards: A Revised Framework, available at http://www.bis.org/publ/bcbs118.pdf.

Basel Committee (2005b). The Application of Basel II to Trading Activities and the Treatment of Double Default Effects, available at http://www.bis.org/publ/bcbs116.pdf.

Basel Committee (2005c). An Explanatory Note on the Basel II IRB Risk Weight Functions, available at http://www.bis.org/publ/irbriskweight.pdf.

Basel Committee (2008). Principles for Sound Liquidity Risk Management and Supervision, available at http://www.bis.org/publ/bcbs144.pdf.

Basel Committee (2009a). Revisions to the Basel II Market Risk Framework, available at http://www.bis.org/publ/bcbs158.pdf.

Basel Committee (2009b). Guidelines for Computing Incremental Risk in the Trading Book, available at http://www.bis.org/publ/bcbs159.pdf.

Basel Committee (2009c). Principles for Sound Stress Testing Practices and Supervision, available at http://www.bis.org/publ/bcbs155.pdf.

Basel Committee (2009d). Analysis of the Trading Book Quantitative Impact Study, available at http://www.bis.org/bcbs/irbriskweight.pdf.

Basel Committee (2009e). Findings on the Interaction of Market and Credit Risk, available at http://www.bis.org/publ/bcbs_wp16.pdf.

Basel Committee (2010a). Sound Practices for Backtesting Counterparty Credit Risk Models, available at http://www.bis.org/publ/bcbs185.pdf.

Basel Committee (2010b). Developments in Modeling Risk Aggregation, available at http://www.bis.org/publ/joint25.pdf.

Basel Committee (2011a). Basel III: A Global Regulatory Framework for more Resilient Banks and Banking Systems, available at http://www.bis.org/publ/bcbs189.pdf.

Basel Committee (2011b). Messages from the Academic Literature on Risk Measurement for the Trading Book, available at http://www.bis.org/publ/bcbs_wp19.pdf.

Basel Committee (2012). Fundamental Review of the Trading Book, available at http://www.bis.org/publ/bcbs219.pdf.

Basel Committee (2013a). Basel III: The Liquidity Coverage Ratio and Liquidity Risk Monitoring Tools, available at http://www.bis.org/publ/bcbs238.pdf.

Basel Committee (2013b). Fundamental Review of the Trading Book: A Revised Market Risk Framework, available at http://www.bis.org/publ/bcbs265.pdf.

Basel Committee (2013c). Principles for Effective Risk Data Aggregation and Risk Reporting, available at http://www.bis.org/publ/bcbs239.pdf.

Basel Committee (2013d). Progress in Adopting the Principles for Effective Risk Data Aggregation and Risk Reporting, available at http://www.bis.org/publ/bcbs268.pdf.

Basel Committee (2014a). Fundamental Review of the Trading Book: Outstanding Issues, available at http://www.bis.org/publ/d305.pdf.

Basel Committee (2014b). A Sound Capital Planning Process: Fundamental Elements, available at http://www.bis.org/publ/bcbs277.pdf.

Basel Committee (2014c). Revisions to the Standardised Approach for Credit Risk, available at http://www.bis.org/bcbs/publ/d307.pdf.

Basel Committee (2014d). Basel III: The Net Stable Funding Ratio, available at http://www.bis.org/publ/d295.pdf.

Bates, T. W., Kahle, K. M., and Stulz, R. M. (2009). Why Do U.S. Firms Hold So Much More Cash than They Used To? *Journal of Finance*, Vol 64 (5), pp. 1985–2021.

Begg, C. B. and Gray, R. (1984). Calculation of Polychotomous Logistic Regression Parameters Using Individualized Regressions, *Biometrika*, 71, pp. 11–18.

Belkin, B., Suchower, S., and Forest Jr. L. (1998). A One-Parameter Representation of Credit Risk and Transition Matrices, *CreditMetrics Monitor*, Third Quarter.

Bensalah, Y. (2000). Steps in Applying Extreme Value Theory to Finance: A Review, Working Paper, Bank of Canada.

Berkowitz, J. (2000). A Coherent Framework for Stress Testing, *Journal of Risk*, 2, pp. 1–11.

Berkowitz, J. (2001). Testing Density Forecasts With Applications to Risk Management, *Journal of Business and Economic Statistics*, 19, pp. 465–474.

Berkowitz, J. and O'Brien, J. (2002). How Accurate Are Value-at-Risk Models at Commercial Banks? *Journal of Finance*, 57, pp. 1093–1111.

Bertsimas D., Brown, D. B., and Caramanis, C. (2011). Theory and Applications of Robust Optimization, *SIAM Rev.*, 53 (3), 464–501.

Bervas, A. (2006). Market Liquidity and Its Incorporation into Risk Management, Technical Paper, Banque de France.

Bhanot, K. (2005). What Causes Mean Reversion in Corporate Bond Index Spreads? The Impact of Survival, *Journal of Banking & Finance*, 29 (6), pp. 1385–1403.

Bianchetti, M. (2012). Two Curves, One Price: Pricing & Hedging Interest Rate Derivatives Decoupling Forwarding and Discounting Yield Curves, available at http://arxiv.org/pdf/0905.2770.pdf.

Björk, T. (1998). *Arbitrage Theory in Continuous Time*, Oxford Press.

Black, F. (1976). Studies of Stock Market Volatility Changes, *Proceedings of the American Statistical Association, Business and Economics Statistics Section*, pp. 177–181.

Black, F. (1976). The Pricing of Commodity Contracts, *Journal of Financial Economics*, 3, pp. 167–179.

Black, F. and Karasinski, P. (1991). Bond and Option Pricing When Short Rates Are Lognormal, *Financial Analysts Journal*, July/August, pp. 52–59.

Black, F. and Scholes, M. (1973). The Pricing of Options and Corporate Liabilities, *Journal of Political Economy*, 81.

Board of Governors of the Federal Reserve System and the Office of the Comptroller of the Currency (2011). Supervisory Guidance on Model Risk Management, OCC 2011–12.

Bollerslev, T. (1986). Generalized Autoregressive Conditional Heteroskedasticity, *Journal of Econometrics*, 31, pp. 307–327.

Bollerslev, T. (1987). A Conditionally Heteroskedastic Time Series Model for Speculative Prices and Rates of Return, *Review of Economics and Statistics*, Vol 69 (3), pp. 542–47.

Bollerslev, T. (1990). Modelling the Coherence in Short-Run Nominal Exchange Rates: A Multivariate Generalized ARCH *Approach, Review of Economics and Statistics*, 72, pp. 498–505.

Bollerslev, T. (1990). Modelling the Coherence in Short-run Nominal Exchange Rates: A Multivariate Generalized ARCH Model, *Review of Economics and Statistics*, 72 (3), pp. 498–505.

Bollerslev, T. and Wooldridge, J. M. (1992). Quasi-Maximum Likelihood Estimation and Inference in Dynamic Models with Time-Varying Covariances, *Econometric Reviews, Taylor and Francis Journals*, 11 (2), pp. 143–172.

Bollerslev, T., Engle, R. F., and Wooldridge, J. M. (1988). A Capital-Asset Pricing Model with Time-Varying Covariances, *Journal of Political Economy*, 96, pp. 116–131.

Box, G. E. P. and Draper, N. R. (1987). *Empirical Model-Building and Response Surfaces*, John Wiley & Sons, Hoboken, NJ

Boyson, N., Helwege, J., and Jindra, J. (2010). Crises, Liquidity Shocks, and Fire Sales at Financial Institutions, Working Paper, Northeastern University.

Bröker, F. and Schweizer, S. (2004). Integrating Rating Migrations, in *CreditRisk$^+$ in the Banking Industry*, Springer Verlag.

Britten-Jones, M. and Schaefer, S. M. (1999). Nonlinear Value-at-Risk, *European Finance Review*, Vol 2 (2), pp. 161–187.

Brockmann, M. and Kalkbrener, M. (2010). On the Aggregation of Risk, *Journal of Risk*, Vol 12 (3).

Brooks, C., Clare, A. D., Dalle Molle, J. W., and Persand, G. (2005). A Comparison of Extreme Value Theory Approaches for Determining Value-at-Risk, *Journal of Empirical Finance*, 12, pp. 339–352.

Bruneton, J. P. (2011). Copula-Based Hierarchical Aggregation of Correlated Risks: The Behaviour of the Diversification Benefit in Gaussian and Lognormal Trees, available at http://arxiv.org /abs/1111.1113.

Brunnermeier, M. K. (2009). Deciphering the 2007–2008 Liquidity and Credit Distress, *Journal of Economic Perspectives*, 23, pp. 77–100.

Burgard, C. and Kjaer, M. (2011). In the Balance, *Risk*, October.

Burgard, C. and Kjaer, M. (2012). The FVA Debate: In Theory and Practice, available at http://papers .ssrn.com/sol3/papers.cfm?abstract_id=2157634.

Burgisser, A. K., Wagner, A., and Wolf, M. (1999). Integrating Correlations, *Risk*, Vol 12 (7), pp. 57–60.

Cai, J. and Thakor, A. V. (2008). Liquidity Risk, Credit Risk and Interbank Competition, Working Paper, Washington University.

Campbell, J. Y., Lo A. W., and MacKinlay, A. C. (1997). *The Econometrics of Financial Markets*, Princeton.

Campello, M., Giambona, E., Graham, J. R., and Harvey, C. R. (2011). Liquidity Management and Corporate Investment during a Financial Crisis, *Review of Financial Studies*, Vol 24 (6), pp. 1944–1979.

Campello, M., Giambona, E., Graham, J. R., and Harvey, C. R. H. (2012). Access to Liquidity and Corporate Investment in Europe during the Financial Crisis, *Review of Finance*, Vol 16 (2), pp. 323–346.

Canabarro, E. and Duffie, D. (2003). Measuring and Marking Counterparty Risk, in *Asset/Liability Management for Financial Institutions*, Institutional Investor Books, London.

Canals-Cerdá, J. J. and Kerr, S. (2015). Credit Risk Modeling in Segmented Portfolios: An Application to Credit Cards, Federal Reserve Bank of Philadelphia, Working Paper No 15-08.

Cantor, R. and Hamilton, D. (2004). Rating Transitions and Defaults Conditional on Watchlist, Outlook and Rating History, Moodys special comments.

Capriotti, L., Lee, S., and Peacock, M. (2011). Real-Time Counterparty Credit Risk Management in Monte Carlo. available at http://ssrn.com/paper=1824864.

Cárdenas, J., Fruchard, E., Koehler, E., Christophe, M., and Thomazeau, I. (1997). VaR: One Step Beyond, *Risk*, Vol 10 (10), pp. 72–75.

Carlehed, M. and Petrov, A. (2012). A Methodology for Point-In-Time–Through-The-Cycle Probability of Default Decomposition in Risk Classification Systems, *Journal of Risk Model Validation*, Vol 6 (3), pp. 3–25.

Carling, K., Jacobson, T., Lindé, J., and Roszbach, K. (2002). Capital Charges under Basel II: Corporate Credit Risk Modeling and the Macroeconomy, Working Paper Sveriges Riksbank No 145.

Cassella, G. and Berger, R. L. (1990). *Statistical Inference*, Duxbury Press.

Castagna, A. (2012). Yes, FVA Is a Cost for Derivatives Desks, available at http://papers.ssrn .com/sol3/papers.cfm?abstract_id=2141663.

Castillaci, G. (2008). Bootstrapping Credit Curves from CDS Spread Curves, available at http://papers .ssrn.com/sol3/papers.cfm?abstract_id=2042177.

Castilacci, G. and Seclari, M. J. (2003). The Practice of Delta–Gamma VaR: Implementing the Quadratic Portfolio Model, *European Journal of Operational Research*, 150, pp. 529–545.

CEBS (2009). CEBS Draft Revised Guidelines on Stress Testing (CP32), available at https://www.eba .europa.eu/documents/10180/37070/CP32.pdf.

CEBS (2010). CEBS Guidelines on Stress Testing (GL32), available at https://www.eba.europa.eu /documents/10180/16094/ST_Guidelines.pdf.

Cech, C. (2006). Copula-Based Top-Down Approaches in Financial Risk Aggregation, University of Applied Sciences Vienna, Working Paper Series No 32.

Cesari, G., Aquilina, J., Charpillon, N., Filipovic, Z., Lee, G., and Manda, I. (2009). *Modelling, Pricing and Hedging Counterparty Exposure*, Springer Finance.

Chari, V. V., Christiano, L., and Kehoe, P. J. (2008). Facts and Myths about the Financial Crisis of 2008, FRB Minneapolis Working Paper No 666.

Chen R. R., Filonuk, W., Patro, D. K. and Yan, A. (2013). Valuing Financial Assets with Liquidity Discount: An Implication for Basel III, *Journal of Fixed Income*, Winter, pp. 1–19.

Chen, W. (2009). Risk-Based Portfolio Optimization Using SAS®, *SAS Global Forum 2009*, Paper 127-2009.

Chen, W. and Skoglund, J. (2012). Cash Flow Replication with Mismatch Constraints, *Journal of Risk*, 14 (4), pp. 115–128.

Chen, W. and Skoglund, J. (2013). An Integrated Stress Testing Framework via Markov Switching Simulation, *Journal of Risk Model Validation*, Vol 7 (2), pp. 3–27.

Chen, W. and Skoglund, J. (2014). Optimal Hedging of Funding Liquidity Risk, *Journal of Risk*, Vol 16 (3), pp. 85–111.

Chen, W., Skoglund, J., and Cai, L. (2012). Planning for Optimal Liquidity Execution, *International Review of Applied Financial Issues and Economics*, Vol 4 (1).

Cheung, Y. W. and Lai, K. S. (1994). Mean Reversion in Real Exchange Rates, *Economic Letters*, 46, pp. 251–256.

Cheung, Y. W. and Lai, K. S. (2000). On the Purchasing Power Parity Puzzle, *Journal of International Economics*, 52, pp. 321–330.

Chishti, A. (1999). Simulation of Fixed-Income Portfolios Using Grids, *Algo Research Quarterly*, 2 (2), pp. 41–50.

Choudhry, M. (2007). *Bank Asset and Liability Management, Strategy, Trading and Analysis*. Hoboken, NJ: Wiley Finance.

Christensen, P. E. and Fabozzi, F. J. (1987). Dedicated Bond Portfolios, in *The Handbook of Fixed Income Securities*, Dow Jones–Irwin.

Christoffersen, P. (1998). Evaluating Interval Forecasts, *International Economic Review*, 39, pp. 841–862.

Christoffersen, P. and Pelletier, P. (2004). Backtesting Value at Risk: A Duration-Based Approach, *Journal of Financial Econometrics*, 2, pp. 84–108.

Christoffersen, P., Diebold, F. X., and Schuermann, T. (1998). Horizon Problems and Extreme Events in Financial Risk Management, *Federal Reserve Bank of New York Economic Policy Review*, 4 (3), pp. 109–118.

Colletaz, G., Hurlin, Ch., and Perignon, Ch. (2013). The Risk Map: A New Tool for Validating Risk Models, *Journal of Banking & Finance*, 37 (10), pp. 3843–3854.

Committee of European Banking Supervisors (2010). Guidelines on Liquidity Cost Benefit Allocation.

Comprehensive Capital Analysis and Review (2014). Comprehensive Capital Analysis and Review 2014: Assessment Framework and Results, available at http://www.federalreserve.gov /newsevents/press/bcreg/ccar_20140326.pdf.

Comprehensive Capital Analysis and Review (CCAR), available at http://www.federalreserve.gov /bankinforeg/ccar.htm.

Cossin, D. and Pirotte, H. (2001). *Advanced Credit Risk Analysis*. Hoboken, NJ: Wiley Series in Financial Engineering.

Cox, D. R. (1972). Regression Models and Life Tables (with discussion), *Journal of the Royal Statistical Society*, 34, pp. 187–220.

Cox, J., Ingersoll, J., and Ross, S. (1985). A Theory of the Term Structure of Interest Rates, *Econometrica*, 53, pp. 385–408.

Cox, J. C., Ross, S., and Rubinstein, M. (1979). Option Pricing: A Simplified Approach, *Journal of Financial Economics*, 7, pp. 229–264.

CreditMetrics manual (1997). J.P. Morgan.

CreditRisk$^+$ manual (1997). available from http://www.csfb.com/creditrisk.

Crnkovic, C. and Drachman, J. (1996). Quality Control, *Risk*, Vol 9 (7), pp. 138–143.

Danielsson, J. and De Vries, C. (1997). Value at Risk and Extreme Returns, FMG Discussion Paper No 273, Financial Markets Group, London School of Economics.

Danielsson, J. and Zigrand, J. P. (2004). On Time-Scaling of Risk and the Square-Root-of-Time Rule, EFA 2004 Maastricht Meetings Paper No 5339.

Daul, S., De Giorgi, E., Lindskog, F., and McNeil, A. J. (2003). The Grouped *t*-Copula with an Application to Credit Risk, *Risk*, 16 (11), pp. 73–76.

Davidson, J. (1994). *Stochastic Limit Theory*, Oxford University Press.

Demarta, S. and McNeil, A. J. (2005). The t Copula and Related Copulas, *International Statistical Review*, 73 (1), pp. 111–129.

Denault, M. (2001). Coherent Allocation of Risk Capital, *Journal of Risk*, 4 (1).

Derman, E. (1996). *Model Risk*, Goldman Sachs, Quantitative Strategies Research Notes.

Derman, E. and Kani, I. (1996). The Ins and Outs of Barrier Options: Part 1, *Derivatives Quarterly*, pp. 55–67.

Dermine, J. and Bissada, Y. F. (2002). *Asset and Liability Management: A Guide to Value Creation and Risk Control*, Financial Times—Prentice Hall.

Dev, A. and Rao, V. (2006). *Performance Measurement in Financial Institutions in an ERM Framework*, Risk Books.

Diamond, D. W. and Dybvig, P. H. (1983). Bank Runs, *Deposit Insurance, and Liquidity, Journal of Political Economy*, 91 (3), pp. 401–419.

Diebold, F., Hickman, A., Inoue, A., and Schuermann, T. (1997). Converting 1-Day Volatility to h-Day Volatility: Scaling by sqrt(h) Is Worse Than You Think, Discussion paper series, no. 97-34, Wharton.

Diebold, F. X., Doherty, N. A., and Herring, R. J. (2010). The Known, the Unknown, and the Unknowable in Financial Risk Management, *Financial Markets and Portfolio Management*, Vol 24 (4), pp. 453–454.

Diebold, F. X., Gunther, T., and Tay, A. (1998). Evaluating Density Forecasts with Applications to Financial Risk Management, *International Economic Review*, 39, pp. 863–883.

Dimakos, X. and Aas, K. (2004). Integrated Risk Modeling, *Statistical Modeling*, 4, pp. 265–277.

Dodd-Frank Act Stress Tests (DFAST), available at http://www.federalreserve.gov/bankinforeg/dfa-stress-tests.htm.

Drehmann M. J. and Nikolau, K. (2009). Funding Liquidity Risk: Definition and Measurement, ECB Working Paper Series, 124.

Drehmann, M., Elliot, J., and Kapadia, S. (2007). Funding Liquidity Risk: Potential Triggers and Systemic Implications, Mimeo, Bank of England.

Duane, M., Schuermann, T., and Reynolds, P. (2014). Stress Testing Bank Profitability, *Journal of Risk Management in Financial Institutions*, 7 (1).

Duffie, D. and Lando, D. (2001). Term Structure of Credit Spreads with Incomplete Accounting Information, *Econometrica*, 69, pp. 633–664.

Duffie, D. and Pan, J. (2001). Analytical Value-at-Risk with Jumps and Credit Risk, *Finance and Stochastics*, 5(2), pp. 155–180.

Duffie, D. and Singleton, K. (1999). Modeling Term Structures of Defaultable Bonds, *Review of Financial Studies*, 12, pp. 687–720.

Duffie, D. and Ziegler, A. (2003). Liquidation Risk, *Financial Analysts Journal*, 59 (3).

Dufour, J.-M. (2006). Monte Carlo Tests with Nuisance Parameters: A General Approach to Finite-Sample Inference and Nonstandard Asymptotics, *Journal of Econometrics*, 133, 443–477.

Dullman, K., Scheicher, M., and Schmieder, C. (2007). Asset Correlations and Credit Portfolio Risk: An Empirical Analysis, Discussion Paper Series 2: Banking and Financial Studies No 13.

Dunsky, R. M. and Ho, T. M. (2007). Valuing Fixed Rate Mortgage Loans with Default and Prepayment Options, *The Journal of Fixed Income*, 16 (4), pp. 7–31.

Efron, B. and Tibshirani, R. (1993). *An Introduction to the Bootstrap*, Chapman & Hall/CRC.

Elton, E. J. and Gruber, M. J. (1995). *Modern Portfolio Theory and Investment Analysis*. New York: John Wiley & Sons.

Embrechts, P., McNeil, A., and Straumann, D. (2001). Correlation and Dependence in Risk Management: Properties and Pitfalls, in *Risk Management: Value at Risk and Beyond*. Cambridge: Cambridge University Press.

Embrechts, P., Mikosch, T., and Klüppelberg, C. (1997). *Modelling Extremal Events for Insurance and Finance*. Berlin: Springer.

Emmer, S., Kratz, M., and Tache, D. (2014). What Is the Best Risk Measure in Practice? A Comparison of Standard Measures, available at http://arxiv.org/abs/1312.1645v3.

Engle, R. F. (1982). Autoregressive Conditional Heteroskedasticity with Estimates of the Variance of United Kingdom Inflation, *Econometrica*, 50, pp. 987–1007.

Engle, R. F. (2002). Dynamic Conditional Correlation: A Simple Class of Multivariate GARCH Models, *Journal of Business and Economic Statistics*, 20, pp. 339–350.

Engle, R. F. and Gonzales-Rivera, G. (1991). Semiparametric ARCH Models, *Journal of Business and Economic Statistics*, 9 (4), pp. 345–359.

Epperlein, E. and Smillie, A. (2006). Cracking VaR with Kernels, RISK, August.

Epperlein, E., Hrabak, S. P., Zhu, W., and Smillie, A. (2010). Back(testing) to the Future: From Market Risk to Counterparty Credit Risk Models, in *Counterparty Credit Risk*. London: Risk Books.

Ernst, C., Stange, S., and Kaserer, C. (2009). Measuring Market Liquidity Risk—Which Model Works Best?, CEFS Working Paper Series, No 2009-01.

Errais, E., Giesecke, K., and Goldberg, L. R. (2010). Affine Point Processes and Portfolio Credit Risk, *SIAM Journal of Financial Mathematics*, 1, pp. 642–665.

European Banking Authority (2014). Methodological Note EU-wide Stress Test 2014, available at https://www.eba.europa.eu/-/eba-publishes-common-methodology-and-scenario-for-2014-eu-banks-stress-test.

European Banking Authority, (2014). Methodological Note EU-Wide Stress Test 2014, April 29.

European Central Bank (2013). A Macro Stress Testing Framework for Assessing Systemic Risks in the Banking Sector, available at http://www.ecb.europa.eu/pub/pdf/scpops/ecbocp152.pdf.

European Central Bank (2013). A Macro Stress Testing Framework for Assessing Systemic Risks in the Banking Sector, Occasional Paper Series No 152, October.

Fabozzi, F. J. (1997). *Fixed Income Mathematics*. New York: McGraw-Hill.

Fallon, W. (1996). Calculating Value-at-Risk, working paper.

Fama and French (1993). Common risk factors in the returns of stocks and bonds, *Journal of Financial Economics*, pp. 3–56.

Federal Reserve (2012). CCAR frequently asked questions, available at http://www.federalreserve.gov/bankinforeg/ccar.htm.

Feuerverger, A. and Wong, C. M. (2000). Computation of Value-at-Risk for Non-Linear Portfolios, *Journal of Risk*, 3 (1), pp. 37–55.

Fiedler, R. (2007). A Concept for Cash Flow and Funding Liquidity Risk, in *Liquidity Risk: Measurement and Management*. Hoboken, NJ: John Wiley & Sons.

Fiedler, R. and Kustner, M. (2011). Counter-Balancing Capacity, white paper, Pelican Consulting.

Financial Services Authority of United Kingdom (2009). Strengthening Liquidity Standards, Financial Services Authority Policy Statement, 09/16 October.

Financial Stability Board (2013). Principles for an Effective Risk Appetite Framework, available at http://www.financialstabilityboard.org/2013/11/r_131118/.

Financial Stability Forum (2008). Report of the Financial Stability Forum on Enhancing Market and Institutional Resilience. Available at http://www.financialstabilityboard.org/wp-content/uploads/r_0804.pdf?page_moved=1.

Finger, C. (1999). Conditional Approaches for CreditMetrics Portfolio Distributions, *Credit Metrics Monitor*, 2 (1), pp. 14–33.

Fisher, R. A. (1956). *Statistical Methods and Scientific Inference*. London: Oliver & Boyd.

Föllmer, H. and Schied, A. (2002). Convex Measures of Risk and Trading Constraints, *Finance Stochastics*, 6 (4), pp. 429–447.

Fons, J. (1994). Using Default Rates to Model the Term-Structure of Credit Risk, *Financial Analysts Journal*, 50, pp. 25–32.

Frey, R., McNeil, A., and Nyfeler, N. (2001). Copulas and Credit Models, *Risk*, 14, pp. 111–114.

Garcia Cespedes, J. C., de Juan Herrero, J. A., Kreinin, A., and Rosen, D. (2006). A Simple Multifactor "Factor Adjustment" for the Treatment of Credit Capital Diversifcation, *Journal of Credit Risk*, 2 (3), pp. 57–85.

Garman, M. (1997). Taking VaR to Pieces, *Risk*, 10, pp. 70–71.

Gatev, E. and Strahan, P. (2006). Banks' Advantage in Hedging Liquidity Risk: Theory and Evidence from the Commercial Paper Market, *Journal of Finance*, 61, pp. 867–892.

Gatev, E., Schuermann, T., and Strahan, P. (2009). Managing Banks Liquidity Risk: How Deposit-Loan Synergies Vary with Market Conditions, *Review of Financial Studies*, 22, pp. 995–1020.

Gemming, G. (2002). Testing Merton's Model for Credit Spreads on Zero-Coupon Bonds, *Financial Econometrics Reseacrh Centre*, Working Paper Series, wp02-08.

Geršl, A., Jakubík, P., Konečný, T., and Seidler, J. (2013). Dynamic Stress Testing: The Framework for Assessing the Resilience of the Banking Sector Used by the Czech National Bank, *Czech Journal of Economics and Finance*, Vol 63 (6), pp. 505–536.

Geske, R. (1977). The Valuation of Corporate Liabilities as Compound Options, *Journal of Financial and Quantitative Analysis*, pp. 541–552.

Gibson, M. (2005). Measuring Counterparty Credit Exposure to a Margined Counterparty, in *Counterparty Credit Risk Modelling*, Risk Books, London.

Gibson, M. S. and Pritsker, M. (2000). Improving Grid-Based Methods for Estimating Value at Risk of Fixed-Income Portfolios, Federal Reserve Board, Finance and Economics Discussion Series, 25.

Giese, G. (2004). Enhanced CreditRisk+, in *CreditRisk+ in the Banking Industry*. New York: Springer Verlag.

Giesecke, K. (2001). Default and Information, Working Paper, Cornell University.

Giesecke, K. (2004). Correlated Default with Incomplete Information, *Journal of Banking & Finance*, 28, pp. 1521–1545.

Gil-Pelaez, J. (1951). Note on the Inversion Theorem, *Biometrika*, 38, pp. 481–482.

Glasserman, P. (2003). *Monte Carlo Methods in Financial Engineering*. New York: Springer.

Glasserman, P. and Li, J. (2005). Importance Sampling for Portfolio Credit Risk, *Management Science*, 50 (11), pp. 1643–1656.

Glasserman, P., Heidelberger, P., and Shahabuddin, P. (2000a). Importance Sampling and Stratification for Value-at-Risk, in *Computational Finance 1999*, MIT Press, pp. 7–24.

Glasserman, P., Heidelberger, P., and Shahabuddin, P. (2000b). Variance Reduction Techniques for Estimating Value-at-Risk, *Management Science*, 46, pp. 1349–1364.

Glasserman, P., Heidelberger, P., and Shahabuddin, P. (2002). Portfolio Value-at-Risk with Heavy Tailed Risk Factors, *Mathematical Finance*, 12, pp. 239–269.

Glasserman, P., Kang, C., and Kang, W. (2013). Stress Scenario Selection by Empirical Likelihood, Office of Financial Research, Working Paper #0007.

Glosten, L., Jagannathan, R., and Runkle, D. (1993). On the Relation Between Expected Values and the Nominal Excess Return on Stocks, *Journal of Finance*, 48, pp. 1779–1801.

Gordy, M. (2000). A Comparative Anatomy of Credit Risk Models, *Journal of Banking and Finance*, 24, pp. 119–145.

Gordy, M. (2003). A Risk-Factor Model Foundation for Ratings-Based Bank Capital Rules, *Journal of Financial Intermediation*, 12 (3), pp. 199–232.

Gordy, M. (2004). Granularity, in *New Risk Measures for Investment and Regulation*. Hoboken, NJ: John Wiley & Sons.

Gordy, M. and Lütkebohmert, E. (2007). Granularity Adjustment for Basel II, Deutsche Bundesbank Discussion Paper, Series 2, No 01.

Gordy, M. B. (2002). Saddlepoint Approximation of CreditRisk+, *Journal of Banking & Finance*, 26 (7), pp. 1335–1353.

Gordy, M. B. (2004). Saddlepoint Approximation, in *CreditRisk+ in the Banking Industry*. New York: Springer Verlag.

Governor Daniel K. Tarullo at the Federal Reserve, speech (May 8, 2014). available at http://www.federalreserve.gov/newsevents/speech/tarullo20140508a.htm.

Grandell, J. (1991). *Aspects of Risk Theory*. New York: Springer Verlag.

Granger, C. W. J. and Ding, Z. (1995). Some Properties of the Absolute Returns: An Alternative Measurement of Risk, *Annales d'Economie et de Statistique*, 40, pp. 67–91.

Granito, M. R. (1984). *Bond Portfolio Immunization*. Lexington, MA: Lexington Books.

Grant, J. (2011). Liquidity Transfer Pricing: A Guide to Better Practice, Financial Stability Institute, Occasional Paper No 10.

Greene, W. H. (1993). *Econometric Analysis*, Prentice-Hall.

Gregory, J. (2009). Being Two-Faced Over Counterparty Credit Risk, *Risk*, February.

Gregory J. (2010). *Counterparty Credit Risk: The New Challenge for Financial Markets*. Hoboken, NJ: John Wiley & Sons.

Grundke, P. (2011). Stress Tests with Bottom-Up Approaches, *Journal of Risk Model Validation*, 5 (1), pp. 71–90.

Grundke, P. (2012). Further Recipes for Quantitative Reverse Stress Testing, *Journal of Risk Model Validation*, 6 (2), pp. 81–102.

Grundlach, M. and Lehrbass, F. (eds) (2004). *CreditRisk+ in the Banking Industry*. New York: Springer Verlag.

Gurrieri, S., Nakabayashi, M., and Wong, T. (2009). Calibration Methods of Hull-White Model, Working Paper, Mizuho Securities, Tokyo.

Haaf, H. and Tasche, D. (2002). Calculating Value-at-Risk Contributions in CreditRisk+, *GARP Risk Review*, 7, July/August, pp. 43–47.

Haaf, H., Reiss, O., and Schoenmaker, J. (2004). Numerically Stable Computation of CreditRisk+, in *CreditRisk+ in the Banking Industry*. New York: Springer Verlag.

Hallerbach, W. (2003). Decomposing Portfolio Value-at-Risk: A General Analysis, *Journal of Risk*, 5, pp. 1–18.

Hamerle, A., Knapp, M., and Wildenauer, N. (2007). Default and Recovery Correlations: A Dynamic Econometric Approach, *Risk*, January, pp. 100–105.

Hart, I. and Ross, M. (1994). Striking Continuity, *Risk*, Vol 7 (6).

Haug, E. G. (2007). *The Complete Guide to Option Pricing Formulas*. New York: McGraw-Hill.

Hawawini, G. A. (ed.) (1982). *Bond Duration and Immunization: Early Developments and Recent Contributions*, Garland Publishing, New York.

He, C. and Teräsvirta, T. (1999). Properties of Moments of a Family of GARCH Processes, *Journal of Econometrics*, 92, pp. 173–192.

Heidorn, T. and Kahlert, D. (2010). Implied Correlations of iTraxx Tranches during the Financial Crisis, Working Paper, Frankfurt School of Finance Management.

Heitfield, E. and Barger, N. (2003). Treatment of Double-Default and Double-Recovery Effects for Hedged Exposures under Pillar I of the Proposed New Basel Capital Accord, White Paper by the staff of the Board of Governors of the Federal Reserve System.

Hill, B. M. (1975). A Simple General Approach to Inference about the Tail of a Distribution, *Annals of Statistics*, 2, pp. 1163–1174.

Homescu, C. (2011a). Adjoints and Automatic (Algorithmic) Differentiation in Computational Finance, available at papers.ssrn.com/sol3/papers.cfm?abstract_id=1828503.

Homescu, C. (2011b). Generic Computing Alternatives for Better Greeks, available at http://papers.ssrn.com/sol3/papers.cfm?abstract_id=1921085.

Hull, J. (2006). *Options, Futures and Other Derivatives*, 6th Edition. New York: Prentice-Hall.

Hull, J. and White, A. (1990). Pricing Interest Derivative Securities, *Review of Financial Studies*, Vol 3 (4).

Hull, J. and White, A. (1994). Numerical Procedures for Implementing Term Structure Models I: Single-Factor Models, *Journal of Derivatives*, 2 (1), pp. 7–16.

Hull, J. and White, A. (1996). Using Hull-White Interest Rate Trees, *Journal of Derivatives*, Spring, pp. 26–36.

Hull, J. and White, A. (2000). Valuing Credit Default Swaps II: Modeling Default correlations, Working Paper, University of Toronto.

Hull, J. and White, A. (2012a). CVA and Wrong Way Risk, *Financial Analysts Journal*, 68 (5), pp. 58–69.

Hull, J. and White, A. (2012b). The FVA Debate, *Risk*, July, pp. 83–85.

Hull, J. and White, A. (2013). LIBOR vs. OIS: The Derivatives Discounting Dilemma, *Journal of Investment Management*, 11 (3), pp. 14–27.

Hull, J. and White, A. (2004). Valuation of a CDO and an *n*th to Default CDS without Monte Carlo Simulation, *Journal of Derivatives*, 12 (2).

Hull, J., Predescu, M., and White, A. (2004). The Relationship Between Credit Default Swap Spreads, Bond Yields, and Credit Rating Announcements, Working Paper, University of Toronto.

Hult, H. and Lindskog, F. (2001). *Multivariate Extremes, Aggregation and Dependence in Elliptical Distributions*, ETH preprint.

Hunsky, R. M. and Do, T. S. Y. (2007). Valuing Fixed Rate Mortgage Loans with Default and Prepayment Options, *Journal of Fixed Income*, 16 (4), pp. 7–31.

ISDA press release (November 3, 2011). ISDA Leads Industry Effort to Standardize the Credit Support Annex.

Israel, R. B., Rosenthal, J. S., and Wei, J. Z. (2001). Finding Generators for Markov Chains via Empirical Transition Matrices, with Applications to Credit Ratings, *Mathematical Finance*, 11 (2), pp. 245–265.

Ivashina, V. and Scharfstein, D. (2010). Bank Lending during the Financial Crisis of 2008, *Journal of Financial Economics*, 97, pp. 319–338.

Jagannathan, R., Ronn, E., and Chen, W. (2011). Pricing Credit-Rated Defaultable Coupon Bonds, *International Review of Applied Financial Issues and Economics*, Vol 3 (3), pp. 574–593.

Jamshidian, F. (1989). An Exact Bond Option Formula, *Journal of Finance*, 44, pp. 205–209.

Jamshidian, F. and Zhu, Y. (1997). Scenario Simulation: Theory and Methodology, *Finance Stochastics*, 1, pp. 43–67.

Jankowitsch, R., Nagler, F., and Subrahmanyam, M. G. (2014). The Determinants of Recovery Rates in the US Corporate Bond Market, *Journal of Financial Economics*, Vol 114 (1), pp. 155–177.

Jarrow, R. and Turnbull, S. (1995). The Pricing and Hedging of Options on Financial Securities Subject to Credit Risk, *Journal of Finance*, 50, pp. 53–85.

Jarrow, R. and Van Deventer, D. (1998). The Arbitrage Free Valuation and Hedging of Demand Deposits and Credit Card Loans, *Journal of Banking and Finance*, 22, pp. 249–272.

Jarrow, R. and Yu, F. (2001). Counterparty Risk and the Pricing of Defaultable Securities, *Journal of Finance*, 53, pp. 2225–2243.

Jarrow, R., Lando, D., and Turnbull, S. (1997). A Markov Model for the Term Structure of Credit Risk Spreads, *Review of Financial Studies*, 10 (2), pp. 481–523.

Jo, J. H. (2012). Managing Systemic Risk from the Perspective of the Financial Network under Macroeconomic Distress, Financial Stability Institute Award Winning 2012 paper.

Jones, E. P., Mason, S. P., and Rosenfeld, E. (1984). Contingent Claim Analysis of Corporate Capital Structures: An Empirical Investigation, *Journal of Finance*, 39 (3), pp. 611–627.

Jorion, P. (1986). Bayes-Stein Estimation for Portfolio Analysis, *Journal of Financial and Quantitative Analysis*, 21, pp. 279–292.

Jorion, P. (2009). *Financial Risk Manager Handbook*. Hoboken, NJ: Wiley.

Jorion, P. (2009). Risk Management Lessons from the Credit Crisis, *European Financial Management*, 15 (5), pp. 923–933.

Josefsson, M. (2004). A Copula-EVT Based Approach for Measuring Tail Related Risk: Applied on the Swedish Market, Master's Thesis, Royal School of Technology.

Kang, L. and Babbs, S. H. (2012). Modeling Overnight and Daytime Returns Using a Multivariate Generalized Autoregressive Conditional Heteroskedsticity Copula Model, *Journal of Risk,* 14 (4), pp. 35–63.

Kashyap, A. K., Rajan, R., and Stein, J. C. (2002). Banks as Liquidity Providers: An Explanation for the Coexistence of Lending and Deposit-Taking, *Journal of Finance,* 57 (1), pp. 33–73.

Kaufmann, R. and Patie, P. (2003). *Strategic Long-Term Financial Risks: The One-Dimensional Case,* RiskLab Report, ETH Zurich.

Kerkhof, J. and Melenberg, B. (2004). Backtesting for Risk-Based Regulatory Capital, *Journal of Banking & Finance,* 28, pp. 1845–1865.

Kocherlakota, R., Rosenbloom, E. S., and Shiu, E. S. W. (1988). Algorithms for Cash Flow Matching, *Transactions of Society of Actuaries,* 40 (1), pp. 477–484.

Kourouma, L., Dupre, D., San lippo, G., and Taramasco, O. (2011). *Extreme Value at Risk and Expected Shortfall during Financial Crisis,* Cahier de recherche du CERAG 2011-03 E2.

Koylouglu, H. U. and Hickman, A. (1998). Reconcilable Differences, *Risk,* October, pp. 56–62.

Krainer, J. and Laderman, E. (2011). Prepayment and Delinquency in the Mortgage Crisis Period, Federal Reserve Bank of San Francisco, Working Paper 2011-25.

Krokhmal, P., Palmquist, J., and Uryasev, S. (2002). Portfolio Optimization with Conditional Value-at-Risk Objective and Constraints, *Journal of Risk,* 4 (2), pp. 43–68.

Kuester, K., Mittnik, S., and Paolella, M. S. (2006). Value-at-Risk Prediction: A Comparison of Alternative Strategies, *Journal of Financial Econometrics,* 4 (1), pp. 53–89.

Kullback, S. M. (1959). *Information Theory and Statistics.* New York: John Wiley & Sons.

Kuritzkes, A., Schuermann, T., and Weiner, S. (2002). Risk Measurement, Risk Management and Capital Adequacy in Financial Conglomerates, Wharton Paper.

Kwan, S. (2009). Behavior of LIBOR in the Current Financial Crisis, FRBSF Economic Letter 2009-04 (January 23).

Lancaster, T. (1990). *The Econometric Analysis of Transition Data.* Cambridge: Cambridge University Press.

Lando, D. (1998). On Cox Processes and Credit Risky Securities. *Review of Derivatives Research,* 2, pp. 99–120.

Larsen, N. H., Mausser, S., and Uryase, V. (2004). Algorithms for Optimization of Value-at-Risk, Financial Engineering, E-Commerce and Supply Chain. New York: Springer, 19–46.

Laurent, J. P. and Gregory, J. (2003). Basket Default Swaps, CDO and Factor Copulas, Working Paper, ISFA Actuarial School, University of Lyon.

Lawrence, C. and Robinson, G. (1995). Liquid Measures, *Risk,* pp. 52–55.

Ledoit, O. and Wolf, M. (2003). Improved Estimation of the Covariance Matrix of Stock Returns with an Application to Portfolio Selection, *Journal of Empirical Finance,* 10 (5), pp. 603–621.

Ledoit, O. and Wolf, M. (2004). A Well-Conditioned Estimator for Large-Dimensional Covariance Matrices. *Journal of Multivariate Analysis,* 88 (2), pp. 365–411.

Lesko, M., Schlottmann, F., and Vorgrimler, S. (2004). Estimation of Sector Weights from Real World Data, in *CreditRisk$^+$ in the Banking Industry.* New York: Springer Verlag.

Levin, A. (2001). Active-Passive Decomposition in Burnout Modeling, *Journal of Fixed Income,* 10 (4), pp. 27–40.

Levin, A. and Davidson, A. (2005). Prepayment Risk- and Option-Adjusted Valuation of MBS—Opportunities for Arbitrage, *Journal of Portfolio Management,* 31 (4), pp. 1–20.

Levy and Levin (1999). Wrong Way Exposure, *Risk,* July.

Li, D. X. (2000). On Default Correlation: A Copula Function Approach, *Journal of Fixed Income,* Vol 9 (4), pp. 43–54.

Litterman, R. (1996). Hot Spots™ and Hedges, *Journal of Portfolio Management,* 22, pp. 52–75.

Litterman, R. and Scheinkman, J. (1991). Common Factors Affecting Bond Returns, *Journal of Fixed Income,* June, pp. 54–61.

Longstaff, F. and Schwartz, E. (1995). A Simple Approach to Valuing Risky Fixed and Floating Rate Debt, *Journal of Finance*, 50 (3), pp. 789–819.

Longstaff, F. A. and Schwartz, E. S. (2001). Valuing American Options by Simulation: A Simple Least-Squares Approach, *Review of Financial Studies*, 14 (1), pp. 113–147.

Lucas, A., Klaassen, P., Spreij, P., and Staetmans, S. (1999). An Analytic Approach to Credit Risk of Large Corporate Bond and Loan Portfolios, Research Memorandum 1999-18, Vrije Universiteit Amsterdam.

Lugannani, R. and Rice, S. (1980). Saddlepoint Approximations for the Distribution of the Sum of Independent Random Variables, *Advances in Applied Probability*, 12, pp. 475–490.

Lundbergh, S. (1999). Modelling Economic High-Frequency Time Series, PhD Thesis, Stockholm School of Economics, Ch. 4: A GARCH Model with Time-Varying Parameters.

Madan, D. B., Carr, P. P., and Chang, E. C. (1998). The Variance Gamma Process and Option Pricing, *European Finance Review*, 2, pp. 79–105.

Manning, M. J. (2004). Exploring the Relationship Between Credit Spreads and Default Probabilities, Working Paper No 225, Bank of England.

Markov, M., Mottl, V., and Muchnik, I. (2004). Dynamic Style Analysis and Applications, Available at SSRN: http://ssrn.com/abstract=1971363.

Markowitz, H. M. (1952). Portfolio Selection, *Journal of Finance* 7, pp. 77–99.

Markowitz, H. M. (1959). Portfolio Selection: Efficient Diversification of Investments. New York: John Wiley & Sons.

Martin, R. and Wilde, T. (2002). Unsystematic Credit Risk, *Risk*, 15, pp. 123–128.

Mashal, R., Naldi, M., and Zeevi, A. (2003). On the Dependence of Equity and Asset Returns, *Risk*, October, pp. 83–87.

Matz, L. (2011). *Liquidity Risk Measurement and Management, Basel III and Beyond*, Xlibris.

McConnell, J. and Singh, M. (1994). Rational Prepayments and the Valuation of Collateralized Mortgage Obligations, *Journal of Finance*, Vol 49 (3), pp. 891–921.

McGinty, L., Beinstein, E., Ahluwalia, R., and Watts, M. (2004). *Introducing Base Correlations, Credit Derivatives Strategy*, JP Morgan.

McMillan, D. G. (2001). Nonlinear Predictability of Stock Market Returns: Evidence from Nonparametric and Threshold models, *International Review of Economics and Finance*, 10, pp. 353–368.

McNeil, A. and Frey, R. (2000). Estimation of Tail Related Risk Measures for Heteroscedastic Financial Time Series: An Extreme Value Approach, *Journal of Empirical Finance*, 7, pp. 271–300.

McNeil, A., Frey, R., and Embrechts, P. (2005). *Quantitative Risk Management*. Oxford: Oxford Press.

McNeil, A. J. and Smith, A. D. (2012). Multivariate Stress Scenarios and Solvency, *Insurance: Mathematics and Economics*, 50 (3), pp. 299–308.

Memmel, C. and Wehn, C. (2006). The Supervisor's Portfolio: The Market Price Risk of German Banks from 2001 to 2004 — Analysis and Models for Risk Aggregation, *Journal of Banking Regulation*, 7, pp. 309–324.

Menkens, O. (2007). Value at Risk and Self–Similarity, in *Numerical Methods for Finance*, Chapman & Hall.

Merton, R. C. (1973). Theory of Rational Option Pricing, *Bell Journal of Economics and Management Science*, 4, pp. 141–183.

Merton, R. C. (1974). On the Pricing of Corporate Debt: The Risk Structure of Interest Rates, *Journal of Finance*, Vol 29 (2), pp. 449–470.

Mikosh, T. (2006). *Non–Life Insurance Mathematics: An Introduction with Stochastic Processes*, 2nd Edition. New York: Springer Verlag.

Mills, T. C. (1999). *The Econometric Modelling of Financial Time Series*. Cambridge: Cambridge University Press.

Mina, J. and Ulmer, A. (1999). Delta–Gamma Four Ways, Working Paper, J.P. Morgan/Reuters.

Modigliani, F. and Miller, M. H. (1958). The Cost of Capital, Corporation Finance and the Theory of Investment, *American Economic Review* 48 (3), pp. 261–297.

Moody's Hybrid Model for Public Firms (2000). Moody's Investor Service, Global Credit Research.

Moody's Investor Service (1997). *Moody's Rating Migration and Credit Quality Correlation*, July, 1920–1996.

Morgan, D. (1998). The Credit Effects of Monetary Policy: Evidence Using Loan Commitments, *Journal of Money Credit and Banking*, 20, pp. 102–118.

Morokoff, W. J. (2003). Simulation Methods for Risk Analysis of Collateralized Debt Obligations, *Simulation Conference, Proceedings of the 2003 Winter* (Volume1).

Neal, R., Rolph, D., Dupoyet, B., and Jiang, X. (2012). Interest Rate and Credit Spread Dynamics, Working Paper, Indiana University.

Nelson, D. B. (1990). Stationarity and Persistence in the GARCH(1,1) Model, *Econometric Theory*, 6, pp. 318–334.

Nelson, D. B. (1991). Conditional Heteroskedasticity in Asset Returns: A New Approach, *Econometrica*, 59, pp. 347–370.

Nelson, D. B. and Cao, C. Q. (1992). Inequality Constraints in the Univariate GARCH Model, *Journal of Business and Economic Statistics*, 10, pp. 229–235.

Neu, P., Leistenschneider, A., Wondrak, B., and Knippschild, M. (2007). Market Developments in Banks' Funding Markets, in *Liquidity Risk: Measurement and Management*, Wiley, Hoboken.

Nickell, P., Perraudin, W., and Varotto, S. (2000). Stability of Rating Transitions, *Journal of Banking and Finance*, 24, pp. 203–227.

Nobelprize (1990). The Sveriges Riksbank Prize in Economic Sciences in Memory of Alfred Nobel 1990, Nobelprize.org., Nobel Media AB, available at http://www.nobelprize.org/nobel.

Nobelprize (1997). The Sveriges Riksbank Prize in Economic Sciences in Memory of Alfred Nobel 1997, Nobelprize.org., Nobel Media AB, available at http://www.nobelprize.org/nobel.

Nyström, K. (2007). On the Rating and Pricing of Mortgage Portfolios through Structured Finance, *Journal of Risk Model Validation*, Vol 4 (1).

Nyström, K. (2008). Harmonic Analysis, Quadratic Forms and Asymptotic Expansions of Risk Measures, *Applied Mathematical Sciences*, 2 (21), pp. 1023–1052.

Nyström, K. and Skoglund, J. (2002). A Framework for Scenario-based Risk Management, available at http://gloria-mundi.com/UploadFile/2010-2/knjs.pdf.

Nyström, K. and Skoglund, J. (2003a). Essentials of Credit Portfolio Management, available at http://www.defaultrisk.com/pp_model_77.htm.

Nyström, K. and Skoglund, J. (2003b). Harmonic Analysis, Quadratic Forms and Risk Management, Working Paper, Department of Mathematics, Umeå University.

Nyström, K. and Skoglund, J. (2005). Efficient Filtering of Financial Time Series and Extreme Value Theory, *Journal of Risk*, 7 (2), pp. 63–84.

Nyström, K. and Skoglund, J. (2006). A Credit Risk Model for Large Dimensional Portfolios with Application to Economic Capital, *Journal of Banking & Finance*, 30, pp. 2163–2197.

O'Kane, D. (2008). *Modelling Single-Name and Multi-Name Credit Derivatives*. Hoboken, NJ: John Wiley & Sons.

O'Kane, D. and Turnbull, S. (2003). *Valuation of Credit Default Swaps*, Fixed Income Quantitative Credit Research, Lehman Brothers.

Owen, A. B. (2001). *Empirical Likelihood*, Chapman & Hall/CRC.

Pengelley M. (2011). CVA Melee, *Risk*, 24 (2), pp. 37–39.

Peura, S. and Soininen, J. (2005). One, Two, Three, Four Types of Default, Working Paper, Sampo Bank.

Pichler, S. and Selitsch, K. (2000). *A Comparison of Analytic VaR Methodologies for Portfolios that Include Pptions, Model Risk, Concepts, Calibration and Pricing*, Rajna Gibson (editor). London: Risk Books.

Piterbarg, V. (2010). Funding Beyond Discounting: Collateral Agreements and Derivatives Pricing, *Risk*, 2, pp. 97–102.

Pritsker, M. (2006). The Hidden Dangers of Historical Simulation, *Journal of Banking & Finance*, 30 (2), pp. 561–582.

Prudential Regulation Authority (2013). A Framework for Stress Testing the UK Banking System, October.

Pykthin, M. (2004). Multi-Factor Adjustment, *Risk*, March, pp. 85–90.

Pykhtin, M. (2009). Modeling Credit Exposure for Collateralized Counterparties, *Journal of Credit Risk*, 5 (4), pp. 3–27.

Pykthin, M. (2012). Model Foundations of Basel III Standardised CVA Charge, *Asia Risk*, August.

Pykthin, M. and Zhu, S. (2006). Measuring Counterparty Credit Risk for Trading Products under Basel II, in *Basel Handbook*, 2nd Edition. London: Risk Books.

Pykthin, M. and Zhu, S. (2007). A Guide to Modeling Counterparty Credit Risk, *GARP Risk Review*, July/August, pp. 16–22.

Pykthin, M. and Rosen, D. (2010). Pricing Counterparty Risk at the Trade Level and Credit Valuation Adjustment Allocations, *Journal of Credit Risk*, 6(4).

Rebonato, R. (2001). *Managing Model Risk: Handbook of Risk Management*, FT-Prentice Hall.

Rebonato, R. (2010). *Coherent Stress Testing: A Bayesian Approach to the Analysis of Financial Stress*. Hoboken, NJ: John Wiley & Sons.

Rebonato, R. and Jackel, P. (1999). *The Most General Methodology to Create a Valid Correlation Matrix for Risk Management and Option Pricing Purposes*, QUARC preprint.

Reiner, E. and Rubinstein, M. (1991). Breaking Down the Barriers, *Risk*, 4 (8).

Reserve Bank of India (2013). Guidelines on Stress Testing, December 2.

Richardson, M. and Smith, T. (1991). Tests of Financial Models in the Presence of Overlapping Observations, *Review of Financial Studies*, 4, pp. 227–254.

Righi, M. B. and Ceretta, P. S. (2013). Individual and Flexible Expected Shortfall Backtesting, *Journal of Risk Model Validation*, 7 (3), pp. 3–20.

RiskMetrics™ (1996). Technical Document, 4th Edition, J.P.Morgan, December.

Rockafellar, R. T. and Uryasev, S. (2000). Optimization of Conditional Value at Risk, *Journal of Risk*, 2 (3), pp. 21–39.

Rockafellar, R. T. and Uryasev, S. (2002). Conditional Value-at-Risk for General Loss Distributions, *Journal of Banking & Finance*, 26, pp. 1443–1471.

Rogge, E. and Schönbucher, P. J. (2003). Modelling Dynamic Portfolio Credit Risk, Working Paper, ABN AMRO Bank and ETH Zurich.

Ron, U. (2000). A Practical Guide to Swap Curve Construction, Working Paper 2000-17, Bank of Canada.

Ronn, E. and Verma, A. (1986). Pricing Risk-Adjusted Deposit Insurance: An Option-Based Model, *Journal of Finance*, 41 (4), pp. 871–895.

Rösch, D. and Scheule, H. (2005). A Multifactor Approach for Systematic Default and Recovery Risk, *Journal of Fixed Income*, 15 (2), pp. 63–75.

Rosenberg, J. and Schuermann, T. (2004). A General Approach to Integrated Risk Management with Skewed, Fat-Tailed Risks, Federal Reserve Bank of New York, Staff Report No 185.

Rousseeuw, P. J. and Molenberghs, G. (1993). Transformations of Non Positive Semidefinite Correlation Matrices, *Communications in Statistics: Theory and Methods*, 22 (4), pp. 965–984.

Rouvinez, C. (1997). Going Greek with VaR, *Risk*, 10 (2), pp. 57–65.

Rowe, D. (1993). Curves of Confidence, *Risk*, November, pp. 52–55.

Rowe, D. (1995). Aggregating Credit Exposures: The Primary Risk Source Approach, in *Derivative Credit Risk*, Risk Publications, pp. 13–21.

Rowe, D. and Mulholland, M. (1999). Aggregating Market-Driven Credit Exposures: A Multiple Risk Source Approach, in *Derivative Credit Risk*, Risk Books, pp. 141–147.

Saa'-Requejo, J. and Santa Clara, P. (1997). Bond Pricing with Default Risk, Working Paper, John E. Anderson Graduate School of Management, UCLA.

Sadefo-Kamdem, J. (2003). Value at Risk and Expected Shortfall for Linear Portfolios with Elliptically Distributed Risk Factors, available at http://arxiv.org/pdf/math/0309211.

Saidenber, M. and Strahan, P. (1999). *Are Banks Still Important for Financing Large Businesses?* Federal Reserve Bank of New York, Current Issues in Economics and Finance 5.

Sarig, O. and Warga, A. (1989). Some Empirical Estimates of the Risk Structure of Interest Rates, *Journal of Finance*, Vol 44 (5), pp. 1351–1360.

Schönbucher, P. J. (2000). Factor Models for Portofolio Credit Risk, *Journal of Risk Finance*, 3 (1), pp. 45–56.

Scherer, B. (2004). *Portfolio Construction and Risk Budgeting*, 2nd Edition. London: Risk Books.

Schuermann, T. (2013). Stress Testing Banks, Wharton Financial Institutions Center, working paper.

Schuermann, T. and Jafry, Y. (2003). Measurement and Estimation of Credit Migration Matrices, Wharton Financial Instititutions Center, Working Paper, 03-08.

Schwartz, E. S. and Torous, W. N. (1992). Prepayment, Default, and the Valuation of Mortgage Pass-Through Securities, *Journal of Business*, 65, pp. 221–239.

Schwartz, E. S. and Torous, W. N. (1993). Mortgage Prepayment and Default Decisions: A Poisson Regression Approach, *Journal of the American Real Estate and Urban Economics Association*, 21, pp. 431–449.

Scopelliti, A. D. (2014). Securitisation and Bank Capital in European Banking: Does Regulation Affect Risk Retention Decisions?, Working Paper, University of Warwick and University of Reggio Calabria.

Selvaggio, R. (1996). Using the OAS Methodology to Value and Hedge Commercial Bank Retail Demand Deposit Premiums, *Handbook of Asset and Liability Management*, Second Edition. New York: McGraw-Hill.

Senior Supervisors Group (2008). Observations on Risk Management Practices during the Recent Market Turbulence. Available at http://www.newyorkfed.org/newsevents/news/banking/2008/rp080306.html.

Serfling, R. J. (1980). *Approximation Theorems of Mathematical Statistics*. New York: Wiley Series in Probability and Statistics.

Shannon, C. E. (1956). The Bandwagon, *IRE Transactions on Information Theory*, 2, pp. 3.

Sharpe, W. F. (1964). Capital Asset Prices: A Theory of Market Equilibrium under Conditions of Risk, *Journal of Finance*, 19 (3), pp. 425–442.

Sharpe, W. F. (1994). The Sharpe Ratio, *Journal of Portfolio Management*, 21 (1), pp. 49–58.

Shephard, N. (1996). Statistical Aspects of ARCH and Stochastic Volatility, in *Time Series Models in Econometrics, Finance and Other Fields*, Chapman & Hall, pp. 1–67.

Shimko, D., Tejima, N., and Van Deventer, D. (1993). The Pricing of Risky Debt When Interest Rates Are Stochastic, *Journal of Fixed Income*, September, pp. 58–65.

Shumway, T. (2001). Forcasting Bankruptcy More Accurately: A Simple Hazard Model, *Journal of Business*, 74 (1), pp. 101–124.

Skoglund, J. (2001). A Simple Efficient GMM Estimator of GARCH Models, SSE/EFI Working Paper Series in Economics and Finance No 434.

Skoglund, J. (2013). Modern Risk-Based Funds Transfer Pricing, *Journal of Performance Management*, 25 (1), pp. 3–24.

Skoglund, J. and Chen, W. (2015). The Application of Credit Risk Models to Macroeconomic Regulatory Stress Testing, working paper, available at SSRN: http://ssrn.com/abstract=2605862.

Skoglund, J. and Chen, W. (2009). Risk Contributions, Information and Reverse Stress Testing, *Journal of Risk Model Validation*, Vol 3 (2), pp. 61–77.

Skoglund, J. and Chen, W. (2011). On the Choice of Liquidity Horizon for Incremental Risk Charges: Are the Incentives of Banks and Regulators Aligned? *Journal of Risk Model Validation*, Vol 5 (3), pp. 37–57.

Skoglund, J. and Chen, W. (2012). Cash Liquidity at Risk, *International Review of Applied Financial Issues and Economics*, 4 (1).

Skoglund, J., Erdman, D., and Chen, W. (2010). The Performance of VaR Models during the Crisis, *Journal of Risk Model validation*, 4 (1), pp. 3–21.

Skoglund, J., Erdman, D., and Chen, W. (2011). On the Time Scaling of Value-at-Risk with Trading, *Journal of Risk Model Validation*, 5 (4), pp. 17–26.

Skoglund, J., Erdman, D., and Chen, W. (2013). A Mixed Approach to Risk Aggregation using Hierachical Copulas, *Journal of Risk Management in Financial Institutions*, 6, pp. 188–205.

Skoglund, J., Vestal, D., and Chen, W. (2013). Credit Valuation Adjustment Tail Risk and the Impact of Wrong Way Trades, *Journal of Risk Management in Financial Institutions*, 6 (3), pp. 280–310.

Smith, D. J. (2012). Valuing Interest Rate Swaps Using OIS Discounting, Boston University School of Management Research Paper No 2012-11.

Smith, R. (1987). Estimating Tails of Probability Distributions, *Annals of Statistics*, 15, pp. 1174–1207.

Sorensen, E. and Bollier, T. (1994). Pricing Swap Default Risk, *Financial Analysts Journal*, 50, pp. 23–33.

Stanton, R. (1995). Rational Prepayment and the Valuation of Mortgage-Backed Securities, *Review of Financial Studies*, 8 (3), pp. 677–708.

Stein, R. M., Das, A., Ding, Y., and Chinchalkar, S. (2010). Moody's Mortgage Metrics Prime: A Quasi-Structural Model of Prime Mortgage Portfolio Losses, Moody's Research Labs, New York.

Sufi, A. (2009). Bank Lines of Credit in Corporate Finance: An Empirical Analysis, *Review of Financial Studies*, 22, pp. 1057–1088.

Supervisory Capital Assessment Program (2009). The Supervisory Capital Assessment Program: Design and Implementation, available at http://www.federalreserve.gov/newsevents/press/bcreg /bcreg20090424a1.pdf.

Supervisory Capital Assessment Program (SCAP), (2009). The Supervisory Capital Assessment Program: Design and Implementation, Board of Governors of the Federal Reserve System, April 24.

Sweeney, R. J. (2000). Mean Reversion in G-10 Nominal Exchange Rates, Working Paper, Georgetown University.

Taleb, N. N. (2007). *The Black Swan: The Impact of the Highly Improbable*, Random House.

Tasche, D. (1999). Risk Contributions and Performance Measurement, Working Paper, Technische Universität Munchen.

Tasche, D. (2000). Conditional Expectation as a Quantile Derivative, Working Paper, Technische Universität Munchen.

Tasche, D. (2006). Measuring Sectoral Diversification in an Asymptotic Multifactor Framework, *Journal of Credit Risk*, 2 (3), pp. 33–55.

Tasche, D. (2007). Euler Allocation: Theory and Practice, available at http://arxiv.org/abs/0708.2542.

Tavakoli, J. (2003). *Structured Finance and Collateralized Debt Obligations*. Hoboken, NJ: Wiley Finance.

Taylor, A. M. and Taylor, M. P. (2004). The Purchasing Power Parity Debate, *Journal of Economic Perspectives*, 18 (4), pp. 135–158.

Thakor, A. (2005). Do Loan Commitments Cause Overlending? *Journal of Money, Credit and Banking*, 37, pp. 1067–1099.

Theil, M. (1969). A Multinomial Extension of the Linear Logit Model, *International Economic Review*, 10, pp. 251–259.

Thomas, L. C., Edelmann, D. B., and Crook, J. N. (2002). Credit Scoring and Its Applications, *SIAM Monographs on Mathematical Modeling and Computation*.

Tirole, J. (2005). *The Theory of Corporate Finance*. Princeton, NJ: Princeton University Press.

Tse, Y. and Tsui, A. (2002). A Multivariate GARCH Model with Time-Varying Correlations, *Journal of Business and Economic Statistics*, 20, pp. 351–362.

Tse, Y. K. (2000). A Test for Constant Correlations in a Multivariate GARCH Model, *Journal of Econometrics* 98, pp. 107–127.

Van Deventer, D. R., Imai, K., and Mesler, M. (2005). *Advanced Financial Risk Management*. Hoboken, NJ: Wiley Finance.

Vasicek, O. (1991). *Limiting Loan Loss Distribution*, KMV Corporation.

Vasicek, O. (2002). Loan Portfolio Value, *Risk,* December, pp. 160–162.

Wang, S. S. (1996). Premium Calculation by Transforming the Layer Premium Density, *ASTIN Bulletin*, 26, pp. 71–92.

Wei, J. Z. (2003). A Multi-Factor, Credit Migration Model for Sovereign and Corporate Debts, *Journal of International Money and Finance*, 22, pp. 709–735.

Westin, R. B. (1974). Prediction from Binary Choice Models, *Journal of Econometrics*, 2, pp. 1–16.

Wieland, J. (2011). Curve Fitting: Efficient Methods for Calculating Solvency Capital, Diplomarbeit in Wirtschaftsmathematik, Universität Ulm.

Wiener, N. (1956). What Is Information Theory? *IRE Transactions on Information Theory*, 2, pp. 48.

Wilson, A. (1997). Portfolio Credit Risk, *Risk* 9, pp. 111–117, and 10, pp. 56–61.

Wong, W. K. (2008). Backtesting Trading Risk of Commercial Banks using Expected Shortfall, *Journal of Banking & Finance*, 32 (7), pp. 1404–1415.

Yu, F. (2003). Default Correlation in Reduced-Form Models, Working Paper, University of California.

Zellner, A. (1962). An Efficient Method of Estimating Seemingly Unrelated Regressions and Tests of Aggregation Bias, *Journal of the American Statistical Association*, 57, pp. 500–509.

Zhou, C. (1997). A Jump-Diffusion Approach to Modeling Credit Risk and Valuing Defaultable Securities, Working Paper, Federal Reserve Board, Washington.

Index

Printed and bound by CPI Group (UK) Ltd, Croydon, CR0 4YY

23/04/2025

14660930-0003